DERWENT LEES

ART AND LIFE

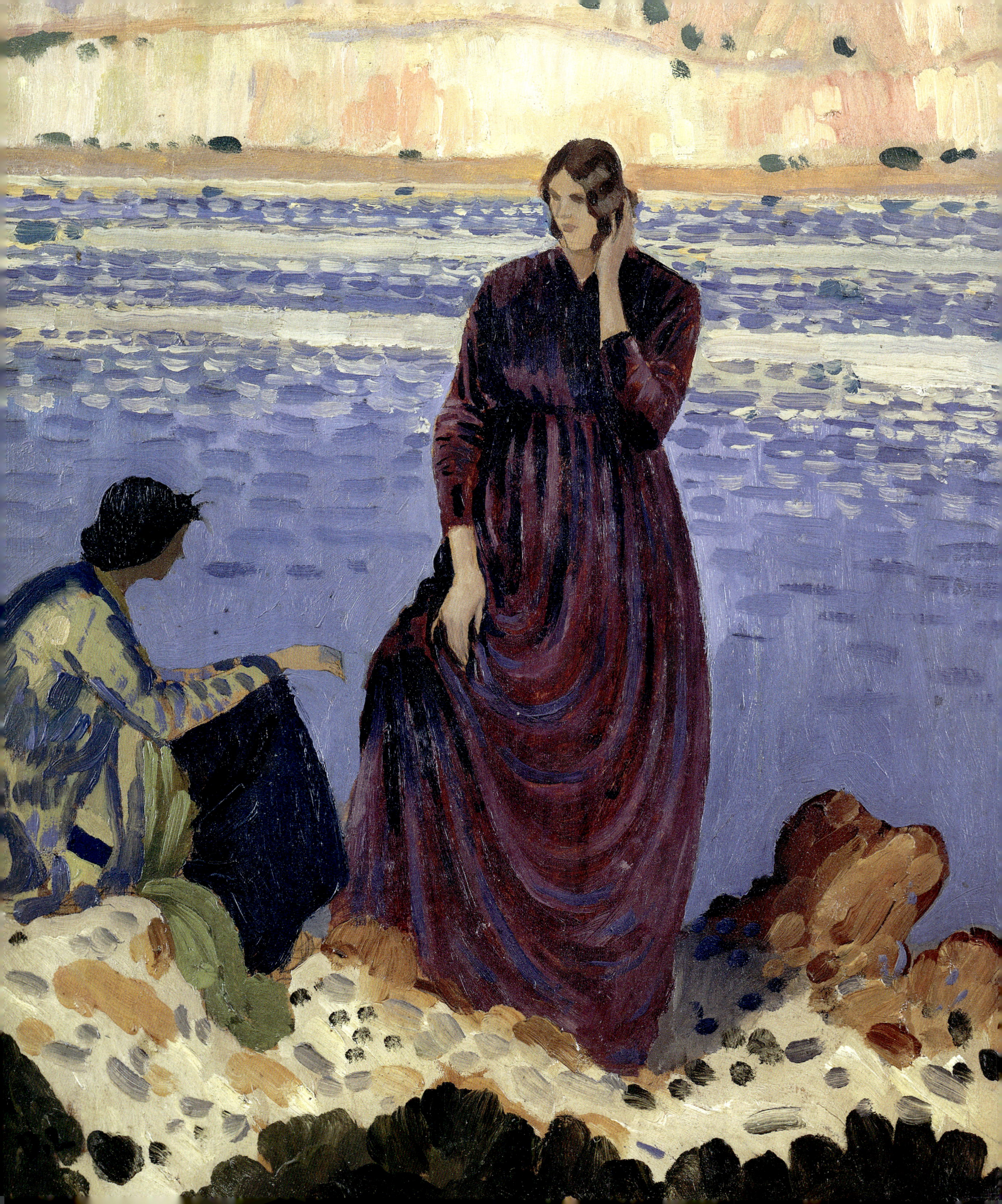

DERWENT LEES

ART AND LIFE

LYNN DAVIES

LUND
HUMPHRIES

First published in 2025 by Lund Humphries

Lund Humphries
Second Home Spitalfields
68–80 Hanbury Street
London
E1 5JL
UK
info@lundhumphries.com
www.lundhumphries.com

ISBN: 978-1-84822-711-8

A Cataloguing-in-Publication record for this book is available from the British Library

Copy edited by Julie Gunz
Designed by Adrian Hunt
Set in Goldenbook and Reforma
Printed in Bosnia and Herzegovina

Front cover: DL11.50 (detail)
Derwent Lees, *A Landscape with Tree*, 1911, Private Collection
Back cover: DL08.12 (detail)
Derwent Lees, *Self Portrait*, c.1908, National Gallery of Victoria, Melbourne
Frontispiece: DL13.40 (detail)
Derwent Lees, *Dorelia and Lyndra, The Blue Pool, Dorset*, 1913, Private Collection

We are grateful for the support of the Museum of Old and New Art, Hobart, Tasmania

MONA

Lund Humphries' EU GPSR Authorised Representative is LOGOS EUROPE, 9 rue Nicolas Poussin, 17000, LA ROCHELLE, France
Contact@logoseurope.eu

MIX
Paper | Supporting responsible forestry
FSC® C118234
FSC www.fsc.org

CONTENTS

PREFACE

Derwent Lees spent his childhood bathed in the light and colours of Australia, then found himself creatively and intellectually accepted into London's early 20th-century art world. Student, then teacher at the Slade School of Art for more than a decade, he was a close friend of Augustus John, James Dickson Innes, Ambrose McEvoy and Philip Wilson Steer – relationships that shaped his artistic practice. He painted in England, Wales and Poland, then rediscovered the resonating light of his childhood in southern France, and an English simulacrum on the Dorset coast. Ultimately, the trauma of war and the loss of friends and love crushed his fragile existence.

This is a tale of connections and acceptance; a story of loss and courage.

Renowned biographer Hilary Spurling wrote that Henri Matisse had 'not escaped the attentions of mythmakers who have invented for him an image that too often reflects the narrowness and banality of the minds from which it came'.[1] This myth-making 'insidiously damaged the painter's reputation. Work has been wrongly dated, crucial connections have been missed, whole sequences of Matisse's artistic development left out of account. Individuals who played key roles in his life and work have been downgraded or passed over altogether.'[2] Derwent was to suffer the same treatment.

This narrative corrects inaccurate accounts and errors that have persisted about Derwent Lees for nearly a century. It provides a comprehensive examination of his life and work, tracing his childhood in Australia and New Zealand, his teaching and artistic growth in England, Wales and France, and culminating in the tragedy of his last decade and his legacy. It is an intimate portrayal of family and friendships, so, where appropriate, first names or nicknames have been used.

More than 450 artworks form the Derwent Lees catalogue raisonné, but only a handful of personal letters and memoirs remain, so I have been measured in my account of his life. Every effort has been made to ensure accurate information is presented; however, inevitably there will be missing pieces and perhaps unforeseen inaccuracies. I have examined the available evidence and resolved many gaps and inconsistencies.

Derwent Lees was the first Australian to paint extensively in the south of France, and the first Australian-born artist to paint in Collioure after Matisse and André Derain's famed Fauvist summer, and in neighbouring Banyuls-sur-Mer, Aristide Maillol's natal village.

I hope that this book underlines that Derwent should be remembered as a talented draughtsman, artist and loyal friend, not as a man defined by mental health challenges or physical disability. For that was not the man at all.

'Dew evaporates
and all our world is dew
so dear, so fresh, so fleeting'

Kobayashi Issa[3]

I dedicate this book to my mother

1 A COLONIAL BOY 1884–1905

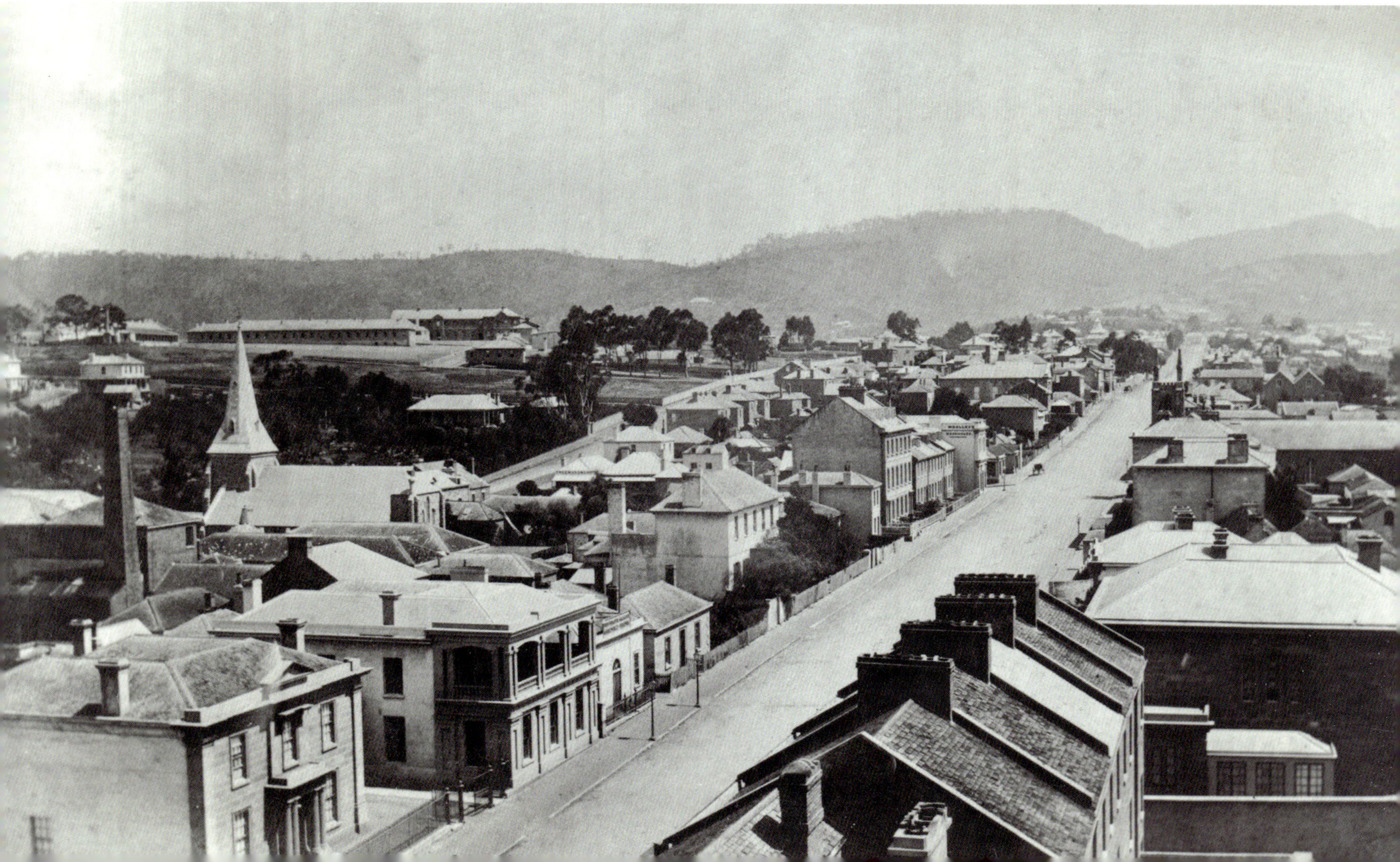

Derwent Lees was born on 14 November 1884, child number ten for Gertrude and William Lees, and the fourth to be born on the rugged island of Tasmania. The family had come from the British colony of Victoria, arriving in Hobart Town in 1879, the capital of what was then also a British colony, and moved into lodgings above the Union Bank where Derwent's father was to be manager. The grand building sat in the heart of the small port city on the shore of the river Derwent.[1] The family rooms on the first floor were perched over the town, directly above the banking chambers.[2]

For William, the aspiring and loyal bank manager, it was a career continuously on the move, constantly responding to the demands of the London directors. He and his wife arrived with six children, but Phillip, the youngest, died soon after. He was ten months old, and the cause of his death, *tabes mesenterica* and diarrhoea, was common. Having lost her infant child, and living comfortably above the busy commercial institution, Gertrude likely busied herself tending to her remaining brood. Two were enrolled in the independent boys' school in the same street,[3] while two boys and an infant girl, three-year-old Olive, were still at home. The younger boys, James, seven, and Noel, a year younger, would have likely played in the city park and bushland along the nearby rivulet.

The Union Bank building occupied the former premises of the Derwent Bank,[4] named after the river on whose western edge the town was built. The Union Bank had purchased the building in 1846. The Derwent Bank soon ceased trading, despite constructing a new building (also called The Derwent Bank) next door which then became the home of the Tasmanian Club, where William was elected a member.[5]

William and Gertrude had married in Victoria in 1867, where their first six children were born. It was in Tasmania that the family was completed, and there was a gentle rhythm to their life on the island for more than five happy years. For William, the name Derwent was indelibly linked to Hobart, and his Tasmanian working and family life. His tenth child was to be a fond reminder of the family's island home.

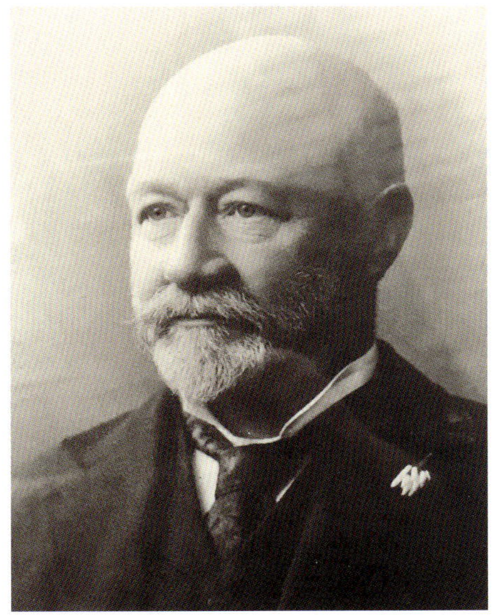

Opposite:
An early view of Macquarie Street, Hobart, c.1890, postcard, State Library Victoria, Melbourne

Union Bank building with its upstairs residence (2nd bottom left), beside the Tasmanian Club (formerly the 'new' Derwent Bank, bottom left)

Above:
William Lees, c.1898, photographer unknown, Ballarat Gold Museum, The Sovereign Hill Museums Association, Ballarat

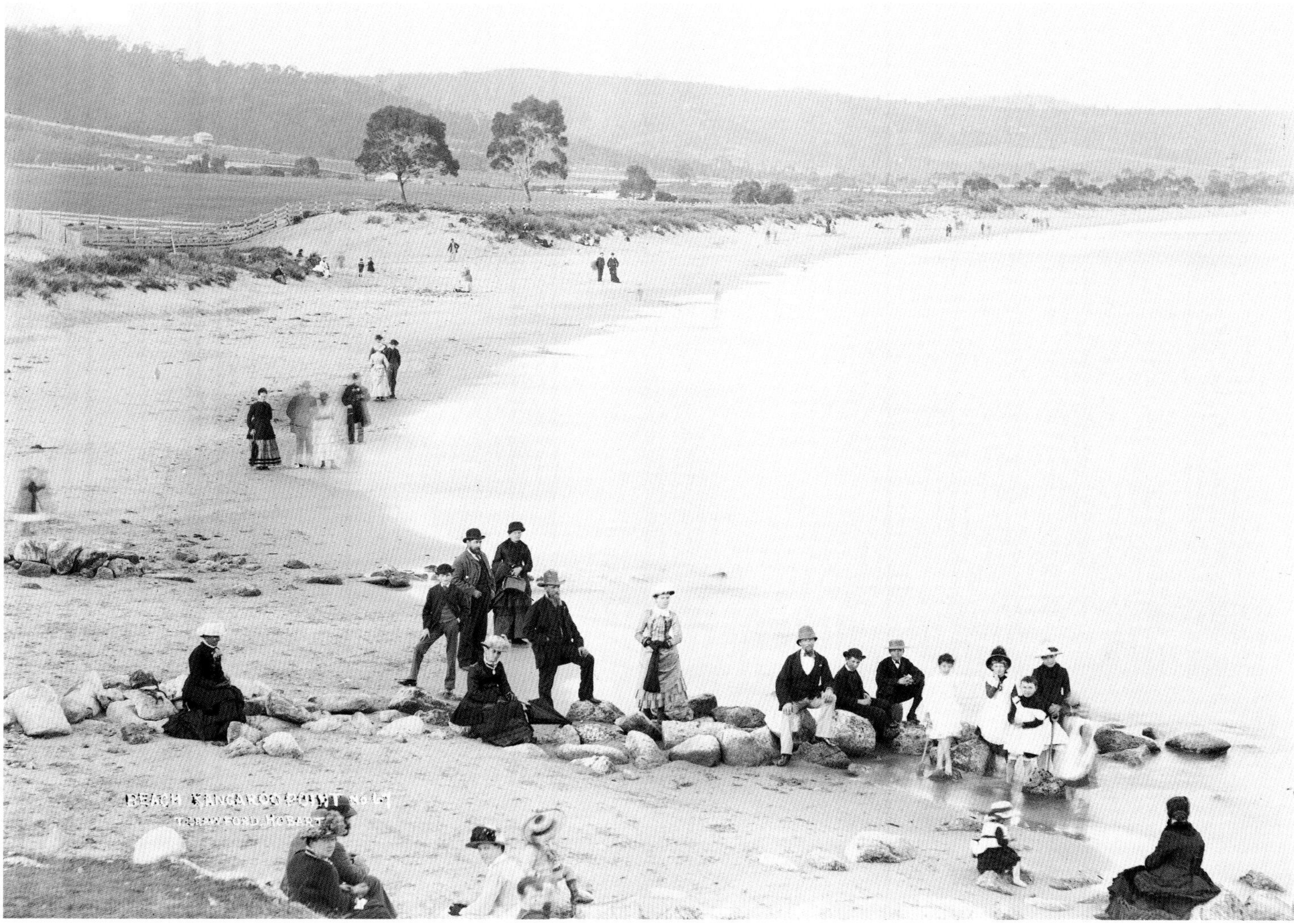

Beach scene, Kangaroo Point, Clarence, c.1900, photographer unknown, Tasmanian Archives and Heritage Office, Libraries Tasmania, Hobart

Derwent's birth was registered in the Hobart district of Clarence, but without a first name. All district entries were recorded a second time on the central Hobart register and this too shows no first name. Gertrude bore four children in Tasmania; two registered with first names, and two without.[6] Both Derwent's birth and his infant brother's death were recorded in Clarence, while the other three births are inscribed in the Hobart register.

Phillip's death and Derwent's birth both happened at the family's weekender, a ten-minute journey by paddle steamer across the drowned river valley of the Derwent from Hobart to Kangaroo Point (later Bellerive), an area popular with British colonists for game hunting. Lodges were built there from the 1840s and, by the time the Lees arrived, it was a much-coveted holiday area of sandy beaches, rocky coves and beachfront reserves. However, during January 1880, when Phillip died, there had been an outbreak of diphtheria, due to nightsoil being thrown into the river beside the local beach.[7] The resulting bacterial soup, coupled with the summer heat, was a deadly mix for the young. Derwent was born four years later, at Kangaroo Point overlooking the Derwent, undoubtedly also contributing to the choice of his name.

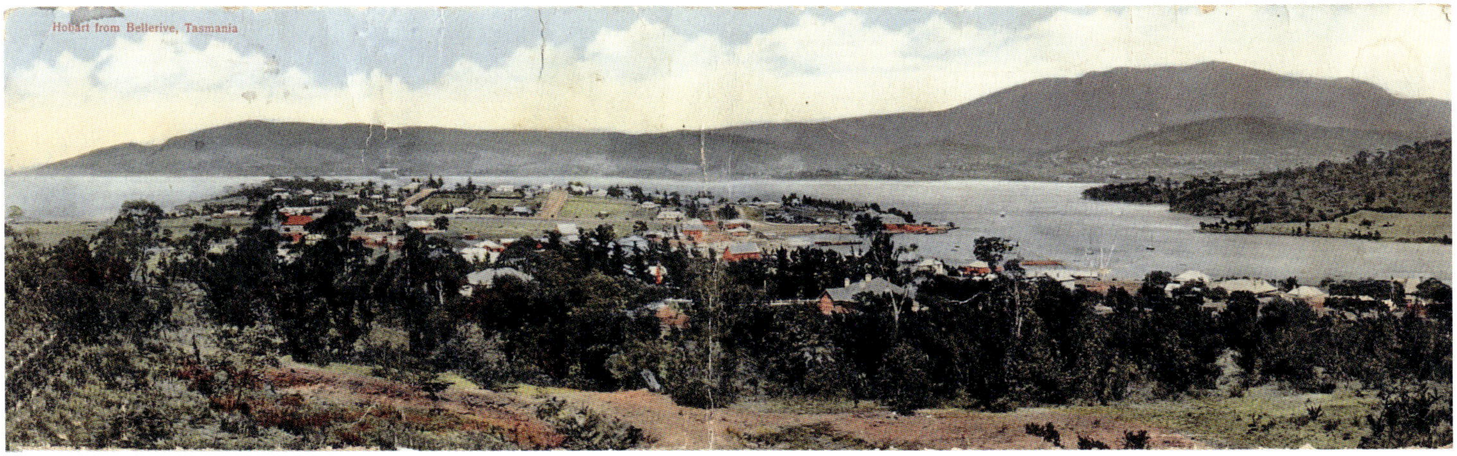

Kangaroo Point, now Bellerive (foreground), with Hobart on the far side of the Derwent River, c.1900, colour-tinted postcard, Tasmania

TO DUNEDIN

Four months later, William negotiated a new contract, and in late March 1885 the family boarded the *Manapouri* bound for Dunedin, New Zealand. The Hobart directors bade William farewell with a 'purse of sovereigns', stating that 'while we congratulate you that your efforts have been acknowledged by your promotion to a larger and more important sphere of labour, we regret the loss of your presence amongst us'.[8]

William would have been delighted with his New Zealand posting, as he was now to live in the city in which his extended family had become well established.[9] His father, William Lowder Lees, had emigrated from Australia in the 1860s. William and Gerte, as she was affectionately known, initially lived above the bank, although with many children ranging in age, it must have been cramped. Gerte advertised for a general servant, a cook, a nurse and a laundress.[10] Quite a staff to support her brood, and they later moved to a larger house.

William was elected as a member of the gentlemen's Dunedin Club upon arrival in the town but was to resign in 1888. The family would again be on the move, back to Victoria, Australia, though deep familial connections would bind them to New Zealand. Some of the family returned to Dunedin in 1891, arriving just weeks before the death of Derwent's grandfather, William Lowder Lees. In the years that followed, Derwent's siblings often returned to visit their New Zealand relations.[11] Derwent's brother Gilbert (1883–1967) would later develop skills in meat exporting in New Zealand and retire there after a successful career in Australia.

The family was struck by tragedy in Dunedin in 1886. Derwent's brother Noel (b.1873) had been ill for some time and, during break at the local school one August day, his heart suddenly failed and he died.[12] A cyst had ruptured, and was followed by massive, anaphylactic shock. He was diagnosed with hydatid disease. A deadly *Echinococcus* parasite lodged in his lungs had taken its toll. British colonists inadvertently spread the infection by feeding infected sheep offal to their dogs. During the late 1880s, records show that the islands of Tasmania and New Zealand had the world's highest rates of hydatid infection.[13]

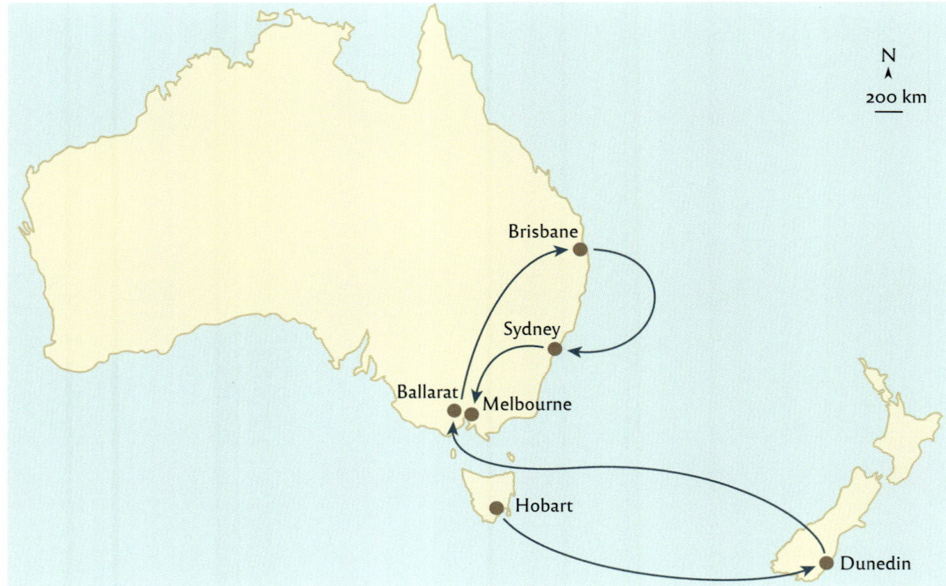

Places where Derwent lived in Australia and New Zealand, 1884–1901

A small white marble stone inside a wrought-iron fence at the local cemetery marks the 12-year-old's passing, beside a memorial to his infant brother Phillip, who had died six years earlier and had been interred in Hobart Town, Tasmania.[14]

MOVING BETWEEN COLONIES

By the end of the following year, the family were back in rural Victoria, where William and Gertrude had met and married.[15] She had emigrated from Dunse in Scotland; he from Kingsland (near Leominster), England. However, their return was to be short-lived. By June 1890, the bank's Ballarat directors reluctantly said farewell to William, who gathered up his family to head to the office in Brisbane, Queensland.[16] The girls attended the private Brisbane Grammar School, and the younger boys were privately tutored. The family lived in salubrious surrounds, paid for by the bank. William worked tirelessly to please the London board, but a financial crisis loomed. The colonies were struggling economically, and 1893 was their toughest year. William's 1890s postings would have been stressful. The Union Bank 'was one of the few banks that survived the "great" crash of 1893 without any suspension of its services'.[17] Added to this, in 1893, Brisbane residents were hit by the worst flood in a century, which caused huge damage. While managing their way through these crises, conversations turned to the impact of federating the Australian colonies.

In April 1894, William accepted a promotion and the Leeses left Brisbane for Sydney,[18] remaining there for more than four years. In April 1898, William, Chief Inspector of the Union Bank of Australia, was made Acting General Manager for Australasia. He, Gerte, and the younger children then made one final move to Melbourne in March 1899, where he took up the position of General Manager, reporting directly to the London directors.[19]

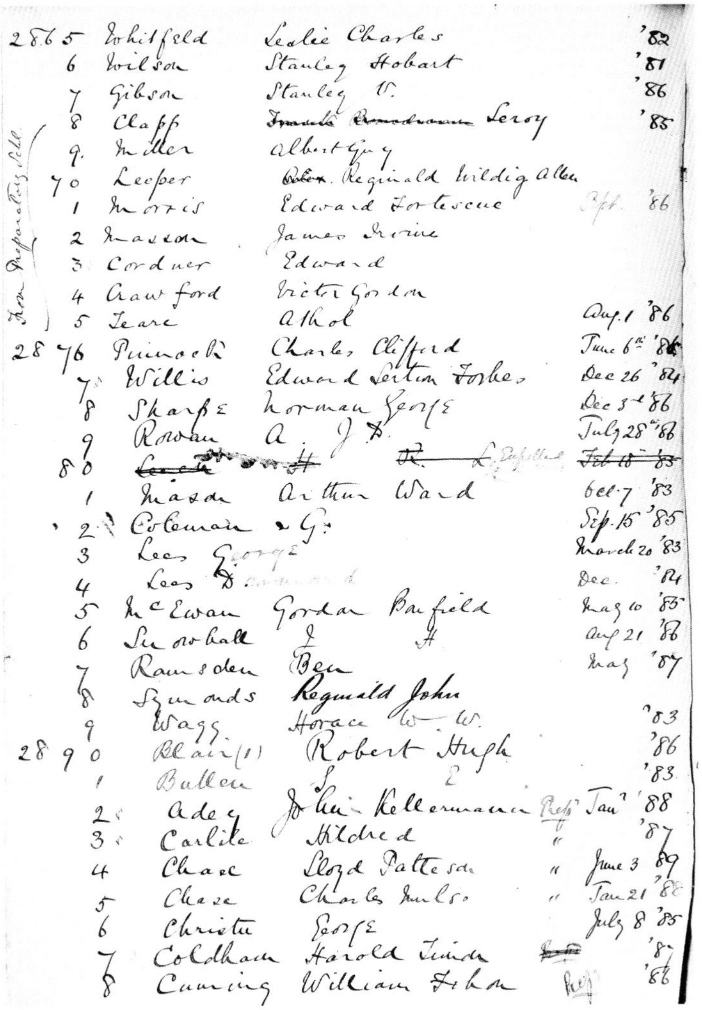

2865	Whitfeld	Leslie Charles	'82
6	Wilson	Stanley Hobart	'81
7	Gibson	Stanley V.	'86
8	Clapp	~~[illegible]~~ Leroy	'85
9	Miller	Albert Guy	
70	Leeper	Robert Reginald Wilding Allen	
1	Morris	Edward Fortescue	Sept. '86
2	Mason	James Irvine	
3	Cordner	Edward	
4	Crawford	Victor Gordon	
5	Teare	Athol	Aug 1 '86
2876	Pinnock	Charles Clifford	June 6th '86
7	Willis	Edward Sutton Forbes	Dec 26 '84
8	Sharpe	Norman George	Dec 3rd '86
9	Rowan	A. J. B.	July 28th '86
80	~~[illegible]~~	~~[illegible]~~	~~Feb 18 '83~~
1	Mason	Arthur Ward	Oct 7 '83
2	Coleman	R. G.	Sep 15 '85
3	Lees	George	March 20 '83
4	Lees	D[illegible]	Dec. '84
5	McEwan	Gordon Banfield	May 10 '85
6	[illegible]	J. H.	Aug 21 '86
7	Ramsden	Ben	May '87
8	Symonds	Reginald John	
9	Wagg	Horace W. W.	'83
2890	Blair	Robert Hugh	'86
1	Bullen	J. E.	'83
2	Adey	John Kellermann	Jan '88
3	Carlile	Mildred	'87
4	Chase	Lloyd Patteson	June 3 '89
5	Chase	Charles Mills	Jan 21 '88
6	Christie	George	July 8 '85
7	Coldham	Harold Linden	'87
8	Cuming	William John	'86

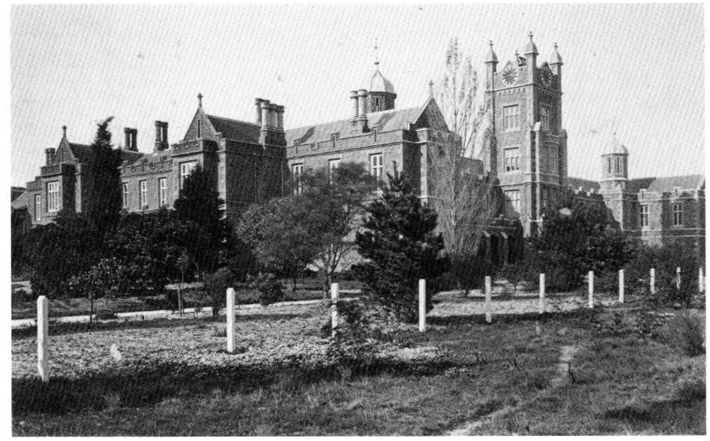

Left:
Melbourne Church of England Grammar School, Student Register, c.1899–1902, Melbourne Grammar School Archives, Melbourne

Incorrect first names for Gilbert and Derwent were added later in different ink

Right:
Melbourne Church of England Grammar School, c.1890, photographer unknown, State Library Victoria, Melbourne

This was Derwent's fifth childhood home. With an upheaval every few years, and older siblings staying behind in towns that they had left, his family was now widely dispersed. Derwent and his older brother Gilbert were both enrolled at the independent boys' Melbourne Church of England Grammar School (MGS) in April 1899. The names G. Lees and D. Lees were scribed in the school's enrolment register at the same time. Two years later, in a different ink, both first names were incorrectly filled out, with G becoming George, and D transformed to Desmond.[20] These clerical errors, including Derwent's incorrect month of birth, were recently uncovered by the school's archivist.

Walter Withers (1854–1914) was the Master of Drawing and Painting at MGS.[21] He was a well-respected artist in both Australia and England, and much liked by his students. Withers had trained in London at the Royal Academy of Arts and the South Kensington schools and later at the Académie Julian in Paris. He mixed in Melbourne with the famed Australian Impressionist artists Frederick McCubbin, Arthur Streeton, Julian Ashton, Tom Roberts and Charles Conder, as an active contributor to the local art scene. They collectively established what became known

William Lees
1839–1913
m. 1867
Gertrude Knox
1843–1900

- William Robert Lees 1868- 1931
- Geoffrey John Lees 1870–1951
- James Harcourt Lees 1872–1910
- Noel Lees 1873–1886
- Olive Mary Lees 1876–1967
- Phillip Amyas Lees 1879–1880
- Phyllis Maud Lees 1880–1952
- Eleanor Gertrude Lees 1881–1957
- Gilbert Lees 1883–1967
- Derwent Lees 1884–1931

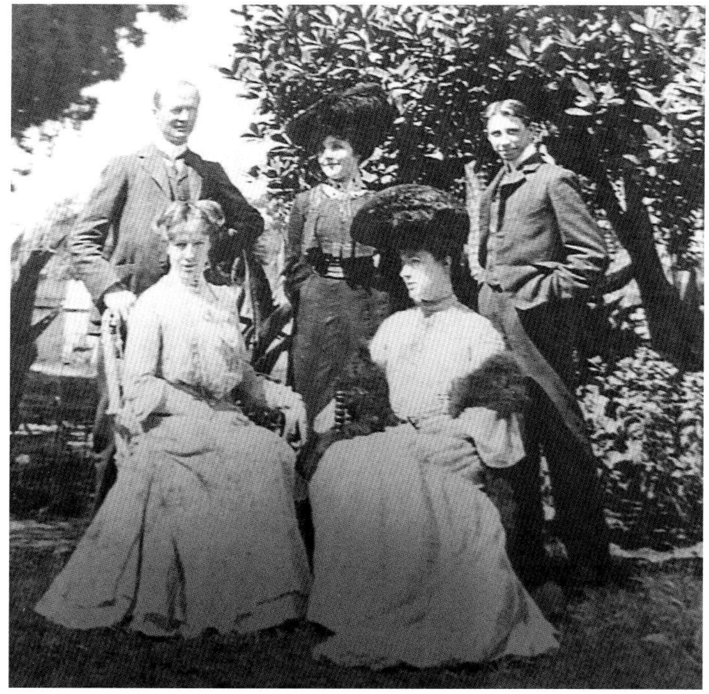

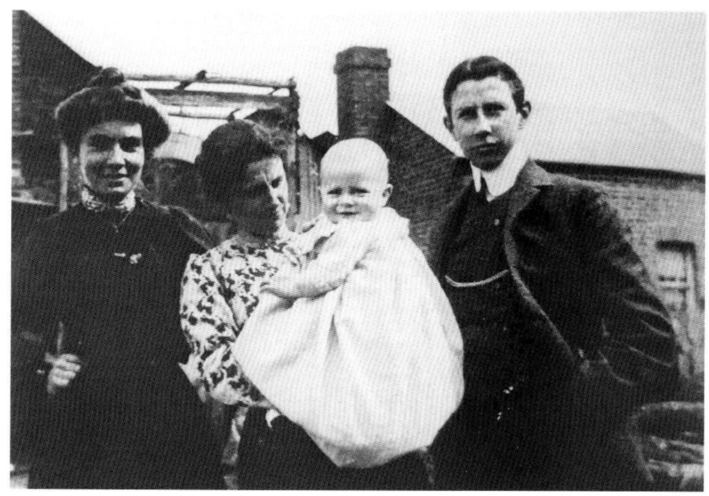

Left:
Derwent Lees's family

Right, above:
Derwent and siblings, c.1902, Private Collection

Geoffrey, Olive, Derwent (back l–r); Eleanor, Phyllis (front l–r); William, James and Gilbert are absent; likely taken at Geoffrey Noel's christening, Adelong, New South Wales

Right, below:
Olive, Alice (known as Essie, Derwent's sister-in-law) holding her son, Geoffrey Noel, Derwent (l–r), c.1902, Private Collection

as the Heidelberg School in Melbourne during the 1890s, focused on working *en plein air* (in the open air). Withers must have encouraged his young student, as it was under him that Derwent's artistic passion first gained recognition with the award of an art prize for 'drawing form'.[22]

Fifty years later, alumni were invited to share memories of their time at the school. In 1947, Gilbert wrote that, 'my principle [*sic*] memory of my period at School is the extraordinary kindness of Mrs Blanch in looking after my young brother, who more or less blew himself up in the Chem. Lab. He recovered to become a painter of note in London before he died.'[23] Mrs Blanch was the headmaster's wife.

The Lees family were strongly linked to MGS. Derwent's father, William, had attended the school's precursor (the Melbourne Diocesan School) in 1851 and, much later, the sons of Derwent's brothers Geoffrey and James were students there.

In September 1900, Derwent's older brother James married in Grenfell, New South Wales, at what was to be the last full family gathering.[24] Derwent turned 16 as he and Gilbert finished their second year at MGS; however, by late 1900, Gerte had fallen severely unwell.

The New Year, 1 January 1901, heralded the birth of the Commonwealth of Australia. The six British colonies formed the new federated nation of Australia, with sovereign links to the United Kingdom. It caused a monumental administrative change at the Union Bank. All responsibility sat with William, who complained to London about difficulties caused by the board's micromanagement. The new Australian Treasury announced the first general conference of Australian banks for May 1901; but by then the directors had called William to a meeting in London. He left Australia in March 1901, never to return.[25]

Gerte had supported her husband through every move over 30 years. She had weathered it all – the constant upheavals, shifting homes and the loss of two children. Unwell for months, if not years, abdominal discomfort and general malaise slowed her pace. In December 1900, a large cyst in her liver burst, causing immediate, acute pain and intestinal paralysis from peritonitis. She was admitted to Melbourne's Homeopathic Hospital but died between Christmas and New Year, on 29 December, at 56 years of age, just days before the formation of the Australian nation. Like Noel, she had contracted hydatid disease. The parasite can live asymptomatically inside the body for years, then grow and kill its host within months. The autopsy showed that the cyst had been present for a long time, nestled amongst necrotic liver tissue, before bursting. The funeral and burial were hurried: a Saturday death then a Sunday burial.[26] Monday was New Year's Eve and the last day of the British Colony of Victoria; Tuesday was New Year's Day 1901, and the new nation celebrated its birth as the Lees family grieved.

MORE TRAGEDY

By the end of the year, Derwent's father had decided to remain in London, and a few weeks short of Christmas 1901 he married a woman some 20 years his junior.[27] Derwent, his youngest, was still a teenager, and the family, now scattered and broken, was only a memory.

During this year Gilbert also moved to England to learn about the meat export trade and did not return until 1907.[28] There was little to hold him to his homeland. By the late 19th century, trade from Australia and New Zealand to Britain in meat, grains and wool was thriving. Inspired by his grandfather, who had forged a successful career in meat processing in New Zealand, he was to learn the ropes in England.

Gilbert was soon joined by his three sisters and Derwent, led by 25-year-old Olive. Following the month-long voyage from Australia to England, the young Lees siblings must have attended their father's second wedding in late November 1901 in London, before returning to Sydney in February 1902.[29] While the rest of the

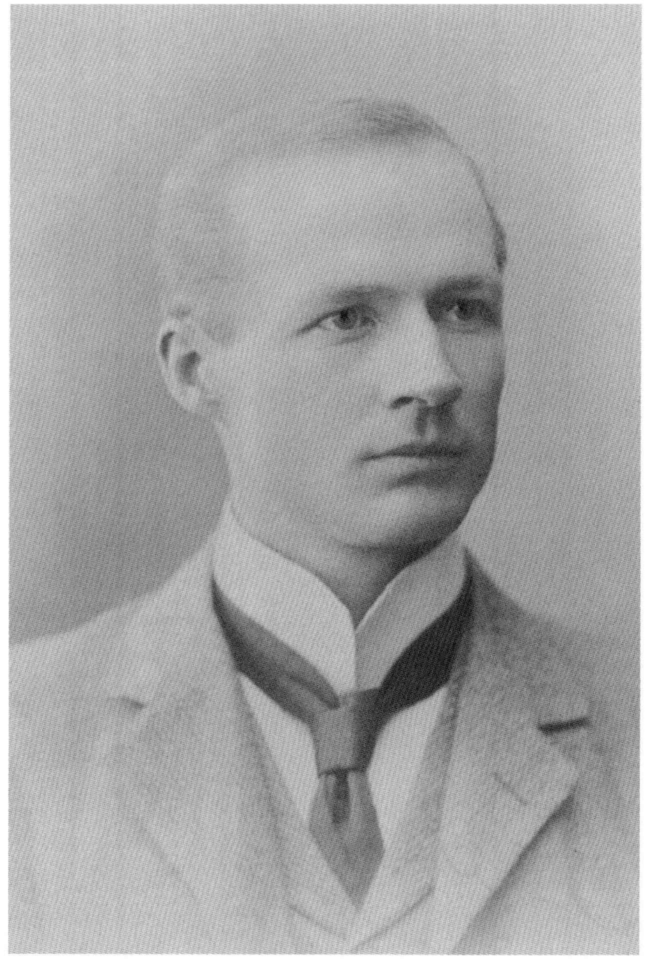

Geoffrey John Lees, c.1900, State Archives Collection, Museums of History New South Wales, Sydney

family was abroad, and just before Christmas 1901, their older brother Geoffrey married in New South Wales. His new wife soon gave birth to a son, Geoffrey Noel Lees – sadly, Geoffrey Noel was also to die young, drowning in a waterhole while swimming with classmates. Derwent's relations still recall their parents telling them that the name Noel had brought the family bad luck.[30]

More tragedy struck in August 1902. Derwent was probably working with his brother James who managed the Melyra Estate, a large Union Bank pastoral property in rural New South Wales, when he had a horse-riding accident. While riding with a friend, he slipped from his saddle, leaving one foot trapped in the stirrup, suffering an injury so severe that his right foot had to be amputated.[31] His brother Geoffrey, a doctor, was called to Sydney in support; the local newspaper noting 'his brother requiring to have an operation performed which might result in the loss of a foot'.[32] In years to come, London friends would comment on the ease with which Derwent could scale fences or walk without anyone knowing he had an artificial foot. Renowned artist Augustus John (1878–1961) said that Derwent entertained friends by wriggling his articulated wooden toes.[33] Perhaps the loss of his foot precipitated his change of career, cementing his father's acceptance of his passion for art. William had a strong work ethic,[34] and Derwent would have been encouraged to attend university, like his older brother. Geoffrey had passed his medical examination at the University of Sydney in 1899 and became a practising doctor in the government's first public hospital, the Coast Hospital, before becoming a devoted rural doctor.[35]

After two years of study, Derwent sat his matriculation exam at the University of Sydney, gaining a pass in March 1905.[36] Despite studying in Sydney, he matriculated as a student of Melbourne Grammar School.[37] The 20-year-old decided to study art at the Slade School of Drawing, Painting and Sculpture at University College London. It was a courageous step for a lone young man who would be viewed as an outsider and an antipodean colonial, but, for Derwent, England represented the centre of modernity and momentum in the creative arts. In July 1905 he boarded the *Suevic* bound for London.[38]

It heralded a new beginning of a life in art, centred on the forms of both landscapes and the human figure. The journey took little more than 40 days, passing South Africa, Tenerife and then Gibraltar, and only a few hundred kilometres west of where Henri Matisse (1869–1954) and André Derain (1880–1954) were painting wild and brightly coloured Fauvist works in Collioure, France. In five years, that same Catalan light and colour, at a climate and latitude similar to his Australian and New Zealand childhood, would also captivate Derwent.

2 THE YOUNG ARTIST 1905–6

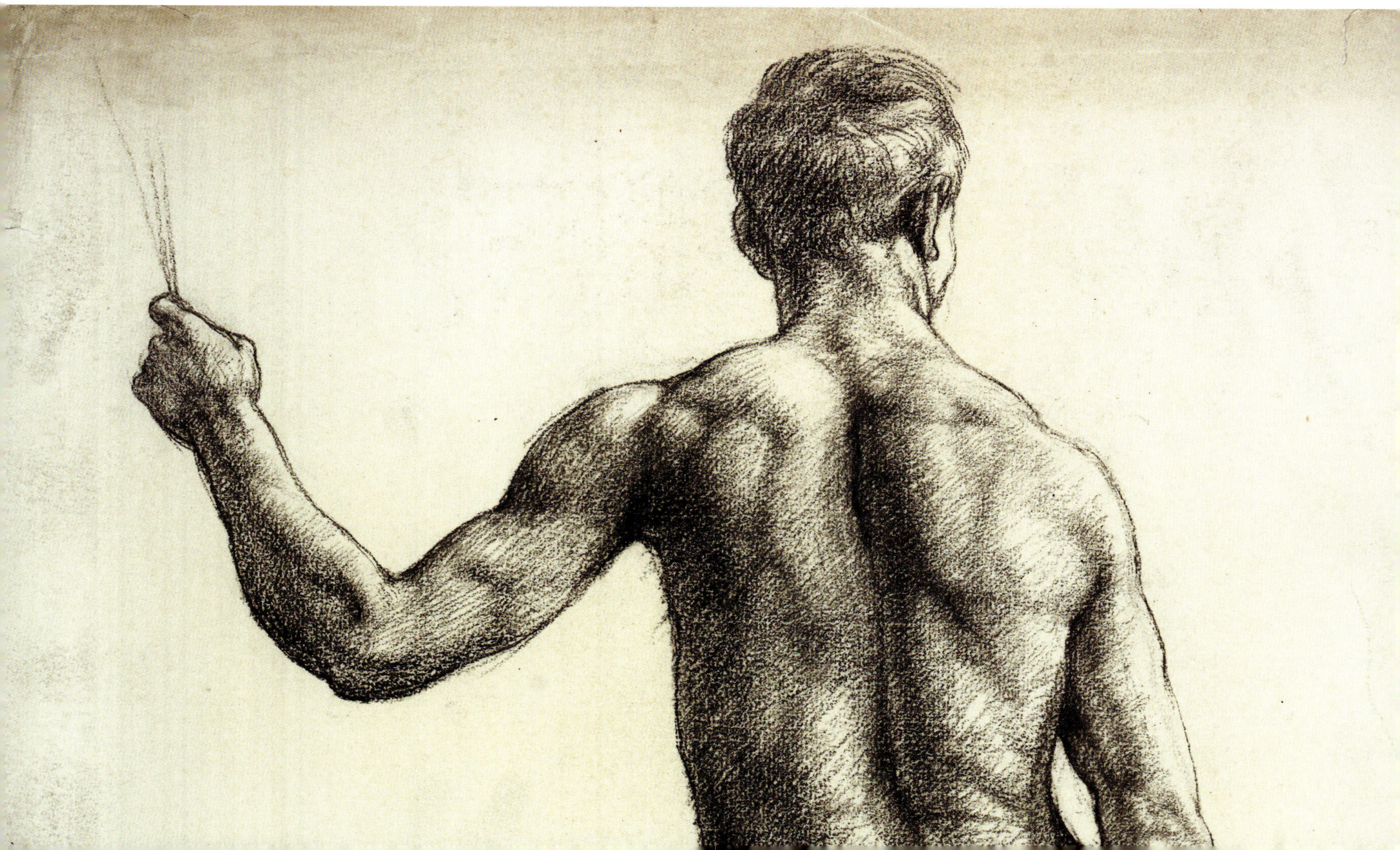

Derwent arrived in London in the summer of 1905 to a city abuzz with vital, creative energies and a rapidly changing art scene. He likely stayed with his brother or father. New galleries and groups proliferated, catalysed by the lasting impact of the Pre-Raphaelite and Aesthetic movements and defiant of the conservative establishment (typified by the Royal Academy that invited only those approved by its membership). A more dynamic and accepting scene was developing. The late-19th-century education reforms had opened the profession of artist to the middle and working classes and now many more young men and women, often financially supported by their families, could train for a career in art.

The academic year at University College London's (UCL) Slade School of Art had three terms, commencing in early October and finishing around the last week of June. To be accepted into the Slade, prospective candidates were required to present a portfolio of work for assessment, and certification of adequate prior schooling. Once approved for admission, tuition fees had to be paid in advance. Students not only had to pay the annual fees, but also provide their own drawing and painting supplies.[1] This, coupled with food and lodging expenses, made life for the would-be artist of meagre means an uncertain and risky path. Derwent missed the start of the 1905 academic year as he had to spend the autumn term preparing his entry portfolio, most likely at art classes in Paris.

He commenced his Slade studies at the start of second term, in January 1906, incorrectly writing his birth date as 15 November 1884 on the application form,[2] perhaps an unimportant detail for a young man starting out with nothing but a yearning to be creative. He was embarking on a precarious career, eschewing the familial path into banking, agriculture or the meat trades. His passion for art must have been evident as his father, despite nearing retirement and with no property assets, paid for Derwent's passage to London, his tuition and a small living allowance.

Derwent entered classes under Professor Fred Brown (1851–1941), Assistant Professor Henry Tonks (1862–1937) and Slade Assistant Walter Westley Russell (1867–1949). Full-time students studied five days a week and a half day on Saturday.

Opposite:
DL07.2 (detail)
Derwent Lees, *A Study of a Male Figure [walking to left, seen partly from behind]*, 1907

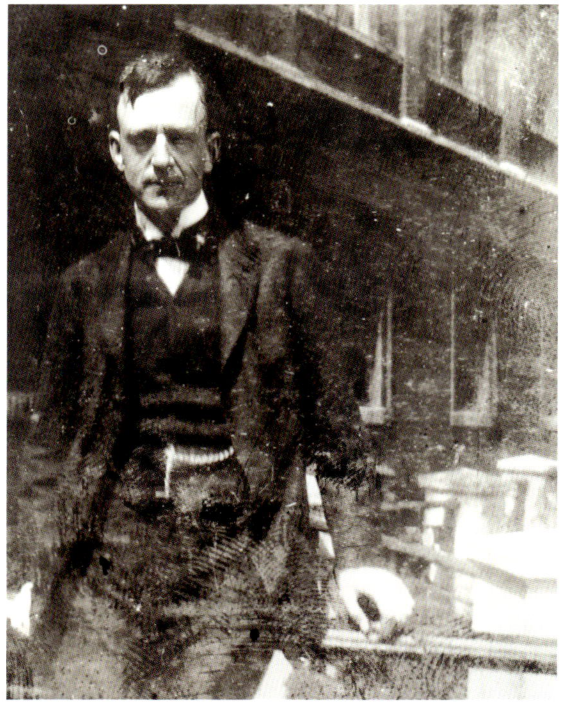

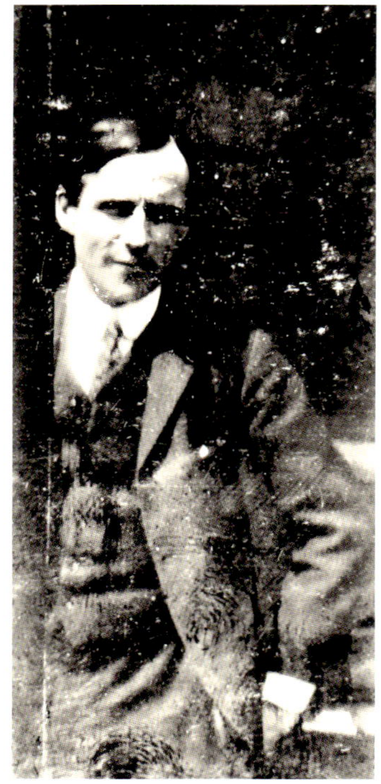

Left:
Henry Tonks, c.1907, UCL Special Collections, University College London

Right:
Walter Westley Russell, c.1907, UCL Special Collections, University College London

Below:
The Slade Antique Room, photographer unknown. In: Gladys Beattie Crozier, 'The Slade School of Art', *Every Woman's Encyclopedia*, v.1, London, 1912

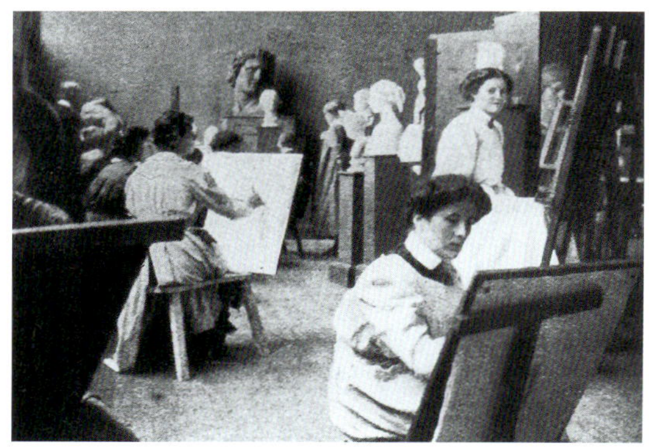

Lessons initially involved drawing busts and statues in the Antique Room, and only once deemed competent could they progress to life drawing. Augustus John recounted that the Antique Room 'was furnished with numerous casts from late Greek, Greco-Roman and Italian Renaissance sculpture' where students drew with a 'stick of charcoal, a sheet of *Michallet* paper and a chunk of bread for rubbing out'.[3] The bread was available for purchase daily at the school's signing-in register. The Antique Room was bitterly cold and some students spent months there, shivering but determined, desperate to render a classical form with enough competence to be allowed to progress to draw from life.

The painting programme, assisted by Philip Wilson Steer (1860–1942), also demanded proficiency in all aspects of drawing before classes could be attended. While life models were the main subject, students also rendered scenes from literary sources and depicted house interiors, music or theatre halls and mythical scenes. The Alhambra Theatre in Leicester Square and the Old Bedford Music Hall were favourite subjects. Regular lectures on perspective, anatomy, sculpture classes and history of art filled out the curriculum, with composition subjects changing monthly. Time was also allocated to examine the works of Old Masters at the National Gallery and the neighbouring British Museum. Students had the summer months to see family or set out on painting trips in Britain or abroad.

A MENTOR AND FRIENDS

The punishing schedule of cast, then life and figure drawing, established by Brown and Tonks, had become a Slade tradition. The understanding and accurate rendering of the proportions of the human body was requisite. This was a skill that Derwent not only mastered but championed.

Tonks had been a practising doctor before relinquishing medicine to join the Slade staff for a career in art as Head of Drawing. He obsessed about the importance of observation and detail in depicting the human form.[4] He was tough but fair, although he was once described berating weeping students with damning criticism. Augustus reported that 'he was a sharp critic and not given to mincing his words', and that he 'had a passion for teaching drawing, and the Slade was his mistress'.[5] Studying muscle layering and movement, contours, bone structure and diagonal shading were central to his teaching method. He expected dedication to build competence and gain hard-won praise. Joseph Hone, his chief biographer, recounted: 'to say that Tonks was an inspiring teacher is to rate his work too low. The first lesson from him might be like a cold douche but after that the student, if he took the douche well, felt that he was being folded under the shadow of a wing. The garrulous and the self-opinionated fared badly.'[6]

James Dickson Innes, c.1912, photographer unknown, Wikimedia Commons

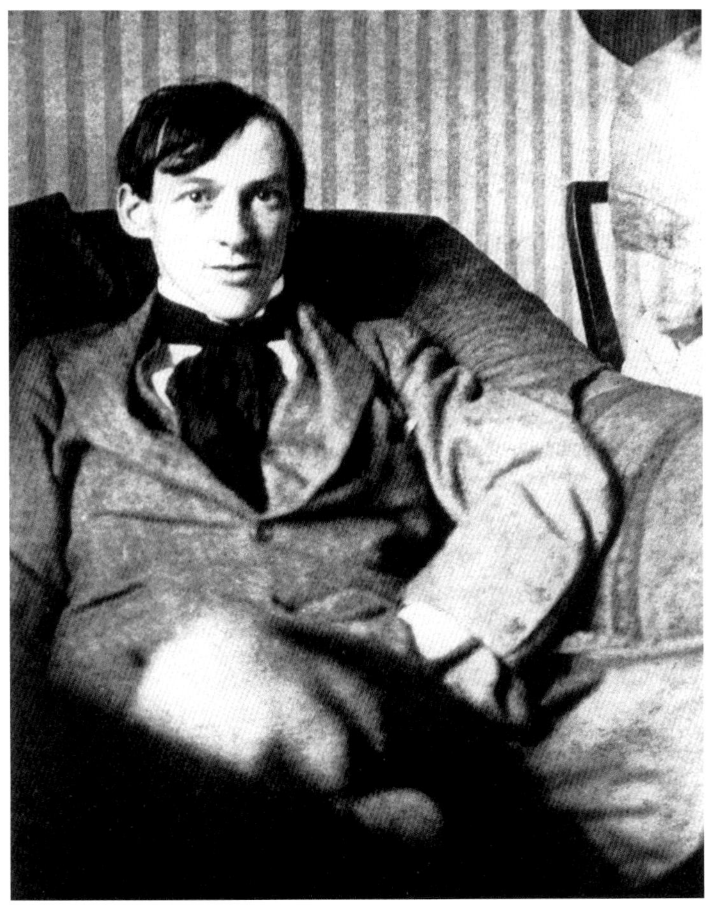

Derwent excelled in this environment. He was awarded a certificate in Drawing and then first prize in Figure Drawing in June 1907 (DL07.1–20, excluding versos). His submission, of at least 17 large figures drawn in a range of poses, is now held at the UCL Art Museum and displays all the hallmarks of Tonks's teaching. Derwent became known for his strong drawing skills, along with classmate and good friend Donald Maclaren (1886–1917), and the older Slade alumnus and later close friend, Augustus John. Despite Tonks's reputation for being a gruff disciplinarian, Derwent was to remain loyal to him, his teaching principles and the Slade throughout his life.

In early 1906, Derwent struck up a friendship with classmate James Dickson Innes (1887–1914), known as Dick. Dick had started at the Slade in Term I in October 1905. A close bond rapidly developed, forging a friendship and artistic partnership that persisted through their most creative years. A close Slade group formed around Derwent, Dick and Maclaren (often called Mac), the latter both two years younger; joined for a time by Derwent's brother Gilbert. This was a heady group of high-energy young men seeking fun, adventure and freedom from the Edwardian social mores that enveloped them.

During these insouciant London years, 'Dick, Mac and Lees', as they were known, lived a bacchanalian life. In a December 1907 letter to Gilbert, by then back in Australia, Dick reminded him of drunken evenings the four had spent together. He reported that during their most recent term he and Derwent 'have been to no Whoer [*sic*] shops, nor have we (I believe) gone in for any fornication whatever'.[7] A year later, however, Dick wrote to artist friend John Fothergill (1876–1957) asking whether Mac's 'sexual infection' was improving, as he was 'covered with shame. It realy [*sic*] was very Hard [*sic*] to be struck down at so inconvenient a time.'[8] Dick's letter to Gilbert also commented on Derwent's caring spirit and strong morals, as Dick found it 'amusing for me in this way to be reporting on your brother as it is he who is always looking after me and instilling virtuous principles into me. Not the other way round as you would imagine from this.'[9]

DANK ROOMS IN FITZROVIA

Like most of their artist friends, the three Slade students based themselves in and around Chelsea and Fitzrovia. At times Derwent and Dick lived in Chelsea's Cheyne Walk by the River Thames, cohabiting with Ronald Gray (1868–1951), an artist and lifelong friend of Tonks. Later, artists and close friends Nora (née Munro; 1892–1948) and Gerald Summers (1886–1969) and Randolph Schwabe (1885–1948) and his wife 'Birdie' (Gwendolyn) would also call Cheyne Walk home, and Slade staffers Walter Russell and Philip Wilson Steer lived close by.

However, it was Fitzrovia, just two blocks from the Slade, that most attracted Derwent and his friends, as 'Fitzroy Street was then a fashionably unfashionable artists' quarter'.[10] Mac moved between numbers 6 and 10 Fitzroy Street and adjacent Charlotte Street. Derwent lodged at 39 Grafton Street, virtually in view of the Slade, and later at 12 and 18 Fitzroy Street and 21 Fitzroy Square. Dick lived at number 8, then 10 Fitzroy Street. In 1908, Dick wrote to Fothergill about one of Derwent's Fitzroy Street digs, explaining that 'he now lives in rather a bad room at 22, next but one to yours'.[11] Their lodgings were often in larger houses, divided into numerous small, dank, rented rooms. Derwent and Augustus also stayed in rooms in Percy Street above the popular Eiffel Tower Restaurant, frequented by local artists, writers and eccentrics.[12] Life was fluid, and moving was commonplace, usually driven by changing financial circumstances. Many lived hand to mouth, with heating, a second set of clothes, or an extra pair of shoes, seen as unaffordable luxuries. 'Fitzrovia . . . was a large, shifting, classeless [*sic*] society of oddly assorted persons linked together by a common interest in painting and sculpture'.[13]

By 1907, the three aspiring artists began to exhibit at the New English Art Club (NEAC), and likely at the Friday Club (early catalogues are untraceable). For Derwent, sales were essential to afford food and lodgings. For Dick, exhibiting supplemented the financial support provided by his parents and his Slade scholarship. Mac was

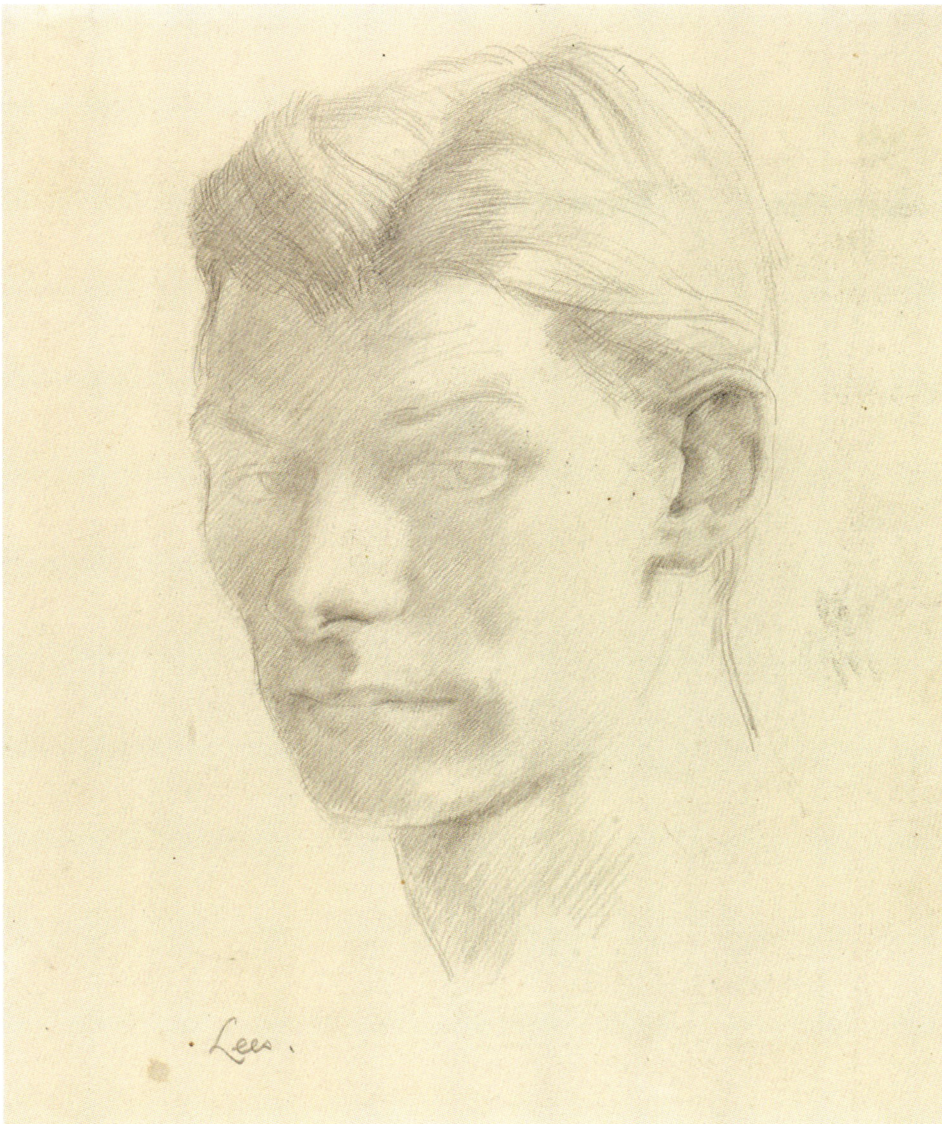

DL07.24
Derwent Lees, *Portrait of Donald Maclaren / Portrait of a Man*, c.1907, pencil on paper, 32.5 x 25 cm, UCL Art Museum, University College London

also a scholarship holder. Derwent's age had precluded him from applying for the same scholarship.

Like Derwent, Mac, who was born in London in 1886, had also suffered family tragedy when his father, an established architect, died when he was just four years old. His training at the Slade was protracted, starting in 1903 yet not completing until 1908, the same year as Dick and Derwent. He won many prizes, including the 1906–7 Melvill Nettleship Prize for Figure Composition.[14] During this period, Derwent completed a pencil portrait of Mac (DL07.24). The two were both talented portraitists, with Mac painting a portrait of his uncle D.S. MacColl (1859–1948, held at the Tate), who became the Keeper of the National Gallery of British Art (now Tate), in 1906. Mac was also an accomplished landscape artist, painting in Guernsey, Devon, Cornwall and Scotland and the Welsh coast.

Both Mac and Derwent would become art teachers and marry, Mac settling in Liverpool, marrying Vernie Violet Williams and having two daughters. He would

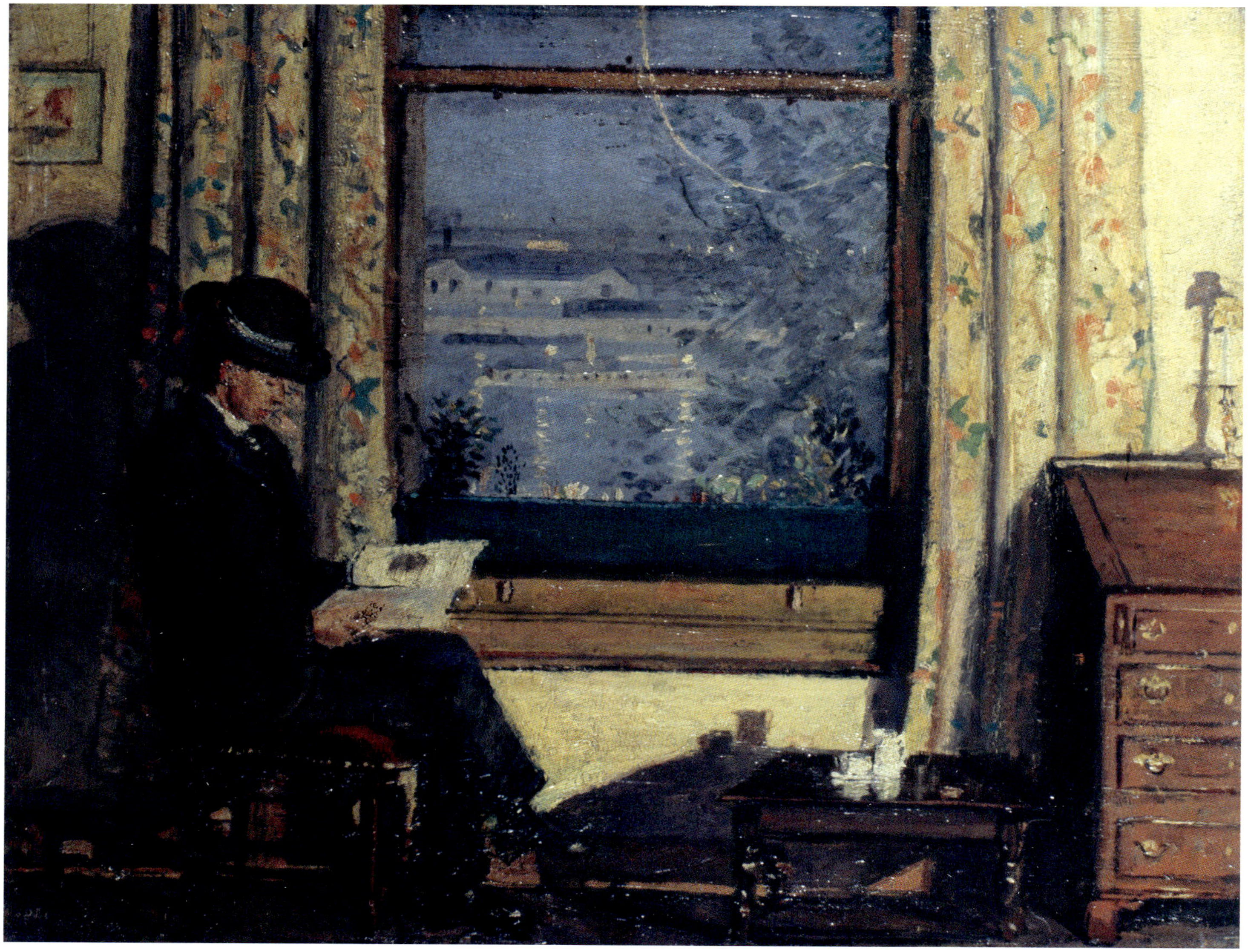

James Dickson Innes, *Moonlight and Lamplight / Portrait of Derwent Lees*, 1907, oil on canvas, 40.6 x 50.8 cm, location unknown

later enlist in the 10th Battalion Liverpool (Scottish) Regiment, leaving for France in March 1917, and dying on the Western Front, 29 June 1917. His name is inscribed on the Slade School's limestone memorial tablet, along with the 14 other staff and students who lost their lives in the Great War.[15]

Derwent also had a close relationship with his brother Gilbert. For 20 years they were constantly together, at the same school, sharing tutors, and giving each other support. Gilbert was in London when Derwent first arrived in 1905, and they may have visited their father's natal village, Kingsland (Herefordshire), which, along with neighbouring Leominster, was revered by the expatriate Lees family. Grandfather William Lowder, who had moved to Australia then New Zealand in the 1860s, as a livestock agent, saw business potential in preserving meat for long-distance transportation. In 1884, a frozen New Zealand leg of lamb arrived in Leominster to much fanfare and was captured in the local newspaper. Sent by William Lowder, it was a gift, clever marketing, and a source of family pride. Gilbert had chosen a similar career path, apprenticed to the meat export trade in London. He would return to the Melbourne office of Gordon Woodroffe in July 1907,[16] and later became the Brisbane manager for Thomas Borthwick & Sons Ltd. In 1913, he married New Zealander Clarice Wood in Christchurch. Their only child John Charles was born in January 1917, but died within two days. Gilbert would retire to New Zealand after working for Borthwick's in Australia for 25 years.[17] Throughout Derwent's life, and despite the great distances between them, he and Gilbert would remain close.

As the 1906 summer drew to a close, Gilbert continued his apprenticeship while the three Slade students prepared for the next academic year. Alice, mother to Dick, now 19, and older brother Jack, rented rooms for the boys in Cheyne Walk. She was at her youngest son's side for much of his time at the Slade. She understood that he was youthful, but also sickly. It was at this address during 1907 that Dick painted *Moonlight and Lamplight*, an interior scene with Derwent posed in hat, suit and tie, reading on a chair beside a window.[18]

Dick created several works here with views over the Thames towards Battersea. He was an artist of extraordinary talent, later lauded for painting with 'great speed and boundless enthusiasm' while 'inspirations came to him suddenly'.[19] A self-assured young man, he was a foil for Derwent and a counter to the latter's lack of confidence. He possessed a certainty and belief that came from being bathed in familial love and support. Dick had been sheltered from much of life's pressures and traumas, unlike Derwent, who had only limited ability to improve his circumstances while a student. The close friends: one, emotionally labile and in a precarious financial situation; the other, financially and emotionally secure but often unwell. It was a fragile existence, but their natural comradeship and creative partnership laid a foundation of trust, despite occasional juvenile intensity. Their strong personalities and creative spirits, somewhat naive, searingly honest and often guileless, drew them together. Much later, after their deaths, artist contemporary and friend Randolph Schwabe described them as 'a bizarre pair'.[20]

A DIFFERENCE IN CHARACTER

By summer 1907, Derwent had completed his second year of studies and received the Slade Figure Drawing prize. He, Dick and Mac bade farewell to Gilbert while making plans for a summer painting trip to Wales, their first *plein air* experience together. Derwent was now settled, and his true character was emerging – loyal, hardworking and mischievous amongst close friends; few felt ill of him.

He was also sensitive and preferred a structured, calm environment. On one rare occasion, his usual affability gave way to defensiveness. Slade classmate and close friend Rudolph Ihlee (1883–1968) was unimpressed with Derwent's behaviour during their Welsh painting trip, where 'Dick, Mac and Lees' were accompanied by fellow students Rudolph and William Clause (1887–1946).

Derwent and Rudolph were very different as men and artists; however, they were good friends at the Slade, and became exhibitors at the same NEAC and Friday Club shows, and jurors on the Friday Club hanging committees. Both were talented portraitists and landscape artists, with Rudolph preferring to paint more architectural townscapes and structured landscapes. By contrast, Derwent's preference was always the female figure or soft, remote-seeming landscapes with few man-made structures, interpreting the world through curves, movement and softened shapes. One was methodical and independent, while the other searched for looseness and freedom, as if to escape the strictures of his mental and academic bounds. Derwent seemed to need the structure demanded by an institution, while Rudolph was content to spend 'eight months of the year "on the road" in the car, pushing on from place to place and painting',[21] with few possessions and responsibilities.

Three decades after their trip, Rudolph recalled that Derwent's 'megalomania and extreme selfishness . . . became very noticeable one summer'.[22] This is the earliest known account of Derwent's shifting moods, although his future wife would say that he could be 'stormy in argument . . . and always nervous and excitable with a curious intensity of utterance'.[23] Schwabe indirectly noted that William Clause, who accompanied them on the 1907 trip, 'had a hectoring manner',[24] so perhaps Derwent was releasing internal pressure if Rudolph and William, forthright in their opinions, made him feel ill at ease. James Trollope, Rudolph's biographer, intimates that Rudolph disliked intensity,[25] and in the 1920s he and fellow artist Edgar Hereford (c.1886–1953) had a notably unpleasant interaction with the passionate and patriotic southern Catalan sculptor Mario Vives.[26]

Rudolph was self-reliant, 'outgoing and spontaneous'.[27] He developed his own style, away from and uninfluenced by the London art scene. Conversely, Derwent needed routine, structure and guiding mentors in his life. Their different characters were however allied by an artistic sensibility, a knowing that the 'creative mind . . . is a human creature born abnormally, inhumanly sensitive'.[28]

Opposite:
Slade Personalities: Derwent Lees with classmates outside the front of the Slade, c.1907. UCL Special Collections, University College London

Previously unidentified photograph showing Matthew Smith, James Dickson Innes, Edgar Hereford and Donald Maclaren (back l–r); Rudolph Ihlee and Derwent Lees (front l–r)

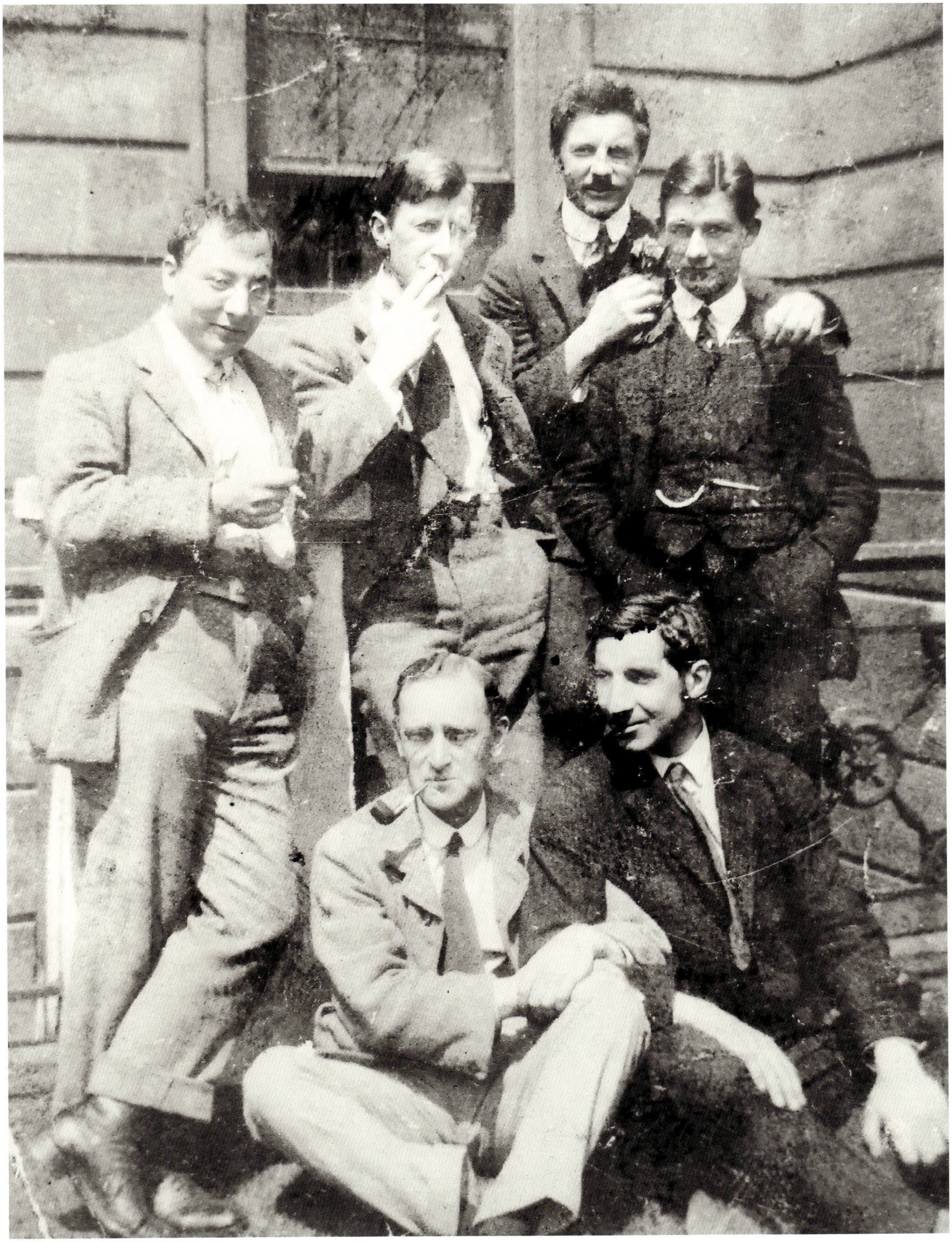

3 MENTORS AND MASTERS 1907–8

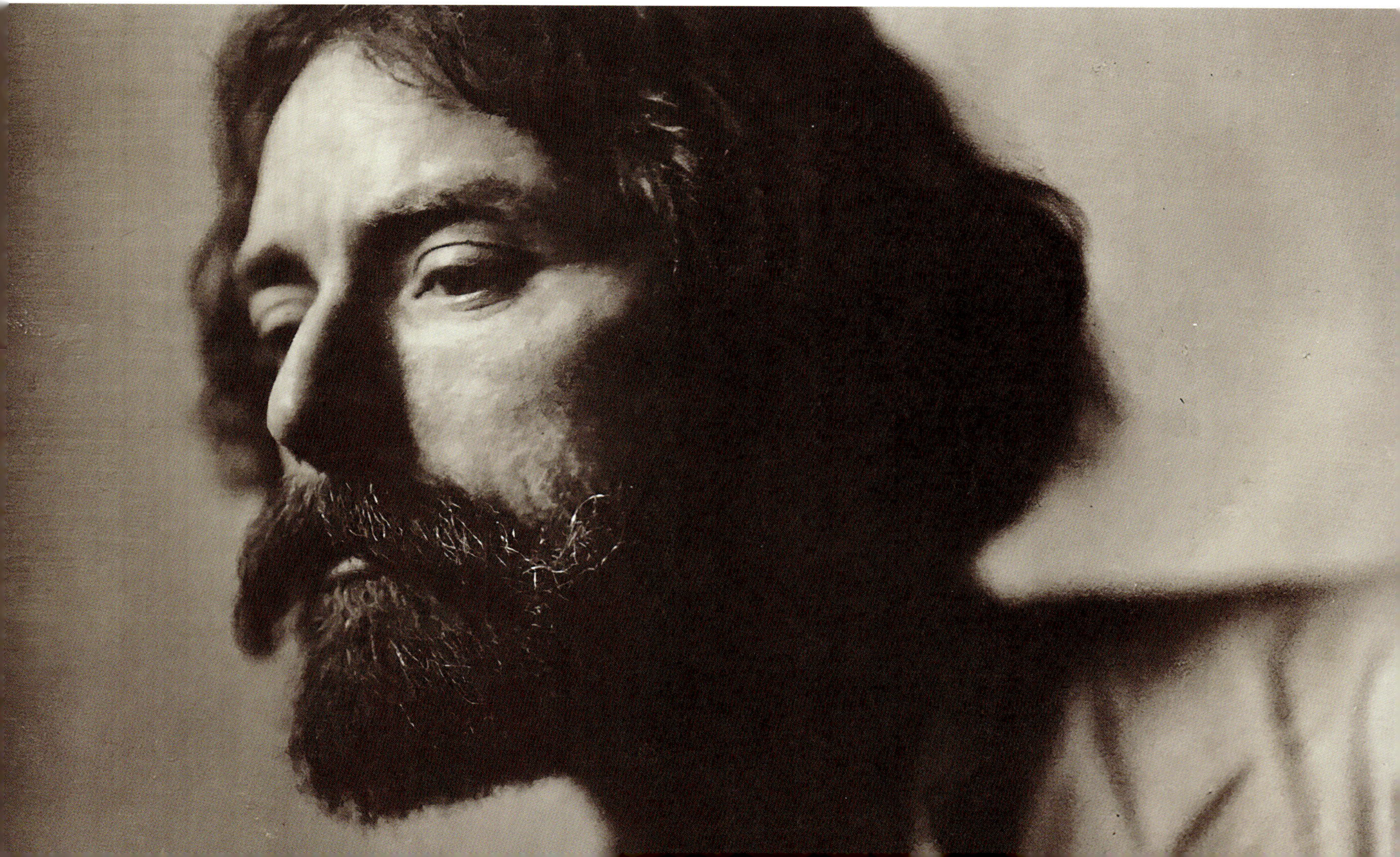

During 1907, painter and printmaker Walter Sickert (1860–1942) rented studio space at 19 Fitzroy Street, where he hosted Saturday afternoon 'at homes' for local artists and writers, to talk art, philosophy and ideas, and sell work to prospective buyers. Everyone contributed a small amount towards rent in return for exhibiting works. Known as the Fitzroy Street Group, these gatherings soon gained renown. Derwent and Dick, whose social and artistic network was growing, were early participants.

As the pair returned for their final year at the Slade, they met Augustus John, either through Fitzrovia connections, or at the Slade, where he had returned to take life drawing classes. Augustus had studied there in the 1890s, but returned to London from Paris in 1907, after his wife Ida died, moving after a short stay in Cheyne Walk to 8 Fitzroy Street (which had housed James Whistler's studio). In December Dick also moved to number 8, a three-minute walk from Derwent's rented room. Dick and Derwent met another local, Slade student and flamboyant raconteur John Fothergill, who 'was not well off; but he was extremely generous, and of an adventurous spirit'.[1] Both Augustus and Fothergill welcomed the adulation of the two younger acolytes. For a time, 8 Fitzroy Street housed Dick and fellow painter Henry Lamb (1883–1960), with Augustus and family on the top floor. Walter Sickert was nearby; Spencer Gore (1878–1914) had his studio at number 21, and Albert Rutherston (1881–1953) and Fothergill were at number 18 – both addresses also home to Derwent on occasion.[2]

However, of all Dick and Derwent's new acquaintances, it was Augustus that stood out. Already an artist of repute, he encouraged the two impressionable students, introducing them to collectors, gallerists and patrons, other artists, writers, models and hangers-on. An exciting and heady mix for the young colonial and his Welsh companion.

In autumn 1907, Derwent exhibited a work for the first time, *The Farm* (DL07.37), at the *39th Exhibition of Modern Pictures* of the New English Art Club (NEAC). Mac exhibited *The Coal Hole* and Dick submitted two works of Chepstow Castle,

Opposite:
Augustus John, 1909, photograph by Jacob Hilsdorf

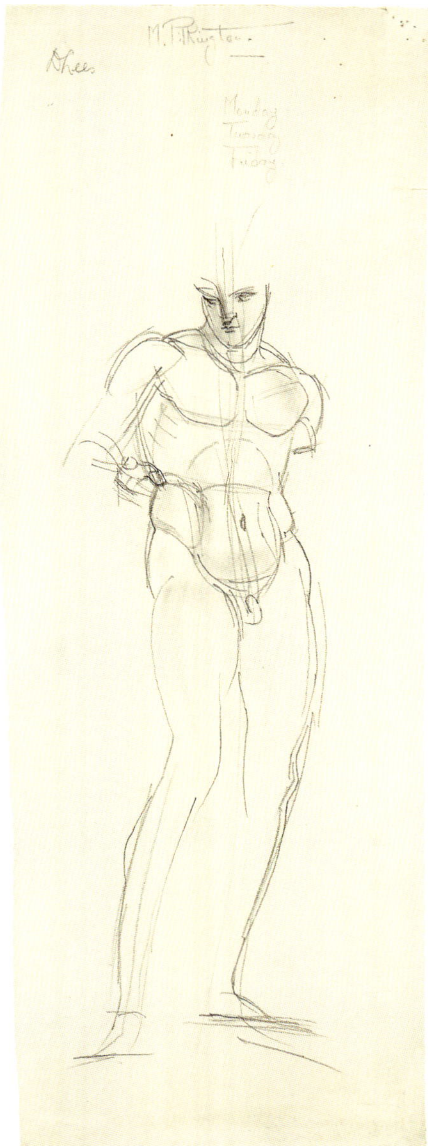

DL08.5
Derwent Lees, *Sketch of a Male Nude*, 1908–13, pencil on paper, 36.8 x 13.4 cm, The Whitworth, University of Manchester

from their first *plein air* trip together. For Derwent and Dick, it was the 'beginning of a pattern of collaboration that continued over the next six years, nurturing the efforts of both artists to develop a more modern style of landscape painting'.[3]

Derwent had few funds and little time to muse or contemplate his art; however, in October 1907 he was thrown a lifeline. Of all the students and graduates, Henry Tonks chose Derwent, though still a student, to be the Slade's only Assistant Drawing Master, reporting directly to him and thereby reducing his own teaching load from three to two days a week.[4] Perhaps Derwent's prize works impressed Tonks. Derwent was diligent and hard-working, but most importantly for Tonks, he was humble and had exceptional drawing talent.

Derwent was now both student and teacher. Head of School, Professor Fred Brown, reported the appointment to the University Council, and at the end of the academic year the position was renewed with more days per week added. For Derwent this was a small but vital term-time wage. Self-disciplined, and more than happy with the rigorous repetition of imparting classical and life drawing techniques, he was now partially self-supporting. Derwent was the youngest Slade staff member by some 20 years, and the first Slade student to join the staff on an ongoing basis since the start of Brown's tenure in 1893. Two anatomical instruction sketches by Derwent (DL08.5–6) were kept by Margaret Pilkington (1891–1974, Slade student 1913–14), later Honorary Director of the Whitworth Art Gallery. Derwent's class days are pencilled at the top of one of the works.

Dick's Christmas 1907 letter to Derwent's brother Gilbert in Australia reported on their financial prospects. Derwent had two commissions for drawings and the Assistant Drawing position one day a week, while Mac was giving painting lessons to 'some young ladey [*sic*] at 10/- a lesson once a week',[5] had sold some works and had his scholarship fund. Dick had both a scholarship and parental support. As the year closed, life was full of promise. The annual Slade Fancy Dress Ball rounded off the year.

By the April 1908 three-week Easter holiday, the young art students found themselves with just months to complete their portfolios to become Slade graduates. There was now a steady rhythm to Derwent's life, but Easter was tough, as Mac's mother died on 9 April. It was Good Friday, and Dick was in France, so Derwent tended to his close friend, who had now lost both parents.

Mac exhibited little over the following year but continued as part-time drawing master to the young daughter of Lord Ribblesdale, leaving London after graduation for Lancashire's Ribble Valley estate. He spent at least a year in the district, including taking time out to visit former Slade colleague and close friend, Gerald Summers, at Stalybridge. In 1910, Mac moved to the village of Bourton, Shrivenham, as artist-in-residence to the Butler family.[6] This was the home of Cyril K. Butler (1864–1936), who was later variously Chairman, Secretary and Treasurer of the Contemporary Art Society, and a patron. During the First World War, Derwent would also stay as artist-in-residence at Bourton House. Mac and Lees both needed a regular salary; both would become art teachers, and would see less of each other after graduation.

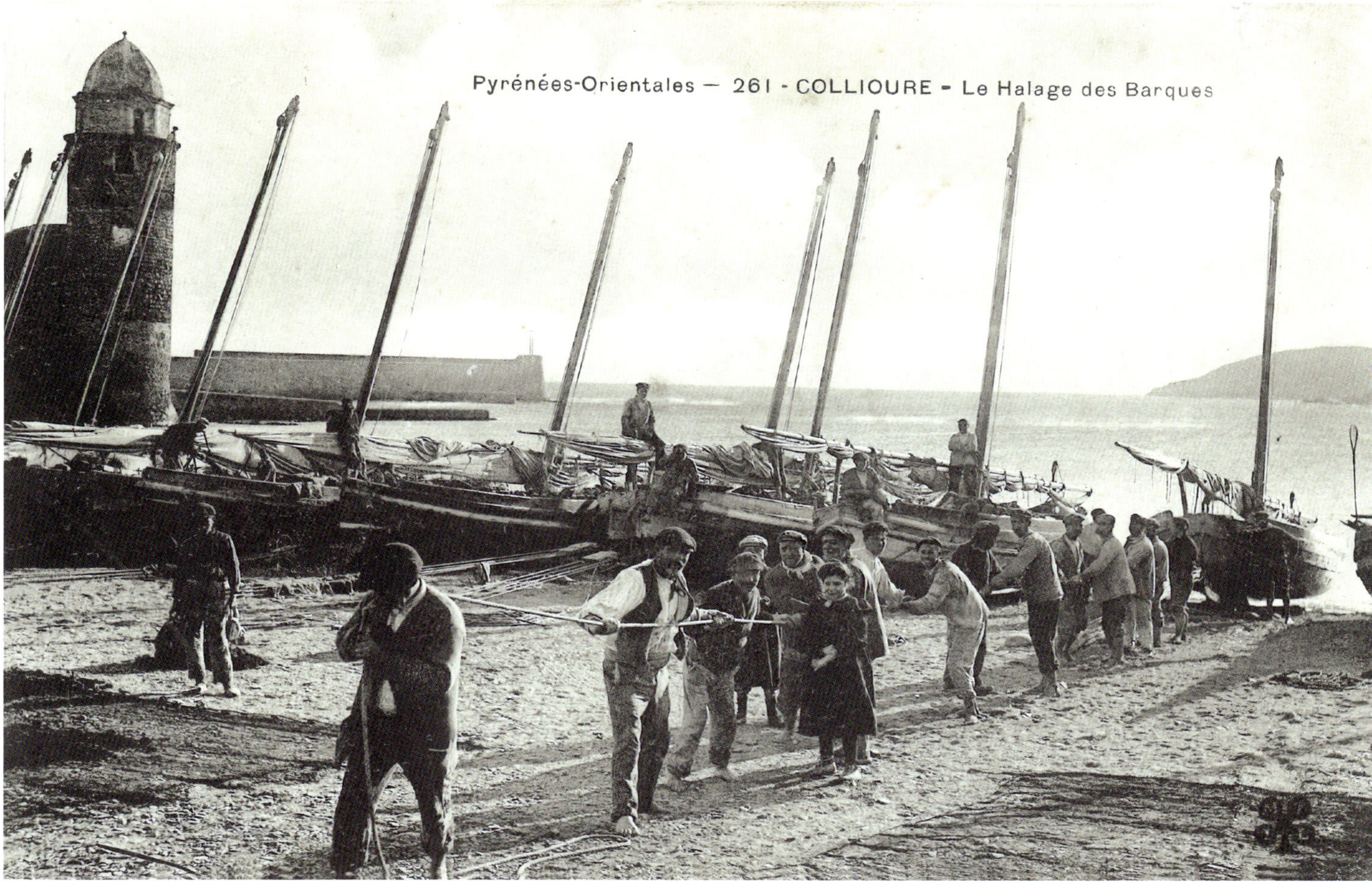

Beaching a Catalan fishing boat, Collioure, c.1905, postcard, France

DICK IN CATALONIA

During the 1908 Easter holiday Dick, accompanied by Fothergill, made his first trip to the south of France, to a region that would ignite in him a deep passion for mountain landscapes. Two years later Derwent would discover the same place, also finding it transformational.

After painting in the Aveyron region around Bozouls, Dick and Fothergill arrived in the coastal village of Collioure in early spring. The weather was variable and the village calm. The villagers, for whom the sea and hills were their livelihood, were setting up for the season, dyeing and mending nets and refitting their *barques* (Catalan fishing boats). Fishing in summer was followed by vineyard work, then winemaking and cork harvesting in autumn and winter, when the dismantled *barques* were beached high beyond the surge of tide and storm. With the first run of migrating sardines, the heavy boats were pulled down to the water's edge, requiring the strength of at least six men, and the beach became a place of work, not pleasure.

The two artists are likely to have met young Mathieu Muxart, just as Henri Matisse had done. Matisse had left Collioure six months before Dick and Fothergill arrived; it had been his third summer in the village since he and André Derain first forged a new art style, to be called Fauvism, based around vibrant colours,

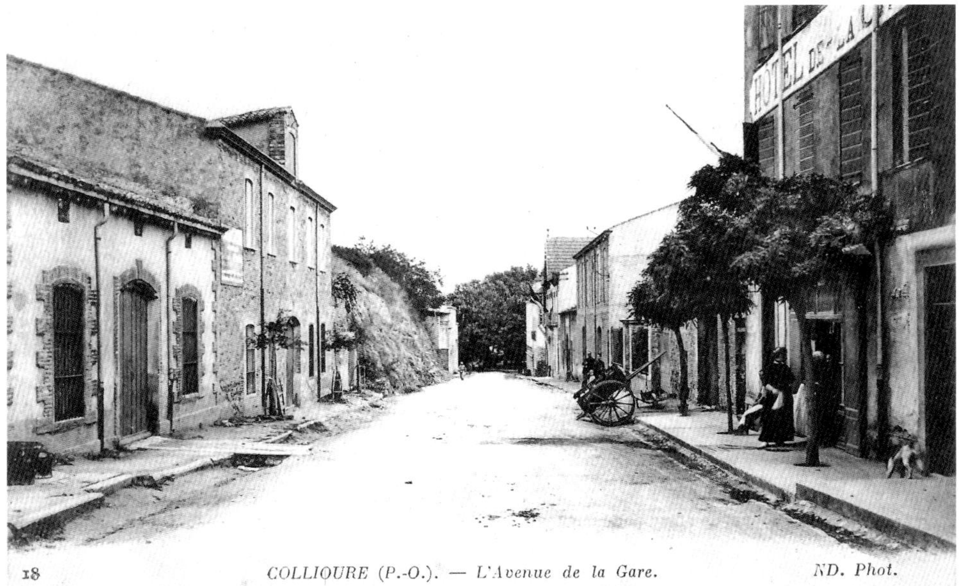

Hotel de la Gare, Collioure, c.1910, postcard, France

strong brushstrokes and bold representational forms. Matisse would visit again, two months before Derwent's arrival in July 1910.[7]

Muxart worked at the village's only hotel, located between the train station and the market square. He acted as Matisse's local guide in 1905, later recounting that he was the first painter to stay at the village's Hotel de la Gare, which previously lodged only travelling salesmen or railway men.[8] Muxart may have shown the two Slade artists around, as Dick's scenes mimic those of earlier visiting artists. He painted at the back of the village on Ernest Py's Ambeille Hill, on the slope by Fort Miradou, on the port's breakwater, and in the former garden of renowned botanist Charles Naudin (1815–99). These well-established painting sites were less than ten minutes from the hotel.[9]

Later, after the First World War, in 1919, Ian Strang (1886–1952), Derwent's close friend and Slade alumnus, would visit the now-famed village, and a few years later Slade classmates Rudolph Ihlee and Edgar Hereford would come to live there, with Hereford painting Naudin's garden, just as Dick, Matisse and Aristide Maillol (1861–1944) had done before him.

Fothergill later quipped that he chose Collioure for his and Dick's 1908 trip because 'it looked so good on the map',[10] but the village had been a well-known artists' haven for at least half a century, with works exhibited in Paris, Perpignan and Barcelona long before Matisse and Derain displayed their revolutionary Fauvist paintings. It seems that Dick and Fothergill were merely following the stir in the wake of the Paris 1905 *Salon d'Automne* exhibition.

Early painters of Collioure included Paul Signac, Adolphe Appian, Henri-Edmond Cross, Henri Manguin, Louis Valtat, Louis Codet, Charles Camoin and Max Monier de la Sizeranne, who exhibited *Le Port de Collioure* in spring 1868 at Paris's Palais des Champs-Élysées along with the Artistes Roussillonnais group. This group consisted of George-Daniel de Monfreid, Louis Bausil, Gustave Violet and Maillol, who became a close friend of Matisse, as well as Maillol's friend Étienne Terrus.[11]

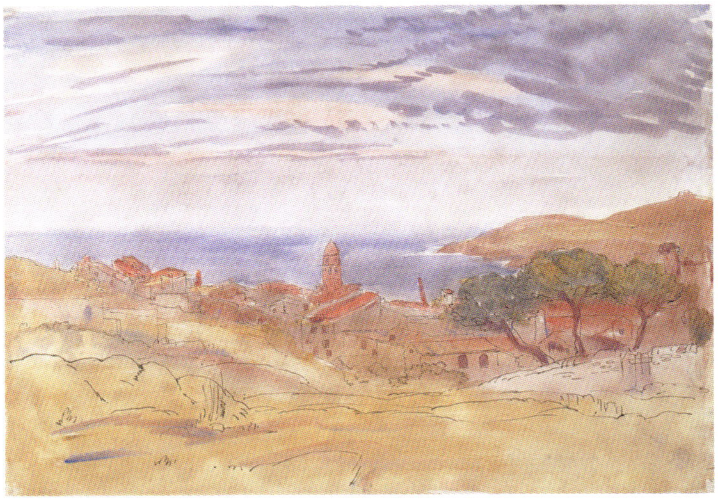

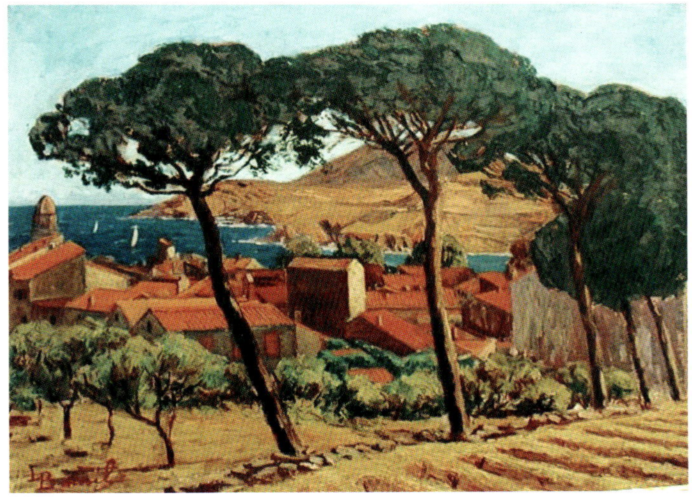

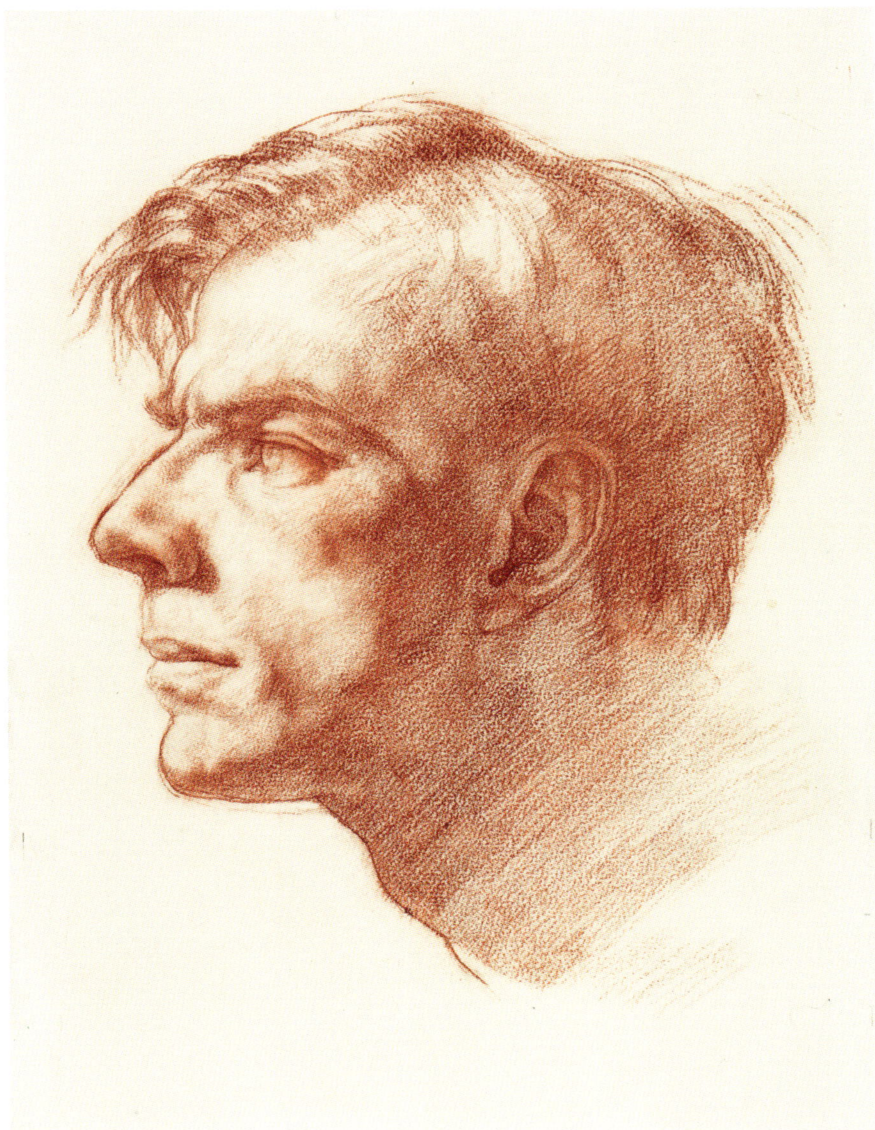

Above left:
James Dickson Innes, *Collioure*, c.1908, watercolour and ink on paper, 27.9 x 38.8 cm, Amgueddfa Cymru – National Museum Wales, Cardiff

Above right:
Louis Bausil, *Collioure*, 1908, oil on canvas, 60 x 81 cm, Private Collection

Right:
DL07.26
Derwent Lees, *Portrait of J.R. Fothergill, Esq. / Portrait Head*, 1907, red chalk on paper, 38.5 x 28.5 cm, UCL Art Museum

Dick's south of France excursion yielded more than a dozen watercolours and oils. Fothergill exclaimed that had they not visited Collioure, 'we might have had in Innes just one more exponent of pale English sunshine and veiled charm'.[12] However, Dick returned to London unwell, then home to Wales, where he was diagnosed with tuberculosis. In June he wrote to Fothergill saying that he was coming to London to see a specialist, but to keep this 'a secret as I only want to see you and Lees'.[13] He had already written to Derwent of his plans while recommending places in Wales where Derwent may like to paint.

Later that year Derwent moved to Dick's former Chelsea house at 125 Cheyne Walk,[14] and for the next few years he would shift back and forth between bohemian Chelsea and Fitzrovia, until he settled at 21 Fitzroy Square.

OF PRIZES, A MODEL AND CLUBS

In late June, 'Dick, Mac and Lees' completed their final student portfolio submissions. Much emphasis was placed on Professor Brown's Summer Competition, for which he set the subjects for a student to 'display all that he has learnt in the school of drawing and painting from the life, of the setting of figures in space, of the design and construction of a picture, and he is afforded also the scope for original imaginative creation'.[15] Augustus had won the 1898 prize, Derwent's friends Randolph Schwabe and Ian Strang were the 1905 recipients, and it was awarded to Dick in 1908. The themes were often repeated, with *Samson Betrayed by Delilah* on Brown's rotating subject list.

One such 1908 student work by Derwent, *Samson and Delilah* (DL08.4), is housed at the Art Gallery of Ballarat, Australia, and the female model in the drawing is Edith Harriet Price (1890–1984), who would later become Derwent's wife. She modelled regularly for Augustus and Derwent from about 1908, initially calling herself Edith Ashley before later settling on Lyndra as her professional name (sometimes misspelt Lindra, Linda, Lynda and Lrndra). It seems her family constantly changed names. Edith's mother had a somewhat cavalier attitude towards her surname, changing from Price to Ashley-Price, then to Pierce after a second marriage. Still later she was Price-Pierce, then Gilbert-Price on occasion, before reverting to Ashley-Price after the war, then back to Price. Edith's oldest sister Alice May Price (1885–1967) was also liberal with her name, marrying using her stage name, Renee Ashley. The surname Ashley was also used by other members of Edith's family on and off until the early 1920s.

Dick and Derwent had now become founding members of the Friday Club, established by Vanessa Stephen (1879–1961), sister of Virginia Woolf and later a key figure in the Bloomsbury Group. This was an art conversation and exhibiting group which she formed in the year they started at the Slade. It was a bold undertaking for a 25-year-old female at the turn of the century. By 1904, she had lost her parents and would soon marry the art critic Clive Bell (1881–1964). The Club's early members were her friends from the Royal Academy schools and the Slade. Initially, it was little more than an informal gathering of young art students; they held talks about art and organised an annual fancy dress dance in Regent Park's Botanical Gardens. Derwent was faithful to the Club for many years, exhibiting with them from 1908 to 1915, and even joining their jury and hanging committee from 1912 to 1914.[16]

Derwent's close friend Essil Elmslie (1880–1952), of whom he drew several portraits and interior figures, became the Club secretary when Vanessa stopped exhibiting in 1913. A letter from Vanessa to Duncan Grant (1885–1978) suggests that Essil was probably already managing the Club's activities by mid-1910, as Vanessa felt that amateur artists were diluting the Club's purpose.[17] Essil was slightly older than Derwent and had studied at the Slade before him, however he likely knew her and her family quite well. Essil's mother was Australian and had married a Scottish sea captain in Australia, and as a young child Essil had visited there. Away from the Slade, Derwent rarely did nude studies, however, in late 1909 and into 1910, he did nude drawings of Essil, a small one of which he inscribed and gave to her (DL09.29), suggesting that they may have been intimates for a time. The two were to remain close friends.

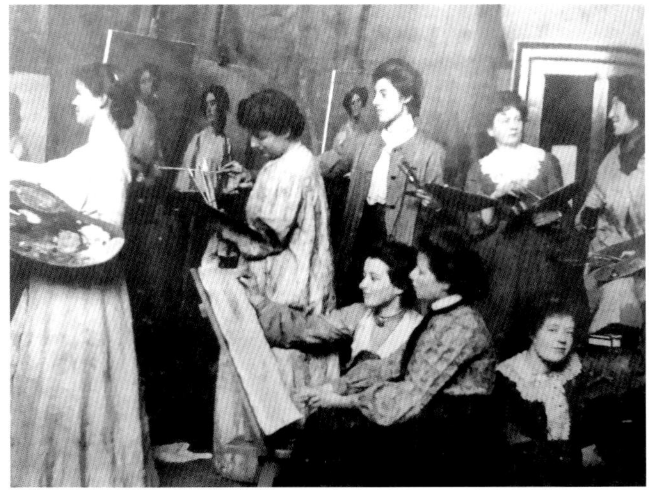

Essil Elmslie in the Slade painting studio, c.1904, photographer unknown

Essil (far left) received 2nd prize in Head Painting, 1901, and the Melvill Nettleship Prize for Figure Composition, 1905

Derwent was loyal, only ever working for one institution, the Slade, and belonging only to the NEAC, the Fitzroy Street Group (which later merged into the London Group) and the Friday Club. He mainly showed his work at the NEAC members' exhibitions, often held at the Chenil Gallery, although he remained in close contact with his Friday Club friends, often displaying works at their exhibitions. Most Friday Club shows were held at the Alpine Club rooms in Mayfair, but during the Club's early years there was a constant hunt for gallery space. This was initially assuaged by New Zealander John Baillie at his London gallery, where, in 1908, Derwent met landscape artist and Club member Robert Bevan (1865–1925). Bevan mounted his first one-man show at the Baillie Gallery in May, followed by the Friday Club's *Exhibition and Paintings of Still Life* in June, where Dick and Derwent hung work alongside artists such as Pierre-Auguste Renoir and Camille Pissarro.[18]

Bevan was also part of Sickert's Fitzroy Street Group 'at homes', fast becoming an increasingly important part of the progressive London artistic scene. Of these gatherings, Albert Rutherston wrote that, 'we had many visitors and a steady sale of work by all of us resulted. Our Saturday afternoons became well-established, too, in the social sense.'[19]

> There was an appetising smell of tea and pigment as you ascended to a glorious afternoon of pictures and of talk. Easels and chairs faced the fireplace with a serried stack of canvases against the wall. Six works or more of an individual painter were extricated in turn, each Fitzroyalist displaying his quota or having it displayed for him by the untiring Gore.[20]

These gatherings, along with the clubs and exhibiting societies, were an economic and social lifeline for many artists, creating links with dealers, gallery owners and collectors. It was a surprisingly successful strategy, borne of financial need, yet fostering an acceptance of artistic differences.

4 A NEW BEGINNING 1908–10

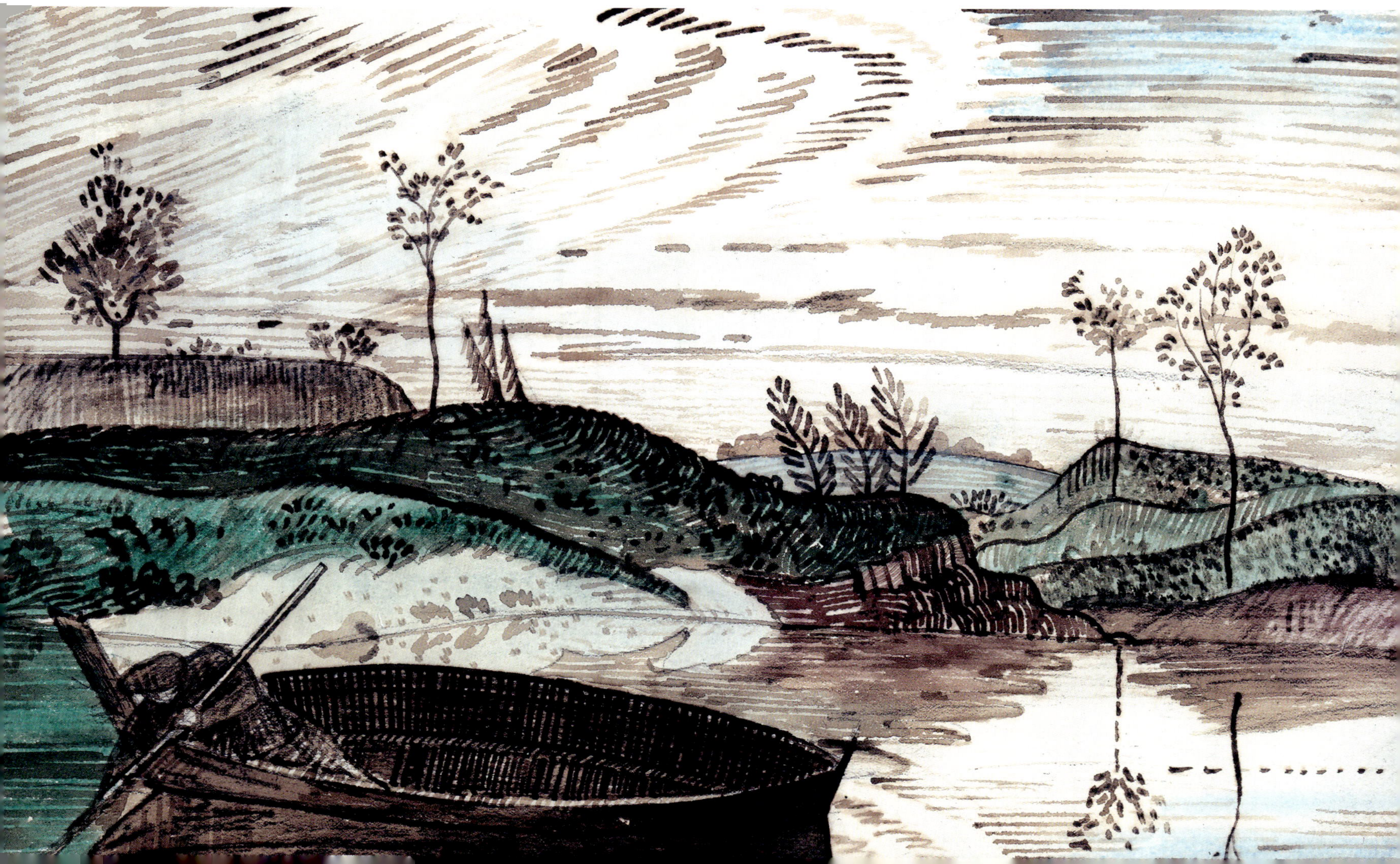

Derwent was now a Slade graduate. During the summer of 1908 he was formally appointed as the Slade's Assistant Drawing Master and in August appeared on the annual staff list.[1] It is unlikely that he worked full time, as he struggled to survive financially even though his Slade wage was augmented by an allowance from his father. Randolph Schwabe later revealed that Derwent 'lived mostly at that time on a small allowance from his father'.[2] His principal free time consisted of the Christmas and Easter term breaks and the long summer holiday, during which he had to paint, sell work and secure commissions to build his reputation.

Derwent spent part of the 1908 holiday season at gallery openings and was regaled by the grandest of public fairs, the immensely popular Franco-British Exhibition in London. More than eight million visitors flocked to over 100 exhibition buildings and pavilions which were connected by ornate arches, bridges, waterways and an artificial lake. He also travelled to France,[3] though with whom or where is unknown. However, a likely work from the trip may be the detailed drawing of Chateau Gaillard at Les Andelys (DL09.37), later pasted into Dick's 1908–9 scrapbook (a portfolio containing a collection of various small drawings and paintings by friends and other artists) held at the Tate. Dick spent much of the summer travelling along the southern English coast, to the Isle of Wight catching up with his brothers.

By late September, both Derwent and Dick were back in London, where Dick reported to John Fothergill that Derwent had 'done some realey [*sic*] wonderfull [*sic*] drawings of himself with a beard (he looks exactley [*sic*] like John and it of cource [*sic*] hides the same defect of receding chin that John's beard does) . . . he has had his beard shaved off, so I did not see him with it'.[4]

The red chalk *Self Portrait* (DL08.12) to which he refers shows a relaxed Derwent sporting a loose scruffy beard, emulating Augustus John in both look and art. The similarity in appearance and style is striking, and Dick hoped that with good health and time, his former classmate would become 'unjohney [*sic*]'.[5] Derwent was heavily influenced by Augustus, to whom he was a willing apprentice. It is thanks to him that the young Australian made his initial steps from controlled, academic drawing

Opposite:
DL09.14 (detail)
Derwent Lees, *The Bsura, Poland / On the Burza River*, 1909

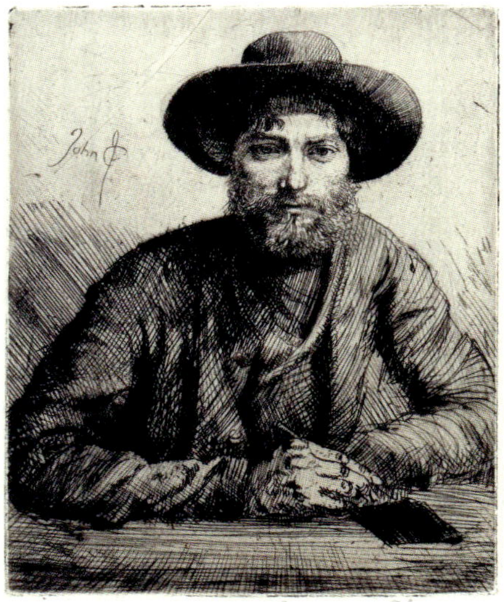

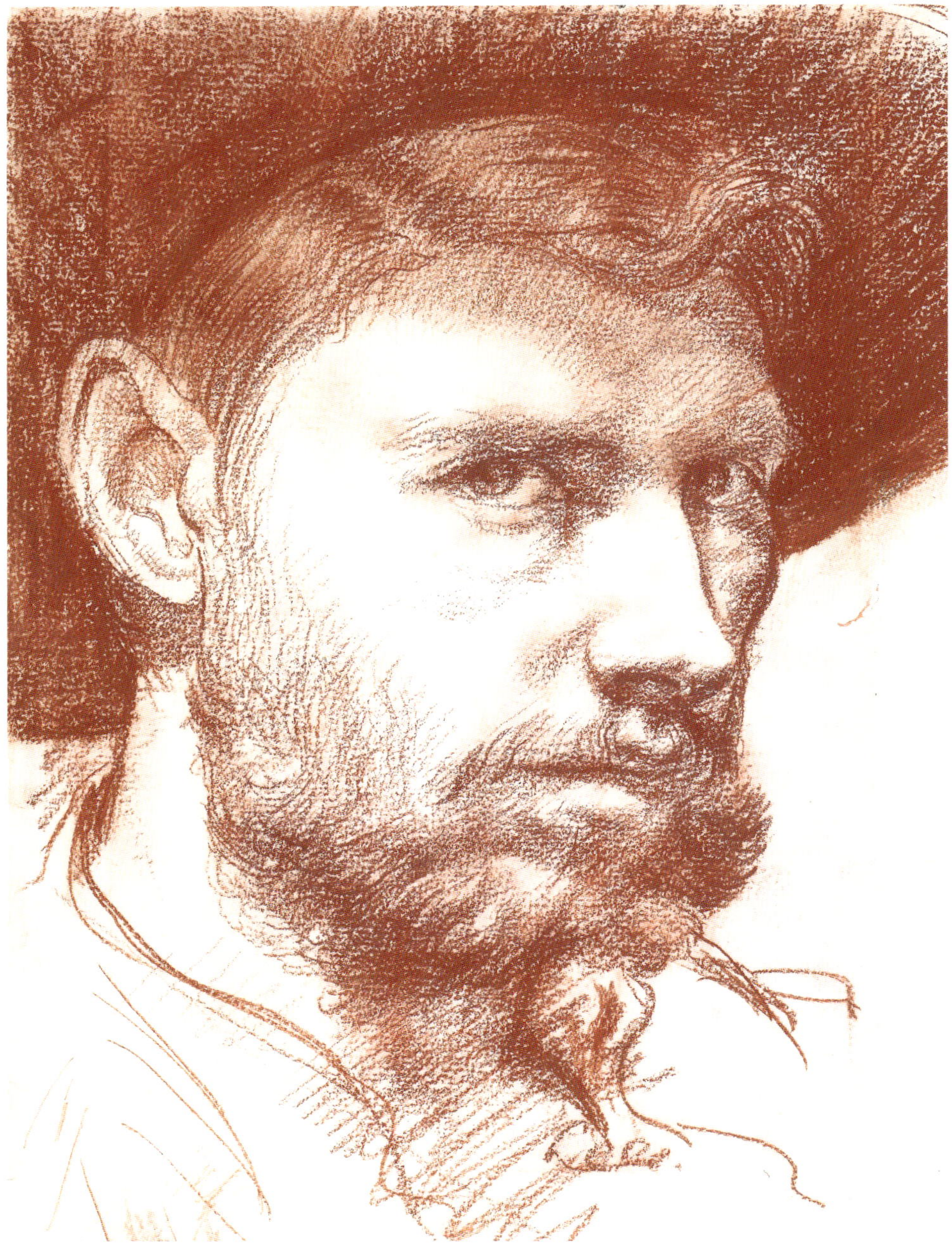

Left:
Augustus John, *Portrait of the Artist: Bust, in a Hat, Etching*, c.1902, etching on paper, 12.6 x 10.4 cm (plate), Fitzwilliam Museum, University of Cambridge

Right:
DL08.12
Derwent Lees, *Self Portrait*, c.1908, red chalk on paper, 26.1 x 22.2 cm, National Gallery of Victoria, Melbourne

to looser, more experimental work. Derwent continued in this role of Augustus's understudy for a decade, their relationship deepening into a friendship of respect and shared intellect.

At the end of the Second World War, some 15 years after Derwent's death, Schwabe, the then Slade Professor, attended a London exhibition, among which was Derwent's 1908 *Self Portrait*. Schwabe wrote in his diary that he 'bought a sanguine self-portrait of Lees, with a beard, for £20, for Australia, supposing that they may be interested in him as Australian-born. The drawing is like, though he did not usually wear a beard.'[6] True to his words, Schwabe offered it to John McDonnell (1904–64), newly appointed London adviser to Melbourne's National Gallery of Victoria, who purchased it through the Felton Bequest. It was a touching gesture for a departed friend; Schwabe quietly suggesting that Australia 'might one day know him'. By then in poor health, Schwabe was to die the following September.

During 1907 and 1908, Derwent had done many portrait studies, one of which was of Fothergill, created at the height of his and Dick's friendship with him. The meticulously detailed work captures the contours and forms of his face in soft iron-red tones. Not long after, a dispute between Fothergill and Dick ended the young artists' association with the older bon vivant. It seems that Fothergill's apparent romantic attraction to Dick had not been reciprocated.

In May 1909, Derwent exhibited the *Portrait of J.R. Fothergill, Esq.* and *Portrait of the Author* (DL07.26, DL08.11) at the New English Art Club (NEAC) exhibition, along with two other drawings from the Song of Solomon (DL09.32–3).[7]

CLOSE COLLABORATIONS

Dick had left academia in mid-1908, only to be offered work back at the Slade in October. He was exhausted from a full summer social and travelling calendar that followed on the heels of his initial diagnosis. He accepted the position, but a relapse soon followed, and he resigned, telling Fothergill that 'I got into such a stale condition at the Slade and this entire change has quite wakened me up again . . . I wrote to him [Professor Fred Brown] thanking him for his patience and tolerance to me and telling him I could not come back to the Slade.'[8] He recuperated at St Ives in Cornwall, his mother at his side.

A detailed ink, watercolour and pastel interior of the Alhambra Theatre, *The Alhambra* (DL08.9, held at the Tate), has been jointly attributed to both Derwent and Dick. However, with further research,[9] it is considered to be a work solely by Derwent, as is the near identical work *The Alhambra London* (DL08.24). The Australian's particular skill in rendering the human form is evident, as well as the complex scene which captures numerous, precisely drawn theatregoers.

In early 1909, Derwent and Dick did collaborate on one work at St Ives (DL09.5, discussed below). Derwent was visiting over Christmas and the New Year, then again at Easter. The ill and often labile Dick wrote to Fothergill after the New Year visit, saying that Derwent 'found me bad tempered but is coming again some time fairly soon so it could not have been very bad. Naturally I thought him rather stupid too. These things always go both ways.'[10] The sentiment was soon forgotten, as Dick's next letter to Fothergill reported that 'I am enormously pleased to hear that Lees gets on so well'.[11] On one trip to visit his consumptive friend, Derwent painted a small watercolour, *Coast at St Ives* (DL09.7), later pasted into Dick's scrapbook. This early, explorative, almost tentative landscape suggests that Derwent still saw himself largely as a draughtsman and assistant drawing master.

Soon after his 1907 return from Paris, Augustus had started regularly drawing the young model Edith Ashley (née Price), scribbling her name under one portrait and a figure work. It was probably at the Slade (where he often visited and sat in on life classes) that he met her, along with Derwent and Dick, while she was possibly modelling there. An early nude study of Edith by Augustus also shows all

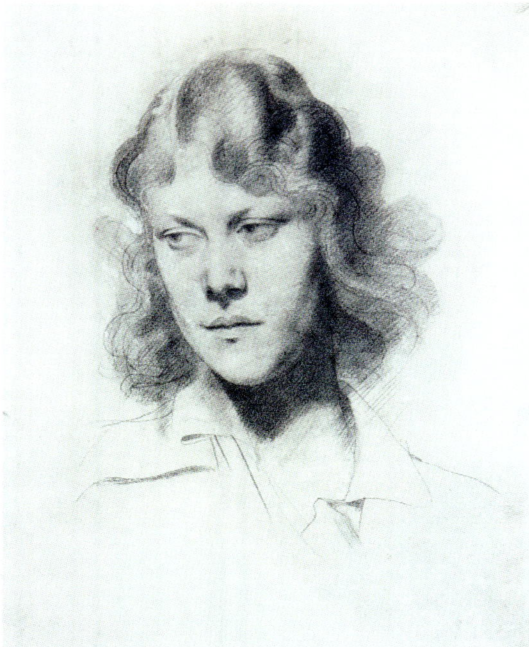

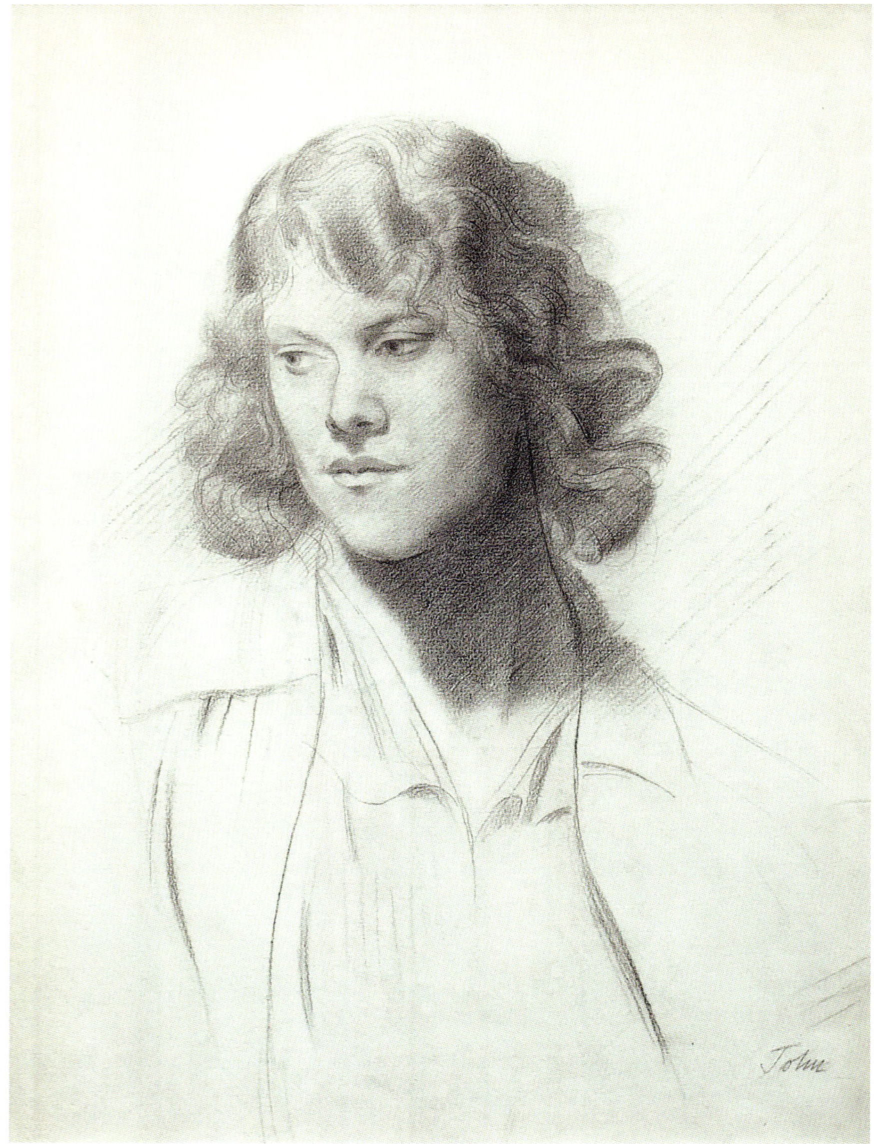

Left:
DL13.68
Derwent Lees, *Portrait Study*, c.1913, pencil on paper, 37 x 28 cm, Private Collection

Right:
Augustus John, *Portrait of Edith Lees*, c.1913, pencil on paper, 34.3 x 24.4 cm, Piano Nobile Gallery, London

the hallmarks of Henry Tonks's teaching. Augustus drew many models during the pre-war years, with some later even taking the train to north Wales from London to pose, partly draped, in the cold mountain air. Others paid their own fare to model at his Dorset home, only to be met by Dorelia McNeill (1881–1969), his common-law wife and life companion, who calmly looked one young beauty up and down and, without a word, sent her straight back to London.[12]

Drawing from life was one of the most coveted subjects in the Slade curriculum. The School spent a generous £150 to £180 annually employing male and female models to pose daily, nude or part-clothed. Edith turned 18 at the start of the 1908–9 academic year, and she would become one of Augustus's and Derwent's principal models for the next five or more years.

Edith had a full, sinuous and youthful figure with an oval face, strong chin and squarish jawline, and long wavy hair. Dick also knew her but loathed drawing the human form. According to Fothergill, he could neither spell nor represent the human figure; 'no life drawings by him remain and the only hint of his skill in this area is a feeble, blocked diagram of a human leg in one letter'.[13]

Augustus and Derwent were accomplished draughtsmen, both revelling in the complexities and subtleties of the human face and body, Derwent drawing 'with his usual studied accuracy'.[14] More than 50 works by Augustus feature Edith, while Derwent was to create more than 70 portraits, sketches or figure works of her. Over a few short years he obsessively portrayed Edith in pencil and ink drawings, oils, etchings and literary illustrations, in portraits, nudes, mythological scenes and as a figure in many of his landscapes. Interestingly none show her ears and very few are nudes. Many of Derwent's early drawings capture his models in upward or side-facing poses, perhaps suggesting a lack of confidence in directly facing his subject.

Through winter 1908 and into the spring of 1909 Dick was trapped convalescing in Cornwall. Derwent spent more time with Augustus and one result of this period was a series of pencil portraits of Edith by both artists (e.g. DL09.24–7). The popular London model Beatrice Stewart also posed for them, as she had for John Singer Sargent. In 1912, she became the figure of Adrian Jones's *Peace Descending on the Quadriga of War* on the Wellington Arch at Hyde Park Corner. Later, around 1913–14, Derwent and Augustus also drew similar pencil portraits of close friend and artist Nora Summers (DL14.22).[15]

The two men explored their mutual love and talent for portraiture and figure composition over several years, even etching self-portraits together after the First World War. Some works are identical in composition, with the same model holding the same pose in the same clothes and light. Some models were friends, some professional sitters, some became lovers. They drew and painted models together on and off until 1914.

While Derwent occasionally sketched and drew Edith until late 1909, then repeatedly from late 1912 (by then she was referring to herself as Lyndra), he also drew other female artist friends – Elsie McNaught (1886–1987; DL09.28), who also drew him, Ethel (DL11.57–60) and Louisa Alice Elder (DL11.55–6, 63), Essil Elmslie (DL09.29, DL11.51–4), 'Hetty' (DL11.62), 'Emma' (DL11.61), Elizabeth Lipczinski (1882–1969; DL11.8, 17, 23–4) and, later, he painted Lady Diana Manners (1892–1986; DL15.9), Grace, Lady Curzon (1879–1958),[16] Lady Louisa Kendall Butler (1872–1944; DL16.13) and Margherita Scott-Ellis, Lady Howard de Walden (1890–1974; DL18.1, 3).

IN CORNWALL

In a series of letters during the first months of 1909, Dick expounded his frustration at being infirm.[17] In moments of petulance, and despite acknowledging his own bad temper, he lashed out at Derwent. In other letters he sang Derwent's praises, making ribald comments about his mate's popularity with the ladies now that he was part of the Slade staff. Dick's fluctuating moods appear to have dominated this period of their relationship.

In one letter before Derwent visited, Dick complained to Fothergill:

> you told me Lees had quite blossomed out since I left London. Unluckily he has already begun to decay in parts . . . he tells me 'it is a great trouble and waste of time to answer invitations' and that he does not see why he should answer me. He then tells me that I am very feeble and that my last letter 'made him vomit'.[18]

Derwent's 'vomit' remark perhaps shows his laconic Australian sense of humour in response to Dick's detailed description of his malady. Dick then wrote that Derwent's work 'is a great improvement one oil painting being very sincere and sound and the w.c.'s [watercolours] are much better . . . he has done some realey [*sic*] wonderfull [*sic*] drawings of himself'.[19]

Dick often made envious snipes at his closest friends. He said of Mac that, 'there realy [*sic*] does seem something lothsome [*sic*] about all the carreying [*sic*] on of his life'.[20] Then he turned to Derwent's need for mentors. Perhaps jealous of his friend's freedom, he irascibly complained to Fothergill about Derwent's social bluntness in 'showing his backside to people', but that 'at least shews [*sic*] that he has given up trying to imitate you'.[21] This referred to the portrait Derwent drew of Fothergill, subsequently hung at the 1909 NEAC show. Fellow artist Albert Rutherston confirmed Fothergill and Derwent's artistic closeness in a letter, saying that he hoped Fothergill and Derwent 'will do some good work'.[22]

There was some truth to Dick's comment about Derwent's mentor-seeking, with the latter turning his attention from Fothergill to Augustus. Despite occasional blunt words, however, their friendship persisted, with Dick ending one letter declaring that he is 'glad Lees is well'.[23] In another, he made positive remarks about Derwent's abilities, while alluding to his friend's fragility, 'I am sure granted health and a little more time he will do some wonder-full [*sic*] stuff'.[24]

Dick and Derwent had a productive time sketching and painting scenes together on the Cornish foreshore. They co-created at least one painting, *The Dancers* (aka *The Sirens*, DL09.5), inscribed and co-signed 'D. Leesinnes 09'. Nubile 'sirens' lure hapless sailors to their doom. This allegorical work, perhaps led by Derwent (who enjoyed literature and philosophical debate and was well versed in the classics from his Australian education), would have been stimulated by their visit to the 'shipwreck coast'. There are two versions of this scene, one with the sirens singing with a bat hovering overhead, a Victorian harbinger of doom (DL09.5). In the second, they beseech a passing boat (a Mediterranean felucca). The latter work (*Drawing – Sirens*, DL09.4), and two preparatory sketches (DL09.2–3; pasted into Dick's student scrapbook held at the Tate)[25] were created by Derwent.

Derwent returned to St Ives during the 1909 Easter break, accompanied by Stephen Stokowski (1883–?), a student living in Fitzrovia who had started at the Slade two years after him.[26] Both Stephen and artist Stanisława de Karlowska (1876–1952), Robert Bevan's wife (whom Derwent had met the previous summer), were born on the outskirts of Lowicz near Warsaw, Poland, and studied at the Cracow School of Art. Mac may have also joined them during a break from his painting master duties. It seems that he and Dick may not have got along so well, as Dick seldom

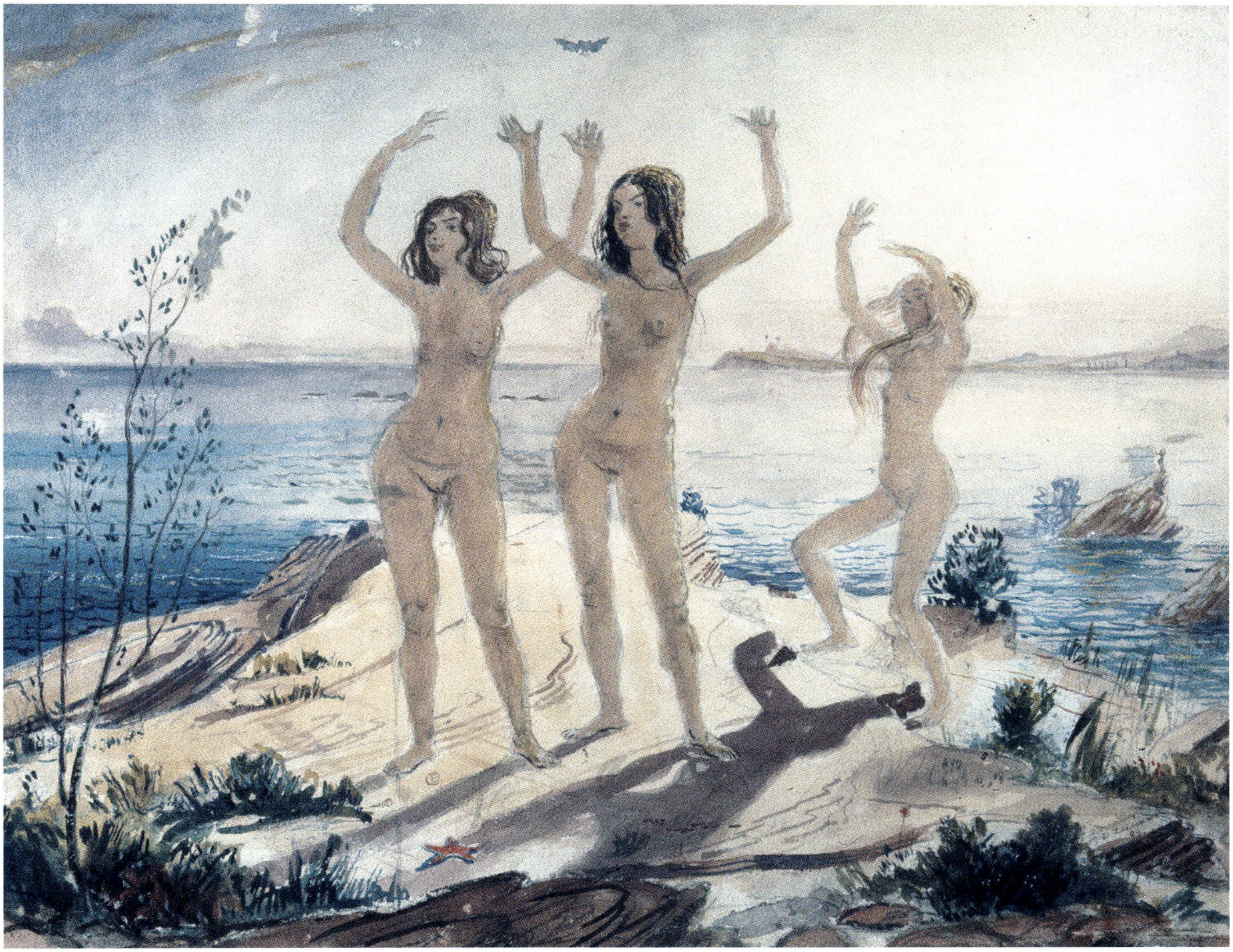

DL09.5
Derwent Lees and James Dickson Innes, *The Dancers / The Sirens*, 1909, watercolour on paper, 38.7 x 48.3 cm, Private Collection

wrote kindly about their former classmate. In June 1908 he scolded Fothergill, saying it was 'unkinde [*sic*] of you to send me the piece of paper Maclaren had been sniveling on', and his 1909 letters are equally unpleasant.[27]

TO POLAND THEN DORSET

By June 1909, Derwent had completed his first full year as the Slade Assistant Drawing Master. He was well liked by students and respected by fellow staff. Effortless in drawing and caring for his students, his generosity of spirit was reciprocated with solid friendships and support. The July 1909 Dean's Report presented to the Professorial meeting noted that 'the Slade School of Fine Art has improved or at least well sustained its standard. A new Assistant, Mr D. Lees, has been appointed.'[28] His position was renewed, and for the first time he had a summer off in which to take an extended painting trip, knowing that he could return to the security of his part-time position. The holiday was punctuated by the mid-August nuptials of his cousin, Hugh Lowder-Lees, in London, which he attended with his father and stepmother. Hugh, born in New Zealand, would return there with his English-born wife. He, like Derwent's brother Gilbert and other family members, worked for the meat exporting firm, Gordon Woodroffe.

The highlight of Derwent's summer was a painting holiday to north-west Poland at the invitation of Stephen Stokowski, probably also accompanying Robert Bevan and Stanisława (Stasia). This was Derwent's first extended painting trip abroad and his first serious move from the classroom to *plein air*, working alongside Stephen around his home village of Sobota, perhaps also mentored by Stasia and Robert. Stasia was renowned for her warmth and generosity, and in London she regularly hosted afternoon teas for artists and friends. Robert, 20 years Derwent's senior, was a friend of Tonks, who was to become Derwent's chief 'life guide'.

For nearly a decade, the Bevans had spent their summers in Poland based at Stasia's parents' estate just north of Lowicz, at Wszeliwy, not far from Sobota. Derwent's paintings from his Polish trip capture riverbank scenes of the Bzura River in pen, ink wash and watercolour (DL09.8–15). The works show a careful observation of rolling clouds, movements of water, gentle undulations of the tilled land and the northern light, slowly breaking free of the rigours of the Slade. There are similarities in his treatment of trees in these works to his Cornish sketches; however, it was at Sobota that he first experimented with multiple works of the same scene, each rendered using different techniques, tones and colours. These beginnings of experimentation ultimately led to a unique style of painting of unusual viewpoints, in softened lines and forms and a distinct colour palette, which would reveal itself most strongly in his watercolours and colourful small oils of southern France and Dorset.

BACK IN LONDON

Derwent now readied himself for the next academic year while applying the finishing touches to works for the winter 1909 NEAC show. The hanging committee approved four of his paintings, of which three were Polish landscapes. Two of these works still carry Percy Young's stamp on the verso (DL09.11, 13). Located directly opposite the School, his business was well positioned as the Slade art materials supplier.

By late 1909, Dick was installed in a studio in Paris with former classmate Matthew Smith (1879–1959), while Augustus was preparing to leave for Provence. During their absence, Derwent spent more time with his Slade colleagues and local artists. Working *en plein air* was actively encouraged by the School. Walter Russell, Derwent's former teacher and Slade staff member since the mid-1890s, often took students on open-air excursions. In 1902, Russell had given drawing and painting classes in Richmond, Yorkshire; however, by 1908, Dorset 'became a particular focus for Slade tutors and students',[29] such that Vanessa Bell wrote to her sister Virginia Woolf in October 1910, having visited Dorset's Corfe Castle, exclaiming that it 'reminded her of Steer and where she expected to see industrious Slade students perched on the hills'.[30] The comment reflected the passion that the Slade's painting stalwart Philip Wilson Steer had for this area, where he regularly painted until late 1909, by which time Derwent was also working there *en plein air*, particularly on watercolours of nudes in landscapes (e.g. DL09.16, 19–22). Derwent also visited locations closer to London, in Sussex and on the Kent coast. His father lived in Folkestone, close to Dover, where he would later paint with Steer. On the northern Kent coast, he drew a detailed work in ink and wash of the Tudor courtier house, Shurland House, on the Isle of Sheppey (DL07.23).

Russell, 20 years Derwent's senior, was a skilled illustrator, etcher and drawing master, as well as an accomplished portrait and landscape painter. Derwent likely accompanied him as his assistant on excursions during his early years on staff. Despite being the youngest and most recent staff member, by 1911 to 1912, he was leading his own *plein air* student excursions, and on one such outing in the spring of 1912, he met up with Dick and fellow artist Frank Slade (1875–1962) in Rye.

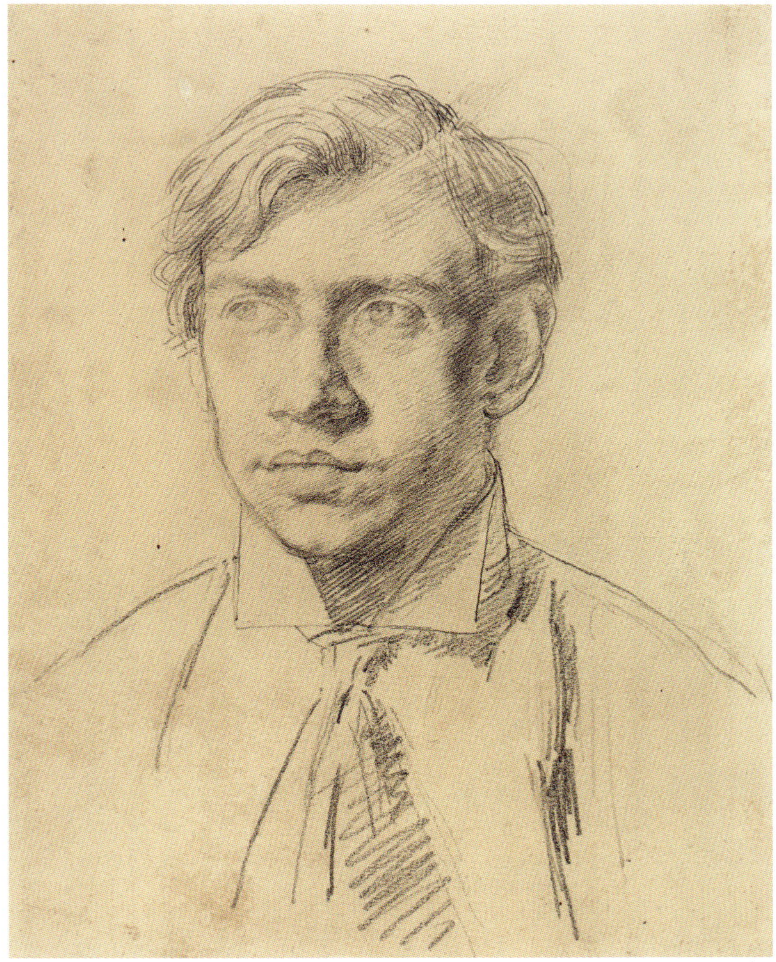

Elsie McNaught, *Portrait of Derwent Lees*, c.1910, pencil on paper, 31.4 x 24 cm, UCL Art Museum, University College London

During 1910, Derwent continued teaching, rendering portraits of female models and artist friends in his free time. He exhibited *Portrait of Young Woman* (DL09.27), painted the year before, and two further portraits of his close friends *Alice* and *Essil*, at a later NEAC show (DL11.56, 51). These works are characterised by softly contoured lines with distinctive diagonal shading, a technique he taught his students, and evident in the 1910 portrait of Derwent by Elsie McNaught. She had enrolled at the Slade while Derwent was still a student but finished her studies under his tutelage in 1911. Elsie was a talented artist and was awarded many prizes. Having produced a pencil portrait of her Assistant Drawing Master,[31] he also drew her (DL09.28). A 'close relationship',[32] perhaps romantic, has been intimated. The two remained good friends for many years, both exhibiting at the same shows, and later painting at Blaenau Ffestiniog in northern Wales at the same time.

In early summer, as Derwent was completing *Girl's Head* (DL09.26) for the next NEAC show, he received tragic news of his brother James that would have echoes for Derwent when he was to reach a similar age. On 18 June 1910 it was a cloudy Saturday in Sydney, Australia. In the mid-afternoon, in popular Centennial Park, people were promenading and picnicking. James, however, was alone. He made his way to bushes by a small reservoir, took out his revolver, and shot himself in the head. The shot rang out and his body was found within minutes. He was well dressed in a grey suit; notes in his pocket were sombre indicators of his employment situation. He was 38, with a wife and three young children living in Cobar, far from Sydney, and he had been alone in the city for some time. The gun lay beside him with one chamber discharged. There was no autopsy. His intention was clear.[33]

5 CONFIDENCE IN A SOUTHERN LIGHT 1910

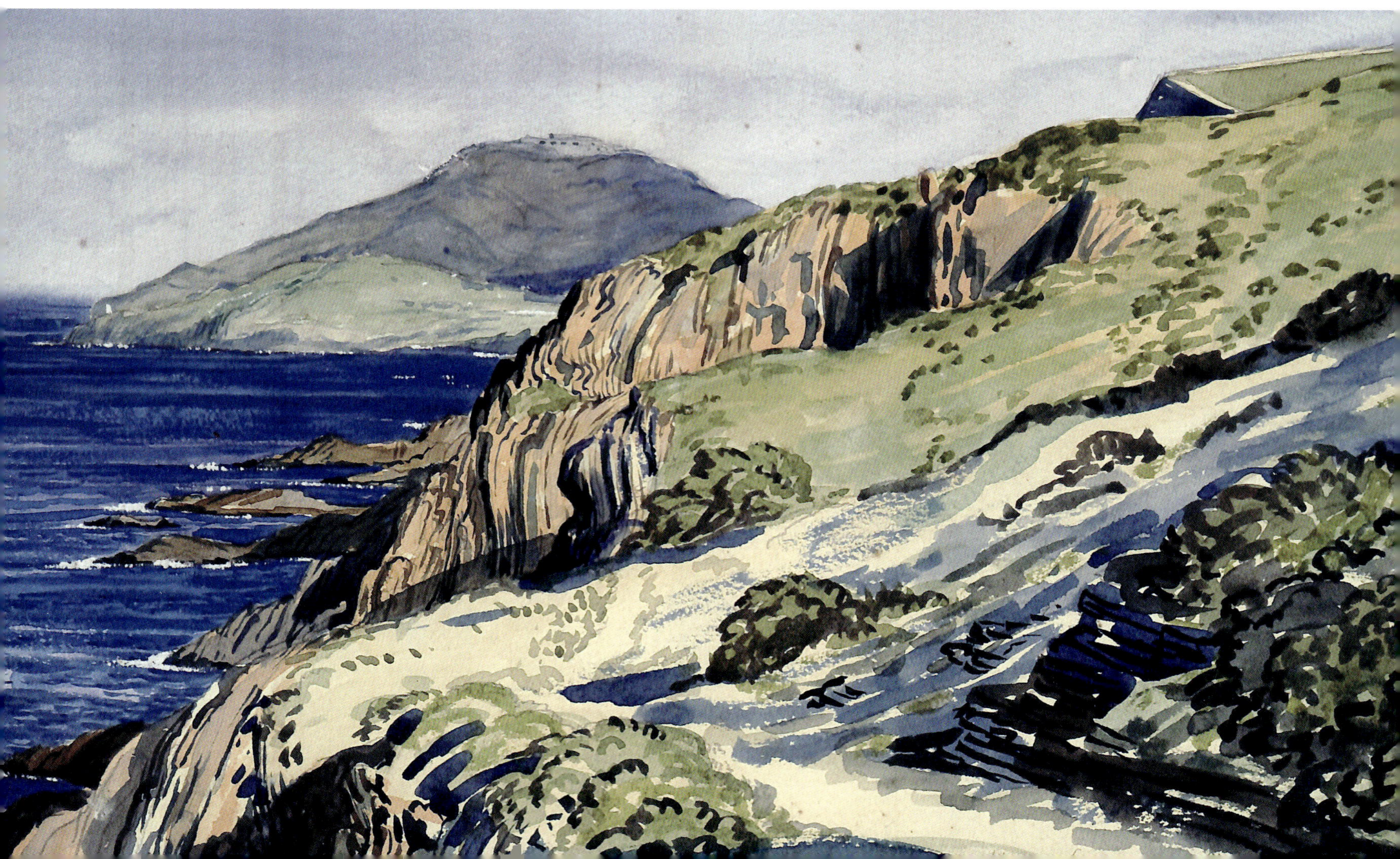

Derwent was now 25 years old, and after three years of tutoring, was ready to experience something new. His assiduous copying of Old Masters, following Henry Tonks's classical approach to drawing, still dominated his work. He in turn instilled the same practice of learning-by-copying in his students, so it is also unsurprising that his early British *plein air* scenes were influenced by his travelling companions. It is likely a lack of confidence in painting outside that resulted in Dick's one-off remark to John Fothergill that Derwent's paintings 'are much better but I tire of seeing my own subjects so many times'.[1] Friend and painting companion Frank Slade would later say that he, Dick and Derwent often worked *en plein air* 'sitting side by side' sketching the same scene.[2] To be fair, Dick had penned his ill-tempered words while unwell in early 1909, and while mirroring subject choice may have been the case for Derwent's early landscape scenes, it was not so for his body of work created in France. Here, a quite different story was to emerge.

During Henri Matisse and André Derain's famed Fauvist summer of 1905, they too worked closely alongside one another. Each later commented how they benefited and drew inspiration from the other.[3] By contrast, Derwent's habit of echoing his friends' subjects resulted in Randolph Schwabe describing it as something to do with his 'peculiar makeup',[4] an insightful remark perhaps reflecting an unresolved sense of identity.

Initially, Dick and Derwent's artistic differences were subtle, however Derwent slowly shifted to an increasingly independent experimentation in scene, technique and palette. Their treatment and movement of brush stroke displayed marked differences. A unique combination of composition, colouration and technique emerged in Derwent's work in the south of France, no doubt catalysed by the light and clarity of viewscape, and encouraged by his travelling companion and colleague Walter Russell. Dick had been staying in Paris but joined Derwent and Russell on a *plein air* painting trip south to Collioure in the summer of 1910.

As the overnight *couchette* rattled its way through the Rhône Valley past Avignon, Derwent would have noticed a remarkable change in light. The lowering, darker hues

Opposite:
DL10.23 (detail)
Derwent Lees, *Collioure / The Sea Coast*, 1910

of the north were dissolved by a brightness that brusquely defined the rolling hills and distant ridges. Then, turning onto the alluvial plains south of Montpellier, the Mediterranean in sight, the crisp luminescence gave an encompassing sharpness to the landforms. Scrubby hills gave way to mountain range after mountain range. He had not experienced such sun since childhood. From his train window, he would have seen blues, violets and purples of mountains touching the sky with purpose.

John Ruskin, artist and polymath, wrote that 'you will never love art well until you love what she mirrors better'.[5] Derwent's art was rooted in his childhood and a deep love of light, mountains and the sea – the essential sun, water and crisp colours of Australia and New Zealand. Arriving in similar, albeit northern, latitudes would have transported him to his home country. In Collioure, Derwent even found familiar southern temperate vegetation from his birthplace at 42°S in Tasmanian blue gum trees (*Eucalyptus globulus*) and silver wattles, now known locally as mimosa (*Acacia dealbata*), species sent as seeds from Melbourne's Botanic Gardens in the 1870s to French botanists Joseph Decaisne and Charles Naudin, later planted in Naudin's experimental Collioure gardens at 42°N.[6]

Collioure local Paul Soulier wrote in his 1902 guidebook that 'the intense light makes it seem like you are entering a new world'.[7] Paul lived next door to the Hotel de la Gare and became a close friend of Matisse. Arriving in May 1905, Matisse had left his wife and daughter with his sister-in-law in Perpignan. They soon joined him and, in July, 25-year-old André Derain arrived, the same age as Derwent when he was to arrive in the village. Madame Rousette, who ran the Hotel de la Gare, was an intimidating presence and initially refused to lodge the scruffy-looking Derain until Matisse smoothed things over.[8] Most of the villagers spoke Catalan and did not identify as French, as 'it was not until the French government came

Summer fishing fleet, Boramar Beach, Collioure, c.1905, photographer unknown, Private Collection

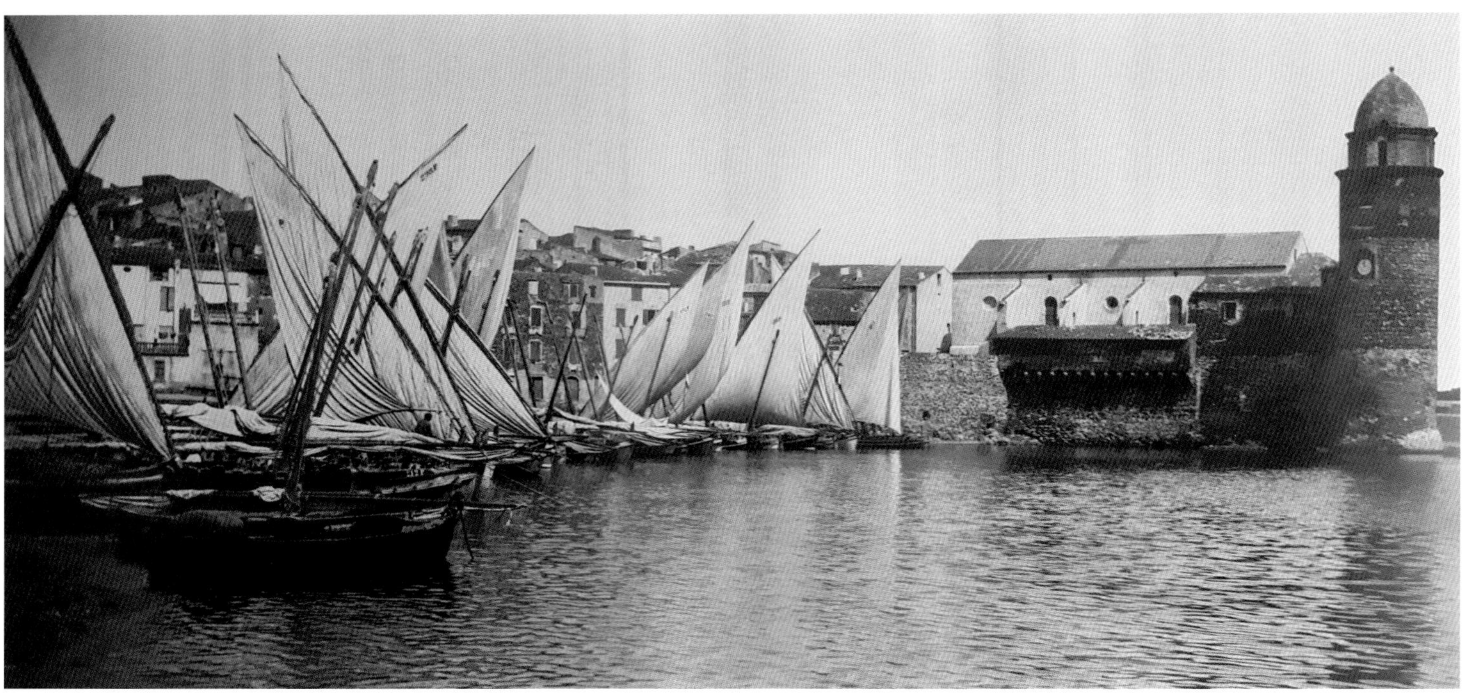

to the Roussillon to recruit soldiers during World War I that many villagers found out which country they were living in',[9] (a confusion accentuated by Roussillon being part of Spain before the separation of Spanish 'Southern' Catalonia from French 'Northern' Catalonia two and a half centuries earlier).

Matisse and Derain captured village life around the port, rocky shorelines, neighbouring cork-oak forests and the Albères mountains which run behind the last four French coastal villages north of the Spanish border: Collioure, Port Vendres, Banyuls-sur-Mer (Banyuls) and Cerbère.

By 1910, when Russell, Derwent and Dick arrived, Matisse was a frequent visitor among an already steady stream of artists. Picasso's model-muse Fernande Olivier wrote to Gertrude Stein in June 1910, explaining that they were spending the summer at Cadaqués in Spain, because Picasso said that 'too many painters were going to Colioure [*sic*]'.[10]

Derwent was the first Australian-born painter to visit Collioure after the renowned 1905 *Salon d'Automne* Paris exhibition in which Matisse and Derain had exhibited their striking Collioure paintings and were labelled *fauves* (wild beasts). Their dramatic, vibrantly coloured works were riotously different to what the French public and art world expected. The term coined by young writer Louis Vauxelles not only stuck, but Matisse later said that 'frankly it was admirable. The name *fauves* was perfectly suited to our feelings.'[11]

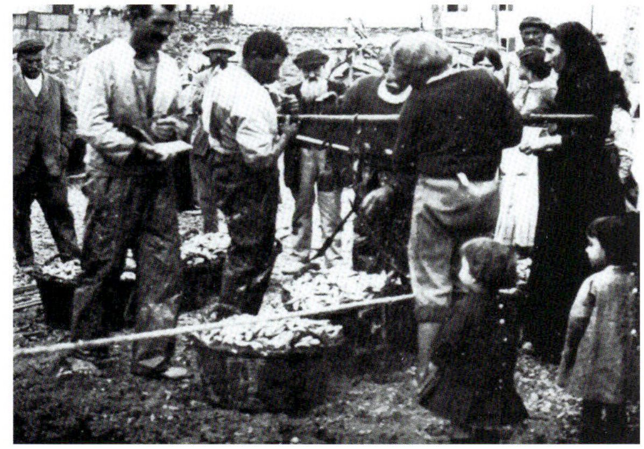

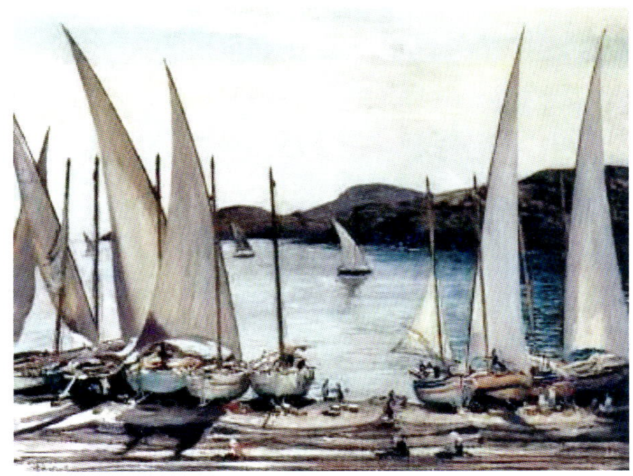

Above:
Derain and Matisse at a Collioure fish auction, 1905, photographer unknown, Private Collection

Derain (front left) sketching, Matisse at centre back

Below:
Walter Westley Russell, *Fishing Boats, Collioure*, 1910, oil on canvas, 71.3 x 91.3 cm, location unknown

OF CLAMOUR AND COLOUR

For Dick, in the summer of 1910 the village was entirely different to the near-empty streets he had experienced with Fothergill in 1908. Sardines pass the coast from mid-May to June, followed by the yearly anchovy run. July was the height of the fishing season, the height of activity and the height of noise.[12] It was hot, the smell of rotting fish guts and fetid nightsoil filling the humid air. Scrapping seagulls and cats were everywhere. Everyone was busy. The small bay was home to about 120 heavy wooden Catalan boats. The village was at a frenetic peak and the loudest cries came from the fishermen, selling their catch as the boats returned (seen in the rare photograph of Matisse and Derain sketching the activity).

The beaches filled with family members, and expectant buyers who hovered, ready to compete for the catch, returning a meagre income for the fishing families. The word *la criée* (fish auction) is derived from the cry of men unloading the baskets spilling over with writhing, silvery fish and passing them to the waiting scales. There and then on the beach, the price per catch was shouted out, haggled and agreed. Prices varied according to the species and the season's abundance. Fish were traded, changed hands and were carted to the salting houses in the narrow streets. The clamour of the day extended through dusk, with the cleaning, gutting, salting, resalting and packing of anchovies and sardines. Work filled the daylight hours and the night – many of the salting houses and associated trades toiled until dawn.[13]

It is likely that the town's fervour drove the two young artists to paint mostly on the village outskirts and inland, while Russell seems to have spent considerable time capturing the port's activities and the fishing fleet.

Away from the ruckus were sweeping vistas to discover. Derwent paid particular attention to the detail and mood of the adjacent hills and rocky coastal landscapes. Some of his works reflect the humid sea air of summer that can mute the palette (DL10.29–32). He captured the violet-purple shaded hills cradling the flushed, green-leafed vines and the rich deep blues of the waters of the Collioure coast. Derwent concentrated on the natural geomorphological form, with only occasional man-made structures appearing in his carefully chosen, accurately depicted landscapes. In a few years, such focal structures would be replaced by the figure of Edith Price.

In Collioure, he discovered a brilliance and nuance of light and shadow and gradually freed himself from the academia that had constrained the development of a personal style. The new colours infused and transformed his palette and it was to be his vital, intuitive use of colour for which Augustus and the critics most complemented him. It was not the primal colour treatment of the *fauves*, but rather colour as close observation, heightened but in sympathy with the key resonances of carefully chosen landscape elements. A different Derwent emerged, with an emphasis on soft form, contour and defined colour *touches*. Derwent as landscape painter was born; a depicter of intimate form and experimenter in colour. He sought emotion in his landscape subject, exploring connection between human form and landform, seeking softness in the *paysage* as if it were a life drawing.

The three men painted the Collioure coast, at either ends of the village, as well as scenes from the neighbouring villages of Port Vendres and Banyuls, short train rides south. From Collioure the artists also walked north, as Matisse and family

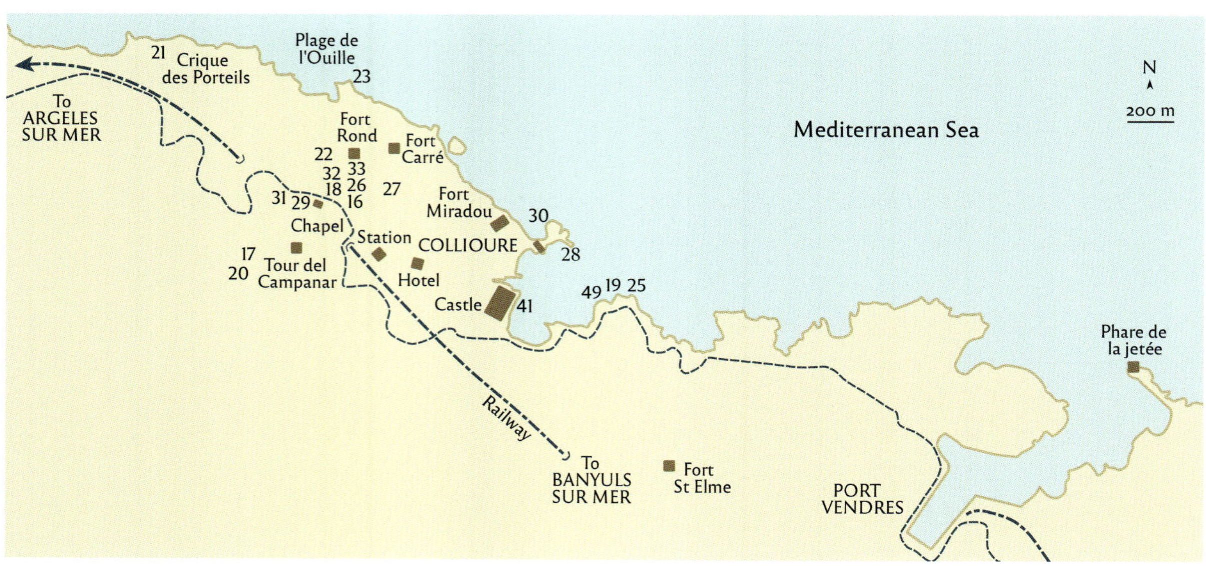

Locations where Derwent painted in Collioure, 1910. Numbers indicate known painting sites; DL10. prefix is not shown; DL12.41 shown as 41

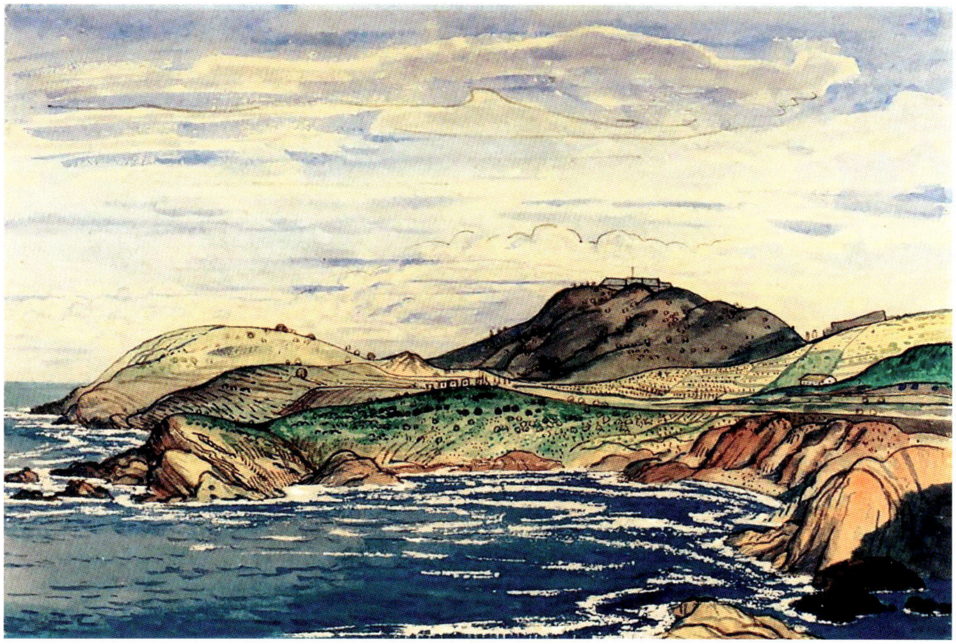

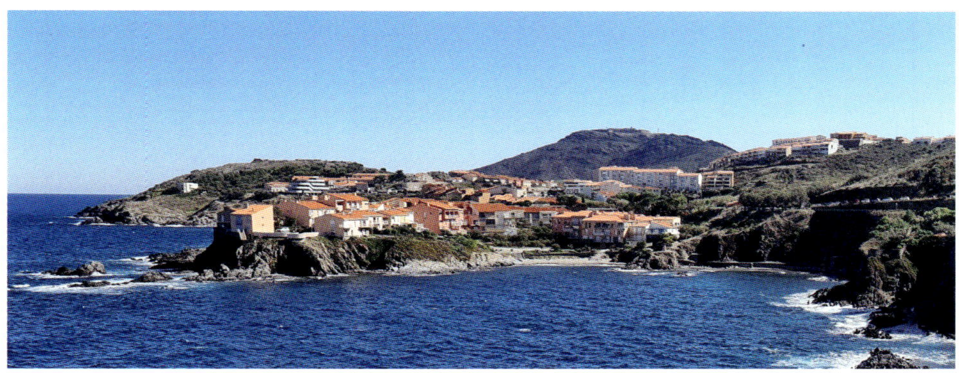

Above:
DL10.25
Derwent Lees, *Mediterranean Bay*, 1910, watercolour and ink on buff paper, 24.7 x 35.5 cm, Private Collection

Right:
Present-day view of DL10.25, Collioure

had done, hugging the inside walls of the train tunnel, to reach the El Ravener creek and the cove of Plage de l'Ouille made famous by Matisse during the summers of 1905 and 1906. They painted along the headlands and beaches further north to the Criques de Porteils in the commune of Argelès-sur-Mer, capturing the Le Racou beach and the vast plain beyond, then returning along the ridge crests. Russell and Dick both painted works here, respectively titled *A Storm* and *The Storm*.

The summer was a turning point for the two younger artists. It marked the beginning of a new pattern of them painting together, yet apart, showing distinct but related scenes from different vantage points, undoubtedly under their former teacher's tutelage. Dick's draft workings of the Canigou mountain-form along the bottom of *Valley Scene, Sunset, Canigou* is likely an example of Russell's mentoring, as the Slade was known for its margin drawing instructions.

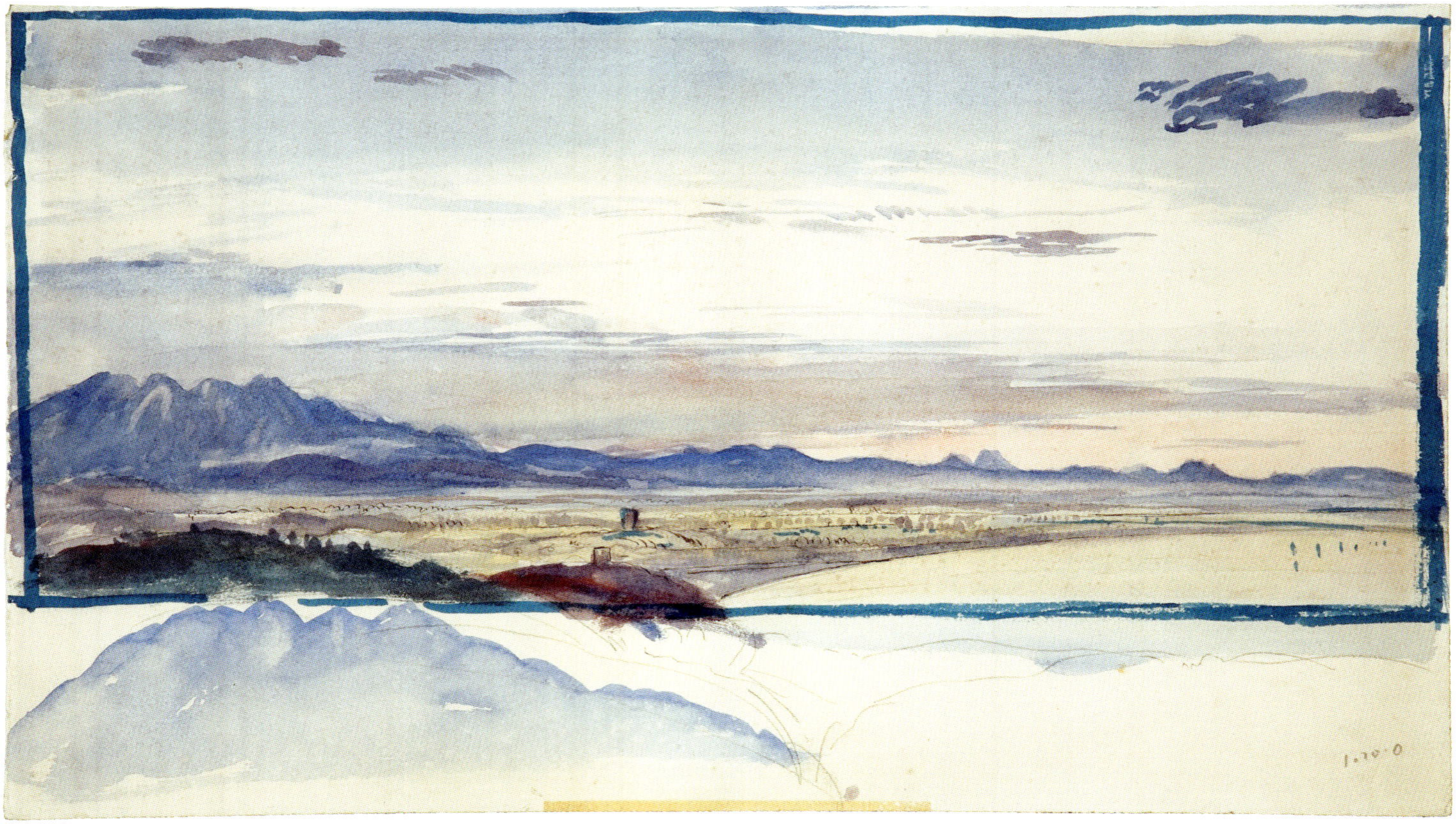

James Dickson Innes, *Valley Scene, Sunset, Canigou*, 1910, watercolour and pencil on paper, 15.6 x 37.8 cm, Bristol Museum and Art Gallery, Bristol

Mt Canigou and the Roussillon Plain, north of Collioure; same location as DL10.32

Dick was attracted to strong, dramatic, natural features. He favoured seascapes or the peaks of Pic Sallfort in the Albères mountains, the distant Mont Canigou and the Corbières range, precursors to his coming fascination with the mountains of North Wales. While Russell preferred to capture the fishing fleet or the large nets drying on the beach, Derwent favoured rolling hills, ridgetops and coastal headlands (DL10.16–36). Derwent's works *Coast at Collioure* (DL10.22) and *Pyrenees and Mediterranean* (DL10.32) were painted from the same vantage point as the two works by Russell and Dick, both titling them *The Pyrenees*. They sketched and painted along the northern ridge beside Fort Rond and the ruins of the chapel above the entrance to the village, facing the coast and the Roussillon Plain, crossed by Hannibal and his elephants 2200 years before.

Derwent completed more than 25 works during the trip, exhibiting nearly half of them at the next two New English Art Club (NEAC) and Friday Club shows. Interestingly he, or the hanging committee, selected coastal or sea works for the exhibitions; his inland viewscapes perhaps deemed less desirable. Russell, like Derwent, hung multiple works at the following NEAC exhibitions (44th winter 1910 and 45th summer 1911) and, again, they showcased littoral scenes. Later in 1910, Russell painted *Fishing Boats, Collioure* (see page 49) and *Drying the Nets, Collioure*, one, a large oil of the beached wooden boats with the blackened nets drying on the sand. Derwent followed suit, titling his work of the same subject *The*

Fishing Fleet, exhibiting it at the 1911 spring NEAC show (DL10.37). During the trip the three artists had sketched and painted on paper, later working up larger oils.

As they headed home to London, it seems certain that they visited Augustus at his rented Provençal villa in Martigues (on the shores of the Etang de Berre near Marseille), where he had been based for much of the year.[14] He had recently shifted to painting oils directly onto small wood panels, allowing him to work more quickly, as the paint dried rapidly. Before the end of September, Augustus also headed back to London. The following summer Derwent and Dick would return in his footsteps to explore the Etang (DL11.26–48, 50), both by then also painting oils on panel.

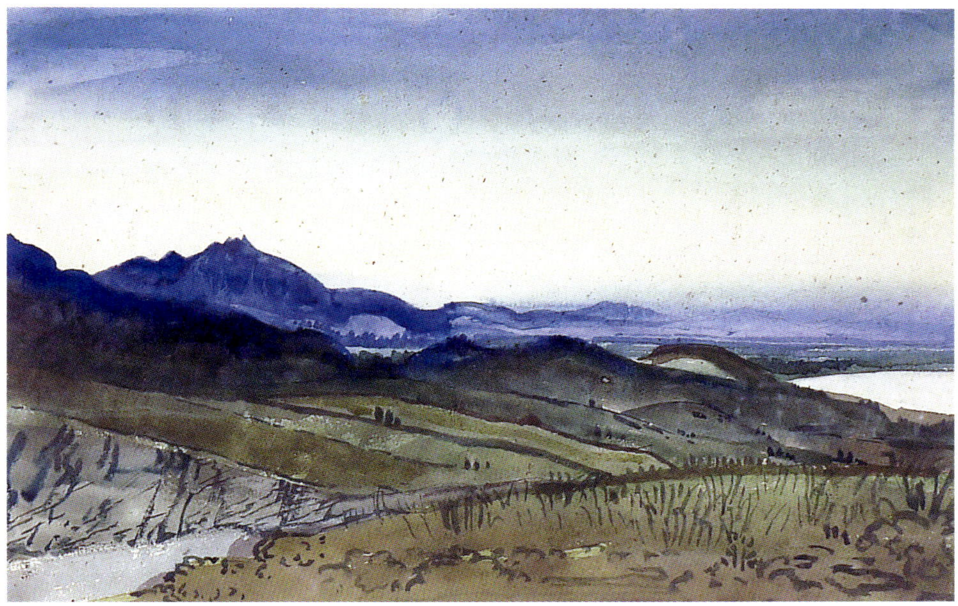

Right:
DL10.32
Derwent Lees, *Pyrenees and Mediterranean*, 1910, watercolour on paper, 22.2 x 35.6 cm, Leeds Art Gallery

Below:
Present-day location of several painting sites by Derwent and Dick, Collioure

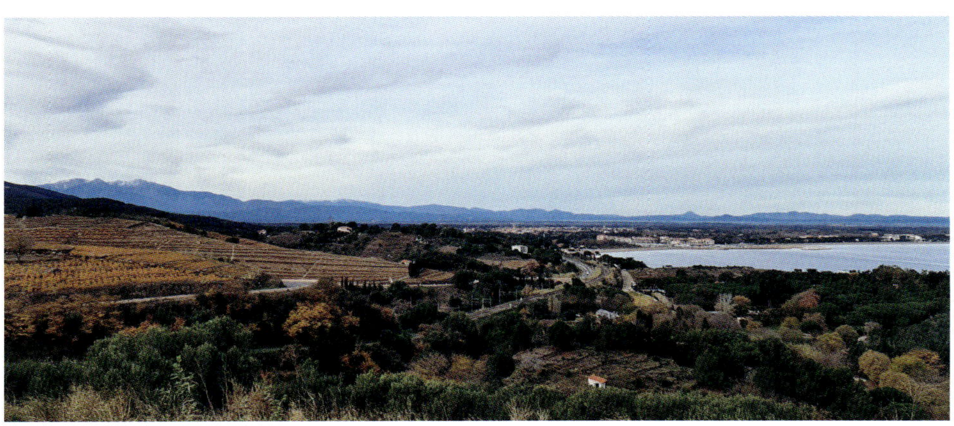

THE CHENIL

The end of the year was full. Augustus and Dick had solo exhibitions at the Chenil Gallery for which to prepare, and Derwent returned to teaching, while exhibiting four paintings of Collioure at the winter NEAC exhibition (DL10.21, 23–5). Six months later, a further five Collioure works were hung at the summer show (DL10.22, 30, 32, 35, 37), preceded by one at the spring show of the Friday Club (DL10.16), with a critic remarking that 'there is good colour in the watercolour landscape of Mr Derwent Lees'.[15]

Following Dick's early 1911 exhibition, Augustus wrote to American art collector, patron and friend John Quinn (1870–1924), suggesting he collect the work of his young friend.[16] Quinn accepted his advice, despite not having seen any of the art. Barely a year later, Augustus recommended Derwent's landscapes, and Quinn would buy at least eight of his works (DL11.6–7, DL12.8, 21, 31, DL13.1, 39, 48). During the year, Derwent and Dick were elected members of the New English Art Club. Their reputations as established artists were firmly on the rise, though life remained precarious.

Gallery exhibitions were 'make or break' for struggling artists, ever hopeful of positive reviews, securing a sale or a commission. The yearly exhibition cycle dominated their calendar. Getting works ready by submission date, waiting for approval from the hanging committee, then framing and adding the finishing touches ready for opening, all this demands intense, nervous energy. Derwent chiefly showed his work at the NEAC's biannual exhibitions; the first in spring or early summer, with the second usually a November or December winter show, often held at the Chenil Gallery. This exhibiting, art-framing and supply business, managed by Jack Knewstub (1872–1959), had opened in 1905 on the Kings Road between Chelsea Town Hall and the Six Bells pub. Exhibitions were mainly held in the upstairs rooms while an etching press room and art supplies shop augmented the revenue. Jack was in his element at 'the Chenil'. He was a true nonconformist who embodied Chelsea and bohemia.[17] His father had been a student of Dante Gabriel Rossetti (1828–82), one of his sisters married William Rothenstein (1872–1945), and another William Orpen (1878–1931). Quinn once remarked that Jack was Augustus's 'private property', as his works were permanently on show at the gallery. Augustus not only used the gallery to sell many of his paintings, but also constructed a large studio at the back of the building. He strongly influenced who exhibited and what collectors, including Lord Howard de Walden, Lady Ottoline Morrell (1873–1938) and Quinn, should buy. The height of the Chenil's success from 1910 to 1914 paralleled the best years of its three most ardent supporters, Augustus, Derwent and Dick.[18] It was later referred to as the Old Chenil Gallery, after new and extended premises, the New Chenil Galleries, opened in 1925. Sadly, this ambitious project rendered the business bankrupt by early 1927.

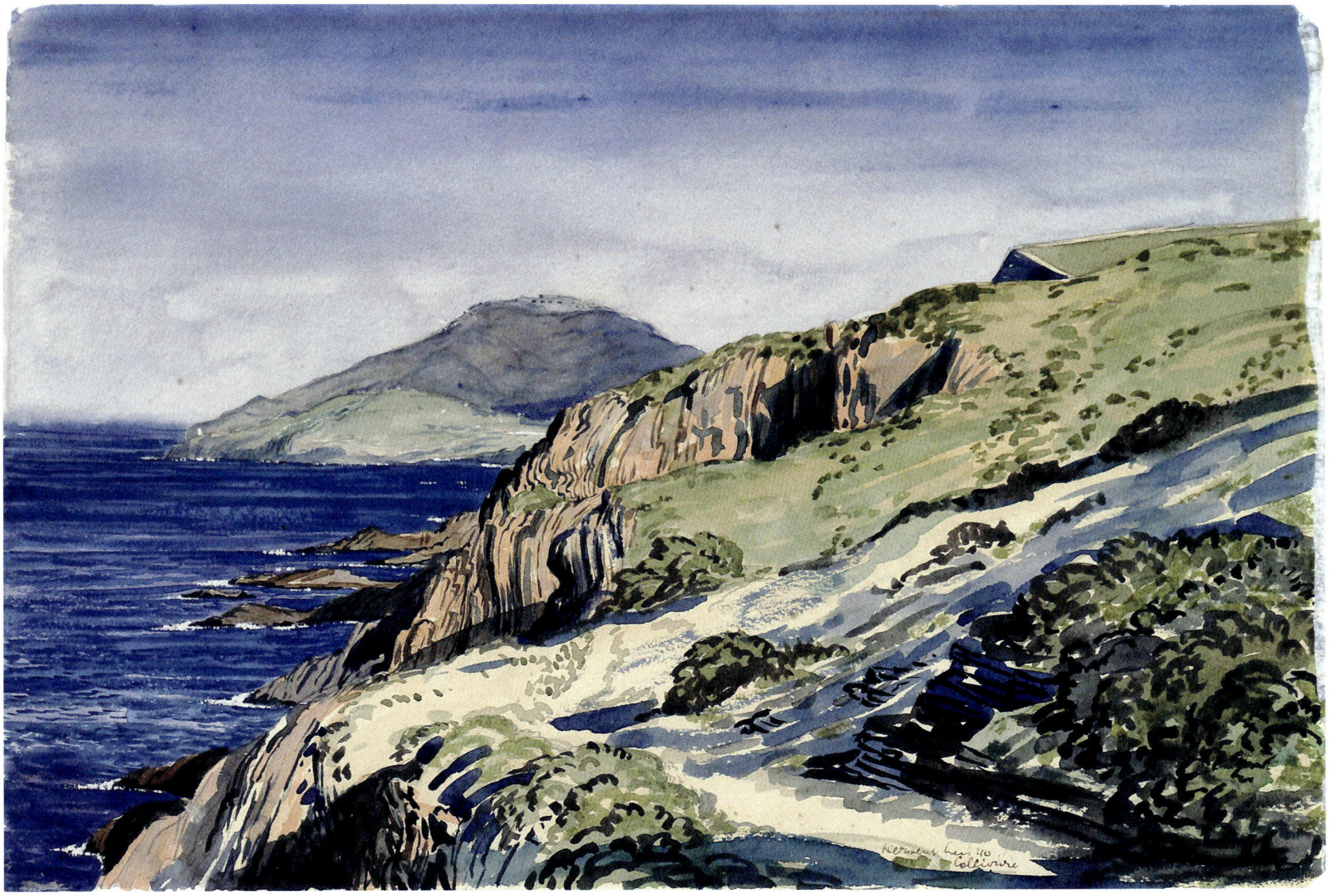

DL10.23
Derwent Lees, *Collioure / The Sea Coast*, 1910, watercolour on paper 25.2 x 35.5 cm, Victoria and Albert Museum, London

6 OF MOUNTAINS AND LAKES 1911

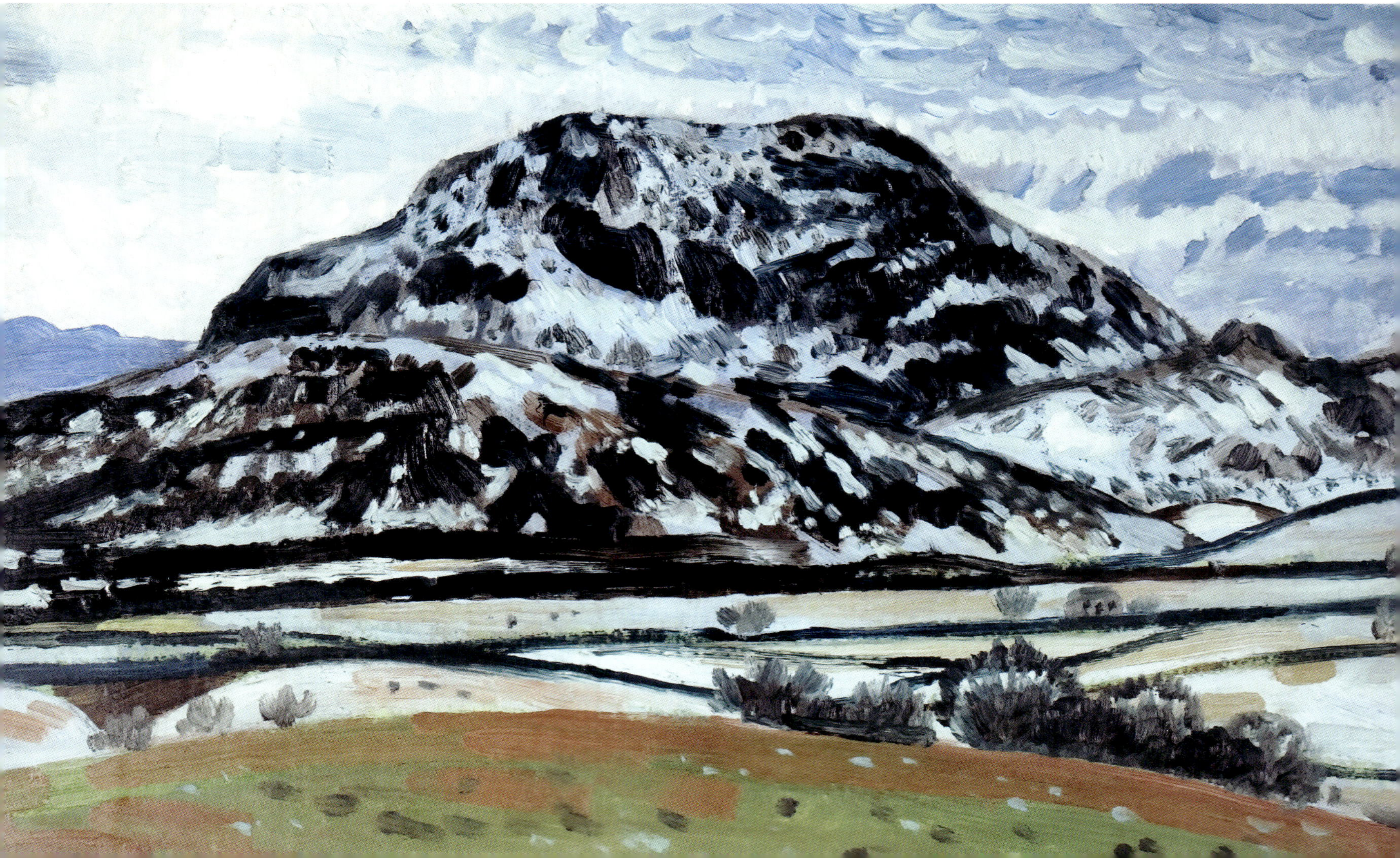

During late 1910, a bond developed between Augustus and Dick around a shared love of Wales, their country of birth, and its northern mountains sculpted by glaciers. Dick's love for mountains developed into a passion focused on the mass of Arenig Fawr in the Migneint area near Bala.[1] He first shared it with Augustus during the winter of 1910, then again in 1911, with Derwent accompanying them (DL11.1–3). In March 1911, Augustus wrote to Dorelia McNeill that 'this is the most wonderful place I've seen',[2] despite 18 months earlier being enthused by the Etang de Berre; 'an enchanting spot this, situated in the water at the mouth of an island sea where it joins the Mediterranean'.[3] He was to remain enthusiastic about the south of France, but was now drawn to Wales. Dick spent every spare moment in the region, leasing a cottage with Augustus at Nant Ddu, which looked across the valley of the Afon Tryweryn to Arenig Fawr.

Derwent enjoyed these Welsh trips, and was increasingly drawn to landscape and figure work, initiated by Augustus. His confidence *en plein air* had grown and his most commercially successful Welsh works were painted when accompanying Dick or Augustus. His oil *Evening* (DL11.6), painted at dusk, overlooking Lake Bala (Llyn Tegid) from above the Pen-y-Bont railway station, was bought by John Quinn, on Augustus's recommendation, and later lent for the famed 1913 American Armory Show in New York.[4]

In Wales, Augustus introduced Derwent to Elizabeth Milne, nicknamed Doonie. Augustus and Doonie's husband, Albert Lipczinski (1876–1974), had become good friends while Augustus was teaching art in Liverpool. Albert was Polish, but his German background meant that during the First World War he was interned, put under house arrest and, despite protests from Augustus, the couple was deported at war's end. In 1911 they stayed at Nant Ddu with their greyhound. Albert was notoriously difficult, and during summer Augustus wrote to Ottoline Morrell saying that Dick was furious about his presence there.[5] Derwent seemed content. It seems he was more comfortable with a few trusted male friends or in the company of women. He preferred to paint women and, after his student days,

Opposite:
DL11.1 (detail)
Derwent Lees, *Arenig Mawr, North Wales / Arenig Manor, North Wales / Arenig Fawr / Landscape*, 1911

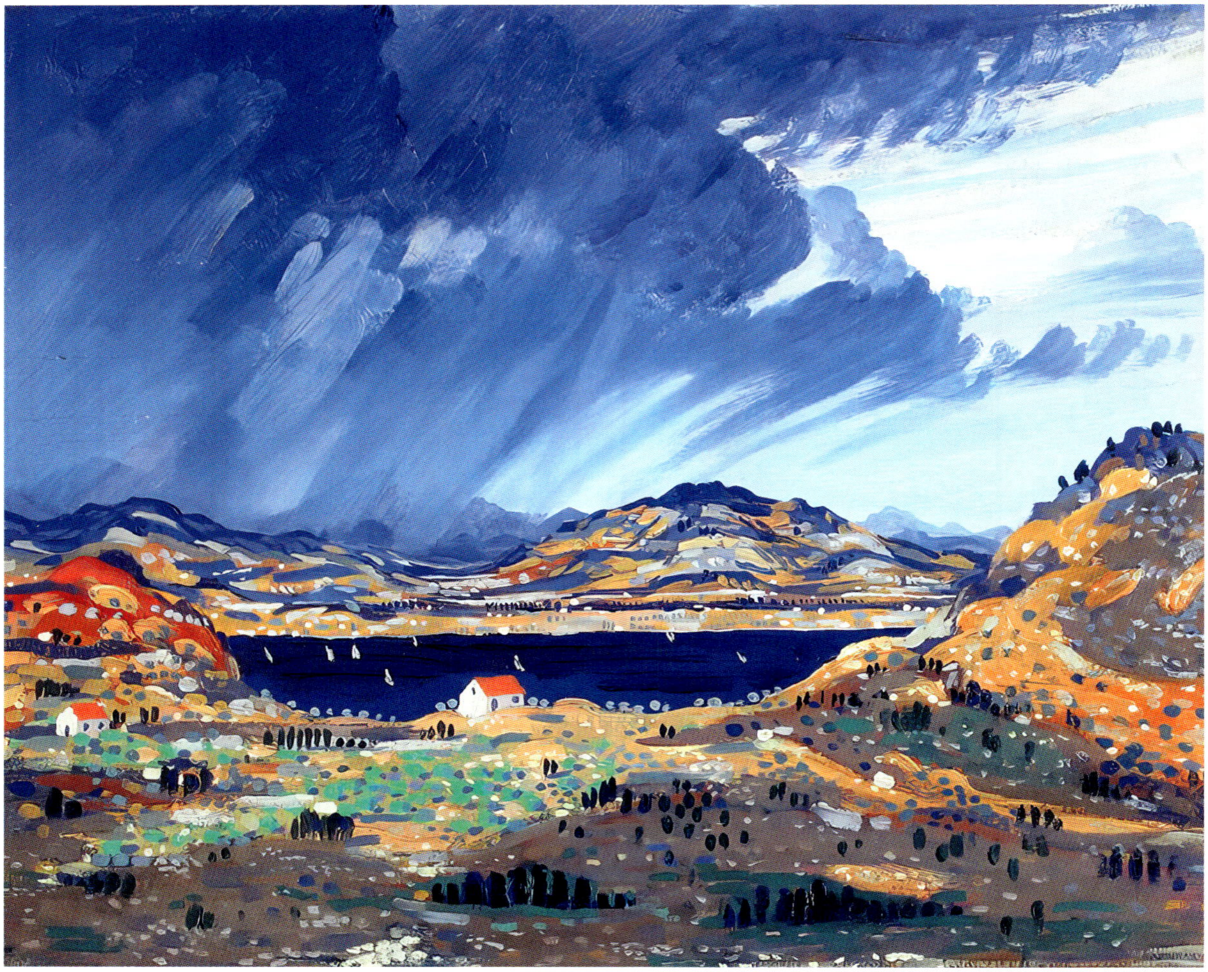

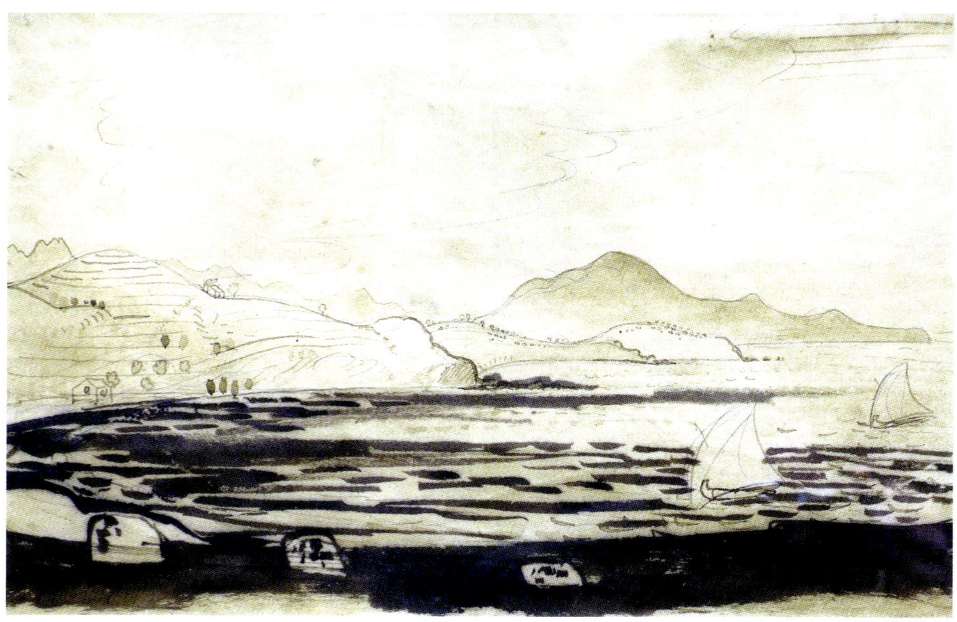

Above:
DL11.29
Derwent Lees, *Approaching Storm, Mediterranean*, 1911, oil on panel, 32.5 x 39 cm, Private Collection

Right:
James Dickson Innes, *Mediterranean Coast, Storm Approaching*, 1911, pen, pencil and wash on mulberry paper, 26 x 37.5 cm, Parc Howard Art Gallery, Llanelli

The Etang de Berre, Istres, depicting the same storm as DL11.29

more than 95 per cent of his portrait and figure subjects were female. During the summer, he produced several drawings including the splendid oil, *Portrait of Elizabeth Lipczinski with her Dog Fanny* (DL11.8), posed on the shore of Llyn Arenig Fawr, under the cliffs of Pen Tyrau. Derwent was to rejoin Augustus and Dick again in northern Wales during winter and into the following year. This rhythm was briefly interrupted by the arrival from Australia of Derwent's older brother Geoffrey and his second wife Naomi, in Easter 1911, for a year-long extended honeymoon, basing themselves in London.

SOUTH TO ISTRES

Two London exhibitions, during the winter of 1910, were to mark a turning point in Derwent's creative practice. *Manet and the Post-Impressionists* was a landmark exhibition organized by Roger Fry at the Grafton Gallery. Fry, an intellectual art critic, was the central promoter of European Post-Impressionism in London before the Great War, particularly through the works of Paul Cézanne, Vincent van Gogh, Paul Gauguin and Maurice Denis, and later, Matisse and Picasso.

The other winter exhibition was Augustus's *Provencal Studies and Other Works* at the Chenil Gallery (Nov–Dec 1910) which showcased more than 45 brightly coloured oils in a loose, expressive manner, many capturing the shores of the Etang de Berre near Marseille.

Derwent was inspired by these exhibitions, and during the summer of 1911, he and Dick returned to the south of France, heading to the shores of the radiant Etang, inland from the Mediterranean. Augustus had been effusive about the Etang and her colours, despite writing to Morrell at the end of his stay saying that 'There are no green fields here'.[6] By then he was craving the rich, moist greens of the British countryside.

Along the lagoon's western shore is the small fishing village of Istres, which became Derwent and Dick's base for capturing the luminous land- and waterscapes. Derwent thrived in the sharp, clear light, blue-green water and wooded rocky hills. He continued exploring painting styles and palettes, producing multiple works from the same location in both watercolour and small oils on panel. The two young men worked along the shoreline below the village, painting mostly from sites above the Plage de la Romaniquette that gave onto the Etang and distant mountains, including Mont Sainte-Victoire. The lagoon is shallow and more temperamental than the Mediterranean, with the *mistral* blowing unceasingly from the Rhône Valley, lifting the waves and rapidly changing the palette of water and skyscapes. Most of their works capture the constantly windswept Etang. Cloud-heads appear and rush, storm shadows form and dissolve. Once

Etang de Berre, Istres, 1907, postcard, Les Amis du Vieil Istres, France

The Plage de la Romaniquette, Istres

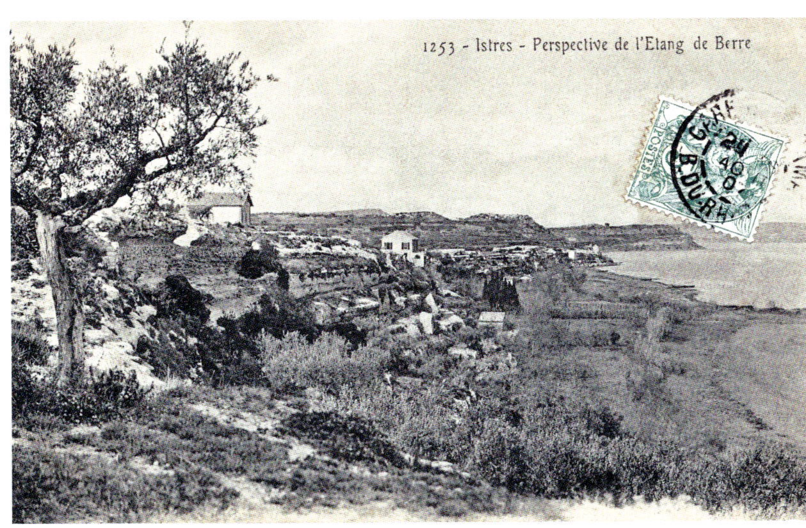

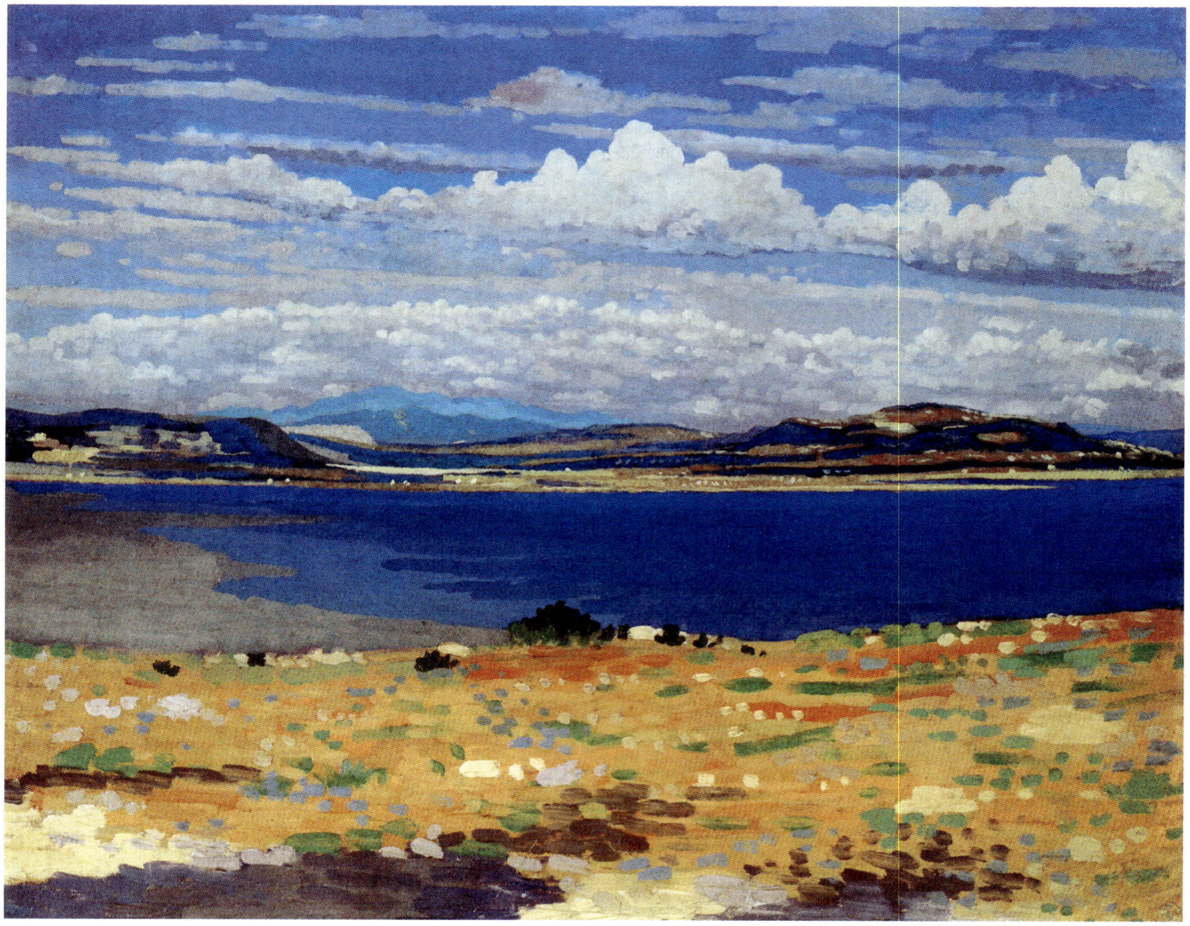

DL11.32
Derwent Lees, *Etang de Berre / A Dorset View / On the Coast, Dorset*, 1911–12, oil on canvas, 60 x 75.5 cm, Private Collection

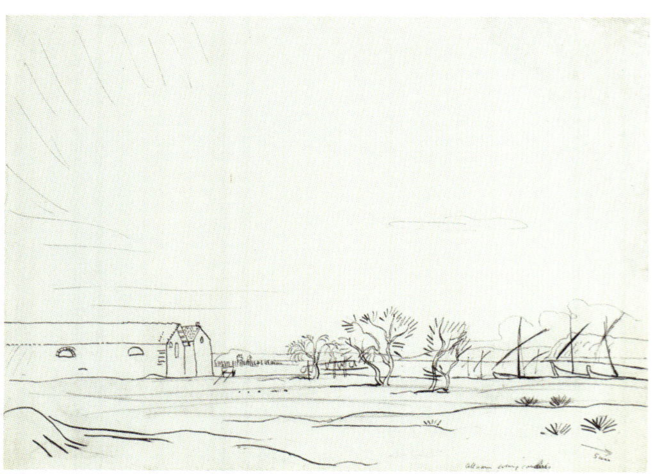

James Dickson Innes, *A Harbour*, c.1911, pen and ink on paper, 26.8 x 36.7 cm, Amgueddfa Cymru – National Museum Wales, Cardiff

Etang de Berre, Istres

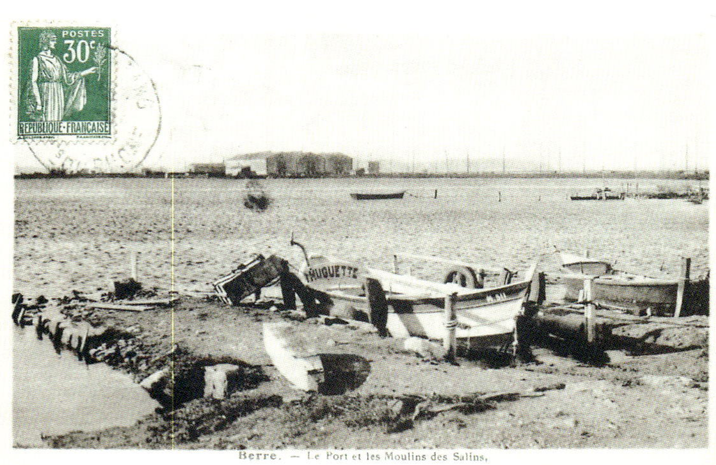

Fishing boats and sheds, Etang de Berre, c.1910, postcard, France

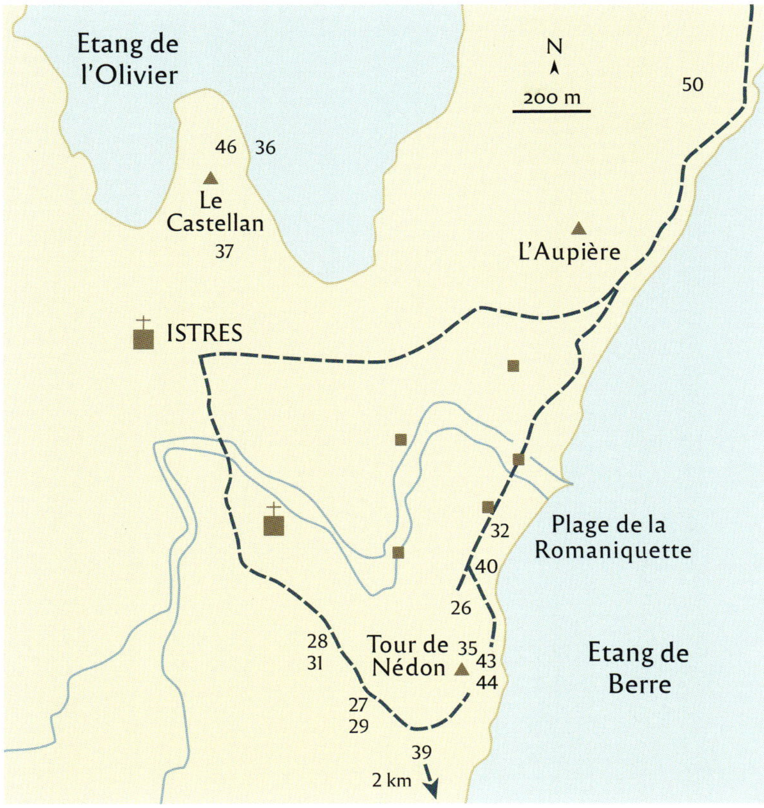

Locations where Derwent painted in Istres, 1911

Numbers indicate known painting sites; DL11. prefix is not shown

again, the young artists painted distinct scenes of the Etang from neighbouring vantage points, including the same summer storm painted at the same time, both creating works named *The Blue Mediterranean* (DL11.47) and *Approaching Storm, Mediterranean* (DL11.29).

Derwent painted the sequence of the storm's movement across the sky and its changing colours from beneath the Tour de Nédon. He and Dick painted olive and pine trees on this shoreline bluff, as well as views of the Etang from Martigues, near where Augustus rented Villa Sainte-Anne. They travelled lightly, often scribbling notes on sketches for later *tableaux* in oil. On one such sketch of beached fishing boats, titled *A Harbour*, Dick scribbled 'all warm evening colours', with an arrow and the word 'sun' indicating the direction of light. The distinctively curved bow of the local boats, captured in ink and wash, definitively placed them on the Etang's shores. Derwent, who ranged widely between the Etang de Berre and its smaller neighbour, the Etang de l'Olivier, painted over 25 landscapes during their stay, most in luminous colours on small panels, curiously omitting any hint of the village of Istres, which closely adjoined several scenes.

Upon their return, Derwent settled back into London life before the start of term. He may have also caught up with Augustus at his new Dorset home, Alderney Manor. Edith Price also stayed there at that time.

Derwent would later exhibit only one painting from his Istres trip at a New English Art Club (NEAC) show (*53rd Exhibition of Modern Pictures*; DL11.31), a commissioned work lent by Sir Cyril Butler, not shown until spring 1915. Perhaps he lacked the funds to pay for framing or had left the works behind during his constant moves to new lodgings. Curiously, as well as not exhibiting his 1911 Istres works, his familiar rounded, flowing signature is replaced on these works by an angular, blocky 'LEES'. They are in marked contrast to his more common, relaxed inscriptions.

OF STYLES AND ATTRIBUTIONS

During 1911, Derwent produced about 65 works. Of the more than 30 landscapes, two thirds were now examples of the oil-on-panel technique. Previously, his open-air works had been in ink or watercolour, often as studies for later oils on canvas. Canvas was traditional, but the oil dried slowly. Applying oils directly onto small panels was easier, with much faster drying times, as previously mentioned in the context of Augustus's work. Wood panel (also known as wood board) was cheaper, compact and easy to cut to any dimension and transport.

All three artists had now shifted mainly to oil on panel. Dick found the move revolutionary, fueling rapid changes in his expression of landscape.[7] Freer to work at whatever pace he wished, he quickly captured new ideas and impressions. Of Derwent's shift to oil on panel and his use of colour, an art critic from *The Times* remarked that 'it is evident that Lees understood the requirements of the small oil painting, as a rather "precious" kind of thing, very well indeed. He seldom fails of decorative completeness, and the enamel-like quality of his pigment is felt to be right for the scale and form.'[8]

There was now a clear and growing divergence between Dick and Derwent's landscapes, with Dick developing an independent painting style, abandoning detailed preliminary studies, a practice Derwent maintained throughout. Until this point, the Slade, and then Augustus, had been the dominant influences in technique, style and medium for the two young artists.

Dick now created more lyrical almost fantastical interpretations, a melange of what was seen and imagined, often with exaggerated features. Ysanne Holt commented of him that there 'can be little doubt that the painter's fantasy of nature was a mental rather than a strictly topographical landscape, one in which the distinctive terrain of north Wales and the south of France would eventually unite'.[9] Dick's winter 1911 output was prodigious, completing nearly 60 oils on panel. Some were scenes worked-up from Wales, others from earlier trips to France, several playfully shift and distort reality, Augustus reflecting that Dick's work 'took on a more poetic colouring with a growing insistence upon pattern which compensated to some extent for his faulty drawing'.[10] Dick improvised beautifully.

This was not Derwent's *modus operandi*. He painted with geomorphological fidelity and with an emphasis on observed detail. He captured the forms of both body and land faithfully, carefully choosing his viewscapes as though containing elements of human form. He would frequently paint the same scene in different chromatic and tonal ranges, experimenting with stronger coloration evocative of Cézanne and Gauguin, within a closely curated context. His emphasis was on contour, colour and occasionally texture, and there was almost no altering of the

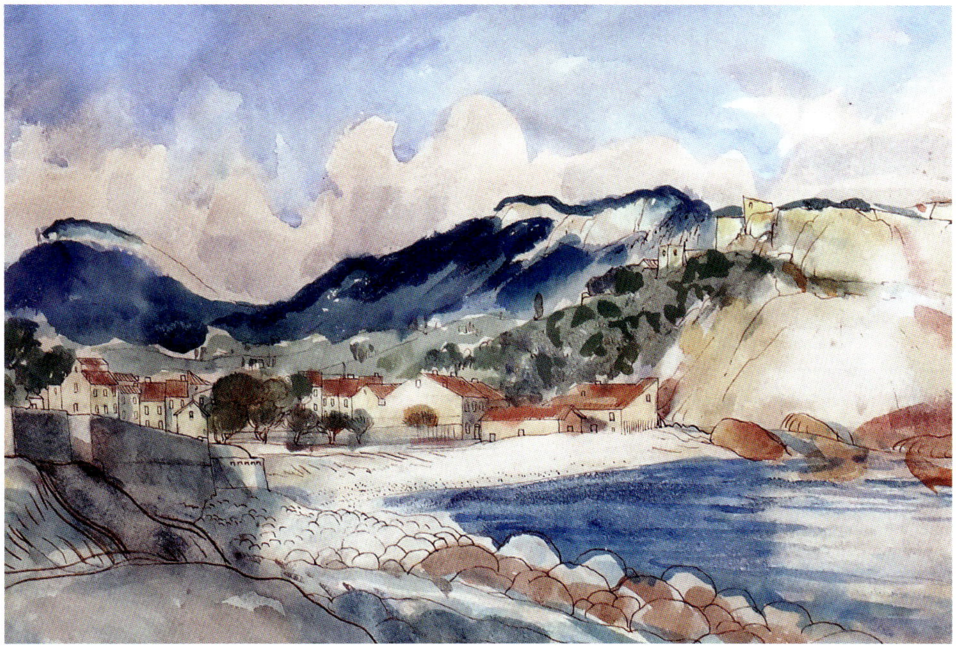

DL14.3
Derwent Lees, *Cassis Village and Bay / Coastal Landscape with a Village in a Cove / A Mediterranean Scene with a Village at the Edge of the Sea / The Bay, South of France / Bay in the South of France / Collioure, 1910 / Seaside Town*, 1914, watercolour, pen and brown ink on paper, 24.1 x 34.3 cm, Private Collection

viewscape. He often produced multiple watercolours or pen and ink studies before a final work in oil.

These distinctions are important when assessing the attribution of the two artists' works. The author has worked with UK art specialists and auction houses to resolve many long-standing inconsistencies and misattributed works. Collaborative research and detailed analysis have resulted in the reattribution from Dick to Derwent of DL08.9 and 24; DL12.4, 5, 10, 12, 35, 36 and 44; DL13.7, 34 and 47; and DL14.3, 32 and 33; as well as the confirmation of the *View of Llanelli* (JDI 102) as a work by Dick. Errors and confusion in attribution (as well as location and date) will continue to present challenges, as stylistic similarities in some of Derwent's works to those of his travelling companions have resulted in a complex legacy of misattributions, title errors and occasional contention.[11] This legacy of errors started during the 1930s, as little was known about the places they visited in France, and with confusion likely added by the artists gifting works to each other.

One example, misattributed to Dick and mistitled *Collioure, 1910*, was in fact painted at a site only visited by Derwent. On the back of the watercolour is a quizzical 'is this by Lees?', lightly scrawled in pencil. Despite this, it was presented to an English auction house in 2022 as being by Dick, of the bay of Collioure, accompanied by an unrelated exhibition history. With conclusive evidence, the auction house sold the watercolour as a work by Derwent. It has been reattributed to him and renamed *Cassis Village and Bay*, 1914 (DL14.3).

Comprehensive analysis indicates that errors in at least one criterion (title, date or signature) have occurred for at least 40 per cent of Derwent's works (see Appendix). He signed, dated or named fewer than 50 per cent of his works. Naming and dating errors have dogged many of his landscapes, with more than one third having been assigned incorrect locations. It is easy to see how this has occurred when comparing his south of France work of Tour Madeloc (DL12.22) with his North Wales works of Moelwyn Mawr (DL14.32–3).

All but a handful of Derwent's landscapes have now been geolocated for this publication through a process of digital mapping and map overlay, archival, pictorial and photographic research, and with drone video capture and on-site visits.

A MANOR AT ALDERNEY

Augustus had discovered the light of Provence in early 1910.[12] Not a year later this was followed by Dick's personal discovery of the northern Welsh landscape, shared with Augustus and Derwent. However, during 1911, Augustus became enraptured once again by something new, this time in southern England. In July, he penned a letter from 'Alderney Manor, Dorset',[13] a place he was to lease for over 15 years. Among acres of scrubby heath and pinewood, he and Dorelia created a bohemian utopia for themselves, their family and friends. Many were to pass through Alderney; some stayed a while, others lived there semi-permanently in one of the caravans, carts or gypsy wagons scattered around the property. There were outbuildings and small cottages, with an oddly designed bungalow as the central focus. Dorelia created a potager and flowerbeds inside the round-walled garden and tended the orchard. They fostered a communal, freer life based on a fundament of acceptance. Dorelia was in her element, as was Augustus. Here, he re-envisioned the south of France, this time conveniently located in England, and not far by train, though just far enough, from London.

At Alderney Manor, along the Dorset coast, in the Purbeck hills, sandy heathlands and nearby water-filled abandoned clay pits, Augustus discovered a simulacrum of the Provençal landscapes and the sunshine and freedom he had found around Martigues, for which he maintained a visceral passion. He revelled in his time in Provence, Wales and London, but found his own nearby version of the Mediterranean in these Dorset heathlands and hills, approximations of the southern French *maquis* scrub, perfumed pinewoods, sand and sea air. This environment would come to transfix Derwent, after also being captivated by the light and colour of southern France in 1910 and 1911.

A series of iridescent blue and green inland pools lay chained above the Dorset coast, their colours shifting with season and weather. The prize among these for both Derwent and Augustus was the Blue Pool, a flooded clay pit at Furzebrook. Its water is intensely coloured with azures, aquamarines and greens due to the suspended clay particles in the water; its contents having been excavated for ball clay, to make tobacco pipes and fine crockery, supplying the famed Wedgewood and Minton pottery factories.[14] Its banks heavily forested today, in the 1910s it was deserted and water-filled, its steep and rolling sandy banks virtually bare, with only a low heathy regrowth of shrubs, wildflowers and the occasional stand of pines.

This varied and dramatic landscape was ideal for working *en plein air*, and in summer, the temperatures, scrubland, local geology and colours, although greener, echoed Provence. This new fantasy played out like a magical stage-set for Augustus

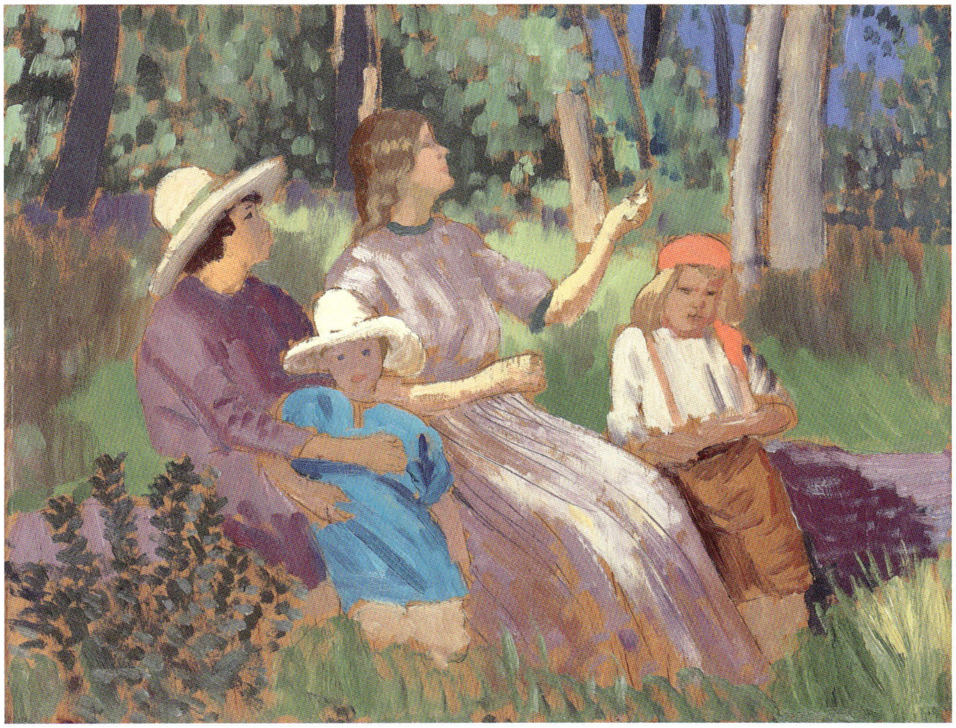

Augustus John, *The Fairy Tale*, c.1912, oil on panel, 30.5 x 39.4 cm, Private Collection

Dorelia and Lyndra (l–r) with Augustus's children, Alderney Manor, Dorset

and his friends' art. 'Purbeck does shine forth like some green and promised land.'[15] Of Augustus and the visiting artists, David Boyd Haycock writes that 'it was here, at a flooded clay pit in 1911 that we see British art breaking free from the shackles of Impressionism and embracing the vibrancy and life and colour of what Roger Fry the year before had dubbed Post-Impressionism. It's all Gauguin and Matisse and the south of France – hardly southern England at all.'[16]

Like Collioure, Purbeck and the Dorset coast had long been frequented by artists. The Slade staff and many of their students had painted there for several years. Scenes among the Purbeck Hills at Creech and Corfe, at Studland Beach, Worbarrow Bay and around the Poole coast became increasingly common. For the next four summers, Derwent would paint at all these locations, shifting effortlessly between landforms and figures, creating joyful, highly coloured scenes.

On the banks of the Blue Pool, in the Alderney garden and in neighbouring heathland, he also painted his muse, posed sometimes casually, sometimes carefully. Edith came to feature as a central figure in Derwent's Dorset works, mostly on her own but sometimes with Dorelia, as well as in works by Augustus. Edith has been mistaken for other models in some portraits and figured landscapes. An unnamed painting by Derwent of Edith in the garden at Alderney was misnamed *Dorelia* (DL13.29), and some works of Edith by Augustus have also been mis-assigned, such as *An Hour at Ower*, a scene showing Dorelia seated in a Dorset landscape with Edith (not Nora Brownsword as has been surmised). Here, Edith again wears her signature white stockings, black shoes and long dress, as in many of Derwent's works.

Soon after taking on the Alderney leasehold, Augustus painted *The Fairy Tale* and *Gypsy in the Sandpit*, which shows Edith playing and talking with Dorelia and her children in the woods and heathland. Augustus's son Caspar identified Edith in *Woman and Child*, c.1911–12:

> One of John's favorite themes during his early career was that of women and children in nature. He generally depicted friends or his own family and often worked on a small scale in a broad, colorful manner. Sir Caspar John, Augustus' second son, has identified the woman in this painting [*Woman and Child*] as Ashley Lees, wife of the painter Derwent Lees. *The wife was at the time a frequent visitor to my father's house, Alderney Manor, in Dorset and he did numerous drawings of her* (letter to the Gallery, 14 Sept 1975). The young boy, Sir Caspar wrote, is probably David, the artist's eldest son.[17]

It was once remarked that Augustus's Provençal and Dorset works transported 'the beholder into a country of sunlight'.[18] A brief period of great creative richness, fostered by Augustus, was ignited here for both men, some claiming it to be their peak.

ROOMS IN LONDON

In the autumn of 1911, Edith Harriet Price turned 21, recording her profession as 'artist model' on the census that year, and living with her mother, now supporting four children. In the same Kensington house were older sister May, an actress; a younger brother, who at 17 was an artist's assistant; a school-aged brother; and a rent-paying boarder. Edith's father had died, or left, when she was barely ten, and her mother had remarried, had another son, and was again widowed or separated.

During the previous year, Edith had seen little of Derwent; she was busy modelling for Augustus, who produced numerous nude studies of her in uninhibited poses. She was then both his model and lover, although he was busy trying to extricate himself from yet another tryst with the wealthy, headstrong Austrian cabaret owner Frida Strindberg. Frida resorted to extreme measures to garner Augustus's attention and, during one encounter, she implored Augustus not to believe stories that Edith had 'been bribed by me not to see you, that I had twice tried to murder her, once by poison, once by pushing her from a cliff' and that it was all 'positively untrue'. In another 1911 letter, Frida pleaded with Augustus to take her back, while referring to his 'girl friend' Edith as 'a silly Kensington girl from a penny novel.'[19]

Despite his continuous string of lovers, Dorelia, his life companion, remained as a true and constant presence at Augustus's side. As a sign of affection, he often gave her pet names. He did not refer to her by her real name Dorothy, but rather Dorelia, and during their many decades together he would sometimes playfully call her 'Relia', 'Ardor' or 'Dodo'.[20]

During the summer of 1911, Augustus had painted the oil *Edyth and Caspar, Dorset Study* at Alderney, later exhibited at the famed American Armory Show. However, it seems that Edith did not like her real name appearing in painting titles (only this example exists). Augustus's version is the only time Edith's name was spelt with a 'y', however, later that year, during or after their short-lived liaison, she started to refer to herself as Lyndra, a name likely coined by Augustus – *llyn* (anglicised to *lyn*) and *dra* from the Welsh meaning deep lake. In awe of her esteemed artist-lover, she continued to use the moniker, Lyndra.

For Derwent, 1911 had been artistically highly varied, with painting trips to northern Wales and Provençal France, and possibly also Dorset. He returned to live at Chelsea's Cheyne Walk, turning 27 at year's end, noting his profession as 'painter' on the census, not teacher, and as New Zealand-born, not Australian. Since his lack of self-identity often led him to emulate those he revered, perhaps he associated with being a New Zealander because of the Lees family roots or because his brother Gilbert had settled there. Maybe it felt reassuring 'to be there too'.

Derwent lived at Cheyne Walk with Dick or other artists, on and off for a number of years. Female artist friends Essil Elmslie and the sisters Alice and Ethel Elder lived close by, with Fairlie Harmar (1876–1945) next door at number 126. Years later, Randolph Schwabe, also a Cheyne resident, would recount that, 'Fairlie H. told me that she has a cook who used to "do for" Derwent Lees'.[21]

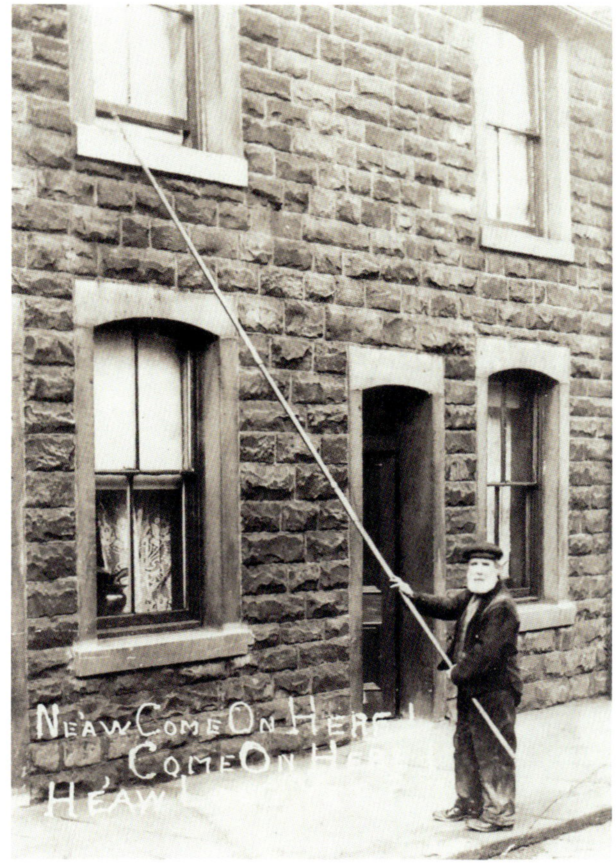

A knocker-upper wakes a client, c.1900, photographer unknown, Red Rose Collections, Lancashire County Council

The head of Derwent's house at number 125 was Henry West, a London lighterman, an important Thames dockside profession. Lightermen guided barges or rowed out into the river in all weather, day or night, in long shifts, to collect goods from ships and bring them back to the quays. The work demanded strength, good health and a deep understanding of the Thames's difficult currents. Like other London dock workers, he likely paid a local 'knocker-upper' to ensure he was at work on time, as his hours were often governed by the tides. Henry supplemented his income by renting out rooms in his house near Battersea Bridge, between the Lindsey and Old Ferry wharves. Chelsea provided cheap accommodation for young artists in the Edwardian era. It was awash with writers and artists' studios and sprawling room-let boarding houses, where sleeping quarters were basic at best. However, in 1911, Derwent was the only registered boarder at the West family home. Perhaps Henry, his wife Elizabeth, and their young daughter provided some semblance of family.

7 MASTERING COLOUR 1912

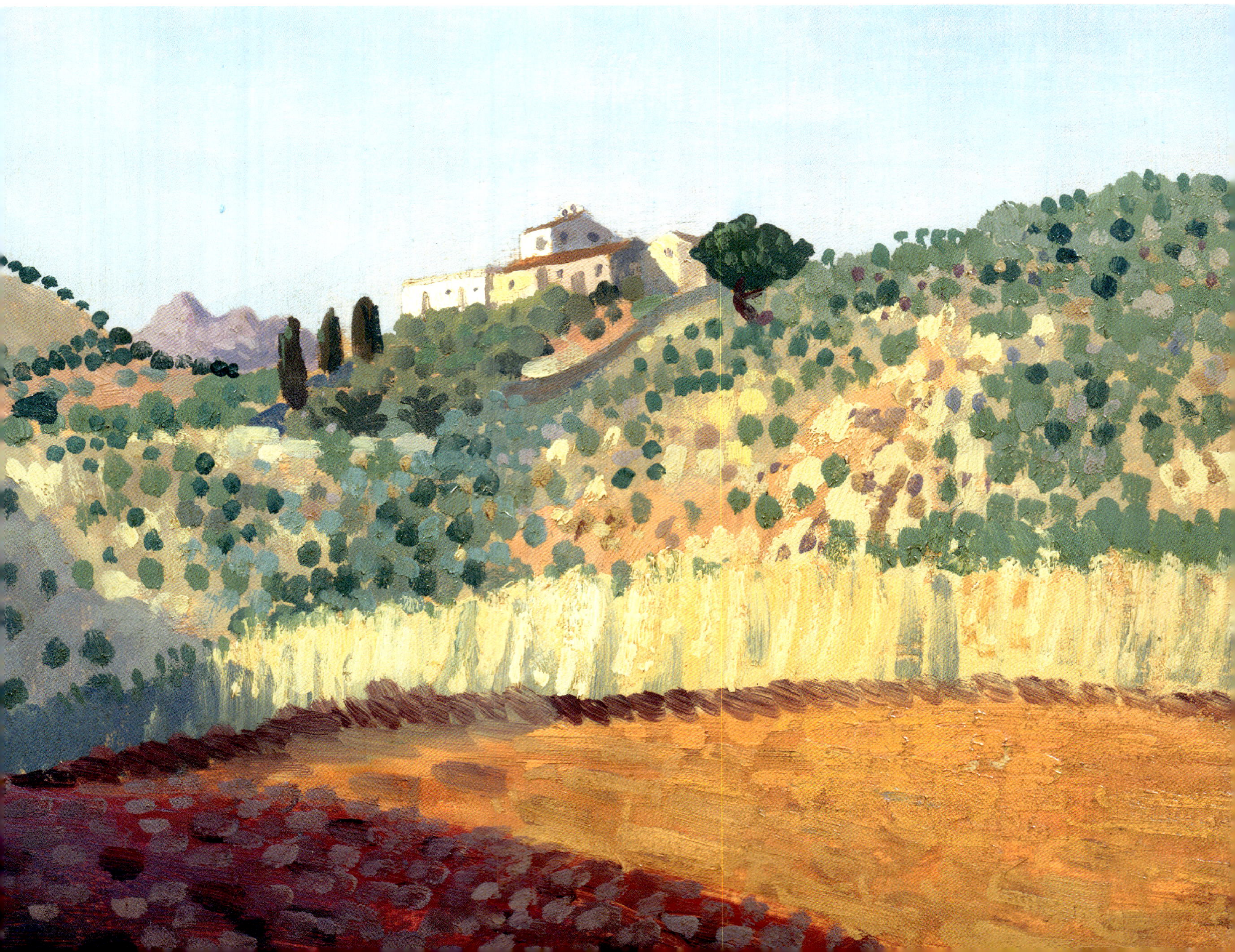

Derwent saw less of Dick during early 1912, apart from a short trip to Hastings and Rye. Dick's tuberculosis was now impacting his daily life, so in May he accepted an invitation from Tommy Scott-Ellis (1880–1946), 8th Baron Howard de Walden, to drive to Spain through France, briefly revisiting French Catalonia,[1] where he, Walter Russell and Derwent had painted two years earlier. The trip was undoubtedly an attempt to improve Dick's condition, with rest stops at sanatoria and spa towns frequented by British aristocrats, European royalty and renowned entertainers. In France, they stayed at the Hotel du Parc at Vernet-les-Bains (a favourite with the often ill Rudyard Kipling, who regularly took the renowned sulphur baths and drank hot sulphurous 'water-cures'), then to Banyuls near the French–Spanish border, before travelling on to the ancient spa town of Ronda in Spain. Here, they stayed at the exclusive Reina Victoria hotel-spa, from whose balcony Dick painted *Afternoon, Ronda*. However, Dick must have preferred the sea to the mountain air and profited from his time in Banyuls while rekindling his passion for the coastal region (now called the Côte Vermeille),[2] for he was to return six months later with Derwent.

Dick and Derwent had met Tommy Scott-Ellis and wife Margherita (Margot) through Augustus. They were active supporters of the arts and avid collectors. In 1910, Tommy had become President of the Contemporary Art Society, whose first purchase was a work by Augustus. Two years on, the Society purchased nine works in oil, one of which was Derwent's *Arenig Mawr, North Wales* (later misinterpreted as *Arenig Manor, North Wales*; DL11.1). Derwent was in good company, alongside Ambrose McEvoy (1878–1927), Vanessa Bell, Duncan Grant and Henry Tonks, whose works were purchased by the Society in the same year. The Society's aim was to 'encourage by purchase and exhibition the more remarkable examples of painters who in any other country would enjoy a certain official patronage. During the last century little or no attempt was made to secure for the nation any vital contemporary painting which has stood the test of time.'[3] The Society would buy three works by the young Australian during his life (also DL14.15, DL15.19).

Opposite:
DL12.26 (detail)
Derwent Lees, *Métairie des Abeilles*, 1912

BY ARENIG FAWR

From 1911 to 1914, Derwent painted often in Wales, chiefly with Dick and Augustus, with fellow artists Ian Strang and Elsie McNaught as occasional company. On some trips, he accompanied Augustus, Dorelia McNeill and Edith, and, for a short time, leased a room or small cottage at Ffestiniog,[4] most likely in the summers of 1912 and 1914. When accompanied by Augustus, Derwent predominantly painted female figures in landscape settings, taking his elder's lead. One critic later remarked that 'There is a lovely piece of colour by the late Derwent Lees, *Figure by Pool Tan-y-Grisiau*, Johnesque of course but individual in colour scheme' (DL14.37).[5] When alone with Dick, he usually painted figureless mountain scenes.

For three years, Dick, Augustus and Derwent followed a rhythm of painting together in Wales, mainly focused around the catchment of the Afon Tryweryn near Bala in the Migneint, then near the slate-mining village of Tanygrisiau below Blaenau Ffestiniog. Derwent painted *Welsh Hills* (DL12.6), a romanticised scene of the now-defunct slate mine and buildings in the Cwmorthin valley above Tanygrisiau, while another, *Tan-y-Bwlch* (DL14.34), shows Edith among rocks above the railway station of the same name. It is one of a dozen works capturing her during the pre-war summer, mostly in scenes around Ffestiniog and Tanygrisiau, and not far from their cottages.[6]

In the wake of Dick's enthusiasm for the mountains of Wales, Derwent also painted numerous scenes around Nant Ddu and the slopes and tarns of Arenigs Fawr and Fach, Pen Tyrau and Moel Llyfnant, sometimes including the Tryweryn stream and the lakes Llyn Tegid (Lake Bala) and Llyn Arenig Fawr. In the wilds of the Migneint and the Moelwyns, the artists had their pick of rolling mountains, creating a mix of often vividly coloured figured and figureless landscapes.

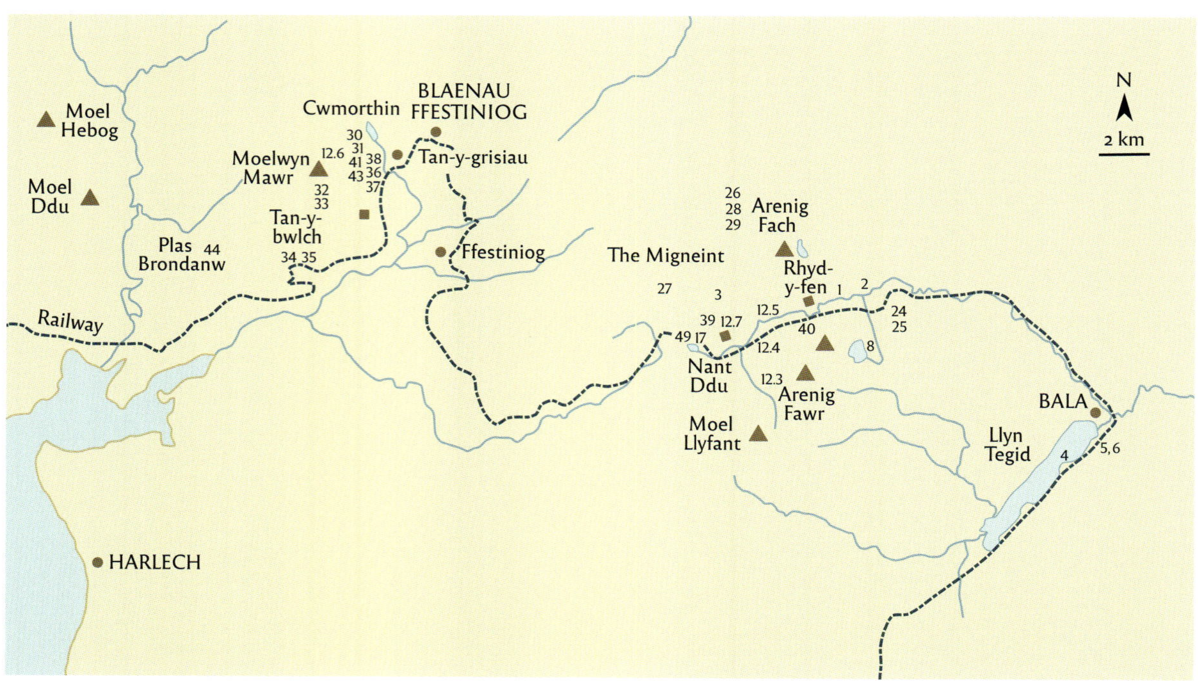

Locations where Derwent painted in North Wales, 1911, 1912 and 1914

Numbers indicate known painting sites, DL11.1–6, 8, 17, DL12.3–7, DL14.24–44; DL11. and DL14. prefixes are not shown

Derwent would later recount their painting rhythm: 'we decided to paint only when the sunlight and moonlight showed us Arenig and her landscape in all of her beauty, we would then immediately paint or draw at great speed and with great energy, this wonder. It is exhausting us all, though it is greatly worth it.'[7]

During this period, Tommy leased Chirk Castle near the Welsh–English border, and here Margot held regular musical and artistic gatherings. Many artists stayed at Chirk, often commissioned to paint the wealthy and generous couple. Margot would later recount in her memoirs that Philip Wilson Steer was 'disgusted' with Augustus for not completing her portrait, despite more than 60 sittings (though he completed it years later).[8] Derwent was also later commissioned to do her portrait, resulting in colourful watercolours (DL18.1, 3) and perhaps an oil.

Although short-lived, the creative output of the three adventurous artists in North Wales from 1910 to 1914 is credited with forming what some refer to as the Arenig School, an art movement of a kind, sparked by Dick and his deep passion for these mountains, which brought a lyrical, post-Impressionist, sometimes Symbolist, always vividly coloured style to the Welsh landscape. This lasted until they were separated by illness and war.

All three men were profoundly affected by what seems to be a childhood resonance with their surrounds and a deep connection with place. In 1939, Eric Newton in 'Pre-War Romanticism: John, Innes and Lees' described their relationship as a 'brotherhood', in which 'each one of the three had his contribution to make . . . it was John who created the characters, Innes who furnished the landscape backgrounds and Lees who stylised the whole'. Upon seeing their works together at the 1939 exhibition celebrating this brotherhood, he remarked that 'the lasting impression left by the exhibition is one of glowing, unhesitant colour'.[9]

While the three friends had established a comfortable painting collaboration and camaraderie, with Dick remaining faithful to the wild and remote landscape of Wales, Augustus and Derwent's passion became increasingly recentred on Dorset, their beloved substitute for the south of France.

PICNICS AND ROAD TRIPS

The annual Slade picnic was an important part of the School's social calendar, capping off the end of Term II. The 1912 picnic photograph shows a neat, clean-shaven Derwent in an oversized blazer beside Charles Koe Child (1868–1935), the Slade administrator. Little more than a decade earlier, the picnic photo had captured Augustus with William Orpen beside Augustus's artist sister Gwen (1876–1939), the Rothensteins and Albert Rutherston in a wagon-cart.

In the 1912 photograph, Adrian Allinson (1890–1959) sits in the front row with his dog. A student at the Slade from 1910, he befriended Mark Gertler (1891–1939, front row, fourth from left) and Christopher Nevinson (1889–1946, front row, third from left), all three of whom were taught by Derwent and became respected artists. At the School, they formed their own group, The Coster Gang, dressing like costermongers in an eccentric ensemble.[10] Adrian finished his studies in June

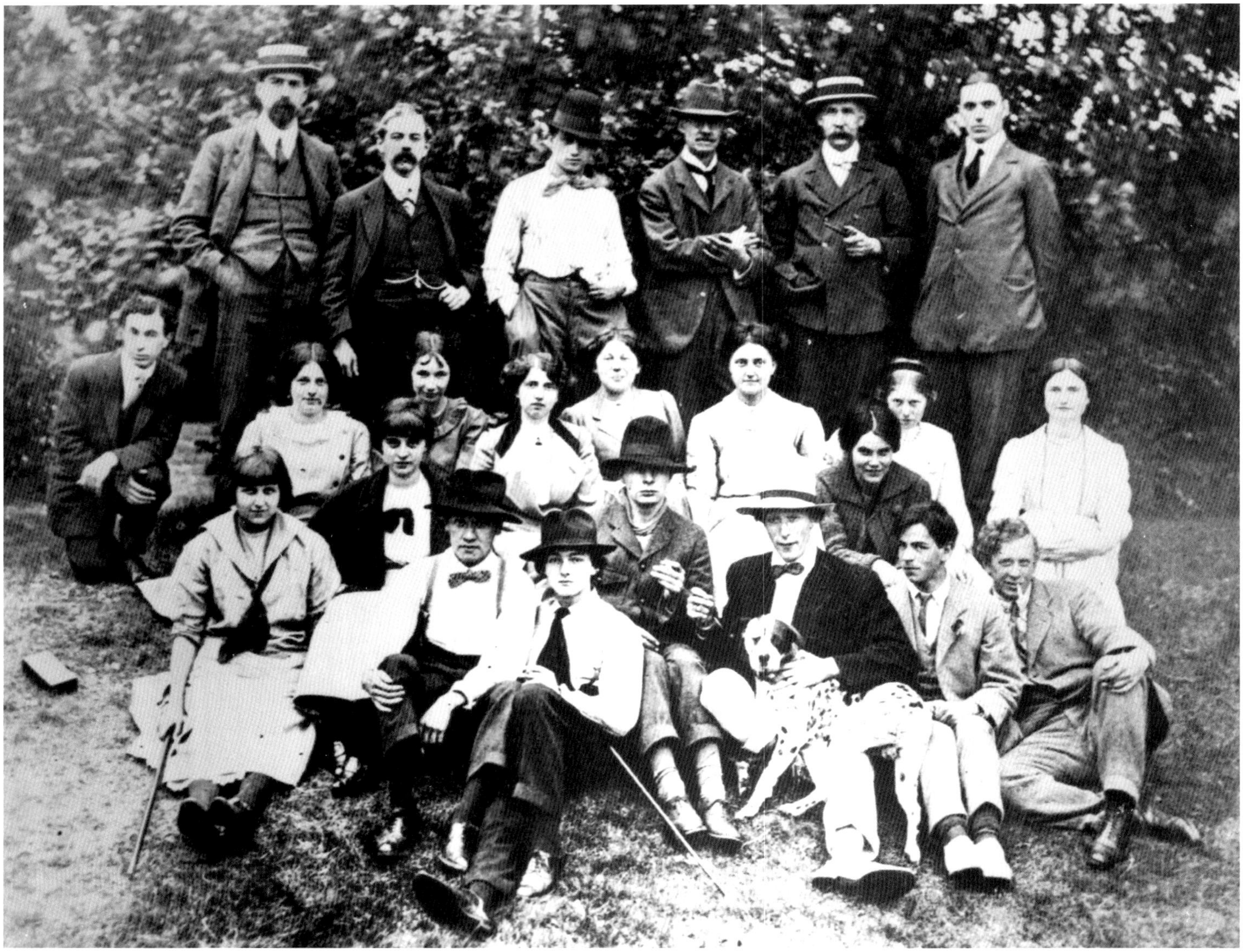

1912, and submitted a light-hearted, but clever and perceptive, caricature of the staff, *The Happy Family*, for exhibition through the New English Art Club (NEAC).

Unsurprisingly, given the Club's close associations with the Slade, the work was rejected, but the depiction is telling. Steer, an 1886 NEAC founding member, is portrayed as the rotund *pater familias*, and indeed many former students felt that Steer 'was the brains of' the Slade.[11] Tonks, Head of Drawing, pushes an ageing Professor Fred Brown in a pram, a nod to his loyalty to the institution, and his support for Brown. Steer is captured as the central figure, holding 'an adolescent' Russell, now Assistant in Painting and long-term staff member, by the hand. Russell in turn guides young Derwent, Assistant in Drawing and faithful *protégé*, by a lead. The youngest and most recent staff member, Derwent is the smiling, dependable and accommodating puppy, revealing both the staff and students' opinion of him as loyal, compliant and personable. In a sign of affection, 'Derwent the puppy' is given the same black-spotted fur as Adrian's own beloved dog.

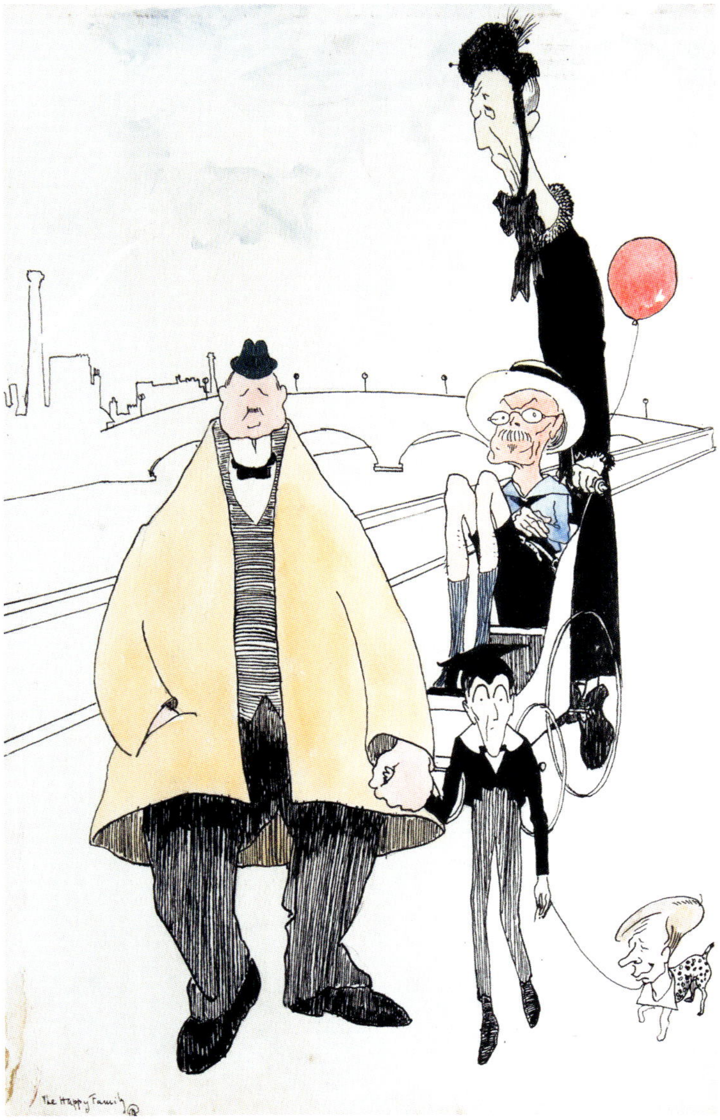

Opposite:
The Slade School Picnic, c.1912, photographer unknown, Tate, London. Derwent in the back row, far right

Left:
Adrian Allinson, *The Happy Family*, 1911–12, pen, ink and watercolour on panel, 32.3 x 22.8 cm, Chris Beetles Gallery, London

Philip Wilson Steer holds Walter Russell's hand, who in turn leads Derwent 'the puppy'. Henry Tonks pushes Professor Fred Brown in a pram

Derwent and Dick met fellow artist Frank Slade through Augustus, to whom he was related through marriage (Frank's brother Edgar had married Jessie McNeill, Dorelia's sister, and Augustus was also close to Frank's brother, Charles). Frank and his wife Hannah, also an artist, spent their summers on the English coast at Rye. Dick based himself there during late spring of 1912 and, before the long summer break, Derwent arrived with Slade students in tow. After a short stay, Derwent later rejoined Frank and Dick, and the three artists sketched around Rye, Pett Level and Guestling. Frank recalled that 'we walked one day to the White Hart at Guestling sketching. Dick, Lees and I decided to sketch Pett Level from the field opposite. We each did a sketch sitting side by side.'[12]

Dick was now frequently unwell, but this did not stop him suggesting an extended trip with Derwent and Frank. Their first stop was the Birmingham City Art Gallery to view the much-promoted Dante Gabriel Rossetti drawings. The Gallery was closed when they arrived, but they gained access thanks to Derwent's Slade School status and '. . . with Professor Lees we got in and were allowed to see the works'.[13] From here, they went in search of new Welsh painting sites, taking trains, cars and old wagons on a hectic painting tour. They sketched and painted mountains, castles, streams, lakes and trees, finishing at Nant Ddu cottage, where Augustus was ensconced with a group of friends and models. Strang also joined them. He sketched a sickly Dick, completing a portrait in oil the following year. Dick continued to push himself, but his body no longer kept up with the demands placed on it.

During the year, he and Derwent had also painted the southern Pembrokeshire coast, near Tenby, where Augustus was born, and along the Gower Peninsula close to Dick's natal town, Llanelli.

Back in London, Derwent had moved to Fitzroy Square in January 1912, where he remained through the first part of the coming war. His rooms, on the second floor at number 21, had a small studio space and overlooked the square. According to Frank, 'Derwent Lees lent me his studio in Fitzroy Square where Innes had been living with him and painting some of his interiors. One time Dick became ill and had to stay in bed. The studio was only just across the passage so we could look after him well.'[14] Derwent painted scenes of the studio as well as views of the square from the front room. His Van Gogh-like drawing of his studio with chair (held by the British Council, DL12.14), surely inspired by Roger Fry's curated London Post-Impressionist exhibitions, shows the same chair seen in a later, unfinished portrait of his wife painted during the war (DL15.29).

It is highly likely that Derwent attended the mid-September nuptials of close friends and former Slade classmates, Nora Munro and Gerald Summers. They married at Chelsea's Old Church and then headed off for a year-long honeymoon abroad. A shift was happening in Derwent's group of friends. Many were settling down, some marrying fellow artists. Derwent was 27 and his older friends, Fred (1866–1916) and Hannah Mayor (1871–1947), the Bevans, the Slades and the McEvoys, had married more than a decade earlier, but now his contemporaries were finding partners. Randolph Schwabe married Slade graduate 'Birdie' (Gwendolyn) Jones. Donald Maclaren (Mac) married Violet, while in April 1913, the same month as Schwabe's wedding, his brother Gilbert married Clarice Wood in New Zealand.

Derwent was a decent prospect. His artistic reputation was on the rise, and he held a contracted position for much of the year, augmented by his father's allowance. Augustus, by contrast, lived a more bohemian lifestyle, with regular trysts and liaisons, despite living with Dorelia, his model-muse and common-law wife – a strong, determined woman. He was an established artist with solid patronage, so he could afford to be wild and eccentric. Derwent, however, was single, with both limited funds and patronage.

As Nora and Gerald prepared to tie the knot in London, Dick collapsed in Ireland at Coole Park, home of Slade graduates Robert and Margaret Gregory.[15] Robert was just a year or so from apparently starting an affair with Nora.[16] Dick's health alarmed those close to him. He returned to London, and during autumn fluctuated between anger, desperation, overwork and heavy drinking. Days, if not weeks, passed of heavy depression, his energy low and often bedridden.[17] His teeth now gone, he ate little.

A SOUTH OF HILLS AND GARDENS

Six months earlier Dick had returned from his restorative trip to French and Spanish sanatoria, only to be confronted by Britian's wettest and coldest summer in 200 years. The 1912 summer was calamitous for the sick, especially for those with lung conditions. The only solution was to head south again. Derwent, likely Dick's 'carer-companion', accompanied him once again to take in the crisp Mediterranean air.

Despite tuberculosis severely impacting Dick's daily life, the pair left London to spend the winter-term break at Banyuls, a coastal village south of Collioure in France. The regional climate, with its sunny skies and recuperative sea air, was considered one of the country's best for rheumatic and respiratory sufferers, including the tubercular. Close to the Spanish border, they alighted from the train above the Baillaury River, which snakes out from the Albères mountains. The village was home to Aristide Maillol, a close friend of Matisse and Montfreid, and an active member of the Artistes Roussillonnais.

December was cool in Banyuls, but the sky was brilliant blue, with the village bathed in crisp, clear light. Paul Soulier's 1902 booklet reported that the botanist Charles Naudin's measurements of sunlight hours showed the region to be six times sunnier than northern France,[18] with more sunlight in December than in April, when Dick had first visited the region. The winter light is sharper, as summer humidity can mask the clarity of distant views, evident in several of Derwent's 1910 works. In winter 1912 his colour palette was transformed.

A severely unwell Dick worked no more than a 10-minute walk from the Hotel des Bains et de la Plage and now rarely completed works *en plein air*.[19] However, he still managed to sketch and paint a handful of oils in his familiar pink and russet brown tones. By contrast, Derwent ventured considerable distances, exploring the town's hinterland using the dry riverbed and adjacent ridges as thoroughfares (DL12.26).

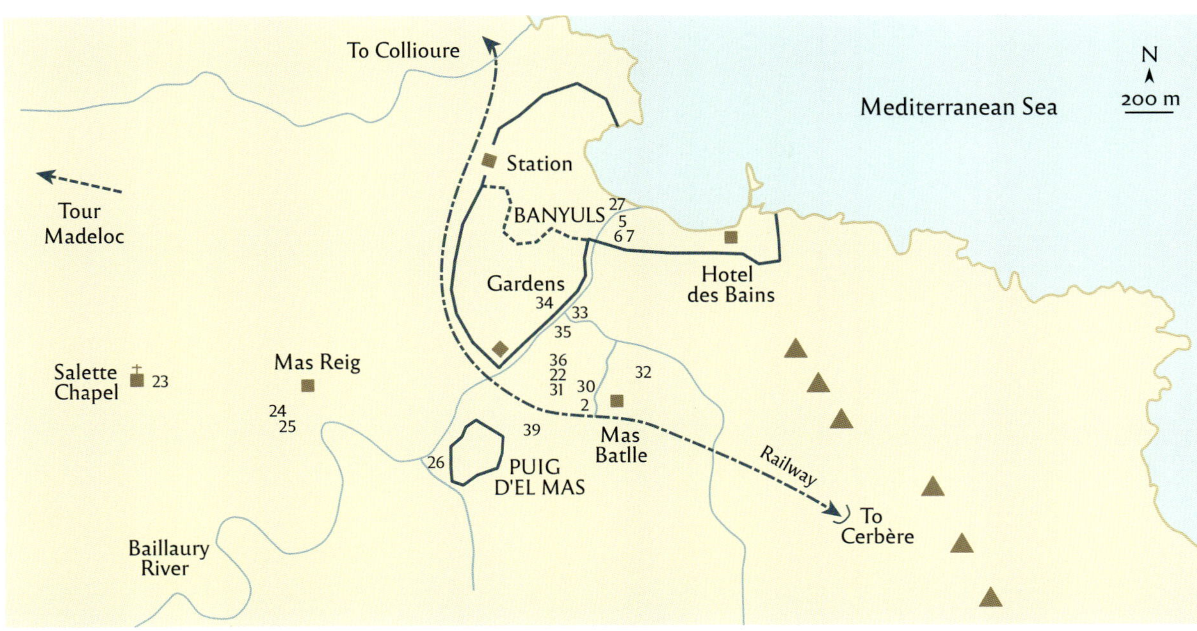

Locations where Derwent painted in Banyuls, 1912–1913 Numbers indicate known painting sites, DL12.22–39, DL13.2, 5–7; DL12. and DL13. prefixes are not shown

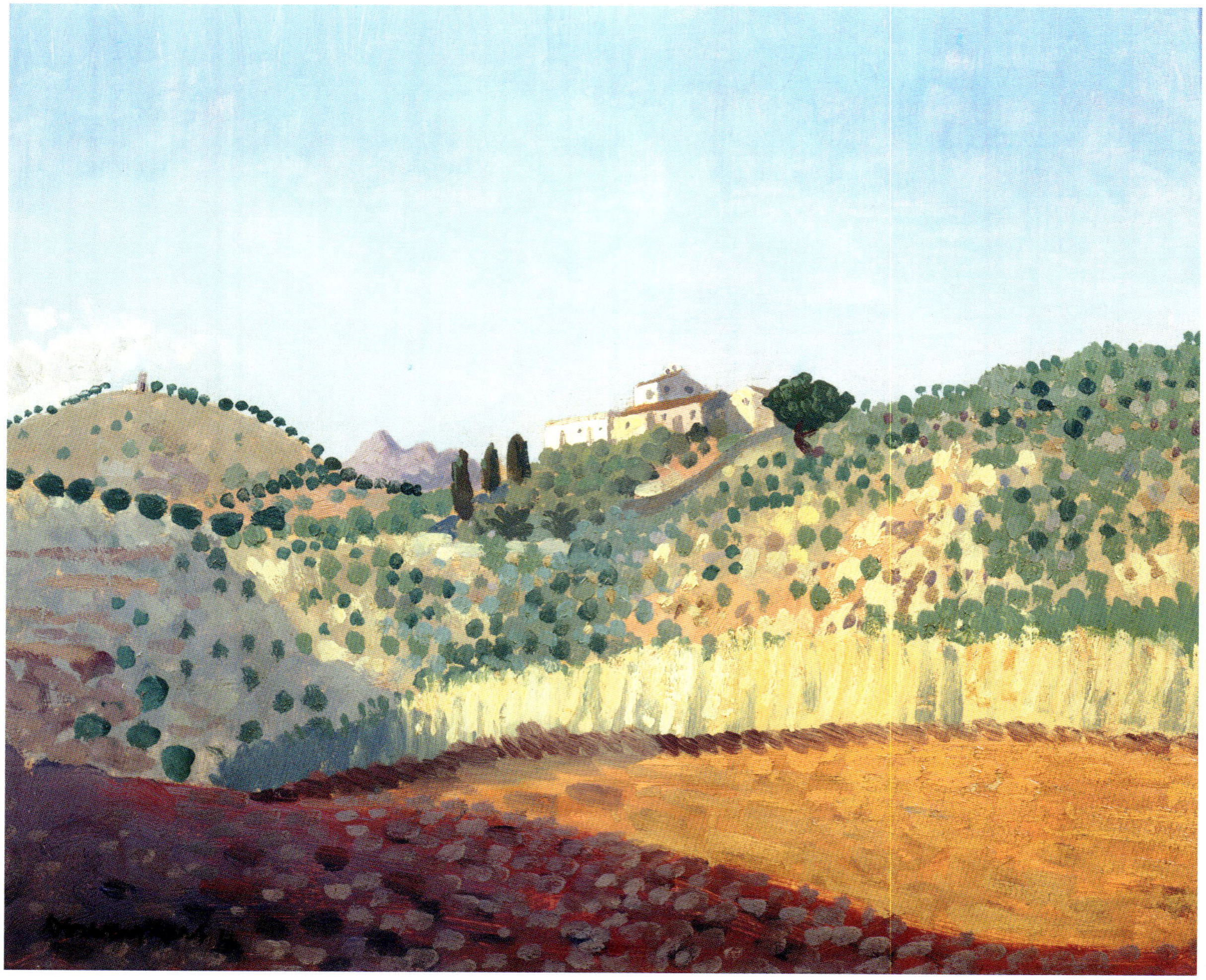

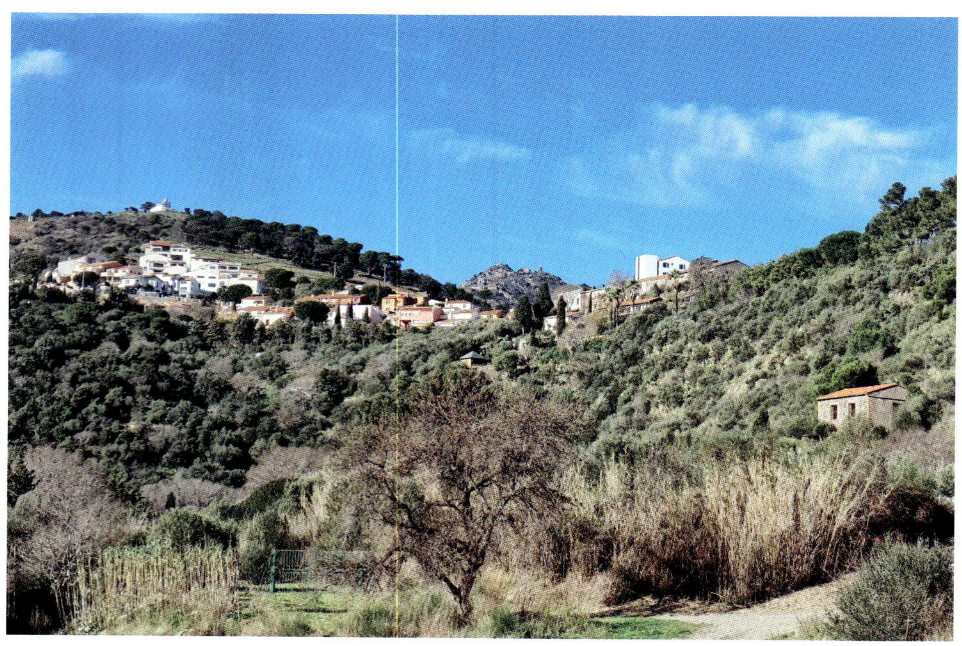

Above:
DL12.26
Derwent Lees, *Métairie des Abeilles*, 1912, oil on panel, 33 x 40.6 cm, Tate

Right:
Present-day view of Mas Reig, Banyuls
See DL12.26

He walked from the bridge below the hamlet of Puig del Mas and discovered the picturesque Mas Batlle with its ancient tower, tucked below the railway line. He painted half a dozen scenes around this *mas* (Catalan farmhouse), and another ten along the riverbank. The winter season is evident, with yellowed river reeds, silvery dormant olive groves and the red- and yellow-leafed vines with brown ochres among the rampant *friche* (dry scrub). He then headed north, crossing the river, and climbing to the ridgetop houses and towers of Mas Reig to paint two further scenes, one later erroneously titled *Spanish Landscape* (DL12.24), then mounted the steep ridge to the small chapel above to sketch *The Blue Hills* (held at the Art Institute of Chicago for the past century, DL12.23). With his wooden prosthetic foot, and the steep, unforgiving terrain, it seems likely he took a donkey to explore these slopes, perhaps the one depicted in *Donkey at Mas Reig, Banyuls* (DL12.25).

In the years that followed, Derwent's vivid Banyuls landscapes, all in sharp, lively colours echoing the bright Australian palette, drew the best reviews of his career. Art critic C. Lewis Hind would write that 'it was Lees who influenced Innes in the flat Japanesy, high-keyed type of landscape', and that the two were part of the Slade's 'Decorative Painting Landscapists'.[20] Derwent's large *Banyuls* oil is a shining example (DL13.2). The painting shimmers in a kaleidoscope of bright enamel blues, oranges and greens. Held at the Southampton City Art Gallery, at its centre is the iconic Mas Batlle, surrounded by sparkling silver olive trees. The palette and the background hills are resonant of the sharp, eastern Australian landscape.

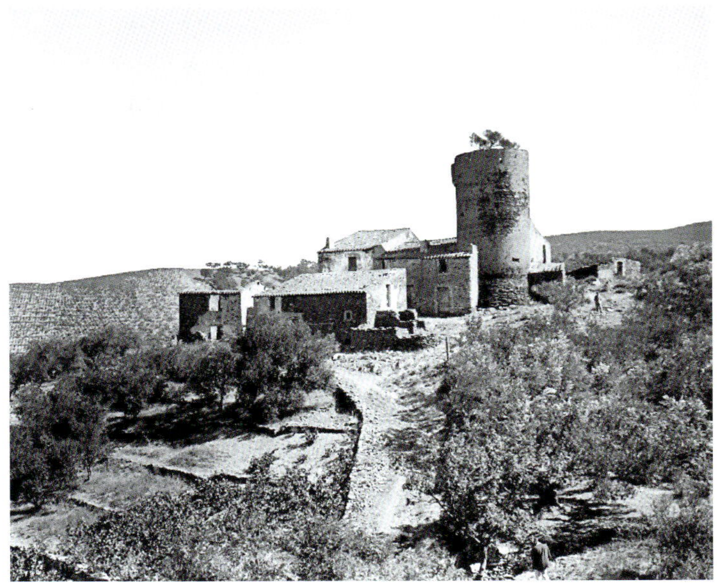

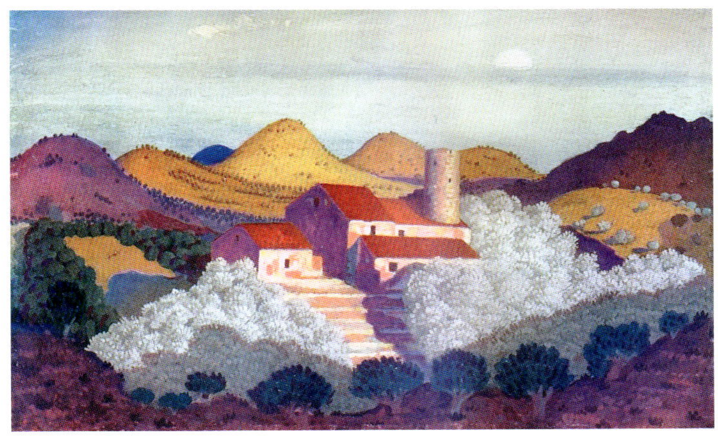

Above:
Mas Batlle, Banyuls, c.1920, postcard, France

Below:
DL12.30
Derwent Lees, *Mas Catalan / Sunset Near Collioure / Sunset, South of France / Sunset, Collioure / Sunset, Colliure*, 1912, oil on panel, 24 x 37.7 cm, Redfern Gallery

Derwent's unique colour palette and style are evident throughout this trip, the works full of luminous yellows, orange, glowing greens and blues, contrasting markedly with Dick's crimson, blush pink and brown tones. These distinctive elements are captured in both Banyuls and Forcalquier, a Provençal village in the Basses Alpes that they visited on the same trip. Derwent's fidelity to the geomorphology and vegetation distinguishes his landscapes from those of his companion and shows that he never fully escaped his Slade training, deliberately or otherwise. By this time, Dick's style had a more playful looseness, and in Banyuls he 'invented his harmonious warm world', giving an 'olive tree a decorative sinuousness that Lees' attention to detail could never allow'.[21] Later, an observant art critic would note that 'when one looks from a distance at Mr Derwent Lees' effects of bold masses, it is curious to discover that actually each minute tree is separately outlined'.[22]

Derwent concentrated on fidelity of scene and luminosity of colour, while Dick's landscapes exhibited a more visionary, quixotic approach.[23] Dick was spontaneous, thriving on rapidly capturing a scene, 'swift in the manner he worked in oil, sometimes slapdash with rapid small brushstrokes and unfocussed when it came to detail'.[24]

Derwent was measured; he liked to study, reflect and cogitate before his final work-up in oil, most often after preparatory watercolours.

Derwent remained faithful to Tonks's training, reinforcing the importance of mastering 'the direction of a contour'. As Tonks's biographer explained, 'The word "outline" did not exist for him, and he would not allow it'.[25] Derwent's work captured the difference between contour and outline, championing Tonks's teaching. However, with no distractions, and when liberated by the intensity of the light, Derwent discovered in Banyuls and Istres (and later again in Cassis) a freedom to express a wider range of coloration and texture, all within the confines of close observation. He demonstrated a tactile, almost sensual response to this southern temperate landscape, enhanced by unusual and judicious choices of scene, never the postcard view.

Derwent was the most prolific early 20th-century painter of Banyuls and the Tour Madeloc massif, with Maillol and his lifelong friend Jozsef Rippl-Ronai (1861–1927) also capturing the local *paysage*. Curiously, in Derwent's works, while remaining true to nature, he is highly selective, avoiding and even eliminating certain man-made elements. For the most part, he deliberately avoids village views, preferring a single or small cluster of structures, as his central foreground focus. His composition is chromatically structured, aligning with his pedagogic design principles of fore-, mid- and background, like a theatre stage set. In Banyuls he removes the man-made medieval stone Tour Madeloc atop the massif in all but one work. For him, it was too powerful an element to form part of the background layer. Interestingly, Dick mostly did the same.

Bursting out of Derwent's Banyuls paintings are the region's Christmas-time riches. The lemon, orange and clementine trees are in full fruit. Renowned for its orangeries, the long street behind the Banyuls waterfront is still called the Rue des Orangers. Derwent's works: *Le Faubourg – Banyuls*, *'Le Mas' Banzals*, *Village Scene*, *Mountain at Banyals*, *The Little Gardens* and *Pear Tree in Blossom* (DL12.27, 33–5, DL13.5–6) capture the abundance of citrus in the market gardens. A creative joy bursts through these paintings, though at least five were later incorrectly renamed, rendering it impossible to appreciate their collective local significance until now. Most of these works, created in the Banyuls *faubourg* (suburb) of market gardens, capture the citrus groves and water wells, with the small hilltop Salette chapel and Tour Madeloc in the background.

The late Professor Albert Callis, a Banyuls local, recounted that as a young boy the gardens 'evoked a lot of memories for me. To get to school we followed the riverbank path by the gardens . . . and when it was the season, in winter, the oranges glowed in the trees and invited us to steal them.'[26]

Citrus fruit gave the local women a meagre but important income. Dick and Derwent's arrival in December 1912 was at the height of the *transbordeuses* (female cross-border workers) season. These local women travelled daily to Cerbère, the neighbouring border village. Trains could not travel from Spain into France as the rail track gauges differed. The women worked in long, back-breaking shifts, moving hundreds of tonnes of luxury citrus from Spanish to French carriages. Women were chosen, as it required careful handling to prevent spoilage of the much-coveted cargo, which was then sold in Paris, Brussels, Berlin and Russia. Using handmade straw

Right:
Les Transbordeuses at Cerbère, moving citrus fruit from Spanish to French trains, c.1920, postcard, France

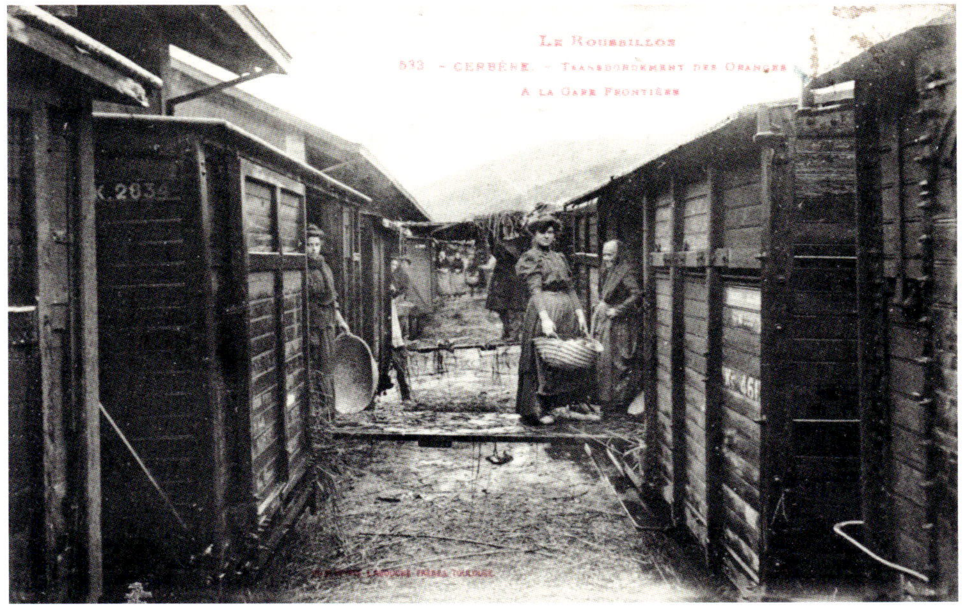

Below:
DL12.27
Derwent Lees, *Le Faubourg – Banyuls / Le Faubourg – Banyals / Spanish Landscape*, 1912, oil on panel, 33.5 x 41 cm, Private Collection

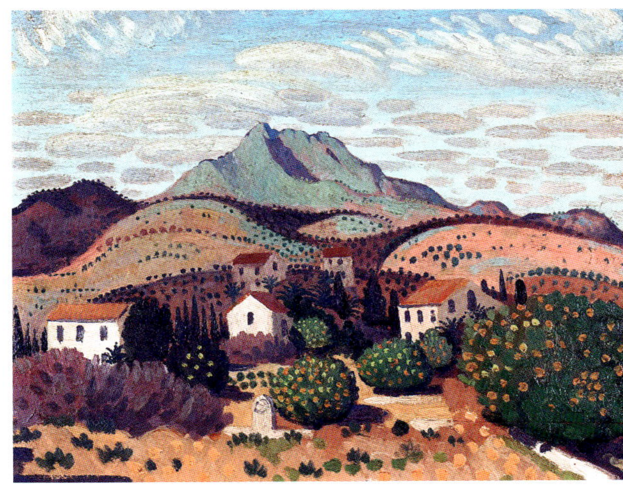

baskets, they carried the fruit across narrow gangplanks from one train carriage to another. Each 20-kg basket was carefully stacked, placing long dry reeds from the local riverbeds between them to create airflow.

The work was hard and relentless. In 1906, they had had enough of the meagre 75 centimes shared between five women per wagon load, and after a year of demands for better pay, they formed one of the earliest female working-class unions and held France's first entirely female strike. They did not succeed, but sowed the seed of years of activism that still stirred during Derwent and Dick's stay.

On the journey south in December, the two young artists had first travelled east from Avignon, visiting the Provençal hilltop towns of Les Baux and Forcalquier to arrive in Digne-les-Bains. Dick sketched Les Baux, a village Augustus had savoured in 1910, in a similar style to a drawing he would do in Banyuls, while Derwent painted *Landscape in the Alpilles* (DL12.16). However, it was in Raoul Dufy's (1877–1953) village of Forcalquier in the Basses Alpes that the young artists found grand panoramic views. From the Citadel at the town's summit, Derwent painted the mountains of the Luberon to the south with the Chapel of St Pancrace, on its remnant volcanic cone, in the foreground (DL12.17). Then followed a broad mountainscape looking east across the valley of the Durance River to the snow-capped Alps and Montagne du Cheval Blanc in the far distance (*Cheval Blanc, Basses Alpes*, erroneously later titled *Italian Landscape with the Alps Beyond*, DL13.1), and a view through the pine trees to the valley below (*Trees, Provence*, DL12.20).

Dick painted the same panorama, *Landscape, Southern France*, from a slightly lower point on the same hill. Another of Derwent's oils, mistitled *Church in a Landscape* (DL12.19), shows the hilltop Citadel seen from an adjacent ridge to the south-east. Not far from Forcalquier is Digne-les-Bains, known for its ancient

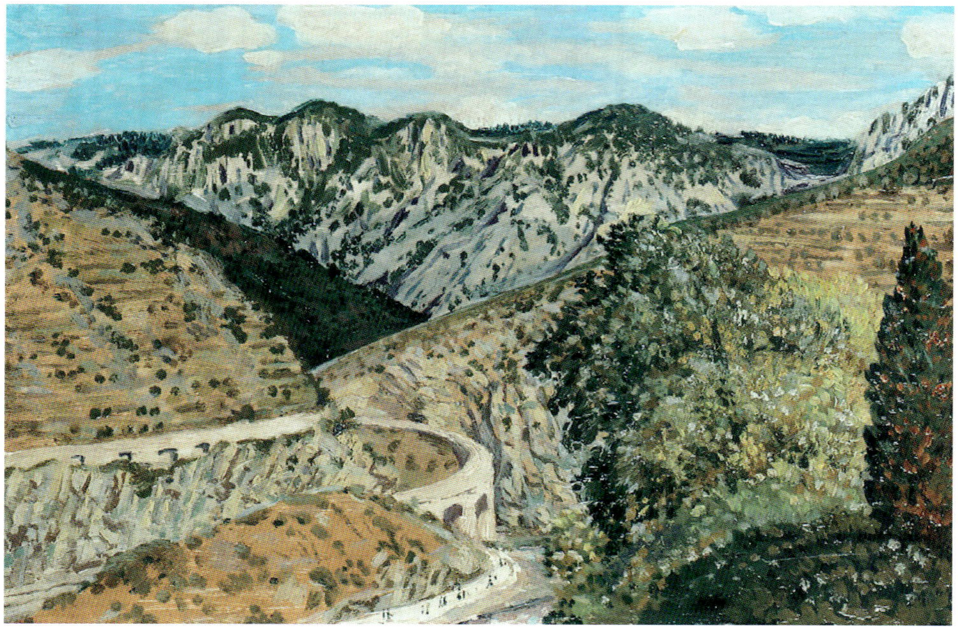

Left:
DL13.4
Derwent Lees, *Mountain Pass / Landscape / Mountainous Landscape*, c.1913, oil on panel, 24.8 x 35.5 cm, Private Collection

Below:
Axat viaduct, Aude Valley, France, c.1910, postcard, France
Painted by Derwent, see DL13.4

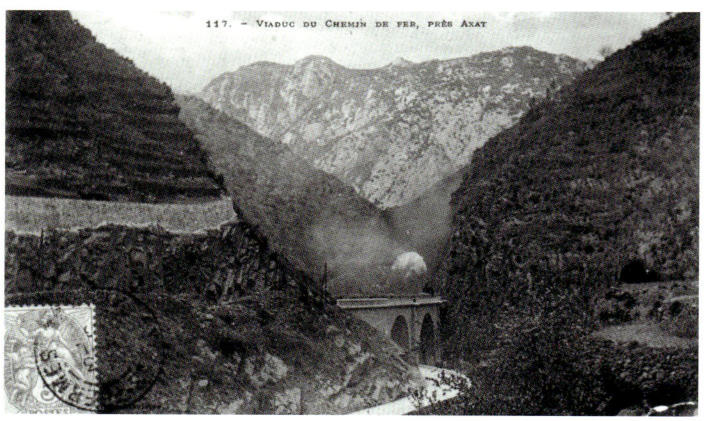

thermal baths, and no doubt the reason for their trip east from Avignon. Long celebrated for its spa-sanatorium and clear air, Dick would have taken the curative waters. From the ridge-top chapel above the spa, Derwent painted a panoramic oil, across the Haute-Bleone valley to the Montagne du Cheval Blanc, a white-limestone peak in the French Pre-Alpes (DL12.37).

It was not a relaxing trip for either artist. Dick's sickly, depressed state must have preyed on his companion. Augustus, upon seeing the two in Marseille on their return in January 1913, said that Dick 'looks rather dejected, and that Lees doesn't appear to be well yet'.[27] Derwent was undoubtedly flattened after nearly a month with his gravely ill companion.

A comparison of their painting sites in Banyuls and Forcalquier shows that Derwent spent most of his time alone and, on their way north, he took a scenic day trip from Perpignan on the *train-rouge* into the low Pyrenees. Near the end of the line, he painted the iconic viaduct of Axat in the Aude river valley, now titled *Mountain Pass* (DL13.4).

Later, Augustus would write that Dick had visited him from 'the Basses-Pyrenees where he had been working',[28] suggesting that Dick may have joined Derwent's excursion, though he 'had had a very dissipated time at Perpignan and was quite run down'.[29]

Dick painted little on the 1912 to 1913 winter trip, while Derwent's output was impressive, painting more than 30 works. It was his most productive painting holiday abroad. Back in London, he continued working on further oils and magazine illustrations, inspired by his French Catalan experience.

This was the last time the two were to travel abroad together, a dejected finale for the timid but lively Australian and his free-spirited Welsh mate. Inspired by the

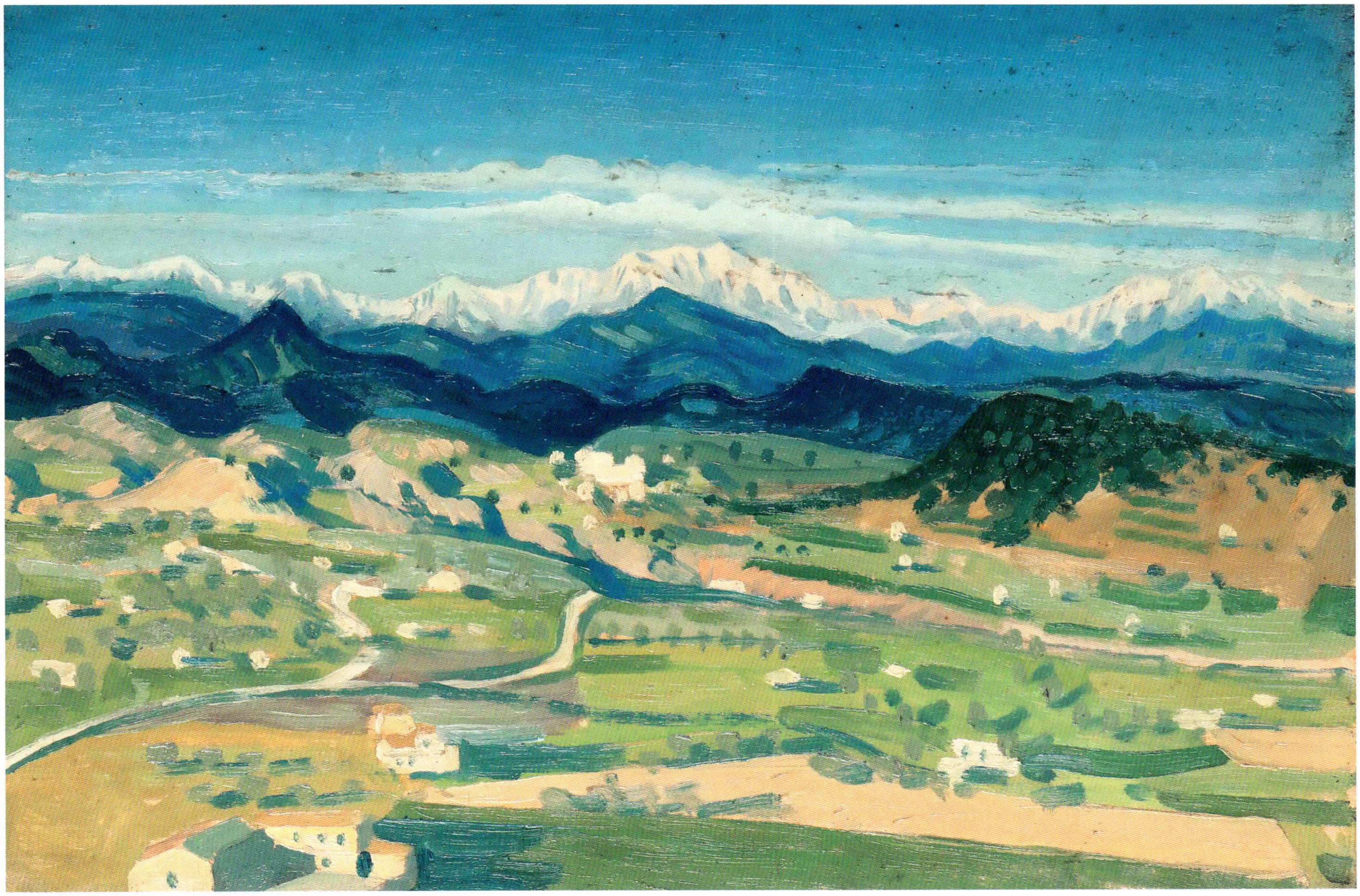

light and latitude of southern France, and in the footsteps of the French 'masters', they had painted in Matisse and Derain's Collioure, Maillol's home village of Banyuls, Dufy's Forcalquier, and also around Istres/Martigues, well-trodden by many before them.

They had both planned to spend time with Augustus near his French villa, but Derwent saw him only briefly in Marseille, returning to London to teach Term II classes. Dick spent a few weeks with Augustus and Dorelia, until they too could no longer cope with him. His disease was running rampant. In early February 1913, Augustus wrote to Quinn saying that 'the company of a sick man gets on one's nerves in the end' and that 'he is insupportable . . . and appears to be going off his head and stutters dreadfully'.[30] Dick was packed off back to London.

DL13.1
Derwent Lees, *Cheval Blanc, Basses Alpes*, 1913, oil on panel, 27.9 x 38.1 cm, Private Collection

8 REACHING HIS PEAK 1913

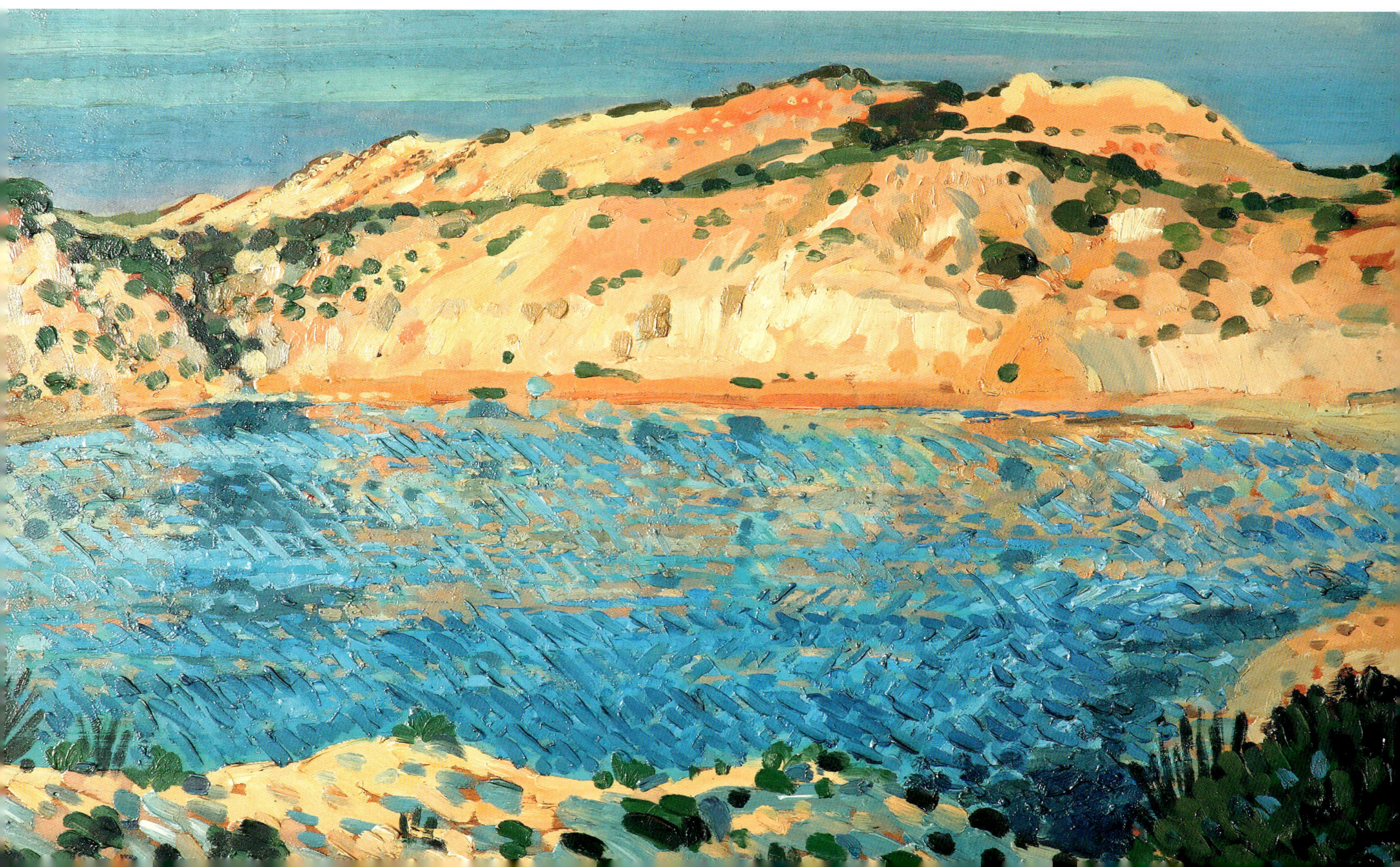

Unlike most of his social group, Derwent had to work during the Slade terms, and supplement his part-time salary by selling paintings. Life was good but money scarce. His teaching position afforded him introductions and invitations to soirées, weekends away and painting holidays. He was, for the first time in his life, flush with friends, an interesting and diverse group of artists and collectors who liked and respected the 28-year-old. Thanks to Augustus and his connections, Derwent's works were shown at the 1913 inaugural American International Exhibition of Modern Art in New York (known as the Armory Show). Augustus helped American art collector John Quinn choose works for his personal collection and for the show.

The huge and controversial Armory Show debuted in New York in February 1913 to an American public ill-accustomed to the new ways of using colour and form. Modern art had arrived, and the reaction was strong. It was a great success and moved to Chicago and Boston in the following months. Three of Derwent's paintings, *Evening*, *A Sullen Day* and *Lowering Clouds* (DL11.6–7, DL12.8), were among 79 pieces lent to the show by Quinn from his personal collection.[1] He was not only the single biggest lender to the Armory, and instrumental in its organisation, but also became the biggest purchaser from the show.

Only three Australian-born artists, each unknown to the other, exhibited at the Armory, as well as Charles Conder (1868–1909), a naturalised Australian born in England. Each had emigrated as young men to pursue careers in art: Derwent to London, Francis McComas (1874–1938; also Tasmanian-born) to the USA, and Frank Nankivell (1869–1959) to Japan and then the USA. None returned to live in their country of birth. On the eve of Australia's nationhood in 1899, art critic Alfred Daplyn wrote that there was 'no question that in Australia an artist, however gifted, has little to look forward to; in the old world the rewards are necessarily greater'.[2]

The year 1913 was highly productive for Derwent; his work was artistically rich and enormously varied. He created etchings, published three sketches in literary-art magazines, exhibited pen and ink washes, pencil portraits, watercolours and

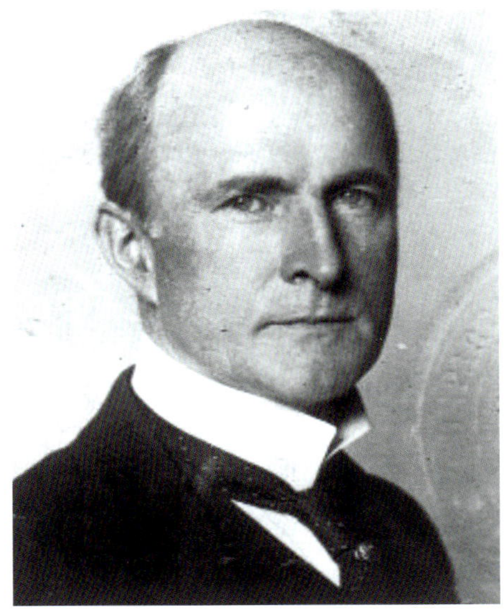

Opposite:
DL13.45 (detail)
Derwent Lees, *The Blue Pool / Reflections in Water*, 1913

Above:
John Quinn, c.1913, photographer unknown, John Quinn Papers Collection, Archives & Manuscripts, New York Public Library

oil landscapes from France, England and Wales, and received several commissions. His star was rising.

Soon after his return from southern France, with the Tour Madeloc massif still resonating in his mind, he was invited to submit drawings to two magazines. Like others in his circle, he keenly embraced such early 20th-century experiments in art and literature. He contributed three simple drawings, based on earlier sketches, one for *Rhythm* (DL09.19) and two for the inaugural issue of the *Blue Review* (DL13.8, 9), published in May by John Middleton Murry and Katherine Mansfield, two of London's literary modernists.

Derwent was a reader, schooled in the classics and well-educated in Australia, with French, Latin and Ancient Greek on the Melbourne Grammar School curriculum. He would have appreciated, if not contributed to, the intellectual drive behind the magazines. And in predictable Derwent style, he felt compelled to fashion himself as 'more literary' in his contributions. For the first and only time in his life, the submitted drawings for the *Blue Review* displayed his full initials: P.D.L., Peter Derwent Lees.[3] Although known as Derwent, he had been called Peter by his family.[4]

Derwent's literary friends and acquaintances at this time included D.H. Lawrence, Rupert Brooke, Lytton Strachey and George Moore, as well as the Bloomsbury friends whom he had known for many years through Vanessa Bell. Duncan Grant lived at 21 Fitzroy Square before Derwent moved into his rooms in January of 1912, whereupon Derwent wrote to him asking if he could 'remember exactly what you used to pay for these rooms' while also noting that 'there's a young man posing at the Slade now with a good body – that might suit you'.[5] Derwent's future wife later recalled that, at his Fitzroy Square studio, 'occasionally in the company were to be seen figures from the literary world; George Moore had for once perhaps, forsaken Ebury Street, or the bearded Lytton Strachey engaged with Lees in abstruse and technical discussion'.[6] They chatted and gathered at Derwent's studio and at the neighbouring new Omega Workshop, 33 Fitzroy Square, established by Roger Fry, Grant and Bell. Opening its doors in spring, Omega was a 'design workshop dedicated to producing modern domestic ware, including a range of furniture, fabrics, pottery, rugs and even fashion'.[7] Fry strived to advance modernism in an artistic environment that was struggling to change, becoming a self-proclaimed champion of new ideas and styles of artistic expression.

Artistic groupings constantly formed, changed or disbanded in this dynamic environment. They included the Friday Club, the Grafton Group, allegiances borne out of *Rhythm* magazine,[8] the breakaway Camden Town Group and the London Group, which evolved in part from the Fitzroy Street Group. Derwent was liked, well respected and appears to have had connections with them all. Sadly, both *Rhythm* and the *Blue Review* did not last, and Murry's segue into publishing came to a crashing halt by the end of summer. In debt and with no money to pay the printer, publication of the *Blue Review* ceased.

One of Derwent's *Blue Review* drawings (DL13.9) appears to be a public, though personal, declaration of love. A central, distant mountain, now confirmed as Tour Madeloc seen from Banyuls, forms the backdrop for the warmth and light of an idealised southern France. The work shows the same trees behind citrus bushes, the same house, ridges and aspect to the peak and foothills of Tour Madeloc, in the same arrangement and at a location where Derwent had painted several works in Banyuls. Two naked figures nestle in an English flowerbed, gazing at each other. The woman is Edith Price. She wears her signature spotted headscarf seen in other 1913 paintings such as *The Sandhill* (aka *Lyndra in the Pyrenees*, DL13.35, despite its recent incorrect titles, a work painted at the Blue Pool in Dorset). In the *Blue Review* drawing, a peaceful and content Derwent reads to her, with his dark and neatly parted hair, and distinctive cowlick, his prosthetic foot hidden from view. This small drawing captured both the person and the place most important to him; perhaps a dream of sharing southern France, the mountains and cerulean skies with his new love.

During the 1913 Easter holiday, Dick, Derwent and fellow artist Trelawney Dayrell Reed (1886–c.1969) likely visited former Slade classmate Elliott Seabrooke (1886–1950), who had taken a studio in Westmorland, Cumbria. From this trip, Derwent painted *North Yorkshire Moors* (DL13.12), while Trelawney later exhibited *Haweswater Westmoreland*, *Skiddaw Cumberland* and *Waters of Cumbria*.[9]

By April, Dick had recovered slightly, but constant convalescence frustrated him. He was back in London to mount another one-man show at the Chenil Gallery. He exhibited on the ground floor, while the upper rooms were filled with paintings, drawings and etchings by Augustus, Derwent and Ian Strang. All four artists received positive reviews and sales. The *Athenaeum* review singled out Derwent's mainly French works:

> His colour is more definite in its significance, and no less, rather more, luxuriously decorative. No one could wish for more entrancing subjects than these of Mr Lees, or for a finer estimate of the kind of paint, just heavy enough in body, just precise enough in touch, which suits these little oil paintings. Among the best things we should mention the *Etang de Berre* (61), the full, handsome forms of *Mas Catalan* (62), the dim, remote snow on *Welsh Hills* (58), the union of spaciousness with quaint pattern in the *Metairie des Abeilles* (55) and the cool gleam of green, blue, and yellow on the *Cheval Blanc, Basses Alpes*. [exhibition numbers shown][10]

He had pared back his measured approach, remaining faithful to the landscape, yet celebrating stronger, more vibrant colours.

Many years after Derwent's death, Dr John MacGregor would bequeath *Métairie des Abeilles* (DL12.26) to the Tate Gallery (now Tate), along with another work inadvertently assigned the same title. The gallery's 1938–53 British paintings inventory lists the two paintings (5355 and 5356), with the second work recorded by way of ditto marks referring to the work above, and thus interpreted as having the same donor, artist and title. This 'second' watercolour is understood to be *After Sunset* (DL09.15), painted in Poland in 1909, and not in Banyuls France. The Métairie des Abeilles is a Catalan hamlet high up in the hills, and many kilometres inland from Banyuls. Derwent must have seen a road sign marking its direction, as his work DL12.26 is of Mas Reig, located on the hill just behind Banyuls village.

A FATHER'S LEGACY

Ethel Elder and Derwent had known each other for several years, as she lived at 101 Cheyne Walk for over a decade, while he was at number 125. The artists regularly crossed paths from 1907 until Derwent moved to Fitzroy Square. Ethel was young when she first attended the Slade in 1892. Her brother Arthur was an artist, and their sister (Louisa) Alice was also briefly at the Slade, and tutored female students in the Antique Room during 1896–7.[11] Arthur was a friend of Walter Sickert, and part of the Chelsea Art Club, before leaving for America in 1905.[12]

Walter Russell and Derwent both painted portraits of Alice Elder while they lived close to each other in Cheyne Walk, and Derwent drew several pencil portraits of both sisters (DL11.55–60, 63). One work shows an interior scene of Ethel leaning against a fireplace at their 101 Cheyne Walk home in Lindsey House. Perhaps known to them at the time was the fact that the house, as Fairlie Harmar later recounted to Randolph Schwabe, was 'part of Lindsay [*sic*] House . . . The first-floor front room, was Whistler's where he painted *Symphony in White*. She points out that the mantelpiece is the same.'[13] James Whistler's 1864 work *Symphony in White, No.2: The Little White Girl* shows the same fireplace (or another in the house) that Derwent captured 50 years later in the watercolour of Ethel, later mistitled *Portrait of Lyndra, the Artist's Wife* (DL11.60).

Shortly after her father David's death in April 1913, Ethel moved from the family's house to a small, rented room in Chelsea. In 1915, she travelled to Ireland, dying in Wexford in the same year. Eight weeks after the death of Ethel's father, Derwent lost his own father. William Lees had retired to Folkestone on the Kent coast with his second wife and died at the age of 73, on the cusp of Derwent's 1913 summer holidays.

Derwent's small, but essential, living allowance now ceased. William's will, administered from Melbourne, had been carefully crafted to care for his wife and children. He owned no property and left the income from most of his small pension, insurance and share portfolio to his three daughters. All were to remain spinsters. During his life, he had provided his daughters with regular allowances which, upon his death, were replaced by managed lump sums.

Of the four sons, Geoffrey and Gilbert were excluded, as they were financially secure. The two book-end sons, Derwent and oldest brother William Robert, both of whom struggled with financial insecurity, received legacies of £50 each. James's children were left £100 in trust.[14]

Decades later, an Australian London-based curator told Schwabe that she met Derwent's sisters at the 1933 Australian touring exhibition of British Contemporary Art, recounting that their father had left 'everything to his second wife, and the daughters of the first marriage were totally unprovided for. They are now elderly women, leading miserable lives, earning a living as single women do – seamstresses, companions.'[15] These comments appear overly harsh, as William worked hard to ensure his children were well educated, he did care for his daughters with regular allowances during his life and, upon his death, the trust funds gave them a measure of financial security. He had also supported Derwent for a decade, in the pursuit of his chosen career.

During late spring 1913, Derwent accepted an invitation to meet Frank Slade in Rye, along with Dick, Trelawney and Augustus. Frank later said that 'One day, Augustus John, with Dick, Trelawny [*sic*] Reed and Derwent Lees turned up at the caravan. Dick said to me "I am so glad you have not grown a beard." The other three all had one each.'[16] The young acolytes were no doubt emulating Augustus. After a few weeks, the ensemble disbanded and Augustus headed to Alderney, probably with Derwent and Trelawney in tow. Always generous in his encouragement, Augustus admired a painting of Frank's, suggesting he submit it to the next New English Art Club (NEAC) exhibition. Frank took his advice and to his delight it sold quickly. Like Derwent, Trelawney was an Alderney regular, even living there for a time, an eccentric character of independent means, a sometime painter, horticulturist, farmer, poet and archaeologist.

BY A BLUE POOL

The Dorset landscape around Alderney Manor and to the south entranced Derwent. He stayed there frequently, mainly during the 1913 summer in the company of Edith and Dorelia McNeill. He sketched and painted Edith repeatedly in the manor gardens, the neighbouring heathlands and hills, but particularly at the flooded Furzebrook clay pit, the Blue Pool. During the year he created at least 70 works, of which more than 30 were of Dorset, with over 20 paintings around the Blue Pool and Creech (DL13.31–52). Derwent was undoubtedly one of the most prolific painters of the Blue Pool, capturing its fluctuating and uniquely luminous waters and curious landforms.

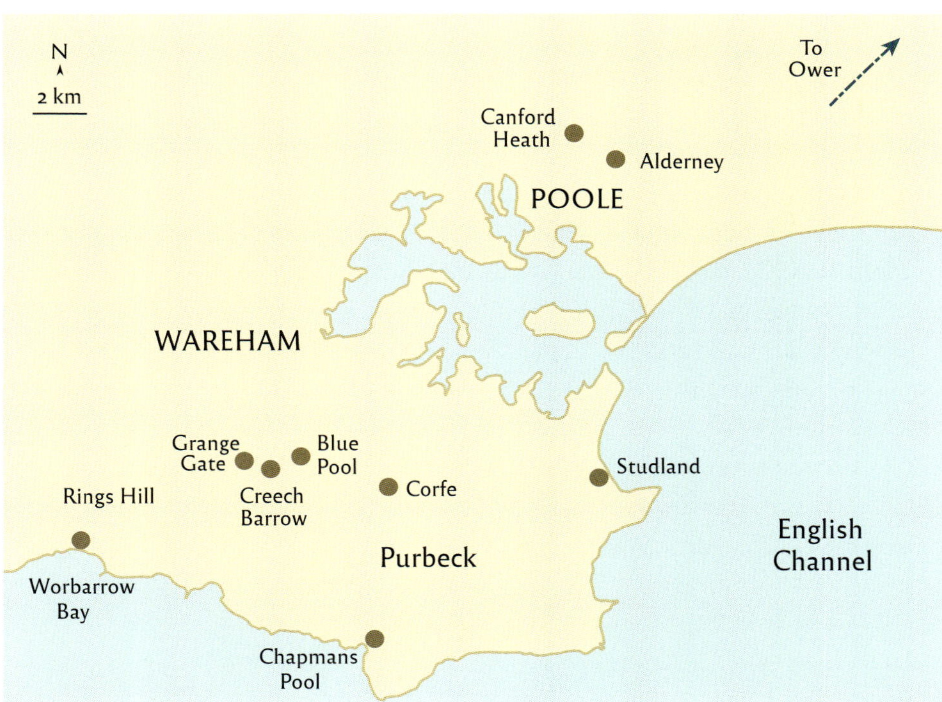

Locations where Derwent painted in Dorset 1909–15

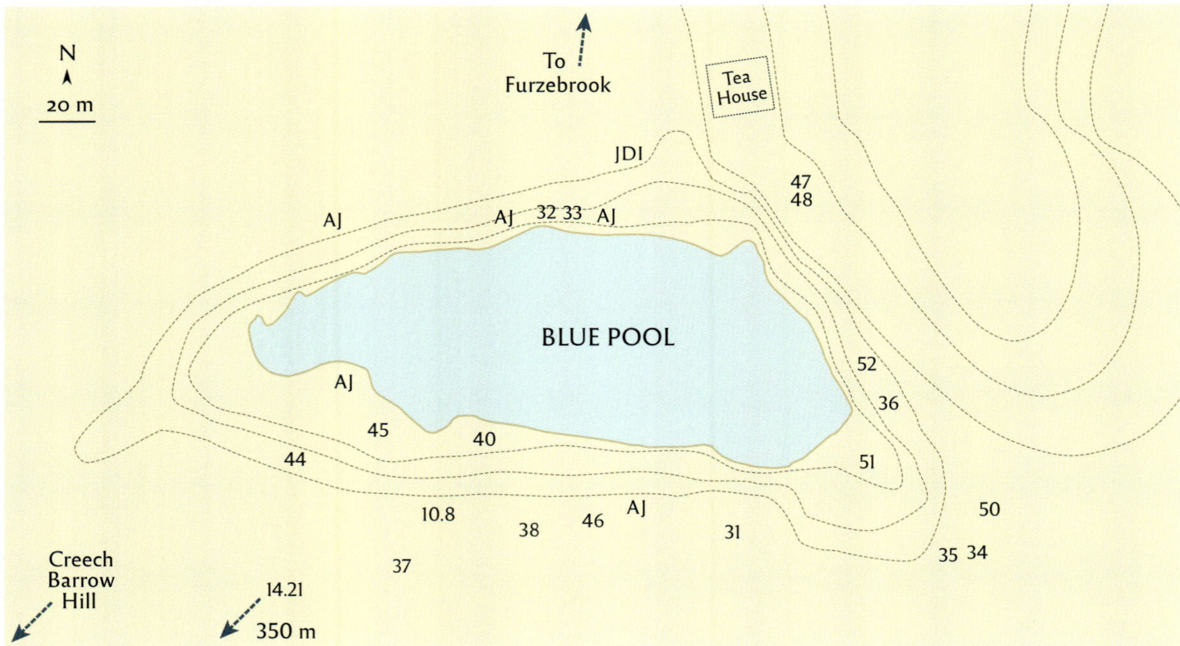

Locations where Derwent painted at the Blue Pool, Dorset Numbers indicate known painting sites, DL10.8, DL13.31–41, 44–52, DL14.21; DL13. prefix is not shown. AJ (Augustus John) and JDI (James Dickson Innes) indicates some of their painting sites

Of the more than a dozen oils of Edith during 1913, eight were at the Blue Pool, and at least one also features Dorelia, set against backdrops of the blue-green water, sandy hillocks and scrubby regrowth of the abandoned clay workings (DL13.38). This Mediterranean-like setting led several of Derwent's works to be misinterpreted as French coastal scenes.

One work, mistitled *Evening, Sun Setting behind Arenig Fach* (DL13.47) and misdated c.1910, is a sunset view of the Blue Pool during the exceptionally low water levels of the late summer drought of 1913, and was erroneously attributed to Dick (who was not at the Blue Pool during the 1913 summer). The painting's location, scene, palette and style, and even the hour and day of the scene, are identical to those of *Reflections* (DL13.48), signed and dated by Derwent, for which it is undoubtedly a preparatory work. Interestingly, the sequence of Derwent's works that year shows the decline in the pool's water levels as the dry season progressed.

Edith also posed in the garden and surrounds of Alderney Manor. Derwent's large, impressive 1913 oils include *The Kitchen Garden* (DL13.28), where Edith holds a spade in the round-walled garden, echoing the powerful 1911 oil by Augustus of Dorelia in the same garden and the same pose. Several paintings by the two artists show that Dorelia and Edith got along well.

Derwent's visits to Alderney probably started in late 1911 and continued until at least late 1915. He had sketched and painted alongside Augustus since 1908, maintaining close ties for more than a decade. Derwent was an agreeable friend, happiest in strong but emotionally safe company. It was Augustus with whom he maintained his longest and most enduring friendship. Similarities in portrait, landscape and figure works attest to a sustained close, shared association from 1908 to 1919. Despite this, Derwent and several other artist friends were seldom mentioned in

Augustus's late-in-life autobiographies. Michael Holroyd explains that Augustus's humility precluded him from recounting stories of those that he had unfailingly encouraged. He generously helped many and 'often he would write enthusiastically about painters' but 'there is no mention of Bomberg . . . and almost none of the other artists upon whose behalf he had secretly exercised himself'.[17] Wildly eccentric, and self-important at times, Augustus was also strong in his praise of others, with a core of kindness and acceptance of difference, both human and artistic.

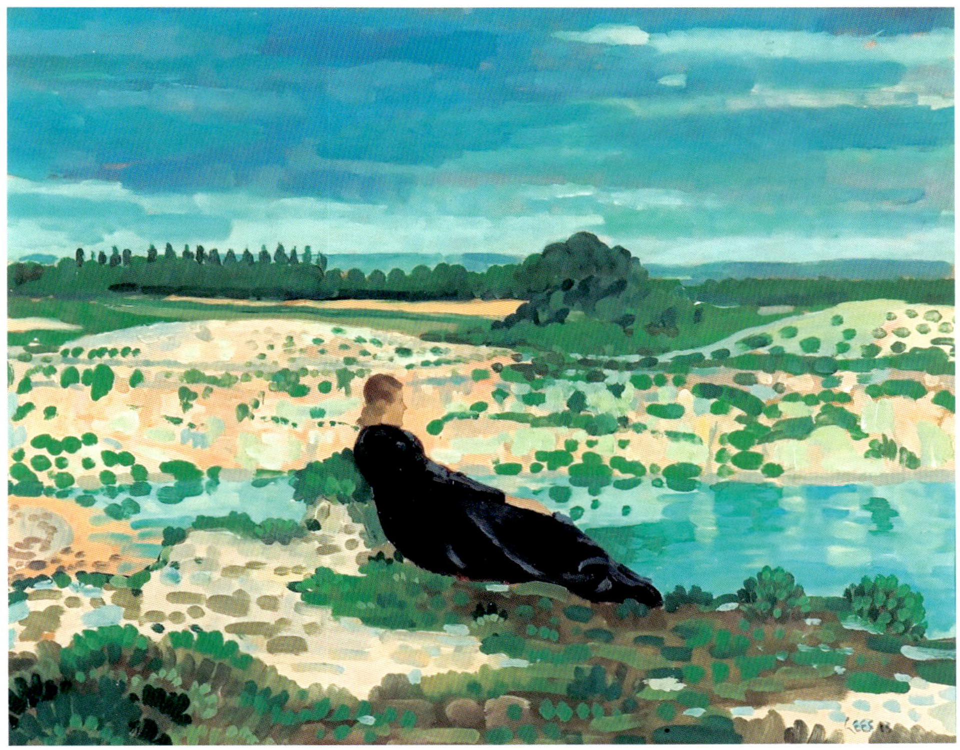

Right:
DL13.38
Derwent Lees, *Lyndra by the Blue Pool, Dorset*, 1913, oil on panel, 39.4 x 50.1 cm, Art Gallery of South Australia, Adelaide

Below:
The Blue Pool, Dorset, c.1910, postcard, England

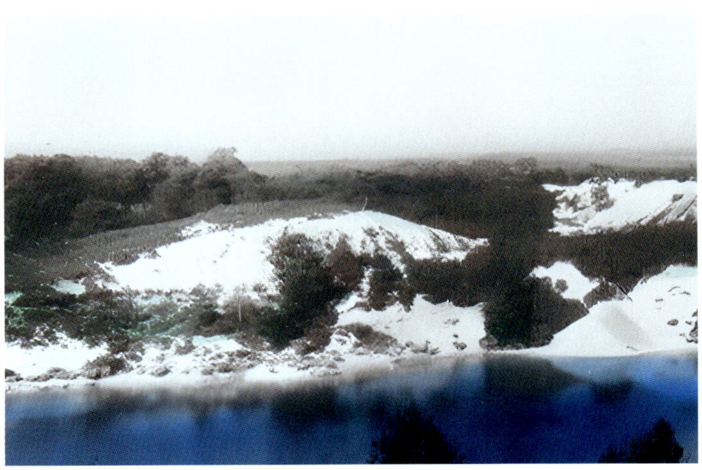

AT FIRST A MODEL

Since 1908, Derwent and Augustus had sketched and painted Edith repeatedly. Apart from life-drawing classes at the Slade, it seems she was a life-model for only them. They drew many closely observed portraits of her with her long, free-flowing hair. By late 1911, she was a regular visitor in Dorset and later in Wales. Her curly tresses were then often pinned into a chignon on the nape of her neck or loosely coiled at the back.

Edith became the subject of 90 per cent of Derwent's landscape figure works. From 1912 onwards, he painted her repeatedly in a range of English and Welsh scenes, especially at the Blue Pool in 1913. Two years later, they would spend the summer with the McEvoys, where she would assume more constrained poses, wearing more conventional clothes.

Edith's family life had been a struggle, with no father to help provide for rent and food. There were few opportunities, and her siblings became artist's assistants or stage performers. In 1906, Australian artist Arthur Streeton (1867–1943) observed that life for women in London's art world was incredibly difficult, particularly so for those of limited means. Faced with isolation and few prospects, Streeton's younger Australian contemporary, Thea Proctor (1879–1966), found herself penniless in London despite her considerable artistic talent. Around the time Derwent started at the Slade, Thea's situation became so wretched that her clothes fell apart and she felt compelled to stop doing portrait commissions and resort to the lower social standing of artist's model.[18]

Also struggling financially, Derwent must have known his two compatriots. Thea lived near Cheyne Walk, and all three exhibited at the same 1910 NEAC show. Years later, back in Sydney, Thea appears to have known Derwent's sister Eleanor (Trixie) Lees, as they regularly attended the same Sydney art exhibitions and parties. Other Australian artists Marjorie Arnold (1884–1940), Bessie Norris (1878–1939) and Mabel Midson (n.d.) also studied at the Slade at the same time as Derwent.

Augustus and Derwent's works of Edith show that, like Thea, she had a very limited wardrobe. For years, in fact, in nearly all portrayals of her, she wore long white socks or stockings and the same small, flat black shoes. Her skirt or dress seldom changed, though the interpretation of its colour often did. *Figure by Pool, Tan-y-Grisiau* (aka *Lyndra in Wales*, DL14.37) and *Lyndra by the Pool* (DL14.36), both painted on the same day in the Cwmorthin valley, show her in the same clothes, however in one her skirt is deep blue and in the other, green.

Soon after her marriage to Derwent, some white clothing and a fashionable hat appeared, but across the years, Edith showed little change in style or dress. Her early family financial situation had been dire, and her wardrobe remained limited.

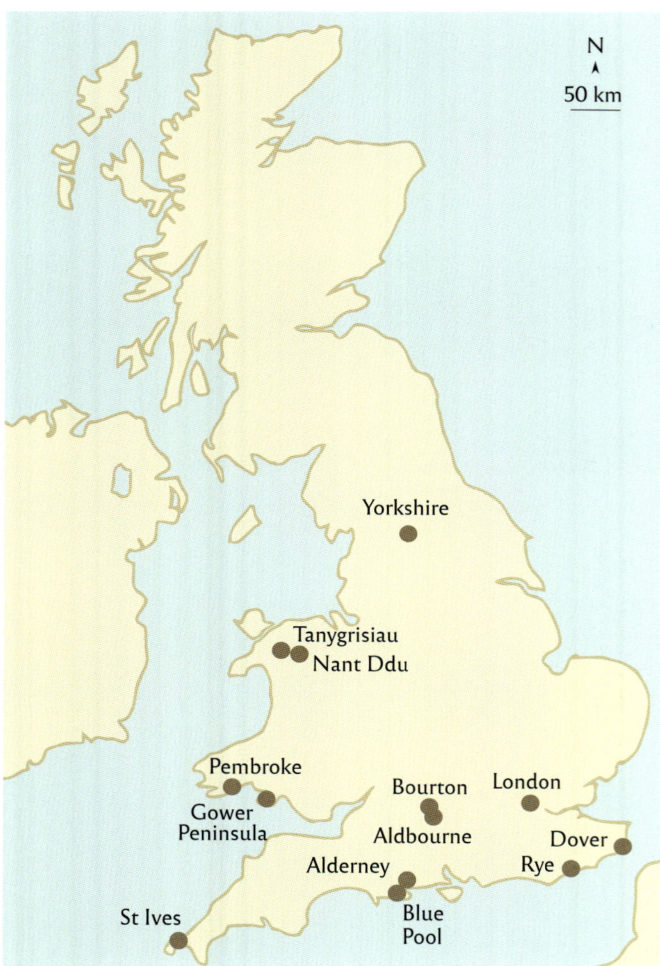

Principal locations where Derwent painted in England and Wales, 1907–23

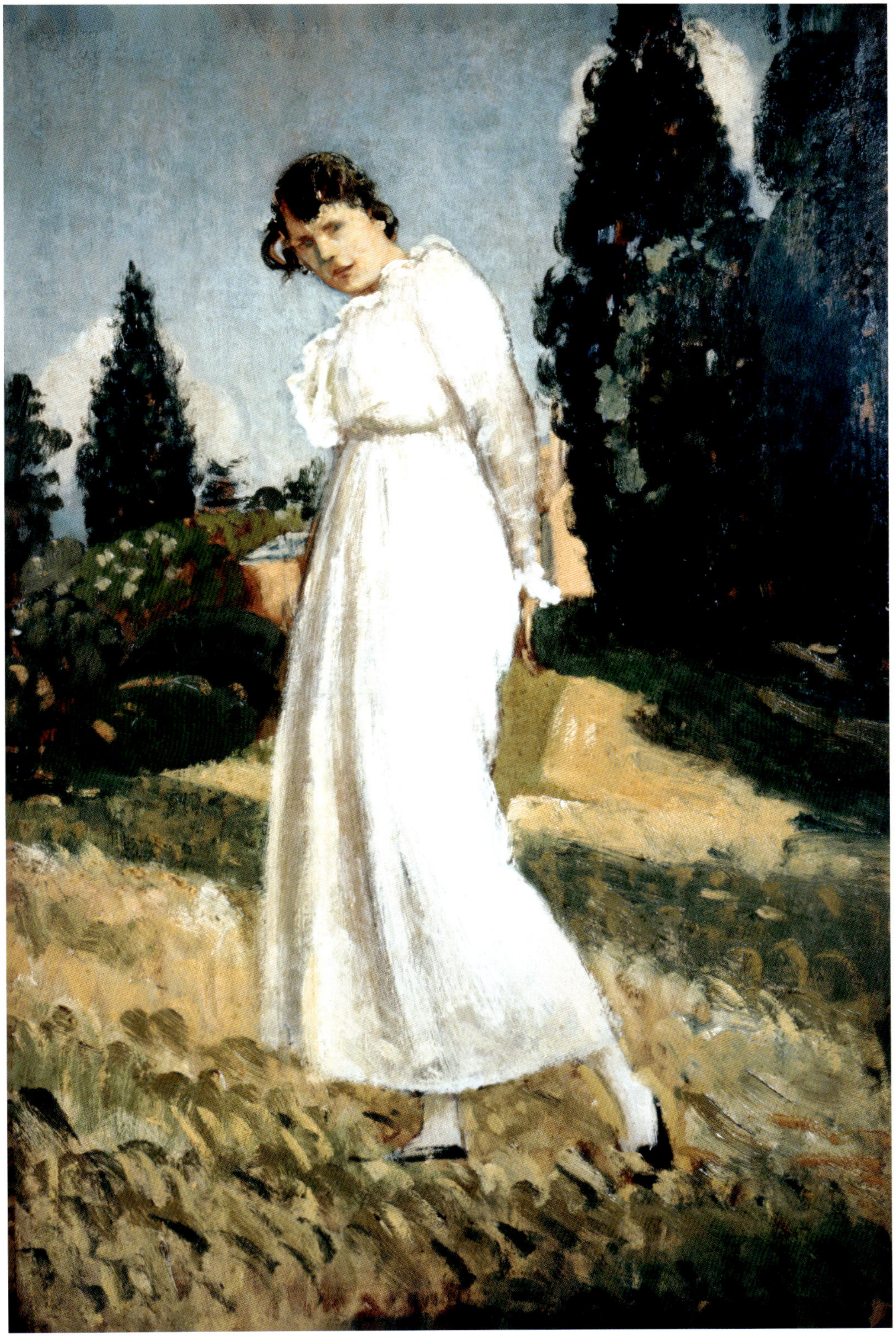

DL13.27
Derwent Lees, *Edith / Lyndra / White Dress*, c.1913, oil on panel, 51 x 32.4 cm, Private Collection

9 MARRIAGE AND SOUTH AGAIN 1913–14

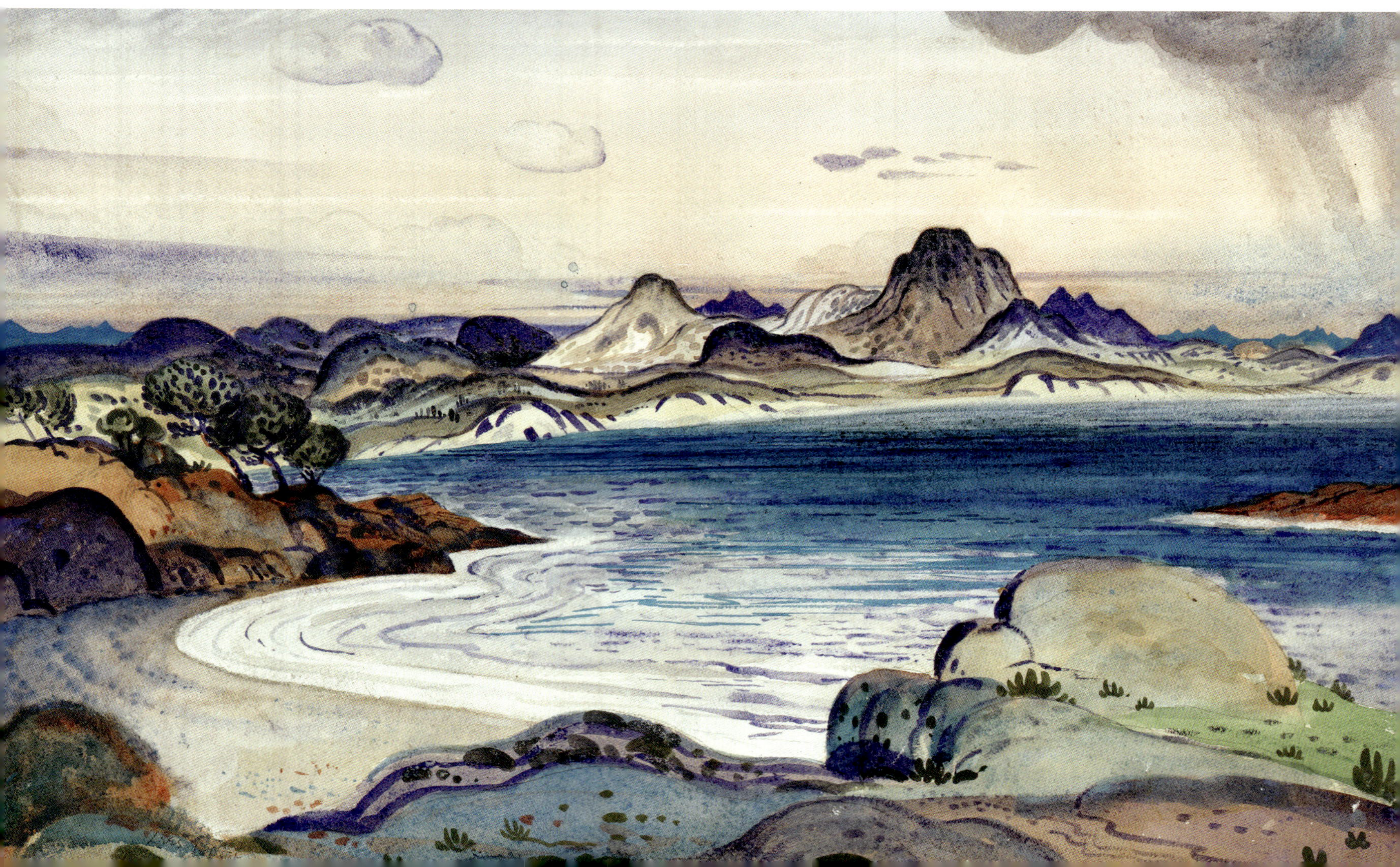

Buoyed by sales and his growing creative prowess, Derwent married his muse. Most of his close friends had settled down, except for Dick, who was now 'rather far gone'.[1] Surrounded by married couples, Derwent followed suit. Unlike most of his friends, he did not marry an artist or lady of social rank, but one more comfortable in gypsy attire and living a bohemian life.

A month after his father's death, on 21 July 1913, Derwent and Edith Price were married in London's St Pancras Registry Office. She was 22, he 28. Ian Strang was best man and Edith's older sister Evelyn was her witness.[2] It was perhaps a hurried decision. Soon after the nuptials, Dick wrote to Augustus that, 'I too was astounded at the Lees marriage. The fact was jumped on me at Waterloo just as I was going to catch the train here – I think I felt rather jealous of him. Well, they both looked very happy and so good luck to them – Ian Strang must have been in great form as best man.'[3] Although Ian mostly lived with his family until his 1933 marriage, from 1911 to 1914 he took a room close to Derwent in Fitzroy Street, accounting for Derwent's closer connection with him and the Strang family. In fact, 'Dick, Mac and Lees' had known Ian from their early Slade student days and had remained good friends.

The married couple spent much of the summer of 1913 in Dorset at the Blue Pool and Alderney Manor. Augustus was often away but was there long enough to capture a tender drawing of a recently married Edith proudly displaying her wedding ring.

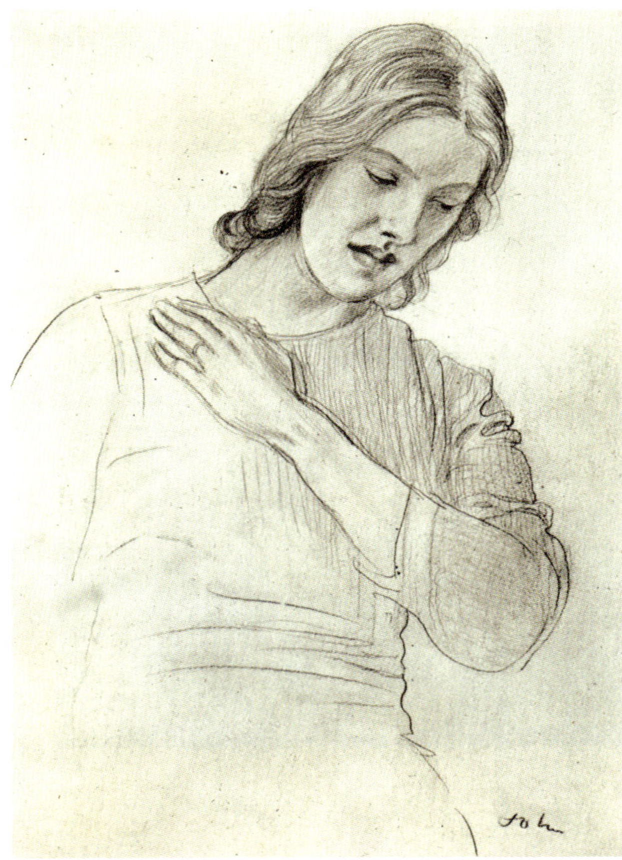

Opposite:
DL14.13 (detail)
Derwent Lees, *La Ciotat / La Ciolat*, 1914

Above:
Augustus John, *Portrait of Mrs Derwent Lees*, 1913, pencil on paper, 33.6 x 24.1 cm, Private Collection

Edith displaying her wedding band

During the year, Derwent also experimented with etchings, no doubt borne out of his closer association with his best man, who was a talented etcher and illustrator, and his father William, a renowned etcher. Derwent created a handful of etched portraits of Edith, some during 1913 and again in 1915, then possibly influenced by Ambrose McEvoy (DL13.24–5, DL15.1). Derwent would have also etched alongside close friend Donald Maclaren, who etched a self-portrait that was printed by the Strangs. Mac dedicated his etching (now held in the British Museum) to David (1887–1967), Ian's printmaker younger brother. This year saw Derwent deepen his friendships with Ian and Mac.

William Strang (1859–1921), talented engraver, printer, lithographer and painter, would have been an accommodating paternal figure for Derwent after the recent loss of his father. William strongly identified with the less fortunate and would have looked kindly upon Derwent's circumstances.[4]

William's painting style at this time differed from Derwent's by an effortless simplicity in line and colour. During the holiday Derwent must have joined the Strangs at an aerial show because he emulated William's oil and etching composition *Aeroplane* in two oils. Derwent's *An Aeroplane Passes* (DL13.54) was exhibited at the winter 1917 New English Art Club (NEAC) exhibition, while *The Sisters in Wales* (DL13.55) has the same structural elements, and even one of the same models, as William's work. Derwent, in the presence of an older artist, knowingly or not, took on the role of experimental understudy, but when alone or with a peer, returned to developing his own style. This was not unusual as he was by far the youngest Slade staff member and spent his working life surrounded by, and taking daily instruction from, older mentors. It must have felt natural being understudy to a mature, more experienced artist, echoing his early family life.

AT THE PEAK

Derwent's productivity peaked in 1913, while close friend Dick's career was waning due to illness. By late 1913 his friends were losing Dick who, despite being gravely ill, departed for the Moroccan coast in October with Trelawney Dayrell Reed.[5] His English poste-restante address, 'c/- Augustus John, Old Chenil Gallery', said much as most of his time at home was spent recuperating at his parents' house or at sanitoria. Upon his departure he asked Augustus to '. . . come and see me when you have time, and please give me news of The Lees when & if you see them'.[6]

By the end of 1913, Derwent had completed more than 40 oils and nearly 30 other works, a substantial accomplishment given his time constraints and recent events. In late December, he mounted his first major show, alongside some drawings by Augustus. Derwent exhibited more than 20 works in the upper rooms at the Chenil Gallery, a mix of landscapes from southern France, Dorset and northern Wales. Edith featured in five of them. The show was well reviewed, with one critic writing that:

> Mr Derwent Lees shows a marked advance on his previous painting. A greater freedom of design and a nicer modulation of paint give to No.34 an arresting force that, added to the luxurious colour which has always been Mr Lees's prerogative, makes it a noteworthy landscape. *Creech Barrow, Dorset* (46), with its finely graded scale of greens and velvety sky, is of similar quality, but the gem of the collection is (No.40) *A Dorset Heath*. It has a happiness of invention, at once perfect and unforeseen,

> which makes it one of the most covetable pictures exhibited in London of recent years. [exhibition numbers shown][7]

Another critic reported his paintings being full of poetry and colour, while the *Yorkshire Evening Post*, which promoted modern painting, suggested one should '. . . spare as much time as you can for . . . the works of Derwent Lees and Augustus John, whose style you may not like, though they are "it" in the new art'.[8]

A telling incident followed the show. Jack Knewstub, manager of the Chenil, had a reputation for paying his artists late; very late. Christopher Nevinson had had an argument with him about his tardiness and for not fairly sharing the proceeds of his sales. William Orpen once aimed a gun at Jack in a rage, shooting a hole through a picture.[9] On completion of his show, Derwent needed the cash. His life, already tough, was now even more pressured. He was married and his father's allowance had ceased. He had to augment his part-time wage as a matter of urgency and sought out Jack at the Chenil. He 'climbed up and got in at the first-floor window, reaching above him to the iron balcony by standing on the sash-bars of the window below and breaking glass as he did so with his wooden foot'.[10] Derwent was 'insistent on cash from his 1914 exhibition – clambering up the outside walls of the gallery and taking on the dealer'.[11] This was, however, business as usual for Jack. Once paid, he and Derwent both returned to the rhythm of Chenil exhibitions, and no further mention is made of the incident.

With his first major show a success, life was on the up. Both the Chenil Gallery and Derwent were at their prime, as was Augustus. Much later, at the celebrated 1939 London exhibition celebrating the three artists' pre-war work, Eric Newton would write that:

> the exhibition at the Redfern Gallery of paintings done in the four years prior to the outbreak of war by Augustus John, J.D. Innes, and Derwent Lees makes one speculate on what constitutes an official brotherhood. Here are the paintings of three men who were, during those four years, no less in tune with one another than Millais, Madox Brown, and Holman Hunt during their first few years after the founding of the pre-Raphaelite Brotherhood . . . It was a brotherhood based on a natural similarity of vision and strengthened by an acquired similarity of technique. Their vision was unashamedly romantic.[12]

These heady years were drawing to a close. The world was trembling on the brink of war, and disease, trauma and poverty would destroy much of what they knew. Both the romance and the brotherhood would soon be inexorably shattered.

CARTOON, CARTONE

In November 1913, while Derwent prepared for his one-man show, the NEAC held its 50th show, exhibiting more than 120 artists. Unsurprisingly, a work by Augustus took pride of place, a large decorative cartoon.

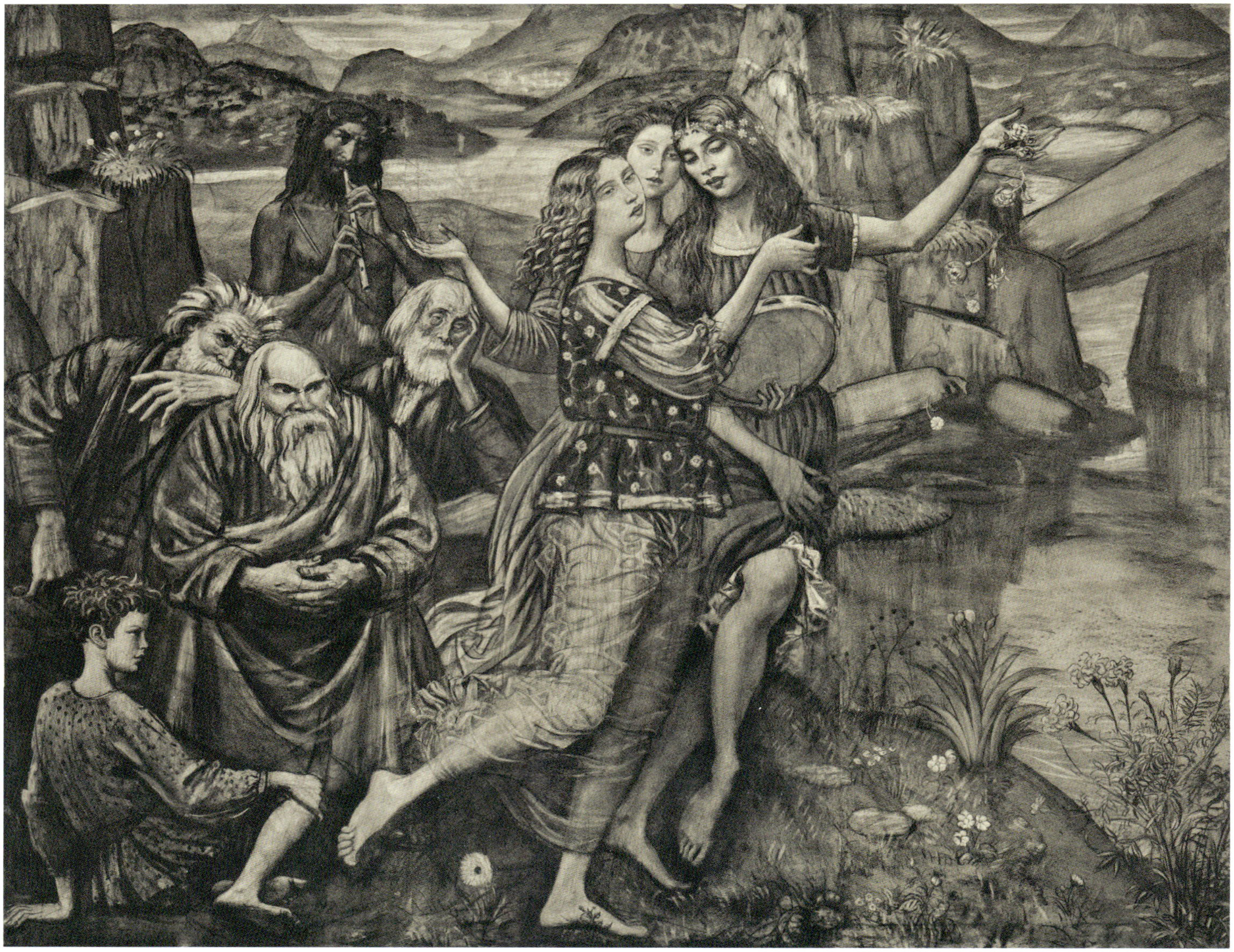

Augustus John, *Flute of Pan*, c.1913, photogravure print of original on chine collé, 27 x 32.6 cm (plate), Amgueddfa Cymru – National Museum Wales, Cardiff

The oversized *Flute of Pan* was first in the catalogue, and first seen on entering the gallery. Art critics were unsure, with one writing that, 'at first the composition seems huddled, but the cross-rhythms and avoidance of facile pose are the reason for this impression. The work is magisterial. It grows upon one, though it is doubtful whether it will ever make the appeal popular.'[13] The allegorical work portrays the classical Three Graces, clothed but gazed on longingly, even lasciviously, by three old men and Pan, all seemingly versions of Augustus himself (further exemplified in a pencil study), and a seated boy (likely one of Augustus's sons). The Graces traditionally represented mirth, elegance, and youth and beauty. Augustus poses them traditionally, dancing amid flowers and the sanctity of nature, with one facing the viewer. This was undoubtedly mischievous, self-referential Augustus at his best, and possibly misunderstood by most that viewed it, but not Derwent. There is no better example of their friendship than Derwent's sophisticated riposte to this work. At the following NEAC show, he presented his own large decoration, *Cartoon – Les Anciennes* (DL14.18).

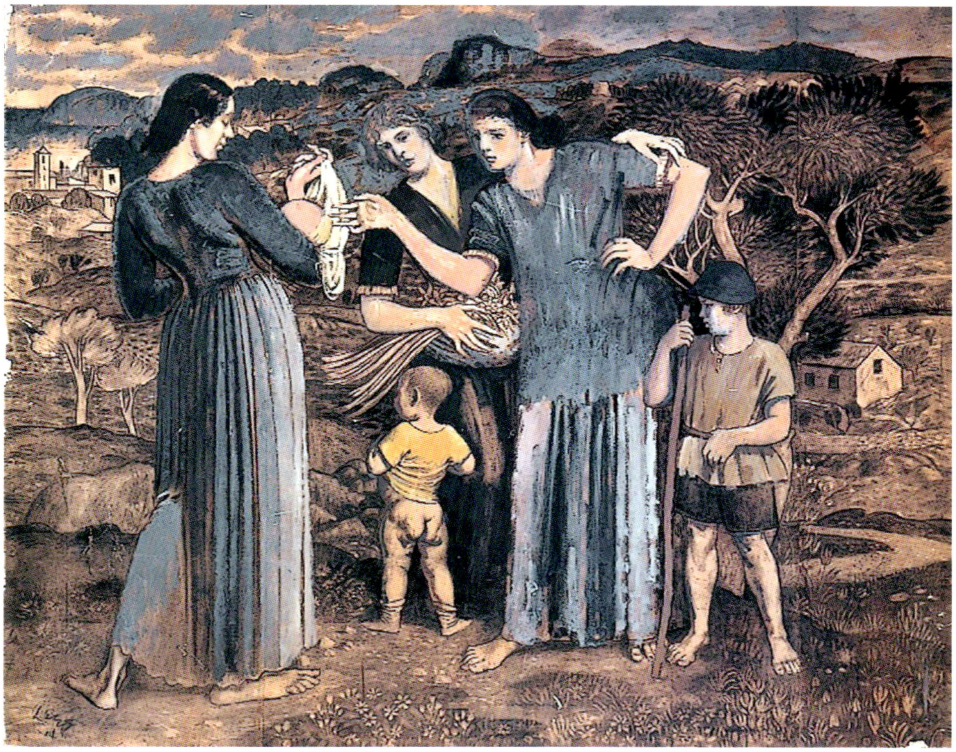

DL14.18
Derwent Lees, *Cartoon – Les Anciennes*, 1914, oil over charcoal on paper glued to canvas, 144.8 x 180.4 cm, UCL Art Museum, University College London

Randolph Schwabe remarked that 'when John sent one of his large charcoal cartoons to the New English Art Club, Lees followed it up, in the Club's next exhibition, by a cartoon similar in size and handling. I am inclined to think that these plagiarisms were not deliberate, but due to his peculiar makeup.'[14] He was partly correct, but Derwent's charcoal work was surely a tongue-in-cheek reply to Augustus's beautiful, classically composed *Flute of Pan*. Derwent's work was not well received, or understood, although *The Westminster Gazette* critic dryly observed that 'I would suggest the drapery be attributed to Mr John'.[15] The composition seems intended as a private joke expressly for Augustus. Four decades after its first showing, London gallery owner Rex Nan Kivell referred to it, saying that 'You may have heard of Augustus John's enthusiastic remarks on it',[16] but in 1914, those who saw it merely as an acolyte's unimaginative copy had missed the point of its creator's dry wit.

Derwent's *Cartoon – Les Anciennes* directly refers to key elements of *Flute of Pan*. Time has passed and the old men and the music are gone. The same three young Graces are now 'mothers with child', their hair now short, the same dresses and tunics now worn and faded, their same aspect, now with more muted expressions, the abode humble and the track worn. The same model from *Flute of Pan* again faces the viewer. It is significant that there are now three infants of different ages. The eldest boy is also no doubt modelled on Augustus's son Robin, as in *Flute of Pan*, dressed in the same but now frayed tunic, belt and shorts. All around are the same daisies and tulips, but now accompanied by a pregnant basket of sheaves and fruit. It had been a fecund spring, and now, the harvest.

The scene is Cassis village, and captures the same mountain backdrop and foreground, cottage and pine tree, as Derwent's watercolour *Landscape – Cassis* (DL14.11), which was possibly a preparatory study.

A cartoon for a decoration is 'a full-scale preparatory drawing for a fresco, oil painting or a tapestry'.[17] Historically, they were drawn as transferable works, and temporarily pinned to a fabric or wall. The word is taken from the Italian *cartone* for thick paper or cardboard. The paper was used for transferring the sketch by blacking the verso, then pinning and tracing it to create an outline of the design on the receiving surface or using multiple pinpricks to create the outline on the wall for later drawing and painting. This process often destroyed the original cartoon.

Augustus's *Flute of Pan* was never transformed into a decoration; instead, a large run of black and white prints was created from the original. John Quinn purchased 50 in early 1914. On inspection, Derwent's cartoon does not have a blackened backing or pinprick outlines. Perhaps it had been commissioned by the art collector Sir Hugh Lane (1875–1915), as were other mural decorations by Augustus, Mac and Ian Strang before the First World War intervened, and which never served their purpose.

Mac exhibited his decoration at the Carfax Gallery in 1913 to curious comments.[18] Commissioned by Sir Hugh for his Dublin art gallery, it seems unlikely to have been delivered. Mac wrote to him in late 1912 regarding its collection, as it was stored at a friend's studio in Thackeray House.[19] Sadly, Sir Hugh would soon die, going down with the RMS *Lusitania* when it was torpedoed by a German submarine during the war, with Mac dying not long after on the battlefield.

Later, Derwent overpainted parts of his *Les Anciennes* in oils of soft ochre, blue and yellow tones, and it seems to have been re-exhibited at the 1916 NEAC show as *Sketch for a Decoration*.

In 1952, Nan Kivell, then Redfern Gallery Director, sent an unsolicited letter to the Slade on Edith's behalf, inviting the School to buy the work. At 150 x 180 cm and mounted on backboard, it was large, and Edith was to be charged storage fees by London frame-makers Alfred Stiles and Sons if she did not relocate it. The Slade did not have funds for the purchase, but agreed to store it, with the provision that Edith could retrieve it at any time if she found a buyer.[20] This unique work remains at the UCL Art Museum, along with a large portfolio of Derwent's 1907 prize-winning student drawings which, despite never leaving the institution in which they were created, were not forgotten. In 1947, Schwabe noted in his diary that he had 'looked through a large number of old Slade prize drawings, including Lees'.[21]

There are similarities between other decorative murals that Augustus and Derwent created which also present a dreamlike parade of classical, statuesque women against a landscape backdrop, often with children in the foreground, showing the persistent influence of the primitive symbolism of French artist Pierre Puvis de Chavannes (1824–1898) that they both also absorbed into their figures of landscapes in Wales. Augustus's *Lyric Fantasy* was one of several murals commissioned by Sir Hugh for his Chelsea home. Augustus often designed the composition using family and friends as models, and while *Lyric Fantasy* was commenced in 1909, it was never displayed nor given a title until 1940. Derwent's *Les Anciennes* was also never transferred to a wall. Another large decoration by Derwent was shown at the

Gieves Art Gallery as *The Little Stranger* in 1928 (DL13.74), and a further preparatory study for a decoration is held by the National Gallery of Australia (DL10.15).

Augustus and Derwent's shared intelligence, humour and love of sensual forms, human and landscape, were at the core of their relationship and mutual respect. Augustus wanted 'fair-weather friends . . . there were two motives behind all Augustus's friendships: inspiration and entertainment. Either they stimulated him when at work, or they induced self-forgetfulness in the intervals between working.'[22] Derwent met both criteria. His combination of intelligence, craftsmanship and tolerance made him an ideal friend. And despite Augustus's hedonistic bent, Derwent's enduring male friends were always open-hearted and genuine. While Augustus was gregarious, uninhibited and intoxicatingly full of life, Derwent was content to remain in the background. Augustus did not like the self-absorbed or egotistical, and neither did Henry Tonks. For Derwent, both friendships were important, as they were to last.

TO CASSIS

Derwent exhibited his oversized cartoon at the summer 1914 NEAC exhibition, along with four landscapes of coastal Provence. These scenes of Cassis, La Ciotat and Cap Canaille are likely to have been created during the Slade mid-term break, when he and Edith purportedly took a trip through France and Switzerland. His one-off inheritance had been paid to him at Christmas 1913, replacing his father's regular allowance, and this may have explained an extravagant honeymoon. Despite these moments of lightness, by late April, talk of war created unrest and the Slade

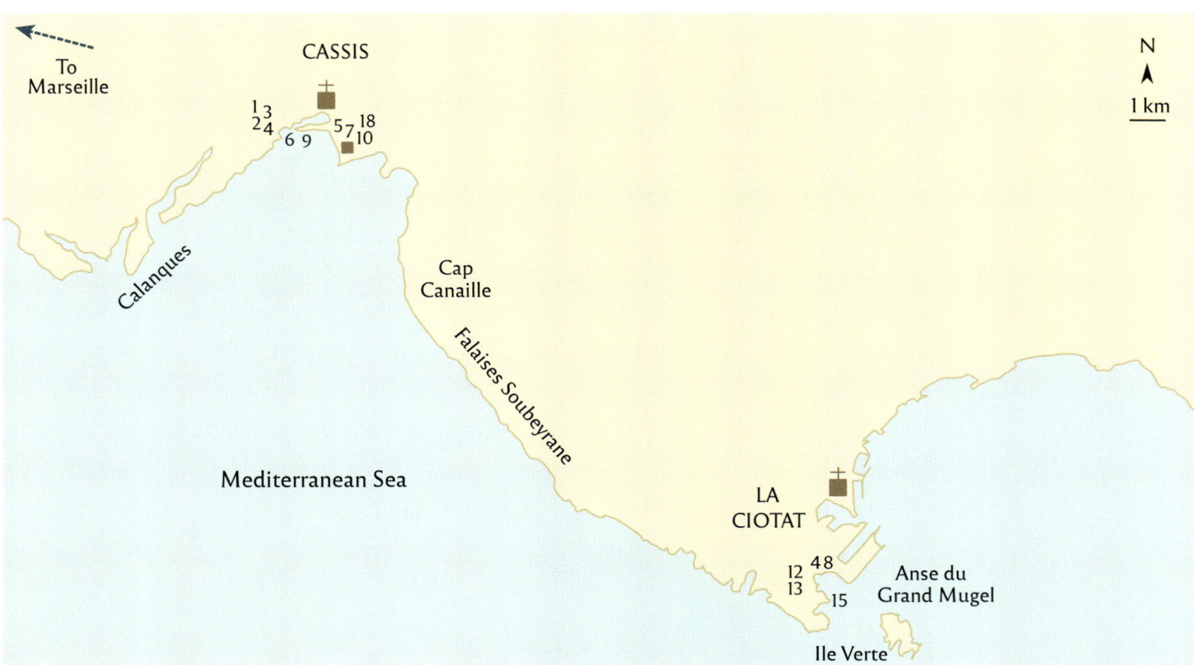

Principal locations where Derwent painted in Cassis and La Ciotat, 1914 Numbers indicate known painting sites; DL14. prefix is not shown

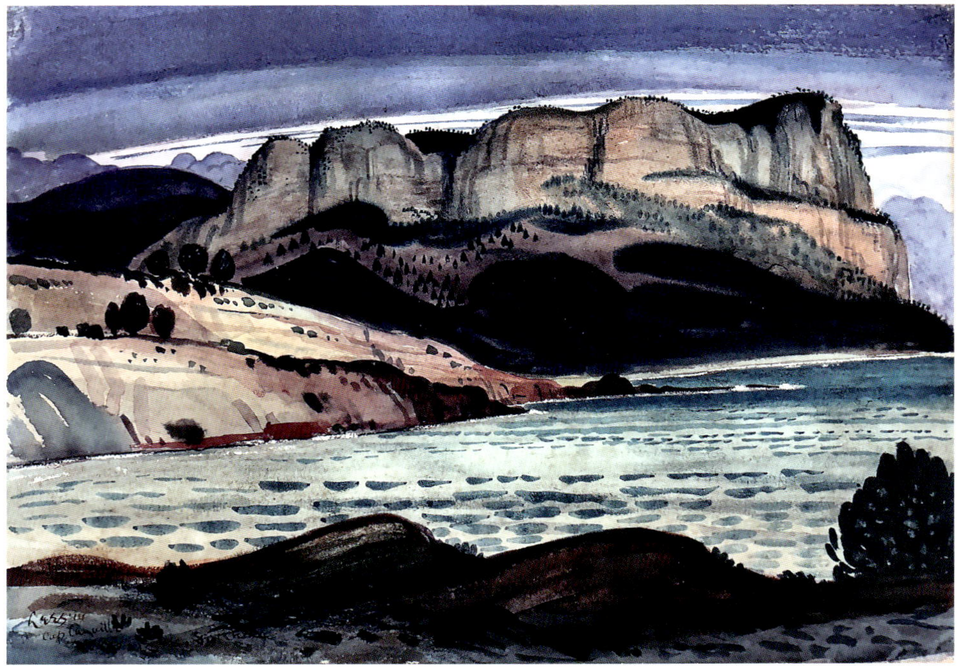

DL14.9
Derwent Lees, *Cap Canaille*, 1914, watercolour, pencil, pen and ink with surface scratching on paper, 25 x 35.5 cm, The Whitworth, University of Manchester

held meetings to consider relocating to Oxford. Despite much discussion, the School decided to remain at Gower Street in London.

It is unknown with whom the Lees travelled to Cassis and La Ciotat, but a letter from Augustus to Dorelia McNeill shows that Derwent was looking for travelling companions. He asked Augustus if he would go to Provence, but he was not keen.[23] Derwent had other friends in his London art circles who were in Cassis in 1914. Ethel Elder and Derwent jointly exhibited works from Cassis and La Ciotat at the summer 1914 and spring 1915 NEAC exhibitions, so she, or Fred and Hannah Mayor, were likely travelling companions. Or perhaps Samuel Peploe (1871–1935), fellow *Rhythm* and *Blue Review* contributor, who also frequented Cassis, first exhibiting works from there in London in March 1914.

Ethel painted the Liautaud Hotel in Cassis and scenes along the Calanque road. Derwent painted the town and port from the same road, as well as Cap Canaille from the breakwater, the clifftop castle ruins and the bay (DL14.1–11).

He and Fred also painted similar watercolour scenes from the port's western entrance. Derwent worked up three watercolour studies at this site for a large scene of the bay in oil (DL14.1–4). This was his modus operandi, with *The Times* remarking of his technique that 'each landscape was an essay, until after many similar studies he was successful'.[24] Fred and Hannah Mayor, both member artists of the Staithes Group and part of Derwent's London art circles, had moved to France in 1902, spending the summers in the north and winters in Cassis.[25]

After Derwent's death, an art critic would single out his French works, revealing that they:

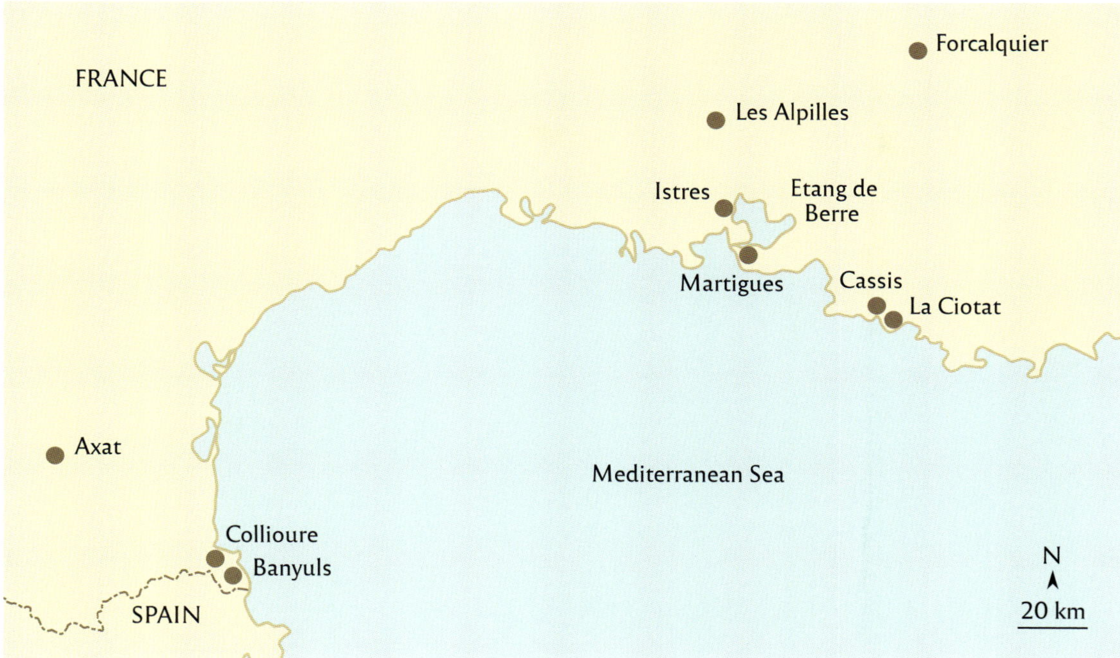

Locations where Derwent painted in southern France, 1910–14

> make their presence felt. In No.126 rich harmonies of blue and green, combined with horizontal pattern in clouds and fields, make it a satisfying watercolour. No.125 *Seascape with Headland Near Cassis*, has a foreboding atmosphere, but on further examination in the forbidding headland pinks and yellows relieve the ominous grey-blues of the water and sky in a remarkable manner. [exhibition numbers shown; No.125 is DL14.9][26]

The small Mediterranean fishing port of Cassis and its mountain backdrop was reminiscent of both Collioure and Banyuls, as was neighbouring La Ciotat, where Derwent painted at least seven works (DL14.12–16, 19, 47). Paul Signac described Cassis to Vincent van Gogh in 1888 as 'some white, some blue, some orange harmonically dispersed in pretty undulations. All around mountains with rhythmic curves.'[27] The words resonate with many of Derwent's joyful paintings from the Cassis area.

During his short career, Derwent completed more than 200 landscapes (those with no figures), of which 60 per cent are of France. Of these, most are from the southern Catalan coast (Collioure, Banyuls, Port Vendres and Argelès) and the remainder from his Provençal trips (Cassis, La Ciotat, Istres and Forcalquier). The 20 or so works produced during his 1914 Cassis–La Ciotat trip represent his last French works. It was his final trip to the colour, light and latitude of his childhood, to the resonating warmth of his remembered 'home'.

He was never to leave Britain again.

10 JOY AND PAIN 1914–15

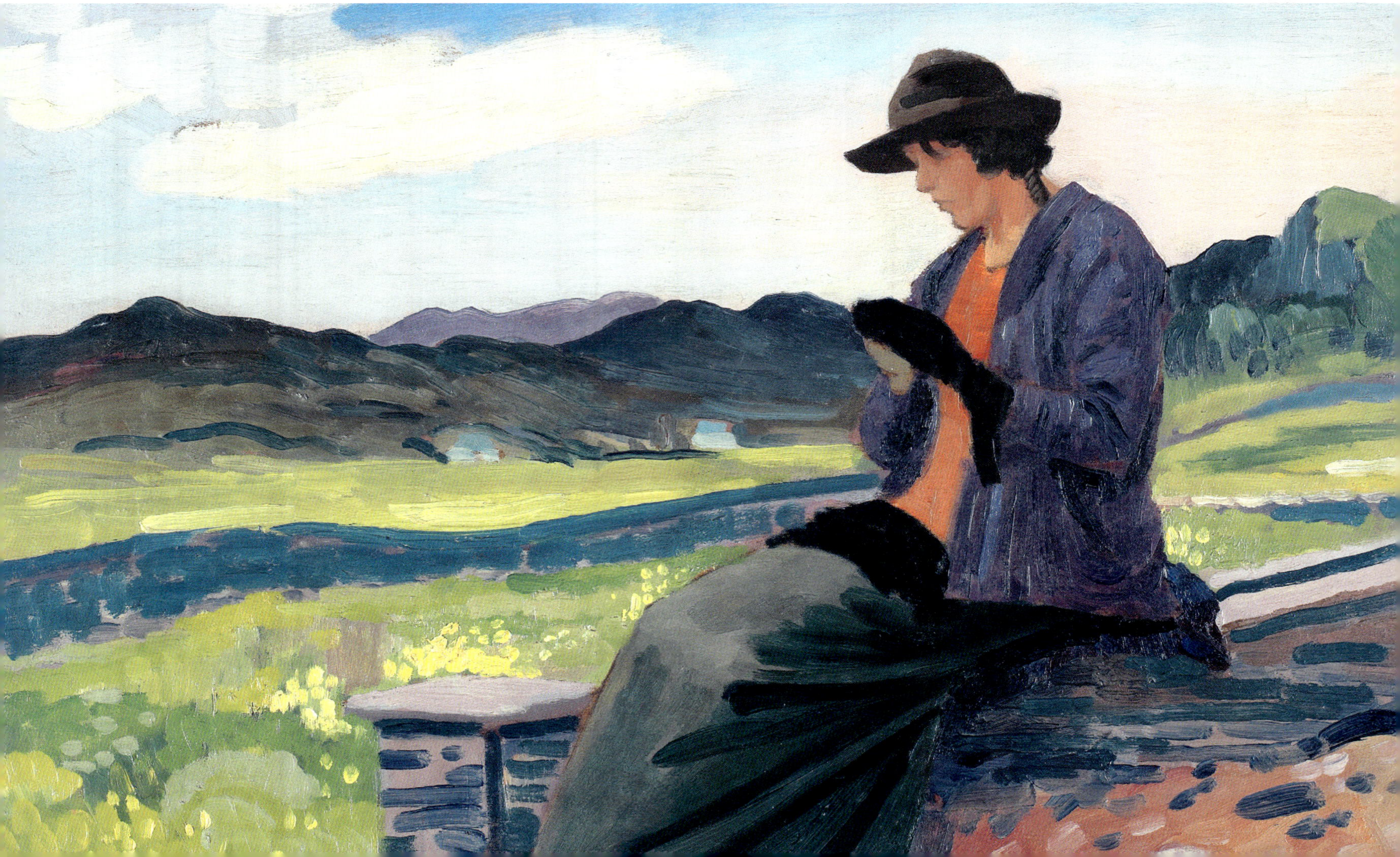

Derwent and Edith spent the spring and summer of 1914 on England's Dorset coast and in northern Wales. During a May long weekend, they set off to Dorset with Nora and Gerald Summers to paint around the Purbeck Hills near Creech and bathe at Chapman's Pool on the coast. During the trip, Derwent gave his friends a watercolour of Worbarrow Bay, complete with a light-hearted inscription in French of an incident with a flat tyre while travelling in Gerald's car (DL14.20). Schwabe later wrote that 'I believe Gerald Summers was the first man who ever drove a car down to Arish Mell',[1] a flat tyre unsurprising on the rough track to the beach.

Over summer the Lees likely caught up with Nora and Gerald again around the Dorset coast, and perhaps also at Alderney, where the Summerses were frequent visitors.

For a time, the two couples travelled in a caravan drawn by two large, old white horses, and Randolph Schwabe also joined them. Derwent and Nora painted together, creating similar watercolour and ink landscapes, often the only distinguishing feature being Nora's tiny but distinct and delicate illustrative elements such as ridgetops lined by minute, neatly inked rows of trees. Derwent used the same elements, but as looser forms. He also likely captured the two women, in pencil and ink, as winsome nudes in a distinctive, simplified style, perhaps as their swimming costumes dried after their swim at Chapman's Pool (DL13.62–3). Gerald painted landscapes too, with a preference for man-made structures such as industrial machinery and quarries.

Augustus and Derwent both drew pencil portraits of Nora holding the same pose (DL14.22). Derwent gave his portrait to Nora and Gerald, and they were to purchase an elaborately framed, richly coloured oil of Edith at the Blue Pool painted the preceding summer (DL13.32).[2]

Life was good, and Derwent's contentment was evident in his art and his inscriptions. Approximately 50 per cent of his landscapes are signed, with his dominant signature a flowing, forward-leaning style mimicking his natural handwriting (variously: full name, surname, first initial and surname, or just initials, often adjusted according

Opposite:
DL14.44 (detail)
Derwent Lees, *Lyndra in Wales*, 1914

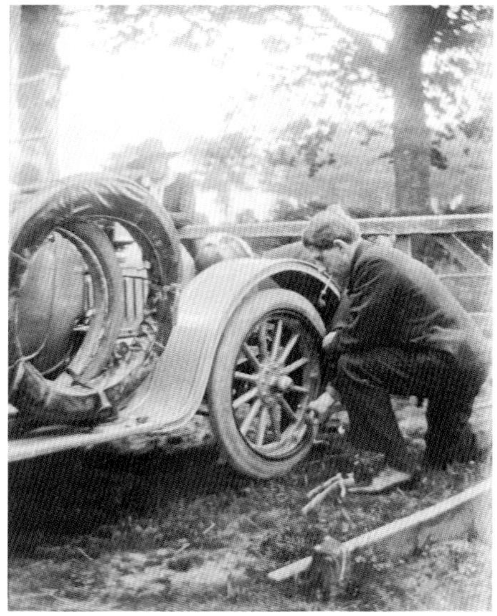

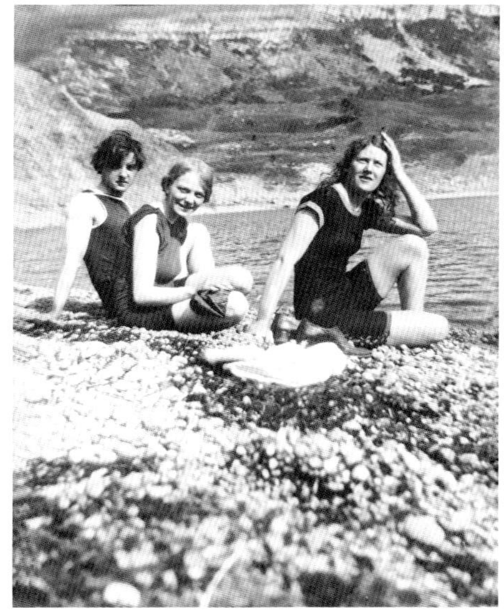

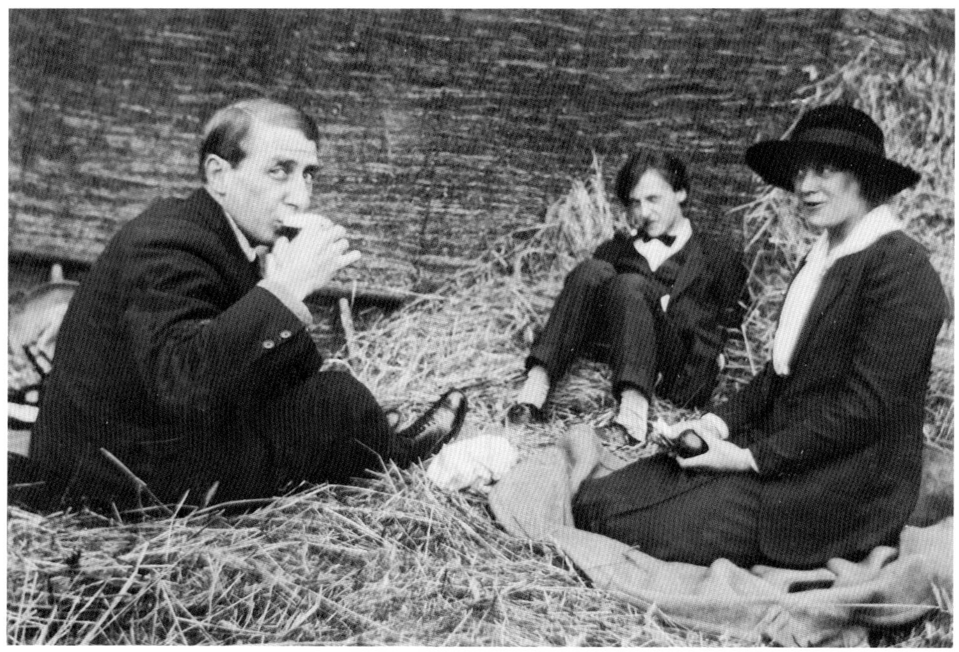

Left:
Derwent fixing a flat tyre on Gerald Summers's car, Dorset, 1914, photograph by Nora Summers, Private Collection

Right:
Lyndra, Nora and Gerald Summers (l–r), Chapman's Pool, Dorset, 1914, photograph possibly by Derwent Lees, Private Collection

Below:
Derwent, Gerald Summers and Lyndra (l–r) having a tea break, Dorset, 1914, photograph by Nora Summers, Private Collection

to medium). When at his happiest, it seems his signature signalled his mood, with an ease and confidence evident in several watercolours. Confident, playful signatures and inscriptions appear on his 1910 Collioure and 1914 Cassis works, and on the 1913 and 1914 Dorset paintings. A light cartouche swirl encircling his surname appears on several works in happier moments.

Derwent's output during the long summer break of 1914 was impressive, with several landscapes and figures in landscapes in Dorset, and at least 20 in North Wales, mostly including Edith. He transformed the Welsh slate-mining landscape into a richly coloured, almost romantic backdrop for her. These large *plein air* works, including *Tan-y-Bwlch*, *Lyndra by the Rocks*, *Lyndra by the Pool*, *Lyndra in Wales*, *Lyndra at Tanygrisiau*, *Lyndra*, *Portrait of a Lady in a Landscape* and *Girl*

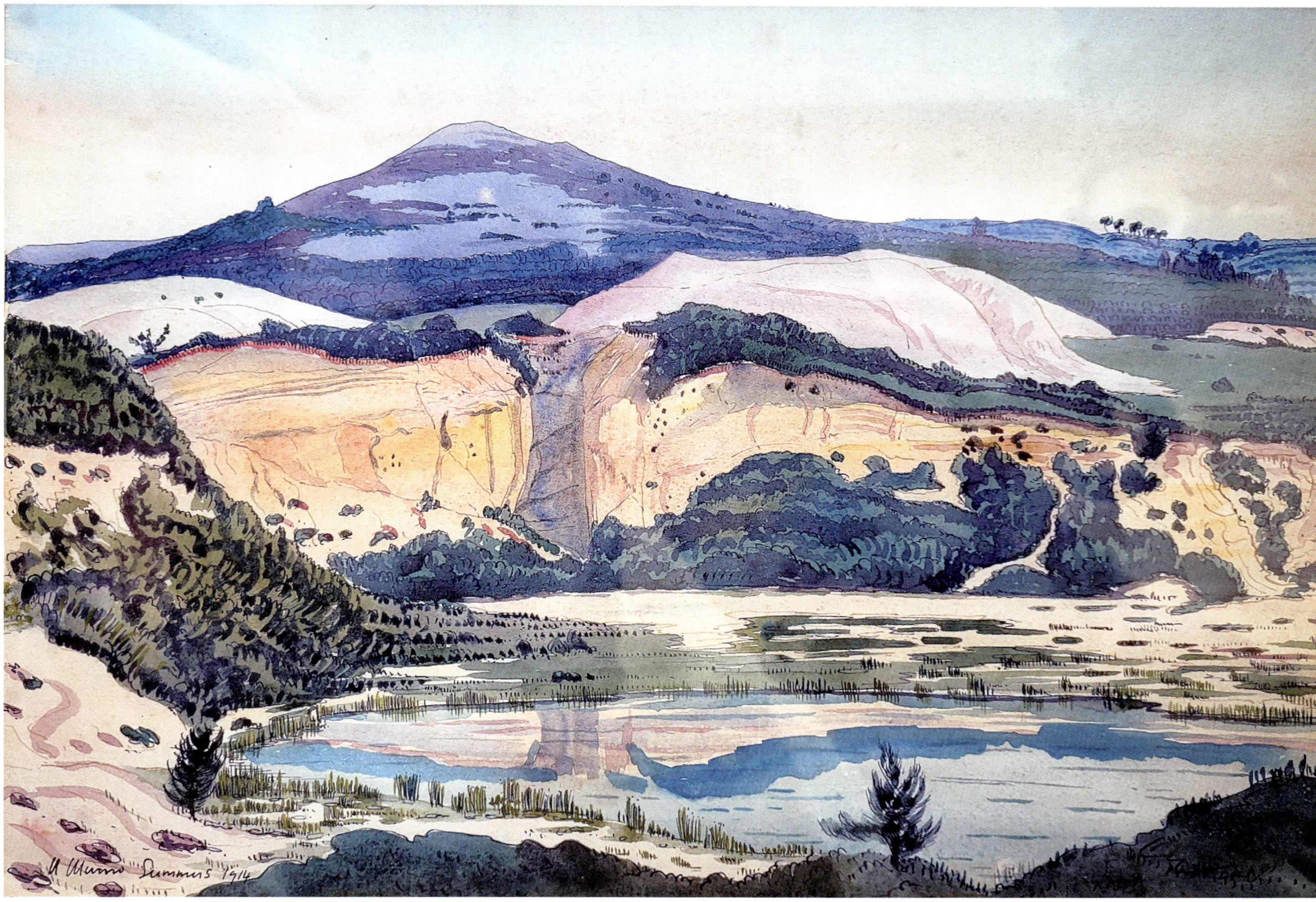

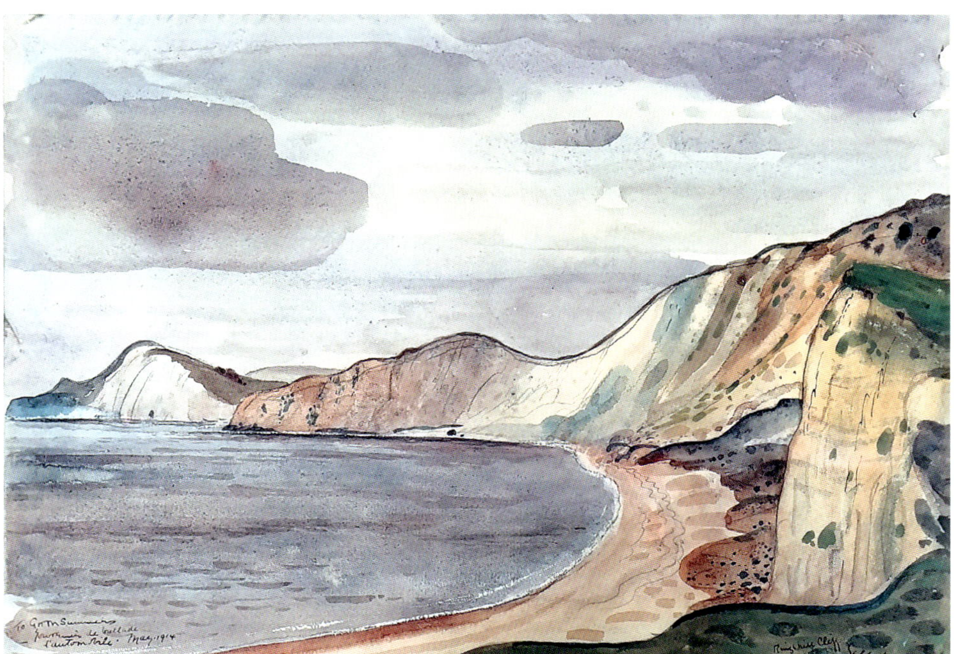

Above:
Nora Summers, *The Blue Pool, Dorset*, c.1914, pen, ink and watercolour, 28 x 39 cm, Private Collection

Left:
DL14.20
Derwent Lees, *Rings Hill Cliff, Dorset*, 1914, watercolour on paper, 25 x 35.5 cm, Private Collection

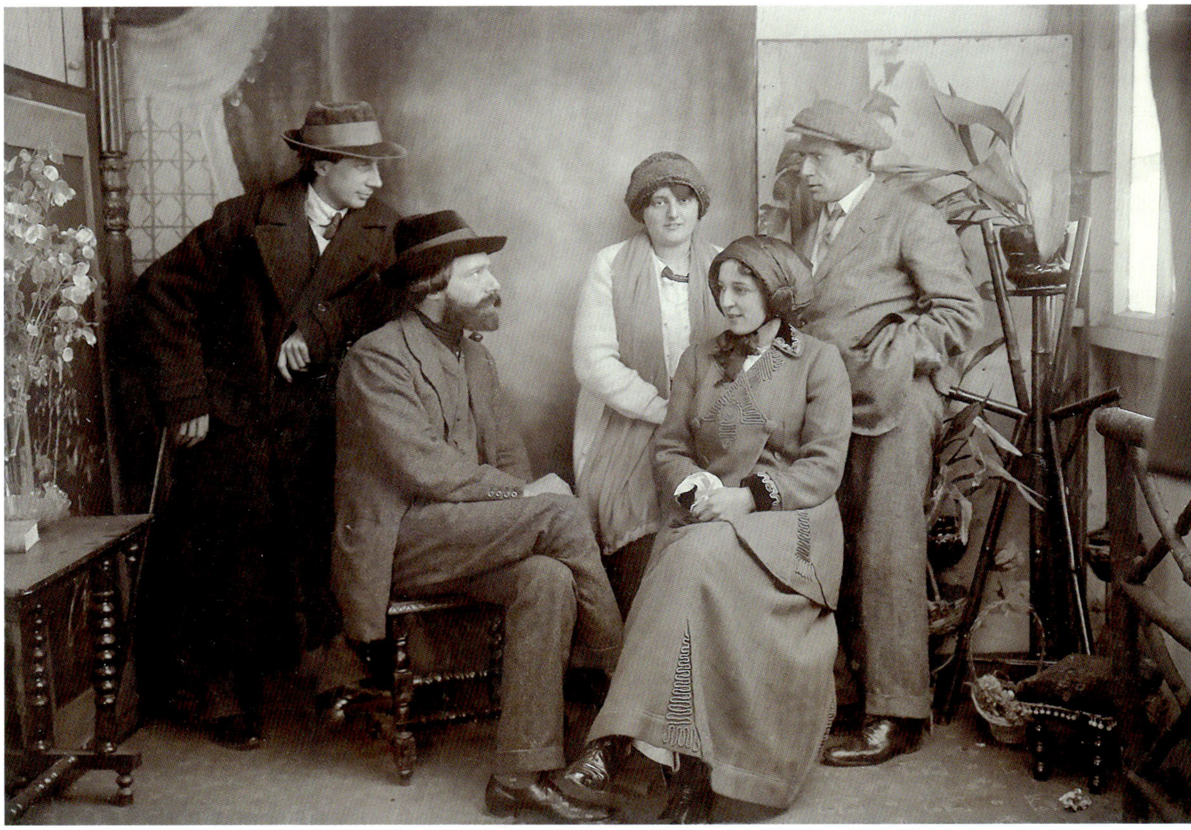

Derwent Lees, Augustus John, Gwendolyn van Raalte, Mr and Mrs Holbrooke (l–r), Trawsfynydd, Wales, c.1914, photograph by R. Meredith & Sons, The Howard de Walden Estate Document Archive, London

in a Black Hat (DL14.34–41), exude a creative confidence, portraying his wife in a wide range of poses and palettes. In many of them, Edith wears her full-flowing, pre-Raphaelite style, dress. Dorelia McNeill 'was known for her free-flowing dress, a style that was influenced by the clothing of John's gypsy friends. She encouraged others within her circle, such as her sister Edie, and Lyndra, the wife of Derwent Lees, to wear similar clothes.'[3]

Edith wears Derwent's hat in several 1914 works, the same hat seen in a rare photograph of him with friends in Wales that summer. Taken at R. Meredith & Sons studio in Trawsfynydd, the photograph shows Derwent with Augustus, the composer Joseph Holbrooke and his wife, and Lady Howard de Walden's sister, Gwendolyn van Raalte (1893–1975), known as Poots.

There was a casual, almost domestic, intimacy between the Leeses and Augustus and Dorelia. In *Lyndra in Wales* (DL14.44), a 1914 oil, she sits on a low wall surrounded by spring flowers; the location identified as near the country house of Plas Brondanw, just over the Moelwyn mountains from Ffestiniog, with Moel Hebog in the distance. Edith later recounted to Maurice Ingram, who bought the painting from the Redfern Gallery in 1937, that it shows her 'darning a pair of Augustus John's socks'.[4] Dorelia was known for making and mending clothes and teaching others. Decades later, Michael Holroyd (Augustus's biographer) spoke to a friend of Dorelia's who mentioned that 'One afternoon I had gone up to Alderney Manor to learn from Dorelia how to "turn a heel", so I could be able to knit socks for my two boys'.[5] In Dorelia's absence, it seems Edith filled that role for Augustus.

In some of Derwent's 1914 late summer Welsh works, Edith has an air of boredom or discontent. She and Derwent appear to have spent much of this time alone. The domestic mood was changing. Augustus would write to Dorelia from the Llwynythyl cottage near Tanygrisiau (that Lord Howard de Walden had purchased for Augustus and friends to use) in late summer explaining that 'the Lees couple seem to be somewhat lost'. The cottage was full, and the ambiance tense. Augustus was irritated by Holbrooke, telling Dorelia that he 'is too horrible' and planned to leave the following day.[6] From now on Augustus was to see less of Derwent; impending war put everyone on edge, but there was more to this comment about the Leeses.

DICK'S DEPARTURE

Dick had again travelled south to the warmth and sea air, accompanied by Trelawney Dayrell Reed, in an attempt to halt the progression of his illness, but his condition worsened. He was ignoring medical advice and 'doing La Bombe', as Augustus described Dick's excessive drinking sessions.[7] In 1914, tuberculosis was a much-feared, highly contagious killer. No one yet understood that neither warmth, sea nor mountain air were curative.

By early summer, he was gravely ill, and Trelawney cabled Dick's family. Accounts differ as to who brought Dick home, some surmising that it was his older brother Jack; however, Augustus wrote in Dick's 1923 memorial exhibition catalogue that his mother travelled to Tenerife to fetch her ailing son. This is supported by a passenger ship record of a Mr and a Mrs Innes, not married, accompanied by a 25-year-old nurse, arriving in Liverpool from Tenerife in the final days of June 1914.[8]

Dick arrived home, and everyone expected him to recover, since he usually recuperated under his mother's care. Fothergill would later write that 'Dick got back to England in 1914 where his mother tried to cure his consumption'.[9] However, within eight weeks he was dead. His friends had not seen him for many months, some for well over a year. In his final weeks he wrote to friends, asking them to visit (as Frank Slade's and Augustus's two surviving letters attest).[10]

No personal correspondence of Derwent's from this time has survived, so it is unknown whether he was beside his friend near the end. There is a tendency to interpret the absence of information as negative evidence of its existence, but it was not a coincidence that Derwent was out of sorts later that summer in Wales, distressed and 'somewhat lost'. Dick's death must have had a profound impact on him.

Dick died on 22 August 1914 in Swanley, Kent, his death certificate poignantly noting that he was 'of no occupation'.[11] Frank said of his close friend that 'inspirations came to him suddenly'.[12] Dick was a vibrant, active and remarkable artist, whose friendship and energy led Augustus to later reminisce that Derwent had 'found in his friend's approach to Nature a means of release from his academic shackles, and with immense will and intelligence strove to adapt himself to a new outlook'.[13]

Derwent had now lost his fifth close connection; first Noel, then his mother, James, his father, and now Dick.

Everyone's focus now turned to the war. Derwent returned to London, reassured by the structure and routine provided by Henry Tonks and the Slade. Classes commenced on 5 October 1914. He settled down after the events of late summer, his mentors Tonks and Augustus being mostly in London. However, Tonks soon registered as a doctor with the British forces and, by January 1915, the UCL Council Minutes recorded his leave of absence for military service.[14] Weeks working at prisoner of war camps in Dorchester and Essex were followed by a spell at a British Red Cross hospital in France. He was, however, home often enough to exhibit alongside Augustus and Derwent at the December 1914 New English Art Club (NEAC) show and at both summer and winter 1915 NEAC exhibitions.

Derwent painted some 50 works in 1914, and 1915 was also to be productive. In February, ever faithful to the Friday Club, he showed four works from northern Wales and Cassis at the Alpine Club Gallery. His former classmate and close friend, Elsie McNaught, also hung work, having spent time in North Wales in the past September and earlier in the year, no doubt catching up with Derwent. Elsie had travelled with her mountaineer cousin, Dorothy Pilley, and their aunt Clara, basing themselves just to the north of Tanygrisiau, mainly around Llyn Dinas.

In May 1915, Derwent put forward a mix of works for the Chenil Gallery's exhibition of *Paintings by Alfred P. Allinson and T. Dayrell-Reed and also others*, and a few weeks later he hung another three at the summer NEAC exhibition. Friend and former neighbour Ethel Elder showed a work from Cassis before leaving for Ireland.

The English-born Australian artist Tom Roberts (1856–1931) showed works at the same summer 1915 exhibition. Born in Dorset, he spent much of his life in Australia. Despite a 30-year age difference, they would have likely crossed paths. They exhibited at two of the same exhibitions, both knew Walter Withers and Charles Conder and both had studied art in the northern hemisphere. Coincidentally, both would die in the same year. The 1915 NEAC exhibition was reported in the Australian and New Zealand papers, which observed:

> Two Australian artists have had their pictures very well hung at the exhibition in London of the New English Art Club. One is Mr Tom Roberts (of Melbourne) who has a beautiful Yorkshire landscape called *Goth and Moor*. The other is Mr Derwent Lees who has three landscapes of Provence; one of them is hung in the place of honour.[15]

In another promising review, an art critic wrote that,

> Mr Derwent Lees, on a smaller scale, displays in his *Étang de Berre, Provence* (115), admirable decorative qualities, powerful colour massively used, and a high standard of definition. Nothing in the exhibition is a better example of the use of paint for purposes of formal design, and by this work Mr. Lees may be considered as having established a place for himself among landscape painters. [exhibition number shown][16]

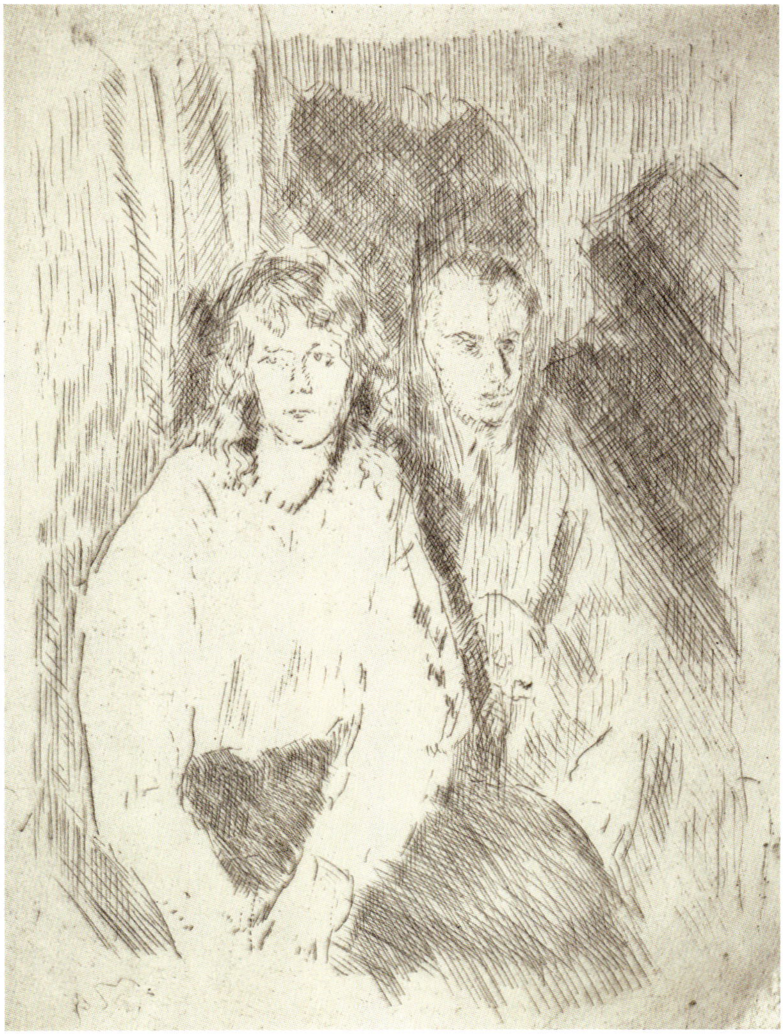

Ambrose McEvoy, *Mr and Mrs Derwent Lees*, c.1915, etching on paper, 20.3 x 15.2 cm (plate), Victoria and Albert Museum, London

AMBROSE

Tonks understood his Assistant Drawing Master well. They had known each other for a decade, and Tonks knew that Derwent needed support. It seems likely that he spoke to Ambrose McEvoy before leaving for the war. Ambrose had been the Slade Assistant since 1913 and, as couples, the Leeses and McEvoys would have seen each other socially. Ambrose's watercolour of *Mr and Mrs Derwent Lees* was chosen for the spring 1915 NEAC show, and the Leeses also spent the summer with him and his family. It seems that they visited Freshford, Ambrose's wife's family village, and Aldbourne, where his brother Charles (1879–1929) had established a theatre, and perhaps also Westcot near Wantage, where Charles had lived. It is likely they also painted in nearby Bourton, Shrivenham, where Ambrose had been artist-in-residence to Sir Cyril Kendall Butler a decade earlier. He had continued doing commissions for the wealthy art patron, painting a Butler family portrait in 1912.[17] Cyril was by now a collector of both Ambrose's and Derwent's works, eventually owning more than 15 by Derwent.

During 1915, Ambrose created an etching based on sketches and the watercolour he had exhibited of the Leeses. Held at London's Victoria and Albert Museum, the small work shows a tentative Derwent seated behind Edith in an interior scene. During the summer the two artists painted alongside each other, with Derwent's oil on canvas *Aldbourne* (DL15.19) capturing an almost identical viewscape to Ambrose's *Morning, Aldbourne* and *View from Aldbourne*. They had a productive holiday, with Derwent painting a dozen landscapes around Aldbourne, and ten works with Edith as a central figure. She appears pensive, perhaps bored, with her hair coiffed into a pinned bob, sometimes wearing a necklace. Gone were the gypsy scarves and flowing dresses. Her clothes and poses contrast markedly with those of Derwent's oils at Alderney Manor earlier in the year.

Derwent's Aldbourne works were primarily on canvas. These were highly praised, with one purchased by the Contemporary Art Society (DL15.19). He also used a sponge for the first time, an Ambrose technique. Years later, Schwabe wrote that Derwent,

> had a remarkable facility, and over and above his very skillful drawings from life, adapted himself, chameleon-like, to the styles of John, Innes and McEvoy. His sudden switch-over from the technique of Innes to that of McEvoy was surprising. It occurred one summer when he had been away in McEvoy's company . . . he turned to the use of sponges and other devices. McEvoy used to put his watercolours repeatedly under the tap, working on them again after each washing. Having seen this practice, Lees did likewise.[18]

Intrigue or lack of confidence perhaps stimulated his desire to experiment with his friend's technique as he played with a range of painting and drawing styles during his short career.

Writing 20 years after this trip, *The Studio* described the two artists' pre-war teaching at the Slade:

> Two newcomers to the staff during the Edwardian period were Ambrose McEvoy, and Derwent Lees. Both had been brilliant students at the Slade; McEvoy the sensitive painter greatly helped that side, while Lees, the gifted draughtsman, supported the all-important drawing. It was a great loss that both died early; Lees . . . although unrecognised during his lifetime, he is now becoming quite a minor master.[19]

Augustus and Ambrose had studied together at the Slade, both becoming fashionable and highly successful portrait artists. Both older and more established than Derwent, they quickly became London society's go-to portraitists; one, whose works of intensity and wildness showed moments of striking creativity; the other, a reliable, highly talented society painter with a distinctive style and technique. During 1915, Ambrose exhibited a portrait of his wife Mary, *Madame*, that was so well received it transformed him into a leading portraitist to the wealthy classes, particularly of women. Derwent also painted aristocratic beauties, such as Lady Louisa Kendall Butler (DL16.13) and Lady Diana Manners (DL15.9). His portraits

Head of a Girl (aka *Portrait Study: Woman with Head Turned to the Right*, DL15.4), *Study of a Young Girl* (DL15.5), *Portrait of a Girl* (DL15.31) and *Lyndra* (DL15.30) all show the strong influence of Ambrose's style, as does *London Public House* (DL15.2), no doubt akin to Ambrose's *Public House*, painted and exhibited in 1915.

In 1915, the patriotic thing to do for the 'at-home' artist was to paint portraits of uniformed soldiers. Derwent made pencil sketches of his friend, Slade graduate and Fitzrovia neighbour Francis Helps (1891–1972; DL15.6), before producing a final work in pencil and a watercolour that was purchased by the British Museum in 1939 (DL15.7). Francis readied himself to depart for the war while Derwent, influenced by Augustus and Ambrose, likely did further portraits of men in uniform. Derwent needed to feel comfortable with his male sitters, and after his student (or Slade teaching) days, his only male subjects were close friends: Donald Maclaren, John Fothergill and Francis. Contemplative in uniform, and painted with warmth and sensitivity, his subject looks to the mid-distance. Francis had started at the Slade in 1908 and volunteered for service in 1915, serving in France until he was discharged in July 1918, unaware of the importance he was yet to have in his former teacher's crumbling life. Francis later taught painting at the Leeds College of Art, his peers describing him as 'a kindly man who loved his painting, but his artistic heart was still in the 19th century'.[20]

WINIFRED

Derwent's Slade contract was renewed for another year, and staff returned for Term I in early October 1915. His commitment to the institution filled most of his waking hours and he was liked by his students. Schwabe later commented that Derwent's 'teaching was highly thought of by his colleagues and by those who came under him'.[21]

Dick once wrote to Fothergill saying that, at the Slade, Derwent was 'the Don Juan of the establishment'.[22] Comfortable in the company of women, he was kind, neatly dressed and charming. Around October, a young female student appears to have fallen under Derwent's spell and, according to the teenager's letters to a friend, he also with her. Winifred Knights (1899–1947) wrote many letters to her close friend Awdrey Clarke, in which she dissected her seemingly flirtatious conversations with her teacher. Although likely nothing more than an Edwardian teenage girl's crush on her teacher, perhaps a mutual attraction did exist. There was a gentleness between the two and, after one of her first term classes, she wrote to Awdrey stating that 'I am falling in love with him' and included a pencil illustration of how she felt when walking home from class that day.[23]

In another, she even described their conversation:

> Lees Its [*sic*] you who do these fairy tale drawings for the Sketch Club.
> WMK How did you guess?
> Lees By the drawing on the side of your board . . . It is a very strange thing . . . that when one is drawing from imagination one invariably gets ones own likeness or at least a part of ones likeness. [punctuation, layout *sic*][24]

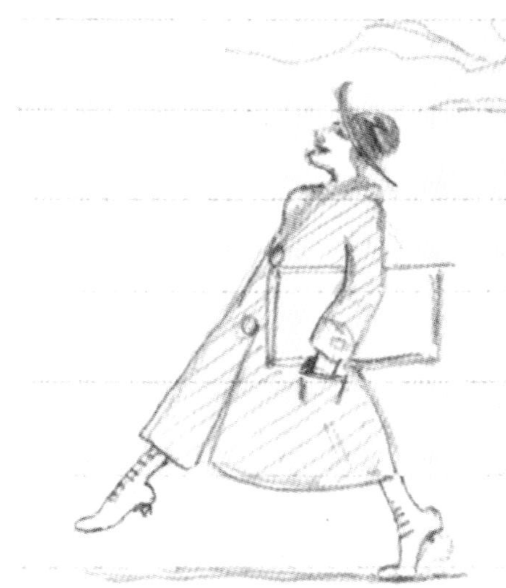

Winifred Knights, *'I went home like this yesterday after it all'*, 1915, pencil on lined paper, Winifred Knights Correspondence, UCL Special Collections, University College London

Illustration in a letter to Awdrey Clarke

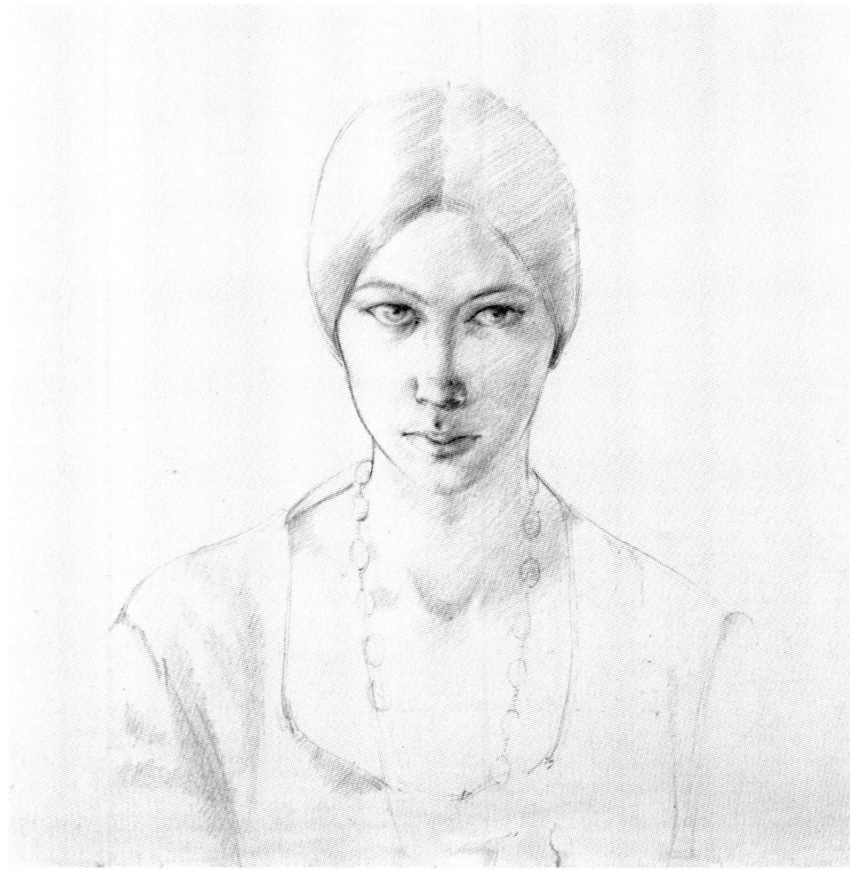

Winifred Knights, *Self Portrait*, c.1916, pencil on paper, 28.3 x 38 cm, UCL Art Museum, University College London

In one late 1915 letter, Winifred sketched an amusing caricature of some of her fellow students and staff which included 'Professor Tonks', 'Professor Mac-Evoy' [*sic*] and 'Professor Lees', entitled *Some Sladites*.

In another, she wrote:

> He marched right up to me just as before only Mac-Evoy [*sic*] was not in the room although he had just left me. The drawing I was doing was a hand . . .
> Well Lees stood behind me as before for about a minute and then said in a very quiet, soft, voice, ahum!! [*sic*]
> 'Let me see this mysterious hand???' [*sic*]
> Well, he [Lees] sat down and began as before saying 'this really is a very good drawing, very good, I like this mysterious effect you have got'
> Really Awdry I could see nothing mysterious in it. Then, 'you have got quite a snaky appearance into that finger.'
> Long gaze, very exciting
> Now this Awdry which happened as he spoke is very difficult to explain so I will draw it if I can [sketch of Derwent on the stool, she on the floor, with an arrow pointing to the word 'Hands!!']
> You see that he sat on the donkey stool, sideways and left a huge space of seat by the drawing board.

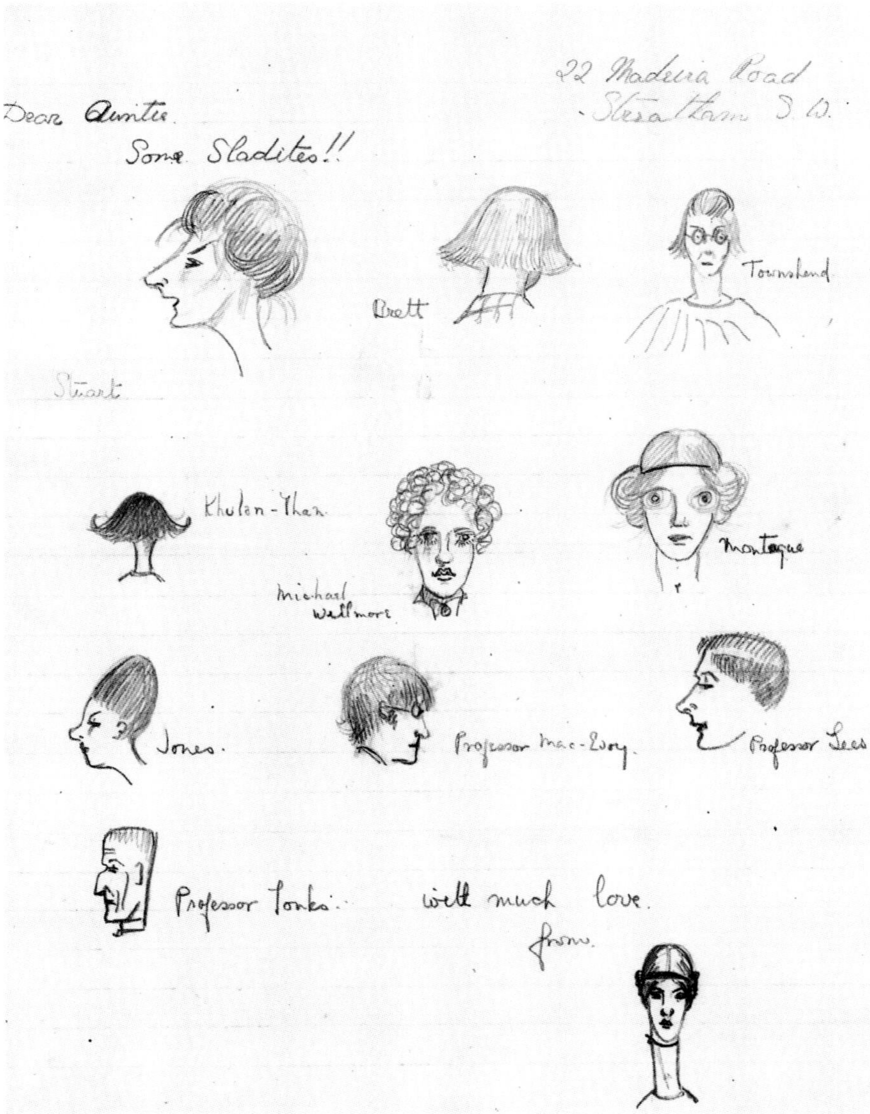

Left:
Winifred Knights, *Some Sladites!!*, 1915, pencil on paper, Winifred Knights Correspondence, UCL Special Collections, University College London

Illustration in a letter to Awdrey Clarke

Below:
Winifred Knights, *Derwent and Winifred Hands Touching*, 1915, pencil on paper, Winifred Knights Correspondence, UCL Special Collections, University College London

Illustration in a letter to Awdrey Clarke

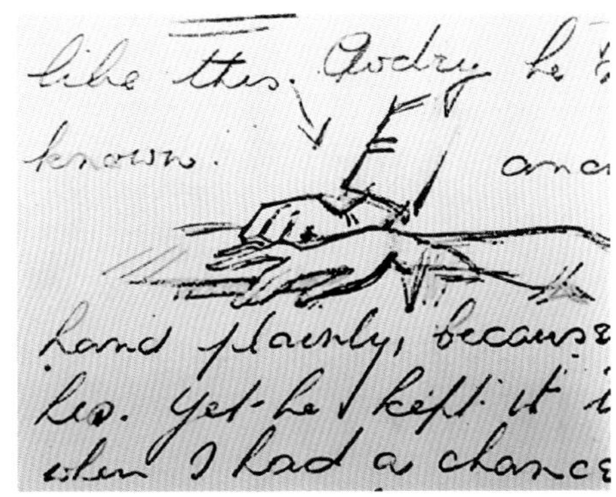

> I who had to sit on the floor ached so there, that I thought there would be no harm in supporting myself by putting up my hand on the seat of the donkey thus: [sketch of her hand on the seat]
> well he began talking away and very soon I became aware that his hand [triple underlined] was touching mine like this [sketch of the hand-touching]. Awdry he must have known and felt my hand plainly, because I felt his. Yet he kept it there and when I had a chance I took mine away when he wasn't looking at me. Well I had a lesson until 4pm on Old Masters. It was a ripping lesson for me you can imagine. [punctuation, layout *sic*][25]

Some letters seem to reveal Derwent's modesty and vulnerability. Winifred wrote: 'Awdry, He can't draw if I stare at him too much. I have some of his drawings that he has done for me lately and they were awful and he knows it because he tried to excuse himself to me' [punctuation *sic*].[26]

Winifred continued glowing about Derwent's drawing instructions well into 1916. In a letter penned that year, she reiterated her attraction towards her drawing teacher, while commenting on his caring nature: 'Lees gave me a ragging about bad contours . . . I felt very sad and must have looked it too for at 3.45 Lees came back and in a very sweet voice told me that it was much better' [punctuation *sic*].[27] Rosanna Eckersley's research of Winifred's time at the Slade indicates that correct Edwardian mores were upheld.[28]

Like Winifred, Derwent peppered his correspondence with drawings. Soon after Derwent's death, Edith shared letters that he had written to her while away on painting trips; words of warmth, self-deprecating humour and concern. Alleyne Zander, then London's Redfern Gallery curator, saw these letters and wrote that Derwent 'was always unhappy at the slightest separation yet contrived to fill the pages with the most amusing little sketches, small satires at his own expense that were to cheer her in his absence'.[29]

Derwent routinely discussed techniques and ideas with individual students, adhering to Fred Brown and Tonks's approach of illustrating teaching points with explanatory sketches in the margins of their work or on a separate piece of paper. This method must have been used by all drawing staff as Gilbert Spencer's biographer, Paul Gough, commented that, based on their training by Tonks and Brown, '[Walter] Russell and Lees communicated their ideas in conversations with students and by marginal drawings on the students' worksheets.'[30]

Neville Lewis, another of Derwent's students during the war, recounted that the Slade's 'teaching staff was about as good as it could be', and that 'Lees was a lively young man with great enthusiasm. He was an excellent draughtsman and I think he would certainly have made a name for himself if he had not died at an early age.' However, during his second year of studies Neville recalled that

> London was becoming more and more gloomy, and people were really depressed. The war was going badly, and it looked as if it would never end. The first zeppelin raids, the falling bombs, together with the banging of anti-aircraft guns and the searchlights swinging their beams in all directions, made Londoners realise they were in the war zone. A strict blackout was enforced.[31]

Neville soon left his studies at the Slade, as did Winifred, who was traumatised after witnessing an explosion in London. She returned to her studies after the cessation of fighting.

FAREWELL TO BOHEMIA

Derwent and Edith's calendar the preceding summer had been full, staying with the McEvoys around Aldbourne, painting in Dorset with Augustus and Dorelia, and then in northern Wales.

More than two years had elapsed since his father's small but regular allowance had gone and Derwent was now supporting Edith as well. It also seems that he may not have been good at budgeting for leaner times. Schwabe gave some insight into his friend's impecunious but impulsive state, saying that when his father's allowance arrived, Derwent 'would sometimes spend most of it on an extravagance, such as a carved frame, and then had to borrow sixpences for cigarettes from his char. She pawned her wedding ring once to help him. He repaid her, of course.'[32] It was a constant battle between hope and despair, but he was clearly decent and trustworthy for a charwoman, hardly well off herself, to pawn her wedding ring to help the penniless artist-teacher.

Understandably the war resulted in a substantial loss of students at the Slade. However, 'unlike the salaries of the Academic Staff in all other departments [the Slade Professor and his Assistants] are largely dependent upon fees',[33] rather than on fixed stipends. This made the Slade Drawing Assistant's life even more precarious. His income from the Slade and also from painting sales had rapidly declined. At the outbreak of war, the revenue from Slade student fees for the 1914–15 academic year was 20 per cent lower than in the preceding year and, by the start of the 1915–16 School year, it had dropped a further 45 per cent.[34] Derwent was on the edge of poverty.

He submitted seven works at the Christmas 1915 NEAC exhibition, hanging new works alongside paintings from 1909, clearly trying to sell as much as possible. The works were well received, one critic admiring his older paintings, with 'Mr Derwent Lees' two impressive designs, *The Bsura, Poland* . . . and *Le Mas aux Oliviers, Roussillon* . . . being, to our mind, the most original contribution amongst the watercolours'.[35]

Additionally, a luminous oil of Aldbourne village was hung (DL15.19), accompanied by a dramatic skyscape, *The Thunder Cloud* (DL15.22), an oil on which Derwent had applied Ambrose's sponge technique. At the public show, a critic noted that: 'an interesting object-lesson in diffuseness and concentration by the painter is provided by "*Aldbourne*" (105), in oils and "*The Bsura, Poland*" (275), and "*Le Mas aux Oliviers, Roussillon*" (279), in water-colour, by Mr Derwent Lees. There is just as much "work" in the oil painting and there are just as many facts in the water-colours' [exhibition numbers shown].[36]

During the year, Edith had been the subject of more than 15 of Derwent's oils, including *The Artist's Wife Reclining* (DL15.26), which captures her relaxing in the Dorset summer heat, and *Lyndra and Charlie* (DL15.28), a painting of Edith with one of Dorelia's donkeys, at Alderney Manor.

Derwent and Edith, active young followers and aspirants of Augustus and Dorelia, emulated them and their lives in look, bohemian lifestyle, and in Derwent's art. There was an ease to their interactions, captured in both artists' works over several years, but this creative kinship was drawing to a close. The summer of 1915 was the last time the couple spent together, possibly the last time Derwent painted at Alderney, and the last year in which Edith appeared in any of his works.

They were still living together at 21 Fitzroy Square, but their few happy years were already coming to an end.

11 THE DECLINE 1916–18

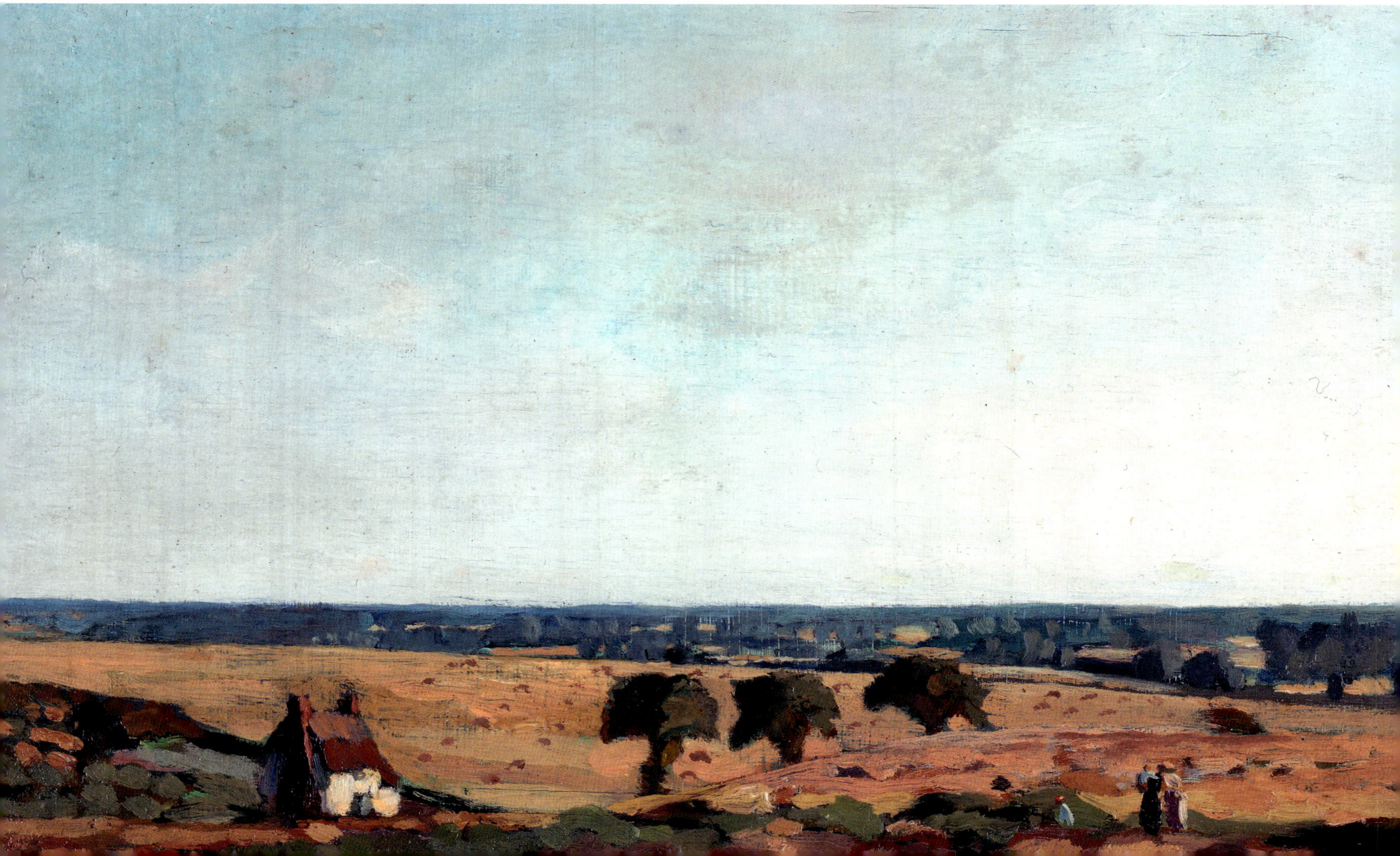

Derwent, Augustus and Henry Tonks showed works in the exhibition of *Some Recent Developments of Modern Art* that opened in January 1916 at the Dowdeswell Gallery. The reviews were good, but January was unexpectedly tough for Derwent. The Slade granted Tonks leave of absence for the period of the war; that leave was now permanent. Tonks left to serve in ambulance units in France and Italy, later returning to military hospitals in England, where he drew pastels of soldiers' facial injuries. He was still a senior member of the Slade staff, but Derwent was no longer under his wing. Derwent's chief mentor and role model, the dogged, loyal and reliable, stern but knowing patriarch of his world, had now gone.

Term had barely finished when Derwent's friends also started leaving for the war. Walter Russell had already gone. Ian Strang was one of Derwent's first close friends to have signed up. He left to serve in the Middlesex and Royal Berkshire Regiments, remaining enlisted until early 1919. Former student, draughtsman and painter Bernard Meninsky (1891–1950), who was to rent a room at the same 18 Fitzroy Street address as Derwent, signed up and left. Francis Helps had also left to serve in the Artist Rifles' Expedition in France in 1915. Derwent's growing friendship with Ambrose McEvoy was interrupted, as he became attached to the Royal Naval Division in 1916, later leaving for a short period at the Western Front with the Royal Marines.

Fred Mayor's asthma was one reason his family had spent their winters in Cassis, where the air was warmer and humid, however, back in London at the outbreak of war, he sought enlistment as a war artist, which required an operation to ameliorate his symptoms. The procedure failed, causing a haemorrhage, and he died. Hannah, his artist wife, was left alone with three young children, and the following year she would lose her son Charles. Despite these tragedies she, like Francis Helps, would come to show profound kindness to an increasingly distraught Derwent.

Augustus did not initially volunteer but became increasingly disappointed at not being involved. After spending time in Ireland in 1915, he returned to England to complete several commissioned works and society portraits. Busy, but not sated,

Opposite:
DL16.9 (detail)
Derwent Lees, *The Vista / Landscape*, 1916

he tried enlisting but, in December 1916, failed the medical due to a bad knee. He was restless, his deafness hampered him, and the war had intensified his feeling of exclusion. Fewer visitors passed through Alderney, and despite Dorelia McNeill living a productive life there, the exuberant Augustus would often escape to London, to portraits, parties and soirées. Derwent saw less of him, and their former fluid artistic interaction fell away. The mood was different. Everything was different.

SEPARATION

By mid-1916, Derwent had left Fitzroy Square for a single, downmarket room at 18 Fitzroy Street; with or without Edith is unclear, but something had profoundly changed between them. He put ten works on show at the early summer New English Art Club (NEAC) exhibition, a large number for him. For the first time, however, there were no new works, only an assortment of pencil portraits, unsold watercolours from earlier painting holidays and a sketch study for a decoration. There were signs of desperation; two works (*Sketch for a Decoration*, likely a reworking of the 1914 *Cartoon – Les Anciennes*, DL14.18, and an unfinished work of his 'estranged' wife) were in pencil and charcoal on paper, then adhered to canvas backboards, and partly overpainted in oil. He was invited to join the selecting jury for the NEAC's twice-yearly exhibitions. This unusual shift to selling vastly varied, unsold, older material, and an attempt to increase his profile by being on the jury, reflected his empty studio and an increasingly tough financial situation.

It seems that Edith had left Derwent during the first half of 1916. She no longer appeared in his works nor holidayed with him. No English electoral registers were published for 1916 and 1917, and with no known personal correspondence, it is not possible to resolve exactly when they separated, but Edith all but vanishes from view for several years.

News of the horrendous carnage at the Front filtered back home. Family and friends were dying in droves on the battlefields and the war had now arrived at home. Londoners had first experienced an aerial bomb attack from the monstrous Zeppelin airships in 1915. With the general fear and alarm, art sales dried up; for who would now buy art? Derwent had no other skill. Along with a decline in patronage, there was an economic depression, a flood of sick and wounded returning servicemen, and a general sense of despair. July 1916 saw the start of the Battle of the Somme where one million were to die. On Saturday 1 July, the deadliest of days, nearly 20,000 British Empire soldiers were lost. London was on edge and Britain on constant alert.

Derwent spent the summer of 1916 under the sheltering wing of Philip Wilson Steer, known by his students as the doyen of the Slade. Steer, the School's modest but kindly part-time painting teacher, came to Derwent's rescue. He had been at the institution since the early 1890s and was the person to whom Tonks deferred when making staff appointments and awarding prizes and scholarships.[1] Steer's life had a constant and invariant rhythm, typified by almost ritualised summer painting holidays. Leonard Greaves remarked that 'few modern painters have lived such an obviously unadventurous life as Wilson Steer, yet . . . he produced fine work

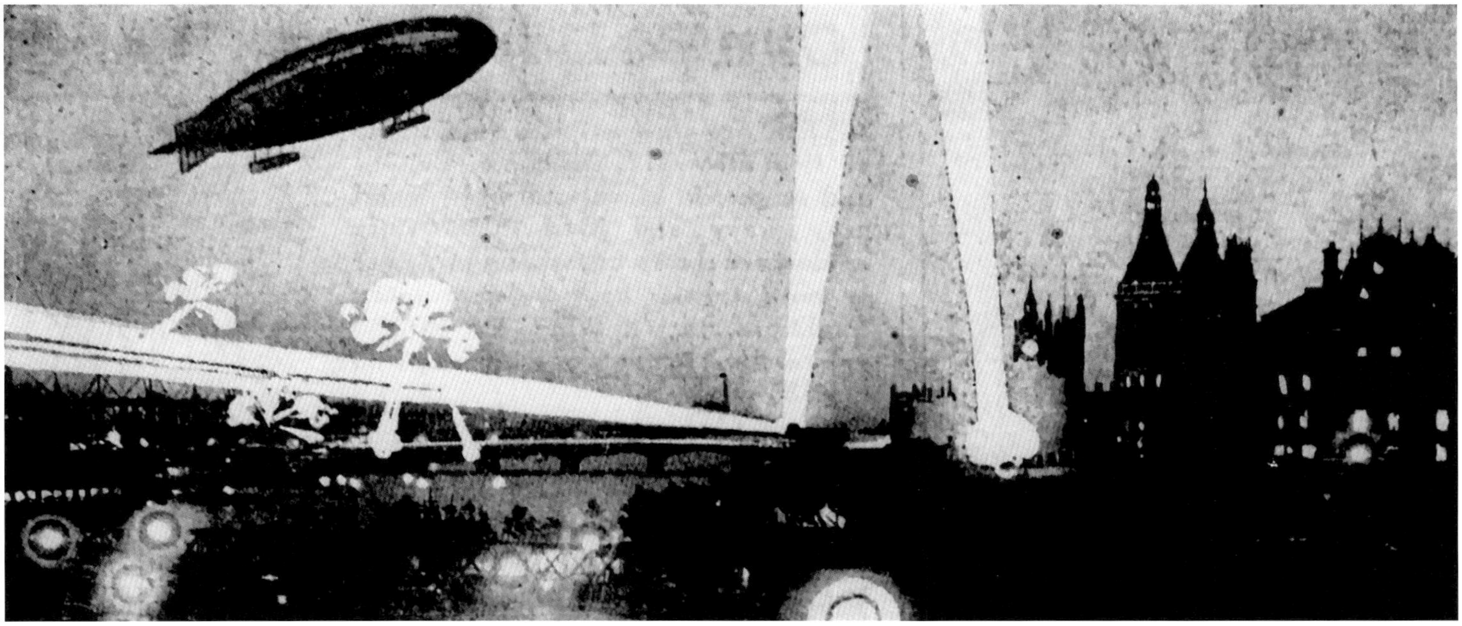

German Airships Shower Hail of Death in Raid on London, England, artist unknown, print, E.W. Scripps, *Seattle Star*, 1 Jun 1915

spreading, as it were, from a static centre'.[2] Steer lived in Cheyne Walk, had known Derwent since his student days, and was a close friend of Tonks, the Mayors and Cyril Butler. For more than a decade, Cyril hosted artists at Bourton House in the village of Bourton near Shrivenham, including Tonks, Ambrose, Augustus, Donald Maclaren, and later Slade student William Roberts (1895–1980). Steer had also done many commissions for the Butler family at the turn of the century.

The resolute bachelor seems to have organised a tranquil summer for Derwent to paint in the quiet surrounds of Bourton. He also most likely organised Derwent's role on the NEAC selecting jury as he was one of the Club's founding members. During the summer Steer painted in the Vale, near Bourton, and at the Howard de Waldens' Chirk Castle.

Ambrose McEvoy's biographer, Lydia Miller, notes that Steer and Tonks were known for not only supporting, but also paternally nurturing those students that were 'possessed with gifts and grit' and 'that Steer could be quite troubled by their mistfortunes [*sic*]'. The two Slade stalwarts judiciously recommended and then 'followed their former students' progress, and were deeply affected by any problems they faced in their careers'.[3]

Cyril Butler was a generous and supportive art patron to many artists, and Ambrose and Derwent were among the younger recipients of his pre- and wartime commissions. A letter from Derwent to Butler, dated 5 June 1916, touches on Derwent's deteriorating mental state, 'I see them [my brothers] and my father in my dreams and nightmares, in my house, in my wife. I see them everywhere but in my paintings.'[4]

The tiny, tree-lined village of Bourton, with its neat lanes of honey-coloured stone cottages, peacefully nestled among wide, rolling fields, created the perfect atmosphere for a productive summer break. Derwent seldom ventured far from his lodgings, painting from his bedroom window above the Bourton House stables, in

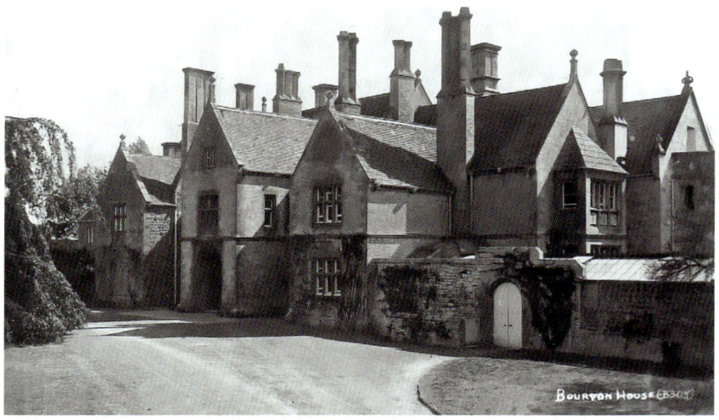

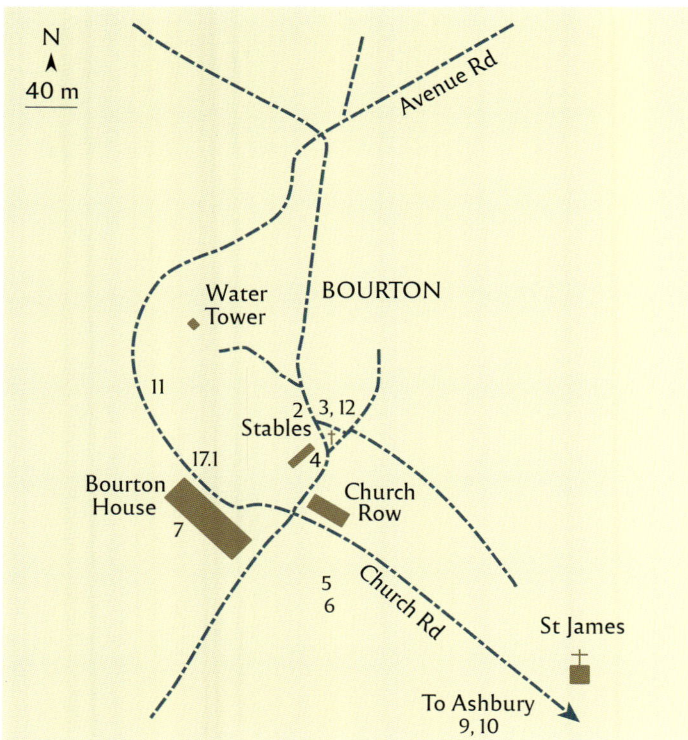

Above:
Bourton House, Bourton, Shrivenham, c.1930, photographer unknown, Shrivenham Heritage Society & the Paul Williams Collection

Former home of Sir Cyril Kendall Butler

Below:
Locations where Derwent painted in and around Bourton, Shrivenham, 1916

Numbers indicate known painting sites, DL16.2–7, 9–12, DL17.1; DL16. prefix is not shown

the grounds, a neighbouring field, and by the ancient medieval cross one minute from the stable door. Only two works were painted further afield, on the Ashbury to Idstone road, 30 minutes by gig from Bourton. Derwent painted a dozen watercolour and oil scenes of the village and the surrounding countryside (DL16.2–12, DL17.1).

Cyril's nephew would later describe some of the art hung at Bourton House, explaining that:

> Wilson Steer was in the dining room with portraits of the family. Sickert and McEvoy filled in the gaps. McEvoy was especially represented and enjoyed painting in the down-land country. Augustus John left endless drawings, many of his high women, along the first-floor passages. Tonks, who was then head of the Slade, had pride of place with a cat playing with a necklace in the library, and a birdcage in the hall. He was frequently there for weekends. Derwent Lees painted the rock garden and the drive before instability intervened to check his course. His pictures of the South of France were also in the music room.[5]

This collection included Derwent's large, impressive oil panorama, *Etang de Berre, Provence* (DL11.31) which, after Cyril's death, was purchased for the Johannesburg Art Gallery in 1948. Cyril had also purchased a few works by Dick and, interestingly, he owned the unsigned and undated *The Alhambra* (DL08.9, formerly attributed to both Derwent and Dick) as well as the co-signed 1909 work, *The Dancers* (aka *The Sirens*, DL09.5).

Cyril became Derwent's chief patron, buying and commissioning many works during his lifetime. Sir Edward Marsh, American lawyer John Quinn, Sir Ivor Spencer-Churchill, Earl of Sandwich, R.G. Micklethwait and Lord Howard de Walden were also important Lees collectors. Sadly, their support was not enough to keep him out of poverty. After Derwent's death, wealthy Bradford wool merchant Arthur Crossland (1880–1956) would become his most prolific collector and likely the only person owning works from the four countries where Derwent painted: England, Wales, France and Poland. He would lend more than a dozen of these works for the 1939 *Modern Drawings and Paintings Lent by Arthur Crossland Esquire* exhibition at the Laing Art Gallery.

In early autumn of 1916, the Slade again provided its familiar structure and shelter, as Derwent accepted his tenth contract as Assistant in Drawing for the coming academic year. He was well-established as the drawing tutor; however, he was struggling with his personal and financial situation. Despite this, his summer

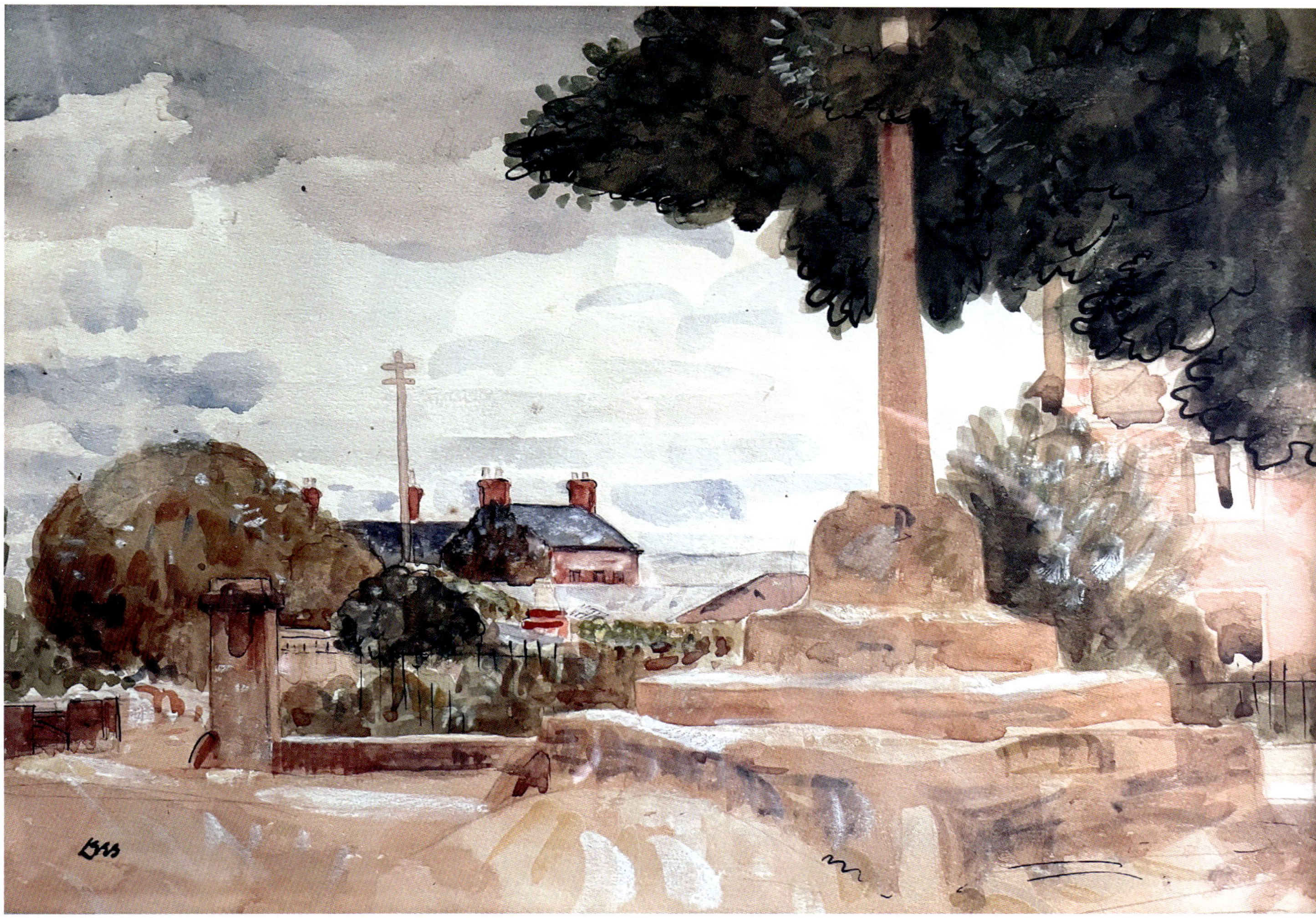

DL16.3
Derwent Lees, *Bourton Cross*,
1916, watercolour and ink on paper,
23 x 33 cm, Private Collection

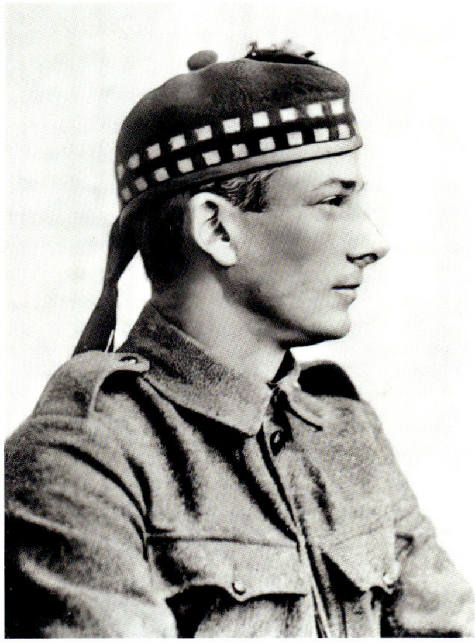

Left:
Donald Maclaren in uniform, c.1917, photographer unknown, Medical School Roll of Honour, 1914–19, UCL Special Collections, University College London

Right:
UCL Slade First World War Memorial Tablet, photograph by UCL Digital Education, UCL Special Collections, University College London

Presented to the Chairman of the Slade Committee, 11 Nov 1921

output was remarkable, and seven of his Bourton works were accepted for the winter NEAC show, along with another three from Banyuls, France and Wales.

This was a strong exhibiting year for Derwent, second only to 1913–14. He produced 20 works for the two 1916 exhibitions, nearly all figureless landscapes. On seeing the ten works at the winter show, Tonks, ever the supporter, wrote to leading British art collector Geoffrey Blackwell that '. . . Derwent Lees has some pretty watercolours worthy of your attention'.[6] Derwent also continued to serve on the NEAC selecting jury.

Derwent must have worked alongside, and been guided by, his former painting teacher during his Bourton summer, as two of his works were in the 'Steer style'. As one reviewer remarked, 'Mr. Lees, whose bent in landscape used to be more severe and stylistic, might well have been under the influence of Mr. Steer when he painted his charming but slightly confused *In a Rock Garden*, the best of his exhibits'.[7] One work, *The Drive* (DL17.1), a richly coloured view of the wooded driveway of Bourton House, was later incorrectly assumed to have been painted at a mental hospital and erroneously redated and renamed *The Drive to the Asylum*.[8]

At the close of Term II, Easter 1917, Derwent's close friend Mac departed for the war. He left Liverpool, his wife and two children, and travelled to Belgium with his regiment. Derwent remained a juror for the summer NEAC exhibition, for which he contributed just one work, *Portrait* (DL17.2), reviewed as 'a very clever portrait of a lady by Mr. Derwent Lees'.[9] Mac was killed in action as Term III came to an end. A shrapnel splinter struck a bomb in his pocket which exploded. He was buried in Hainaut, Belgium.

On 13 June 1917, 14 German planes dropped around 100 bombs on London in the first daylight raid of the war and, on the cusp of the summer holidays, Derwent had a breakdown, later reported to University Council.[10] He was 32, with a catalogue of loss and death behind him: his parents, two brothers, Dick, Ethel Elder, Fred Mayor and now Mac. Without family or close friends around him, and under the intense psychological pressures of the bombing and the war, the sudden impending poverty after five short years of promise, and his wife's abandonment, he crumbled.

A LONG SUMMER

Searchlights routinely tracked across London's night sky, as the Germans switched their air attacks from the slow, looming airships to fixed-wing planes. Blackout orders were issued, further fuelling a sense of powerlessness for the traumatised Derwent. The bombing raids continued throughout the summer. At the end of September, as the Slade commenced its 1917–18 academic year, the Zeppelins and planes made six night-time raids on London in close succession. Many Londoners left; of those compelled to stay, up to 300,000 sought safety from the bombs in underground shelters.

After spending two years agitating to be part of the war, in early September Augustus finally passed his army medical, and was commissioned to serve as war artist to the Canadian Army.

It is unknown what Derwent did during the summer of 1917, but the Slade showed good faith, reappointing him for the coming academic year,[11] however 1917 was the last time his name would appear in journals and newspapers as part of the UCL Slade staff. He would soon disappear from view, and eventually from the art world.

The UCL Council minutes spoke of his desperate attempt to return to teaching in October 1917, later recorded by Tonks as 'useless', and he left the Slade once more. Despite this, Professor Fred Brown reported that Derwent was prevented from resuming work due to ill-health '. . . at present'.[12] They still hoped that he would return, but it was to be impossible. He was broken and would never work again. The School was awarded additional financial support to cover Derwent's absence and in the following months they agreed to continue his full stipend for the entire academic year, with funds to be paid to Mrs Lees. Professor Brown wrote:

> My dear Provost
> I regret to have to tell you that my assistant Mr Lees has not resumed work at the Slade School – he has had a brain attack of some sort or at the mildest a nervous breakdown.
> I have got temporary assistance from Mr Bevan-Petman a late scholar

> and Mr Tonks has offered to come three days a week instead of two.
> I regret also to say that Mr Russell who has been at the front for some time is also suffering and had a nervous breakdown and is invalided home. I hope it is not of a permanent nature but do not know details.
> I am myself fairly well and hope you are also
> Professor Fred Brown [layout *sic*][13]

Unlike Derwent, his friend and former colleague Russell recovered and later resumed his duties at the Slade.

SEEKING REFUGE

Not long after, Tonks was appointed Professor of Slade School, a position he was to hold until 1930 when his successor Randolph Schwabe took the helm. Walter Sickert once remarked about the convivial but often stern man, with his sharp, unrelenting intellect, that 'The Slade was Tonks, and Tonks was the Slade'.[14] It was Tonks who had seen Derwent's potential as a young man of thought, intellect and fine draughtsmanship. He remained dedicated to the Slade and his art practice, alongside his closest friends Steer and painter and author George Moore. They shared a rich social life of frequent evenings of hearty food and carefully curated wine, philosophical and jocular debate. After the war, George published an account of this life in *Conversations on Ebury Street*, where the dinners often took place. Despite his new professorial role, Tonks took further leave as war artist during 1918 and, in the summer of 1919, joined the British expeditionary forces in Russia. By then, Derwent had been long absent from the Slade.

Augustus finally left for France, though not before staging an exhibition at the Chenil Gallery in November. It ran through January 1918, as did the Winter NEAC show, which included one work by Derwent, *An Aeroplane Passes* (DL13.54), painted in happier times. Derwent was no longer part of the NEAC's selecting jury, though remained a Club member. At the end of the year, he (or someone acting on his behalf) and Augustus placed works in a public art sale managed by the London auction house Christie, Manson & Woods.[15]

Derwent, either penniless or no longer able to manage on his own, was taken in by old friend Hannah Mayor. Alone, supporting her two young children, and despite her own trauma, she was to maintain a refuge for those in need: the desperate, lonely and the frightened. Derwent lived (likely renting a room) at Hannah's Kensington home for extended periods during 1917, 1918 and 1919. While the Slade honoured Derwent's contract, and continued to pay his wage, there was no sign of Edith, despite being the recipient of her husband's salary.[16] With extreme financial hardship, the loss of a partner, family and friends, a sense of failure and declining painting sales, it was Derwent's friends who gave him support and a roof over his head.

The guestbook at the Howard de Waldens' medieval Chirk Castle on the Welsh–English border shows that Derwent first arrived on 11 January 1918, initially for a short stay. There are only two entries for him. He returned for a longer three-week stay

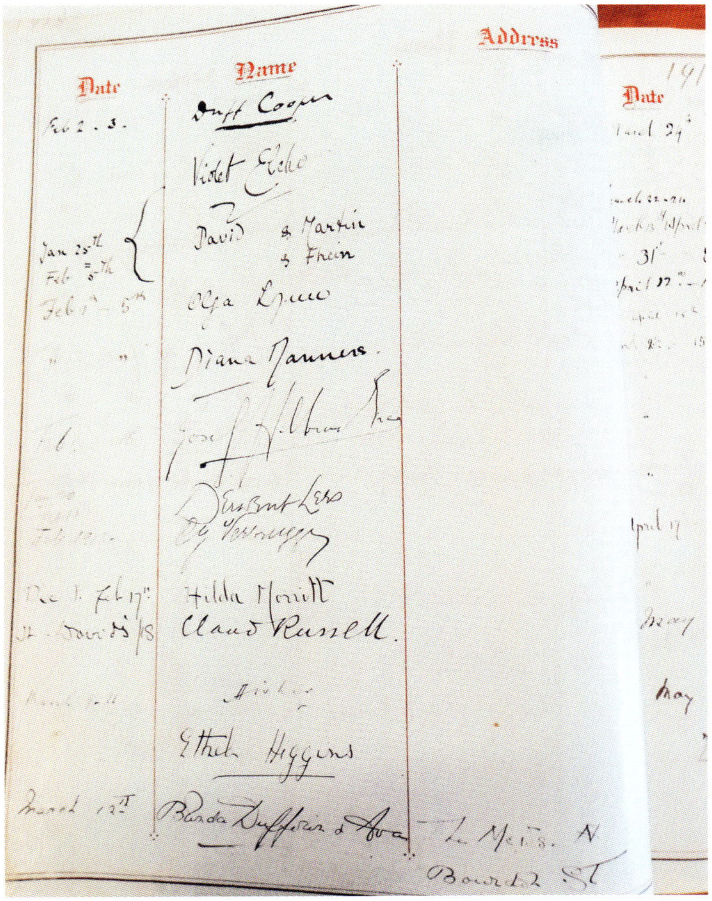

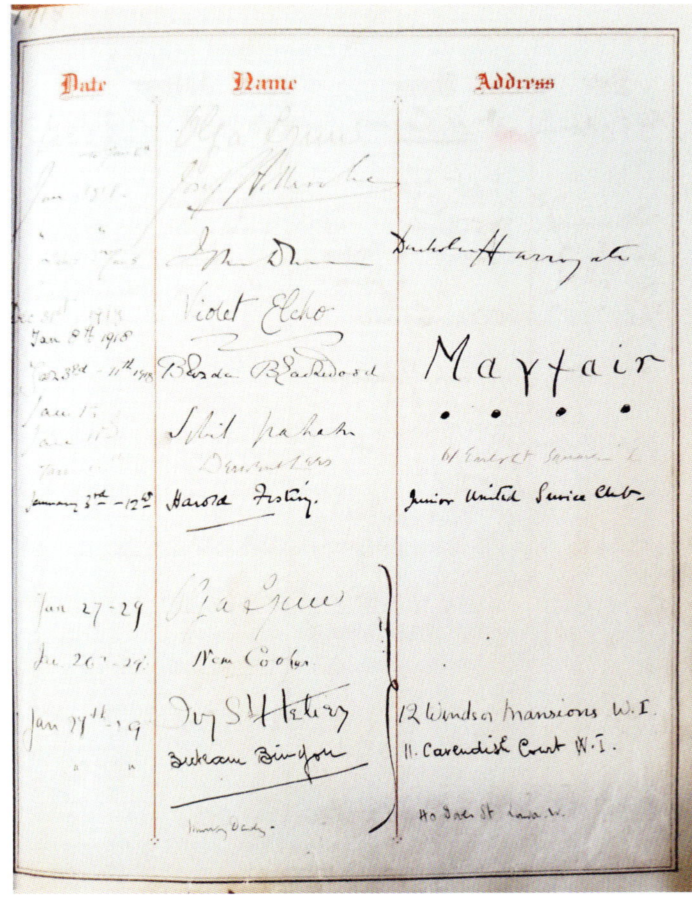

Above left and right:
Chirk Castle Guestbook, 1918, The Howard de Walden Estate Document Archive, London; Chirk Castle Wales, National Trust UK [facsimile]

from 20 January until 11 February but may have stayed longer or perhaps returned.[17] Augustus had brought him there, leaving him in the care of Lady Howard de Walden in a genuine attempt to find someone to look after his frail friend, before leaving to report for deployment to France. Earlier researchers incorrectly postulated that this event occurred before the war, based on Lady Howard de Walden's memoirs, which do not record dates or timelines about Derwent's or his friends' visits.[18]

It was an exceptionally cold winter, and frequent heavy snowfalls fell across Britain. The guestbook registers Derwent's home address as 61 Earl's Court, Kensington, Hannah Mayor's home. Apart from the UCL Council Minutes, Lady Howard de Walden's account and later letters to her are the only known record of Derwent's deteriorating mental state.[19] Just six months earlier, despite being fragile, the Slade felt that he was strong enough to renew his contract for the following academic year, but something critical had happened in 1917. His decline had been rapid.

The night-time London air raids meant that 'blackout darkened streets had become home to all kinds of "thieving and vicing". Conscientious objectors had always been targeted but homosexuals, modern painters, poets and foreigners were now more likely to be branded as potential traitors too . . . and German-born singer Olga Lynn whose real name was Lowenthal, lived in daily fear of being deported.'[20] Olga was one of the guests at Chirk during Derwent's stay. Perhaps Derwent, a 'modern painter', had also been subjected to aggression in the streets. Their friend Rudolph Stulik, the Austrian owner of Fitzrovia's Eiffel Tower Restaurant, had been interned, as had the Lipczinskis.

At Chirk, Derwent was a long way from London, in a place of frenetic and eccentric social activity where he recognised few faces. He asked Lady Howard de Walden whether he was in an asylum.[21] Numerous guests regularly arrived and left the vast and foreboding castle from January to Easter 1918: singers, performers, composers, sportsmen, servicemen, aristocrats and the wife of Lord Howard de Walden's salmon-fishing friend, Harold Morritt. The evenings were full of raucous performances and games. The stage actress and composer Ivy St Helier stayed, along with celebrated Belgian fencer Cyril Verbrugge, Violet, Lady Elcho and her sister Lady Diana Manners, who later married Alfred Duff Cooper, 1st Viscount Norwich, and others, including children and pet dogs. The Howard de Waldens' grandson wrote that:

> Chirk House parties were gloriously eclectic, actors and theatre designers, artists, writers, singers and musicians, mingling with foreign royal families and Tommy's sporting friends. In the evening guests would be ushered to the Music Room for a programme . . . and Margot's sister Poots kept a piano in her bedroom where the more Bohemian guests would gravitate for jazz and carousing.[22]

Lady Howard de Walden later wrote that:

> Augustus produced a young admiring and promising artist called Derwent Lees and left him with me, saying 'he needs a bit of a rest cure and feeding up. I hope you don't mind' . . . this pale young man was terrified of us, of the size of the place and of himself . . . I used to hear a knock on my bedroom door at any hour of the night, and wake up, imagining hearing breathing. And there he stood, quite quietly and said, 'I come to your door for protection, now I will go to bed'. Very un-nerving. And every day I took him for a walk . . . he did paint rather well but was as mad as a hatter.[23]

In the middle of the night, he muttered 'frightened' and 'can't sleep' to Lady Howard de Walden outside her bedroom door in short, staccato speech. Derwent was confused and agitated. He had insight, as he could articulate what was happening, but he was unable to control his emotional state. This remains the only account of the decline in Derwent's mental health after the Slade reported his June 1917 breakdown. Despite his condition, Derwent met his obligation to paint Lady Howard de Walden's portrait.[24] Two watercolours (DL18.1, 3) likely represent Derwent's last completed commissioned portrait studies, although letters reveal that he had another portrait commission during the spring of 1918. In one letter to Lady Howard de Walden, he writes that 'I am to go to Lady Curzon again soon to finish a drawing and I will let you know with what success when it is done', and in another, dated May 1918, he exclaimed that he 'shall attempt to master a drawing of Lady Curzon tomorrow if she can arrange to give me a sitting'.[25]

Following a later stay at Chirk Castle, Derwent thanked Lady Howard de Walden for returning his belongings, confiding that 'I don't know what induced me to leave them – not quite in my right mind. I wonder whether I ever have been.' In this depressed, vulnerable state, with an awareness of his own mental confusion, he disclosed that 'I have been on the point of writing you a long letter that might have let in a great deal of light on many incomprehensible things – it probably wd [*sic*] have been many reams in length but I have thought better of it – at least for the time being – it may have been of little use after all.' Then he asked her, 'Have you had the drawings yet? They should have arrived by now I think!' Later on, he wrote, 'No painting or drawing yet – I can't make up my mind to it'. He was still enjoying his craft, exclaiming that I 'should be very glad indeed to do the "faces"'.[26]

There was a warm exchange between the two and, despite his earlier evident mental fragility at Chirk, Lady Howard de Walden must have liked him and enjoyed his company, as he was invited to return on more than one occasion. In one letter, Derwent thanked her while apologising profusely for not responding to her 'very kind invitation' to join her and friends for a musical recital led by Joseph Holbrooke. He postulated that 'I am, I suppose, too unmusical – to make a concert a success' but 'I am sure I should have enjoyed it'. Derwent concluded, just as he had commenced the letter, by thanking Lady Howard de Walden for her most recent 'invitation to come to Chirk during the week' and suggesting that it 'may tempt me to do so'.[27]

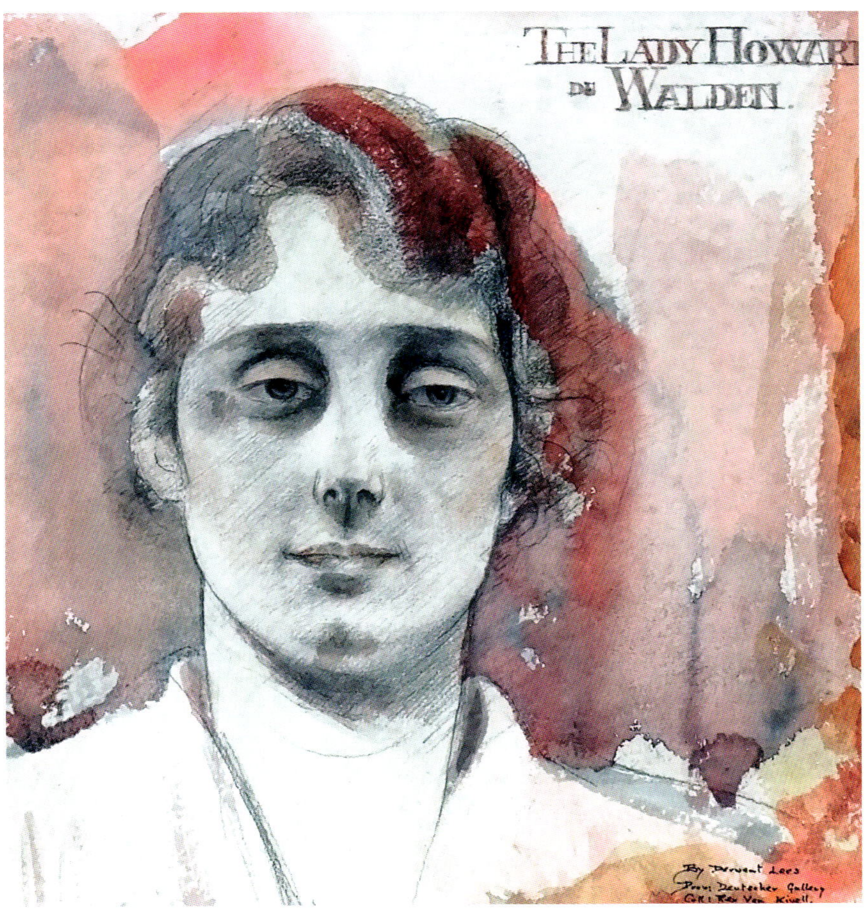

DL18.1
Derwent Lees, *The Lady Howard de Walden*, 1918, watercolour wash and pencil on paper, 35.2 x 25 cm, Private Collection

12 THE ENCLOSED WORLD 1918–28

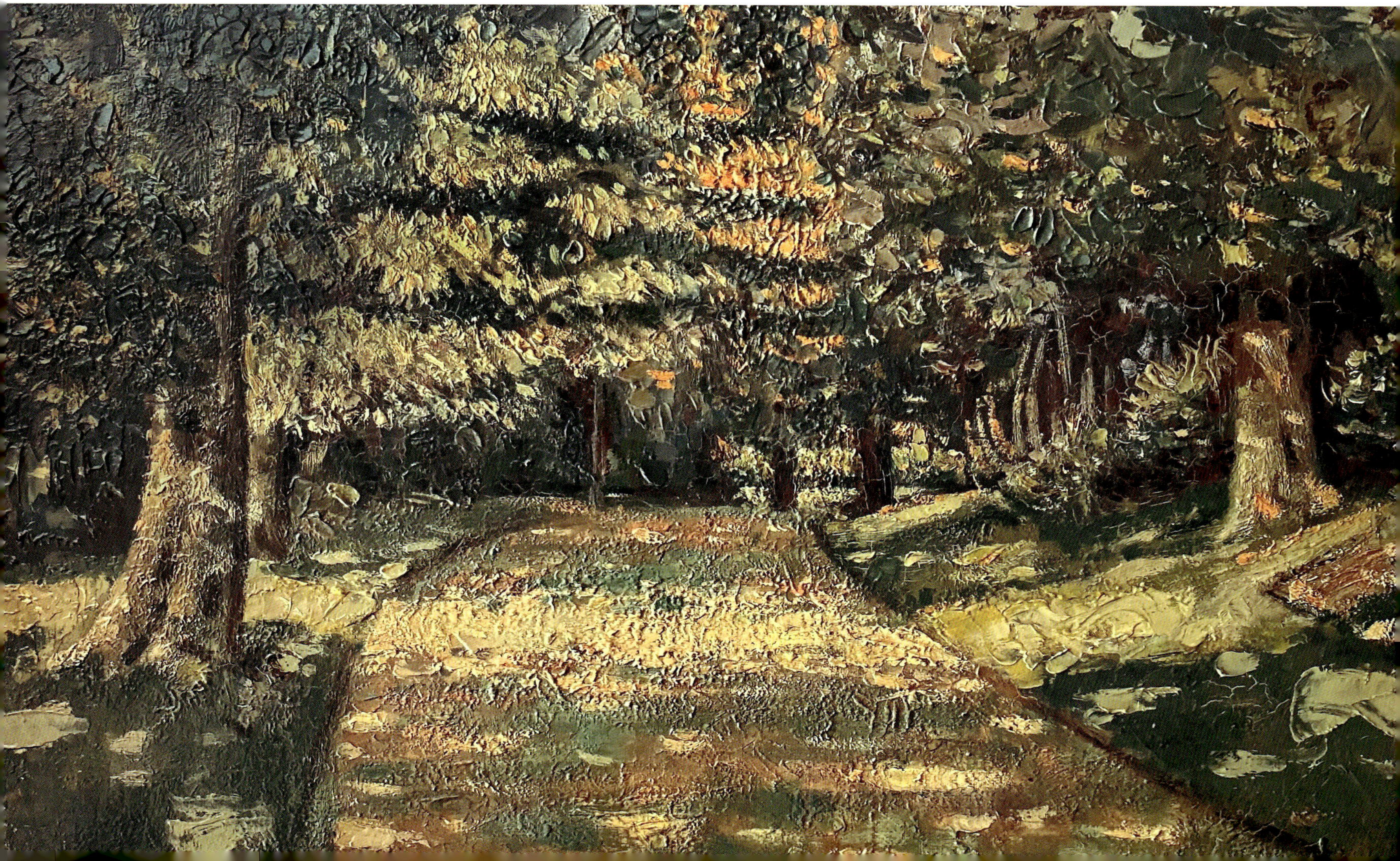

Derwent returned to London and his room at Hannah Mayor's in spring 1918. At Easter, Augustus returned from the war 'in a state of utter confusion'.[1] Unable to cope with what he had experienced in France, he was sent home after creating a fracas during an argument, over which a military court martial was pending. He was considered Britain's most eminent living artist; immensely talented, working alongside Dick, Derwent and others, and living the bohemian gypsy dream. Life had been full of promise; loose and experimental. It was often remarked that 'in these years before the war, John was producing his best work',[2] but Dick was now dead, the war had both ripped apart his and Derwent's romantic, creative lifestyles and killed Donald Maclaren.

The March 1918 UCL Council Minutes reported that Derwent was in severe 'financial straits' due to ill health and reiterated the Slade's commitment to continue his stipend until his academic year contract ceased at the end of June. In recognition of his service, a bonus payment of £30 was recommended to assist him 'until he is fit to return to his work'. Their faith in him and their care and warmth was unbending. Outgoing Professor Fred Brown offered an additional £5 of his own money to assist Derwent, and Henry Tonks also offered funds of his own. They recognised their former colleague's dire financial situation, and that his part-time term wage was not enough for him to recover. The bonus was granted with 'payment being made, under the circumstances, to Mrs Lees'.[3] Whether the funds were spent on Derwent's welfare is unknown, though at least some must have paid for his room at Hannah's.

With the return of soldiers from the Front, the Spanish flu epidemic now hit the capital. Within nine months nearly 20,000 Londoners died. There was a glut of mourning cards, but a shortage of food. Flour and sugar were rationed.

In the early summer of 1918, Tonks, now the Slade Professor, poignantly reported that Derwent 'unfortunately broke down in health in June last year; he made one attempt to begin work again here but it was useless. Reports as to his health are now more favourable.'[4] Friends and colleagues were not giving up on him. In July, former student and neighbour Francis Helps was among the returning servicemen;

Opposite:
DL17.1 (detail)
Derwent Lees,
The Drive / The Avenue / The Drive to the Asylum, 1917

Bernard Meninsky a month later, although emotionally fragile and discharged with a nervous breakdown. Meninsky later committed suicide, but upon discharge in August 1918, he moved to 18 Fitzroy Street, the address recorded by Derwent on his New English Art Club (NEAC) membership form, despite living mostly in Hannah's home. Francis moved into a large boarding house in Charlotte Street, adjacent to Fitzroy Street.

Derwent completed at least one *plein air* landscape during the year, *Shoreline, Dover* (DL18.2), with the caring, steady influence of *pater* Philip Wilson Steer again evident. Steer had a painting commission in Dover and spent much of the summer there, and must have taken Derwent to the Kent coast to paint and recuperate by the sea. Later, at a London Sotheby sale in November 1931, Derwent's *Dover* watercolour was sold with a note stating that it had been exhibited at the National Gallery, Millbank (now Tate) as part of Steer's living retrospective, *Loan Exhibition of Works by P. Wilson Steer*, Apr–Jul 1929; a generous gesture from an old friend.

CLAYBURY

The Slade lost many to the First World War; some temporarily, some permanently. Hannah continued to rent out rooms, so that she could keep her Earl's Court home and educate her children. She had given up painting for now, and she and a handful of friends took care of Derwent. However, his mental state deteriorated further during the winter of 1918, and he was admitted to Claybury Mental Hospital, Redbridge, London, as: 'male patient, admission number 8130'.[5]

Here, he found himself in an immense, labyrinthine institution, a world away from the London he knew. Claybury had been a large family estate with extensive parklands, ponds, pastures and an ancient woodland. It now accommodated more than 2500 patients, of which 1100 were men. Patients were separated by gender and prognosis. Those with a chronic illness were kept apart from those for whom recovery was deemed likely, which included Derwent. Initial treatment for new patients was an abundance of fresh air, quiet and rest. They were placed for one or more weeks in a ward bed on a large open verandah overlooking the grounds. It was winter and the fresh air and calm of Claybury had a beneficial effect. Despite the austere surroundings and unfamiliar regime, Derwent improved. Assessed as well enough for discharge in early 1919, he returned to 61 Earl's Court and Hannah's care.

A CALL TO ETCH

Derwent returned to his familiar surrounds, though Augustus soon left for the Versailles Peace Conference, commissioned to capture the historic moment on canvas, and Tonks departed for Russia in June. By mid-1919, Derwent, still lodging with Hannah, was no longer exhibiting, though retained his NEAC membership. It was to be his final year as a Club member.[6]

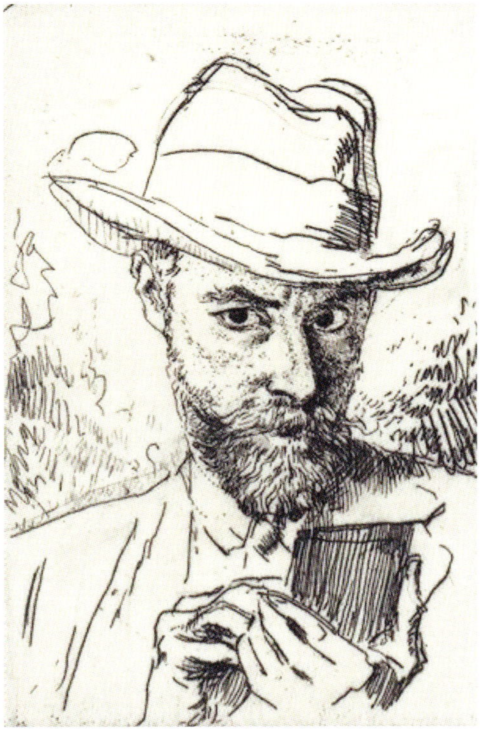

Augustus John, *A Man Etching / Self Portrait in Hat Sketching*, Oct 1919, etching on paper, 14 x 9.5 cm (plate), *Print Collectors Quarterly*, Jul 1931

By September, Augustus had returned to London. His payments from the British and the Canadian forces came to an end, so he threw himself into a new project. He laboured intensely, creating works for what would be his largest exhibition of etchings. October was busy: Augustus was working in his studio, and in the Chenil Gallery etching press room. Derwent was there too.

The show at the Chenil opened in November. Funding had been organised by the country's most celebrated etching and printing specialist, Campbell Dodgson (the British Museum's Keeper of Prints and Drawings), who had encouraged the Museum and the Contemporary Art Society to acquire modern prints and drawings. One etching by Augustus, *A Man Etching*, shows him holding the copper plate in one hand and scribing it with the other. The work was definitively dated in Dodgson's 1919 catalogue raisonné of Augustus's prints, as created in October 1919.[7] Reviews of the more than 125 etchings were enthusiastic.

The two long-time friends, the showman Augustus and the unassuming Derwent, must have worked alongside each other one final time, as Derwent did an etching of himself, in a mirror-image of his loyal friend's self-portrait. His wretched, haunted face stares out at us intensely. Clearly unwell and dispirited, he holds a piercing, unnerving gaze. Prints of *Derwent Lees* (aka *Self-Portrait*, DL19.1) are held in London's National Portrait Gallery and in at least one private collection.

Augustus had comforted the poet Arthur Symons during his 1909 breakdown, and now it appears that he was there again to provide care and support to his Australian friend. He, and their close circle of friends, had been concerned about Derwent's fragile state for a long time, with Christopher Nevinson writing to Augustus in 1913 that 'DL's father has died suddenly; it has affected his already poor health very

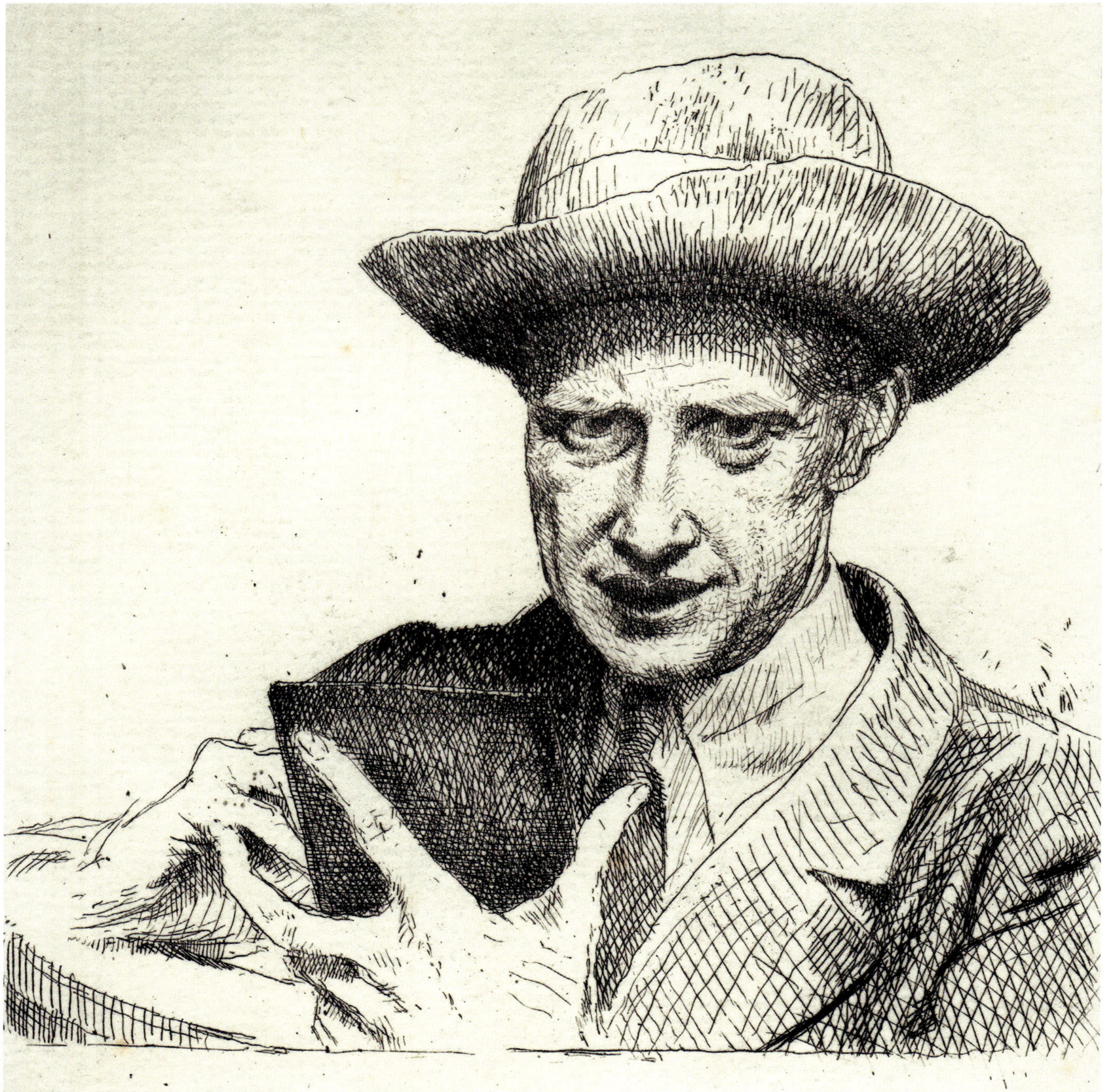

DL19.1
Derwent Lees, *Derwent Lees*, c.1919,
etching on paper, 17.5 x 12.2 cm,
National Portrait Gallery, London

badly indeed. E [Edith] now out of her mind with worry',[8] and earlier that same year Augustus had expressed similar words of concern in a letter to John Quinn.[9]

It is unknown whether Derwent attended the 7 November 1919 gallery opening or exhibited his work, for a fortnight later he was admitted to London's St Pancras Workhouse,[10] presumably as a last resort. It was another exceptionally cold English winter, and he was a long way from the warmth of Hannah's home.

Once again though, a friend was to appear and help him.

BACK TO CLAYBURY

Several details on the registration of Derwent's admission to the workhouse on Friday, 21 November 1919 are incorrect. Francis Helps, the student and friend he had painted in 1915, happened on the distraught Derwent in Fitzrovia and is poignantly recorded on the register as his 'nearest known relative or friend.[11] There was no sign of Edith. Francis must have guessed at the details entered on the register, while helping admit his former teacher, for Derwent's birth year is erroneously marked as 1888 and his address as 4 Fitzroy Street.

Derwent was medically assessed and a fortnight later transferred back into the system that he was never to leave again. At 35 years of age, he was re-admitted to Claybury Mental Hospital on Friday, 3 December 1919, as 'patient 8506'.[12]

Christmas 1919 came and went.

Tonks was now back at the Slade full time; Hannah resumed her art practice, Francis and Meninsky taught art and occasionally exhibited. Augustus was busy, but unlike the pre-war 'glory days' of landscapes and figures, he became more and more a society portrait painter. Art critic Eric Newton remarked at Augustus, Dick and Derwent's 1939 exhibition of pre-war works at the Redfern Gallery that, 'Romanticism in painting did not survive the war. This exhibition shows its fine last flowering.'[13]

Edith remains difficult to track after 1915. After the war, her mother and siblings intermittently added Ashley, and sometimes Gilbert, to their surname. An Edith Price took a room in a London boarding house soon after the cessation of fighting, however in 1921 she was living with her mother and siblings in Kensington, working at a local theatre. By 1926, Edith is confirmed as rooming at her sister Evelyn's house at 99 Warwick Road in London. This address is still marked on the back of some of Derwent's paintings today, becoming Edith's home, or *post-restante* address, for nearly 50 years.

During the summer of 1921 the Goupil Gallery exhibited *Representative Works by some of the Foremost Painters of the Modern British School*. It included Derwent's *Bonnuls – Roussillon* (DL12.43) and Hannah also presented many of her late husband Fred's paintings. Derwent was however no longer in London nor a member of an art club. His work appeared sporadically at galleries over the next decade, until Edith met the person who was to become the principal marketer of her husband's work, Rex Nan Kivell, a man who would put his stamp on Derwent's legacy.

THEN TO WEST PARK

In the spring of 1923, Derwent's brother Gilbert and his wife Clarice arrived in London, registering his sister Phyllis (or Pip to the family), in Sydney, as next of kin.[14] They must have spent time with Derwent and had him assessed for transfer to the new West Park Mental Hospital, south of London. Construction on this 80-acre site had halted during the war. With more than 9 acres of special purpose buildings to construct, electricity to install and a rail link to create, the site was busy and behind schedule, finally opening on 20 June 1924. Derwent was one of the first patients to be transferred there, arriving from Claybury on the 10 July, patient number 85.[15] About 400 patients were admitted annually over the next decade, nearly half of whom recovered and were discharged. The remainder were to die at the facility.[16]

Gilbert must have visited his brother at the Claybury Hospital, as he and Clarice remained in England for four months. During their stay it seems that they took Derwent for a trip during which he painted *A Sussex Landscape* (DL23.1). Perhaps his enthusiasm was reignited upon attending Ambrose McEvoy's first major one-man exhibition of watercolours at the Leicester Galleries during April. Derwent's brother's arrival had been timely, as the Chenil Gallery also mounted a retrospective exhibition of Dick's works, in April. Gilbert knew Dick well from his earlier years in London and would have likely attended the opening, possibly accompanying Derwent on day-release.

As Gilbert and Clarice Lees boarded the steamer for home,[17] London's new Redfern Gallery opened its doors. Derwent's friend Essil Elmslie was appointed gallery manager, a position she held until she married art collector Charles Rutherston in 1925.[18] The Redfern then employed a young New Zealand parvenu who styled himself as Rex de Charembac Nan Kivell, his true name Reginald Nankivell (1898–1977). Despite accumulating considerable wealth, Rex would spend much of his London working life in an unassuming basement apartment in Fitzrovia. He and Edith probably met through Fitzroy art circles, or at the New Chenil Galleries which opened in 1925. Rex was a young, upward-climbing risk-taker, prone to invention, who would take over the Redfern Gallery in 1931. Edith was indigent, in need of cash, and armed with hundreds of her husband's artworks. It was a match of great mutual convenience.

After the First World War, London's art galleries faced substantial hurdles. Declining turnover saw the Grafton, Dore, Dowdeswell and Dowdeswell galleries close, places Derwent had regularly frequented.[19] The National Gallery of British Art (later Tate) had closed in 1916, only reopening in 1921. The Chenil remained open, and its manager Jack Knewstub convinced Augustus that a grander and expanded business, with new gallery spaces, studios and retail shopfront, was the answer to flagging sales. The New Chenil Galleries opened with fanfare in 1925. In 1926, Augustus and his sister Gwen held an elaborate exhibition in the new space, but by year's end, the business collapsed. Augustus could not find anyone to take on the failing enterprise, and the beloved Chenil was no more. Jack left London, and his relationship with Augustus never recovered.

During 1925, Sir Cyril Kendall Butler, who had hosted Derwent at Bourton House in 1916, lent three of Derwent's works for a NEAC retrospective exhibition in London and Manchester. The exhibition closed in early summer, just as Derwent's brother Geoffrey arrived in England with his wife and two children.[20] Geoffrey, his guiding older sibling, had inspired Derwent to continue his studies, thus enabling him to pursue art as a career. He no doubt spent time with Derwent before taking his family on a continental holiday, returning to Australia in July.

NOT FORGOTTEN

Despite his permanent confinement, it appears that Derwent continued to paint at West Park Hospital. He was ill and hospitalised, but not forgotten, and it is likely that friends visited him. Daytime excursions were encouraged for a specific class of patients, with some free to walk unsupervised around the grounds or permitted to leave the facility on parole. A West Park report from the time said of the parolees that a 'large measure of freedom is much appreciated, and the privilege is practically never abused'.[21]

During his first visit to the light and sun of French Catalonia in 1910, Derwent had painted an evocative summer watercolour overlooking Collioure. In 1927, well-known collector Francis Falconer Madan wrote to the Director of the Tate (then the National Gallery, Millbank) Charles Aitken, proposing the purchase of Derwent's *Landscape at Collioure* (DL10.16). It was assessed by the Trustees and subsequently bought through the gallery's Art Collections Fund. The painting shows the old northern entrance to the village, with Fort Miradou, the waterfront castle, the hilltop Fort St Elme above Collioure, and Fort Béar above Port Vendres to the distant south. It is one of three watercolour versions of this scene, each markedly different in chromatic range (DL10.26, DL10.33).

A year later, following the Tate's purchase, the Contemporary Art Society, led by Sir Cyril Kendall Butler, Lord Howard de Walden and Sir Ivor Spencer-Churchill, purchased Derwent's watercolour *Seascape* (aka *La Ciotat, South of France*, DL14.15). The three men were collectively to own more than 20 of Derwent's works.

London's Victoria and Albert Museum held a Samuel Palmer retrospective exhibition in October 1926. The catalogue of the *Exhibition of Drawings, Etchings & Woodcuts by Samuel Palmer and other Disciples of William Blake* was illustrated with more than 50 works. The exhibition finished later in 1926 and, soon after, Derwent painted a tiny pastoral landscape heavily influenced by Palmer, redolent with drama and resignation. Despite having been a *plein-air* landscape artist, this small work seems to be all he could manage in his declining condition. Dated 1927, the subject, style and even the title, *Pastoral* (aka *Day's End*, DL27.1), emulated Palmer's *The End of the Day* and *The Herdsman*, recorded in the exhibition's catalogue. It is possible that Derwent visited the exhibition, as his colours and brushwork are true to Palmer's, and perhaps worked from the catalogue. The work also echoes the palette and compositional elements of Palmer's *Tityrus Restored to His Patrimony*. While completing *Day's End*, Derwent's former colleague and close friend Ambrose McEvoy, still in high demand after his career peak in 1924 and having created a massive body of work, contracted pneumonia. Ambrose died in January 1927 at the age of 48, apparently exhausted from overwork.

OF EDITH

Ambrose, like many of Derwent's friends, had shown care for his Australian contemporary. Less than a year before Ambrose's death, the Slade administrator Charles Koe Child received a letter from Edith asking for financial help. He in turn wrote to Ambrose, seeking Edith's address and explaining her request. Ambrose replied:

> Dear Child
> Mrs Lees's address is 99 Warwick Rd SW 5. I should think that she should be able to get something from the A.F.B.I. [The Artists' Benevolent Fund Institution]
> I will get into communication with her about it. Have you any idea what she wants? Is it an allowance a lump sum or work? Will you let me have a line here. I have to go away but I shall be back early next week.
> Yours ever
> Ambrose McEvoy [layout *sic*]

A comment written in red pencil across the top of the letter suggests that this was not the first time Edith had sought assistance. It reads, 'Mrs Derwent Lees Grant from Artists Benev. Fund 1926? She might possibly raise questions again.'[22] In February 1926 Edith replied and, amongst comments on her personal hardship, she thanked Child, noting her own difficulties since the termination of the Slade's salary in July 1918. Derwent is not mentioned in these letters.

> 99 Warwick Rd SW 5
> 7-2-26
> Dear Mr Child
> Thank you so much for your letter. Will you please thank Professor Tonks for me it is exceedingly kind of him in trying to help me on account of my health this last year has been a particularly trying one. The reaction I suppose of fighting against giving in and I have tryed [*sic*] very hard since 1918. I find things are getting more difficult for me each year and for this reason I shall be most grateful if The Artists Benevolent Fund could possibly help me even though I am not a widow. I was bitterly disappointed last Nov when I lost some work which I do like apart from the financial side it does help me to forget. I lost it because at the time I had rheumatism in my eyes and was unable to see. My place was filled in the same day. They never wait for you. I am just getting over a chill and feel better so if you would call to see me I could call at the Slade any time convenient to you.
> With all my thanks
> Yours very truly
> Edith Lees [layout *sic*][23]

A month later, the Slade received an update.

> 99 Warwick Rd S.W. 5
> 9-3-26
> Dear Mr Child
> I have heard from the Artists Benevolent Fund and the Council have very generously granted me a £100 to be paid quarterly. The first payment I received yesterday evening a cheque for £25 – I am most awfully grateful as it will relieve things considerably. Will you please convey my gratitude to Professor Tonks.
> You have been extremely kind in trying so hard to help me the result of which you see has not been in vain.
> Thanking you for your kindness and the trouble you have taken in making everything so explicit.
> Yours V. [*sic*] sincerely
> Edith Lees [layout *sic*][24]

This last letter was in response to the Slade's application to the Artists' Benevolent Fund on Edith's behalf. Edith had a roof over her head, and two married sisters close by who financially wanted for little. Intriguingly, few non-university, personal administrative letters from this period were retained for the Slade records by Child, yet he felt it important to keep Edith's correspondence on file. Perhaps it related to the internal departmental margin comment about her 'raising questions again'. Regardless, Edith received funds of £100.

13 END AND AFTERMATH 1928–67

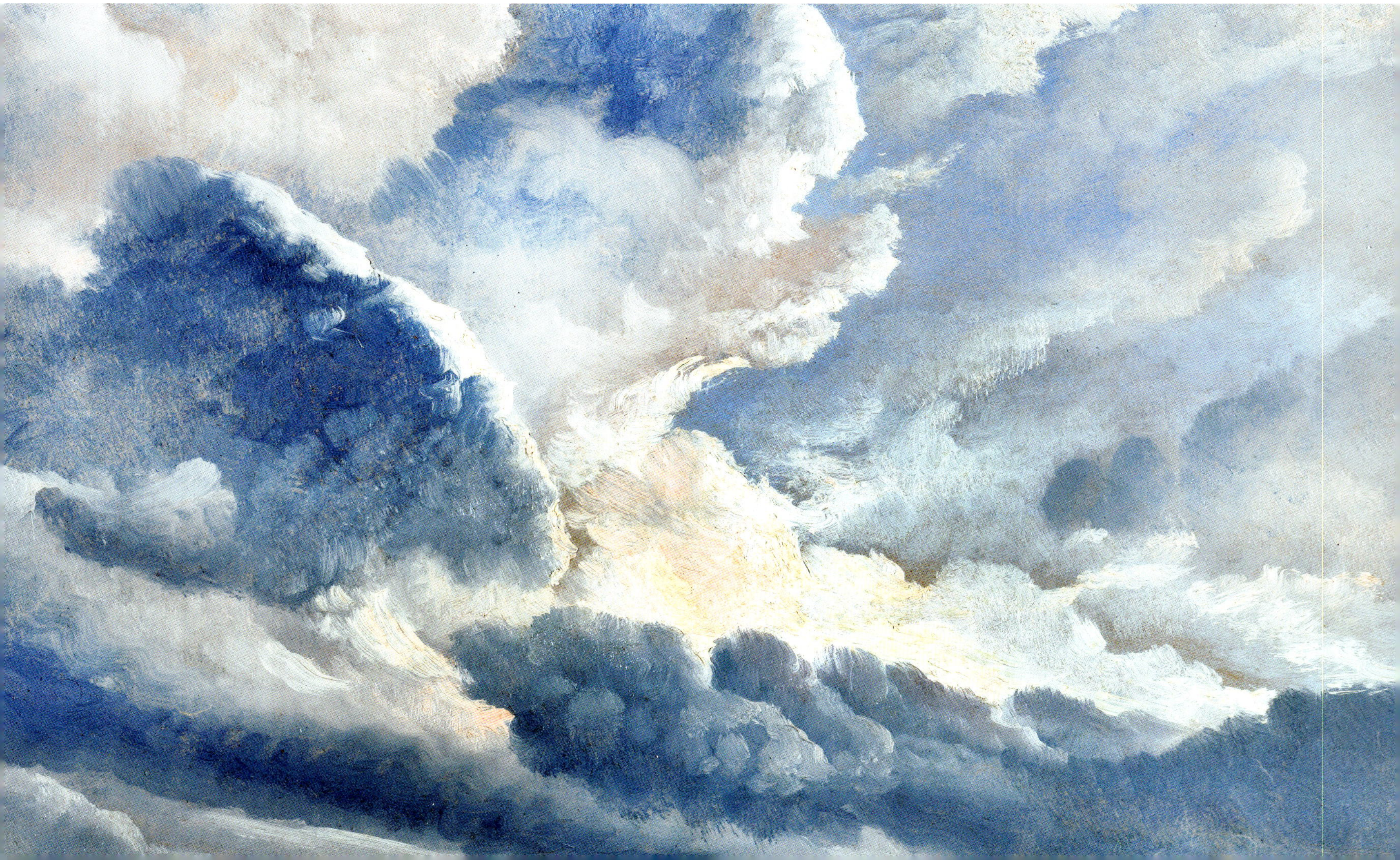

Derwent's siblings were worried about their youngest brother. Gilbert was granted leave for remote work in late 1928, and he and Clarice left Brisbane for England once again.[1] They stayed in London for several months. Gilbert was back in the city in which he had first trained for the meat industry 25 years earlier. In November, several of Derwent's paintings were shown at the Gieves Gallery. *The Times* admired them:

> Mr. Derwent Lees's work, always of great interest, is well represented at an exhibition at the Gieves Art Gallery . . . chiefly contains his landscapes, and these admirably illustrate the artist's sensibility, which showed itself chiefly in a feeling for almost flat patterns, enhanced by the elegance of his brush strokes, and in his colour . . . Mr. Lees's figure studies should by no-means be neglected, since in these his command over line can best be appreciated.[2]

The Lees siblings must have been extremely concerned about Derwent, for as Gilbert returned to Australia, their sister Eleanor, known as Trixie, appears to have also set sail for England.[3] Like her other sisters, she was single, living as a stenographer in Sydney. If indeed Trixie did make the 1929 journey, she would have arrived in summer and been the last family member to see Derwent, before returning home in October as the American stock market crashed, triggering the start of the Great Depression.

THE HAND OF REX NAN KIVELL

Alleyne Clarice Zander (1893–1958), an Australian curator and artist, arrived in London in 1929. Initially working with Rex Nan Kivell as the Redfern Gallery secretary,

Opposite:
DL15.22 (detail)
Derwent Lees, *The Thunder Cloud*, 1915

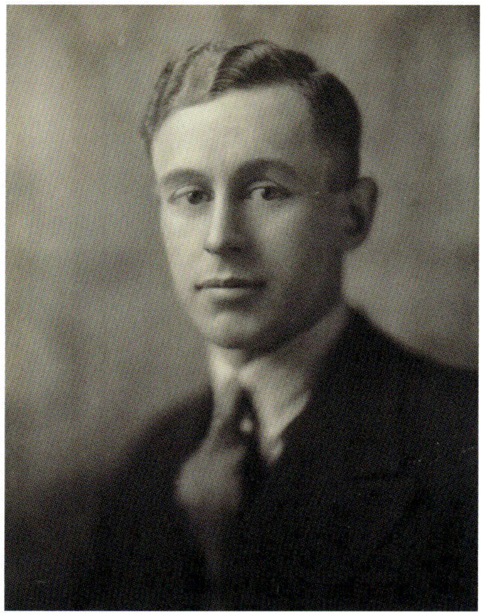

Portrait of Rex Nan Kivell aged 30, London, 1930, photograph by Fenwick Cutting, The National Library of Australia, Canberra

she became gallery manager when Rex took over the business in 1931. Edith was now in possession of most of Derwent's artworks, a potential trove for Rex, but her knowledge of her husband's life story and painting trips was uneven and limited. It was during these years that details of Derwent's childhood and his painting titles and trips became a melange of mismatched and incorrect facts, some invented, others artfully marketed. Many painting locations and titles were created from scratch, with a bias to the few places where Edith knew he had painted; Dorset, North Wales and the Cassis–Provence region. The errors have been compounded by several unsubstantiated details of his life. Until now, a century later, with details repeated like 'whispers down the lane', threads of the fabric of who he was, and from whence he came, were lost, buried or distorted.

Very few, in fact merely a tenth, of his works portraying Edith were exhibited in Derwent's lifetime, despite having painted or sketched her at least 100 times and being desperately in need of money by mid-war. He had emptied his studio of works for his final exhibitions; a mix of unrelated sketches and paintings, so when husband and wife parted ways, it appears that Edith kept nearly all his works of her. Half his Welsh and Dorset oils portraying Edith, and at least 20 of his most notable oil paintings of her, were never exhibited by him. Of his more than 450 traced works, Derwent exhibited fewer than 100. After his death, three-quarters were put up for sale, many featuring his model-muse-wife. Edith preferred to present herself as Lyndra in the works of her sold after his death. Only one work used her true name (DL13.27). Entitled *Edith*, this large oil painting was chosen by Derwent for his only 'one-man' show at the end of 1913, the year he married his love.

More than 200 works by Derwent were to pass through Rex's hands between 1930 and the 1960s, and it is with him that much of the misinformation about Derwent's works, and the misattribution of works between Derwent and Dick, occurred.

In April 1930, the Redfern Gallery staged an exhibition of Derwent's works, in which it seems he played no role. Sadly, this was his only genuine one-man show, as his earlier 1913–14 Chenil Gallery exhibition had also displayed works by other artists, in particular Augustus. Undoubtedly, the works exhibited in 1930 would have been presented by Edith, those she had kept when the couple parted. Art critics even commented that an oddly garbed, single woman appeared in many works, which was of course the Edith of Derwent's pre-war Welsh and Dorset landscapes. Later in the year Rex lent *Lyndra at the Pool* (DL13.36) for the winter New English Art Club (NEAC) show, where, curiously, Derwent was now an exhibiting non-member with his contact address as 'The Redfern Gallery'.

Of the 1930 show, reviewers repeated the same sentiment about the artist's absence. In *The Observer*, Paul George Konody wrote that, 'Derwent Lees whose untimely disappearance in 1918, due to an incurable mental affliction is to be greatly regretted. An exhibition of Derwent Lees's last available pictures is now being held at the Redfern Gallery in Bond-street.'[4] Other magazines echoed the same message; Derwent was 'regrettably stricken with an incurable mental affliction'.[5] These were but the first to be exhibited of over 200 works in Edith's hands. Some works have her sister's Warwick Road address on the verso, and Evelyn is even named as the seller of an early student work by Dick (perhaps given to Derwent), later resold through the Redfern Gallery. Rex became the principal overseer, architect and manager of Derwent's legacy, and plans were afoot for even larger exhibitions.

While examining another artist, researchers Frances Carey, Anton Griffiths and Stephen Coppel found that Rex 'entailed a cavalier disregard for the artist's intentions'.[6] Nathaniel Williams, Nan Kivell's biographer, also remarked that Rex 'was known to be fluid with the truth'.[7] Rex was soon to market Derwent to his country of birth as the 'unknown' Australian modernist painter, with a large quiver of his works to sell.

THE FINAL RELEASE

Derwent Lees died on Saturday, 28 March 1931 at West Park Hospital in Epsom, Surrey, at 46 years of age. His death certificate records the cause of death as 'exhaustion from mania', with no post-mortem requested.[8] His family was far away, and he was summarily buried on 2 April 1931 with no gravestone.[9]

Obituaries celebrated the talented and sensitive artist, but it was not long before exhibition catalogues and articles erroneously claimed that he had painted in Italy, Croatia, Spain and the Crimea; was born in 1885 in Melbourne or Brisbane; grew up in the bush; attended university in Melbourne and had lost a leg. Later still, claims arose that his name was Desmond; that he had commenced his Slade studies in 1905, becoming a staff member in 1908; had a mental breakdown before the First World War, and stopped painting upon his hospitalisation.[10] All of this was untrue.

His death was tragic. When he was admitted to hospital 11 years earlier, Derwent's initial diagnosis was 'schizophrenia'. However, in 1917, this term was used for a wide range of psychoses, mal-controlled nervous states, manic depressive and bipolar disorders. Patients were often institutionalised for temporary, passing states of mental disquiet and disorders, and, at the end of the First World War, the understanding of the type of mental collapse Derwent suffered was limited. There is no evidence that alcohol or drug use were contributing factors in his decline, and schizophrenia commonly manifests earlier in life. Upon reviewing Derwent's medical registers, archival material relating to his breakdown (that followed a successful working life), and consulting specialist physicians, it is much more likely that he had a depressive or related bipolar illness. The West Park Hospital medical registers from 1924 until his 1931 death record his condition as 'chronic mania' and, sadly, it was not until the 1940s that lithium carbonate became a life-changing treatment for mania. Derwent's early life trauma and emotional sensitivity, coupled with extreme financial hardship and personal losses during the war, were likely sufficient to trigger his mid-1917 breakdown, from which he was unable to recover. The registers corroborate this assessment, classifying both the cause of his condition and its continuation as being 'prolonged mental stress'.[11]

At a dinner in the mid-1930s, Alleyne told Slade Professor Randolph Schwabe that 'there was no madness in the family: Derwent was quite unlike the others, who are sane and commonplace'.[12] This comment, however, was based on a single encounter with Derwent's sisters at a Sydney exhibition and it seems plausible that some of the other male siblings also experienced intense emotional states by their early thirties. Derwent's brother James married in 1900, and worked on rural Australian properties, moving five times in as many years. By 1910 he was unwell, unemployed and a long way from his wife and young children. After hospitalisation in Sydney, he took a single room at Mrs Mary Saville's boarding house near the sea at Coogee, and that June had shot himself in the head.[13] Documents in his pockets revealed that he was 'worried of late' and looking for work.[14] Whether his suicide was driven by financial, health or emotional reasons is unknown, however it is documented that this risk is higher in untreated bipolar or related depressive disorders.[15]

Much of their oldest brother William Robert Lees's working life is untraceable, but he too was unemployed by his mid-thirties and may have been unwell. He travelled to England in the early 1900s looking for work, but returned to Australia in 1904 as a single, unemployed 35-year-old. Later he found work in the Western Australian gold mines but died a few weeks after Derwent of miner's silicosis in the Wooroloo Sanatorium.[16] Silicosis dogged the miners of the Australian gold rush and is a horrendous way to die: 'belying the wealth from gold was the human misery associated with the mining industry – the sudden, devastating accidents and the ongoing prevalence of the miners' phthisis epidemic'.[17] While the specific cause of their disquiet or maladies is unknown, it remains that the three siblings, William, James and Derwent, lost their livelihoods at the same age, in what should have been the prime of their working lives.

THE CROWDED PLOT

Derwent's mother Gertrude had given birth to ten children. One child had died in infancy, one in childhood, one by suicide and now her youngest, of 'exhaustion from mania'. Of those that remained, few had children. Phillip was buried in a public grave in southern Tasmania, his older brother Noel in a family plot in New Zealand, Gertrude in Melbourne, their father in England.

Derwent was buried in a private, unmarked plot at Merton Cemetery in Surrey.[18] He was not buried in a public grave like most deceased inter-war patients from West Park Hospital. It seems that his siblings or friends provided the funds for the dedicated plot, as the hospital Register of Deaths includes a note 'bury by friends', suggesting that family, friends or Edith arranged and paid for his burial.[19]

Strangely though, Derwent is not lying alone. Another lies beside him. Edith, at 40 years old, is the registered contact for the burial plot, which had space reserved for her eventually to rest beside her late husband. However, she gave or sold her 'space' to a man Derwent never knew, nor he him.

Derwent was buried on 2 April 1931. A man of the same age, Joseph Chambers, was buried beside him on 14 April 1932.[20] Joseph had died in a London Poor Law infirmary, his will leaving his small estate to an Alice May Corne. Born Alice May Price, she was Edith's older sister, and lived above Joseph's apartment in the basement of a house in Earl's Court. Joseph lived there for many years, with Alice living upstairs with her much older husband Surtees. Joseph had signed his will leaving everything to Alice in 1920, 12 years before his death. It seems that they had been close for a long time.

Alice was an actress and used her stage name Renee Ashley when she married her musical director husband in 1906. Like her mother, she changed names with disconcerting fluidity, referring to herself as either Alice May Corne, Renee May Corne, May Ashley-Price, May Price or Miss Gilbert Price. At the time of their marriage, Surtees was nearing 50 but Alice was only 20, the same age as Joseph. After Joseph's death, she moved into his basement apartment, while Surtees remained upstairs until he died in 1939.[21]

Thus, Derwent lies alongside the long-time former intimate, perhaps lover, of his wife's sister. Once again it appears that Edith's priorities did not include Derwent.

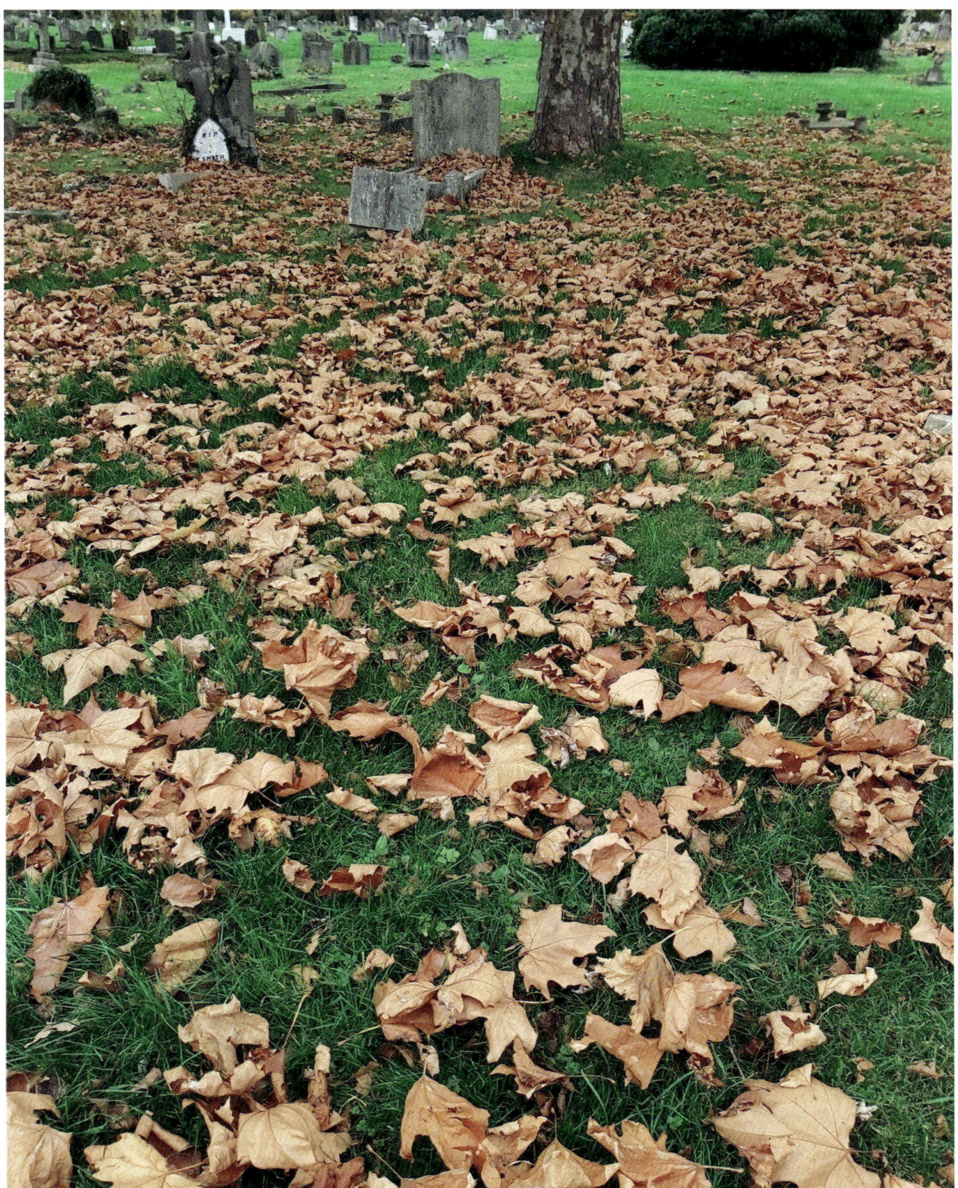

Derwent's unmarked grave, Merton Cemetery, Surrey, 2021, photograph by Stephen R. Johnson, The Friends of Horton Cemetery, and the Reverend Vicar, Horton Parish, Epsom

EDITH AND REX

April 1932 was a busy month for Edith. As Joseph was being buried beside Derwent, she received word that a letter had arrived at the Redfern Gallery from Australia, forwarded by the Slade. It was likely from her sister-in-law Clarice Lees, who had visited London with Gilbert and knew some of Derwent's friends. Derwent's family and the Slade did not know Edith's address, despite her living at or using her sister's address for at least a decade. The Slade, however, knew of her close ties to the Redfern. Edith penned a short thank you on custom-printed 99 Warwick Rd letterhead to Professor Schwabe, sending her regards to Mrs Schwabe, and requesting that further correspondence be sent directly to her Warwick Road address.[22]

Within a year, Edith was living in Venice, no doubt aided by monies left in her late husband's account and through connections he had forged in London's art circles, and perhaps by painting sales. Arriving in late 1932 or 1933, she stayed for three or more years.[23] Schwabe and his wife met her during a short trip to Italy in spring 1935, after arriving in Venice on Friday, 5 April. Three days later, Schwabe wrote in his diary about 'Edith Lees, who is giving English lessons in Venice, and who lives in the Abbazia'.[24]

Edith must have also contributed a work to the politically contentious 1936 Venice Biennale. Despite Britain not officially exhibiting that year, due to their concern about Mussolini's invasion of Abyssinia, her late husband's work *Dorset Scene* (DL13.49) was shown. The British committee permitted English citizens resident in Venice at the time to exhibit works in an unofficial capacity. Works by 27 artists were shown in the Biennale's English stand. It seems Edith later returned to Venice, staying at the exclusive Hotel Europa e Brittania on the Grand Canal, a stone's throw from St Mark's Square.

Edith had presented Rex with a portfolio of Derwent's works to sell, and the marketing campaign commenced less than a year after the artist's death. Several biographical pieces followed, many littered with errors. This was probably a result of Rex's cursory inspections of the landscapes and Edith's lack of knowledge about Derwent's travels, leading to many persistently misinformed painting locations and landscape titles titles (see Appendix).

Derwent's art was first shown in Australia as part of the 1933 *Exhibition of British Contemporary Art* which opened in Melbourne in March, then Sydney. Around 20 April, Derwent's sisters visited the Sydney exhibition and met Alleyne. As a result, the Australian newspapers amended some previously published incorrect biographical details. Despite this, a year later back in London, Rex held the first of two memorial exhibitions, with catalogue and marketing text riddled with mistakes. More than 30 further exhibitions with selections of his works at, or loaned by, the Redfern Gallery were to follow over the next three decades.

By 1936, Edith had returned to London. She reacquainted herself with the Redfern Gallery staff and its newly appointed manager, Mrs Ala Story. From a wealthy Austrian family, Ala had worked earlier as the gallery's assistant. She was well connected and confident in business, and in late 1938 she left the Redfern to take over the Stafford Gallery in St James Place. Edith now had two galleries vying for her late husband's art, and in the following year, both Ala and Rex exhibited Derwent's works at their respective galleries. In Ala's publicity, she wrote that Derwent's

> widow discovered two folios of drawings this year. Mrs Story catalogued and hung them in July . . . they are nearly all dated between 1914 and 1918. Only one bears any evidence of being executed during a war. A painting of a soldier in khaki is called 'Artist in 1915'. The rest are drawings of models (rather John-like): sketches of studios, of public houses and music halls and of romantically wistful young ladies.[25]

Meanwhile, the *Liverpool Daily Post* explained that, at the late September exhibition opening of

> Derwent Lees at the subterranean Stafford Gallery . . . The drawings by Lees were discovered bundled up in an attic. They belong definitely to the Slade School style of 1914 or 1915, but are full of genuine expression and touched, in high degree, with that blend of precision and sensitiveness which marks the best work of this period. 'A Room in Chelsea', 'The Old Bedford,' and 'Elsie McKnight' [*sic*] may be selected.[26]

However, Ala's fortunes changed and, as the talk of another war neared, she left England for the USA. Edith retreated to the calm of her sister May's Ashley Cottage on the Sussex coast at West Wittering, that her husband Surtees (who died that year) had purchased a decade earlier.

Rex and Edith continued their commercial relationship for at least 30 years, selling Derwent's oeuvre until the mid-1960s, by which time its value, along with his reputation, had grown substantially, and Edith had shifted to signing her letters as 'Edith Derwent Lees'.[27]

Rex had arrived in London on war leave in 1917, the same year as Derwent's breakdown. Rex was then just 18, Derwent was 32 and never met the man who would put a stamp on his legacy. One born in New Zealand then living a fabricated life, the other in Australia with his life posthumously reinvented for him. Neither returned to their country of birth; Rex perhaps to avoid the discovery of his invented past, Derwent without the means or reason to return home.

AFTER THE END

Upon visiting the Sydney April 1933 exhibition, Derwent's sisters said that they had not seen their brother in many years, and that it was the first time they had seen his paintings as 'he never painted Australian scenes' and it was 'the first of his work to be exhibited in his native land'.[28] They never met Edith, and on viewing her in *The Orange Skirt* (DL13.26), 'one quaintly called the portrait "introduction to a new relation"'.[29] *The Bulletin* noted that, of all of the visitors, 'Two of the most looked upon, were two of Derwent Lees' sisters, they themselves were keen gazers at their brother's *Orange skirt*, a portrait study'.[30]

The sisters remained faithful followers of their brother's works. At a Sydney 1939 exhibition, opened by Lord Wakehurst, *The Sydney Morning Herald* reported that 'another spectator was Miss Trixie Lees who takes a special interest in painting, because her brother, the late Derwent Lees, was a well-known artist. Several of his pictures are included in a loan exhibition from the Tate Gallery London which will be shown in Melbourne.'[31]

When Derwent's last sibling died in 1967, Edith was still living at 99 Warwick Road in London. She was the sole beneficiary of her husband's estate. At 78, she had not only outlived all Derwent's siblings but also her own full siblings.

While Alleyne and Rex were the first to bring Derwent's works to the Australian public's attention, much credit must go to Australian-born, former Second World War Monuments Officer, John McDonnell. As London advisor for the National Gallery of Victoria's Felton Bequest from 1947 to 1964, he judiciously sought out quality art for its collection, from the Old Masters to the modern, including three by Derwent (DL14.41 and two through the Felton Bequest, DL08.12, DL13.33). Poignantly, one of his first acquisitions, guided by friend and advisor, then Slade Professor Randolph Schwabe, was Derwent's 1908 sanguine *Self Portrait*, purchased in April 1947.

Today Derwent's artworks are held in some 50 public institutions, spread across more than 30 cities, in eight countries.

Derwent Lees was a keenly intelligent, loyal, hard-working and talented artist. He was courageous, generous and sensitive. Crippled by a lack of self-identity and a misunderstood malady, for a fleeting moment he found acceptance, connections and perhaps a meaningful way to escape the grief of his deep losses. With a growing artistic confidence and maturing style, he was bound for greater things, but cut down by tragic circumstance, his disappearance dwarfed by the roll call of the dead from the First World War.

British art critic Frank Rutter observed at Derwent's 1934 Redfern Gallery retrospective that,

> emphatic design, clarity of colour, and a glow of light are qualities which distinguish these attractive small landscapes by Derwent Lees . . . influenced by stronger characters, Derwent Lees might have developed much further had he been able to go on painting in his later years, and, though his career was cut short when he was in a period of transition, his remaining works command respect by their sincerity and accomplishment.[32]

With shifts in artistic trends and the stigma of mental illness, his name was to fade. Yet, as Theodore Roosevelt proclaimed in Paris in 1910, 'credit belongs to the man who is actually in the arena, whose face is marred by dust and sweat and blood; who strives valiantly; who errs, who comes short again and again'.[33]

Opposite:
DL12.20 (detail)
Derwent Lees, *Trees, Provence*, 1912

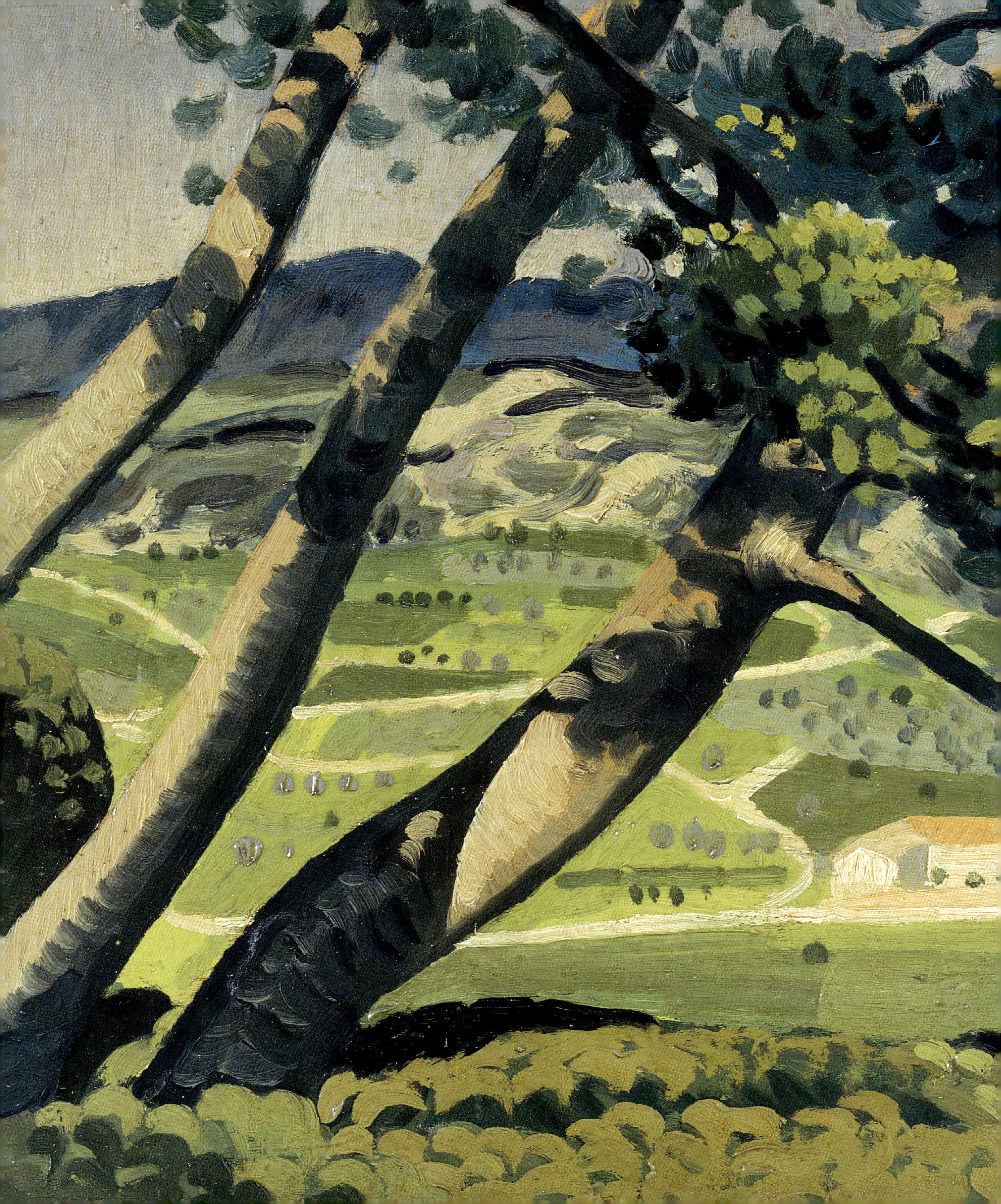

APPENDIX: LANDSCAPE GEOLOCATION

Derwent's landscapes have proved invaluable to my research, providing a rich library anchoring the artist in time and place. Accurately geolocating them is vital in revealing aspects of his creative practice, life story and artistic associations. His landscapes were frequently untitled, and early gallerists often assigned incorrect locations, borne out of a lack of knowledge of his travels or errors created from misreading submitted handwritten gallery note-cards. Nearly half of Derwent's works have incorrect titles or dates, and only about one in ten has a signature, date and title. More than a century later, having passed through multiple galleries and auction houses, many of his works became disassociated from their original subject, date or place of creation.

The following examples of landscape location errors and the geolocation methodology were compiled by Professor Peter Davies.

ENGLISH AND WELSH LANDSCAPES

Many of Derwent's works in England and Wales were given the wrong location, with several untitled landscapes mistaken as being from France; French works were also misinterpreted as Welsh – and vice versa.

A view of Lake Bala, Wales, was mistitled *The Blue Pool, Dorset* (DL11.5) due to a presumed resemblance to Dorset's Blue Pool, while a view of the *Purbeck Hills* (DL13.42) in Dorset was mistitled *Aldbourne Landscape*. A scene of the Bourton House driveway in Shrivenham was misnamed *The Drive to the Asylum* (DL17.1), yet it was commissioned and named by Cyril Butler as *The Avenue* (Bourton House drive led directly onto The Avenue, Bourton). A so-called *View across Roofs, Aldbourne, Wiltshire* (DL16.4) in fact looks towards St James' Church in Bourton, Shrivenham, from the window of the Bourton House stables. *Studio in Fitzroy Street* (DL12.14) is a scene of Derwent's Fitzroy Square studio, with some even assuming it to be Walter Sickert's Fitzroy Street studio.

The Yellow Skirt (DL14.34) is now re-assigned its original title *Tan-y-Bwlch*, as its original label and exhibition attest, and consistent with the site's landform.

Evaluation of the geomorphology, rocks and vegetation helped to reveal that some scenes were from the Purbeck heathlands, and not in France. Distinctive blues, yellows and purples of heathland flowers, especially heather and broom, also characterise these Dorset scenes. *Lyndra Seated on a Sandy Bank* (DL13.31) appeared in later catalogues as *Near Cassis*, despite being painted on the regenerating heathland slope overlooking the Blue Pool, Dorset, and *Lyndra in the Pyrenees* (aka *The Sandhill*, DL13.35) was painted against a backdrop of the Blue Pool's spoil mounds, not French mountains. A scene of spoil mounds and pines overlooking the Blue Pool was mistitled *Mediterranean Landscape* (DL13.51). *Women at La Ciotat* (DL13.37) is also of the Blue Pool, not from Provence, and several untitled scenes of women bathing or washing 'by the sea', were also on the Blue Pool shore.

FRENCH LANDSCAPES

Many works created in France were variously mistitled as from Wales or England, as well as from Spain, Italy, Belgium, Croatia and 'Yugoslavia' – countries Derwent never visited.

The large oil *On the Coast, Dorset* (DL11.32) is of Etang de Berre at Istres. Two works mistitled in the 1930s as *Evening Wales*, and another work titled *Welsh Hills* and exhibited as such in 1968 and 1982, are views from Collioure, France (DL10.29, DL10.31, DL10.32). Seven untitled landscapes painted in Istres and Banyuls in France were mistitled in the 1930s *A Landscape in Spain* (DL11.37), *Scene in Spain* (DL11.40), *Spanish Village* (DL12.24) and *Spanish Landscape* (DL12.27, DL12.32, DL13.3), leading to misconceptions that he painted in Spain. The inventively titled *Italian Landscape with the Alps Beyond* (DL13.1), a scene of the French Alps from Forcalquier, led to the incorrect assumption that he painted in Italy. The original title, *Cheval Blanc, Basses Alpes*, also led to a belief that he painted in Switzerland.

Many works were given the wrong French location, with a particular emphasis on being Provençal, or from Cassis or Collioure, all places well known to mid-century British gallerists. 'Provence' was added to many titles during the 1930s (likely for commercial reasons), and a scene of the Collioure coastline was mistitled *La Ciotat, Provence* (DL10.25). *Vineyards Collioure* (DL10.18) was wrongly retitled *Provencal Landscape*, and a headland at Istres (DL11.38) as *Coast at Collioure*, despite the distinctive geology of the two areas. The title *Forcalquier from the Alps* (DL12.17), misread from the inscription *Forcalquier Basses Alpes*, is a view from the hilltop citadel in the Basses Alpes region.

Derwent himself misnamed the *Mas Reig* farmhouse in Banyuls as *Métairie des Abeilles* (DL12.26), a farmstead much further inland. *The Little Gardens* (DL13.5), also painted in Banyuls, was posthumously mistitled *The Little Gardens, Cassis*. A study for *A Bay, the South of France, Cassis* (DL14.4) was mistitled *View of Banyuls* (DL14.1), and a similar work by Derwent was mistitled *Collioure, 1910* (DL14.3) and misattributed to James Dickson Innes.

Many errors resulted from misinterpreting Derwent's flowing cursive writing and non-English place names, notably for works from France, Poland and Wales. *La Ciotat* was often misinterpreted (DL14.12, DL14.13), with one work later retitled *Lake* (DL14.15, the registrar having read the letters 'LaC' as lake in French. Others from the coastal village became *La Ciolat*, *Crotat* and even *Cavtat*, the latter leading to a misconception that he painted in the then Yugoslavia.

Several of Derwent's and James Dickson Innes's scenes north of Collioure have been mistaken for the coastline of Croatia or of Wales, despite clear differences in vegetation and landform, different orientations to the setting sun, and the pervasive valley mist of the River Tet being misinterpreted as a coastal bay. Such examples emphasise the importance of on-site visits, coupled with an understanding of natural history, and local knowledge.

Scenes at Banyuls were misspelled as Banyals, Banyales, Bonnuls, Bannuls and Banyons, and *Creech Barrow* (DL13.43) Dorset, as Crich Barrow, Crech Barrow and Crick Barrow. *The Bsura River* (DL09.8) was misspelled from its homonym Bzura by Derwent, then to Beura and Burza (DL09.14); *Argelès, Mediterranean* (DL10.21) was transformed to Angles and Angeles, and *Arenig Mawr* (DL11.1) to *Arenig Manor*.

Claims also arose that Derwent travelled in Russia based on his 1909 works from central Poland, in the then Russian-controlled region of the 'Kingdom of Poland'.

GEOLOCATION METHODS

The geolocation and mapping of painting sites was done by Professor Peter Davies AM, an applied research ecologist, who also integrated science into his art practice. Formerly the University of Tasmania's School of Creative Art's inaugural 'scientist-in-residence', he has co-created a large-scale land-art installation in Australia and was an art history student at the University of Grenoble, France, in the 1970s. Peter brought his natural history, geomorphological, scientific mapping and data skills to the project, enhanced by digital and on-site field work. Site identification also benefited greatly from a dedicated group of English, Welsh and French volunteers (see Acknowledgements, Geolocation).

Close examination of Derwent's works, archival research, liaison with archivists, galleries and museums, science and art specialists, local geographic knowledge, drone flights, on-site visits and contributions by volunteers has clarified the majority of his landscape locations, greatly helped by his fidelity to landscape features. Each landscape, including those with figures, was subject to the following procedure:

- Careful evaluation of: physical and vegetative aspects of the scene; sun direction, angle and point of view, and elevation relative to key features; the nature of the scene's geology and geomorphology; the distribution, type and colour of vegetation; and the location and type of man-made structures.
- Examination of relevantly dated photographs from collections, books, postcards and online archives, including aerial photographs.

- Evaluation against related works by James Dickson Innes, Augustus John, Ambrose McEvoy and Walter Westley Russell.
- Scoping locations using Google Earth, Google Maps Street View, online geographic archives (Geoportail.fr, Geograph.org.uk), maps and landscape visualisation tools (MapTiler®, ReliefMaps®, v.1.9.4).
- Consideration of season and effects on vegetation and human activity, and proximity to transport and other painting sites, in the context of Derwent's known travels.
- Visiting the sites and exploring them from various viewing angles and aspects.

Specific regional information included:

Banyuls & Collioure – Historic photographs and information, maps and postcards were sourced from local historians (Professor Albert Callis, André Guerné, Alexis Aloujes and Albert Hermandez) and advice was provided by Le Blog des Amoureux de Banyuls as well as repeated on-site visits.

Istres, Forcalquier & Cassis – Historic photographs, postcards and advice were provided by Les Amis du Viel Istres.

Blue Pool, Dorset area – Historical and ecological information was provided by David Beeson and Gabriel Summers. Online visualisation was combined with several on-site visits to the Blue Pool, Creech and Grange, and comparison with related works by Augustus John, James Dickson Innes and Nora Summers.

Bourton & Idstone area – Local and historical knowledge, still and drone photographs, and maps were enthusiastically provided by Neil B. Maw of the Shrivenham Heritage Society.

North Wales – Site scoping was supplemented by comparisons with compositions by James Dickson Innes and Augustus John, along with historical photographs of the Migneint and Tanygrisiau areas. Historical and local site knowledge was kindly provided by Keith Bowen, John Appleby and the Friends of Cwmorthin, kindly supplemented by Dr Sarah Munks and Rick Crossland.

FURTHER READING

Beckett, Jane, and Cherry, Deborah, *Edwardian Era*, Phaidon, London, 1987

Clarke, Gill, *Randolph Schwabe*, Sansom & Co., Bristol, 2012

Clarke, Gill (ed.), *The Diaries of Randolph Schwabe: British Art 1930–48*, Sansom & Co., Bristol, 2016

Haycock, David Boyd, *Brilliant Destiny: The Age of Augustus John*, Lund Humphries, London, 2023

Holroyd, Michael, *Augustus John: A Biography*, Holt, Rinehart & Winston, New York, 1975

Holt, Ysanne, *British Artists and the Modernist Landscape*, Ashgate, Aldershot, England, 2003

Hoole, John, and Simons, Margaret, *James Dickson Innes (1887–1914)*, Lund Humphries, London, 2013

Lew, Henry, *Imaging the World*, Hybrid Publishers, Ormond, Australia, 2018

Ragenaud, Virginie, *The Colors of Catalonia: In the Footsteps of Twentieth-Century Artists*, GemmaMedia, Boston, MA, 2012

Robins-Gruetzner, Anna, *Modern Art in Britain 1910–1914*, Merrell Holberton, London, 1997

Shone, Richard, *Bloomsbury Portraits: Vanessa Bell, Duncan Grant, and their Circle*, Phaidon, Oxford, 1976

Yarker, Gwen, *Inquisitive Eyes: Slade Painters in Edwardian Wessex*, Sansom & Co., Bristol, 2016

Yu, Mengting, *London's Women Artists, 1900–1914: A Talented and Decorative Group*, Springer, Singapore, 2020

NOTES

ABBREVIATIONS

UCL – University College London, England
UCL SC – University College London Library Services; Special Collections – includes materials from UCL Records, UCL Archives and UCL Digital Collections

PREFACE

1. Spurling, Hilary, *The Unknown Matisse: A Life of Henri Matisse*, v.1, Hamish Hamilton, London, 1998, p.xxi.
2. ibid., p.xxii.
3. Kobayashi Issa, poet and lay Buddhist priest, penned this haiku following the death of his daughter c.1814. This interpretation was translated into English by Peter Beilenson.

1. A COLONIAL BOY

1. The Union Bank building (16 Macquarie Street) was demolished c.1970. It was sited at present-day 134 Macquarie Street, Hobart, Australia.
2. William Lees is listed in the 1879 Hobart Town Post Office Directory living at 16 Macquarie Street; Tasmanian Government, Hobart Gazette, Valuation Roll 1881 and 1884 list the Union Bank and house, the upstairs residence.
3. Libraries Tasmania, Tasmanian Archives, Australia, Hutchins School Hobart Admissions Register, 1879, NS36/1/1.
4. 'Union Bank. Century of Service', *The Mercury* (Hobart), 1 Sep 1937, p.14.
5. Bennison, Peter, *The Tasmanian Club*, Artemis, Tasmania, 2011, pp 55–7.
6. Libraries Tasmania, Tasmanian Archives, Australia, Register of Births, RGD33 – [Phyllis] Lees, 29 Aug 1880; Eleanor Lees, 8 Oct 1881; Gilbert Lees, 20 Mar 1883; [Derwent] Lees, 14 Nov 1884.
7. Libraries Tasmania, Tasmanian Archives, Australia, Register of Deaths – Hobart, Phillip Lees, RGD35, 20 Jan 1880; *The Mercury* (Hobart), 24 Jan 1880, p.3.
8. *Evening Star* (Dunedin), 6841, 4 Mar 1885, p.2; *The Mercury* (Hobart), 26 Feb 1885, p.2.
9. *Evening Star* (Dunedin), 6840, 3 Mar 1885, p.3.
10. ibid., 6881, 27 Mar 1885, p.3.
11. Victoria, Australia, Unassisted Passenger Lists, 1839–1923, 6 Nov 1891, online at ancestry.com.
12. *Evening Star* (Dunedin), 6989, 24 Aug 1886, p.2.
13. O'Hern, Jennifer and Cooley, Louise, 'A Description of Human Hydatid Disease in Tasmania in the Post-Eradication Era', *Medical Journal of Australia*, 199(2), Jul 2013, p.117; 'Frightening Toll of Hydatid Disease in New Zealand', *Upper Hutt Leader*, 20 Mar 1958, p.6.
14. Otago Region, New Zealand, Cemetery Records, site 1560.
15. *Evening Star* (Dunedin), 7371, 17 Nov 1887, p.3.
16. *The Argus* (Melbourne), 20 Jun 1890, p.6.
17. 'Union Bank. Century of Service', *The Mercury* (Hobart), 1 Sep 1937, p.14.

18. *The Telegraph* (Brisbane), 24 Apr 1894, p.5.
19. *New Zealand Mail*, 14017, 16 Feb 1899.
20. Victoria, Australia, Melbourne Grammar School Archives, Enrolment Register, 1889.
21. *The Melburnian*, 18.1, 1893, p.26.
22. ibid., 25a.1, 6 Apr 1900, p.3.
23. ibid., 72.2(1), 1947 p.135.
24. *The Australasian*, 29 Sep 1900, p.45.
25. *Ovens & Murray Advertiser* (Victoria), 2 Mar 1901, p.12; *The Leader*, 2 Mar 1901, p.24.
26. *The Argus* (Melbourne), Deaths, 31 Dec 1900, p.1; Colony of Victoria, Melbourne, Australia, Deaths in the District of South Melbourne, 1900, no.11212, Gertrude Lees.
27. Diocese of Westminster, London, England, Parish of St Saviour, Pimlico, Marriage Records, 27 Nov 1901, p.123.
28. *The Courier Mail* (Brisbane), 1 Aug 1936, p.17.
29. UK and Ireland, Outward Passenger Lists, 1890–1960, 10 Feb 1902, Southampton, online at ancestry.com.
30. Derwent Lees descendants, personal communication, 2021–4.
31. Morris, Richard (Morris & Son, Woodbridge, Suffolk), personal communication, 2024, unpublished letter from Derwent Lees to Christopher Nevinson, Mar 1912 (courtesy of private collector).
32. *Adelong and Tumut Express and Tumbarumba Post* (New South Wales), 15 Aug 1902, p.2.
33. Holroyd, Michael, *Augustus John: The New Biography*, Vintage, London, 1997, p.355.
34. *The Brisbane Courier* (Queensland), 3 Dec 1891, p.6.
35. *The Telegraph* (New South Wales), 22 Dec 1899, p.8.
36. University of Sydney, Australia, Calendar Archive, 1905, p.262.
37. *The Sydney Morning Herald Telegraph* (New South Wales), 17 Mar 1905, p.7.
38. Western Australia, Crew and Passenger Lists, *Albany*, 20 Jul 1905, online at ancestry.com; *The Australian Star* (New South Wales), 7 Jul 1905, p.5; Lew, Henry, *In Search of Derwent Lees*, self-published, Melbourne, 1996.

2. THE YOUNG ARTIST

1. Clarke, Gill, *Randolph Schwabe*, Sansom & Co., Bristol, 2012, p.17.
2. UCL SC, Registry Record, 1906, no.1520, Derwent Lees, UCLCA/4.
3. John, Augustus, *Chiaroscuro*, Jonathan Cape, London, 1952, pp 40–41.
4. Clarke, Gill, 2012, op.cit., pp 18–19.
5. John, Augustus, 1952, op.cit., pp 41–2.
6. Hone, Joseph, *The Life of Henry Tonks*, Heinemann Ltd, London, 1939, p.74.
7. Derwent Lees's descendants, family collection, letter from James Dickson Innes to Gilbert Lees, 20 Dec 1907; Lew, Henry, 'J.D. Innes and Derwent Lees: New Highlights of their Early Friendship', *Australian Antique Collector*, 1998, pp 120–22.
8. Tate Archive, letter from James Dickson Innes to John Fothergill, 1908–9, TGA 7121.8.
9. Derwent Lees's descendants, family collection, letter from James Dickson Innes to Gilbert Lees, 20 Dec 1907.
10. Rothenstein, William, *Men and Memories*, Faber & Faber, London, 1931, p.332.
11. Tate Archive, letter from James Dickson Innes to John Fothergill, 1908–9, TGA 7121.2.
12. Shone, Richard, *Bloomsbury Portraits: Vanessa Bell, Duncan Grant and their Circle*, Phaidon, Oxford, 1976, p.210; the restaurant changed its name to the White Tower c.1938–43.
13. Lilly, Marjorie, *Sickert: The Painter and his Circle*, Elek, London, 1971, p.136.
14. The UCL award was named after Slade student Henry Melvill Nettleship, who died aged 21 during his second year of studies and whose cousin Ida Nettleship was Augustus John's future wife.
15. UCL Slade School of Fine Art Memorial Tablet, unveiled on Armistice Day at UCL, London, 1921. See p.122.
16. *The Pastoralists Review*, 17(5), Jul 1907, p.98.
17. *The Telegraph* (Brisbane), 1 Aug 1936, p.26; Harrison, Godfrey, *Borthwicks*, Hazel, London, 1963.
18. Hoole, John, and Simons, Margaret, *James Dickson Innes (1887–1914)*, Lund Humphries, London, 2013, p.31; Rothenstein, John, *Modern English Painters*, Eyre and Spottiswoode, London, 1956, p.65.
19. Tate Archive, Slade, Frank, 'James Dickson Innes: Memories of Dick Innes', unpublished, 1958, TGA 937.1, p.6.
20. Hoole, John, and Simons, Margaret, op.cit., p.32.
21. Clarke, Gill (ed.), *The Diaries of Randolph Schwabe: British Art 1930–48*, Sansom & Co., Bristol, 2016, p.226.
22. ibid.
23. *The Herald* (Melbourne), 18 Jun 1932, p.22.
24. Clarke, Gill, 2016, op.cit., p.175.
25. Trollope, James, *Rudolph Ihlee: The Road to Collioure*, Lund Humphries, London, 2022, p.19.
26. Carroitg, Jean, 'C'était hier à Collioure, Argelès et autres lieux', *Massana*, 59, 1996, p.48.
27. Trollope, James, op.cit., p.54.
28. Harris, Theodore, *Pearl S. Buck: A Biography*, v.2: *Her Philosophy as Expressed in Her Letters*, Methuen, London, 1971, p.217.

3. MENTORS AND MASTERS

1. Rothenstein, William, op.cit., p.343.
2. Shone, Richard, 1976, op.cit., p.65; Hoole, John, and Simons, Margaret, op.cit., pp 31, 35.
3. Hoole, John, and Simons, Margaret, op.cit., p.26.
4. UCL SC, Calendar 1908–9, July 1908, Dean's Report, p.xcvii.
5. Derwent Lees descendants, family collection, letter from James Dickson Innes to Gilbert Lees, 20 Dec 1907; Lew, Henry, 1998, op.cit., p.122.
6. England, Census 1911, Donald Maclaren, online at ancestry.com.
7. Matamoros, J., et al., *Matisse-Derain: Collioure 1905*, Gallimard, Paris, 2005, pp 285–7.
8. Spurling, Hilary, op.cit., p.301.
9. ibid., p.361.
10. Fothergill, John, *James Dickson Innes*, Faber & Faber, London, 1946, p.8.
11. Spurling, Hilary, op.cit., pp 374–5.
12. Fothergill, John, op.cit., p.8.
13. Tate Archive, letter from James Dickson Innes to John Fothergill, June 1908, TGA 7121.1.
14. London, England, Electoral Registers, 1832–1965, 1908, online at ancestry.com.
15. Aitken, Charles, 'The Slade School of Fine Arts', *Apollo*, 3(13), 1 Jan 1926, p.3.
16. Shone, Richard, *Burlington Magazine*, 117, 1975, pp 278–84.
17. ibid.; Tate Archive, letter from Vanessa Bell to Duncan Grant, 24 Jun 1910, TGA 20078/1/44/3.
18. Shone, Richard, 1975, op.cit.
19. Rutherston, Albert, *Burlington Magazine*, 8(83), 1943, p.205.
20. Fergusson, Louis, *The Studio*, 1930, p.111, in Shone, Richard, 1976, op.cit., p.65.

4. A NEW BEGINNING

1. UCL SC, Calendar 1908–9, Departments and Staff, Faculty of Arts, p.xxxiii.
2. Schwabe, Randolph, unpublished diary entry, 25 Nov 1937 (courtesy of Gill Clarke).
3. Derwent Lees descendants, family collection, letter from James Dickson Innes to Gilbert Lees, 20 Dec 1907.
4. Tate Archive, letter from James Dickson Innes to John Fothergill, 1908–9, TGA 7121.2.
5. ibid., TGA 7121.7.
6. Clarke, Gill, 2016, op.cit., p.511.
7. Galleries of the Royal Society of British Artists London, *41st Exhibition of Modern Pictures*, exh.cat., New English Art Club, May 1909, nos 220, 232, 239, 254.
8. Hoole, John, and Simons, Margaret, op.cit., p.58, in Tate Archive, letter from

James Dickson Innes to John Fothergill, TGA 7121.7.
9. Hoole, John, and Simons, Margaret, op.cit., p.48; personal communication with John Hoole, 2023–4.
10. Tate Archive, letter from James Dickson Innes to John Fothergill, 15 Jan 1909, TGA 7121.4.
11. ibid., TGA 7121.7.
12. Holroyd, Michael, 1997, op.cit., p.374.
13. Hoole, John, and Simons, Margaret, op.cit., p.30.
14. ibid., p.68.
15. Nora and Gerald Summers's descendants, personal communication, 2022–4.
16. It is not known if this drawing was completed, but Derwent refers to it in letters to Lady Howard de Walden. The Howard de Walden Estate Document Archive, London, letters (1918; May 1918 incomplete) from Derwent Lees to Lady Howard de Walden, HDWF 6/106–107.
17. Tate Archive, Letters from James Dickson Innes to John Fothergill, 1908–9, TGA 7121 series.
18. ibid., TGA 7121.8.
19. ibid., TGA 7121.2.
20. ibid., TGA 7121.7.
21. ibid., TGA 7121.8.
22. Tate Archive, letter from Albert Rutherston to John Fothergill, TGA 7121.28.
23. Tate Archive, letter from James Dickson Innes to John Fothergill, 15 Jan 1909, TGA 7121.4.
24. ibid., TGA 7121.7.
25. Tate Archive, Innes, James Dickson, Sketchbook (scrapbook), TGA 200814.
26. Spelling variants: Stowkowski in UCL SC, Calendar, 1908–9, p.470; Stokowski in UCL SC, Calendar, 1909–10, p.510; Stephen Stokowski in UCL SC, Registry Record, 1907–8, UCLCA/4.
27. Tate Archive, letter from James Dickson Innes to John Fothergill, June 1908, TGA 7121.1.
28. UCL SC, Calendar 1908–9, Dean's Report, p.xcvii.
29. Yarker, Gwen, *Inquisitive Eyes: Slade Painters in Edwardian Wessex*, Sansom & Co., Bristol, 2016, p.16.
30. Spalding, Frances, *Vanessa Bell*, George Weidenfeld & Nicolson, London, 1983, p.90.
31. McNaught, Elsie, 'Portrait of Derwent Lees', UCL Art Museum, LDUCS-6510.
32. Yu, Mengting, *London's Women Artists, 1900–1914: A Talented and Decorative Group*, Springer, Singapore, 2020, p.80.
33. *Grenfell Record & Lachlan District Advertiser*, 22 Jun 1910, p.2; *The Sunday Sun* (Sydney), 19 Jun 1910, p.5; Sydney, Australia, Registers of Coroners Inquests, 1903–11, James Harcourt Lees.

5. CONFIDENCE IN A SOUTHERN LIGHT

1. Holroyd, Michael, 1997, op.cit., p.355, in Tate Archive, letter from James Dickson Innes to John Fothergill, 1908–9, TGA 7121.2.
2. Tate Archive, Slade, Frank, op.cit., p.2.
3. Spurling, Hilary, op.cit., pp 317–27.
4. Schwabe, Randolph, 'Reminiscences of Fellow Students', *Burlington Magazine*, 82(478), 1943, p.9.
5. Ruskin, John, *The Eagle's Nest*, George Allen, London, 1872, Lecture III, p.51.
6. Amigo, Jean-Jacques, 'Charles-Victor Naudin (1815–1899) sa vie, son œuvre, son séjour à Collioure et à la Villa Thuret', *Naturalia Ruscinonensia, Société d'Histoire naturelle de Perpignan et des Pyrénées-Orientales*, Histoire des Sciences, Fascicule, Feb 1999, pp 3–52.
7. Sériziat, Charles-Victor-Émile, and Soulier, Paul, *Collioure et ses Environs*, Livre d'histoire, Paris (1st edn 1902), 2005, pp 100–1.
8. Spurling, Hilary, op.cit., p.316.
9. Raguenaud, Virginie, *The Colors of Catalonia: In the Footsteps of Twentieth-Century Artists*, GemmaMedia, Boston, MA, 2012, p.4.
10. ibid., p.165.
11. Whitfield, Sarah, *Fauvism*, Thames & Hudson, London, 1996, p.91.
12. Martinet, M., 'La Pêche sur les Côtes du Roussillon', *La Revue Scientifique*, 39, 1887, p.659.
13. Spurling, Hilary, op.cit., p.302; Francois Desclaux, Collioure, personal communication, 2022.
14. Holroyd, Michael, 1997, op.cit., p.307.
15. *The Athenaeum*, 4349, 4 March 1911, p.195.
16. New York Public Library, USA, Archives & Manuscripts, John Quinn Letterbooks, 1902–24, cable from John Quinn to Jack Knewstub, 3 Feb 1911.
17. Helmreich, Anne, and Holt, Ysanne, 'Marketing Bohemia: The Chenil Gallery in Chelsea', *Oxford Art Journal*, 33, 2010, p.48.
18. ibid., p.52.

6. OF MOUNTAINS AND LAKES

1. Davies, Brian, 'James Dickson Innes', 2020, online at www.llanellich.org.uk, p.5.
2. Holroyd, Michael, 1997, op.cit., p.354.
3. ibid., letter from Augustus John to Lady Ottoline Morrell, p.316.
4. *International Exhibition of Modern Art*, exh.cat., Association of American Painters and Sculptors, New York, 1913, p.42.
5. Holroyd, Michael, 1997, op.cit., letter from Augustus John to Lady Ottoline Morrell, p.361.
6. ibid., letter from Augustus John to Lady Ottoline Morrell, 5 Aug 1910, p.326.
7. Hoole, John, and Simons, Margaret, op.cit., p.90.
8. *The Times*, 13 Apr 1934, p.12.
9. Holt, Ysanne, *British Artists and the Modernist Landscape*, Ashgate, Aldershot, 2003, p.62.
10. John, Augustus, *Augustus John: Autobiography*, Jonathan Cape, London, 1975, p.227.
11. Lew, Henry, *Imaging the World*, Hybrid, Ormond, Australia, 2018, pp 210–11; Lew, Henry, *Australian Genesis and Exodus*, Hybrid, Melbourne, 2023, pp 82–5.
12. Holroyd, Michael, *Augustus John, A Biography*, Holt, Rinehart & Winston, New York, 1975, p.327.
13. University of Liverpool, England, Archives, letter from Augustus John, 11 Jul 1911, D207/40/52.
14. Stanier, Peter, *Dorset's Industrial Heritage*, Twelveheads Press, Truro, 1989, pp 9, 30.
15. Haycock, David Boyd, 'Impressions of Wessex', *Apollo*, Apr 2016, p.92.
16. ibid.
17. Albright-Knox Art Gallery, *Painting and Sculpture from Antiquity to 1942*, Rizzoli International, New York, 1979, p.480.
18. *The Times*, 9 Jan 1911, p.11.
19. Holroyd, Michael, 1975, op.cit., p.401.
20. ibid., p.147.
21. Schwabe, Randolph, unpublished diary entry, 25 Nov 1937 (courtesy of Gill Clarke).

7. MASTERING COLOUR

1. Hoole, John, and Simons, Margaret, op.cit., p.127.
2. Côte Vermeille (meaning Vermillion Coast), first coined in 1912, described the five southern coastal Roussillon villages: Argelès-sur-Mer, Collioure, Port Vendres, Banyuls-sur-Mer and Cerbère.
3. The Contemporary Art Society, UK, Annual Report, List of Purchases, 1911.
4. Rowan, Eric, and Stewart, Carolyn, *An Elusive Tradition: Art and Society in Wales 1870–1950*, University of Wales Press, Cardiff, 2002, p.75; Fairclough, Oliver, Hoozee, Robert, and Verdickt, Caterina (eds), *Art in Exile: Flanders, Wales and the First World War*, Pandora, Antwerp, 2002, p.28. In 1914 Lees likely stayed at the cottage Lord Howard de Walden had purchased for Augustus John, Joseph Holbrooke and friends to use: personal communication with Thomas Seymour (Lord Howard de Walden's grandson), 2024.
5. 'Summer Exhibition of Modern Art at the Goupil Gallery', *Apollo*, 14(80), 1 Aug 1931, p.124.

6. King, Averil, 'Man of the Mountains', *Country Life*, 2 Mar 2016, p.62; Davies, Brian, op.cit., pp 1–8; Rowan, Eric, *Some Miraculous Promised Land*, Mostyn Gallery, Llandudno, 1982, p.4.
7. Morris, Richard (Morris & Son, Woodbridge, Suffolk), personal communication, 2024, unpublished letter from Derwent Lees to [?], c.1911–13 (courtesy of private collector).
8. Scott-Ellis, Margherita, Lady Howard de Walden, *Pages from My Life*, Sidgwick and Jackson, London, 1965, p.139.
9. Newton, Eric, 'Pre-War Romanticism: John, Innes and Lees', *The Sunday Times*, 12 Feb 1939, p.10.
10. Skipwith, Peyton, 'Adrian Allinson. A Restless Talent', *The Connoisseur*, 1978, pp 264–73; *A Century of British Art: 1900–1945*, exh.cat., Chris Beetles Gallery, London, Sep 2021.
11. Hoole, John, and Simons, Margaret, op.cit., p.22.
12. Tate Archive, Slade, Frank, op.cit., p.2.
13. ibid.; Hoole, John, and Simons, Margaret, op.cit., p.131.
14. Tate Archive, Slade, Frank, op.cit., p.5.
15. Hoole, John, and Simons, Margaret, op.cit., p.134.
16. Murray, Peter, 'Behind the Lines', *Art Lives*, 2014, pp 120–21; Nora and Gerald Summers's descendants, personal communication, 2022.
17. Schwabe, Randolph, 1943, op.cit., p.6.
18. Sériziat, Charles-Victor-Émile, and Soulier, Paul, op.cit., pp 100–1.
19. Hoole, John, and Simons, Margaret, op.cit., p.141.
20. Hind, C. Lewis, *Landscape Painting, from Giotto to the Present Day*, Scribner, New York, 1924, pp 301–2.
21. Hoole, John, and Simons, Margaret, op.cit., p.143.
22. *The Hampshire Advertiser and Southampton Times*, 12 Oct 1935, p.5.
23. Hoole, John, and Simons, Margaret, op.cit., p.143.
24. ibid., p.99.
25. Hone, Joseph, op.cit., p.75.
26. Vetterlein-Marsenach, France, and Vetterlein, Ulrich, *Banyuls-sur-Mer: quand un village se raconte*, Les Presses Littéraires, Saint-Estève, 2010, p.210, text translated from the original French work.
27. Holroyd, Michael, 1997, op.cit., pp 395–6; Holroyd, Michael, 1975, op.cit., letter from Augustus John to John Quinn, Feb 1913, pp 421–2.
28. John, Augustus, 1952, op.cit., p.205.
29. Holroyd, Michael, 1975, op.cit., letter from Augustus John to John Quinn, Feb 1913, p.422.
30. ibid.

8. REACHING HIS PEAK

1. Quinn, John, *Collection of Paintings, Water Colors, Drawings and Sculpture*, Pidgeon Hill Press, New York, 1926, p.20.
2. Daplyn, A.J., *Australasian Art Review*, 1 May 1899, p.14.
3. *The Blue Review: Literature, Drama, Art, Music*, 1(1), May 1913, p.43b.
4. Derwent Lees's descendants, personal communication and family photographs, 2021–4.
5. Tate Archive, letter from Derwent Lees to Duncan Grant, 28 Jan 1912, TGA 20078/1/333.
6. Zander, Alleyne, *The Herald* (Melbourne), 18 Jun 1932, p.22.
7. Marks, Arthur, 'A Sign and a Shop Sign', *British Art Journal*, 13(1), 2012, pp 18–36.
8. *Rhythm: Art Music Literature Monthly*, 2(14), 1913, p.47.
9. Trelawney exhibited these paintings at the Chenil Gallery London, see *Paintings by Alfred P. Allinson and T. Dayrell-Reed and also others*, exh.cat., London, May 1915.
10. *The Athenaeum*, 17 May 1913, p.566.
11. Christian, Jessica, *Wyn George: Traveller and Artist*, Dovecote Press, Wimborne, 2013, p.25.
12. Falk, Peter, *Who Was Who in American Art*, Sound View Press, Madison, CT, 1985, p.184; Fielding, Mantle, *Mantle Fielding's Dictionary of American Painters*, ed. Glenn Opitz, Apollo, Poughkeepsie, NY, 1986, p.255.
13. Clarke, Gill, 2016, op.cit., p.151.
14. Victoria, Australia, Public Records Office, Wills and Probate Records, 1913, no.552, William Lees.
15. Clarke, Gill, 2016, op.cit., p.192.
16. Tate Archive, Slade, Frank, op.cit., p.4.
17. Holroyd, Michael, 1997, op.cit., pp 343–4.
18. *The Strand Magazine*, 29(172), Apr 1905, pp 411–13.

9. MARRIAGE AND SOUTH AGAIN

1. New York Public Library, USA, Archives & Manuscripts, John Quinn Letterbooks, 1902–24, letter from Augustus John to John Quinn, 8 May 1913.
2. District of St Pancras, London, England, Marriage Records, 21 Jul 1913, no.115, Lees and Price.
3. National Library of Wales, letter from J.D. Innes to Augustus John, 4 Aug 1913, NLW 2278 1D, fols 143–5; Hoole, John, and Simons, Margaret, op.cit., p.154.
4. National Galleries Scotland, biography of William Strang, online at www.nationalgalleries.org/art-and-artists/features/william-strang, accessed 2024; Macmillan, Duncan, 'William Strang | William Morris', *The Scotsman, Arts and Culture*, 1 Nov 2014, online at www.scotsman.com/arts-and-culture/visual-arts-review-william-strang-william-morris-1521878, accessed 2024.
5. Tate Archive, letter from Augustus John to James Bolivar Manson, 14 Nov 1913, TGA 806/1/445, p.2.
6. National Library of Wales, letter from J.D. Innes to Augustus John, 4 Aug 1913, NLW 2278 1D, fols 143–5; Hoole, John, and Simons, Margaret, op.cit., p.154.
7. *The Athenaeum*, 4495, 20 Dec 1913, p.734.
8. *The Yorkshire Evening Post*, 1 Apr 1914, p.5; *Sheffield Daily Telegraph*, 2 Apr 1914, p.7.
9. Holroyd, Michael, 1975, op.cit., p.420.
10. Schwabe, Randolph, 1943, op.cit., p.9.
11. Helmreich, Anne, and Holt, Ysanne, op.cit., p.51.
12. Newton, Eric, op.cit., p.10.
13. Huneker, James, *Ivory Apes and Peacocks*, Charles Scribner & Sons, New York, 1915, p.260.
14. Schwabe, Randolph, 1943, op.cit., p.9.
15. *The Westminster Gazette*, 25 May 1914, p.3.
16. UCL Art Museum, letter from Rex Nan Kivell to the Slade School, 18 Apr 1952, LDUCS-5519.
17. Wickham, Annette, 'Art History 101: What is a Cartoon?', *Royal Academy of Arts*, London, 1 Sep 2015, online at www.royalacademy.org.uk/article/daniel-maclise-what-is-a-cartoon, accessed June 2022.
18. *The Athenaeum*, 4451, 15 Feb 1913, p.13.
19. National Library of Ireland, letter from Donald Maclaren to Sir Hugh Lane, 27 Nov 1912, MS 35,823/6/4/5.
20. UCL Art Museum, letter from Rex Nan Kivell to the Slade School, 18 Apr 1952, LDUCS-5519.
21. Schwabe, Randolph, unpublished diary entry, 17 Jan 1947 (courtesy of Gill Clarke).
22. Holroyd, Michael, 1997, op.cit., p.201.
23. Tate Archive, Holroyd, Michael, Research Notes 1910–23, TAM 21C, no.123.
24. 'Gieves Gallery Exhibition', *The Times*, 8 Nov 1928, p.14.
25. Hannah and Fred Mayor's descendants, personal communication, 2022–3.
26. *Evening Star* (Dunedin), 21721, 16 May 1934, p.2.
27. Van Gogh Museum, Amsterdam, Netherlands, letter from Paul Signac to Vincent van Gogh, 12 Apr 1889, online at vangoghletters.org, accessed May 2022.

10. JOY AND PAIN

1. Clarke, Gill, 2016, op.cit., p.204.
2. Nora and Gerald Summers's descendants, personal communication, 2022–4.
3. Gray, Anne, and Galbally, Ann, *The*

Edwardians: Secrets and Desires*, exh.cat., National Gallery of Australia, Canberra, 2004, p.48.

4. *Fitzwilliam Museum Cambridge Catalogue of Paintings*, v.III: *British School*, Cambridge University Press, Cambridge, 1960, p.151 – *Lyndra in Wales*, verso inscription: communication from Edith Lees to (Edward) Maurice Ingram, 1937.
5. Holroyd, Michael, 1997, op.cit., p.374.
6. Tate Archive, Holroyd, Michael, Research Notes 1910–23, TAM 21C, no.124; Lord Howard de Walden owned the Llwynythyl cottage: personal communication with Thomas Seymour (Lord Howard de Walden's grandson), 2024.
7. Tate Archive, Holroyd, Michael, Research Notes, 1910–23, TAM 21C, no.122, c.1913.
8. The Chenil Galleries, *Watercolour Drawings and Paintings by the late James Dickson Innes, Memorial Exhibition*, exh.cat., London, 1923, p.3; UK and Ireland, Incoming Passenger Lists, 1878–1960, Yeoward Line, *Andorinha*, Las Palmas to Liverpool, 28 Jun 1914, online at ancestry.com.
9. Fothergill, John, op.cit., p.6.
10. Tate Archive, Slade, Frank, op.cit.; John, Augustus, 1952, op.cit., pp 205–6.
11. County of Kent, England, Deaths in Sub-District of Farningham, Registration District Dartford, death certificate, James Dickson Innes, 22 Aug 1914, no.391.
12. Tate Archive, Slade, Frank, op.cit., p.6.
13. John, Augustus, 1975, op.cit., p.230.
14. UCL SC, Council Minutes, 1914–16, item 76, 12 Jan 1915, p.52, UCLCA/4.
15. *Darling Downs Gazette* (Queensland), 7 Jul 1915, p.4.
16. *The Athenaeum*, 4570, 29 May 1915, p.488.
17. Holroyd, Michael, 1997, op.cit., p.135; England and Wales, Electoral Registers, 1832–1932, Lower Bourton, 1905, online at ancestry.com; *The Early Years of the New English Art Club, 1886–1918*, 10 Jul–25 Aug 1952, exh.cat., City Museum and Art Gallery, Birmingham, 1952, *The Family of Sir Cyril Butler*, no.57, p.27.
18. Schwabe, Randolph, 1943, op.cit., p.9.
19. *The Studio*, 132, Oct 1946, p.116.
20. Tibbetts, Susan, 'Tom Hudson. A Study of his Vision for Art Education', PhD thesis, University of Huddersfield, England, 2014, p.14.
21. Schwabe, Randolph, 1943, op.cit., p.9.
22. Hoole, John, and Simons, Margaret, op.cit., p.51.
23. Llewellyn, Sacha, *Winifred Knights*, Lund Humphries, London, 2016, p.28, in UCL SC, Winifred Knights Correspondence, letter from Winifred Knights to Awdrey Clarke, 1915.
24. Eckersley, Rosanna, 'A Study of Winifred Knights 1915–1933', PhD thesis, University of East Anglia, England, 2015, p.43, in UCL SC, Winifred Knights Correspondence, letters from Winifred Knights to Awdrey Clarke 1915–16.
25. UCL SC, Winifred Knights Correspondence, letters from Winifred Knights to Awdrey Clarke, Oct [?] 1915.
26. Eckersley, Rosanna, op.cit., p.63.
27. Llewellyn, Sacha, op.cit., p.30.
28. Eckersley, Rosanna, op.cit., p.56.
29. *The Herald* (Melbourne), 18 Jun 1932, p.22.
30. Gough, Paul, *Gilbert Spencer: The Life and Work of a Very English Artist*, Yale University Press, New Haven, CT, 2024, p.41.
31. Lewis, Neville, *Studio Encounters: Some Reminiscences of a Portrait Painter*, Tafelberg-Uitgewers, Cape Town, 1963, pp 13–14, 18.
32. Schwabe, Randolph, unpublished diary entry, 25 Nov 1937 (courtesy of Gill Clarke).
33. UCL SC, Council Minutes, 1914–16, UC Committee Meeting, 2 Nov 1915, report of budget sub-committee, p.22, UCLCA/4, UC Committee Meeting, 4 Jul 1916, reports of the budget sub-committees, Item B, p.69, UCLCA/4.
34. ibid.
35. *The Athenaeum*, 4597, 4 Dec 1915, p.424.
36. *The London Evening Standard*, 13 Dec 1915, p.10.

11. THE DECLINE

1. Greaves, Leonard, *Journal of the Royal Society of Arts*, 4745, 1947, p.516.
2. ibid.
3. Miller, Lydia, 'Ambrose McEvoy (1877–1927): A "Painter of Excellence" Shaped by Artistic Influences', PhD thesis, University of York, England, 2021, p.61, in McEvoy Estate Papers, letter from Charles Cheston to Mrs Hett (Anna McEvoy), 3 Dec 1946.
4. Morris, Richard (Morris & Son, Woodbridge, Suffolk), personal communication, 2024, unpublished letter from Derwent Lees to Cyril Butler, 5 Jun 1916 (courtesy of private collector).
5. Butler, Richard A., Baron, *The Art of the Possible: The Memoirs of Lord Butler*, Hamish Hamilton, London, 1971, p.12.
6. Hone, Joseph, op.cit., p.125.
7. *The Athenaeum*, 4612, Dec 1916, p.613.
8. Butler, Richard A., op.cit., p.12.
9. *The Builder*, 112(3879), Jun 1917.
10. UCL SC, College Committee File 4, letter from Professor Brown to the Provost, 1917, UCLCA/4.
11. UCL SC, Council Minutes, Item 163 (and Appendix III), 5 Jun 1917, p.62, UCLCA/4.
12. UCL SC, Council Minutes, Item 7 (B), 17 Oct 1917, p.4, UCLCA/4.
13. UCL SC, College Committee File 4, letter from Professor Brown to the Provost, 1917, UCLCA/4.
14. Lilly, Marjorie, op.cit., p.116.
15. *The Field*, 1 Dec 1917, p.796.
16. UCL SC, Council Minutes, Item 126 (D), 5 Mar 1918, p.37, UCLCA/4.
17. National Trust UK, Chirk Castle Guestbook, 1918. Earlier reports incorrectly placed Derwent at Chirk Castle in 1914, not January 1918, thus erroneously reporting the mental breakdown event prior to June 1917.
18. Lady Howard de Walden, op.cit., p.146.
19. The Howard de Walden Estate Document Archive, London, letters (1918; May 1918 incomplete) from Derwent Lees to Lady Howard de Walden, HDWF 6/106–107.
20. Mackrell, Judith, *Flappers: Six Women of a Dangerous Generation*, MacMillan, London, 2013, p.47.
21. Lady Howard de Walden, op.cit., p.146.
22. Seymour, Thomas, *My Grandfather, a Modern Medievalist*, National Trust, Swindon, 2012, p.22.
23. Lady Howard de Walden, op.cit., p.146.
24. ibid.
25. The Howard de Walden Estate Document Archive, London, letters (1918; May 1918 incomplete) from Derwent Lees to Lady Howard de Walden, HDWF 6/106–107.
26. ibid.
27. ibid.

12. THE ENCLOSED WORLD

1. Holroyd, Michael, 1997, op.cit., p.434.
2. ibid., p.397.
3. UCL SC, Council Minutes, Item 126 (D), 5 Mar 1918, p.37, UCLCA/4.
4. UCL SC, Council Minutes, Report by Prof. Henry Tonks, Appendix A, 4 Jun 1918, p.2, UCLCA/4.
5. Redbridge Museum and Heritage Centre, Claybury Hospital Records, List of Male Patients 1921–6.
6. De Laperriere, Charles Baile (ed.), *New English Art Club Exhibitors 1886–2001*, v.III: *L–Q*, Hilmarton Manor Press, Calne, 2002.
7. *The Print Collector's Quarterly*, 18(3), Jul 1931, p.280, entry 136, *A Man Etching*.
8. Morris, Richard (Morris & Son, Woodbridge, Suffolk), personal communication, 2024, unpublished letter from Christopher Nevinson to Augustus John, Jul (?) 1913 (courtesy of private collector).
9. Holroyd, Michael, 1975, op.cit., letter from Augustus John to John Quinn, Feb 1913, pp 421–2.
10. St Pancras, London, England, Workhouse Admission and Discharge Records, 1764–1930, arrival 21 Nov 1919, discharge

3 Dec 1919, online at ancestry.com.
11. ibid.
12. Redbridge Central Library, England, Claybury Mental Hospital, List of Male Patients admitted.
13. Newton, Eric, op.cit., p.10.
14. *Personal Notes from Home*, lix(17770), 23 May 1923, p.2.
15. Surrey History Centre, England, West Park Hospital, Male alphabetical register, Jun 1924–Dec 1962, ref.7329/1/1, Admission register, 24 Jun 1924–6 Jan 1931, ref.6366/5/7, Male patients medical register, transfers nos 1–1581, 1924–7, ref.6423/7/7, Civil register, Jun 1924–Jan 1925, ref.6294/7/9.
16. Johnson, Bryan, *West Park Hospital Epsom, Surrey: The First Sixty Years*, London, 1969, p.2.
17. UK and Ireland, Outward Passenger Lists, 1890–1960, Cunard Line, *Aquitania*, 1 Sep 1923, Southampton, online at ancestry.com.
18. *The Guardian*, 30 Dec 1927, p.4.
19. *Architectural Review*, 55, 1 Mar 1924, p.328.
20. Western Australia, Crew and Passenger Lists at Fremantle from London, *Orama*, 28 Jul 1925, online at ancestry.com.
21. Johnson, Bryan, op.cit., p.5.
22. UCL SC, Letters to and from Edith Lees, Ambrose McEvoy and Koe Child, 1926, UCLCA/4/1/2/2/1.
23. ibid.
24. ibid.

13. END AND AFTERMATH

1. *The Telegraph* (Brisbane, Queensland), 30 Nov 1928, p.14; 6 Apr 1929, p.13.
2. 'Gieves Gallery Exhibition', *The Times*, 8 Nov 1928, p.14.
3. UK and Ireland, Outward Passenger Lists, 1890–1960, *Baradine*, 10 Aug 1929, Liverpool, online at ancestry.com.
4. *The Observer*, 13 Apr 1930, p.14.
5. *The Connoisseur*, Jan–Jun 1930, p.400.
6. Carey, Frances, Griffiths, Anton, and Coppel, Stephen, *Avant-Garde British Printmaking*, British Museum, London, 1990, p.21.
7. Williams, Nathaniel, 'Sir Rex Nan Kivell and the NLA Collection' [interview transcript], National Library of Australia, 8 Apr 2019.
8. Registration District Epsom, Surrey, England, Records of Death, 28 Mar 1931, Derwent Lees.
9. Horton Cemetery records, courtesy of Stephen R. Johnson, The Friends of Horton Cemetery and the Reverend Vicar, Horton Parish, Epsom, Surrey, England.
10. *The Studio*, 104, Jul–Dec 1932, pp 236–7; Redfern Gallery, *Augustus John, J.D. Innes, Derwent Lees Paintings 1910–1914*, Feb–Mar 1939, exh.cat., Redfern Gallery, London, 1939, p.5; Redfern Gallery, *Memorial Exhibition Derwent Lees*, Apr–May 1934, exh.cat., Redfern Gallery, London, 1934; *Art in Australia*, Feb 1933, pp 22–4; *Illustrated Catalogue of the Loan Collection of Contemporary British Art*, 31 May–30 Jun 1935, exh.cat., Brown Prior & Co., Melbourne, 1935, p.21; Deutsher Galleries, *Colonial and Impressionist Paintings*, exh.cat., Deutsher Galleries, Armadale, Melbourne, 1978, p.1.
11. Surrey History Centre, England, West Park Hospital, Male alphabetical register, Jun 1924–Dec 1962, ref.7329/1/1, Admission register, 24 Jun 1924–6 Jan 1931, ref.6366/5/7, Male patients medical register, transfers nos 1–1581, 1924–7, ref.6423/7/7, Civil register, Jun 1924–Jan 1925, ref.6294/7/9, Register of deaths, male, 1 Jan 1931–2 May 1939, ref.6366/5/17; Draaisma, Douwe, 'Lithium: The Gripping History of a Psychiatric Success Story', *Nature*, 572, 29 Aug 2019, pp 584–5; Pope, Harrison, and Lipinski, Joseph, 'Diagnosis in Schizophrenia and Manic-Depressive Illness', *Archives of General Psychiatry*, 35, 1978, pp 811–28; personal communication with medical physicians, 2022–4.
12. Clarke, Gill, 2016, op.cit., p.192.
13. Randwick City Council, New South Wales, Australia, Local Studies Library records, 2022.
14. *Grenfell Record & Lachlan District Advertiser*, 22 Jun 1910, p.2; *The Sunday Sun* (Sydney), 19 Jun 1910, p.5; Sydney, Australia, Registers of Coroners Inquests, 1903–11, James Harcourt Lees.
15. Dome, Peter, Rihmer, Zoltan, and Gonda, Xenia, 'Suicide Risk in Bipolar Disorder: A Brief Review', *Medicina*, 55 (8), Jul 2024, p.403.
16. *The West Australian* (Perth), 25 May 1931, p.1.
17. Collins, Yolande, and Kippen, Sandra, 'A Social Disease with Medical Aspects', *Journal of Australasian Mining History*, 6, 2008, pp 70–89.
18. Personal communication with, and site visits by, Stephen R. Johnson, The Friends of Horton Cemetery and the Reverend Vicar, Horton Parish, Epsom, Surrey, England.
19. Surrey History Centre, England, West Park Hospital, Register of deaths, male, 1 Jan 1931–2 May 1939, ref.6366/5/17.
20. Personal communication with, and site visits by, Stephen R. Johnson, The Friends of Horton Cemetery and the Reverend Vicar, Horton Parish, Epsom, Surrey, England.
21. *The Stage*, 23 Feb 1906; England, Census, 1911, Corne, online at ancestry.com; England and Wales, Electoral Registers, 1832–1932, 45 Philbeach Gardens, London, 1931, 1932, online at ancestry.com; 'Will of Joseph Chambers', signed Blackpool, 7 Oct 1920, online at ancestry.com; various British newspaper clippings (subject Corne).
22. UCL SC, letter from Edith Lees to Slade Professor Schwabe, 27 Apr 1932, UCLCA/4/1/2/2/1.
23. *News* (Adelaide), 29 Nov 1933, p.4; *The Herald* (Melbourne), 24 May 1934, p.30.
24. Schwabe, Randolph, unpublished diary entry, 8 Apr 1935 (courtesy of Gill Clarke); Clarke, Gill, 2016, op.cit., p.196.
25. *Nottingham Journal*, 26 Sep 1939, p.2.
26. Gordon, Jan, 'Art in War-Time', *Liverpool Daily Post*, 3 Oct 1939.
27. Southampton City Art Gallery, England, Lees file, letter from Edith Lees to the Gallery, Dec 1949.
28. *The Daily Telegraph* (Sydney), 20 Apr 1933, p.5; *The Herald* (Melbourne), 24 May 1934, p.30, and 21 Mar 1933, p.2; *Art in Australia*, 3rd series, 49, 15 Apr 1933, p.7.
29. *The Daily Telegraph* (Sydney), 20 Apr 1933, p.5.
30. *The Bulletin*, 26 Apr 1933, p.29; *Sydney Mail*, 3 May 1933, p.14.
31. *The Sydney Morning Herald*, 5 Aug 1939, p.11.
32. *The Sunday Times*, 5792, 15 Apr 1934, p.7.
33. Roosevelt, Theodore, 'Citizenship in a Republic' [speech], Sorbonne, Paris, France, 23 Apr 1910.

CATALOGUE RAISONNÉ

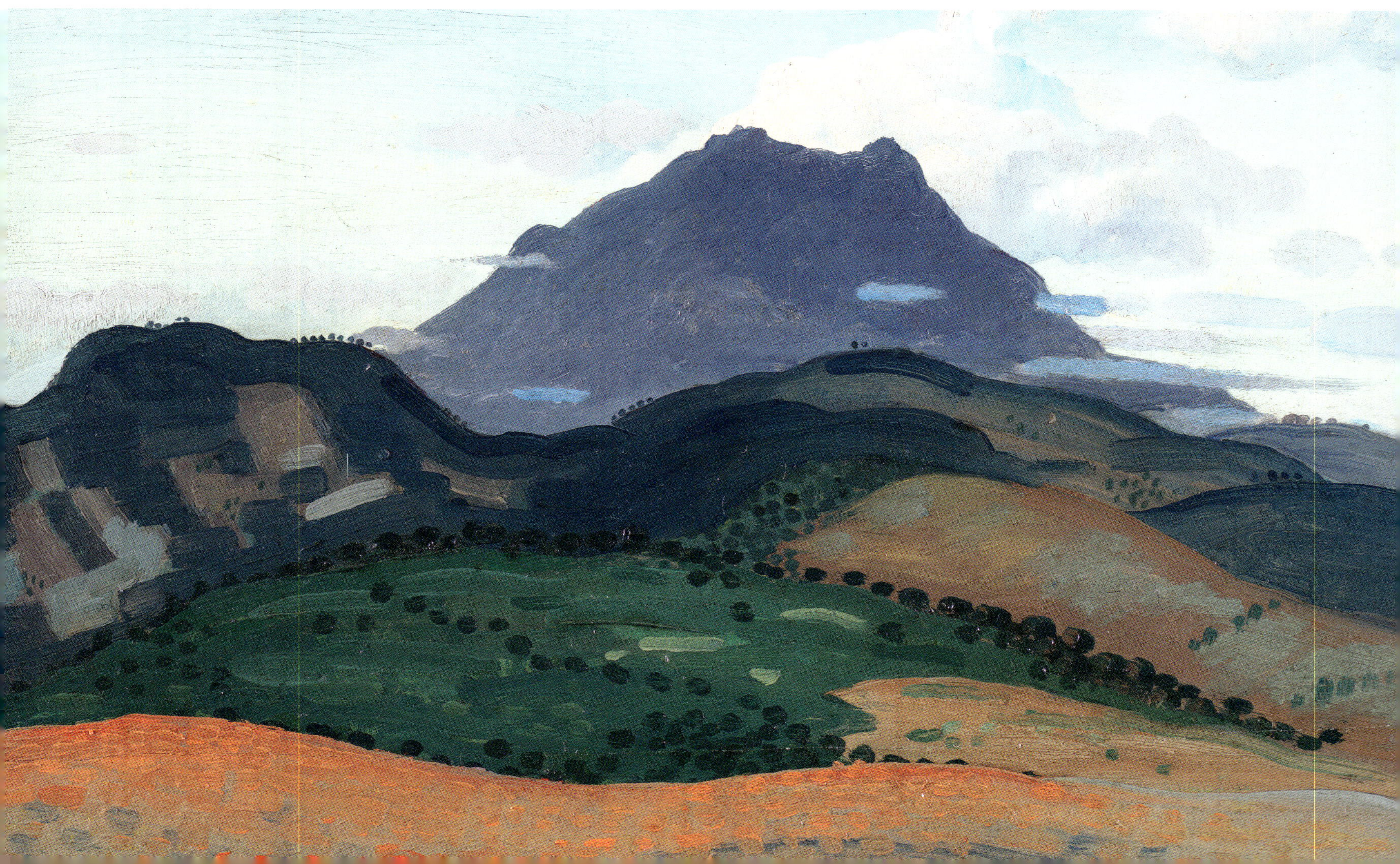

This catalogue is an annotated listing of Derwent Lees's known artworks based on the best available evidence. A multidisciplinary approach has resulted in a wealth of documentary material and evidence to support the catalogue records. These entry records have been derived from detailed examination of the works, their provenance and inscriptions, digital mapping, on-site visits, and extensive use of literature (books, articles), archival (memoirs, photographs, letters) and other primary source materials (including exhibition catalogues).

There are more than 450 known works by Derwent Lees, of which two thirds remain in private collections. Tracing information about these, and the works on paper, continues to be a challenge. Previously 'unseen' works will undoubtedly appear on the market and the catalogue will expand as new works and information become available. The catalogue is dynamic and future research may result in amending or merging some records, as many works were given generic titles or titles that changed through time. Particular difficulties occur where multiple works (on the same medium and with similar dimensions) have been given indistinguishable or the same titles.

All works have been assessed against established inclusion criteria based on demonstrable provenance and exhibition history; congruity of subject, style, palette, inscriptions, locations and dates; consistency with biographic events; and ordination and correlation of dimensions, media and inscription, by date.

My heartfelt thanks to Peter Davies for his exhaustive work on landscape geolocation, data compilation and analysis, and assistance with the catalogue.

Thank you to John Hoole for his generosity in warmly sharing his art history knowledge and research of James Dickson Innes and his works, and for working collaboratively to resolve and reattribute several 'Innes–Lees' artworks. Peter and John – I much enjoyed the rich, and often revelatory, exchange of ideas around 'Innes–Lees' travels, works and geolocation.

Corrections and additions to the catalogue are welcome.

DL12.22 (detail)
Derwent Lees, *Tour Madeloc in the Pyrenees / In the Pyranees*, 1912

GUIDE TO CATALOGUE RECORDS

All works have been assigned a unique identifier (*DLyy.nn*). DL signifies the work was created by Derwent Lees, *yy* signifies the 20th-century year (or first of a year range) in which the work was created, *nn* is the unique number within year or year range of creation.

*DLyy.nn** indicates that no image has been traced.

*DLyy.nn*** indicates that a work has not been illustrated for image quality reasons, despite an image having been traced.

The title is either the earliest assigned title (often by Lees) or a new title when an incorrect or highly misleading one has been given. Many commissioned works were not given formal titles. Variant titles are included.

Dates of works are those inscribed by Lees or, where absent, are assigned based on all available evidence, with an estimated year or year range provided. Previously assigned incorrect year dates have been excluded.

ins: denotes known inscriptions and signatures on the work with the position abbreviated as: l.l., l.r., l.c., l.c.r., c.l., c.r., u.l., u.c., u.r., v. (respectively, lower left, lower right, lower centre, lower centre right, centre left, centre right, upper left, upper centre, upper right, on verso).

Dimensions are presented as height x width. These often vary depending on how a work has been measured (unframed, framed, mount depth, folded paper, etc.), with those deemed the most appropriate cited.

prov: and *exh:* provide the provenance and the exhibition history. Some gaps exist in sales and exhibition records. Records of auction sales or sale-exhibitions are recorded in the provenance. Exhibition history includes exhibitions by public institutions and the principal commercial galleries and dealers of Lees's works. Key literature is included in a few records.

notes: give any additional information, including:

Reattributed denotes works reattributed against the inclusion criteria, mostly between Derwent Lees and James Dickson Innes (JDI), and in consultation with John Hoole (Hoole, John, and Simons, Margaret, *James Dickson Innes (1887–1914)*, Lund Humphries, London, 2013).

Unresolved record denotes that no image has been traced and there is insufficient data to determine whether it is a unique work or should be merged with an existing record.

(?) denotes uncertain record data.

[ ] denotes supplementary information.

CATALOGUE IMAGES

More than 280 reproductions of Derwent Lees's artworks are included. They are ordered by DL identifier and mostly placed near their corresponding catalogue record. Where images appear in the biographic section, the relevant page number is noted in the catalogue record. Not all images could be included in this publication.

INSTITUTIONS AND PEOPLE ABBREVIATIONS

The names of institutions and people may vary according to the year the work was purchased or exhibited.

Bridget McDonnell Gallery	Bridget McDonnell Gallery, Carlton, Victoria, Australia
Butler, Cyril K.	Also C.K. Butler, Cyril Kendall Butler and Sir Cyril K. Butler, KBE
CAS	Contemporary Art Society, London
Chenil Gallery	Chenil Gallery London, including the New Chenil Galleries
Christie's London/ Melbourne	Christie's London or Melbourne, including Christie, Manson & Woods
Deutscher/Deutsher	Deutscher Fine Art, including Deutsher Galleries, Deutscher and Hackett, Melbourne
Ingram, Maurice	Also Edward Maurice Berkeley Ingram, CMG, OBE
JDI	James Dickson Innes
Laing	Laing Art Gallery, Newcastle upon Tyne
Lyndra	Also known as Edith Ashley, Edith Price, Edith Lees, Mrs Edith Lees
NEAC	The New English Art Club, London
NGV	National Gallery of Victoria, Melbourne
RISD	The Museum of Art, Rhode Island School of Design, Rhode Island
Sotheby's	Sotheby's, including Sotheby's & Co., Sotheby and Company, Sotheby Parke Bernet, London (Sussex, New York, Melbourne and Olympia, London rooms are also noted)
Spink	Spink, including Spink & Son Ltd, London and Sydney
Tate	Tate, including Tate Britain and Tate Modern, formerly Tate Gallery, National Gallery of British Art, Millbank
Thos. Agnew & Sons	Thos. Agnew & Sons, London, including Thomas Agnew & Sons, London
UCL Art Museum	University College London Art Museum, Gower Street, London
V&A	Victoria and Albert Museum, London

SELECTED EXHIBITION AND CLUB ABBREVIATIONS

The names of the institutions are consistent with the year in which the work was purchased or exhibited.

NEAC 39th 1907	NEAC, London, *39th Exhibition of Modern Pictures*, autumn 1907
NEAC 41st 1909	NEAC, London, *41st Exhibition of Modern Pictures*, May 1909
NEAC 42nd 1909	NEAC, London, *42nd Exhibition of Modern Pictures*, winter 1909
NEAC 43rd 1910	NEAC, London, *43rd Exhibition of Modern Pictures*, summer 1910
NEAC 44th 1910	NEAC, London, *44th Exhibition of Modern Pictures*, winter 1910
NEAC 45th 1911	NEAC, London, *45th Exhibition of Modern Pictures*, summer 1911
Armory Show	Association of American Painters and Sculptors, 69th Regiment Armory, New York, Chicago, Boston, *International Exhibition of Modern Art*, Feb–May 1913
Chenil 1913	The Chenil Gallery, London, Apr–May 1913
NEAC 49th 1913	NEAC, London, *49th Exhibition of Modern Pictures*, summer 1913
Chenil 1913–14	The Chenil Gallery, London, *Drawings by Augustus John, Paintings by Derwent Lees and other Works*, Dec 1913–Jan 1914
Whitechapel 1914	Whitechapel Art Gallery, London, *Twentieth Century Art. A Review of Modern Movements*, May–Jun 1914
NEAC 51st 1914	NEAC, London, *51st Exhibition of Modern Pictures*, Jun–Jul 1914
NEAC 52nd 1914	NEAC, London, *52nd Exhibition of Modern Pictures*, winter 1914
Chenil 1915	The Chenil Gallery, London, *Paintings by Alfred P. Allinson and T. Dayrell-Reed and also others*, 1915
NEAC 53rd 1915	NEAC, London, *53rd Exhibition of Modern Pictures*, spring 1915
NEAC 54th 1915	NEAC, London, *54th Exhibition of Modern Pictures*, Dec 1915
NEAC 55th 1916	NEAC, London, *55th Exhibition of Modern Pictures*, summer 1916
NEAC 56th 1916–17	NEAC, London, *56th Exhibition of Modern Pictures*, winter 1916
NEAC 57th 1917	NEAC, London, *57th NEAC Exhibition*, summer 1917
NEAC 58th 1917	NEAC, London, *58th NEAC Exhibition*, winter 1917
Goupil 1922	The Goupil Gallery, London, *The Goupil Gallery Salon*, Nov–Dec 1922
NEAC 1925	NEAC, *Retrospective Exhibition 1886–1924*, Manchester, Jan–Feb; London, Apr–May 1925
Goupil 1926	The Goupil Gallery, London, *The Goupil Gallery Salon*, Oct–Nov 1926
Quinn 1927	American Art Association, New York, *Paintings and Sculptures: The Renowned Collection of Modern and Ultra-Modern Art formed by the late John Quinn*, sale and exhibition, Feb 1927
Slade 1927	University College London, Slade School of Art, London, *Centenary Celebrations, Exhibition of Works of Art by Teachers and Students of The Slade School 1871–1927*, Jun–Jul 1927
Redfern 1930a	The Redfern Gallery, London, *Derwent Lees Retrospective Exhibition*, Apr 1930
Goupil 1930	The Goupil Gallery, London, *The Goupil Gallery Salon*, Nov 1930
Redfern 1930b	The Redfern Gallery, London, *Oils by Contemporary Artists*, Dec 1930–Jan 1931
Redfern 1931a	The Redfern Gallery, London, *Contemporary Artists. Etchings, Drawings, Watercolours*, Feb 1931
Redfern 1931b	The Redfern Gallery, London, *British Watercolours and Drawings by Modern Artists*, Jun 1931
Goupil 1931a	The Goupil Gallery, London, *Summer Exhibition of Modern Art*, Jun 1931
Redfern 1931c	The Redfern Gallery, London, *Summer Salon*, Aug–Sep 1931
Goupil 1931b	The Goupil Gallery, London, *The Goupil Gallery Salon*, Nov 1931

Redfern 1932	Redfern Gallery, London, *Recent Contemporary Oils also the last Spirit Pictures by the late Charles Sims, R.A.*, Jun–Jul 1932
British Contemporary Art 1933	Clarice Zander (Redfern Gallery), *Exhibition of British Contemporary Art*, Newspaper House Melbourne; Blaxland Gallery Sydney, Mar–Apr 1933
Redfern 1933	The Redfern Gallery, London, *Colour Prints. Also Selected Oils by Matthew Smith, Walter Sickert, Derwent Lees, Cedric Morris, R.O. Dunlop, George Bissill, Basil Jonzen*, Jun–Jul 1933
Redfern 1934	The Redfern Gallery, London, *Derwent Lees 1885–1931 Retrospective Exhibition*, Apr–May 1934
Empire Art 1934–5	Empire Art Loans Collection Society, *The Loan Collection of Contemporary British Art*, New Zealand Jun–Jul 1934; Adelaide Feb 1935; Melbourne May–Jun 1935
Redfern 1935	The Redfern Gallery, London, *Summer Exhibition*, Jul–Sep 1935
Redfern 1937	The Redfern Gallery, London, *Watercolours and Drawings by R.O. Dunlop, Derwent Lees, Tom Nash, Anthony Slade, Ethel Walker, Clifford Web, Ethelbert White*, Mar 1937
Redfern 1938	The Redfern Gallery, London, *French and English Paintings, Watercolours and Drawings*, Jun 1938
Empire Art 1939	Empire Art Loans Collection Society, *Exhibition of 20th Century British Art, Collection J*, Adelaide, Perth, Sydney, Melbourne, Brisbane, 1939
Laing 1939	*Modern Drawings and Paintings Lent by Arthur Crossland Esquire*, Laing Art Gallery, Newcastle upon Tyne, 1939
Redfern 1939a	The Redfern Gallery, London, *Augustus John, J.D. Innes, Derwent Lees Paintings 1910–1914*, Feb–Mar 1939
Redfern 1939b	The Redfern Gallery, London, *French and English Pictures*, Mar–Apr 1939
Redfern 1939c	The Redfern Gallery, London, *French and English Pictures*, Apr–May 1939
Redfern 1939d	The Redfern Gallery, London, *Summer Exhibition*, Jul–Sep 1939
Stafford 1939	Stafford Gallery, London, *Watercolours and Drawings by Derwent Lees (from 1914 to 1918)*, Sep–Oct 1939
Redfern 1941a	The Redfern Gallery, London, *Summer Exhibition*, 1941
Redfern 1941b	The Redfern Gallery, London, *Exhibition of the Collection of Paintings formed by the late Maurice Ingram*, Oct 1941
Redfern 1943	The Redfern Gallery, London, *Summer Exhibition*, Aug–Sep 1943
Redfern 1944a	The Redfern Gallery, London, *Christopher Wood, V. Khmeluk, Derwent Lees*, Mar–Apr 1944
Redfern 1944b	The Redfern Gallery, London, *Summer Exhibition, French and English Paintings, Drawings, Prints*, 1944
Redfern 1945a	The Redfern Gallery, London, *Michael Ayrton, Christopher Wood, also French and English Paintings, Drawings, Prints*, Feb–Mar 1945
Redfern 1945b	The Redfern Gallery, London, *Summer Exhibition*, Jun–Sep 1945
Redfern 1946a	The Redfern Gallery, London, *Paintings and Drawings by English Artists 1895–1945*, Feb–Mar 1946
Redfern 1946b	The Redfern Gallery, London, *Summer Exhibition*, Jul–Sep 1946
Redfern 1946c	The Redfern Gallery, London, Nov 1946
Wakefield 1947–9	British Council, London, *Contemporary British Prints and Drawings selected from The Wakefield Collection*, Hobart, Melbourne, Adelaide, Perth, Australia, London, 1947; Hamilton, Waikato, Rotorua, Auckland, Wellington, Waipukurau, Takapuna, Dannevirke, Napier, Wanganui, New Zealand; Brisbane, Sydney, Australia, 1948; Suva, Fiji, Rotorua, New Zealand, 1949
Redfern 1947a	The Redfern Gallery, London, *Derwent Lees, Elsa Vaudrey, Michael Rothenstein, Bryan Wynter*, Apr–May 1947
Redfern 1947b	The Redfern Gallery, London, *Summer Exhibition*, Jul–Sep 1947
Redfern 1948	The Redfern Gallery, London, *Summer Exhibition*, Jul–Sep 1948
Redfern 1949	The Redfern Gallery, London, *Summer Exhibition*, Jun–Oct 1949
Birmingham City Gallery 1952	Birmingham City Museum and Art Gallery, *The Early Years of the New English Art Club, 1886–1918*, loaned by the Redfern Gallery, Jul–Aug 1952
Redfern 1952	The Redfern Gallery, London, *Summer Exhibition*, Jul–Aug 1952
Redfern 1954	The Redfern Gallery, London, *Summer Exhibition*, Jul–Aug 1954

Redfern 1955	The Redfern Gallery, London, *Summer Exhibition*, Jul–Aug 1955
Redfern 1958	The Redfern Gallery, London, *Patrick Heron, Derwent Lees, Paul Olds and The Abstract Influence 1910–1950*, Feb 1958
Redfern 1961	The Redfern Gallery, London, *Summer Exhibition*, Jun–Aug 1961
Redfern 1963	The Redfern Gallery, London, *Summer Exhibition*, Jun–Sep 1963
Redfern 1964	The Redfern Gallery, London, *Summer Exhibition*, 1964
Redfern 1966	The Redfern Gallery, London, *Summer Exhibition*, Jun–Sep 1966
Redfern 1967	The Redfern Gallery, London, *Summer Exhibition*, Jun–Sep 1967
Redfern 1968	The Redfern Gallery, London, *Summer Exhibition*, Jun–Sep 1968
Redfern 1969	The Redfern Gallery, London, *Summer Exhibition*, Jun–Sep 1969
Fine Art Society 1971	The Fine Art Society London, *The Slade Tradition 1871–1921: A Centenary Contribution*, Oct–Nov 1971
Deutsher 1978	Deutsher Galleries, Melbourne, *Derwent Lees (1885–1931)*, Nov–Dec 1978
Deutscher 1982	Deutscher Fine Art, Melbourne, *Colonial and Impressionist Paintings*, Mar–Apr 1982
Mostyn Art Gallery 1982–3	Mostyn Art Gallery, Llandudno and the Welsh Arts Council, *Some Miraculous Promised Land: J.D. Innes, Augustus John and Derwent Lees in North Wales 1910–1913*, Jul 1982–Jan 1983; and the Welsh Arts Council Gallery, Cardiff; the Mappin Art Gallery, Sheffield
Edwardian Art 1987	Stoke-on-Trent City Museum and Art Gallery, *An Exhibition from the Collections of the Cities of Bradford, Hull, and Stoke-on-Trent*, 1987
Sane 1997	Sane Australia, *Derwent Lees: The Forgotten Australian*, Carrick Hill Trust, Adelaide, Mar–Apr 1997; McClelland Gallery, Melbourne, May–Jun 1997; Sir Hermann Black Gallery, University of Sydney, Jul 1997; Customs House Gallery, University of Queensland, Brisbane, Aug–Oct 1997

1907

DL07.1
A Study of a Male Figure [left arm raised], 1907
ins: l.l.: D. Lees
Black chalk on paper
62.4 x 47.8 cm
prov: UCL Art Museum
notes: First Prize Figure Drawing

DL07.2
A Study of a Male Figure [walking to left, seen partly from behind], 1907
ins: l.r.: Lees
Black chalk on paper
61.5 x 47.2 cm
prov: UCL Art Museum
notes: First Prize Figure Drawing

DL07.3
A Study of a Male Figure / Standing Male Nude / Study of a Male Figure, Standing, Holding a Staff, 1907
ins: l.l.: Lees
Black chalk on paper
62.3 x 38.5 cm
prov: UCL Art Museum
exh: UCL Art Museum, Strang Print Room, Prized Drawings: A Selection from the Slade 1897–1953 Nov 2006–Mar 2007
notes: First Prize Figure Drawing

DL07.4
A Study of a Male Figure / Standing Male Nude, 1907
Black chalk on paper
57.4 x 38.2 cm
prov: UCL Art Museum
notes: First Prize Figure Drawing

DL07.5
A Study of a Male Figure [walking to right, right arm raised], 1907
ins: l.r.: D. Lees
Black chalk on paper [MBM France watermark]
62.6 x 44.5 cm
prov: UCL Art Museum
notes: First Prize Figure Drawing

DL07.6
A Study of a Male Figure, 1907
ins: l.l.: Lees
Black chalk on paper
62.2 x 48.8 cm
prov: UCL Art Museum
notes: First Prize Figure Drawing

DL07.7
A Study of a Male Figure [standing, arms folded, seen partly from behind], 1907
ins: l.l.: Lees; v.: [black chalk drawing]
Black chalk on paper
61.6 x 43 cm
prov: UCL Art Museum
notes: First Prize Figure Drawing

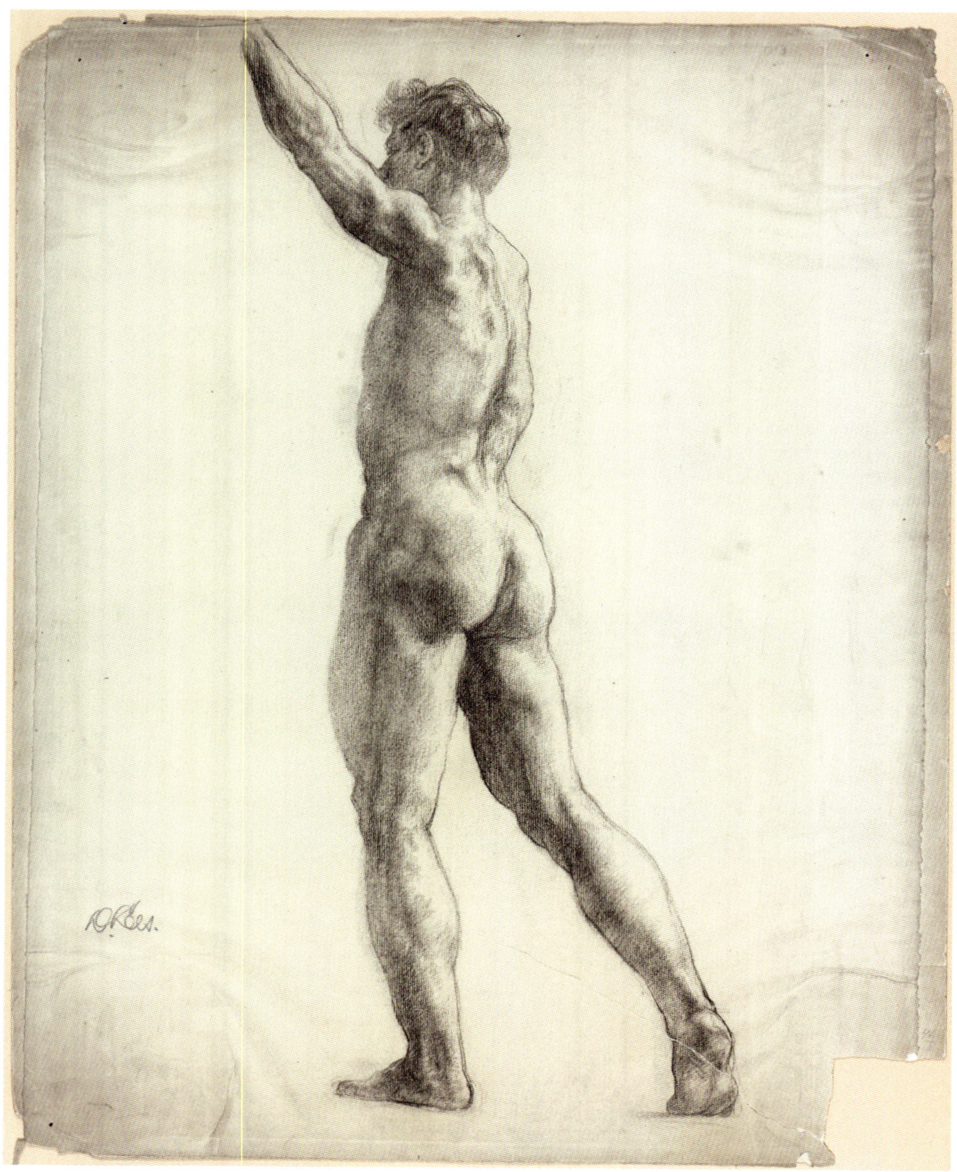

DL07.1

DL07.8
A Study of a Male Figure, 1907
ins: v.: [black chalk drawing]
Black chalk on paper
61.6 x 43 cm
prov: UCL Art Museum
notes: verso of DL07.7

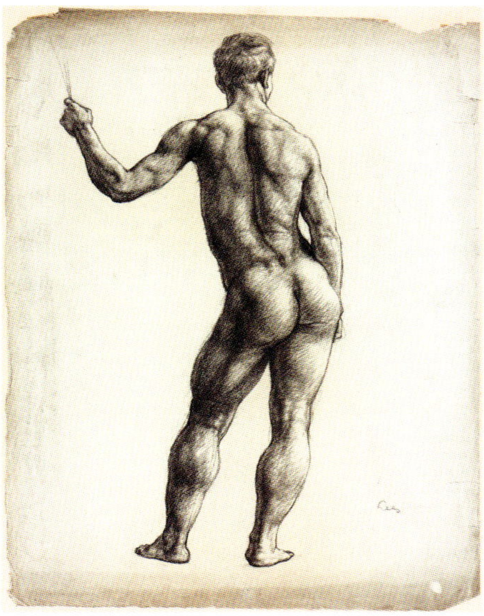

DL07.2

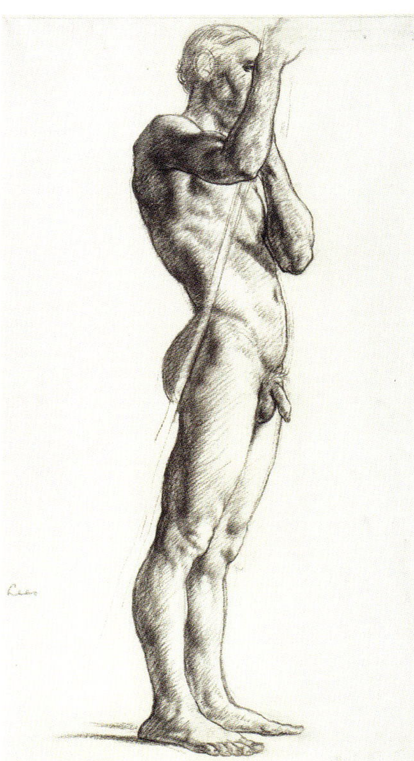

DL07.3

DL07.9
A Study of a Male Figure [standing, seen from behind, left hand to hip], 1907
Black chalk on paper
62.8 x 45 cm
prov: UCL Art Museum
notes: First Prize Figure Drawing

DL07.10
A Study of a Male Figure [standing, seen from behind, left leg bent], 1907
Black chalk on paper
61.4 x 49.7 cm
prov: UCL Art Museum
notes: First Prize Figure Drawing; in Slade School of Art, *The Slade: A Collection of Drawings and Some Pictures done by Past and Present Students of the London Slade School of Art mdccccxciii–mdccccvii*, Richard Clay & Sons, London, 1907, plate 72

DL07.11
A Study of a Male Figure [standing, facing, grasping staff], 1907
ins: u.l.: Lees; v.: [black and red chalk drawing]
Black chalk on paper [Michallet watermark]
62.5 x 43.5 cm
prov: UCL Art Museum
notes: First Prize Figure Drawing

DL07.12
Studies of a Crouching Figure, 1907
ins: v.: [black chalk drawing]
Black and red chalk on paper [Michallet watermark]
62.5 x 43.5 cm
prov: UCL Art Museum
notes: verso of DL07.11

DL07.13
A Study of a Male Figure [seated, seen partly from behind, and a small study of the same figure], 1907
ins: l.r.: D. Lees
Black chalk on paper [Michallet watermark]; Black ink [small study]
63 x 46 cm
prov: UCL Art Museum
notes: First Prize Figure Drawing

DL07.14
A Study of a Male Figure [seen from the side], 1907
ins: l.l.: Lees
Black chalk on paper [MBM watermark]
62.6 x 47.3 cm
prov: UCL Art Museum
notes: First Prize Figure Drawing

DL07.15
A Study of a Male Figure / Standing Male Nude, 1907
Black chalk on paper
60.6 x 29.5 cm
prov: UCL Art Museum
notes: First Prize Figure Drawing

DL07.16
A Study of a Female Figure [seated to right, seen partly from behind], 1907
ins: u.r.: Lees
Black chalk on paper
62.5 x 42 cm
prov: UCL Art Museum
notes: First Prize Figure Drawing

DL07.17
A Study of a Female Figure [seen from the side], 1907
ins: l.l.: Lees
Black chalk on paper
52.9 x 48 cm
prov: UCL Art Museum
notes: First Prize Figure Drawing

DL07.18
Study of a Female Figure / Standing Female Nude, 1907
ins: u.r.: Lees; v.: [black chalk drawing]
Black chalk on paper
62.2 x 41.3 cm
prov: UCL Art Museum
notes: First Prize Figure Drawing

DL07.19**
Study of a Seated Male Figure, 1907
ins: v.: [black chalk drawing]
Black chalk on paper
62.5 x 41.3 cm
prov: UCL Art Museum
notes: verso of DL07.18

DL07.20
A Study of a Female Figure [standing to left, arms raised], 1907
ins: l.r.: Lees
Black chalk on paper
62.3 x 47 cm
prov: UCL Art Museum
notes: First Prize Figure Drawing

DL07.21
Standing Male Nude, c.1907
ins: l.r.: Lees; v.: [red chalk drawing]
Black chalk on paper
62.9 x 48.5 cm
prov: UCL Art Museum

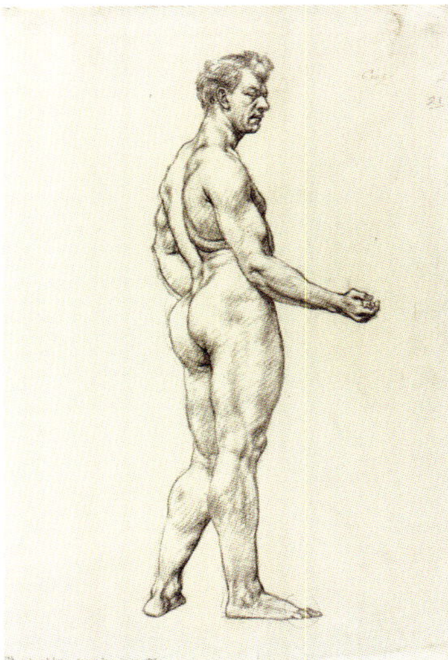

DL07.4

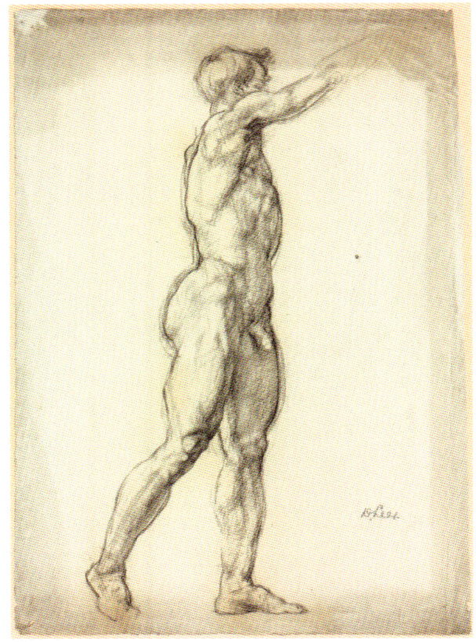

DL07.5

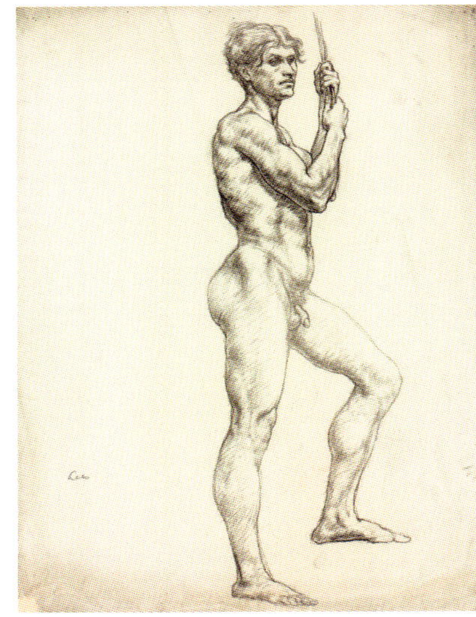

DL07.6

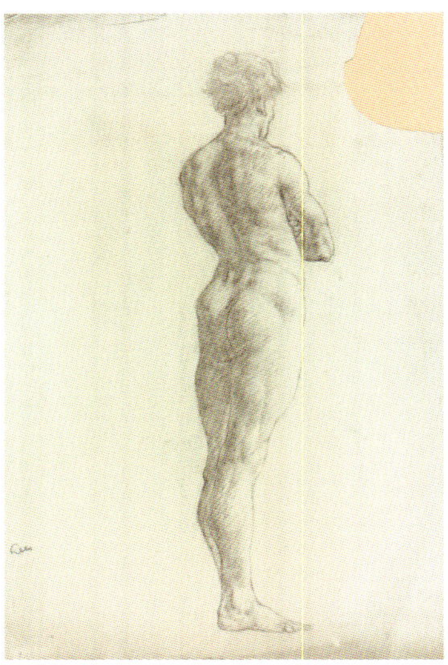

DL07.7

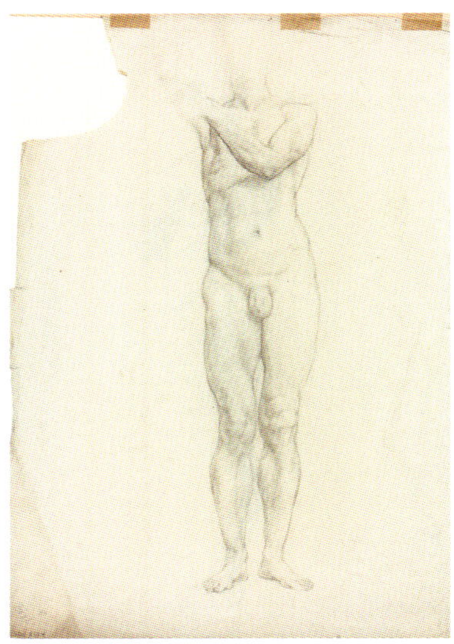

DL07.8

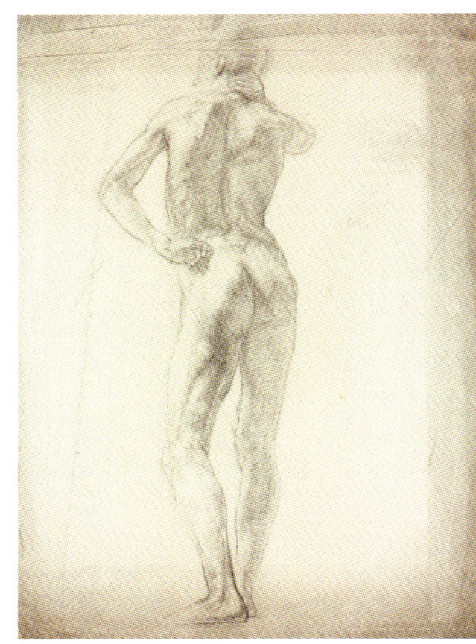

DL07.9

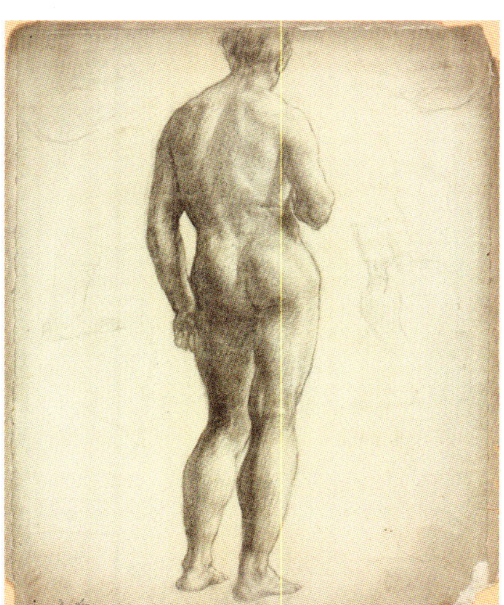

DL07.10

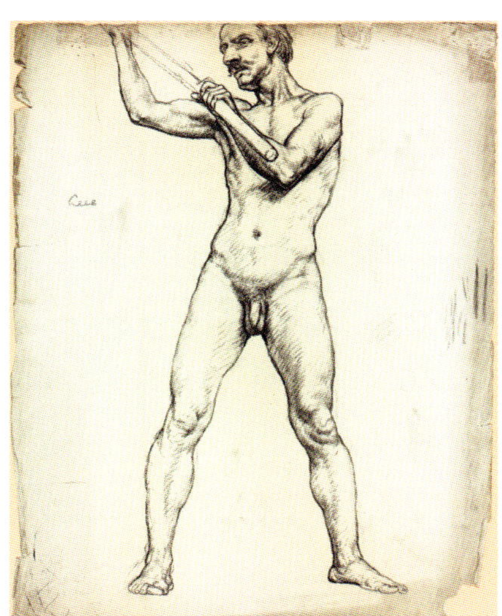

DL07.11

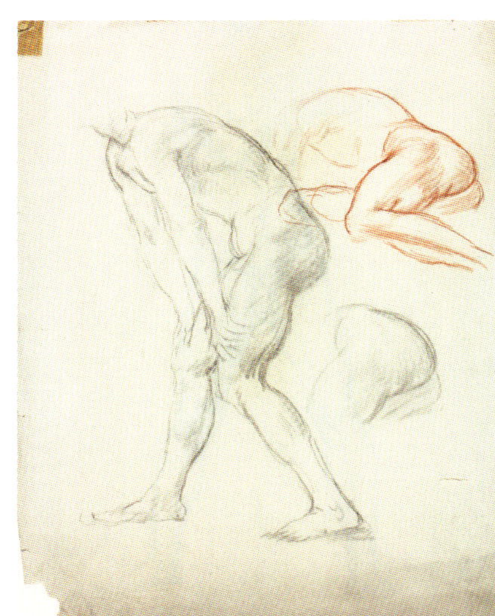

DL07.12

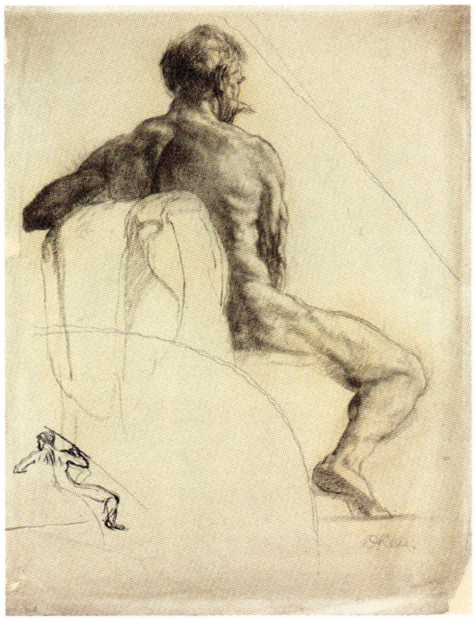

DL07.13

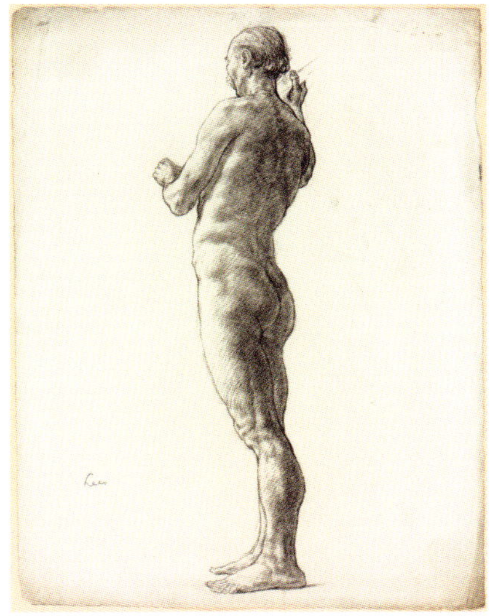

DL07.14

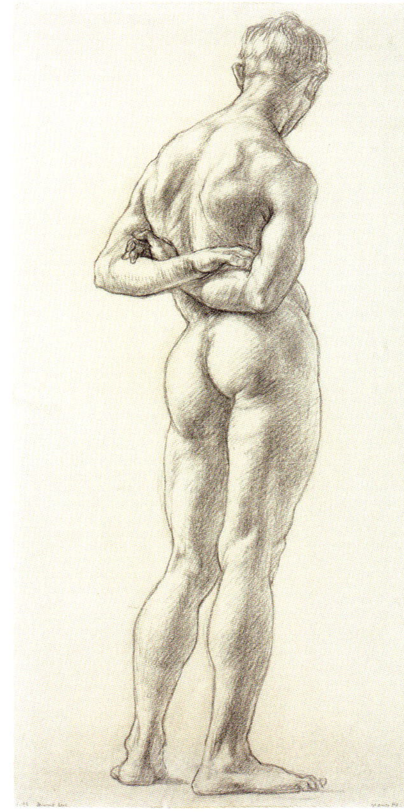

DL07.15

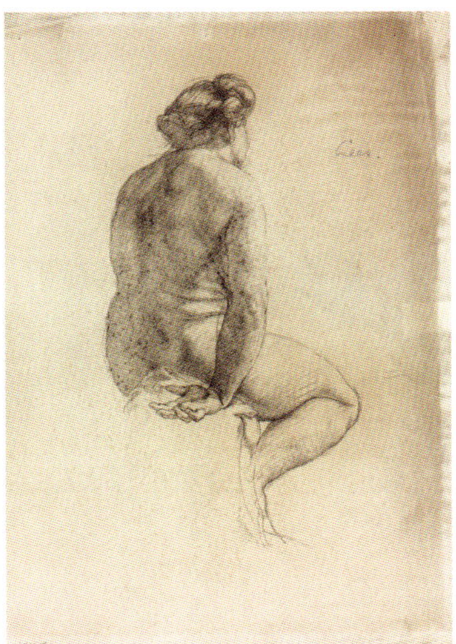

DL07.16

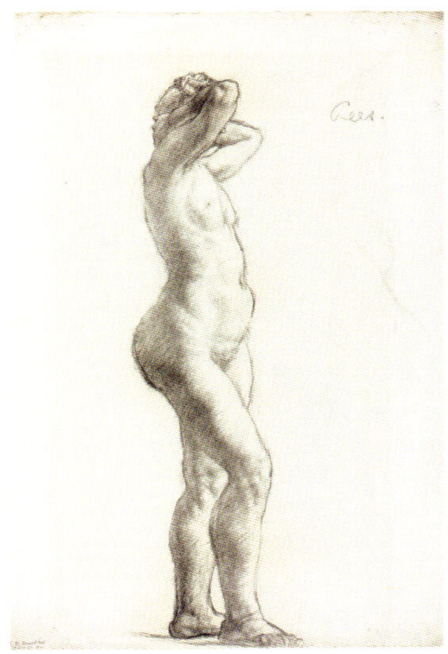

DL07.18

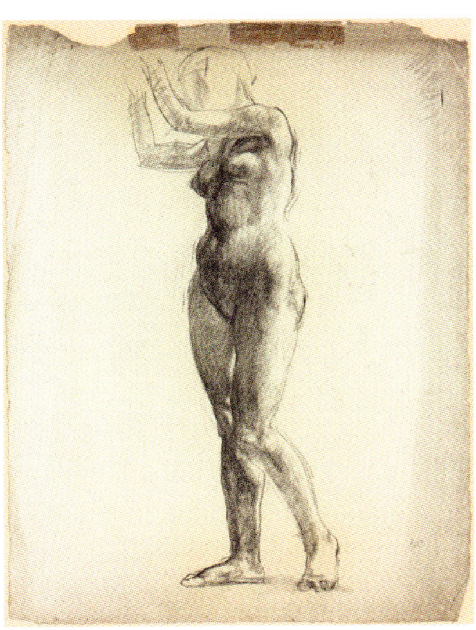

DL07.20

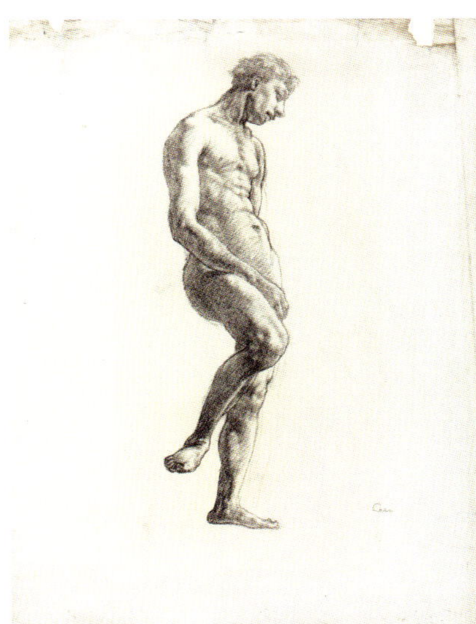

DL07.21

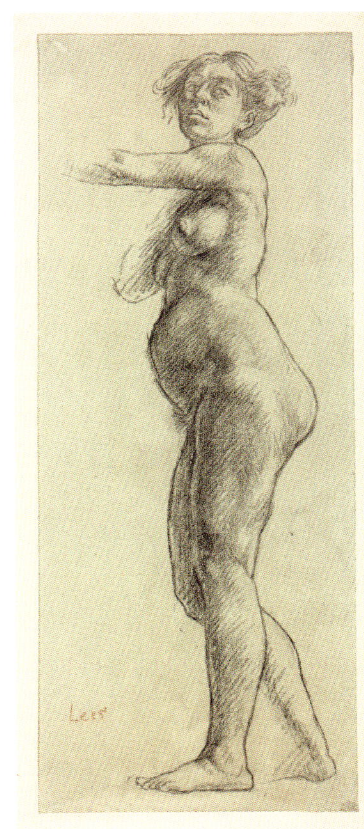

DL07.17

DL07.22**
Drawing of a Head, c.1907
ins: v.: [black chalk drawing]
Red chalk on paper
62.9 x 48.5 cm
prov: UCL Art Museum
notes: verso of DL07.21

DL07.23
Landscape with Buildings / Country House in a Landscape / Country House and Farm in an Autumnal Landscape, 1907–9
ins: l.l.: Lees
Brown ink wash and pen on buff paper
20.3 x 30.5 cm
prov: Arthur Crossland 1939–56; Christie's London Feb 1956 (58, 2nd of 2 in the lot); Thos. Agnew & Sons 1956; Christie's London Jul 2008 (528), 2011 (575); Bonhams 3, Kidlington May 2013 (112); Woolley & Wallis, Salisbury Mar 2015 (407)
exh: Laing 1939 (115 or 167)
notes: Shurland House on the Isle of Sheppey, Kent

DL07.24 (see p.23)
Portrait of Donald Maclaren / Portrait of a Man, c.1907
ins: l.l.: Lees
Pencil on paper
32.5 x 25 cm
prov: UCL Art Museum

DL07.25
Study of a Woman's Head, 1907–8
ins: l.r.: Lees
Pencil on paper
24.1 x 16.5 cm
prov: Gorringe's, Lewes Jul 2003 (1532); Private Collection

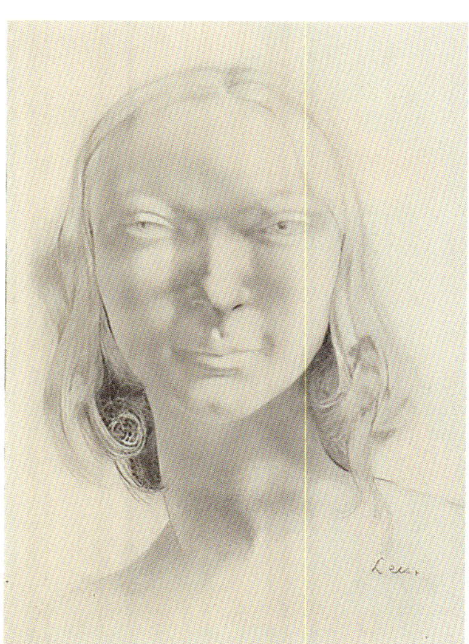

DL07.25

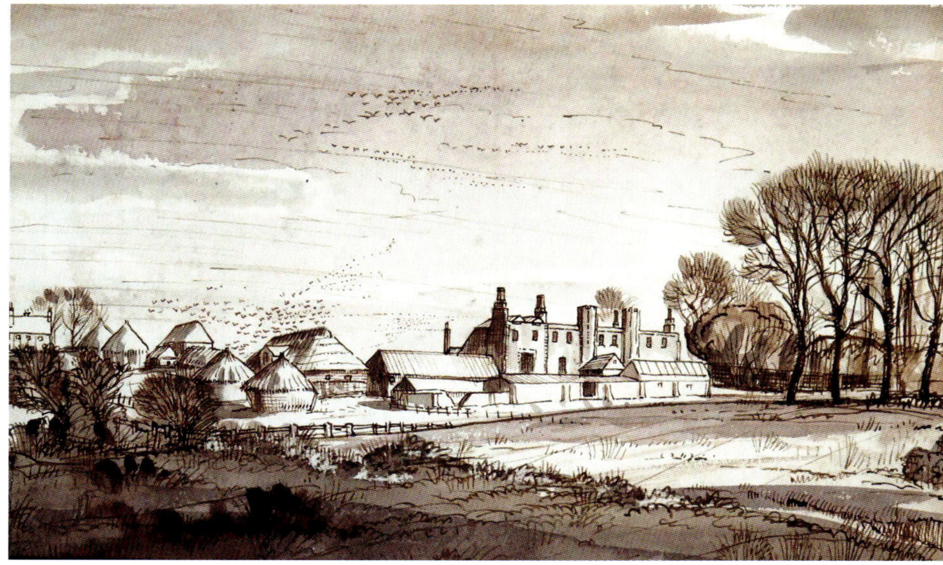

DL07.23

DL07.26 (see p.33)
Portrait of J.R. Fothergill, Esq. / Portrait Head, 1907
ins: v.: [black chalk drawing]
Red chalk on paper
38.5 x 28.5 cm
prov: UCL Art Museum
exh: NEAC 41st 1909 (220)
notes: In Slade School of Art, The Slade: A Collection of Drawings and Some Pictures done by Past and Present Students of the London Slade School of Art mdcccxciii–mdccccvii, Richard Clay & Sons, London, 1907, p.218, plate 94; The Studio, 132, Oct 1946, p.121

DL07.27**
Two Sketches of a Head [one crossed out], 1907
ins: v.: [red chalk drawing]
Black chalk on paper
38.5 x 28.5 cm
prov: UCL Art Museum
notes: verso of DL07.26

DL07.28*
An Extensive Landscape / Landscape, 1907–9
ins: [signature]
Watercolour, ink wash and pen on buff paper
21.5 x 30.5 cm
prov: Arthur Crossland 1939–56; Christie's London Feb 1956 (58, 1st of 2 in the lot); Thos. Agnew & Sons 1956; Christie's London Dec 1963 (8); Sotheby's London May 1979 (61)
exh: Laing 1939, as 'Landscape' (167)

DL07.29*
A Farmstead / Landscape / Farm Buildings in a Landscape / Farm Buildings at Dusk, 1907–9
Watercolour on buff paper
21.5 x 30.5 cm
prov: Arthur Crossland 1939–56; Christie's London Mar 1956 (59, 2nd of 2 in the lot); Piccadilly Gallery, London 1956; Sotheby's London Jun 1979 (37); Christie's London Nov 1981 (70)
exh: Laing 1939 (115)

DL07.30*
Landscape / A Village, 1907–9
Watercolour on paper
21.5 x 30.5 cm
prov: Arthur Crossland 1939–56; Christie's London Mar 1956 (59, 1st of 2 in the lot); Piccadilly Gallery, London 1956
exh: Laing 1939 (183)

DL07.31*
Seated Nude, 1907–11
ins: u.l.: [signature, date]
Pencil on paper
32 x 30 cm
prov: Belgrave Gallery, London 1981; Deutscher 1982; Leonard Joel, Melbourne Aug 1993 (790); Gregson Flanagan Fine Art, Perth Nov 1994 (236); Private Collection

DL07.32*
Two Seated Nudes, 1907–13
Ink and pencil on paper
29.2 x 22.9 cm
prov: Rex Nan Kivell; Deutsher 1978; Private Collection
exh: Deutsher 1978 (11)

DL07.33*
Nude / Standing Female Nude, 1907–11
Pencil on paper
34.5 x 17.5 cm
prov: Redfern Gallery; John and Edward Barkes; Bridget McDonnell Gallery 1989; Brian Dunlop 1997
exh: Bridget McDonnell Gallery 1989 (16); Sane 1997 (33)

DL07.34*
Seated Nude, 1907–11
Pencil on paper
36 x 30 cm
prov: Deutscher 1982; Leonard Joel, Melbourne Aug 1993; Gregson Flanagan Fine Art, Perth Mar 1996 (188); Private Collection

DL07.35*
Reclining Nude, 1907–13
Ink on paper
22.7 x 35.5 cm
prov: Rex Nan Kivell; Deutsher 1978; Private Collection
exh: Deutsher 1978 (28)

DL07.36*
Girl Bending, 1907–13
Ink and wash on paper
25.2 x 30.2 cm
prov: Rex Nan Kivell; Deutsher 1978; Private Collection
exh: Deutsher 1978 (6)

DL07.37*
The Farm, 1907
Watercolour or pencil on paper
exh: NEAC 39th 1907 (100)
notes: Location of work unknown

1908

DL08.1*
Mlle Claude de Laucheere, 1908–16
Watercolour or pencil on paper
34.3 x 24.1 cm
prov: Lady Kendall Butler; Sotheby's London May 1946 (17, 1 of a pair)
notes: Location of work unknown

DL08.2*
Mlle de Laucheere, 1908–16
Watercolour or pencil on paper
34.3 x 24.1 cm
prov: Lady Kendall Butler; Sotheby's London May 1946 (17, 2 of a pair)
notes: Location of work unknown

DL08.3*
Portrait, 1908–18
Watercolour and pencil on paper
prov: Redfern Gallery 1934
exh: Redfern 1934 (48)
notes: Unresolved record

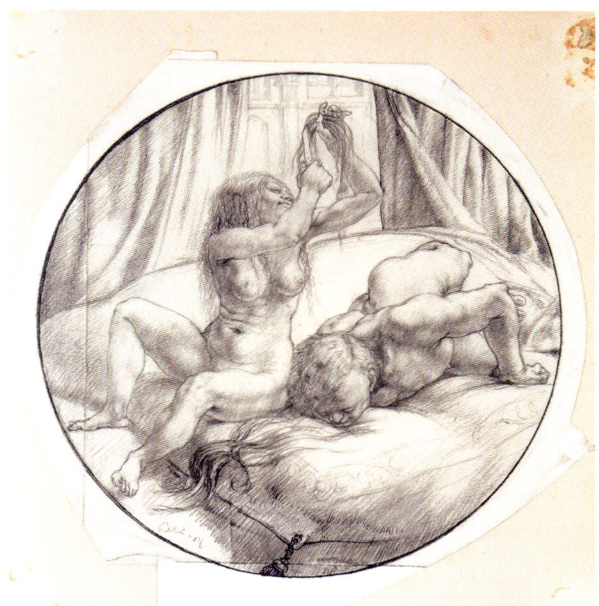

DL08.4

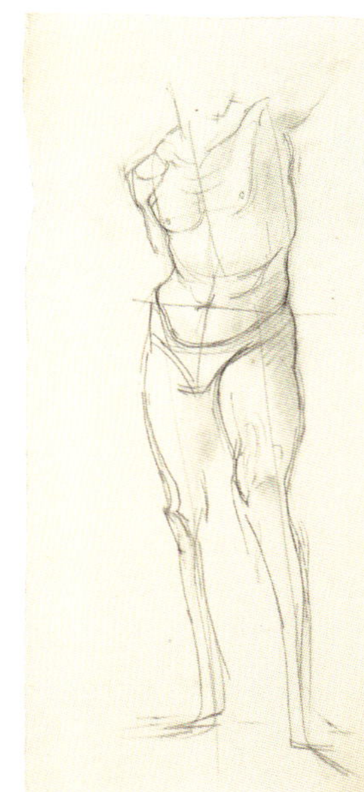

DL08.6

DL08.4
Samson and Delilah, 1908
ins: l.l.: Lees – 08
Pencil, pen and ink on paper, on card
37 x 36.5 cm; diameter 27.6 cm
prov: Rex Nan Kivell; Deutsher 1978; Art Gallery of Ballarat, purchased 1978
exh: Deutsher 1978 (24); Ballarat Fine Art Gallery, Margaret Rich, *From the Beginnings of European Settlement: A Collection of Australian Watercolours and Drawings, 1800–1983* 1983; Sane 1997 (26); Art Gallery of Ballarat, *The Naked and the Nude* Sep–Dec 2008; Baillieu Library, The University of Melbourne, *Radicals, Slayers and Villians* Oct 2014–Feb 2015

DL08.5 (see p.30)
Sketch of a Male Nude, 1908–13
ins: u.l.: D Lees; u.c.: M. Pilkington. Monday Tuesday Friday
Pencil on paper
36.8 x 13.4 cm
prov: Margaret Pilkington 1913–14; Friends of the Whitworth, gifted to The Whitworth, University of Manchester 1992

DL08.6
Sketch of a Male Nude, 1908–13
Pencil on paper
29.7 x 13.1 cm
prov: Margaret Pilkington 1913–14; Friends of the Whitworth, gifted to The Whitworth, University of Manchester 1992

DL08.7
Standing Woman Lifting Skirt / Girl Lifting Skirt / Girl Raising Skirt, c.1908
Watercolour, gouache, ink and pen on paper
35.5 x 25.4 cm
prov: Rex Nan Kivell; Deutsher 1978; National Gallery of Australia, Canberra, purchased 1979
exh: Deutsher 1978 (15); Sane 1997, loaned by the National Gallery of Australia (41)

DL08.8*
Woman Playing Harp, 1908–18
Watercolour and ink on paper
29.1 x 22.8 cm
prov: Rex Nan Kivell; Deutsher 1978
exh: Deutsher 1978 (16)
notes: Unresolved record

DL08.9
The Alhambra, c.1908
Watercolour, graphite, ink and pastel on paper
32.4 x 20.3 cm
prov: Cyril K. Butler; Redfern Gallery; CAS, gifted to Tate 1941
exh: Tate Britain, *Camden Town Drawings* Nov 2011–May 2012
notes: Related to DL08.24; reattributed to DL in consultation with John Hoole, formerly attributed to DL and JDI

DL08.10**
Study of Geoffrey Chaucer, 1908–9
ins: l.c.: Done by D Lees [on scrapbook page]
Watercolour and pen on paper
[37 x 54 cm – open scrapbook]
prov: JDI c.1908–9; Christina Bargery; Tate, purchased Jun 2008
exh: Tate, *Reception, Rupture and Return: The Model and the Life Room* Apr–May 2015, *Tate Archive is 50* Oct 2020–May 2024
notes: Pasted into JDI's scrapbook

DL08.11*
Portrait of the Author, 1908–9
Watercolour on paper
exh: NEAC 41st 1909 (254)
notes: Location of work unknown

DL08.12 (see p.38)
Self Portrait / Lees, c.1908
ins: l.c.: Lees
Red chalk on paper
26.1 x 22.2 cm
prov: Redfern Gallery 1930, 1947; Randolph Schwabe; NGV (through the Felton Bequest) purchased 1947
exh: Redfern 1930a (38), 1947a; NGV, *The Naked Face: Self-Portraits* 2010–11; NGV, Gallery 7 2014–15

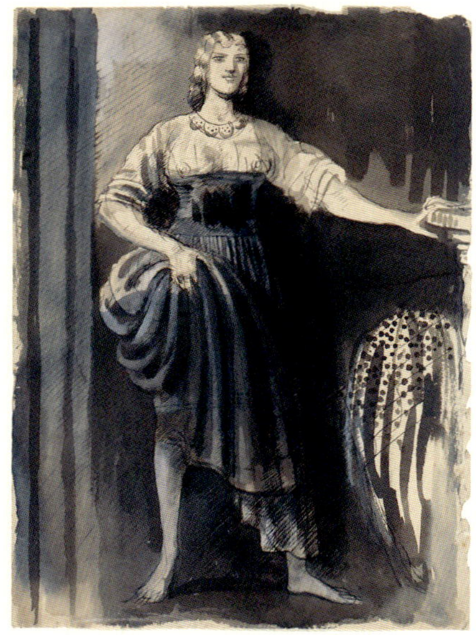

DL08.7

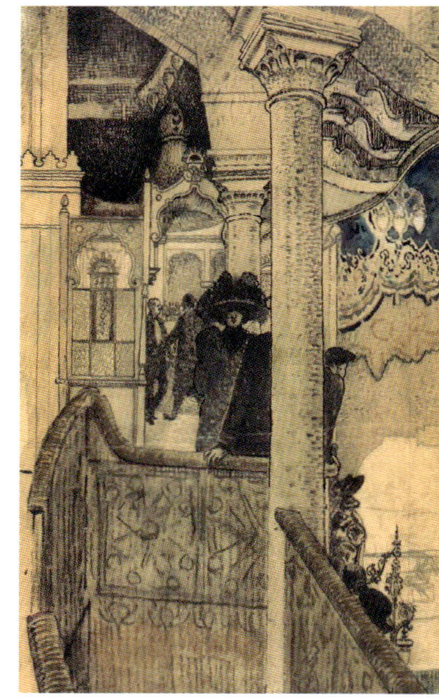

DL08.9

DL08.13*
A Nude Study: Sanguine / A Study of a Female Nude, 1908–9
ins: v.: [signature, inscription]
Red chalk on paper
32.4 x 25.4 cm
prov: Dowdeswell and Dowdeswell, London; Christie's London Feb 1917 (80); Sotheby's London Dec 1971 (40)

DL08.14*
A Room in Chelsea / The Artist's Room in Chelsea, 1908–11
ins: v.: [signature]
Pen, ink and wash on paper
24 x 37 cm
prov: Mrs Edith Lees; Thos. Agnew & Sons Sep–Oct 1990 (67); Christie's London Apr 1995 (39)
exh: Stafford 1939

DL08.15*
Head of a Woman, 1908–12
Pen and ink on paper
14.6 x 10.8 cm
prov: Sotheby's London '1979A', Jan 1980 (10)
notes: Unresolved record

DL08.16*
Two Portrait Studies, 1908–18
Pencil on paper
50.8 x 35.7 cm
prov: Rex Nan Kivell; Deutsher 1978; Private Collection
exh: Deutsher 1978 (38)

DL08.17**
Portrait Study, 1908–13
Pencil on paper
50 x 35.6 cm
prov: Rex Nan Kivell; Deutsher 1978; Private Collection; Leonard Joel, Melbourne Jun 2025 (4215)
exh: Deutsher 1978 (32)
notes: Likely 1913

DL08.18*
Portrait Study, 1908–18
Pencil on paper
50.7 x 35.7 cm
prov: Rex Nan Kivell; Deutsher 1978; Private Collection
exh: Deutsher 1978 (34)

DL08.19*
Portrait Study, 1908–18
Pencil and wash on paper
50.6 x 35.5 cm
prov: Rex Nan Kivell; Deutsher 1978; Private Collection
exh: Deutsher 1978 (19)

DL08.20*
Portrait Study, 1908–18
Pencil and wash on paper
50.9 x 35.5 cm
prov: Rex Nan Kivell; Deutsher 1978; Private Collection
exh: Deutsher 1978 (44)

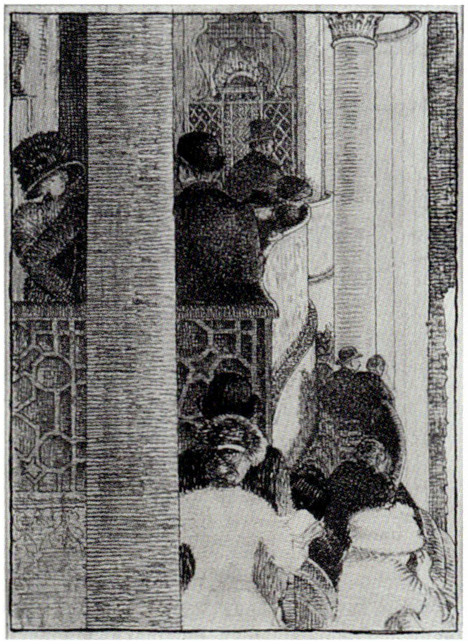

DL08.24

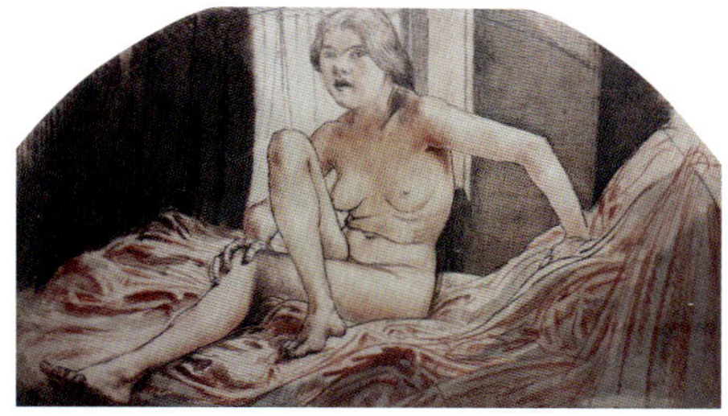

DL08.25

DL08.21*
Portrait Study, 1908–18
Pencil and wash on paper
35.6 x 25.4 cm
prov: Rex Nan Kivell; Deutsher 1978; Private Collection
exh: Deutsher 1978 (17)

DL08.22*
Portrait Study, 1908–18
ins: [signature]
Pencil and wash on paper
47 x 29.6 cm
prov: Rex Nan Kivell; Deutsher 1978, 1979; Private Collection
exh: Deutsher 1978 (39)

DL08.23*
The Old Bedford, 1908–11
prov: Mrs Edith Lees
exh: Stafford 1939
notes: Old Bedford Music Hall, Camden Town

DL08.24
The Alhambra London, c.1908
Pen, ink and pencil on paper
17.5 x 12 cm
prov: Redfern Gallery Sep 1942; Lt Col. J. Bramwell Jones, thence by gift and descent; Lawrences Auctioneers Crewkerne Jan 2025 (352)
exh: Eisteddfod Genedlaethol Cymru, Llandybie, Wales, *Arddangosfa'r Gymru Newydd* (*New Wales Exhibition*) 1944, loaned by Lt Col. J. Bramwell Jones (24)
notes: Related to DL08.9; reattributed in consultation with John Hoole, formerly attributed to JDI

DL08.25
Morning (Female Nude), c.1908
Pen, ink, red conte and/or coloured chalks on paper
36 x 50.5 cm
prov: Mervyn Levy 1967; Herbert Art Gallery & Museum, Coventry
notes: Related to DL08.4

1909

DL09.1
Three Girls, c.1909
ins: l.c.: Done by D Lees [on scrapbook page]
Ink on paper
[37 x 54 cm – open scrapbook]
prov: JDI c.1908–9; Christina Bargery; Tate, purchased Jun 2008
exh: Tate, *Reception, Rupture and Return: The Model and the Life Room* Apr–May 2015, *Tate Archive is 50* Oct 2020–May 2024
notes: Pasted into JDI's scrapbook

DL09.2
Nude Study for 'Sirens', c.1909
Pencil on paper
[37 x 54 cm – open scrapbook]
prov: JDI c.1908–9; Christina Bargery; Tate, purchased Jun 2008
exh: Tate, *Reception, Rupture and Return: The Model and the Life Room* Apr–May 2015, *Tate Archive is 50* Oct 2020–May 2024
notes: Pasted into JDI's scrapbook

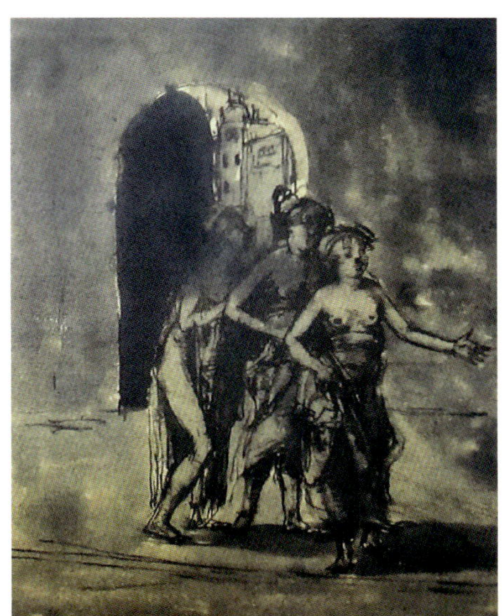

DL09.1

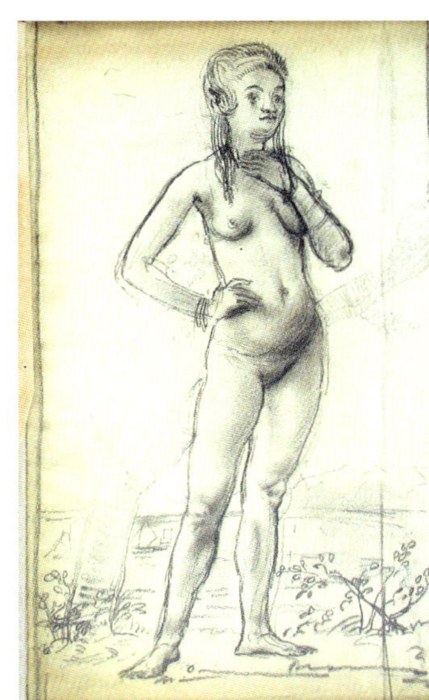

DL09.2

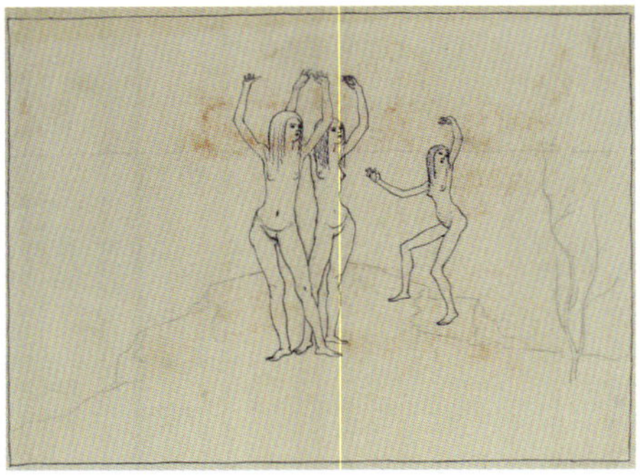

DL09.3

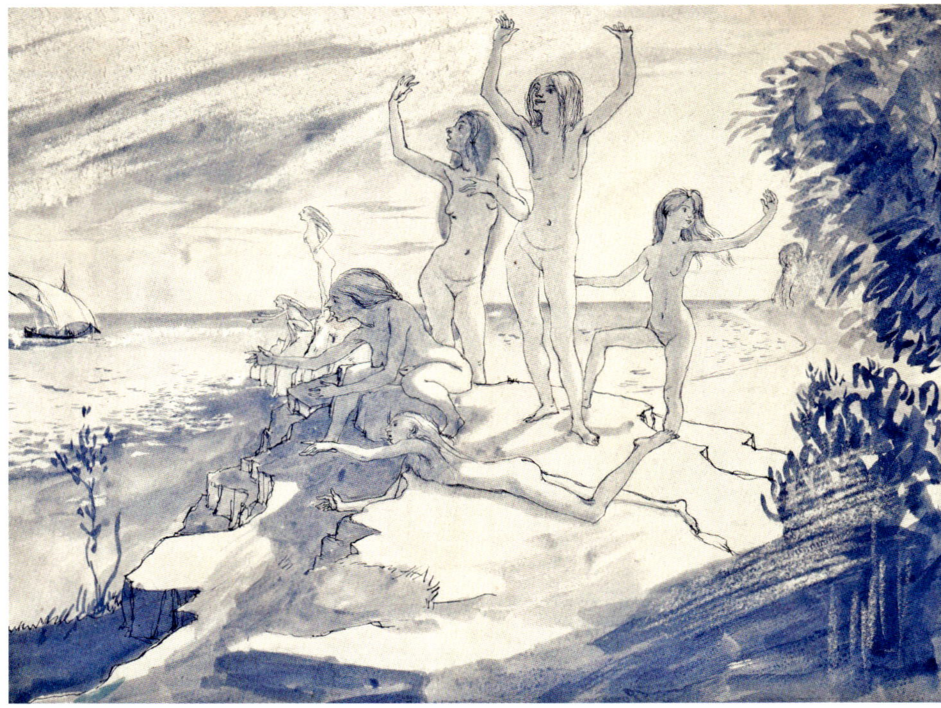

DL09.4

DL09.3
Sketch Study for 'Sirens', c.1909
ins: l.l.: D Lees [on scrapbook margin]
Pencil on paper
[37 x 54 cm – open scrapbook]
prov: JDI c.1908–9; Christina Bargery; Tate, purchased Jun 2008
exh: Tate, *Reception, Rupture and Return: The Model and the Life Room* Apr–May 2015, *Tate Archive is 50* Oct 2020–May 2024
notes: Pasted into JDI's scrapbook

DL09.4
Drawing – Sirens / Sirens on a Clifftop, 1909
ins: v.: Drawing – Derwent Lees [on label]
Pen, blue ink and wash with scratching on paper
25 x 33 cm
prov: Wyndham T. Vint; Christie's London Oct 2013 (399); Panter and Hall London 2022; Private Collection

DL09.5 (see p.43)
The Dancers / The Sirens / Three Nude Girls on Sea Shore, 1909
ins: l.r.: D. Leesinnes 09 [co-signed]
Watercolour on paper
38.7 x 48.3 cm
prov: Cyril K. Butler; Redfern Gallery 1939; Capt. G. Crawshay; Ralph Edwards; Lord Crickhowell, thence by descent
exh: Chenil Gallery 1923 (100) (?); Redfern 1930a, as 'The Dancers', 'composite picture by Lees and Innes', loaned by Cyril K. Butler (31), 1939a (120); Graves Art Gallery, Sheffield, Glynn Vivian Art Gallery, Swansea, National Library of Wales, Aberystwyth Mar–May 1961, loaned by Ralph Edwards (69); Southampton City Art Gallery 1977–8 (36); Mostyn Art Gallery 1982–3 (61)
notes: By DL and JDI; rocky outcrop at Man's Head, St Ives

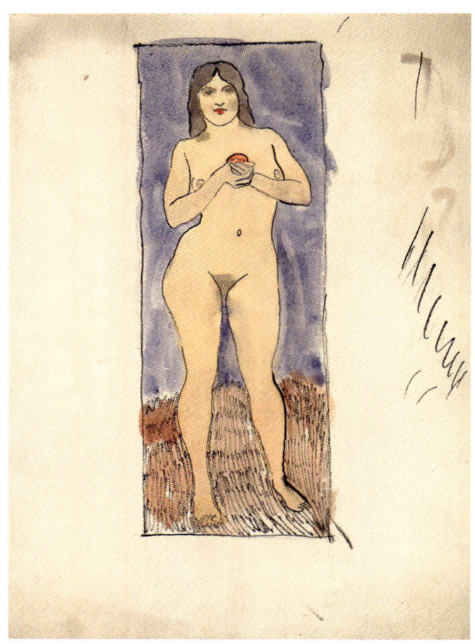

DL09.6

DL09.6
Eve Holding the Apple / Eve, c.1909
ins: u.r., c.r.: [multiple pen and brush strokes]
Watercolour, pencil, pen and ink on paper
35.5 x 25.4 cm
prov: Rex Nan Kivell; Deutsher 1978; National Gallery of Australia, Canberra, purchased 1979
exh: Deutsher 1978 (46); Sane 1997, loaned by the National Gallery of Australia (40)

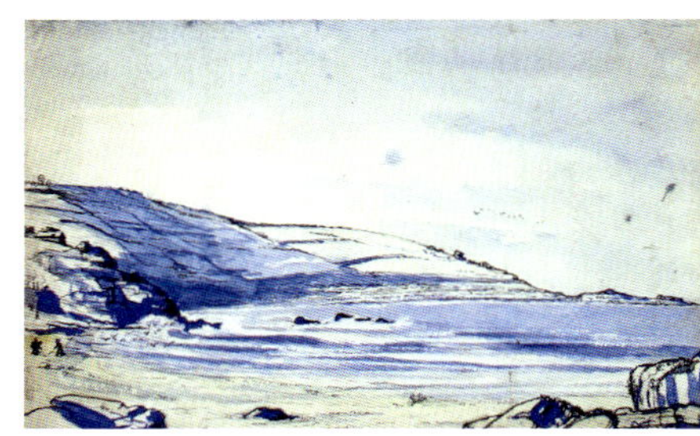

DL09.7

DL09.7
Coast at St Ives, c.1909
Watercolour and pencil on paper
[37 x 54 cm – open scrapbook]
prov: JDI c.1908–9; Christina Bargery; Tate, purchased Jun 2008
exh: Tate, *Reception, Rupture and Return: The Model and the Life Room* Apr–May 2015, *Tate Archive is 50* Oct 2020–May 2024
notes: Pasted into JDI's scrapbook; Porthmeor Beach, Cornwall

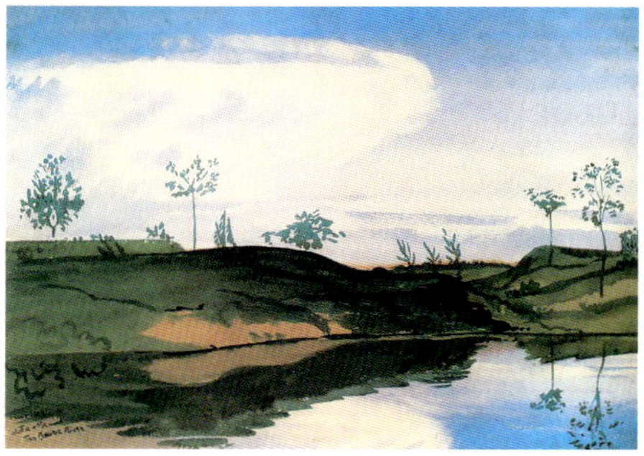

DL09.8

DL09.8
Sobota, Poland, The Bsura River / The Beura River, Poland / The Beura River, Sobota, Poland, 1909
ins: l.l.: Lees 1909 Sobota – Poland The Bsura River
Watercolour and ink body colour on paper
22.9 x 30.5 cm
prov: Redfern Gallery 1944, 1945; Private Collection; Sotheby's London Apr 1967 (24); J.O. Stanley Clarke; Sotheby's London Mar 1973 (46); Thos. Agnew & Sons 1973 (18); Sotheby's London Apr 1986 (504); Christie's London May 1989 (15); Spink 1990 (15)
exh: Redfern 1944a (45), 1945b (477)
notes: Bzura River, Poland

DL09.9
Landscape / A Landscape in Poland / Evening Landscape, Poland, 1909
Watercolour and ink wash on paper
22.3 x 31.2 cm
prov: Redfern Gallery 1944, 1952, 1961, 1964; Private Collection; donated to RISD 2016
exh: Redfern 1944a (50); Birmingham City Gallery 1952, loaned by the Redfern Gallery (170); Redfern 1961 (250), 1964 (408)
notes: Sobota, Poland

DL09.10
Cumulus Clouds / Solota, Poland / Landscape, 1909
ins: l.l.: Derwent Lees 1909 'Sobota' Poland
Watercolour on paper
23.5 x 31.1 cm
prov: Thos. Agnew & Sons Jan–Feb 1957 (108), Mar 1957 (113), Jun–Jul 1968 (93); Private Collection 1971; donated to RISD 2016
exh: NEAC 42nd 1909 (231); Fine Art Society 1971, on loan (46)
notes: Bzura River, Sobota, Poland

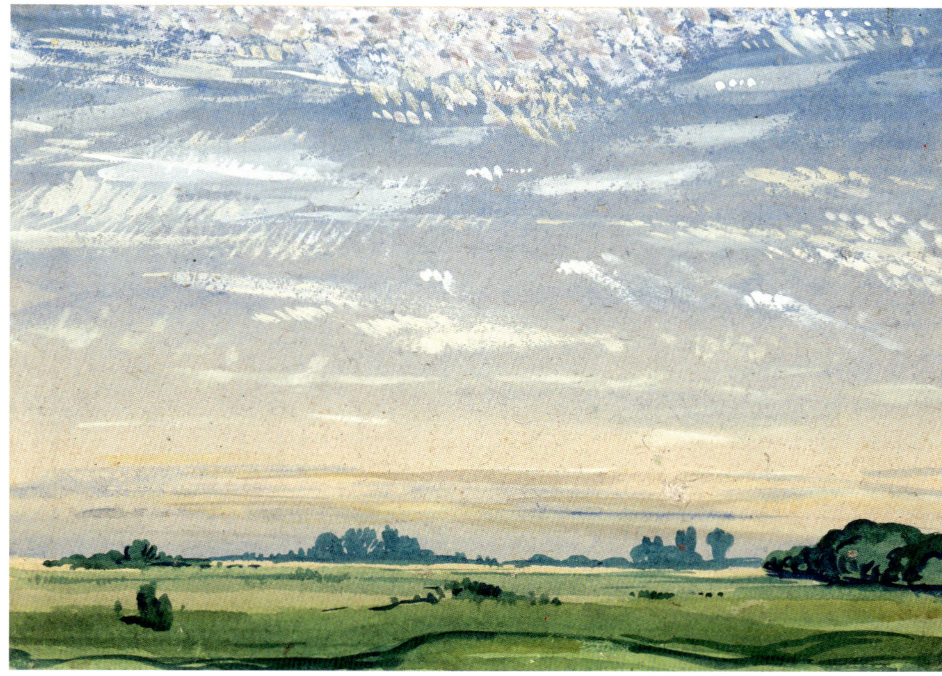

DL09.9

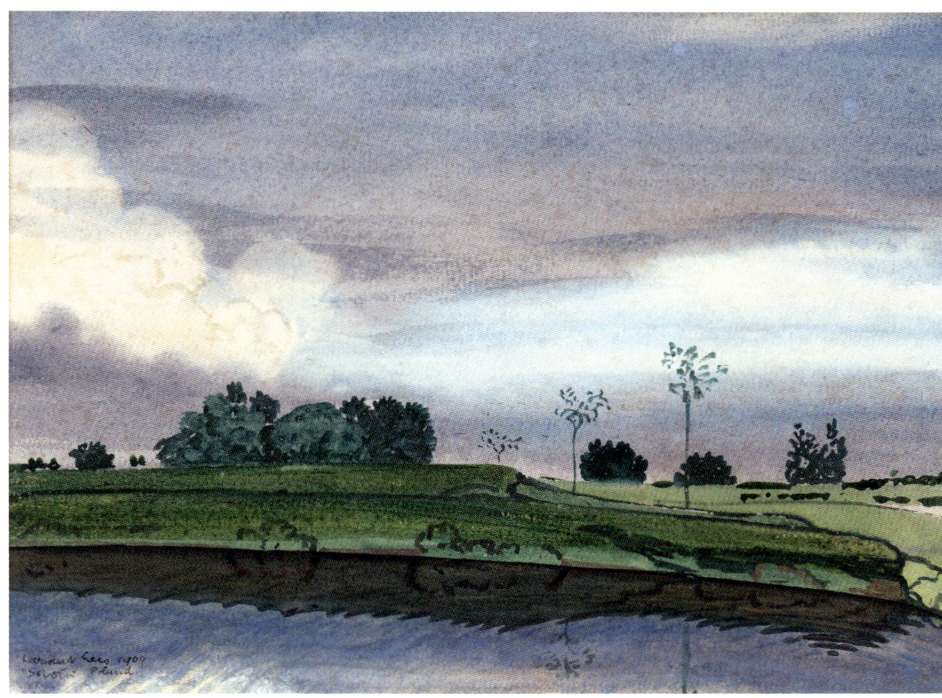

DL09.10

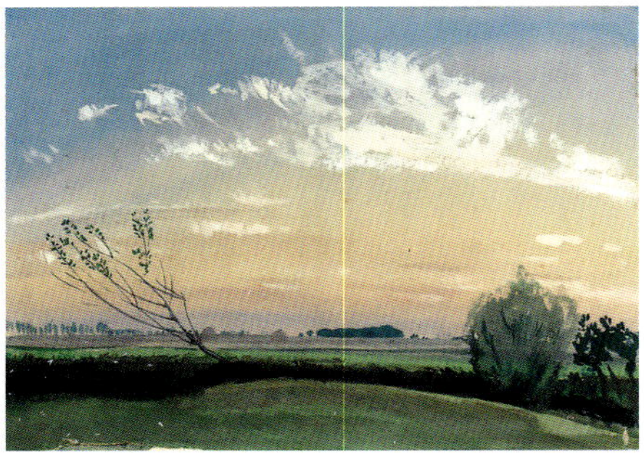

DL09.11

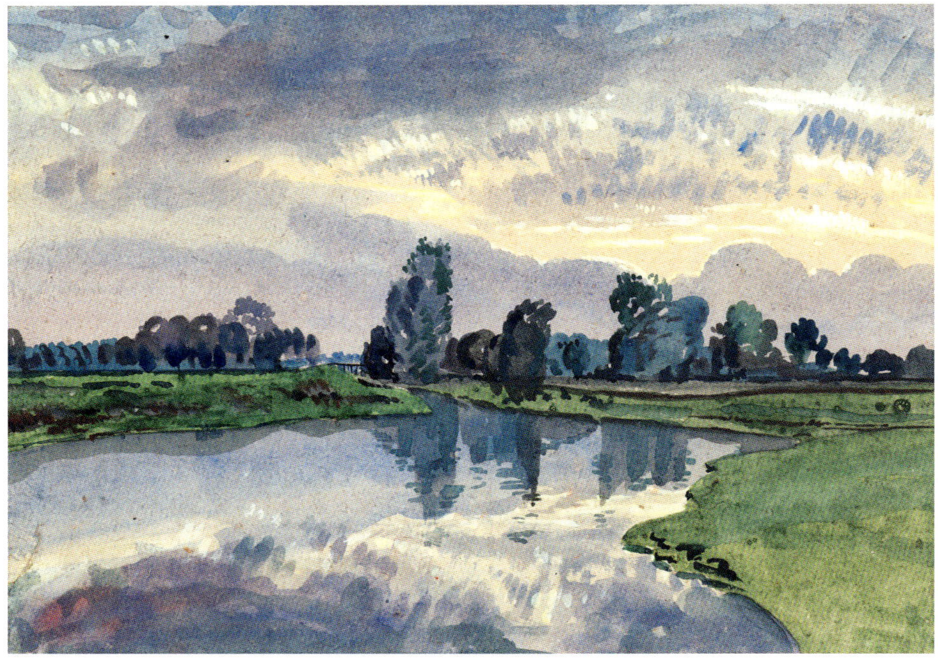

DL09.12

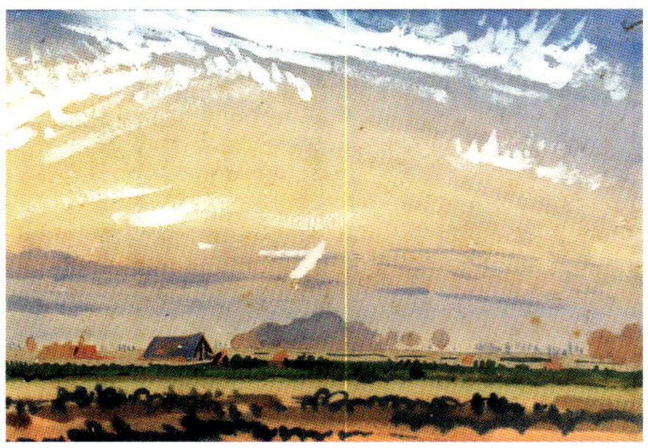

DL09.13

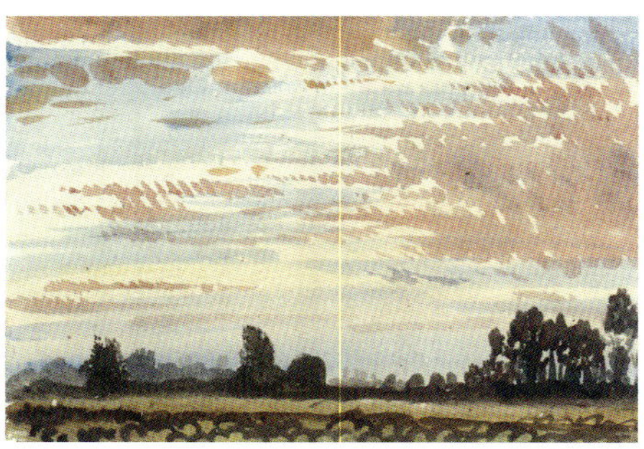

DL09.15

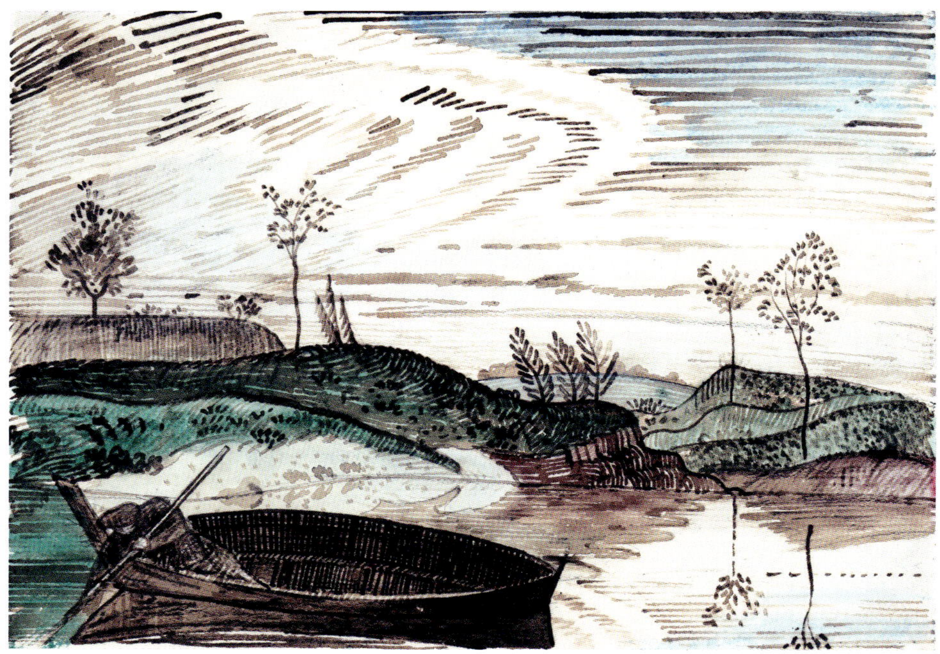

DL09.14

DL09.11
Landscape, 1909
ins: v., l.r.: Percy Young London [stamp]
Watercolour on paper
23 x 31.9 cm
prov: Dr John MacGregor; gifted to Royal Albert Memorial Museum and Art Gallery, Exeter 1929
notes: Near Sobota, Poland

DL09.12
A River in Poland / The Creek / A River Scene / On the River, 1909
Watercolour on tan paper
21.7 x 30.4 cm
prov: Arthur Crossland; Christie's London Feb 1956 (12, 1st of 2 in the lot); Thos. Agnew & Sons 1956 (31885), Jan–Feb 1957 (116), Mar 1957 (117), Jun–Jul 1968 (105); Private Collection; donated to RISD 2016
exh: NEAC 42nd 1909 (225)
notes: Bzura River, Sobota, Poland

DL09.13
A Camp Site, 1909
ins: v., l.r.: Percy Young London [stamp]
Watercolour on paper
22.2 x 31 cm
prov: Dr John MacGregor; gifted to Royal Albert Memorial Museum and Art Gallery, Exeter 1929

DL09.14
The Bsura, Poland / On the Burza River, 1909
Watercolour and ink on paper
25 x 35.2 cm
prov: Charles Rutherston 1916; gifted to Manchester City Art Gallery 1925
exh: NEAC 54th 1915 (275); Manchester City Art Gallery 1925; Arts Council of Great Britain, London, 1946; Arts Council, London, *A Selection of Paintings and Drawings from the Rutherston Collection* 1955
notes: Bzura River, Sobota, Poland

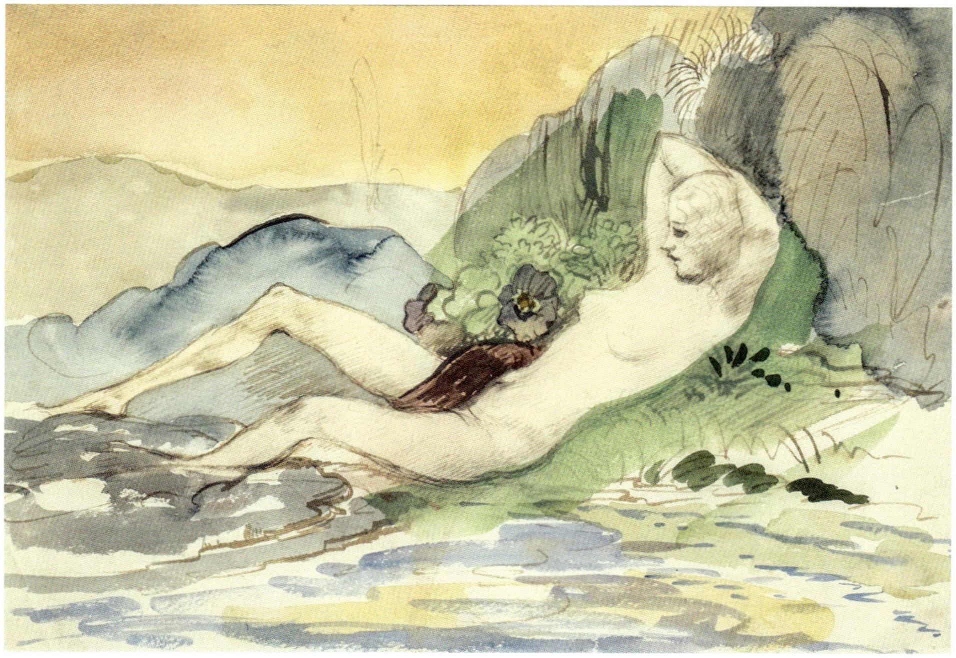

DL09.16

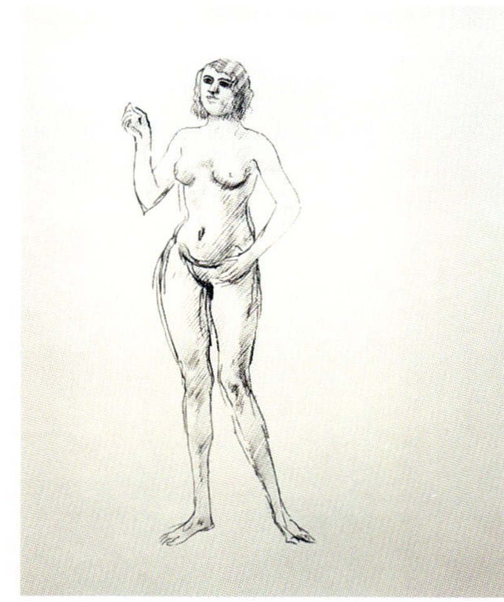

DL09.17

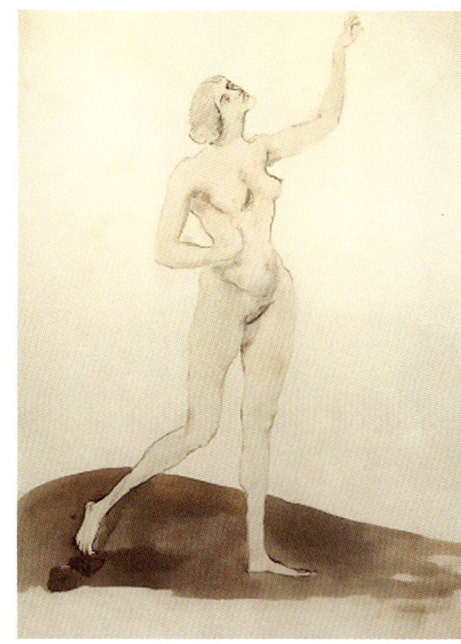

DL09.18

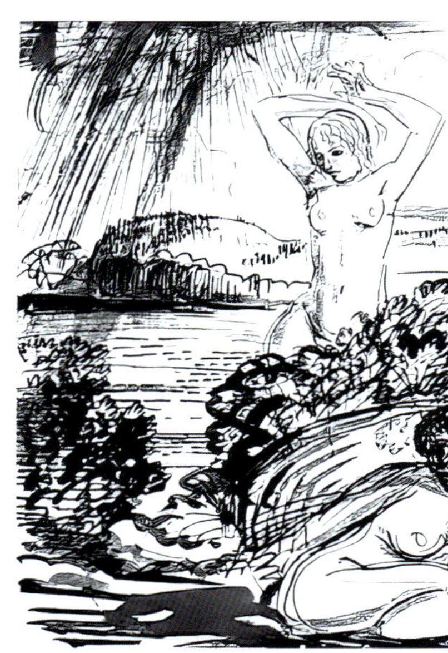

DL09.19

DL09.15
After Sunset / Métairie des Abeilles / Landscape, 1909
Watercolour on paper
22.9 x 30.5 cm
prov: Chenil Gallery Collection; Dr John MacGregor, bequeathed to Tate 1942
exh: NEAC 42nd 1909 (285)
notes: Mistakenly accessioned in 1942 as 'Metairie des Abeilles' (no.5356); Sobota, Poland

DL09.16
Reclining Nude, 1909
Watercolour and ink on paper
25 x 35.5 cm
prov: Redfern Gallery 1945; Deutsher 1978; Leonard Joel, Melbourne Nov 1988 (29); Masterpiece Gallery, Hobart 1998; Private Collection
exh: Redfern 1945b (327); Deutsher 1978 (12)
notes: By the lake at Grange Gate, Creech, Dorset

DL09.17
Standing Nude, 1907–9
Ink on paper
28 x 15 cm
prov: Redfern Gallery; John and Edward Barkes; Bridget McDonnell Gallery 1996, 2024
exh: Bridget McDonnell Gallery 1996

DL09.18
Standing Nude, c.1909
Watercolour wash and ink on paper
35.3 x 25.3 cm
prov: Redfern Gallery; John and Edward Barkes; Bridget McDonnell Gallery, from the estate of Lisé Sigetty-Bates, 2012

DL09.19
A Design, 1909–13
Print on paper
15.5 x 9.3 cm
prov: In J. Middleton Murry (ed.), *Rhythm: Art Music Literature Monthly*, 2(14), 1913, p.475

DL09.20
Two Seated Nudes / Two Female Seated Nudes / Two Girls, c.1909
Watercolour and pencil on paper
35.5 x 34.6 cm
prov: Christie's London May 1989 (16), Sep 1989 (283); Spink 1990 (2); Christie's London May 1994 (137)

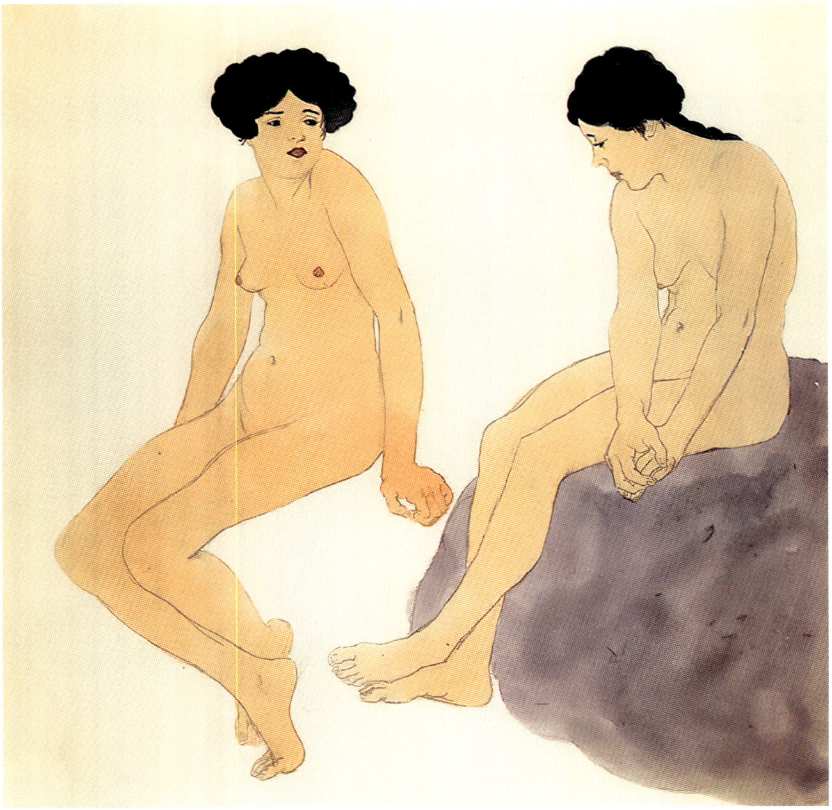

DL09.20

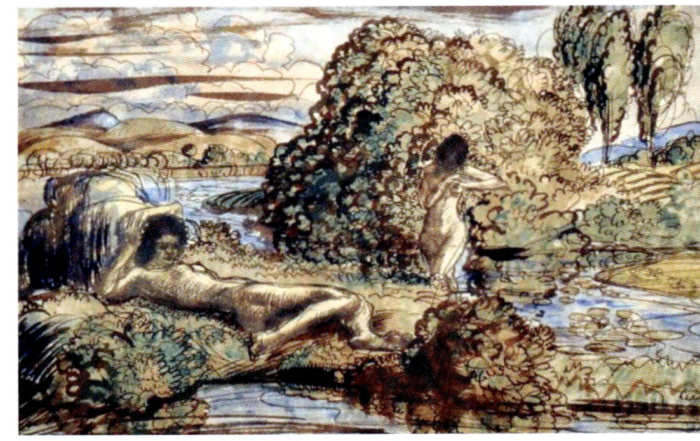

DL09.21

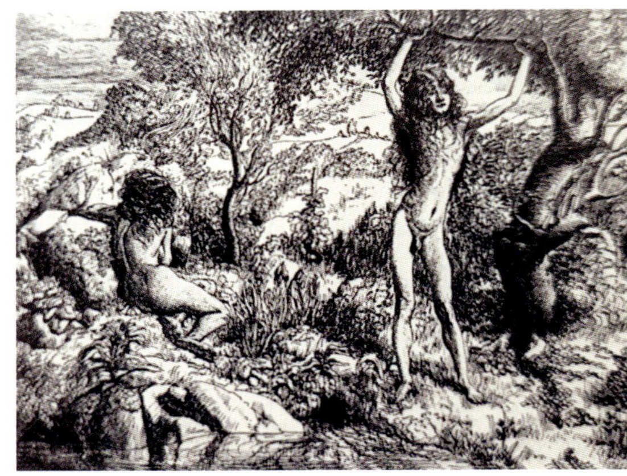

DL09.22

DL09.21
The Bathers / A Sketch of Naked Figures by a Lake, 1909
ins: l.r.: Lees 09
Watercolour, gouache, brush and brown ink on paper
20 x 31 cm
prov: Redfern Gallery; R.H. Kitson; Christie's London Jun 2001 (187); John Nicholson's, Haslemere Apr 2018 (293); Private Collection
exh: Redfern 1939a, collection of R.H. Kitson (128)
notes: Lake at Grange Gate, Creech, Dorset

DL09.22
Rise Up My Love, My Fair One, 1909
ins: l.r.: [signature] 09
Pen and ink on paper
28 x 38 cm
prov: Anthony D'Offay Ltd, London; Fine Art Society; Christie's London Mar 1986 (1 of a set of 4), as 'Four Illustrations' (305); Peter Nahum, London 1986; Daniel Katz Gallery, London 1986; Sotheby's London Jul 1989 (121, 1st of 2 in the lot); Private Collection
notes: Relates to DL09.31, DL09.32 and DL09.33

DL09.23*
Mythological Scene, 1909–10
Ink on paper
25.5 x 20.5 cm
prov: Rex Nan Kivell; Deutsher 1978; Private Collection
exh: Deutsher 1978 (27)

DL09.24**
Seated Nude, c.1909
ins: [signature]
Pencil on paper
17.8 x 17.8 cm
prov: Christie's London Nov 1987, Sep 1989 (144)
notes: Lyndra

DL09.25
Nude Study, c.1909
Pencil on paper
22 x 22 cm
prov: Redfern Gallery; Bridget McDonnell Gallery 2024 (1538)
notes: Lyndra

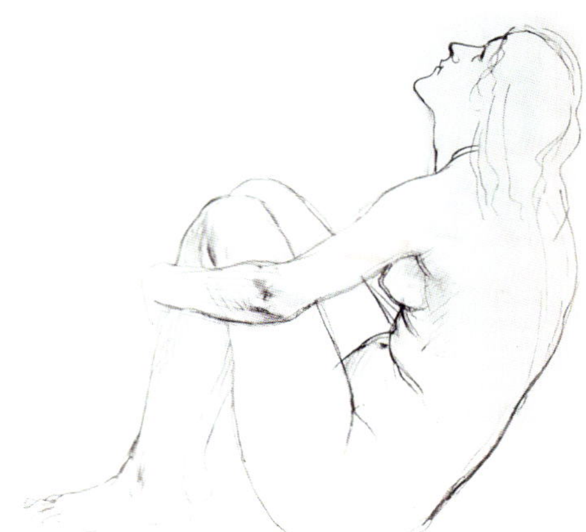

DL09.25

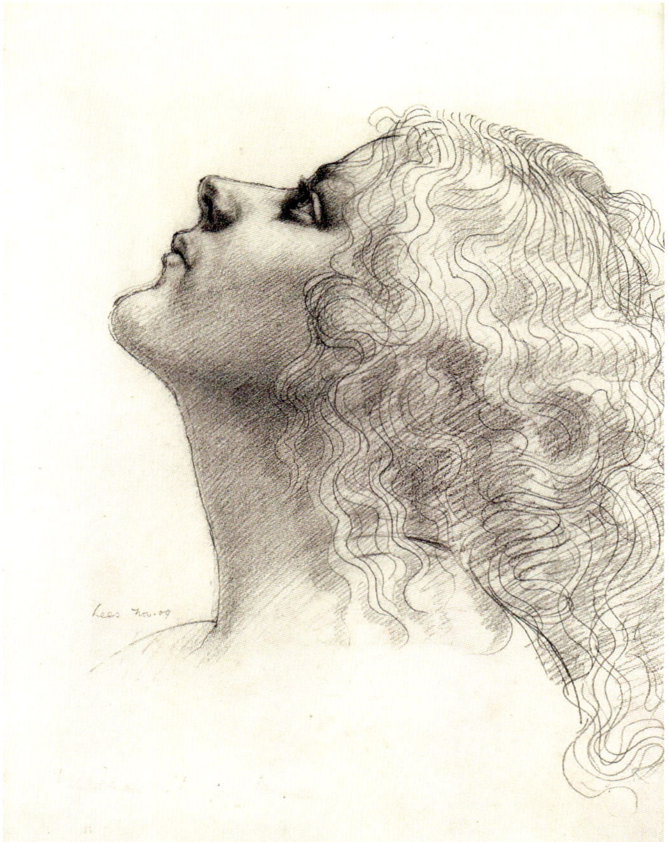

DL09.26

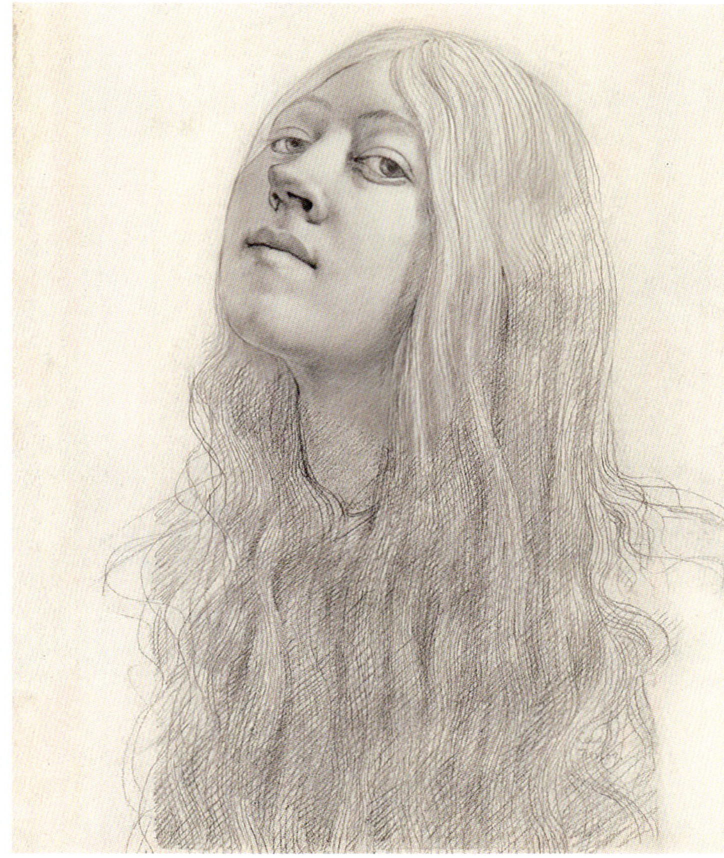

DL09.27

DL09.26
Girl's Head / Girl in Profile / Lyndra, 1909
ins: l.l.: Lees Nov. 09
Pencil on paper
33 x 24.8 cm
prov: Sotheby's London Sep 1994 (?); Lawrences Auctioneers, Crewkerne 2010; The Maas Gallery, London 2021–4
exh: NEAC 43rd 1910 (25) (?); Piano Nobile, London, *Augustus John and the First Crisis of Brilliance* Apr–Jul 2024 (22)

DL09.27
Portrait of a Girl with Long Hair / Portrait of Young Woman / Girl with Long Hair, 1909
ins: l.r.: Lees Nov 09
Pencil on paper
34.8 x 25.3 cm
prov: Redfern Gallery 1944, 1945; Queensland Art Gallery | Gallery of Modern Art, purchased 1954
exh: NEAC 42nd 1909 (173) (?); Redfern 1944b (191), 1945b (419); Sane 1997, loaned by Queensland Art Gallery (30)
notes: Lyndra

DL09.28*
Elsie McNaught / Elsie McNaughton, 1909–11
Pencil on paper
prov: Mrs Edith Lees
exh: Stafford 1939

DL09.29
Study of a Nude Woman, 1909
ins: u.l.: To Miss Elmslie from – Lees. 09
Watercolour and pencil on paper
24.7 x 36.7 cm
prov: Gifted to Essil Elmslie by DL 1909; Charles Rutherston, gifted to Manchester City Art Gallery 1925
notes: Essil Elmslie (later Rutherston)

DL09.30
Girl Sitting, c.1909
ins: v.: [signature]
Watercolour wash and pencil on paper
23 x 38 cm
prov: Bridget McDonnell Gallery 1995, Jul 2008; Private Collection
exh: Bridget McDonnell Gallery Dec 1995 (40)

DL09.31**
Naked Youth Dancing, c.1909
ins: [signature]
Pen and ink with white on paper
28 x 35 cm
prov: Christie's London Mar 1986 (1 of a set of 4), as 'Four Illustrations' (305); Peter Nahum, London 1986; Daniel Katz Gallery, London 1986; Sotheby's London Oct 1996
notes: Relates to DL09.22, DL09.32 and DL09.33

DL09.32**
Illustration to Song of Solomon / Judgement in the Hareem / Embracing Couple, c.1909
ins: l.l.: Lees
Pen, ink and watercolour on paper
28 x 36 cm
prov: Christie's London Mar 1986 (1 of a set of 4), as 'Four Illustrations' (305); Peter Nahum, London 1986; Daniel Katz Gallery, London 1986; Sotheby's London Jul 1989 (121, 2nd of 2 in the lot), Oct 1996
exh: NEAC 41st 1909 (232)
notes: Relates to DL09.22, DL09.31 and DL09.33

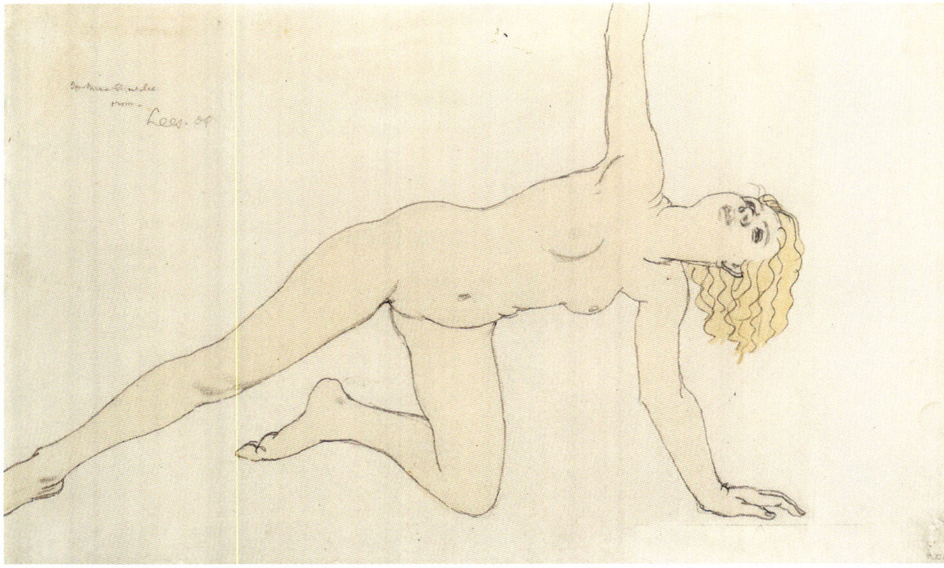

DL09.29

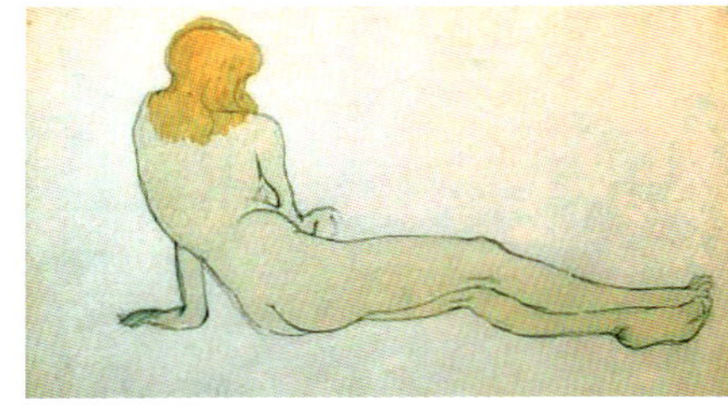

DL09.30

DL09.33**
Illustration to Song of Solomon / Illustration: Egyptian Scene / Youth Asleep, c.1909
ins: l.l.: Lees
Pen and ink on paper
27.9 x 37.5 cm
prov: Anthony D'Offay Ltd, London; Fine Art Society; Christie's London Mar 1986 (1 of a set of 4), as 'Four Illustrations' (305); Peter Nahum, London 1986; Daniel Katz Gallery, London 1986; Sotheby's London Jul 1989, Oct 1996
exh: NEAC 41st 1909 (239)
notes: Relates to DL09.22, DL09.31 and DL09.32

DL09.34*
Reclining Nude, 1909
ins: [signature] '09
Conté on paper
25.3 x 35.7 cm
prov: Rex Nan Kivell; Deutsher 1978; Belgrave Gallery, London; Sotheby's London May 1981 (99, 1st of 3 in the lot); Deutscher 1982; Leonard Joel, Melbourne Jul 1985; Bonhams and Goodman, Sydney; Private Collection
exh: Deutsher 1978 (5)

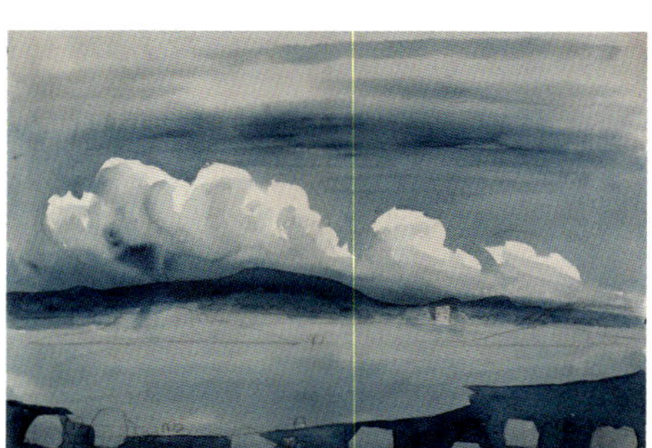

DL09.38

DL09.35*
A Model, 1909–13
prov: Mrs Edith Lees
exh: Stafford 1939
notes: Unresolved record

DL09.36*
Altenahr / Alternahr, near Bonn, Germany – Beside the River Ahr, 1909
ins: Altenahr
Watercolour, pencil, heightened with white on paper
14.5 x 21 cm
prov: Sotheby's London Apr 1980 (94)
notes: Unresolved record

DL09.37**
Chateau Gaillard Normandie, 1908–9
ins: l.r.: Castle Gail(^l)ard Normandie D Lees [on scrapbook page]
Pencil on paper
[37 x 54 cm – open scrapbook]
prov: JDI c.1908–9; Christina Bargery; Tate, purchased Jun 2008
exh: Tate, *Reception, Rupture and Return: The Model and the Life Room* Apr–May 2015, *Tate Archive is 50* Oct 2020–May 2024
notes: Pasted into JDI's scrapbook

DL09.38
Lake at Grange Gate, Dorset / View over a Lake or River Estuary, c.1909
ins: v.: Derwent Lees
Watercolour, pencil on paper
24.1 x 34.3 cm
prov: John Russell-Taylor; Abbott and Holder, London mid-1970s, 2024 (13470)
notes: Preparatory study; Creech, Dorset

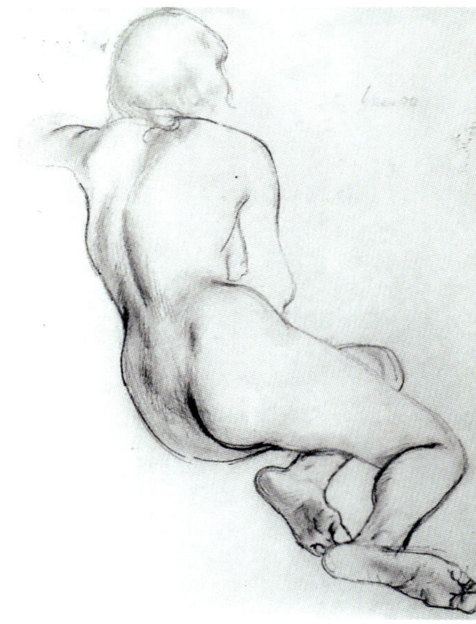

DL09.40

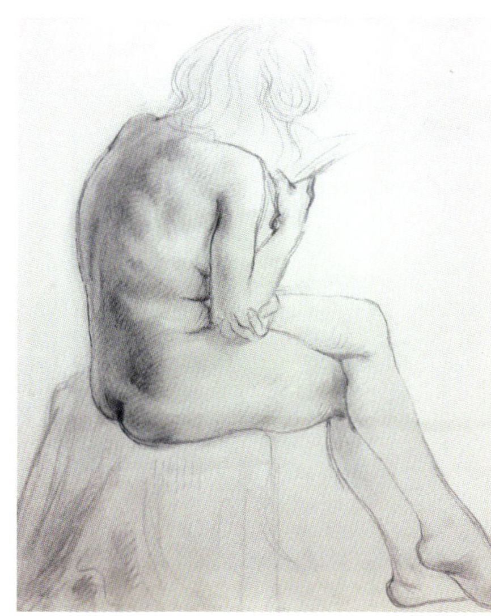

DL09.47

DL09.39**
Nude Dancer / Dancing Nude, c.1909
Ink and wash on paper
42 x 25 cm
prov: Redfern Gallery; John and Edward Barkes; Bridget McDonnell Gallery 1994; Private Collection
exh: Bridget McDonnell Gallery Jul 1994 (14)

DL09.40
Seated Nude, c.1909
ins: u.r.: Lees 09
Pencil on paper
26.5 x 21.5 cm (?)
prov: Redfern Gallery; Bridget McDonnell Gallery 1992, 1996; Private Collection
exh: Bridget McDonnell Gallery Mar 1992 (21), Dec 1996

DL09.41**
Pensive Woman, c.1909
ins: c.r.: Lees
Watercolour and pencil on paper
32.5 x 19 cm
prov: John and Edward Barkes; Bridget McDonnell Gallery 1992; Private Collection
exh: Bridget McDonnell Gallery Feb 1992; Private Collection

DL09.42*
Nude in Armchair, c.1909
Pencil on paper
47 x 33.7 cm
prov: Rex Nan Kivell; Deutsher 1978; Private Collection
exh: Deutsher 1978 (45)

DL09.43*
Nude Model Reading, c.1909
Ink on paper
47.8 x 31.6 cm
prov: Rex Nan Kivell; Deutsher 1978; Private Collection
exh: Deutsher 1978 (14)

DL09.44*
A Woody Landscape / Landscape
Watercolour on paper
21.6 x 30.5 cm
prov: Arthur Crossland 1939–56; Christie's London Feb 1956 (12, 2nd of 2 in the lot); Thos. Agnew & Sons 1956 (33903), Jan–Feb 1957 (113), Jun 1964 (102)
exh: Laing 1939 (82)

DL09.45*
The Polish Plains
Watercolour on paper
21.6 x 30.5 cm
prov: Arthur Crossland; Thos. Agnew & Sons Jan–Feb 1957 (115)
notes: Unresolved record

DL09.46*
Head of a Youth, c.1909
Red crayon on blue paper
29.8 x 21.6 cm
prov: Christie's London Jul 1988
notes: Unresolved record

DL09.47
Nude Reading a Book, 1909
ins: Lees 09
Pencil on paper
27.9 x 22.2 cm
prov: Sotheby's London, Jul 1969 (15); Agnews, London Jun–Jul 1970; Herbert Art Gallery & Museum, Coventry
exh: The Minories, Colchester Jan–Feb 1978

1910

DL10.1**
Nude, 1910
ins: l.r.: Derwent LEES 1910
Conté on paper
37.5 x 18.5 cm
prov: Redfern Gallery; Bridget McDonnell Gallery 1989; Private Collection (USA); Bonhams and Goodman (Bay East Auctions), Sydney May 2009 (140); Private Collection
exh: Bridget McDonnell Gallery May–Jun 1989 (10)

DL10.2*
Nude Study / Seated Nude, c.1910
ins: l.r.: [signature]
Conté on paper
26 x 22 cm
prov: Leonard Joel, Melbourne Nov 1978 (1155); Deutscher 1982; Leonard Joel, Melbourne Jul 1987 (526), Nov 1987 (856); Private Collection

DL10.3*
The Embrace, 1910–11
ins: [signature] 1910
Red chalk, pen, ink and coloured wash on paper
21 x 47 cm
prov: Nora (née Munro) and Gerald Summers, thence by descent to Mrs M. Summers; Sotheby's London Mar 1979 (42)
notes: Two female figures, green wash (personal communication with Gabriel Summers, 2024)

DL10.4*
Head of a Pensive Woman, c.1910
Red chalk on paper
33 x 29.2 cm
prov: Anthony D'Offay Ltd, London; Fine Art Society; Phillips, London 1997; Christie's London Sep 1997

DL10.5
The Awakening / The Wakening, 1910
ins: l.l.: Derwent Lees 1910 [written twice]; v.: The Awakening Derwent Lees
Watercolour and ink on paper
25.2 x 35.4 cm
prov: Rex Nan Kivell; Deutsher 1978; National Gallery of Australia, Canberra, purchased 1979
exh: Deutsher 1978 (41); Sane 1997, loaned by the National Gallery of Australia (34)

DL10.6
Sleeping Woman / Repose / Reclining Nude / Nude Lying on the Grass, 1910–13
ins: l.l.: Lees
Watercolour and ink on paper
25.4 x 35.6 cm
prov: Rex Nan Kivell; Redfern Gallery 1930; W. Maxwell Bolton; Sotheby's London Jul 1964 (93); Christie's London Oct 1974 (18), 1976; Joseph Brown Gallery, Melbourne spring 1976 (51); Deutsher 1978, 1982; Christie's Melbourne May 1991; Deutscher 1992; Christopher Day Gallery, Paddington; Christie's London Nov 1995; Christie's Melbourne Apr 1998 (366); Leonard Joel, Melbourne Nov 2005; Christie's London Jul 2008 (247); Artemis Auctions Aug 2009 (251); Mossgreen, Sydney 2010; Peter Walker Fine Art, Adelaide 2017; Private Collection
exh: NEAC 55th 1916 (168); Redfern 1930a (40); Deutsher 1978 (9); Deutscher Fine Art Melbourne Oct 1992 (29)

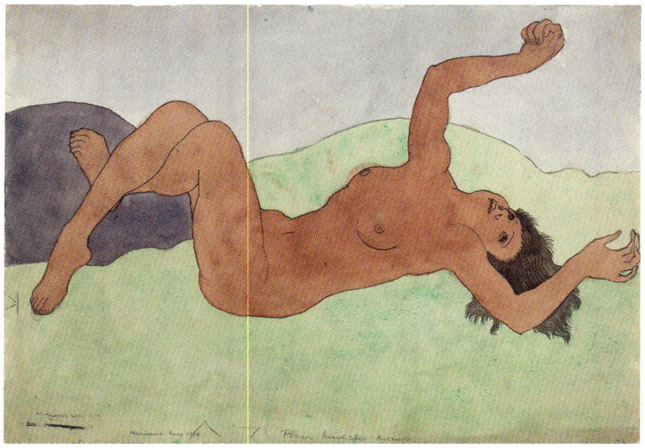

DL10.5

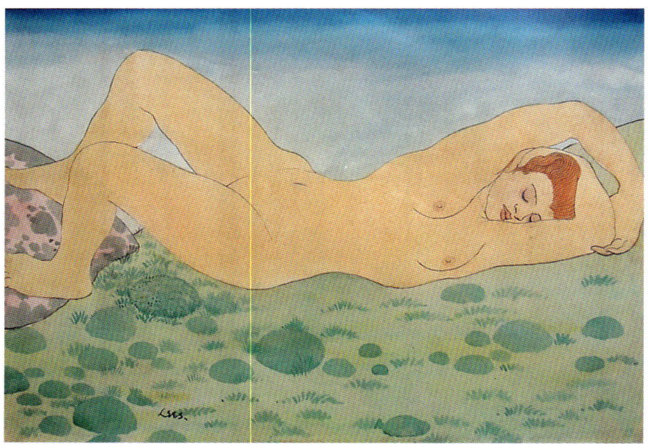

DL10.6

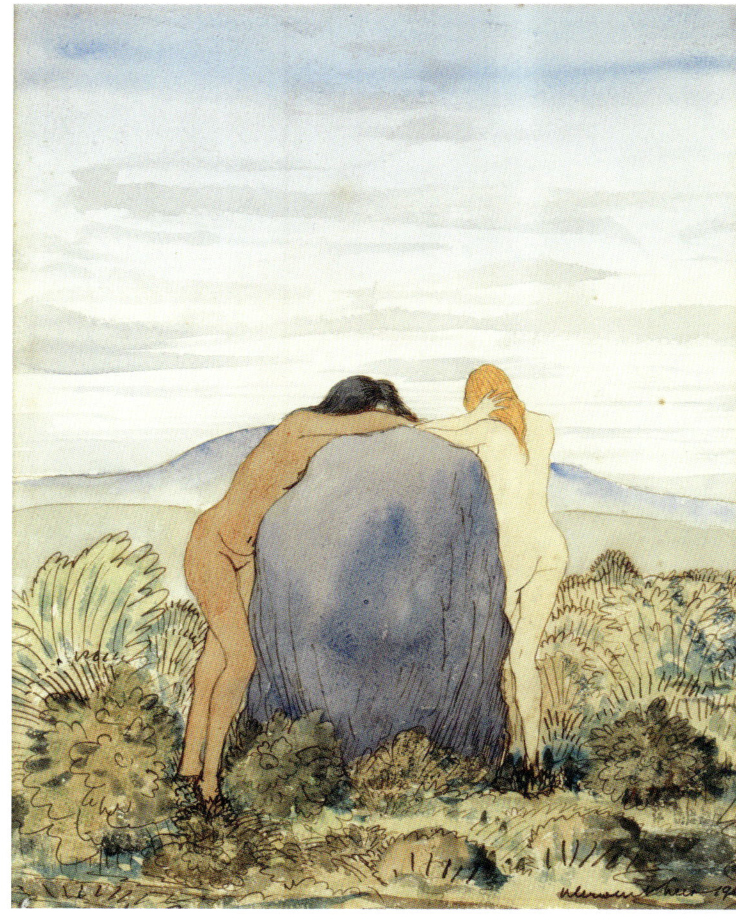

DL10.7

DL10.7
Two Nudes in Landscape / Two Female Nudes, Leaning against a Rock, 1910
ins: l.r.: Derwent Lees 1910; u.c.: Derwent Lees 1910 [in pencil], [window mount aperture marked in pencil at left edge]
Watercolour, pen and ink on paper
30.5 x 24 cm
prov: Sotheby's London Jul 1964 (92); W. Maxwell Bolton; Christie's London Oct 1974 (17); Lucy Johnson Historic + Modern, Burford; Private Collection; Deutscher 1982; Private Collection; Deutscher 2008; Charles Nodrum Gallery, Melbourne; Museum of Old and New Art (Mona), Tasmania, purchased 2022
exh: Deutscher Fine Art Melbourne Jul 1982 (43); Deutscher and Hackett Melbourne, Apr 2008 (228); Museum of Old and New Art (Mona), Hobart, *Monanisms* Nov 2022–4
notes: Grange Heath near Creech, Dorset; likely same models as in DL10.8

DL10.8
Bathers at the Blue Pool / Bather, The Blue Pool / Bathers: The Blue Pool, Dorset, c.1910
ins: v.: u.l.: 35; u.r.: [illeg.]; Derwent Lees / Galley picture [pencil]; Redfern Gallery label, typed c.: Bather, the Blue Pool/ DERWENT LEES
Watercolour and pencil on woven paper
35.4 x 25.2 cm
prov: Redfern Gallery 1946–8; Mr and Mrs J.B. Priestley 1950–51; Redfern Gallery 1952, 1954; Queensland Art Gallery | Gallery of Modern Art, purchased Mar 1954
exh: Redfern 1946b (528); 1947b (525), 1948 (602); Birmingham City Gallery 1952, loaned by the Redfern Gallery (169); Sane 1997, loaned by Queensland Art Gallery (31)
notes: Blue Pool, Dorset; likely the same models as in DL10.7

DL10.9
The Bathers, 1910–13
ins: l.r.: LEES
Ink and brush on paper
15.5 x 25.5 cm
prov: Redfern Gallery 1930; Admiral Sir Charles Madden; Redfern Gallery 1963; Christie's London Jul 1973 (262); John and Edward Barkes; Bridget McDonnell Gallery 1990; Private Collection 1997
exh: Redfern 1930a (39); Bridget McDonnell Gallery Dec 1990 (14); Sane 1997 (38)

DL10.10
Youth and Old Age / Youth and Age / The Red Dress, 1910
ins: l.l.: Lees; v.: [signature, title]
Watercolour wash and pencil on paper
29.2 x 25.4 cm
prov: Christie's London Jul 1988 (190); Sandra Lummis Fine Art, London; Bernard Kelly; Lyon and Turnbull, London Jan 2025 (220)
exh: Friday Club, London 1911

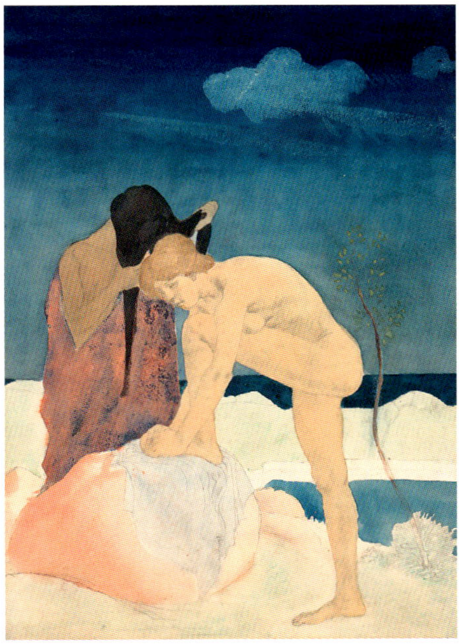

DL10.8

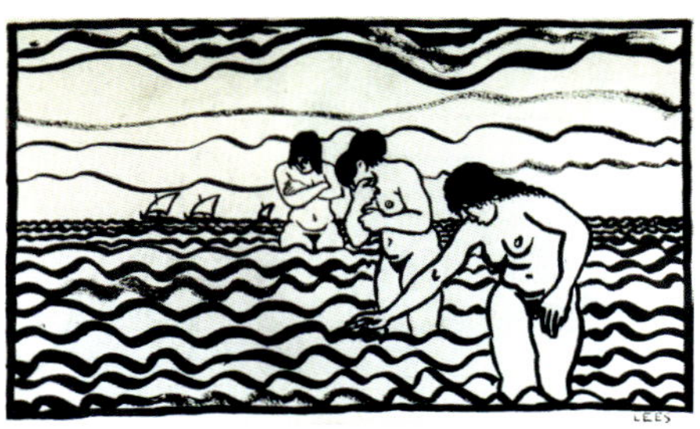

DL10.9

DL10.11**

Over the Hills to Bagdad / Women in Flowing Robes / Two Bedouin Women, 1910
ins: l.l.: Lees
Pencil and wash on paper
28 x 25.4 cm
prov: Phillips, London Jul 1980 (23); Bonhams 3, Oxford Nov 2009 (90)
exh: Friday Club, London 1911

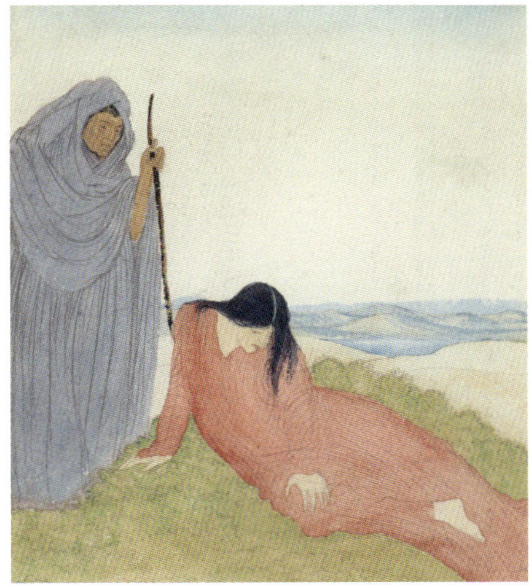

DL10.10

DL10.12*

Portrait of St Anthony, c.1910
Ink and wash on paper
47.5 x 37.5 cm
prov: Rex Nan Kivell; Deutsher 1978; Private Collection
exh: Deutsher 1978 (20)

DL10.13

St Anthony, Unfinished Study / Standing Nudes (Study) / Adam and Eve / The Temptation of St Anthony, c.1910
ins: v.: Derwent Lees [pencil]
Oil on panel
50 x 29 cm
prov: Redfern Gallery 1934, 1958; Bridget McDonnell Gallery 1986; Private Collection
exh: Redfern 1934 (36), 1958 (31); Bridget McDonnell Gallery Apr–May 1986 (12); Sane 1997 (1)

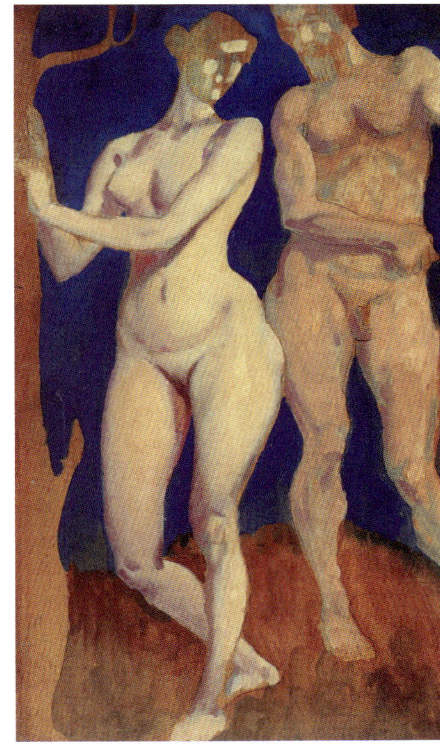

DL10.13

DL10.14*

Sketch Design for a Decoration, 1910–16
Watercolour on paper
exh: NEAC 55th 1916 (162)
notes: Unresolved record

DL10.15

Mythological Scene, 1910–12
Pencil, pen and ink on paper
18.2 x 35.5 cm
prov: Rex Nan Kivell; Deutsher 1978; National Gallery of Australia, Canberra, purchased 1979
exh: Deutsher 1978 (10); Sane 1997, loaned by the National Gallery of Australia (27)

DL10.16

Landscape at Collioure / Collioure, 1910
ins: l.l.: Lees Collioure 1910 Roussillon
Watercolour and gouache on paper
22.5 x 34 cm
prov: Arthur Clifton (Carfax Gallery); Francis Falconer Madan, purchased 1923, then presented to the National Gallery of British Art, Millbank (now Tate) through the National Art Collections Fund 1927
exh: Friday Club, London 1911, as 'Collioure' (52)
notes: Beside Fort Rond, Collioure, facing south; location as in DL10.26 and DL10.33

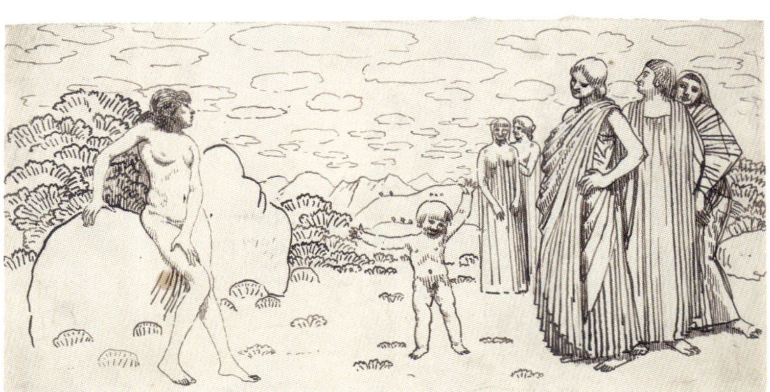

DL10.15

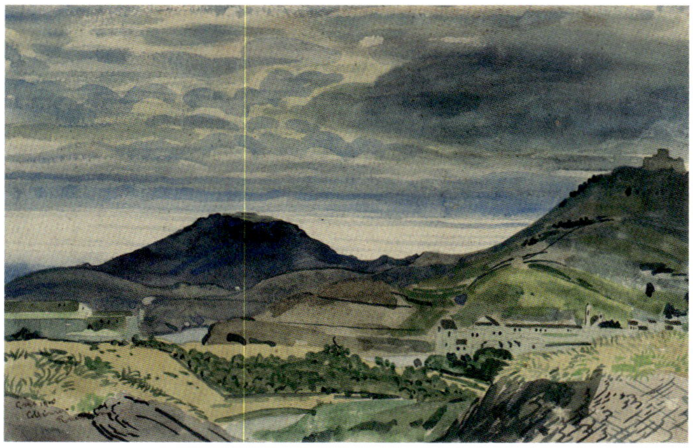

DL10.16

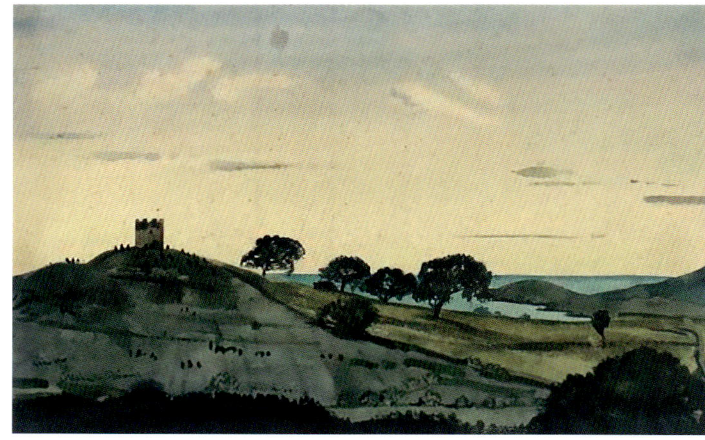

DL10.17

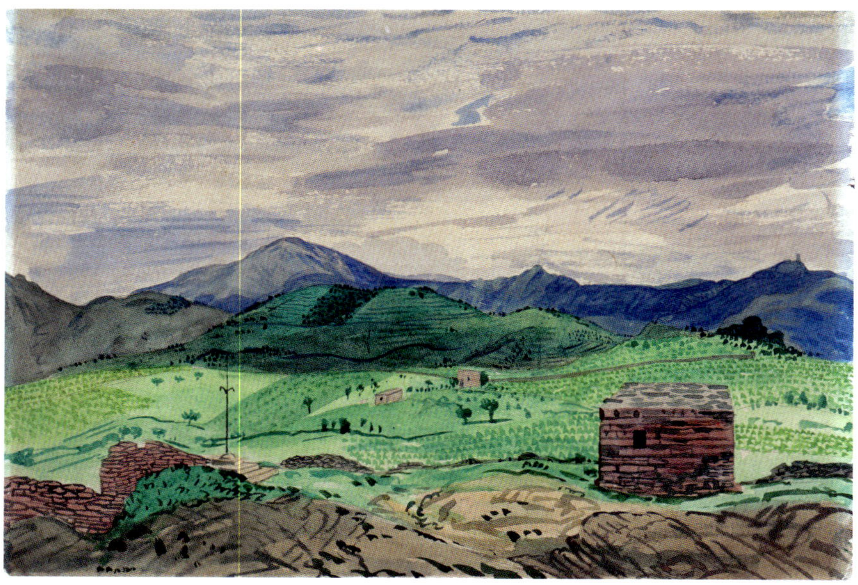

DL10.18

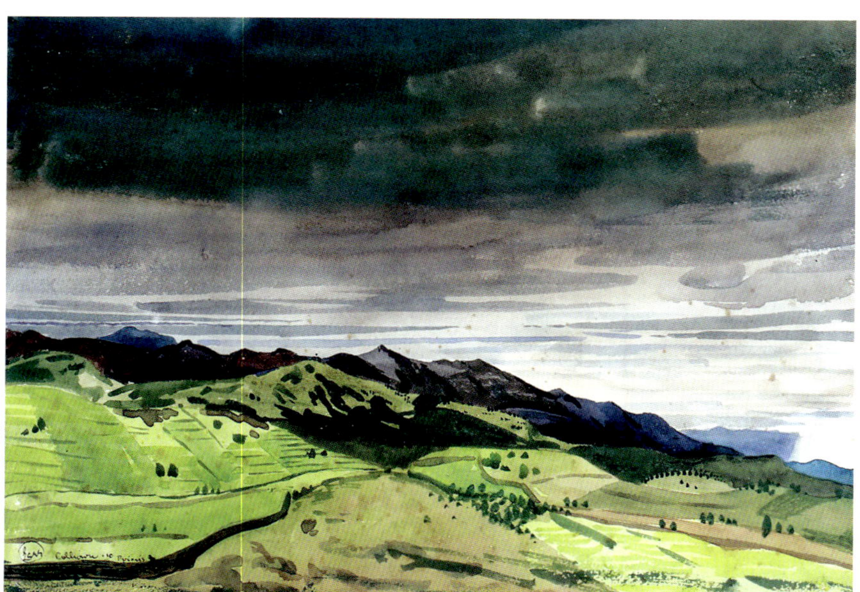

DL10.20

DL10.17
Collioure, Pyrenées / Colieure (Pyrenees) / Collioure, 1910
ins: l.l.: Lees 1910 Collioure – Pyrénées
Watercolour and bodycolour on buff paper
24 x 35.5 cm
prov: Goupil Gallery 1931 (?); Redfern Gallery 1932; Nora and Gerald Summers, thence by descent to Mrs M. Summers; Sotheby's London Mar 1979 (41); Christie's London Jun 2005 (96)
exh: Goupil 1931a (11); Redfern 1932 (16); NEAC summer 1945, as 'Colieure (Pyrenees)' (177) or DL10.20
notes: Torre del Campanar (Tour Vieille), Collioure

DL10.18
Vineyards Collioure / Provencal Landscape / Landscape with Mountains, 1910
ins: u.c.: Derwent Lees [pencil]
Watercolour and ink on paper
25 x 36 cm
prov: Redfern Gallery 1934; Sotheby's London Apr 1971 (69); Fine Art Society 1971 (M8810); Private Collection; donated to RISD 2016
exh: Redfern 1934 (40); Fine Art Society 1971 (47)
notes: Chapelle de Les Forques and Torre del Campanar (Tour Vieille), Collioure; location beside DL10.29

DL10.19
The Fortified Town, Roussillon / Collioure / Collioure – The Royal Castle, 1910
Watercolour and pencil on paper
25.4 x 35.5 cm
prov: Redfern Gallery 1963; Fine Art Society 1979, Feb 2000; Private Collection
exh: NEAC 54th 1915 (175); Redfern 1963 (337)

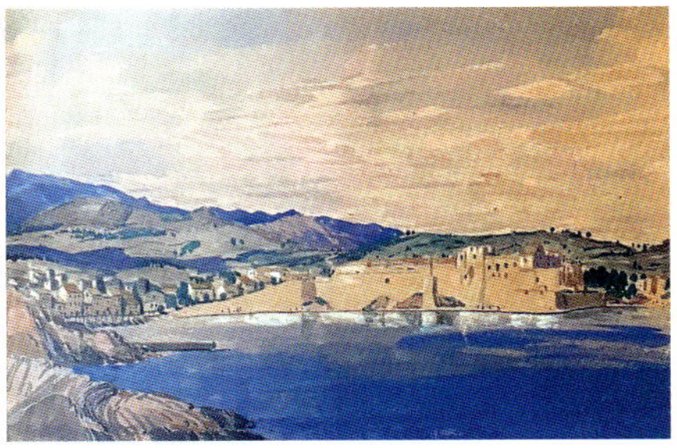

DL10.19

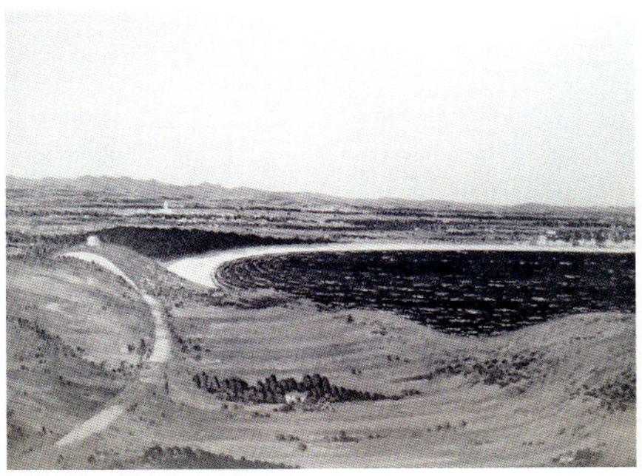

DL10.22

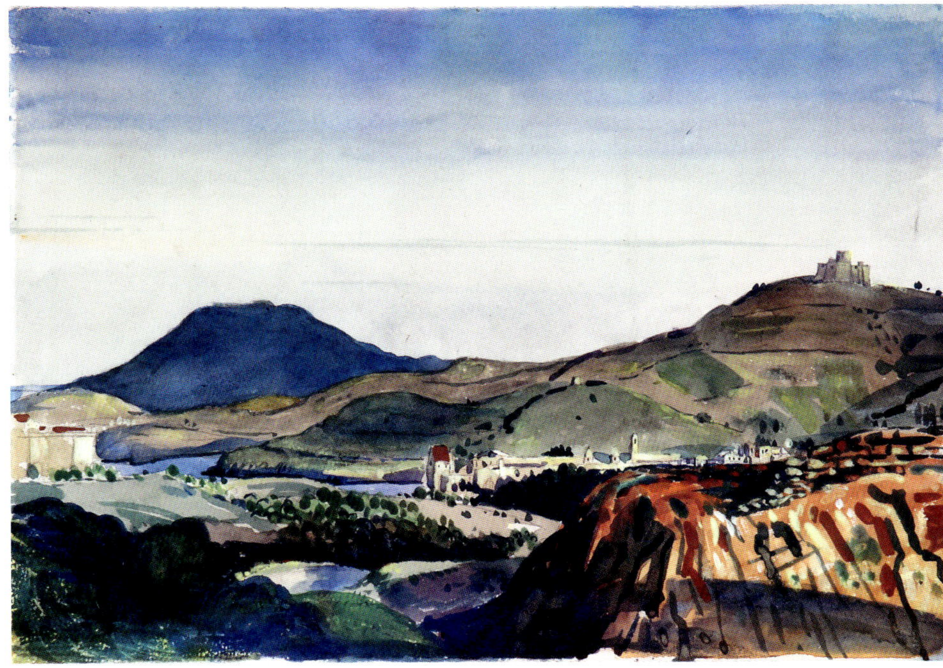

DL10.26

DL10.20
Near Collioure in the Pyrenees / Colliou̇re, Pyrenées, No.2 / Colieure (Pyrenees), 1910
ins: l.l.: Lees [in cartouche] Collioure. 10 Pyrénées
Watercolour on paper
24.5 x 34.5 cm
prov: Mrs Clifton (Carfax Gallery); Goupil Gallery 1931; Thos. Agnew & Sons Feb–Mar 1956 (101); Sir David Scott 1959; Sotheby's London Nov 2008 (180)
exh: Goupil 1931a (129); NEAC summer 1945, as 'Colieure (Pyrenees)' (177) or DL10.17
notes: Albères mountains from Puig d'Ambeille, Collioure

DL10.21**
Argelès, Mediterranean / Argeles / Angles / Angeles / Argelès, Pyrenees, 1910 / Angeles, Pyrenees / South of France, 1910
ins: l.l.: Derwent Lees. 1910 / Argeles Pyrenees
Watercolour, pen and black ink on paper
24 x 35.5 cm
prov: Sir Michael Sadler 1939; Leicester Galleries, London 1944; Prof. M.J. Stewart; Phillips, London Jan 1993; Christie's London Jun 1994 (107A); Lawrences, Crewkerne Jan 2003; Bonhams 3, London, Jun 2003
exh: NEAC 44th 1910 (287); British Contemporary Art 1933 (74); Redfern 1939a, collection of Sir Michael Sadler (129); Leicester Galleries, London *Selected Paintings, Drawings, and Sculpture from the Collection of the late Sir Michael Sadler* Jan–Feb 1944 (136)
notes: Roussillon Plain and the Corbières range from Anse du Porteil, Argelès

DL10.22
Coast at Collioure / The Bay, Cassis, South of France, 1910
Oil on canvas
50.8 x 60.9 cm
prov: W. Wallis; R. G. Micklethwait; Christie's London Jun 1933 (112); Sotheby's London Nov 1933 (45); Malcolm; Sotheby's London Dec 1963, collection of W. Wallis (41)
exh: NEAC 45th 1911 (4)
notes: 1930s ownership order unclear; the Roussillon Plain and railway line from Collioure to Argelès

DL10.23 (see p.55)
Collioure / The Sea Coast (?), 1910
ins: l.r.: Derwent Lees. 10 Collioure
Watercolour on paper
25.2 x 35.5 cm
prov: Piccadilly Circus Galleries, London; V&A, purchased 1963
exh: NEAC 44th 1910 (289) (?)
notes: Fort Béar and coast, Collioure

DL10.24*
Hannibal's Plain, Pyrenees, 1910
Watercolour on paper
exh: NEAC 44th 1910 (285)
notes: Unresolved record

DL10.25 (see p.51)
Mediterranean Bay / La Ciotat / La Ciotat, Provence, 1910
ins: l.l.: Lees [in pencil]
Watercolour and ink on buff paper
24.7 x 35.5 cm
prov: Redfern Gallery 1939, 1943; Mr and Mrs J.B. Priestley 1946–51; Martyn Gregory, London; Christie's London, *The Martyn Gregory Collection of British Art* Mar 2022 (179); Private Collection
exh: NEAC 44th 1910 (180); Redfern 1939a (117), 1943 (245); Martyn Gregory, London, *A Foray into the 20th Century: Works by British Artists* Apr–May 2015 (40)
notes: Fort Béar and La Mauresque from Collioure

DL10.26
Collioure / Collinante, 1910
ins: l.l.: [D?] Lees 1910 Collioure Roussillon
Watercolour and pencil on paper
25.4 x 35.5 cm
prov: Goupil Gallery 1922 (?); John William Buxton Knight and family, Leeds Art Gallery (through the Bilbrough Bequest, no.482), purchased 1923
exh: Goupil 1922 (2); Leeds Art Gallery 1929, as 'Collinante', p.41; Welsh Arts Council 1982–3 (6)
notes: Beside Fort Rond, Collioure, facing south; location as in DL10.16 and DL10.33

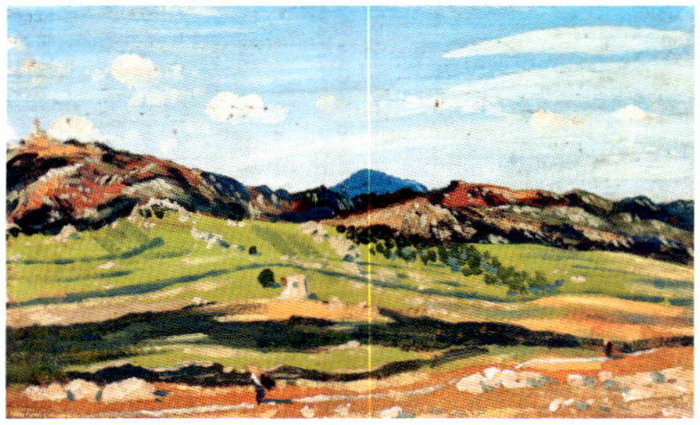

DL10.27

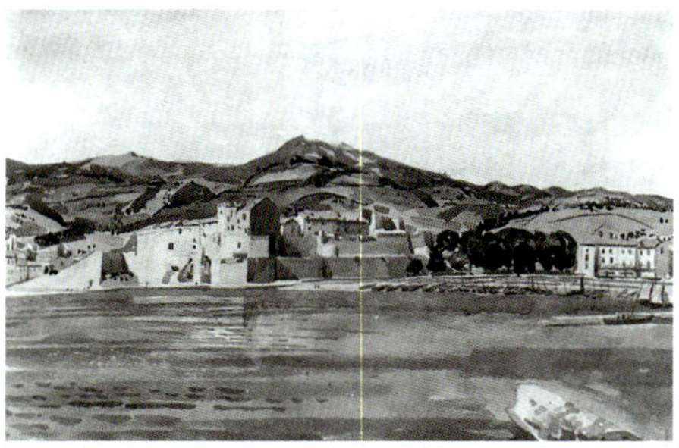

DL10.28

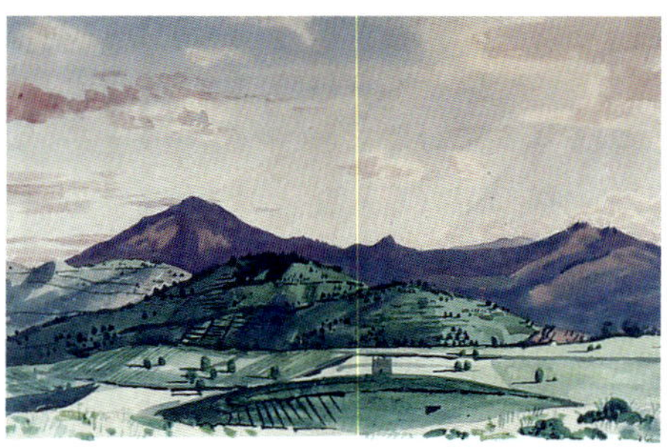

DL10.29

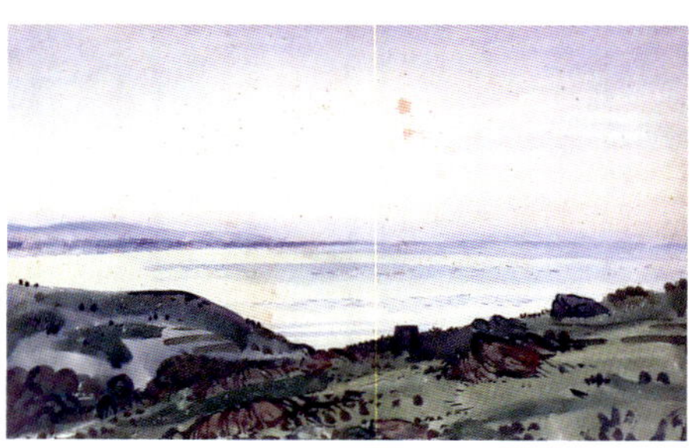

DL10.31

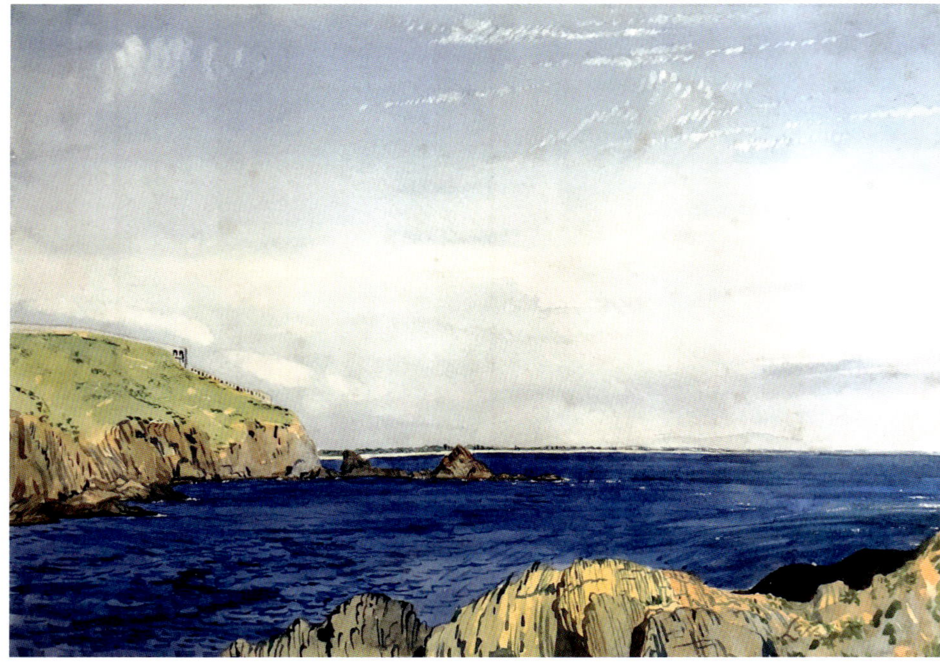

DL10.30

DL10.27
Tour de La Massane, Collioure / Mountainous Landscape, 1910–11
ins: [signature]
Oil on card
25 x 35 cm
prov: Lord Henry Cavendish-Bentinck (?); Sotheby's London May 1933 (94); Burrows; Private Collection 1930s, thence by descent; Sotheby's London Mar 2016 (112), Sep 2019 (164)
notes: Tour de La Massane, the Albères mountains and Torre del Campanar (Tour Vieille) behind Collioure

DL10.28
Port Romanesque, Roussillon, 1910
ins: l.r.: D Lees 1910
Watercolour and pencil on paper
25.4 x 35.5 cm
prov: Sir Edward Marsh; Leicester Galleries, London; Lord Reigate, thence by descent
exh: NEAC 54th 1915 (274)
notes: Collioure harbour from the breakwater

DL10.29
Hills behind Collioure / Evening Wales, 1910
Watercolour on paper
23.2 x 33.8 cm
prov: Redfern Gallery 1933; purchased by the Leeds Art Collections Fund, donated to the Leeds Art Gallery (in memory of Mr and Mrs J.E. Town) 1933
exh: Mostyn Art Gallery 1982–3, as 'Evening Wales' (54)
notes: Torre del Campanar (Tour Vieille), Collioure from the Chapelle de Les Forques; location beside DL10.18

DL10.30
Mediterranean Scene / Les Cottes (?), 1910
ins: l.r.: Lees 10
Watercolour on paper
25.2 x 35.4 cm
prov: Piccadilly Circus Galleries, London; V&A, purchased 1960
exh: NEAC 45th 1911 (75) (?)
notes: From Chapelle St Vincent, Collioure

DL10.31
Coast North of Collioure / Evening Wales / The Welsh Coast at Evening, 1910
Watercolour on paper
22.4 x 34 cm
prov: Redfern Gallery 1930, 1933; purchased by the Leeds Art Collections Fund, donated to the Leeds Art Gallery (in memory of Mr and Mrs J.E. Town) 1933
exh: Redfern 1930a, as 'The Welsh Coast at Evening' (28); Temple Newsam House, Leeds, *Acquisitions of the Leeds Art Collection Fund 1913–1949* 1968 (18050/18080); Mostyn Art Gallery 1982–3 (55)
notes: From Collioure facing the Corbières range; location as in DL10.29

DL10.32
Pyrenees and Mediterranean / Welsh Hills, 1910
Watercolour on paper
22.2 x 35.6 cm
prov: Redfern Gallery; Herbert Morton Hepworth, bequeathed to Leeds Art Gallery 1943
exh: NEAC 45th 1911, as 'Pyrenees and Mediterranean' (39); Mostyn Art Gallery 1982–3, as 'Welsh Hills' (56)
notes: Mont Canigou and the Roussillon Plain from Collioure

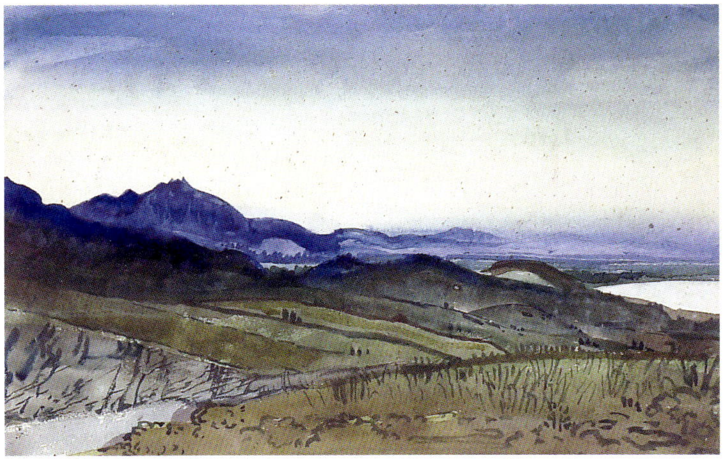

DL10.32

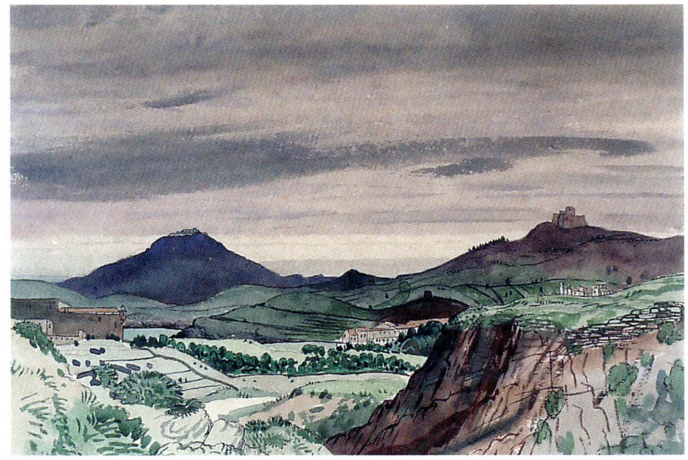

DL10.33

DL10.33
Collioure, 1910
ins: l.l.: Derwent Lees 10 Collioure
Watercolour on paper
24.9 x 36.1 cm
prov: Herbert Morton Hepworth; bequeathed to Leeds Art Gallery 1943
exh: Mostyn Art Gallery 1982–3 (53)
notes: Beside Fort Rond, Collioure, facing south; location as in DL10.16 and DL10.26

DL10.34**
A Continental Mountain Landscape, 1910–12
ins: [signature]
Watercolour and pencil on paper
33 x 44.3 cm
prov: Anderson & Garland Auctioneers, Newcastle upon Tyne Jun 2008 (47); Private Collection
notes: Mont Canigou from Prades, Roussillon

DL10.35*
Port Vendres, France, 1910
Watercolour on paper
exh: NEAC 45th 1911 (48)
notes: Unresolved record

DL10.36*
Mediterranean Coast / Mediterranean / A Mediterranean Bay, 1910–14
Watercolour on paper
22.8 x 32.4 cm
prov: Redfern Gallery 1934; R.H. Kitson; Christie's London, May 1966, collection R.H. Kitson (201)
exh: Redfern 1934 (45), 1939a, collection of R.H. Kitson (130)

DL10.37*
Fishing Boats at Evening / The Fishing Fleet (?), 1910
Watercolour on paper
prov: Sotheby's Sussex Oct 1992
exh: NEAC 45th 1911, as 'The Fishing Fleet' (181)
notes: Location of work unknown

DL10.38*
Mediterranean Coast / Mediterranean, 1910–14
Watercolour on paper
prov: Redfern Gallery 1930; Earl of Sandwich 1930s
exh: Redfern 1930a (21); British Contemporary Art 1933 (78); Redfern 1939a, collection of the Earl of Sandwich (116)

DL10.39*
Seated Nude, 1910–12
ins: [signature]
Pen, ink and grey wash on paper
34.3 x 22.2 cm
prov: Christie's London May 1965 (23); Sanders 1965; Christie's London Jul 1973 (53)

DL10.40*
Colliore / Collioure, c.1910
Watercolour and pencil on paper
24 x 35.5 cm
prov: Christie's London Jul 1940; Collard; Frank Aldous Girling; Arthur Tooth & Sons, London Jan 1973 (13); Fine Art Society 1978; New Grafton Gallery, London Oct–Nov 1980 (27)
exh: Fine Art Society London, *Watercolours 1780–1950s* Apr–May 1978 (40)

DL10.41*
The Coast at Collioure, c.1910
Watercolour on paper
24.1 x 35.5 cm
prov: V.D. Wethered 1927–47; Sotheby's London Jun 1947, property of V.D. Wethered (131); Brown and Phillips, London 1947
exh: Slade 1927, loaned by V.D. Wethered (317)

DL10.42*
A View in Provence / Provence / In Provence, 1910–14
Watercolour on paper
prov: Redfern Gallery 1930, 1933, 1939
exh: Redfern 1930a (30); British Contemporary Art 1933 (75); Redfern 1939a (124)

DL10.43*
Colliore / Colliore, 1910
Watercolour on paper
prov: Redfern Gallery 1933; Maurice Ingram; Redfern Gallery 1941–6
exh: British Contemporary Art 1933 (80); Redfern 1941b, collection of the late Maurice Ingram (82), 1943 (229), 1944a (42), 1944b (349), 1945b (429), 1946b (368)

DL10.44*
Pays Chimérique, 1910–13
exh: Friday Club, London 1915 (18)
notes: Unresolved record

DL10.45*
Mediterranean / Mediterranean Coast / Mediterranean Landscape, 1910–14
Watercolour on paper
22.9 x 33 cm
prov: Redfern Gallery 1944; Thos. Agnew & Sons Feb–Mar 1956 (107), Jan–Feb 1957 (111), Mar 1957 (114); Private Collection; Christie's London Mar 1986 (303)
exh: Redfern 1944a (52), 1944b (376)

DL10.46*
Landscape, Collioure / Landscape, South of France / South of France, 1910
Watercolour on paper
prov: Redfern Gallery 1934, 1939, 1945
exh: Redfern 1934 (42), 1939a (127), 1945a (215)

DL10.47*
Colliure Bay / The Bay, Collioure, c.1910
Watercolour on paper
prov: Thos. Agnew & Sons Feb–Mar 1956 (113); Christie's London Feb 1980 (65); Sotheby's London Jan 1986 (180)
notes: Unresolved record

10.48*
Pyrenees, c.1910
Watercolour on paper
prov: Redfern Gallery; R.H. Kitson
exh: Redfern 1939a, collection of R.H. Kitson (114)

10.49
Citadel at Collioure, Roussillon / The Citadel, Collioure, 1910
ins: l.l.: Lees 1910 Citadel. Collioure, Roussillion
Watercolour on paper
24.7 x 35.5 cm
prov: Carfax Gallery, London; Redfern Gallery 1934, 1963; Leicester Galleries, London; The Mount Trust; Thos. Agnew & Sons Jan 1973, collection of The Mount Trust (21); Christie's London May 1973 (39)
exh: Redfern 1934 (46), 1963 (336)

DL10.50*
Massane, Pyrenees / Masserne, Pyrenees / Massere, Pyrenees, 1910
Watercolour on paper
prov: Goupil Gallery 1922; Lord Howard de Walden 1934; Redfern Gallery 1939
exh: NEAC 55th 1916 (150); Goupil 1922 (10); Redfern 1934, loaned by Lord Howard de Walden (52), 1939a (123)
notes: The Massane hill sits in the Albères mountains behind Collioure

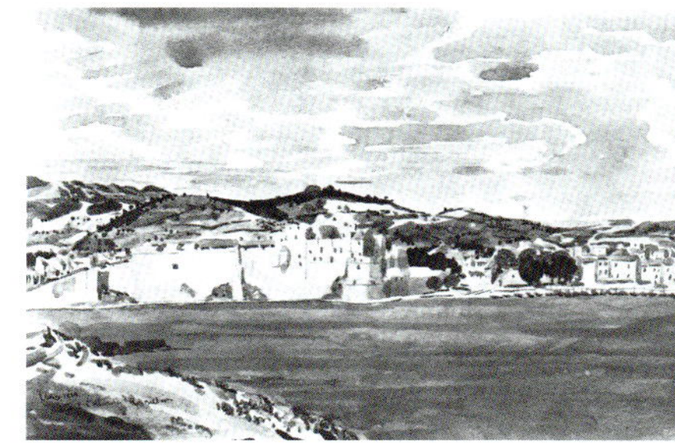

DL10.49

1911

DL11.1
Arenig Mawr, North Wales / Arenig Manor, North Wales / Arenig Fawr / Landscape, 1911
ins: l.r.: LEES 1911
Oil on panel
24.5 x 35 cm
prov: Charles Aitken purchased for the CAS 1912; gifted by the CAS to Stoke on Trent City Museum and Art Gallery (now Potteries Museum and Art Gallery) 1924
exh: Whitechapel 1914, loaned by the CAS (367); Edwardian Art 1987 (58); Potteries Museum and Art Gallery, May–Sep 1989, *Collected Works Presented by the Contemporary Art Society* Feb–Apr 2003, *Passion for Painting* Jul–Aug 2004, *Minerals Make Mountains* Nov 2011; Museum of Modern Art, Machynlleth, Wales, *James Dickson Innes 1887–1914: Arenig* Sep–Nov 2014, loaned by Potteries Museum and Art Gallery
notes: Rhinog Fawr from Bronaber, North Wales

DL11.2
Welsh Landscape in Winter / Snow on Welsh Mountains, c.1911
Oil on panel
25.2 x 35.5 cm
prov: Chenil 1913–14; Brook Street Art Gallery, London Jan 1935 (19); Roland, Browse & Delbanco Gallery, London 1951; Glynn Vivian Art Gallery, Swansea, purchased 1951
exh: Chenil 1913–14 (61); The National Library of Wales, Aberystwyth and the Arts Council of Great Britain, London, *The Artist in Wales* May–Sep 1952; Mostyn Art Gallery 1982–3, loaned by Glynn Vivian Art Gallery (57); National Gallery of Wales, *Art in Exile* Dec 2001, loaned by Glynn Vivian Art Gallery (35); National Museum and Gallery Cardiff, Museum voor Schone Kunsten, Ghent, Hannema-de Stuers Fundatie, Heino, *Art in Exile – Flanders, Wales and the First World War* 2002; Museum voor Schone Kunsten, Ghent, *British Vision – Observation and Imagination in British Art 1750–1950* 2007–8; Glynn Vivian Art Gallery, *Swansea Stories* Sep 2019–Mar 2020
notes: Rhinog Fawr from Bronaber, North Wales

DL11.3**
Welsh Hills / Welsh Hills in Winter, c.1911
Oil on panel
25.4 x 35.5 cm
prov: Redfern Gallery 1930, 1934, 1946; Mr and Mrs J.B. Priestley 1946–51; Sotheby's London Dec 1970 (58); Arthur Tooth & Sons, London Oct–Nov 1974 (4); Spink; Christie's London Nov 1996 (5)
exh: Redfern 1930a (35), 1934 (33), 1946a (44)
notes: Mounts Y Foel and Arenig Fach, North Wales

DL11.4
Landscape at Bala, Merioneth, Wales / Storm on the Coast / Coast Scene, c.1911
ins: v.: Derwent Lees
Oil on panel
25.5 x 34.5 cm
prov: Arthur Crossland 1939–56; Christie's London Mar 1956 (157, 2nd of 2 in the lot); F.B.C. Bravington 1956; Thos. Agnew & Sons 1968 (9); Spink 1979; Christie's London Jun 1995 (108); Private Collection
exh: Mostyn Art Gallery, *The Native Land* 1979, loaned by Spink & Son Ltd
notes: Llyn Tegid (Lake Bala), North Wales

DL11.5
Llyn Tegid, Merionethshire / The Blue Pool, Dorset, 1911
ins: l.l.: LEES 1911
Oil on panel
25 x 36 cm
prov: Sir Edward Marsh 1934; Maurice Ingram 1939, bequeathed to the CAS 1941, thence gifted to the Ferens Art Gallery, Hull 1946
exh: Redfern 1934, loaned by Sir Edward Marsh (18), 1939a, collection of Maurice Ingram (107), 1941b, collection of the late Maurice Ingram (4); British Council, *Cairo, International Exhibition* 1947 (15); City of Bradford, Cartwright Hall, *Jubilee Exhibition* 1954 (215); Leeds University

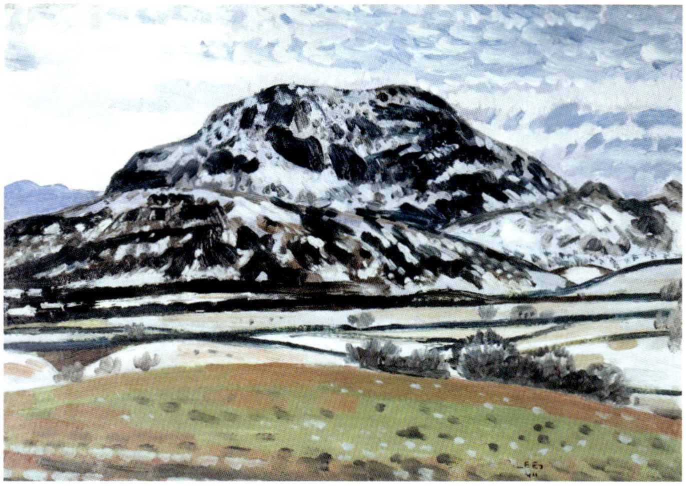

DL11.1

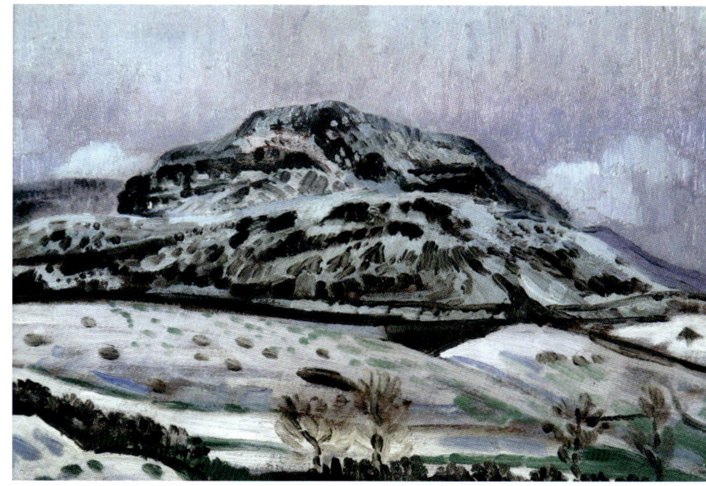

DL11.2

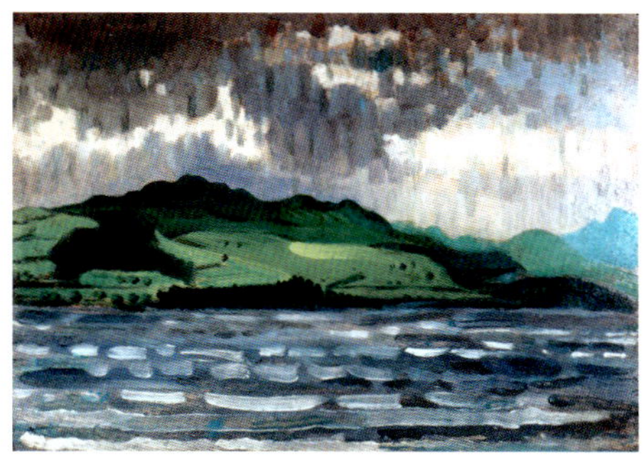

DL11.4

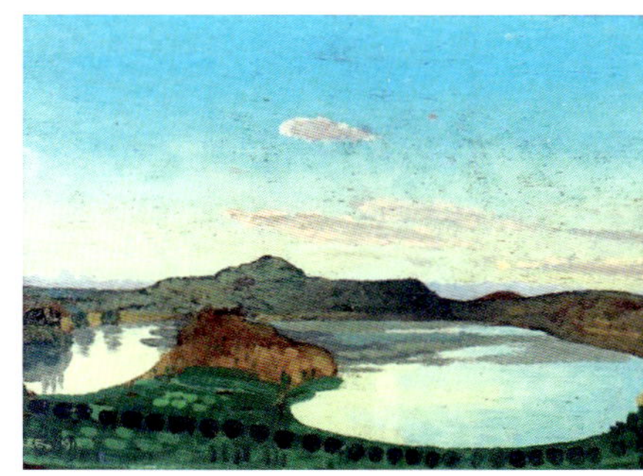

DL11.5

1963; Museum & Art Gallery Service for Yorkshire, *Gifts to Yorkshire Galleries by the Contemporary Art Society*; Edwardian Art 1987, loaned by the Ferens Art Gallery (59); Cartwright Hall, Bradford, and Ferens Art Gallery, Hull Jun–Aug 1987 (59); Ferens Art Gallery, *From Steer to Spencer* Jun–Sep 2000; Ferens Art Gallery, *From Victorian to Edwardian* Jun–Sep 2009; Ferens Art Gallery, *Monet in Mind* Jun 2021
notes: Llyn Tegid (Lake Bala) from above Pen-y-Bont railway station, North Wales

DL11.6
Evening / Lake at Sunset, 1911
Oil on canvas
40 x 49.5 cm
prov: John Quinn Collection 1913; E.J.G. Deordan 1927; Sotheby's New York Mar 1972 (80); Mayor Gallery, London; Government Art Collection, London, purchased 1972
exh: Armory Show 1913, Armory Building Gallery G, New York (105), Chicago (215), Boston (554), loaned by John Quinn; Quinn 1927 (212); Government Art Collection Exhibition, Fine Art Society London Aug 1981; British Embassy, Mexico City (c.1984–2002); British Embassy, Paris (c.2003–13); HM Treasury, London 2015–17; Foreign Secretary's Residence, London 2017–18; 11 Downing Street, London 2020–24
notes: Location as in DL11.5

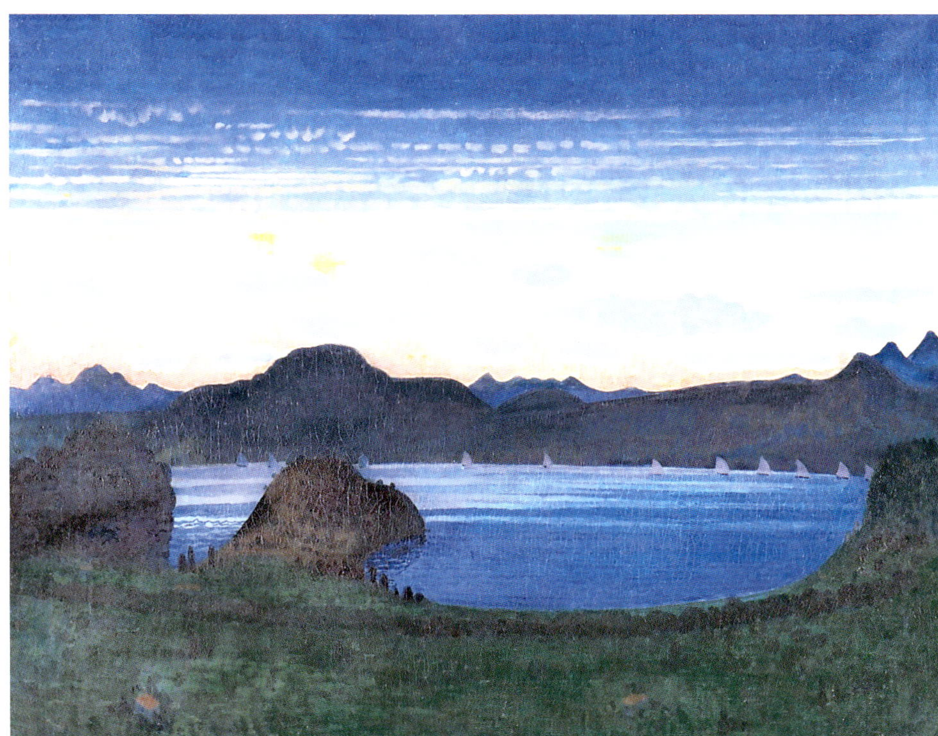

DL11.6

DL11.7*
A Sullen Day, 1911
Oil
35.5 x 45.7 cm
prov: John Quinn Collection 1913; S. Lustgarten 1927
exh: Armory Show 1913, New York, loaned by John Quinn (555); Quinn 1927 (69)
notes: In Quinn 1927 sale catalogue, 'Neo-primitive rendering in imaginative colors, of enamel texture, of a deep blue shaded lake enclosed by majestic mountains; in the left foreground a flowering shrub; under a blue sky, with heavy, rolling clouds tinged with the glow of the sun', p.33

DL11.8
Portrait of Elizabeth Lipczinski with her Dog Fanny / Portrait of Elizabeth Lipczinski with her Dog Fanny, an Italian Greyhound, at Nant Duu [sic] in the Shadow of Arenig Fawr, Wales, c.1911
Oil on panel
46.2 x 30.2 cm
prov: William Waters 1989; Peter Nahum, London 1989; William Waters 1989; Christie's London Oct 2024 (170)
notes: Reattributed from Augustus John to DL by Peter Nahum et al. 1989; shore of Llyn Arenig Fawr, North Wales

DL11.9*
A Mountain Lake, Wales / Lake in Wales / Mountain Lake, 1911–14
Watercolour on paper
prov: Redfern Gallery 1934, 1939
exh: NEAC 55th 1916 (163); Redfern 1934 (39), 1939a (125)

DL11.10*
Welsh Mountains, 1911–14
Oil on panel
25.5 x 35.5 cm
prov: Redfern Gallery 1930, 1932; Gerald Summers 1939; Sotheby's London May 1984
exh: Redfern 1930a (36), 1932 (17), 1939a, collection of Gerald Summers (104)

DL11.11*
Welsh Mountains / Welsh Mountain Landscape, 1911–14
Oil
prov: Lord Ivor Spencer-Churchill 1939
exh: British Contemporary Art 1933 (64); Empire Art 1939, loaned by Lord Ivor Spencer-Churchill (68)

DL11.12*
Distant Hills / Welsh Mountains, 1911–16
Oil
prov: Redfern Gallery 1930, 1939, 1958 (?)
exh: Redfern 1930a (15), 1939a (31), 1939b (15), 1958 (46)
notes: Unresolved record

DL11.13*
North Wales, 1911–14
Oil
prov: Redfern Gallery 1933, 1934, 1939
exh: Redfern 1933 (95), 1934 (3), 1939a (27)
notes: Unresolved record

DL11.14*
Wales, 1911–14
Oil
prov: Redfern Gallery 1934
exh: Redfern 1934 (7)
notes: Unresolved record

DL11.15*
Cale and Farm Buildings / Kale and Farm Buildings, c.1911
Watercolour on paper
22.2 x 31.1 cm
prov: Christie's London May 1974 (214), Oct 1974 (147); Dandleson 1974
notes: Location of work unknown

DL11.16*
Blossom, c.1911
ins: l.l.: Lees
Oil on canvas
28.5 x 32.5 cm
prov: Deutscher 1982; Leonard Joel, Melbourne Aug 2000 (402); Private Collection
notes: Unresolved record

DL11.17
Girl in a Landscape / Lyndra in Green Dress / Gypsy Girl in a Landscape / A Girl in the Welsh Mountains / Landscape with Young Girl, c.1911
ins: l.r.: LEES [partially visible, wiped]
Oil on canvas
76.5 x 49 cm
prov: Chenil Gallery 1913–15; Redfern Gallery 1930, 1945; Mrs B.L. Goodwin; Christie's London Mar 1993 (25A), Oct 1993; Private Collection
exh: Chenil 1913–14 (34); Whitechapel 1914, loaned by the Chenil Gallery (381); Chenil 1915 (92); Redfern 1930a (33), 1945b (200); Sane 1997 (8)
notes: Elizabeth Lipczinski; shore of Llyn Tryweryn, with Moel Llyfnant in background, near Nant Ddu, North Wales

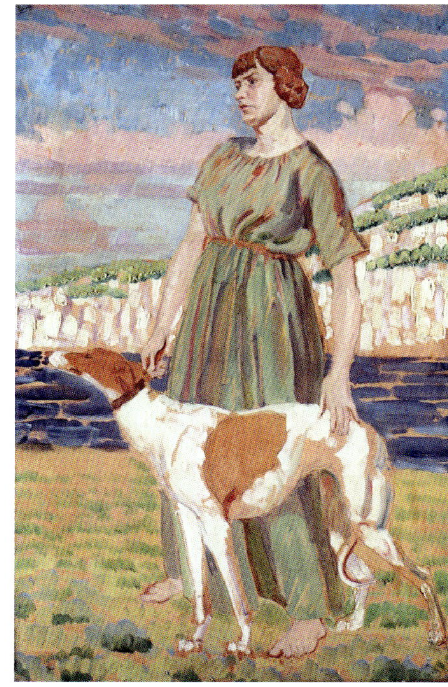

DL11.8

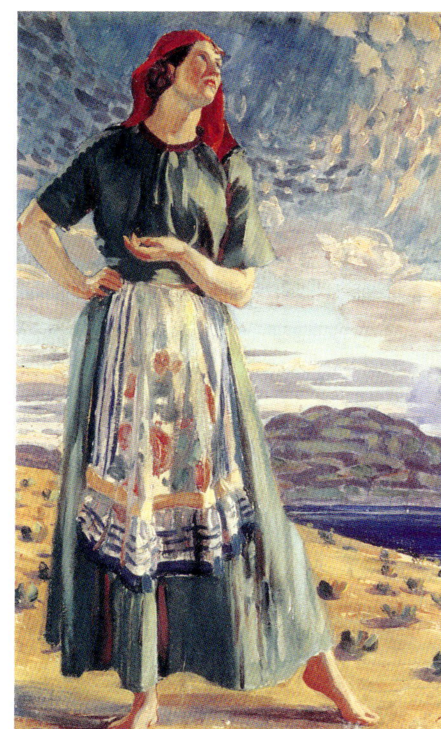

DL11.17

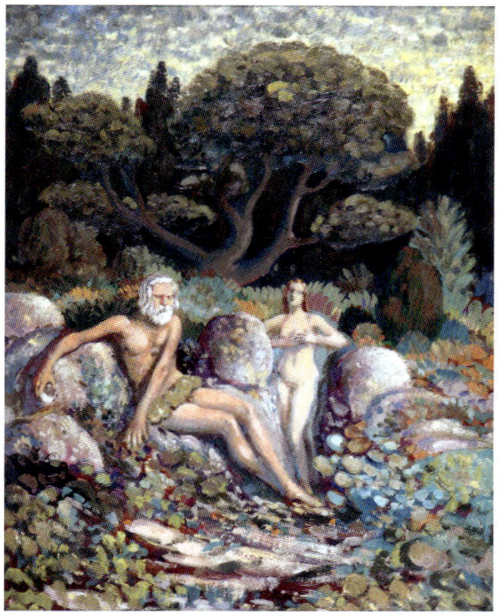

DL11.20

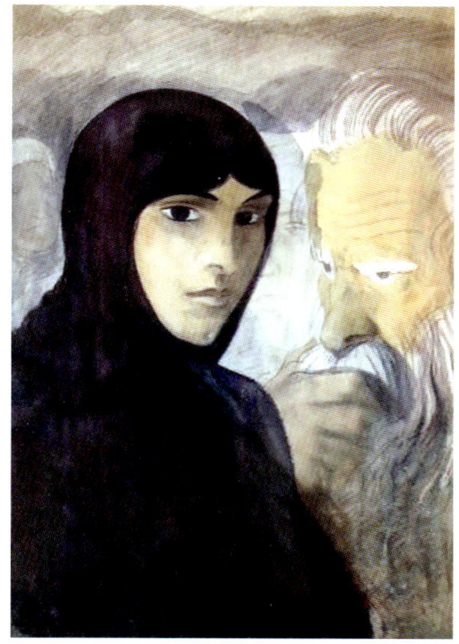

DL11.21

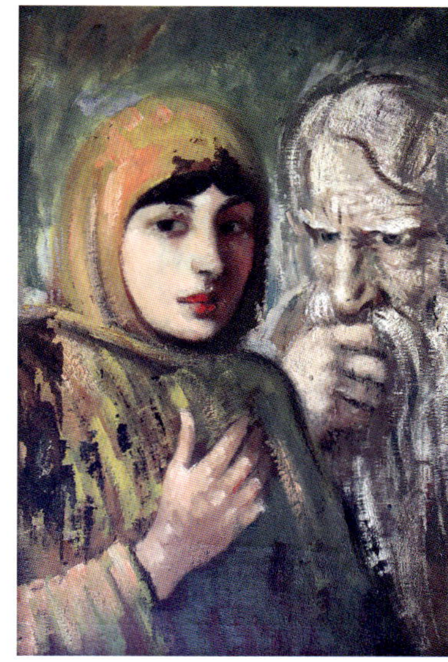

DL11.22

DL11.18**
Figures in a Landscape / Three Gypsy Women, c.1911
Oil on panel
38 x 24.2 cm
prov: Christie's London Mar 1998 (123)

DL11.19*
Figures in a Welsh Landscape / Two Figures in an Irish Landscape (?), c.1911
ins: [signature]
Watercolour and pencil on paper
28 x 24 cm
prov: Mrs Edith Lees 1939; Christie's London Jul 1969 (316) (?)
exh: Redfern 1939a, loaned by Edith Lees (126)

DL11.20
A Woodland Idyll, c.1911
Oil on panel
50.9 x 39.5 cm
prov: Robert H. Jackson; Manchester Art Gallery, purchased 1933
exh: Barbican Gallery, London, *The Last Romantics* Feb–Apr 1989, loaned by Manchester Art Gallery

DL11.21
Russian Peasants, c.1911
ins: v.: [signature, title]
Watercolour on paper
50 x 34.5 cm
prov: Redfern Gallery; John and Edward Barkes; Bridget McDonnell Gallery 1988; Private Collection
exh: Bridget McDonnell Gallery Feb–Mar 1988 (18)

DL11.22
Russian Peasants, c.1911
Oil on canvas
61 x 41 cm
prov: Redfern Gallery 1934; R.E. Abbott (now Abbott and Holder), London; Winifred-Coombe Tennant, purchased 1953, thence by descent
exh: Redfern 1934 (37)

DL11.23
The Yellow Cap / Two Gypsy Women, c.1911
ins: v.: THE YELLOW CAP DERWENT LEES
Watercolour, bodycolour, gouache, brush and black ink on paper
48.3 x 34.3 cm
prov: Redfern Gallery 1944; Phillips, London Jan 1988; Christie's London Jan 1991 (18), Nov 2001 (122)
exh: Redfern 1944a (43)
notes: Studies of Elizabeth Lipczinski (?)

DL11.24
Four Heads / Four Classical Heads / Study of Heads, c.1911
ins: l.l.: Lees
Pencil on paper
47 x 33.6 cm
prov: Dowdeswell and Dowdeswell, London; Christie's London Feb 1917 (78); Arthur Crossland 1939–56; Christie's London Feb 1956 (57, 2nd of 2 in the lot); Piccadilly Gallery, London 1956; Sotheby's London May 1979 (59); Parkin Fine Art, London; Brighton & Hove Museum and Art Gallery, purchased 1979
exh: Laing 1939 (16)
notes: Studies of Elizabeth Lipczinski (?)

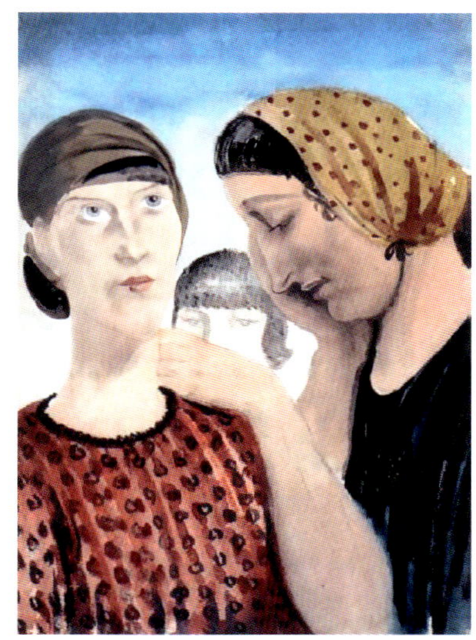

DL11.23

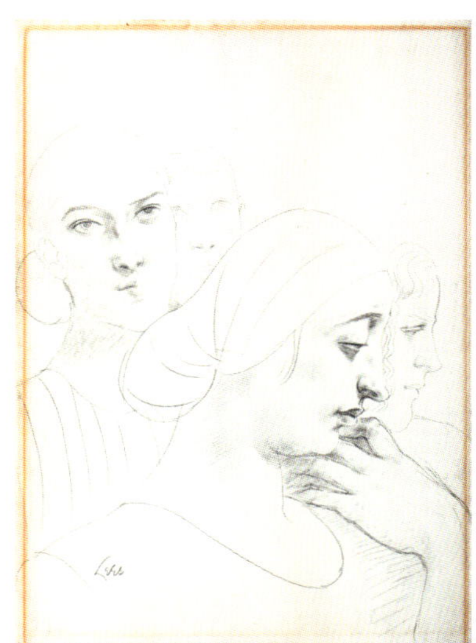

DL11.24

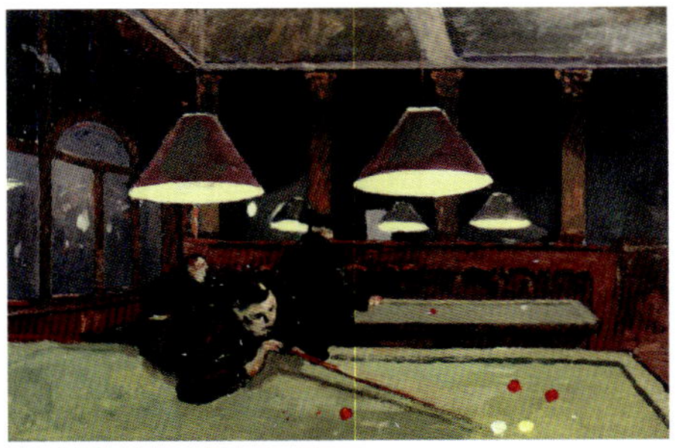

DL11.25

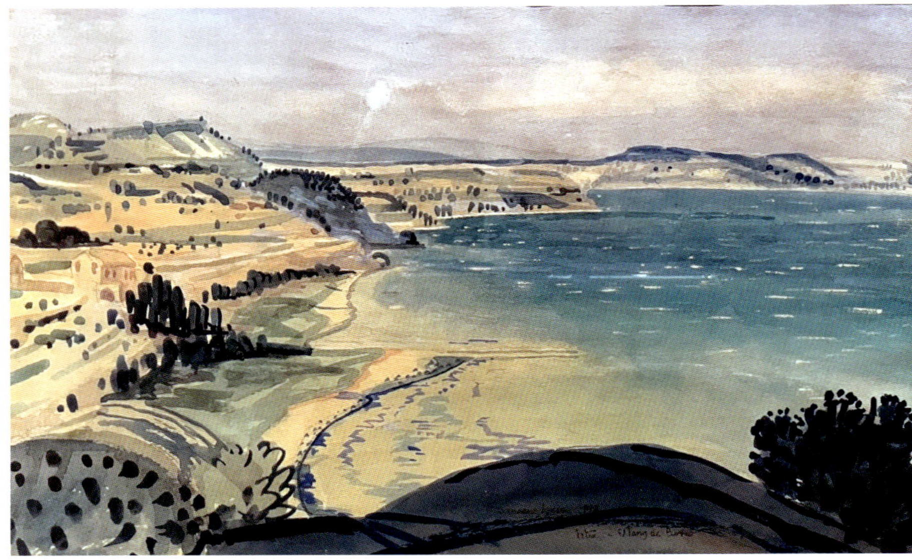

DL11.26

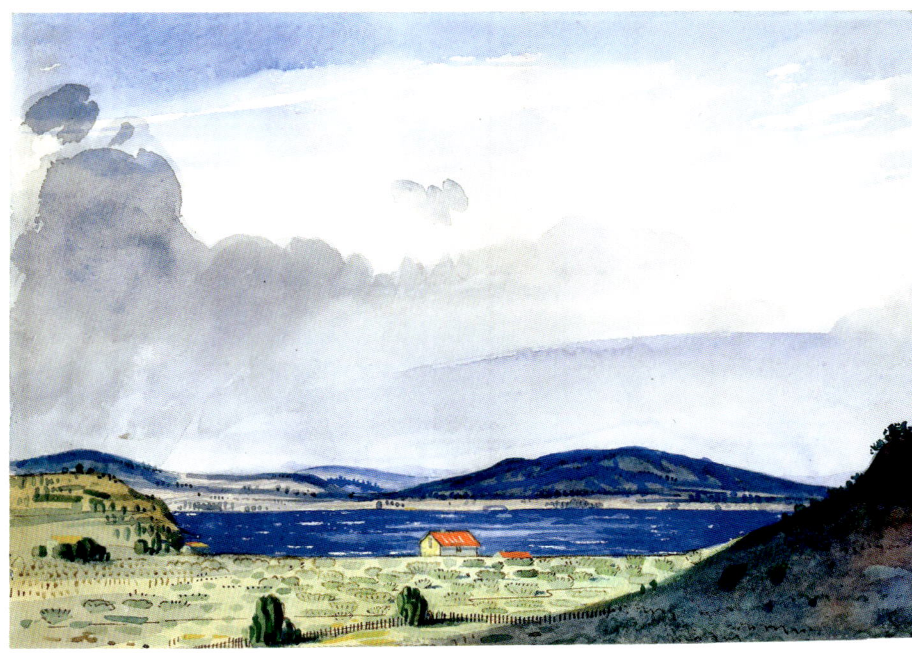

DL11.27

DL11.25
The Billiard Players / The Billiard Room / Billiards Room, The Old Tottenham / The Snooker Players / The Billiard Hall, c.1911
ins: l.l.: Lees
Oil on canvas
40.5 x 61 cm
prov: Redfern Gallery 1947–69; D'Offay Couper Gallery, London 1972; Sotheby's London May 1987
exh: Redfern 1947a (15), 1958 (42), 1961 (251), 1963 (333), 1964 (405), 1966 (272), 1967 (315), 1968 (206), 1969 (194)

DL11.26
Istres – Etang de Berre / Etang de Belle / Isle Etang de Belle, 1911
ins: l.c.r.: Derwent Lees 1911 Istres – Etang de Berre
Watercolour and ink on paper
21 x 33.5 cm
prov: Leicester Galleries, London Jul 1951 (2); Sir E. Beddington-Behrens 1951; Christie's London Jan 1999 (123); Roddy Meagher QC; Lawsons, Sydney 2019 (108); Robin Gibson Gallery, Sydney 2019
exh: Leicester Galleries, London, *Artists of Fame and Promise I* Jul 1951 (2)
notes: Plage de la Romaniquette, Istres

DL11.27
Etang de Berre / Etang de Beurre, 1911
ins: l.r.: Lees 11
Watercolour and ink on paper
22.7 x 31.2 cm
prov: Redfern Gallery; CAS purchased 1944, donated to British Museum 1945
exh: Redfern 1944a (46)

DL11.28
Distant View of Lakeside Buildings / Dorset Coast, 1911
ins: l.l.: LEES – 1911
Oil on panel
24.8 x 35.5 cm
prov: Redfern Gallery 1934; Maurice Ingram 1939; Redfern Gallery 1941; Christie's London Dec 2015 (75)
exh: Redfern 1934 (30); Tate 1940, loaned by Maurice Ingram (157); Redfern 1941b, collection of the late Maurice Ingram (32)
notes: Similar style and location to DL11.32, which was previously titled 'On the Coast, Dorset'; Etang de Berre, Istres

DL11.29 (see p.58)
Approaching Storm, Mediterranean, 1911
ins: [inscription]; v.: [label] Approaching Storm, Mediterranean
Oil on panel
32.5 x 39 cm
prov: Redfern Gallery 1933; Lord Alington 1934, 1939; Bonhams London Mar 2007; Woolley & Wallis, Salisbury Apr 2007, Apr 2008 (675), Dec 2018 (76); Denys Wilcox Fine Art (The Court Gallery, Taunton); Private Collection
exh: Redfern 1933 (86), 1934, loaned by Lord Alington (8), 1939a, loaned by Lord Alington (45)
notes: Location as in DL11.28

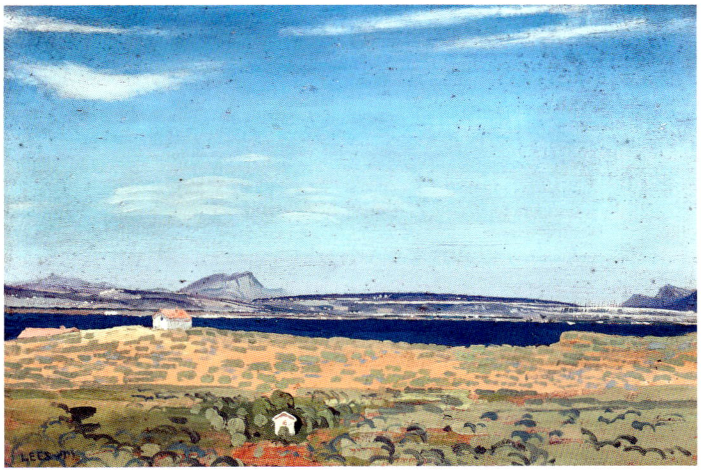

DL11.28

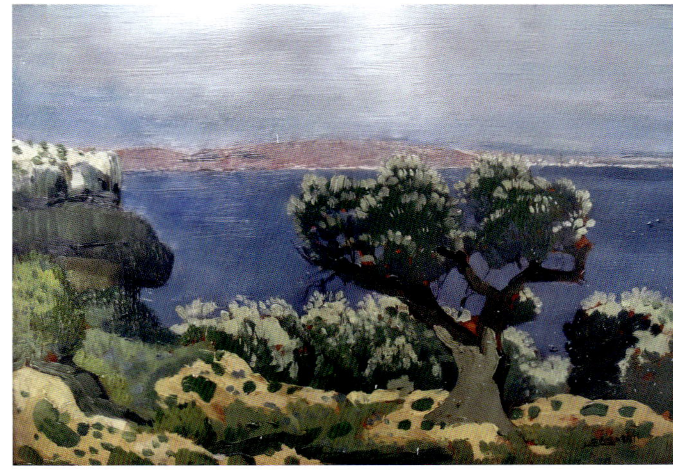

DL11.35

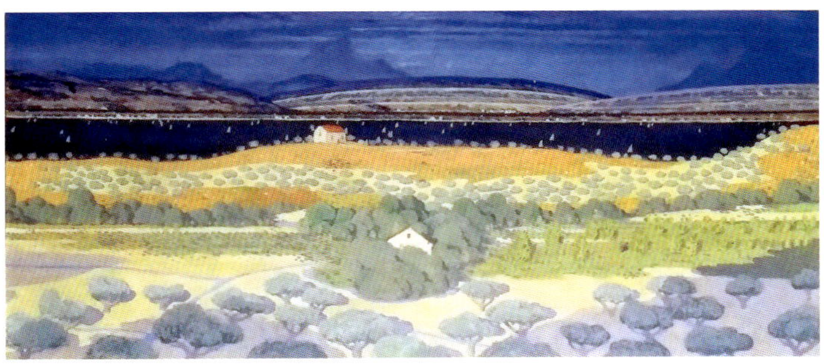

DL11.31

DL11.30*
Storm on the Welsh Coast / Rainstorm off the Welsh Coast / Storm at Sea off the Italian Coast, c.1911
Oil on canvas
60.9 x 76.1 cm
prov: Redfern Gallery 1958; Sotheby's London Feb 1972 (67); Christie's London Dec 1974 (105), 1976
exh: Redfern 1958 (48)

DL11.31
Etang de Berre, Provence / Etang de Berre / Provence / Etang de Beurre, 1911–12
Oil on canvas
59.6 x 74.9 cm
prov: Chenil Gallery 1913; Cyril K. Butler 1915; Lady Kendall Butler; Sotheby's May 1946 (43); Adams Brothers Gallery, London 1946; purchased by P.A. Hendricks (curator) for the Johannesburg Art Gallery, South Africa, 1948
exh: Chenil 1913 (61); NEAC 53rd 1915, loaned by Cyril K. Butler (115); NEAC 1925, loaned by Cyril K. Butler, Manchester (104), London (93); Slade 1927, as 'Provence', loaned by Cyril K. Butler (320); Johannesburg Art Gallery 'British Modern' Oct 1986; Johannesburg Art Gallery, *Europe 20th Century* Sep 1990
notes: Location as in DL11.28

DL11.32 (see p.60)
Etang de Berre / A Dorset View / On the Coast, Dorset, 1911–12
Oil on canvas
60 x 75.5 cm
prov: Christie's London May 1919 (124); Chenil Gallery, London; Earl of Sandwich; Browse & Darby, London 1981; Private Collection
exh: Art Gallery of South Australia, Adelaide, *Bohemian London* 1997, as 'On the Coast, Dorset' (43)
notes: Plage de la Romaniquette, Istres

DL11.33*
Etang de Berre, Provence / Etang de Beurre, 1911
Oil
prov: Redfern Gallery 1939, 1946
exh: Redfern 1939a (46), 1939b (46), 1946a (34)
notes: Location of work unknown

DL11.34*
Mediterranean Coast, c.1911
Oil on panel
prov: Redfern Gallery 1937 (?), 1939 (?); Ralph Smith, Sydney 1965; Private Collection
exh: Redfern 1937 (21), 1939a (101); Art Gallery of New South Wales, Sydney, *The Private Collector: A Loan Exhibition from 25 Sydney Collections* Sep 1965 (36)

DL11.35
On the Mediterranean Coast / Mediterranean Coast, 1911
ins: l.r.: LEES. 1911
Oil on panel
24 x 35.6 cm
prov: Ernest Marsh 1934; Christie's London Nov 1988 (350); Private Collection
exh: Redfern 1934, loaned by Ernest Marsh (35)
notes: On the Tour de Nédon, Istres

DL11.36**
View across the Etang de Berre / Landscape / A Bay Scene / The Lake Istres / View across a Lake, South of France, 1911
ins: l.l.: LEES. 11
Oil on panel
25.5 x 35.5 cm
prov: Arthur Crossland 1939–56; Christie's London Mar 1956 (155); Piccadilly Gallery, London 1956; Sotheby's London Nov 1962 (118), Mar 1973 (47); Private Collection; Sotheby's London Jul 1987 (111)
exh: Laing 1939, as 'Landscape' (197), later sold as 'A Bay Scene'
notes: L'Etang de l'Olivier, Le Castellan, Istres

DL11.37**
View at Istres / A Landscape in Spain / Landscape / Extensive Landscape, 1911
ins: l.r.: Lees [date]
Oil on panel
24.8 x 35.6 cm
prov: Arthur Crossland 1939–56; Christie's London Feb 1956 (156); F.B.C. Bravington 1956; Thos. Agnew & Sons 1985 (10); Sotheby's London Sep 1992; Private Collection
exh: Laing 1939 (311); Sane 1997, loaned by Dr Elliot Rubenstein (20)
notes: From Le Castellan, Istres

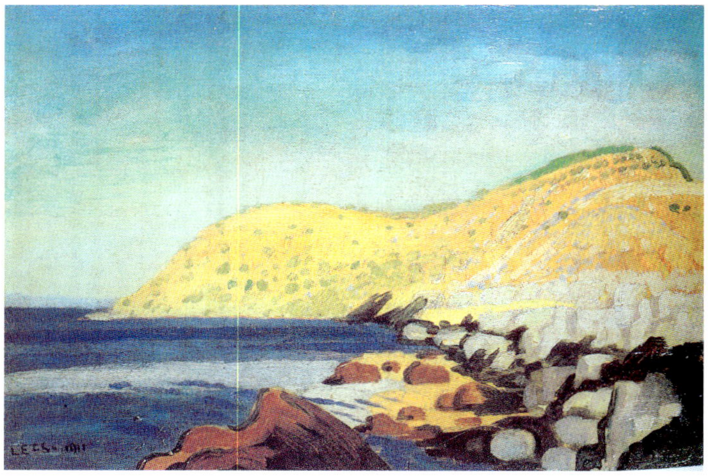

DL11.38

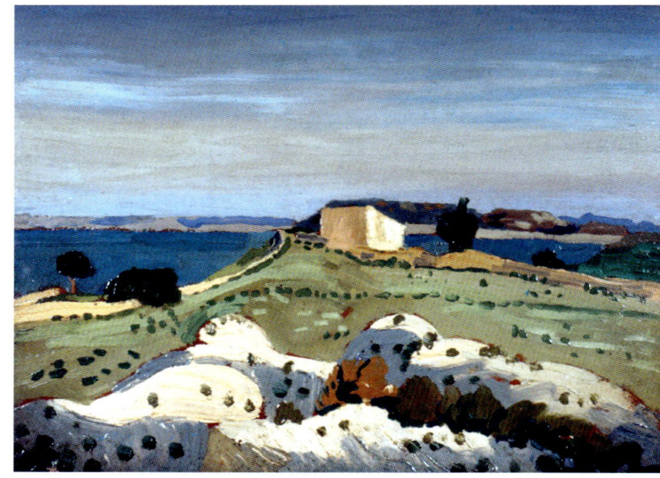

DL11.39

DL11.38
Headland at Istres / Coast at Collioure / Coastal Landscape, Southern France, 1911
ins: l.l.: LEES. 1911; v.: Lees
Oil on panel
25.3 x 35.5 cm
prov: Redfern Gallery 1952, 1954, 1955; Sotheby's London Jul 1967 (48); Thos. Agnew & Sons Oct–Nov 1969 (25); Fine Art Society 1971; Christie's London Nov 1988 (349), Jun 1991 (94), Jun 1996 (38)
exh: Redfern 1952 (295), 1954 (111), 1955 (183); Fine Art Society 1971, as 'Coastal Landscape, Southern France' (45)
notes: Headland near Istres, Etang de Berre

DL11.39
Hilltop at Istres / Near Cassis / Cassis Landscape / Near Cassis, South of France, 1911
Oil on panel
25.5 x 35.5 cm
prov: R.G. Micklethwait; Sotheby's London Nov 1933 (40); Redfern Gallery 1934–47; Mr and Mrs J.B. Priestley 1947–Sep 1951 (later Mrs D.A. Bannerman); Sotheby's London Dec 1970 (56); Fine Art Society 1971; Sotheby's London Apr 1986 (502), May 1988; Christie's London Jun 1990 (245); Private Collection
exh: Redfern 1934 (28); 1943 (25), 1944a (81), 1947a (40); Fine Art Society 1971 (40); Fine Art Society Edinburgh, *British Landscape Painters* Nov–Dec 1973 (55); Piano Nobile, London, *Augustus John and the First Crisis of Brilliance* Apr–Jul 2024 (30)
notes: Etang de Berre from l'Aupière, Istres

DL11.40
Ruin at Istres / Cottage above Cassis / Scene in Spain / A Spanish Landscape, 1911
ins: l.l.: LEES. 1911
Oil on panel
31.7 x 39.3 cm
prov: Arthur Crossland 1939–56; Christie's London Mar 1956 (154); Ackermann's, London 1956; Browse & Darby, London, Jun–Jul 1989 (4)
exh: Laing 1939, as 'Scene in Spain' (307)
notes: Above Etang de Berre, Istres

DL11.41*
View in Provence / Provence, 1911–12
ins: [signature]
Oil on panel
29.8 x 35.5 cm
prov: R.G. Micklethwait; Sotheby's London Nov 1933 (39); Redfern Gallery 1934
exh: Redfern 1934 (24)

DL11.42
Trees in Provence / Trees, Provence, 1911
ins: l.l.: LEES. 1911; v.: Derwent Lees
Oil on panel
25.4 x 35.6 cm
prov: Gieves Art Gallery, London 1928; Sotheby's London Feb 1971 (39); Ashcroft or Ashton (190); Phillips, London Jun 1989 (63); Bonhams London Mar 2023 (3)
exh: Gieves Art Gallery, London Nov 1928
notes: Istres

DL11.43
Olive Trees near Collioure / Olive Grove, 1911
ins: l.l.: LEES 1911
Oil on panel
25.1 x 35.6 cm
prov: Arthur Knyvett-Lee 1934, thence by descent; Christie's London Mar 2016 (108);

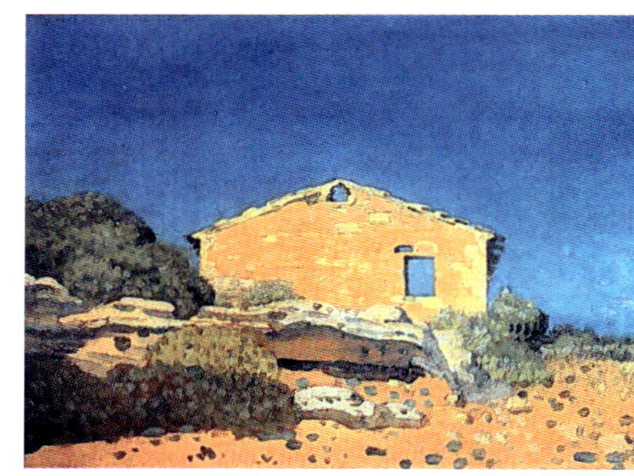

DL11.40

Browse & Darby, London 2016
exh: Redfern 1934, loaned by Arthur Knyvett-Lee (20)
notes: Tour de Nédon, Istres

DL11.44
The Olive Tree, 1911
Oil on panel
25.1 x 35.6 cm
prov: Redfern Gallery 1930; Arthur Knyvett-Lee, thence by descent; Christie's London Mar 2016 (103)
exh: Redfern 1930a (14)
notes: Tour de Nédon, Istres

DL11.45**
The Olive Trees / Trees, Provence, 1911
ins: l.l.: LEES
Oil on panel
22.9 x 35.6 cm
prov: Redfern Gallery 1930, 1934; Private Collection, sold 2006; Private Collection
exh: Redfern 1930a (18), 1934 (32)
notes: Tour de Nédon, Istres

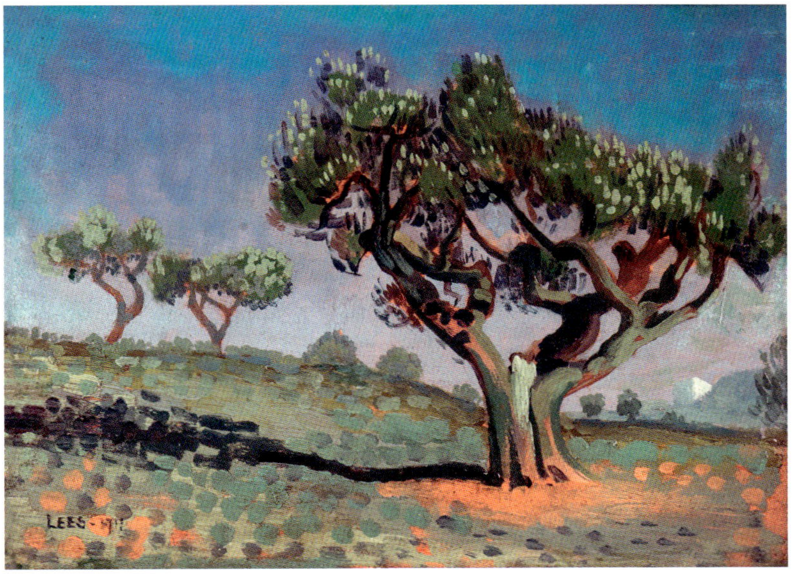

DL11.42

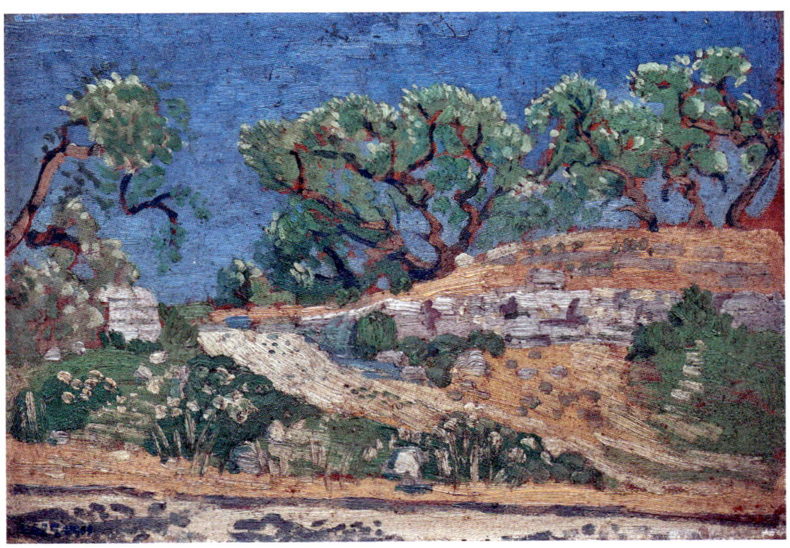

DL11.43

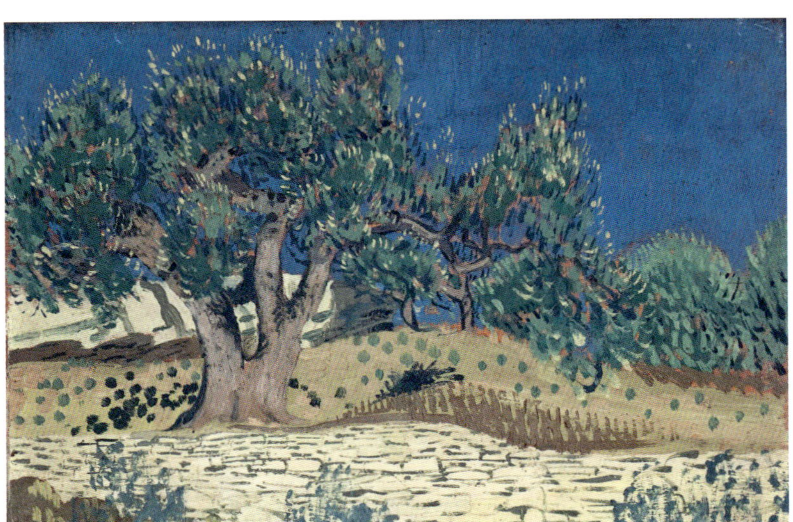

DL11.44

DL11.46**
Olive Trees, Provence, c.1911
ins: l.r.: D LEES. 11
Oil on canvas
38 x 48 cm
prov: Redfern Gallery 1934, 1947; Woolley & Wallis, Salisbury Oct 2001, Mar 2002; Denys Wilcox Fine Art (The Court Gallery, Taunton) Mar 2002; Private Collection
exh: Redfern 1934 (12), 1947a
notes: Le Castellan and Etang de l'Olivier, Istres

DL11.47
The Blue Mediterranean, 1911
ins: l.l.: LEES 1911
Oil on panel
26 x 36 cm
prov: Redfern Gallery 1930; Lord Ivor Spencer-Churchill; Arthur Knyvett-Lee family; Canterbury Auction Galleries Nov 2020; Christopher Kingzett Fine Art, London 2022
exh: Redfern 1930a (7)
notes: From Villa Sainte-Anne, Martigues

DL11.48*
Sea Coast / Seascape / The Blue Sea, c.1911
Oil
prov: Redfern Gallery 1930, 1939, 1947, 1948
exh: Redfern 1930a (11), 1939a (109), 1947b (53), 1948 (134)
notes: Unresolved record

DL11.49*
The Black Shawl, c.1911
ins: v.: [signature, title]
Watercolour, ink and wash on paper
49 x 34 cm
prov: Redfern Gallery; Deutscher 1982; John and Edward Barkes; Bridget McDonnell Gallery 1988; Christie's Melbourne Apr 1991 (76); Private Collection
exh: Bridget McDonnell Gallery Feb–Mar 1988 (20)

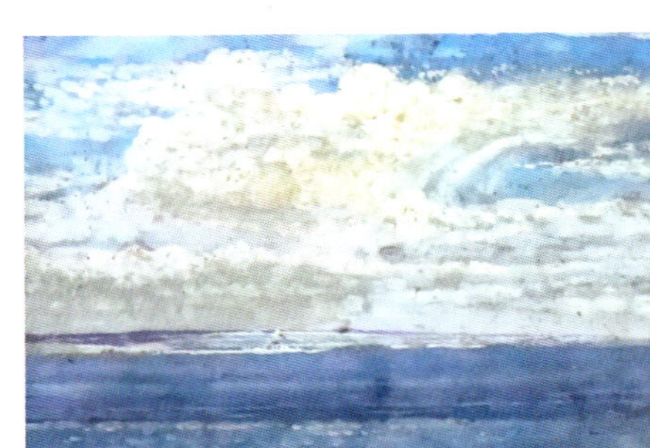

DL11.47

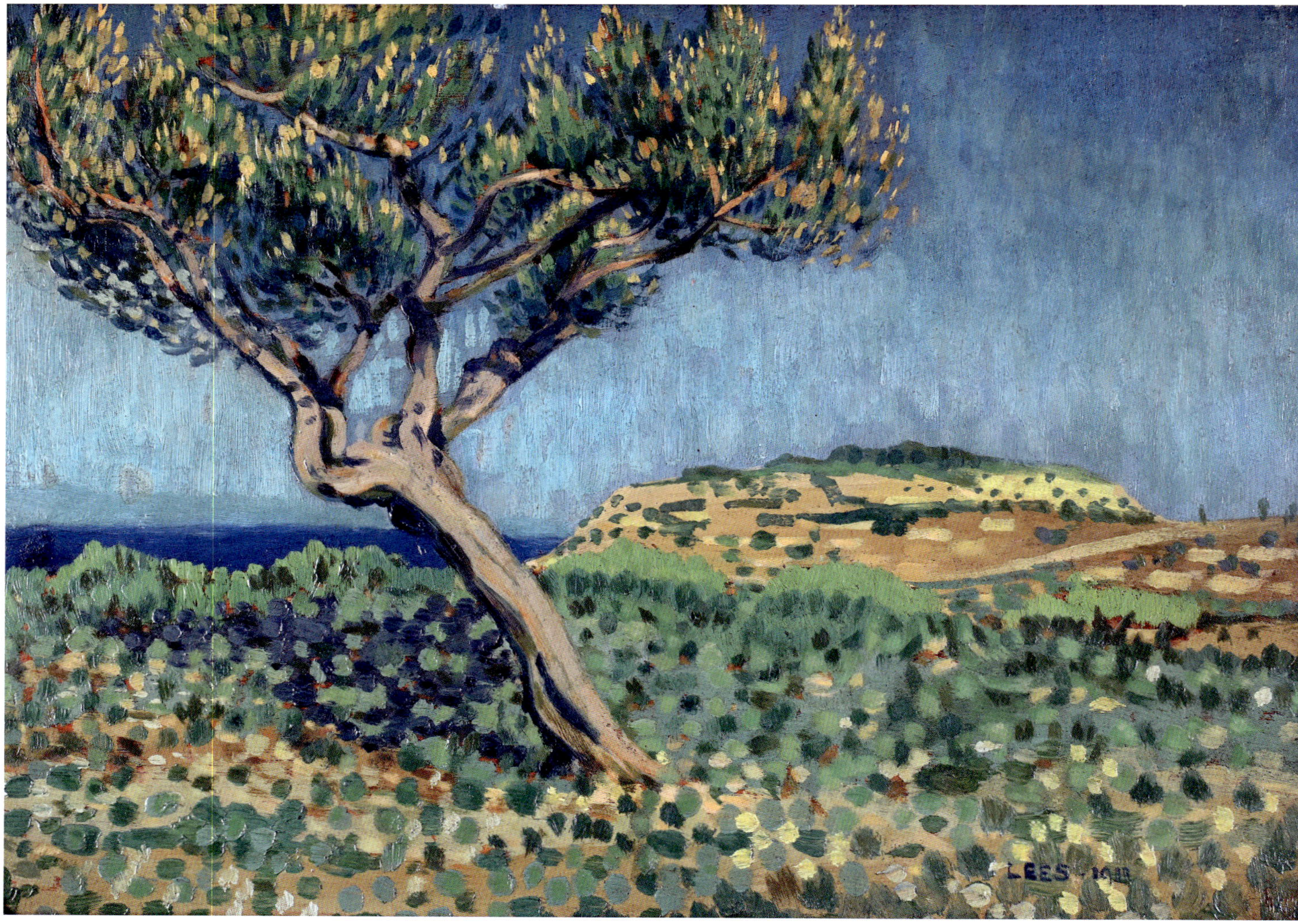

DL11.50

DL11.50
A Landscape with Tree / A Tree amongst Dunes, 1911
ins: l.r.: Lees. 1911
Oil on panel
25.5 x 35 cm
prov: Arthur Crossland; Christie's London Mar 1956 (157, 1st of 2 in the lot); F.B.C. Bravington 1956; A. Brocklebank; Sotheby's London Dec 1968 (257); Thos. Agnew & Sons 1968 (30387); Private Collection; Dreweatts, Newbury Jul 2024 (97)
notes: Istres

DL11.51
Portrait of Essil Elmslie / Essil, 1911
ins: l.r.: D.L. 11
Pencil on paper
21.7 x 26.8 cm
prov: Essil Elmslie, thence by descent to Jeanette Powell (née Rutherston); gifted to Manchester Art Gallery 1953
exh: NEAC 45th 1911 (67); NEAC summer 1922; Manchester Art Gallery, *The Rutherston Loan Scheme 1925–70* 1970; Sheffield Museums Trust and York Museums Trust, *Beyond Bloomsbury: Life, Love and Legacy* (many venues inc. Millennium Gallery) Nov 2021–Feb 2022, York Art Gallery Mar–Jun 2022
notes: Essil Elmslie (later Rutherston)

DL11.52
Essil Elmslie Reading / Woman Reading, 1911
Pencil, pen and ink on paper
20 x 19.5 cm
prov: Rex Nan Kivell Collection; Deutsher 1978; National Gallery of Australia, Canberra, purchased 1979
exh: Deutsher 1978 (7)
notes: Essil Elmslie (later Rutherston)

DL11.53
Essil Elmslie Sewing / Study of a Woman Seated in a Basket Chair and Sewing, 1911
ins: u.l.: Derwent Lees. 1911
Pencil and ink on paper
23.9 x 25.1 cm
prov: Christie's London Oct 1964 (46); Ashmolean Museum, Oxford, purchased 1964
notes: Essil Elmslie (later Rutherston)

DL11.54
Portrait of Mrs Charles Rutherston, c.1911
Pencil and black chalk on paper
29 x 22.5 cm
prov: Mrs Essil Rutherston (née Elmslie), gifted to the CAS 1939; thence gifted to Manchester Art Gallery 1940

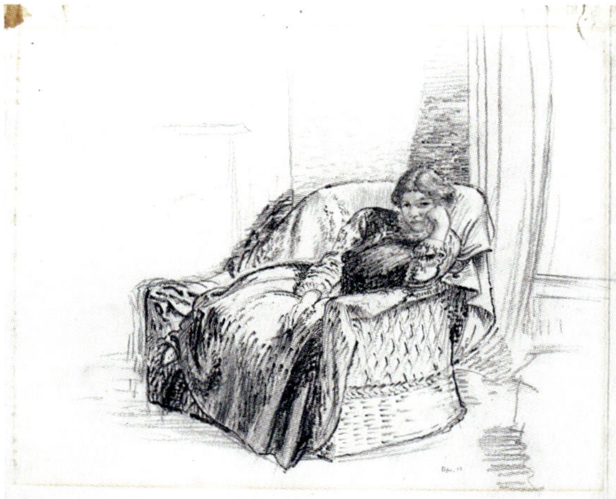

DL11.51

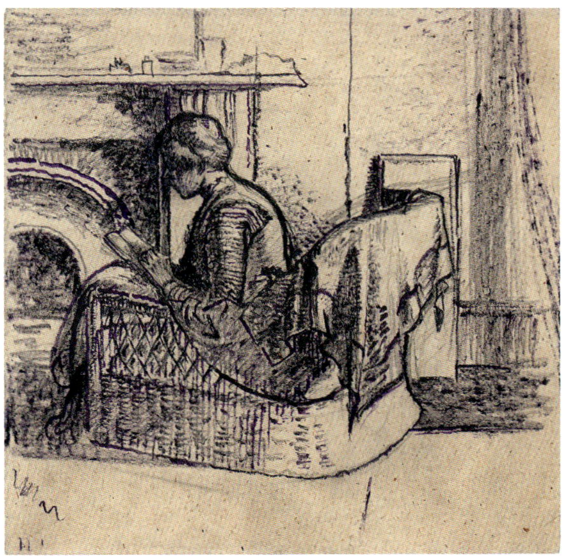

DL11.52

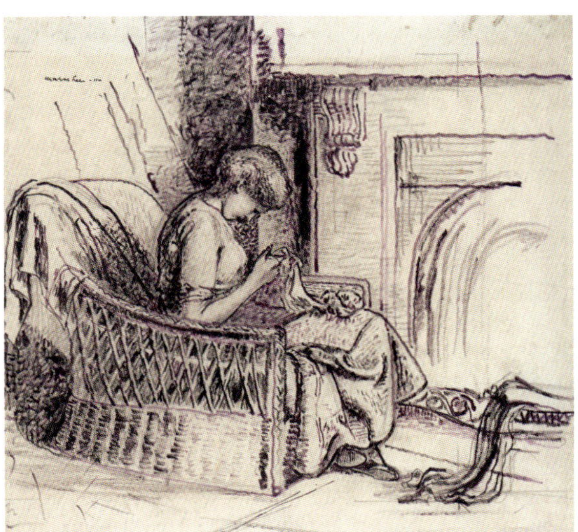

DL11.53

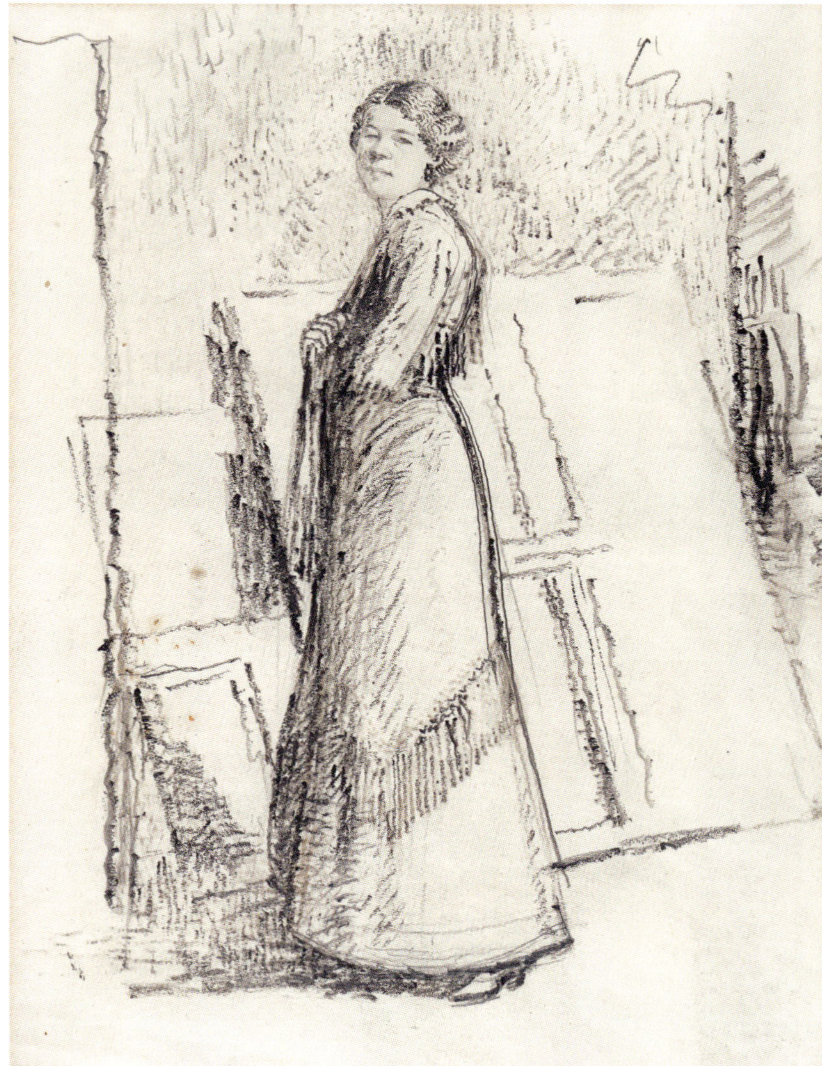

DL11.54

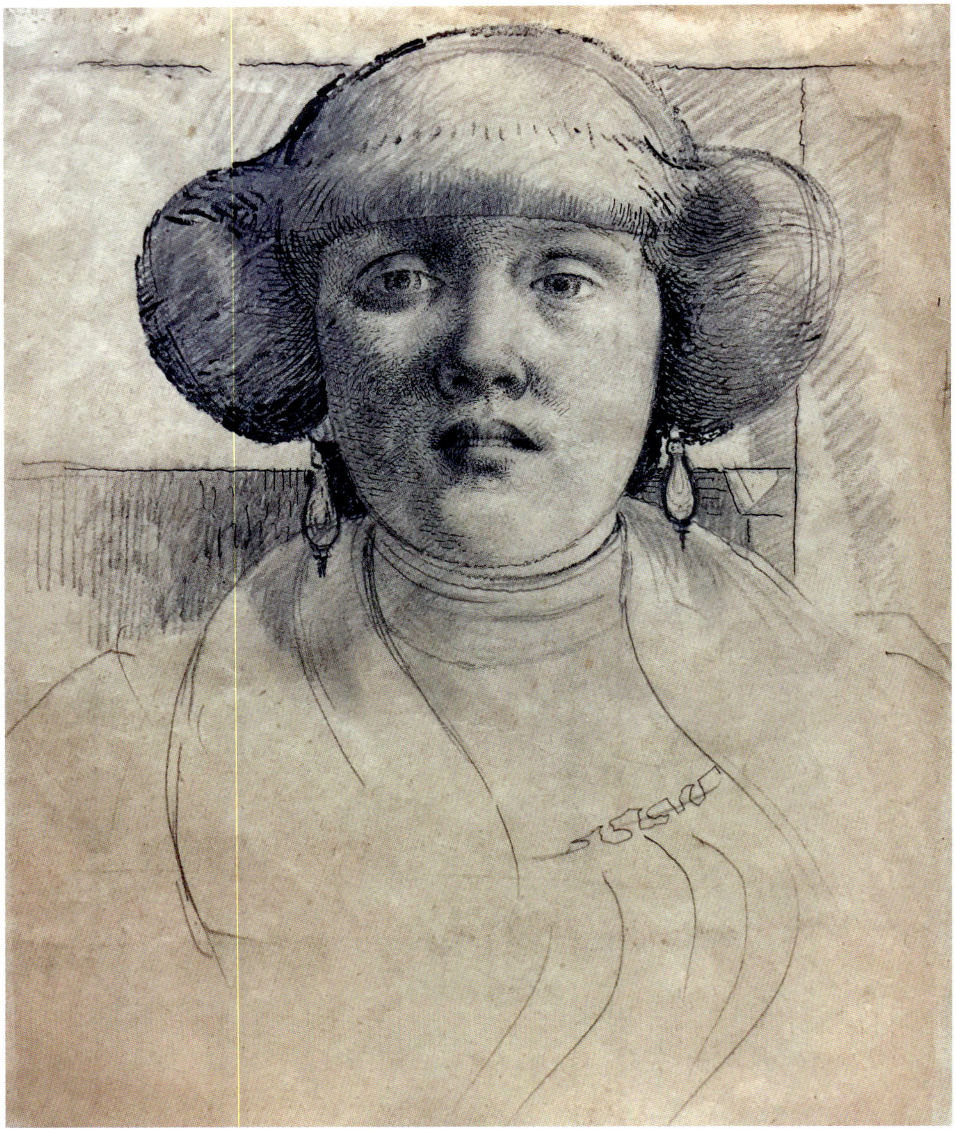

DL11.55

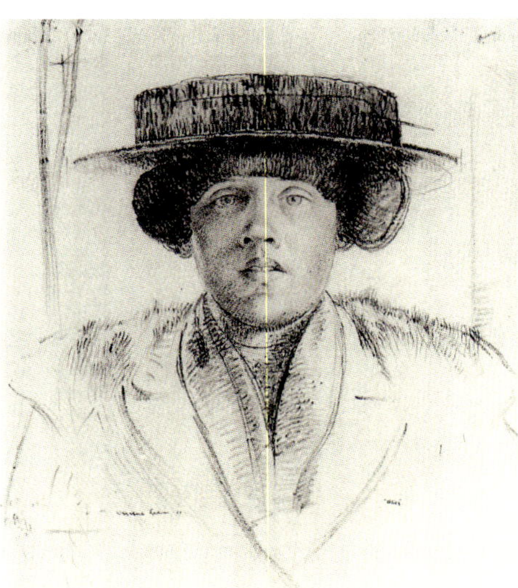

DL11.56

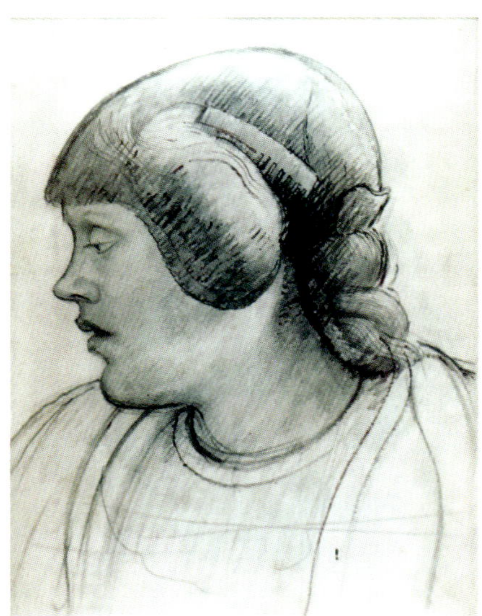

DL11.63

DL11.55
Portrait of Alice Elder / Head of a Woman / Portrait Study of a Woman, 1911
Pencil, pen and ink on paper
32.8 x 27.9 cm
prov: Arthur Crossland; F.B.C. Bravington 1956; Sotheby's London Jul 1967 (49); R. Holland; gifted to Laing by the Friends of the Laing Art Gallery 1967

DL11.56
Alice, 1911
ins: l.l.: Derwent Lees. 11; l.r.: 'Alice'
Pencil and chalk on paper
29.2 x 24.2 cm
prov: Redfern Gallery; Sir Brinsley Ford, purchased Sep 1942; The Ford Collection; Augustine Ford, on loan to The National Trust, Basildon Park
exh: NEAC 45th 1911 (125); Royal Albert Memorial Museum, Exeter, *Exhibition of Works of Art from the Ford Collection, courtesy of Brinsley Ford* 1946
notes: Alice Elder; in B. Ford et al., *The Ford Collection*, v.II: *Sir Brinsley Ford*, The Walpole Society 60, Walpole Society, Leeds, 1998, pp 91–376, fig.153

DL11.57
Portrait of Ethel Elder / Portrait of Ethelreda / Portrait Study of a Young Woman, c.1911
ins: l.l.: Lees
Pencil and white chalk on paper
46.8 x 31.8 cm
prov: Peter Nahum Ltd, London May–Jun 1987; Bloomsbury Auctions, London Jul 2004

DL11.58
Ethelreda (Portrait of a Girl) / Portrait Study / Study of a Young Woman, c.1911
ins: l.l.: Lees
Pencil and watercolour wash on paper
47.3 x 30 cm
prov: Rex Nan Kivell; Deutsher 1978; Joseph Brown Gallery, Melbourne 1981, gifted to The University of Melbourne by Dr Joseph Brown 1982
exh: Deutsher 1978 (43); Joseph Brown Gallery, Melbourne, Sep 1981; Sane 1997, loaned by The University of Melbourne Art Collection (29)
notes: Ethel Elder

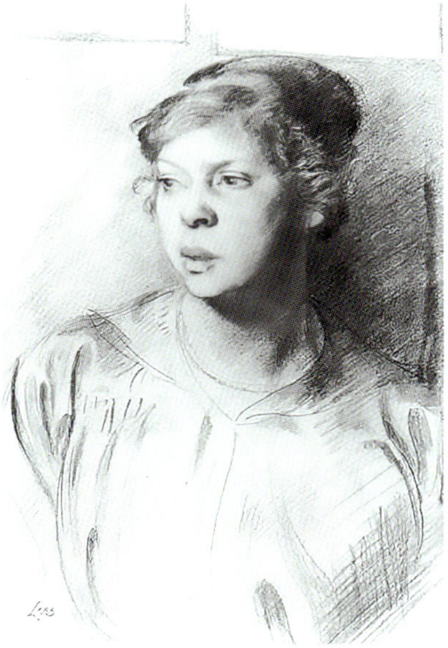

DL11.57

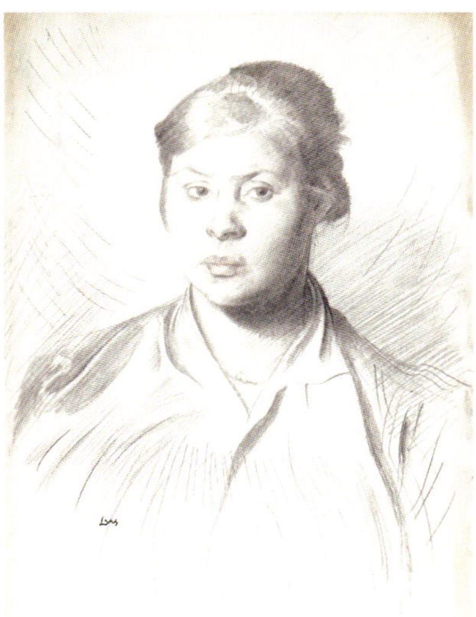

DL11.58

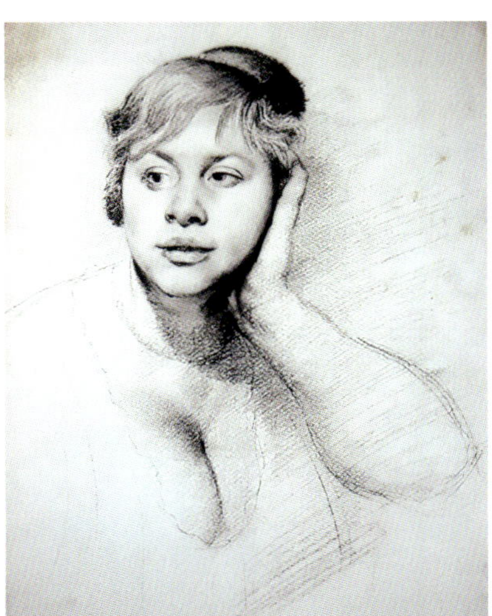

DL11.59

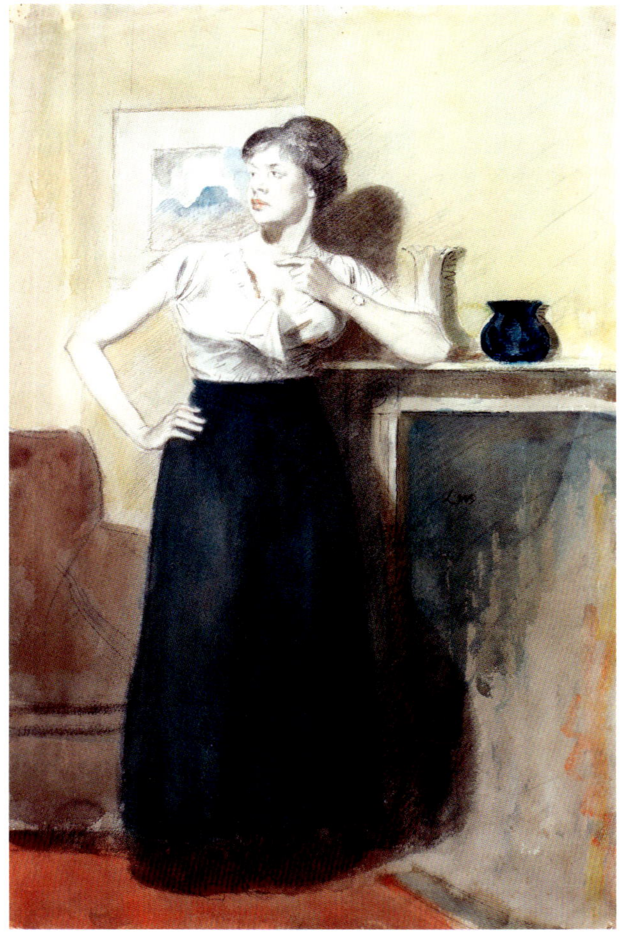

DL11.60

DL11.59
Portrait of Ethel Elder / Ethelreda / Portrait of Ethelreda, c.1911
ins: v.: [signature, inscription]
Pencil and wash on paper
45 x 34.5 cm
prov: Redfern Gallery; Rex Nan Kivell Collection; Deutsher 1976–8; Belgrave Gallery, London; Sotheby's London May 1981 (101); Geoff K. Gray, Sydney Jun 1982 (7); Deutscher-Menzies Fine Art, Melbourne Aug 2002 (241); Private Collection
exh: Deutsher 1978 (26); Sane 1997 (28)

DL11.60
Ethel Elder Standing by Mantlepiece / Studio, Fitzroy Square (Woman Standing by Mantelpiece) / Portrait of Lyndra, the Artist's Wife, c.1911
ins: c.r.: Lees; v.: Lyndra
Watercolour, pencil, pen and ink on paper
46.8 x 29.8 cm
prov: Mrs Edith Lees 1931–9; Bloomsbury Auctions, London Jul 2004; Maas Gallery, London 2022; Private Collection
exh: Stafford 1939

DL11.61*
Emma, c.1911
Pencil on paper
prov: Redfern Gallery 1944, 1949
exh: Redfern 1944b (375)

DL11.62*
Hetty, c.1911
Pencil on paper
prov: Redfern Gallery 1944, 1945, 1949
exh: Redfern 1944b (377), 1945b (426)

DL11.63
Portrait of a Girl, 1911–15
Pencil on paper
26.4 x 31.5 cm
prov: Rex Nan Kivell; Deutsher 1978; John and Edward Barkes; Christopher Day Gallery, Sydney; Bridget McDonnell Gallery 1990; Private Collection
exh: Deutsher 1978 (23); Bridget McDonnell Gallery Dec 1990 (13)
notes: Alice Elder

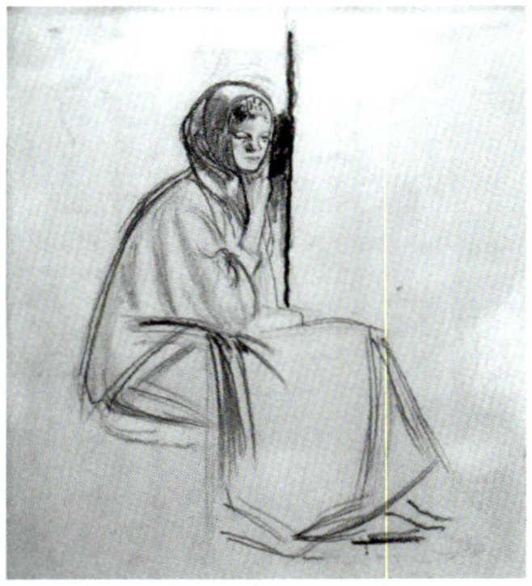

DL11.67

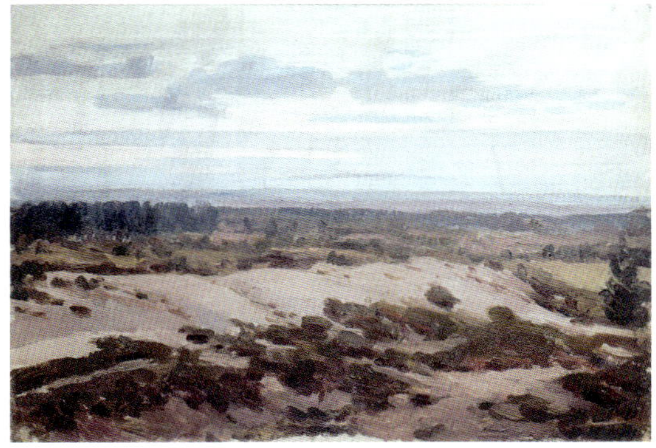

DL11.71

DL11.64*
Family Group / The Family, 1911–15
Ink and wash on paper
37.2 x 25.2 cm
prov: Rex Nan Kivell; Deutsher 1978; Private Collection
exh: Deutsher 1978 (13)

DL11.65*
Nude in Armchair / Nude Seated in an Armchair, c.1911
Ink, brush, pencil and Chinese white on grey paper
51 x 35.5 cm
prov: Rex Nan Kivell; Deutsher 1978; Belgrave Gallery, London; Sotheby's London May 1981 (100)
exh: Deutsher 1978 (36)

DL11.66*
Nude in Armchair, c.1911
Ink and pencil on paper
24.4 x 25.5 cm
prov: Rex Nan Kivell; Deutsher 1978; Private Collection
exh: Deutsher 1978 (42)

DL11.67
Study of a Girl Seated / Girl Sitting, 1911–15
ins: v.: [signature]
Pencil and black wash on paper
25 x 40.7 cm
prov: Rex Nan Kivell; Deutsher 1978; Private Collection; Bridget McDonnell Gallery 1994; Private Collection
exh: NEAC 55th 1916 (103) (?); Deutsher 1978 (4) (?); Bridget McDonnell Gallery Dec 1994 (33)

DL11.68*
Girl Seated / Seated Girl / A Seated Figure of a Girl, 1911–15
prov: Dowdeswell and Dowdeswell, London; Christie's London Feb 1917 (3, 1st of 2 in the lot); Redfern Gallery 1930 (?)
Pencil on paper
exh: NEAC 55th 1916 (24); Redfern 1930a (3)
notes: Unresolved record

DL11.69*
Head of a Girl, 1911–15
Pencil on paper
35 x 24.2cm
prov: Dowdeswell and Dowdeswell, London; Christie's London Feb 1917 (3, 2nd of 2 in the lot), Jun 1979
notes: Unresolved record

DL11.70*
Girls in Galway / Women of Galway / Galway Peasants, c.1911
Watercolour on paper
prov: Redfern Gallery 1945, 1961, 1964
exh: Redfern 1945b (468), 1961 (249), 1964 (407)

DL11.71
Creech Heath, Dorset / Extensive Landscape, c.1911
ins: l.r.: LEES
Oil on canvas
50 x 70 cm
prov: Morris & Son, Woodbridge, Suffolk 2024

1912

DL12.1*
Level Fields, c.1912
ins: [signature]
Oil on panel
31.7 x 39.3 cm
prov: Chenil Gallery 1915; Redfern Gallery 1930; Lord Henry Cavendish-Bentinck (?); Sotheby's London May 1933 (93); Burrows 1933
exh: Chenil 1915 (88); Redfern 1930a (12)

DL12.2*
Portrait of Beatrice Stewart / Portrait of Beatrice Stuart, c.1912
ins: l.l.: Initials
Pencil on paper
24 x 17 cm
prov: Fine Art Society Nov 1971; J. S. Maas & Co., London; Private Collection; Sotheby's Melbourne Nov 1996 (246A)

DL12.3
View North from Arenig Fawr / Cumberland Hills / Landscape, possibly Nant Ddu, Wales, c.1912
ins: l.l.: LEES
Watercolour on paper
25.5 x 35.5 cm
prov: Sotheby's London Nov 1931 (91); Walter Beecroft 1931; Wyndham T. Vint; Christie's London Jun 2002 (277), Dec 2004 (93); The Albany Gallery, London, Vint Estate, 2011; Olympia Auctions, London Mar 2018 (216), Sep 2020 (123); Abbott and Holder, London 2023 (7439)
exh: Bradford District Museum, *Wyndham Theodore Vint Collection*; Cartwright Memorial Hall, Bradford, *Modern Paintings and Drawings* 1956
notes: From the northern slopes of Arenig Fawr

DL12.4
The Foot Bridge / The Approaching Rainstorm / Stormy Evening, North Wales, c.1912
Watercolour, pen and ink on paper
26.5 x 37.5 cm
prov: Redfern Gallery 1930, 1939; Thos. Agnew & Sons; Sotheby's London Nov 1972, as 'The Approaching Rainstorm' by DL (55); Sotheby's Olympia, London Sep 2006, as 'Stormy Evening, North Wales' by JDI (6)
exh: Redfern 1930a, as 'The Foot Bridge' by DL (37); British Council, Johannesburg, *Empire Exhibition* 1936; British Council Fine Arts Committee, 1939, as 'Stormy Evening, North Wales' by JDI (168)
notes: Reattributed in consultation with John Hoole (formerly JDI 166); near Nant Ddu, towards Arenig Fawr

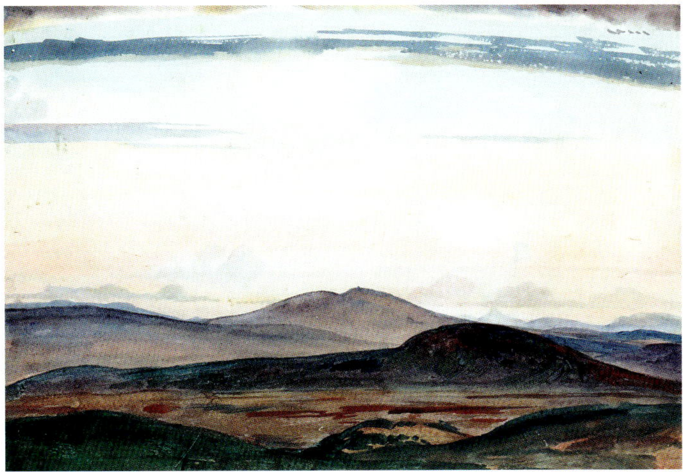

DL12.3

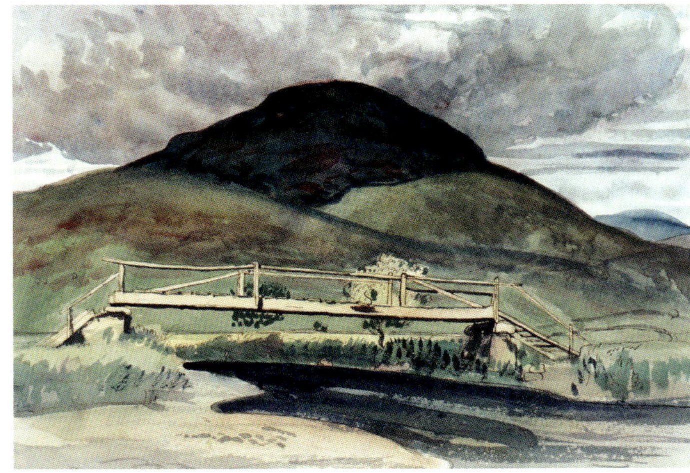

DL12.4

DL12.5
Mount Arenig, North Wales / Welsh Mountains, c.1912
Oil on canvas
33.6 x 43.8 cm
prov: Mrs Euphemia Grove (née Forrest, then Lamb); Dr and Mrs Christopher Turton, thence by descent; Private Collection; Christie's London 16 Nov 2007
notes: Reattributed in consultation with John Hoole (formerly JDI 196); Arenig Fach from near Nant Ddu

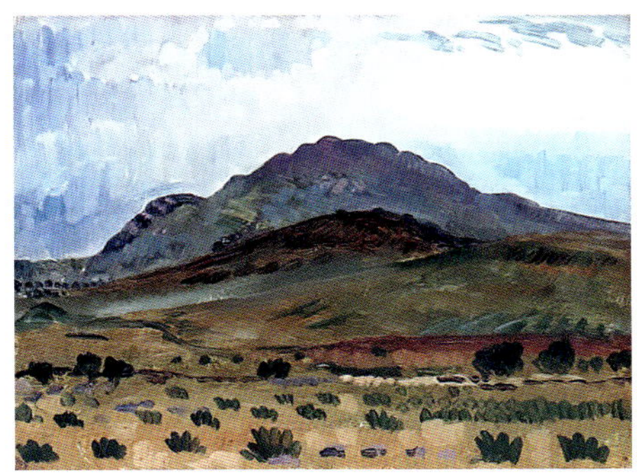

DL12.5

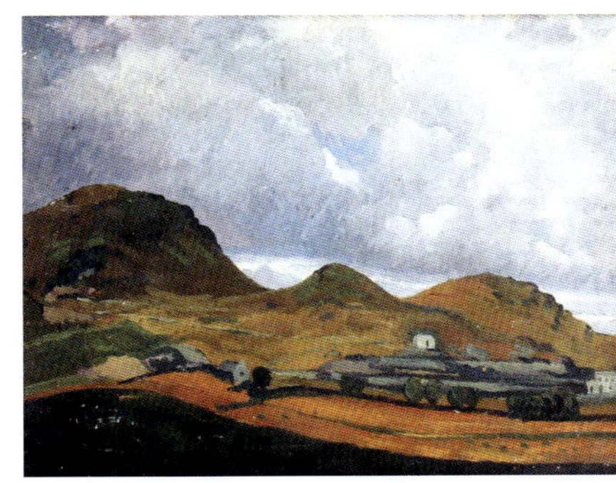

DL12.6

DL12.6
Welsh Hills, 1912–14
Oil on panel
31.5 x 40 cm
prov: Chenil 1913; Sotheby's London Mar 1932 (138); Riddle & Couchman, London 1932; Christie's London Jun 1933 (113, 1st of 2 in the lot); Dr John MacGregor 1933; Royal Burgh of Ayr Collection, purchased c.1971; Maclaurin Gallery, Ayr 1992; Rozelle House Galleries, Ayr 1992
exh: Chenil 1913 (58); Rozelle House Galleries Sep 1978
notes: Cwmorthin slate quarry, Tanygrisiau, North Wales; possibly linked to DL14.30

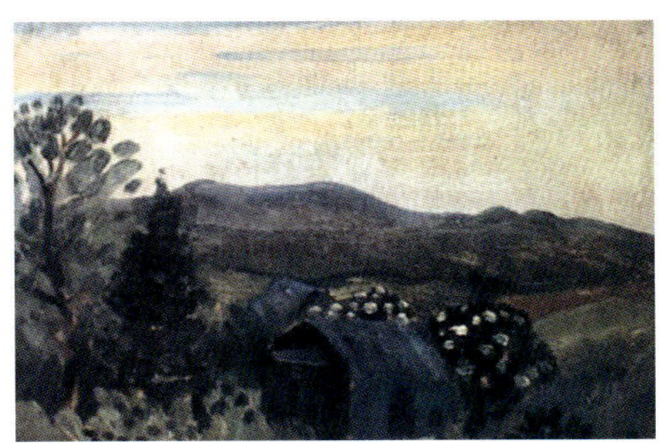

DL12.7

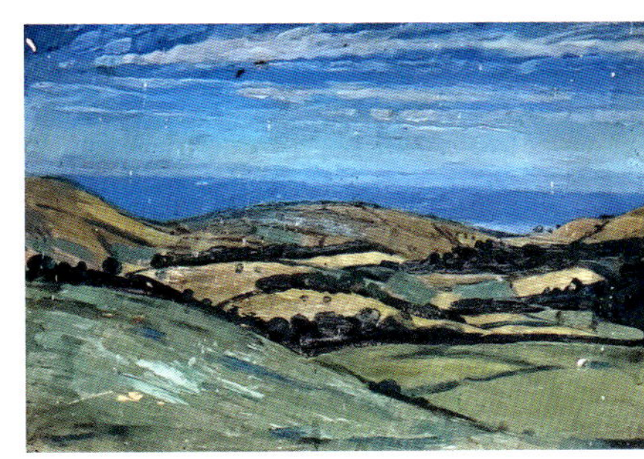

DL12.9

DL12.7
The Blue Hut, 1912–14
Oil on panel
23 x 33 cm
prov: Redfern Gallery 1937, 1939; Piccadilly Gallery, London; Dr Sidney Charles Lewsen; Sotheby's London Mar 1995; Private Collection
exh: Redfern 1937 (1), 1939a (105)
notes: Arenig Fawr, Moel Llyfnant from Rhyd-y-Fen Inn, North Wales

DL12.8*
Lowering Clouds, 1912
Oil on canvas
29.2 x 34.3 cm
prov: John Quinn Collection 1912
exh: Armory Show 1913, loaned by John Quinn, New York (553), Chicago (214), Boston (104)

DL12.9
Pembroke Coast / Welsh Coast / Dorset Coast, c.1912
ins: v.: Derwent Lees 1912; v.: Property of a Lady [on Christie's label]
Oil on panel
22.8 x 32.4 cm
prov: Redfern Gallery 1934, 1947; Leicester Galleries, London; Arthur Tooth & Sons, London Apr–May 1971 (5), Jun–Jul 1972 (23); Christie's London Jun 1983 (41), Nov 1995 (106); Sloane Street Auctions, London Sep 2022 (151); Private Collection
exh: Redfern 1934 (11), 1947b (17)

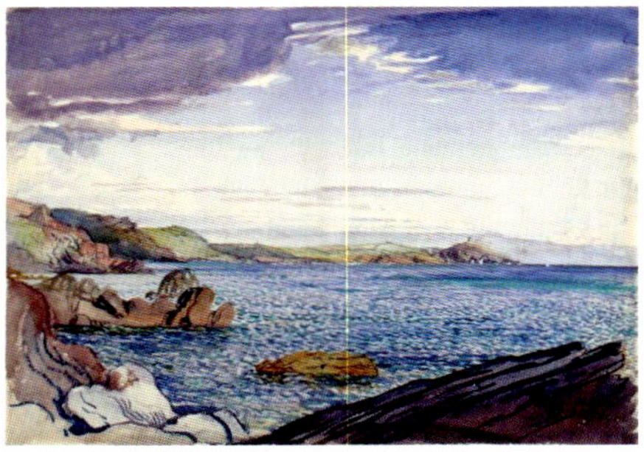

DL12.10

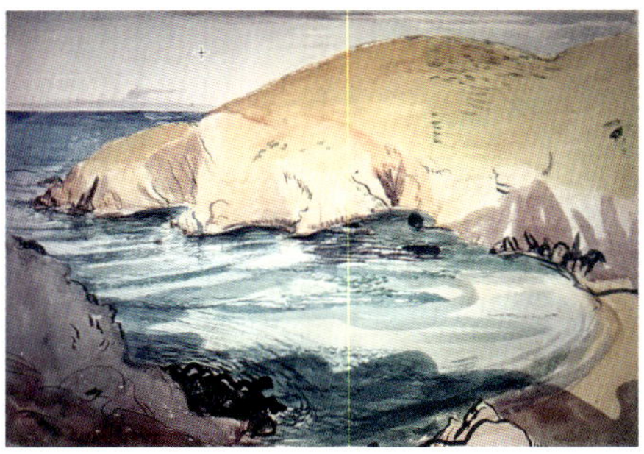

DL12.12

DL12.10
Coastal Scene / Coast of Wales, c.1912
Watercolour and pencil on paper
25.2 x 35.4 cm
prov: Redfern Gallery 1934; Nora Summers (née Munro), bequeathed as 'Coastal Scene' by JDI to Walker Art Gallery, Liverpool 1949
exh: Redfern 1934 (41); Empire Art Loans Exhibitions Society, Australia and New Zealand, *British Watercolours 1850–1914* 1952–3; Castle Museum, Norwich, *Modern Movement in British Watercolour Painting* 1957–8 (34)
notes: Reattributed in consultation with John Hoole (formerly JDI 137)

DL12.11*
The Pine Tree, c.1912
prov: Chenil Gallery 1913–14
exh: Chenil 1913–14 (54)
notes: Unresolved record

DL12.12
Bay on the Welsh Coast / The Bay, Dorset / Coast of Wales (Study), c.1912
Watercolour, pen and pencil on paper
25.4 x 34.9 cm
prov: Redfern Gallery; Mrs E. Grove (née Forrest, then Lamb), thence by descent; Redfern Gallery 1958 (?); Dr and Mrs Christopher Turton, thence by descent; Christie's London 13 Mar 1981
exh: British Contemporary Art 1933, as 'The Bay, Dorset' (76) (?); Redfern 1958 (49)
notes: Reattributed in consultation with John Hoole (formerly JDI 138); Three Cliffs Bay, Gower Peninsula, Wales; location of work unknown

DL12.13*
Studio Door, Fitzroy Square, c.1912
Pencil on paper
prov: Mrs Edith Lees 1931–9
exh: Stafford 1939
notes: Unresolved record

DL12.14
Studio in Fitzroy Square / Studio in Fitzroy Street, c.1912
Pen and ink on paper
45.8 x 30.5 cm
prov: Mrs Edith Lees 1931–9; British Council Fine Arts Committee, London 1939
exh: Stafford 1939; V&A 1947; Wakefield 1947–9, Australia, New Zealand, Fiji (36); British Council, Southampton City Art Gallery, *Camden Town Group* 1951; British Council, Museum of Modern Art, Oxford, Norwich Castle Museum, Southampton, *A Terrific Thing British Art 1910–16* 1976–7; British Council, Castle Museum, Norwich, and Camden Arts Centre, London, *The Camden Scene* Feb–Mar 1979; British Council, *The Painters of Camden Town 1905–1920* 1988
notes: DL's 21 Fitzroy Square studio

DL12.15
A London Square / Fitzroy Square / Fitzroy Square from Sickert's Studio, 1912
ins: l.l.: Lees. 12
Oil on canvas
36 x 30.5 cm
prov: Redfern Gallery 1930, 1939; Mr and Mrs J.B. Priestley 1942–Sep 1951; Redfern Gallery 1958; Robertson & Bruce Ltd, Dundee; Bonhams London Nov 2013 (14)
exh: Redfern 1930a (32), 1939a (29), 1958 (44)
notes: From DL's 21 Fitzroy Square studio

DL12.16*
Landscape at Avignon / Landscape near Avignon / Landscape in the Alpilles, 1912
Watercolour and pen on buff paper
22 x 34 cm
prov: Redfern Gallery 1930, 1933; Wilfrid A. Evill; Sotheby's London Mar 1973, Nov 1980 (171)
exh: Redfern 1930a (41), 1933; British Institute of Adult Education, Brighton Art Gallery and Museum, *Wilfrid Evill Memorial Exhibition* 1965 (98)
notes: In *The Connoisseur*, 'admirably treated in yellows and light browns', Jan–Jun 1930, p.401

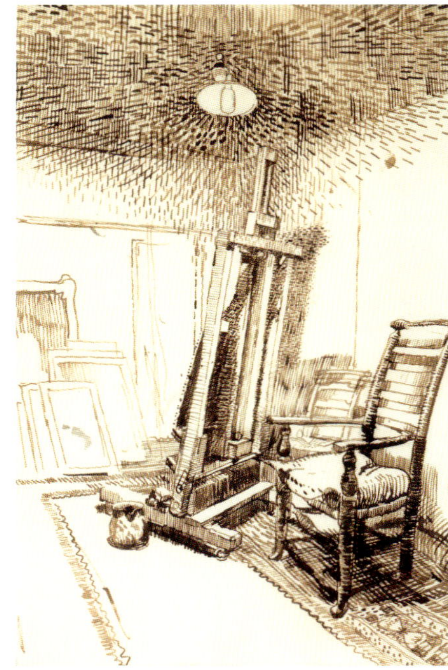

DL12.14

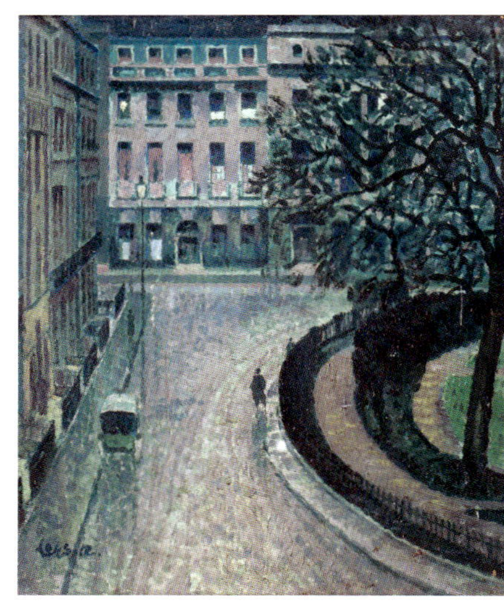

DL12.15

DL12.17
Forcalquier Basses Alpes – Provence, 1912
ins: l.l.: Lees 1912 Forcalquier Basses Alpes – Provence
Watercolour wash and ink on paper
25 x 35.8 cm
prov: Christie's South Kensington Jan 1982 (149); Philip Bacon Galleries, Brisbane; Private Collection
exh: Sane 1997 (35)
notes: Chapelle St Pancrace from Forcalquier Citadel

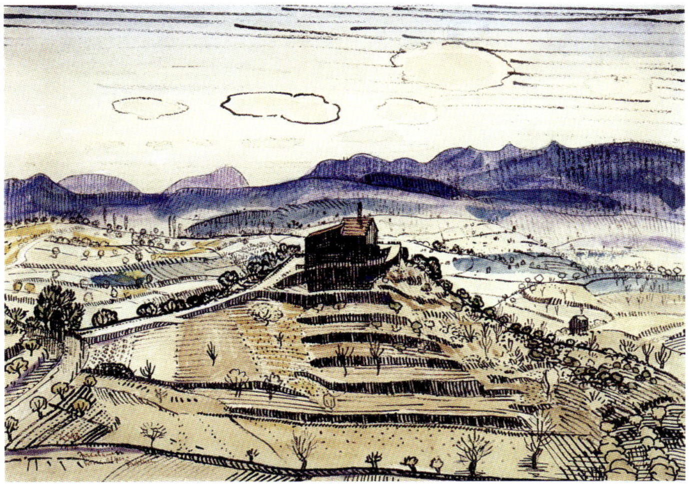

DL12.17

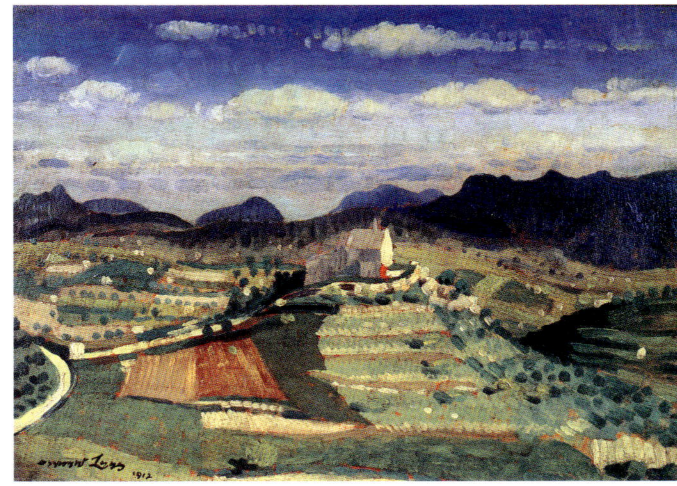

DL12.18

DL12.18
Forcalquier, Basses Alpes / Countryside around Cassis / Landscape near Cassis, 1912
ins: l.l.: Derwent Lees 1912
Oil on panel
25.4 x 34.9 cm
prov: Mrs McLean; Fine Art Society 1971; John and Edward Barkes; Bridget McDonnell Gallery Jun 1989; Private Collection
exh: Fine Art Society 1971 (44); Sane 1997 (13)
notes: Location and viewscape as in DL12.17

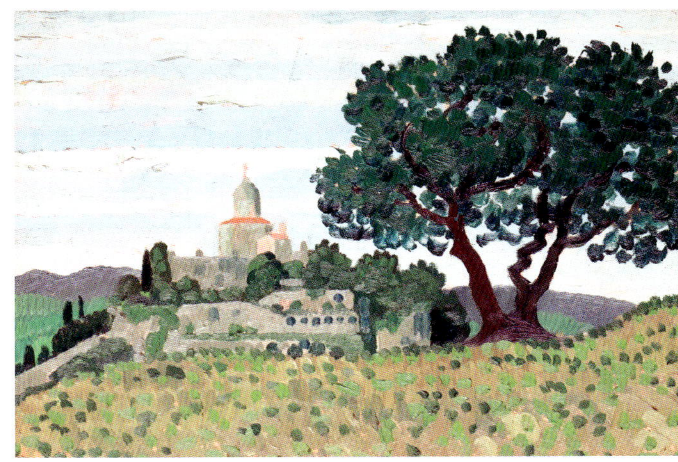

DL12.19

DL12.19
The Citadel, Forcalquier / A Spanish Landscape / Church in a Landscape, 1912
Oil on panel
24.8 x 34.9 cm
prov: Arthur Crossland 1939–56; Christie's London Mar 1956 (156); J. Leger & Son Gallery, London 1956; Christie's London Mar 2016 (110)
exh: Laing 1939 (236)

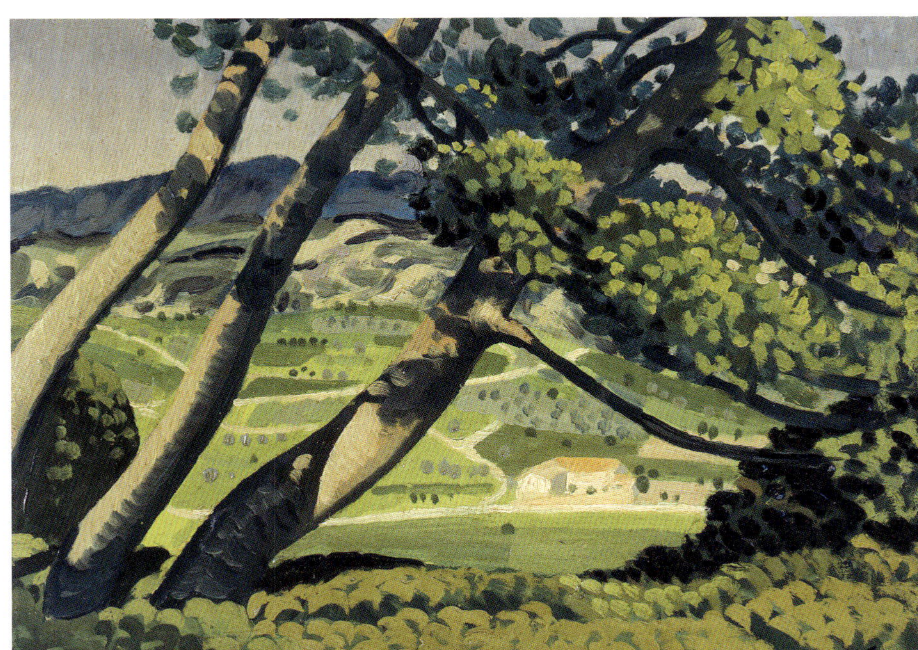

DL12.20

DL12.20
Trees, Provence, 1912
ins: l.r.: Derwent Lees 1912
Oil on panel
25 x 35.5 cm
prov: Redfern Gallery 1934; Thomas Balston; gifted to the Ashmolean Museum, Oxford 1959
exh: Redfern 1934 (21)
notes: From the ridge east of Forcalquier Citadel

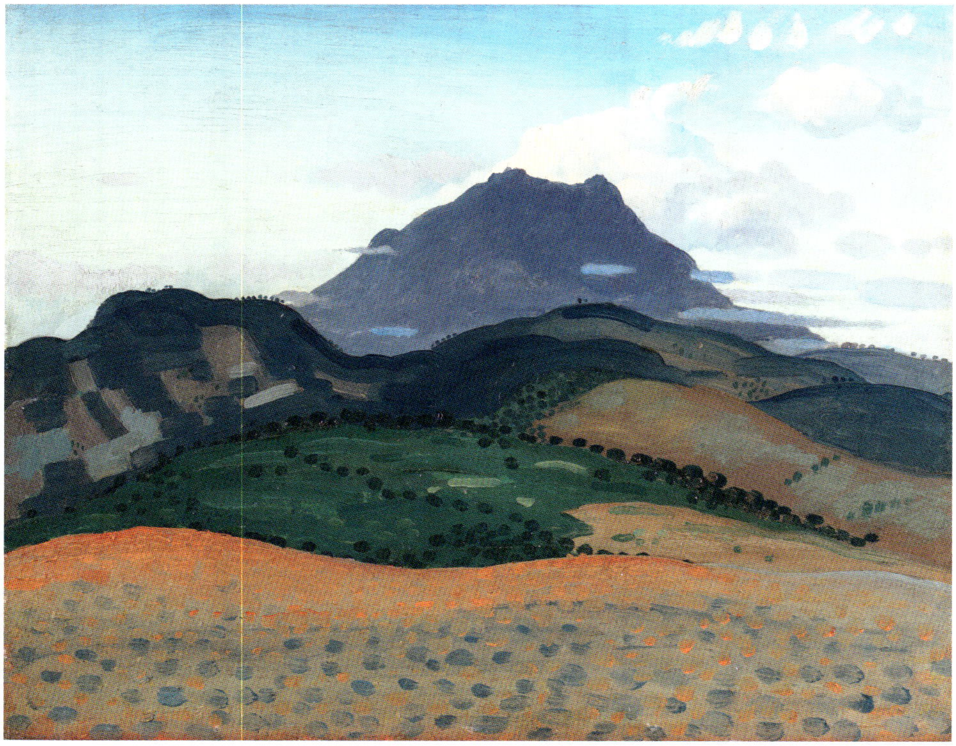

DL12.22

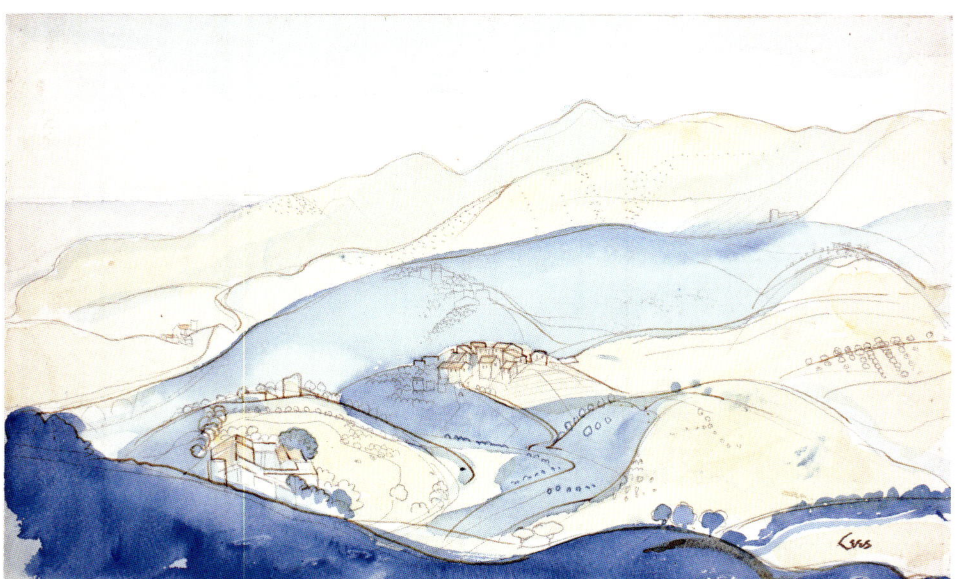

DL12.23

DL12.21*
The Blue Hills / Blue Hills of the South, 1912
ins: l.r.: Derwent Lees 1912
Oil on panel
24.8 x 34.3 cm
prov: John Quinn Collection c.1913–27; Dexter M. Ferry Feb 1927; Redfern Gallery 1930; Lord Henry Cavendish-Bentinck 1931, thence by descent to Lady Bentinck; Christie's London Apr 1940 (142); Listowel 1940
exh: Quinn 1927 (317); Redfern 1930a (4)
notes: In Quinn 1927 sale catalogue, 'A starry blue sky, with a clear full moon; buildings surrounded by a primitively arranged olive grove, and a range of blue mountains in the background. To the left, a massive olive tree', p.126

DL12.22
Tour Madeloc in the Pyrenees, 1912
Oil on panel
32.4 x 40.6 cm
prov: Redfern Gallery 1943; Roland, Browse & Delbanco Gallery, London 1979 (13); Browse & Darby, London 1990; Yale Center for British Art (through the Paul Mellon Fund), purchased 1990
exh: Redfern 1943 (114); Yale Center for British Art, *Twentieth Century Paintings and Sculpture* Jan–Apr 2000; Yale Center for British Art, *Edwardian Opulence*, Feb–Jun 2013
notes: From Mas Batlle vineyard, Banyuls; same scene as DL12.36

DL12.23
The Blue Hills, 1912
ins: l.r.: Lees
Watercolour, graphite, pen and brown ink on cream wove paper laid on ivory board
22.3 x 35.2 cm
prov: William Marchant & Co., London (Goupil Gallery) c.1924; Robert Allerton; gifted to the Art Institute of Chicago 1925
exh: Art Institute of Chicago, *Modern Drawings*, Dec 1926; Art Institute of Chicago, *A Century of Progress: Exhibition of Paintings, and Sculpture*, Jun–Nov 1933 (914)
notes: Puig del Mas and Mas Reig, from the Chapel of Notre-Dame de la Salette, Banyuls

DL12.24
Mas Reig, Banyuls / Spanish Landscape / Spanish Village, 1912
ins: l.l.: Derwent Lees 12
Oil on panel
32.5 x 40.4 cm
prov: Christie's London Apr 1929 (109, 2 in the lot); H.A. Bougers; Christie's London Oct 1974 (215); Ridley 1974; Joseph Brown Gallery, Melbourne; National Gallery of Australia, Canberra, purchased 1976
exh: Sane 1997, loaned by the National Gallery of Australia (14)
notes: Mas Reig, Banyuls

DL12.25
Donkey at Mas Reig, Banyuls / Landscape / Donkey in a Mediterranean Landscape, 1912
ins: l.r.: Lees [twice]
Pencil, pen, black ink and grey wash on paper
24.2 x 34.3 cm
prov: Redfern Gallery 1946–7; Christie's London Mar 1986, Oct 2008 (45), Jan 2012 (431)
exh: British Institute of Adult Education, London (catalogue not traced); Arts Council of Great Britain, London, *British Watercolours and Drawings* 1948 (26)
notes: From the hilltop Mas Reig farmhouse stable, Banyuls; location as in DL12.24

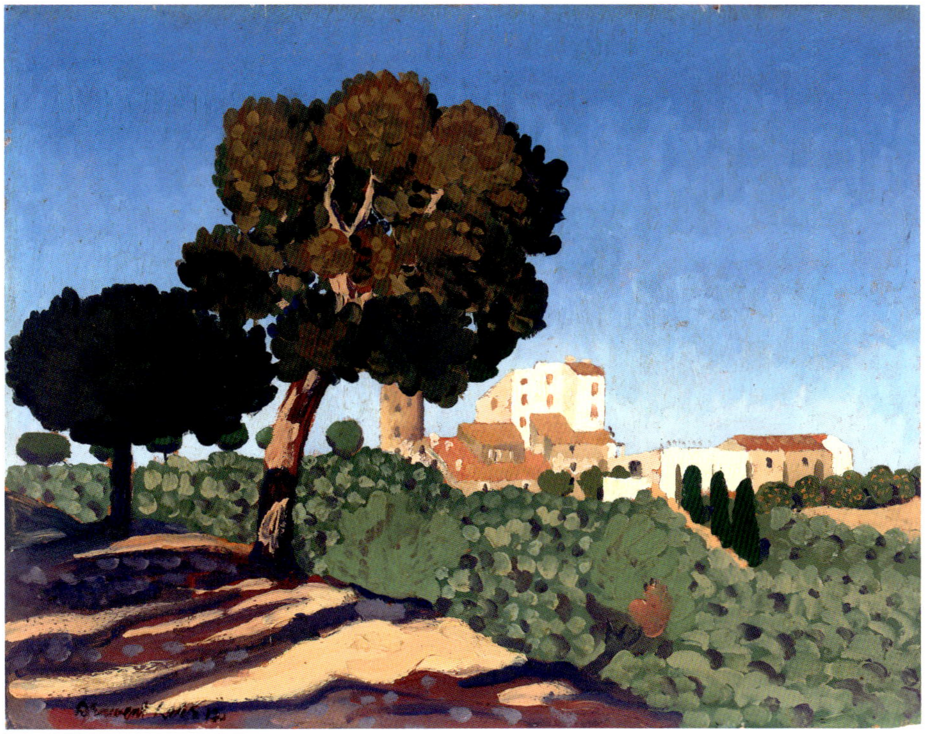

DL12.24

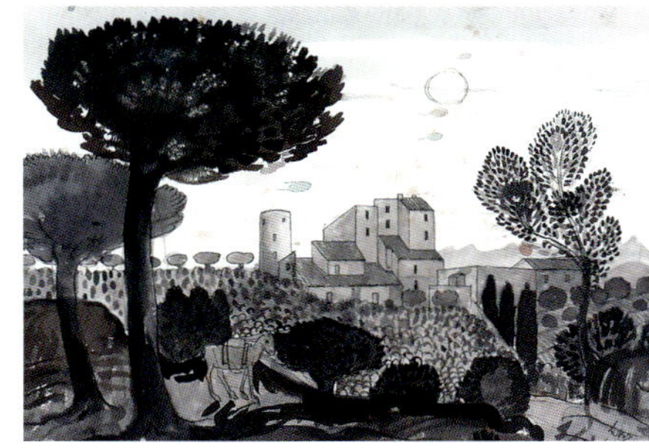

DL12.25

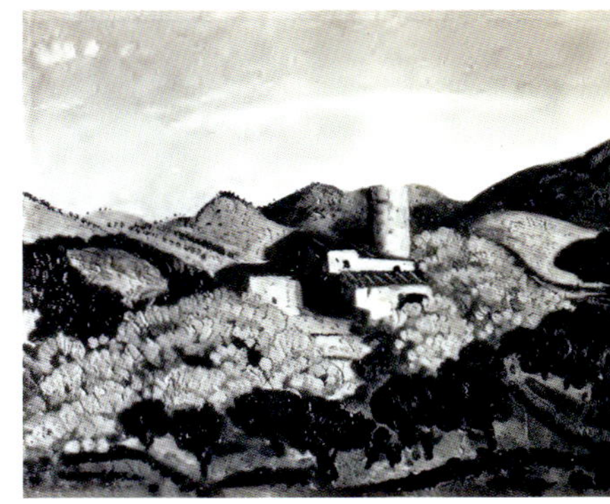

DL12.31

DL12.26 (see p.76)
Métairie des Abeilles / Metaire des Abeilles / Les Metairies D'Abeilles, 1912
ins: l.l.: Derwent Lees 12
Oil on panel
33 x 40.6 cm
prov: Chenil Gallery 1913–14; Sotheby's London Mar 1932 (137); Riddle & Couchman, London 1932; Christie's London Jun 1933 (113, 2nd of 2 in the lot); Dr John MacGregor 1933, bequeathed to Tate 1942
exh: Chenil 1913 (55), 1913–14 (57); Tate Oct 2022–25
notes: Mas Reig and Tour Madeloc peak from the Baillaury River, Banyuls

DL12.27 (see p.79)
Le Faubourg – Banyuls / Le Faubourg – Banyals / Spanish Landscape, 1912
ins: v.: [The Tate Gallery label]
Oil on panel
33.5 x 41 cm
prov: Arthur Tooth & Sons, London Sep 1932; Sir Anthony and Lady Hornby 1963, thence by descent; Sotheby's London Nov 2023 (156); Private Collection
exh: NEAC 49th 1913, as 'Le Faubourg Banyals' (202); Tate, *Private Views* Apr–May 1963, as 'Spanish Landscape', loaned by Sir Anthony Hornby (79)
notes: Tour Madeloc and houses along the Baillaury River, Banyuls

DL12.28*
View of a Village in Italy (Blick auf eine Ortschaft in Italien), c.1912
Oil on panel
32 x 22.5 cm
prov: Kunst & Auktionshaus Ruef, Landshut, Germany Mar 1993
notes: Unresolved record

DL12.29*
Le Mas aux Oliviers, Roussillon, 1912
Watercolour on paper
exh: NEAC 54th 1915 (279)
notes: Location of work unknown

DL12.30 (see p.77)
Mas Catalan / Sunset Near Collioure / Sunset, South of France / Sunset, Collioure / Sunset, Colliure, 1912
Oil on panel
24 x 37.7 cm
prov: Chenil Gallery 1913; R.G. Micklethwait; Sotheby's London Nov 1933 (43); Redfern Gallery 1934; Maurice Ingram 1939; Redfern Gallery 1941, 1946
exh: Chenil 1913 (62); NEAC 49th 1913 (244); Redfern 1934 (26), 1939a, collection of Maurice Ingram (44), 1941b, collection of the late Maurice Ingram (2), 1946b (195)
notes: In *Studio International* [full page illustration], 108, Jul–Dec 1934, p.15; Mas Batlle, Banyuls

DL12.31
Olive Farm (Banyules 1912), 1912
ins: l.l.: Derwent Lees 12
Oil on panel
35.5 x 43.1 cm
prov: John Quinn Collection; Dexter M. Ferry 1927
exh: Quinn 1927 (318)
notes: In Quinn 1927 sale catalogue, 'Mountainous landscape, with a building in the valley surrounded by glistening olive trees; under a clear blue sky', p.126; Mas Batlle, Banyuls

DL12.32
The Round Hill, Banyales / Spanish Landscape / Mountainous Landscape with a Hillock in the Foreground, 1912
Oil on panel
32 x 40 cm
prov: Chenil Gallery 1913–14; Lord Henry Cavendish-Bentinck (?); Sotheby's London May 1933 (95); Burrows; Spink Jun 1989 (41); Hove Museum & Art Gallery, Brighton (with assistance from the V&A Purchase Grant Funds), purchased 1989
exh: Chenil 1913–14 (62); Brighton & Hove Museum, permanent display 2002–6
notes: From Mas Batlle facing south-east, Banyuls

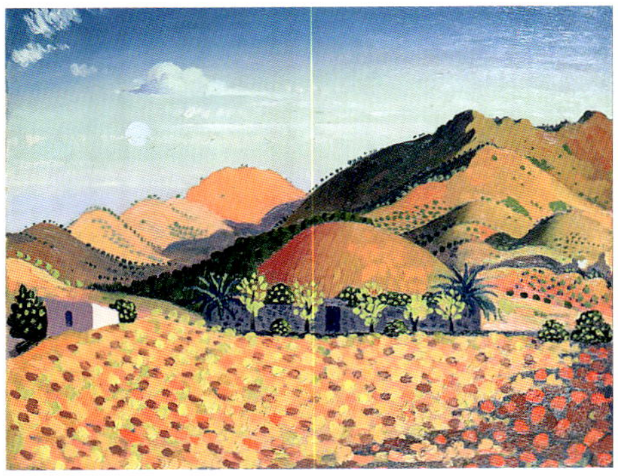

DL12.32

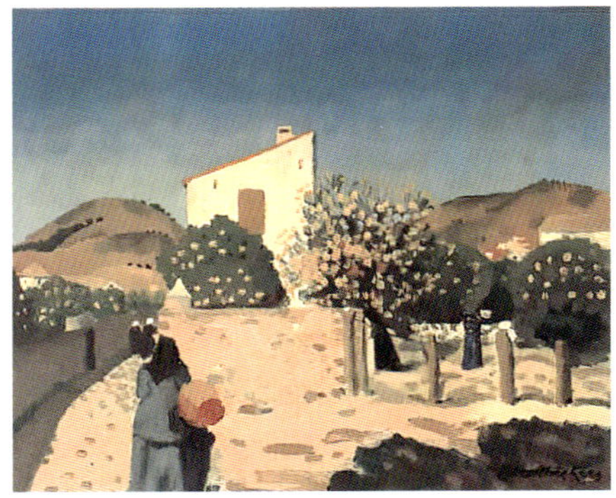

DL12.34

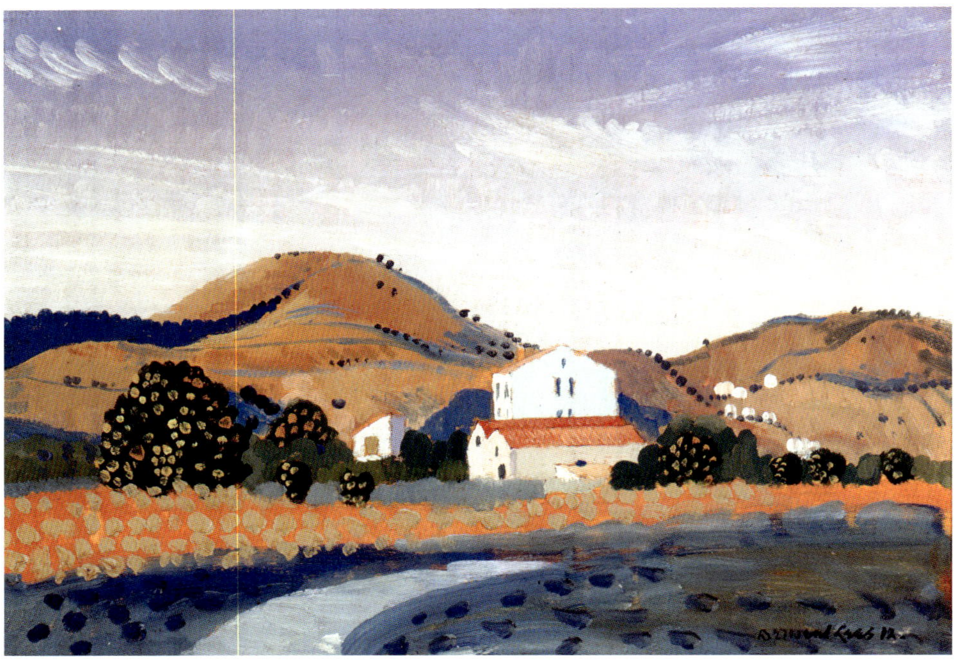

DL12.33

DL12.33
'Le Mas' Banzals / Landscape, The Round Hills / The Round Hill / Landscape, South of France, 1912
ins: l.r.: Derwent Lees 12
Oil on panel
24.9 x 35.5 cm
prov: Sotheby's London Mar 1932 (145); Arthur Tooth & Sons, London; Sir Edward Hayward 1935; bequeathed to the Collection of the Carrick Hill Trust, Adelaide (Hayward Bequest) 1983
exh: NEAC 56th 1916–17 (54); Art Gallery of South Australia, Adelaide, *Bohemian London* 1997 (41); Sane 1997, loaned by Carrick Hill (11)
notes: Rue des Orangers from the Baillaury River, Banyuls

DL12.34
Village Scene / Fruit Trees, 1912
ins: l.r.: Derwent Lees 12
Oil on panel
24.8 x 35.5 cm
prov: R.G. Micklethwait; Sotheby's London Nov 1933 (41); Redfern Gallery 1933; Sotheby's London May 1988 (30)
notes: Rue des Orangers, Banyuls; house as in DL12.33

DL12.35
Mountain at Banyals / Tour Madeloc, 1912
Watercolour on paper
31.8 x 45.7 cm
prov: Spink 1977–8
exh: NEAC 56th 1916–17 (149); Southampton City Art Gallery, as 'Tour Madeloc' attributed to JDI, 1977–8 (111)
notes: Reattributed in consultation with John Hoole (formerly JDI 317); Tour Madeloc from Banyuls, study for DL13.7

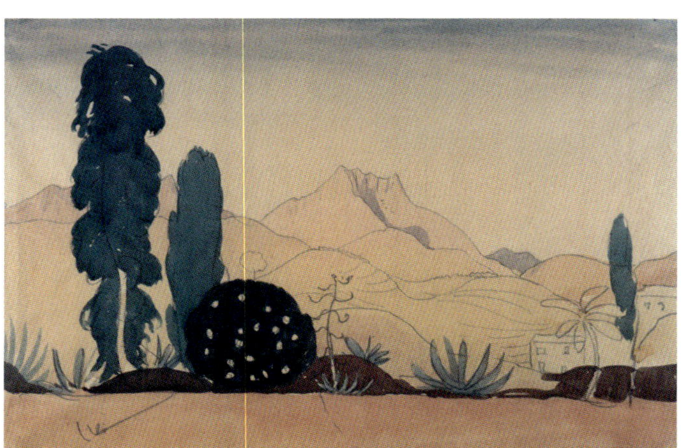

DL12.35

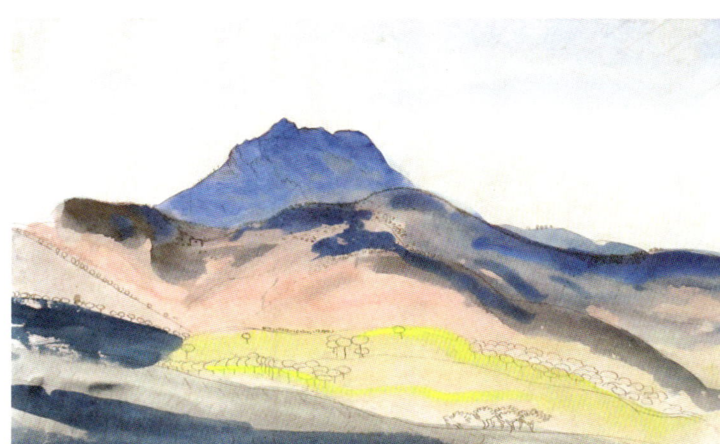

DL12.36

DL12.36
Tour Madeloc, Banyuls / Arenig, North Wales, 1912
Watercolour on paper
22.9 x 34.3 cm
prov: Redfern Gallery; Mr and Mrs J.B. Priestley 1946–51 (?), attributed to JDI; Mrs D.A. Bannerman (formerly Mrs Priestley) 1976; unknown auction house 2015 (28); Martyn Gregory, London 2015
exh: Graves Art Gallery, Sheffield, Glynn Vivian Art Gallery, Swansea, National Library of Wales, Aberystwyth Mar–May 1961, loaned by Mrs D.A. Bannerman (59)
notes: Reattributed in consultation with John Hoole (formerly JDI 287 A); Tour Madeloc from Mas Batlle vineyards, Banyuls, study for DL12.22

DL12.37
Mountainous Landscape / Mountain Landscape, 1912
Oil on panel
25 x 35 cm
prov: Arthur Crossland; Christie's London Feb 1956 (158, 1st of a pair); F.B.C. Bravington 1956; Sotheby's London, Dec 1968 (258); Thos. Agnew & Sons 1968 (30388); Private Collection; Dreweatts, Newbury Jul 2024 (100)
notes: Montagne du Cheval Blanc, Pre-Alpes from Digne-les-Bains

DL12.38*
Little Vineyard, c.1912
Oil
exh: NEAC 49th 1913 (253)
notes: Unresolved record

DL12.39
Old Banyuls / Vineyard, Provence, c.1912
ins: l.l.: Lees
Watercolour, gouache and ink on paper
22.5 x 35 cm
prov: Redfern Gallery; Thos. Agnew & Sons 1967 (126); John and Edward Barkes; Bridget McDonnell Gallery 1992; Private Collection
exh: NEAC 55th 1916 (137); Bridget McDonnell Gallery Aug–Sep 1992
notes: Puig del Mas, Banyuls

DL12.40*
Spanish Landscape, c.1913
Oil on panel
33 x 40.6 cm
prov: Arthur Crossland 1939–56; Christie's London Feb 1956 (155); F.B.C. Bravington 1956; Sotheby's London Jul 1967 (47); Thos. Agnew & Sons 1967
exh: Laing 1939 (310); Bradford 1954 (253)
notes: Unresolved record

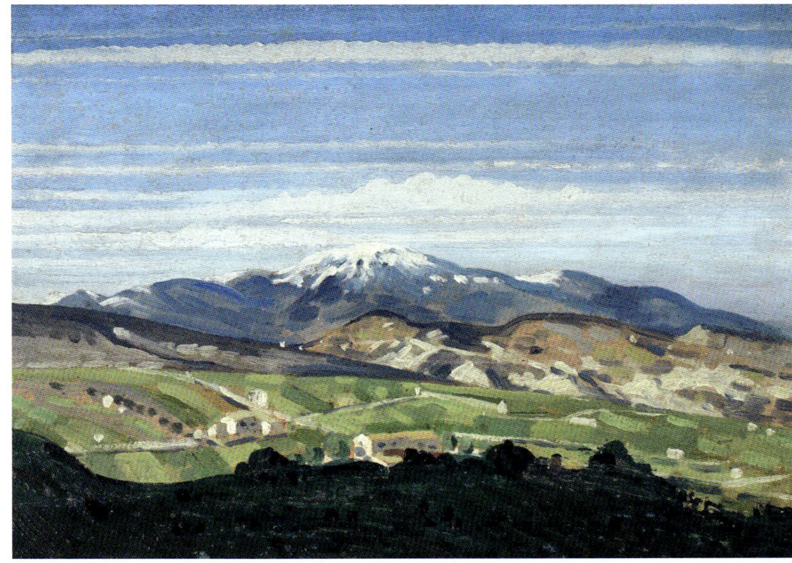

DL12.37

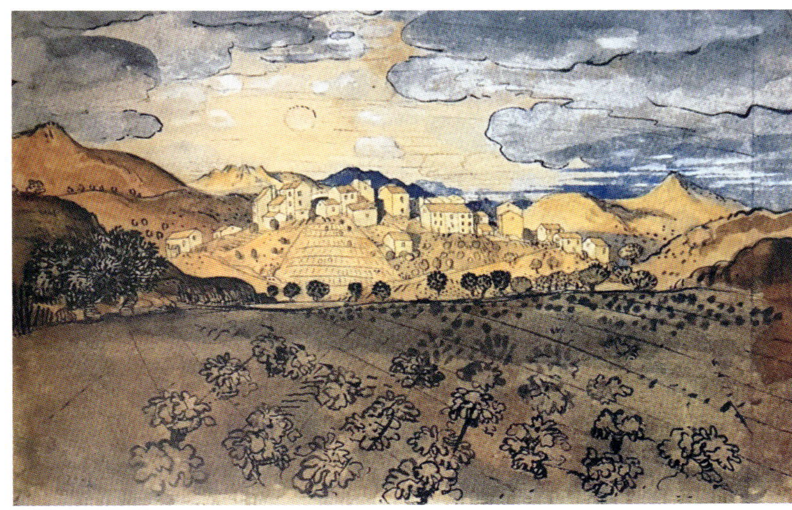

DL12.39

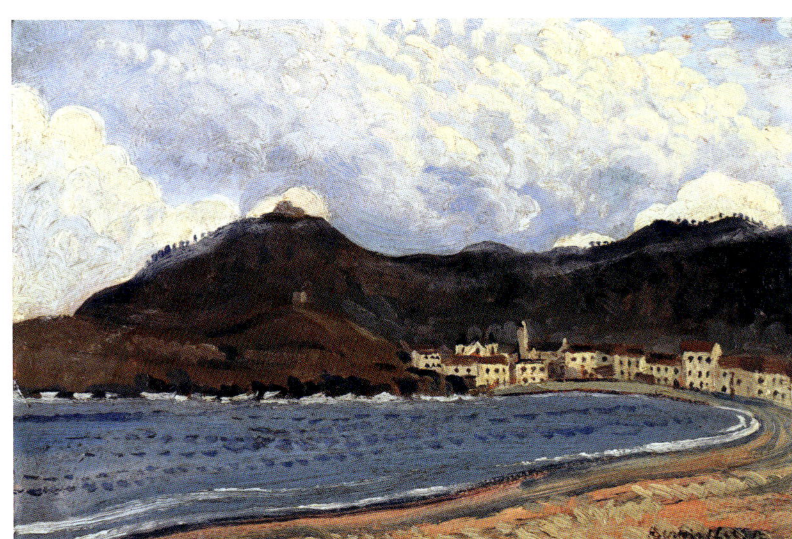

DL12.41

DL12.41
Collioure / The Bay of Collioure, 1912
ins: l.r.: Derwent Lees 12
Oil on panel
25 x 35.5 cm
prov: Redfern Gallery 1934, 1939, 1943; Sotheby's London Nov 1962 (117); Thos. Agnew & Sons Oct–Nov 1967 (20), Apr 1969 (30966); Christie's London, as 'The Bay of Collioure', Oct 1979 (63); Private Collection; Dreweatts, Newbury Jul 2024 (98)
exh: Redfern 1934 (10), 1939a (103), 1943 (84); Sherborne House, Sherborne, 2004 (26)

DL12.42*
The Round Hill, Banyuls, 1912
ins: [signature] 1912
Oil on panel
23.5 x 35.5 cm
prov: R.G. Micklethwait; Sotheby's London Nov 1933 (42); Redfern Gallery 1934
exh: Redfern 1934 (17)

DL12.43*
Bonnuls – Roussillon, 1912–13
Oil on panel
[small]
prov: Goupil Gallery 1921
exh: Goupil Gallery, London, *Representative Works by some of the Foremost Painters of the Modern British School* Jun–Jul 1921 (11)
notes: In C. Lewis Hind, *Landscape Painting, from Giotto to the Present Day*, Scribner, New York, 1924, 'Bonnuls-Roussillon, by Derwent Lees is still and hot, and the heat-filled sky and the arid, yellow land, with dumpy hills, give the impression of a place where only the sun shines, where no wind blows, and no rain falls . . . nature is controlled into a pattern', p.302

DL12.44*
Round Hill, South of France / The Round Hill, Bozouls / The Round Hill, Bozouls, South of France, c.1912
Pen, ink and watercolour on mulberry paper
23 x 35 cm
prov: D.E.H. Pratt; Sotheby's June 1981 (99)
exh: Eisteddfod Genedlaethol Cymru, Llandybie, Wales, *Arddangosfa'r Gymru Newydd* (*New Wales Exhibition*) 1944, loaned by D.E.H. Pratt (4); Graves Art Gallery, Sheffield, Glynn Vivian Art Gallery, Swansea, National Library of Wales, Aberystwyth Mar–May 1961, loaned by D.E.H. Pratt (93)
notes: Reattributed in consultation with John Hoole (formerly JDI 78)

DL12.45*
The Green Valley, 1912
ins: [signature] 1912
Oil on panel
24.1 x 34.3 cm
prov: Christie's London May 1965 (95); Fine Art Society London 1965

1913

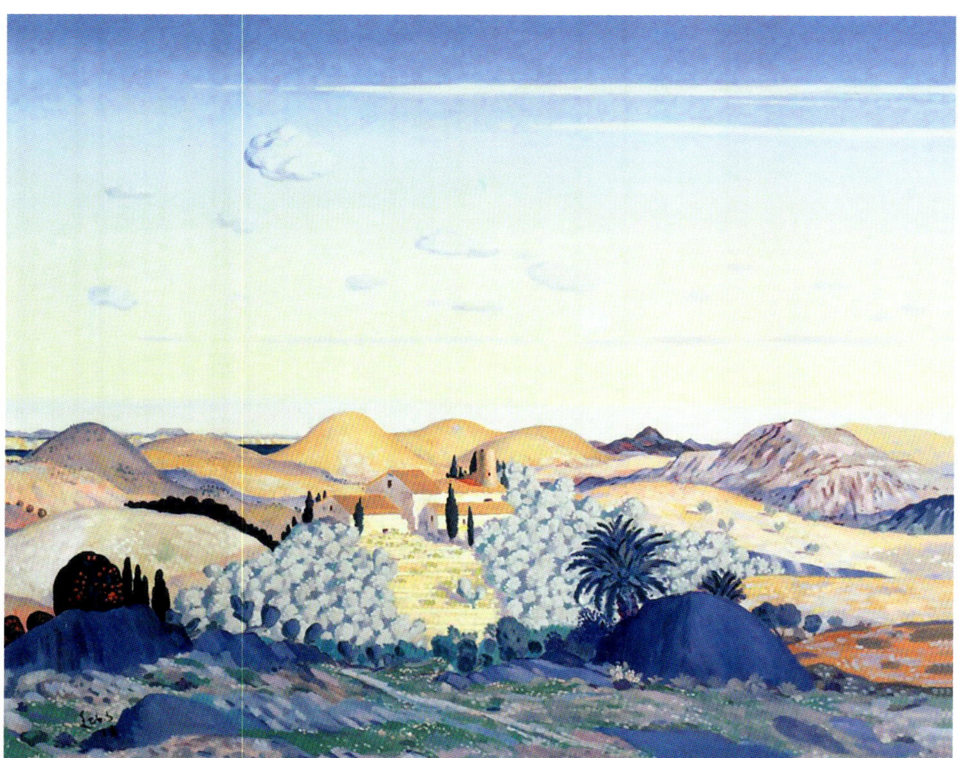

DL13.2

DL13.1 (see p.81)
Cheval Blanc, Basses Alpes / Italian Landscape with the Alps Beyond, 1913
ins: l.l.: Derwent Lees 1913
Oil on panel
27.9 x 38.1 cm
prov: Chenil Gallery 1913; John Quinn Collection; Ferargil Galleries, New York 1927; Christie's London Dec 2015 (78); Private Collection
exh: Chenil 1913; Quinn 1927 (49)
notes: The Alps and Vansoler Plateau from the Forcalquier Citadel

DL13.2
Banyuls / Bannuls, Roussillon / Banyuls – Roussillon / Banyons, Provence, 1913
ins: l.l.: Lees 1913
Oil on canvas
79 x 94.7 cm
prov: Cyril K. Butler 1915; Redfern Gallery 1939, 1944, 1947, 1948; Southampton City Art Gallery (through the Frederick William Smith Bequest), purchased Dec 1949
exh: NEAC 53rd 1915, loaned by Cyril K. Butler (136); Redfern 1939a (38); Melbourne Town Hall and the Herald Weekly Tribune, Melbourne, Queensland National Art Gallery and the Courier-Mail, Brisbane, Hobart Museum and Art Gallery, Hobart, *French and British*

Contemporary Art 1939–44, loaned by the Redfern Gallery (37); Redfern 1944a (47), 1947a, 1948 (104); Royal West of England Academy, Bristol, *British Painters in France* May–Jun 1953 (90); Exeter Art Gallery, *Contemporary Paintings from Southampton Art Gallery* Apr 1955 (14); Worthing Art Gallery, *Modern Paintings from Southampton Art Gallery* Apr–May 1957 (20); Plymouth City Art Gallery, *The Camden Town Group and Related Pictures* May–Jun 1974 (35); Southampton City Art Gallery, *Camden Town to Euston Road* Nov–Dec 2014, *Landscape Unbound* Nov 2022–Mar 2023
notes: Mas Batlle, Banyuls

DL13.3*
Spanish Landscape / A Mountainous Landscape in Spain, c.1913
Oil on panel
21.6 x 33 cm
prov: Arthur Crossland 1939–56; Christie's London Feb 1956 (157); F.B.C. Bravington 1956
exh: Laing 1939 (231)

DL13.4 (see p.80)
Mountain Pass / Landscape / Mountainous Landscape, c.1913
Oil on panel
24.8 x 35.5 cm
prov: Arthur Crossland 1939–56; Christie's London Feb 1956 (158, 2nd of a pair); F.B.C. Bravington 1956; Private Collection; Christie's London Nov 1988 (348); Fine Art Society 1989–2006; Bonhams London Mar 2006 (13); Private Collection
exh: Laing 1939 (200)
notes: Railway viaduct, Axat, France

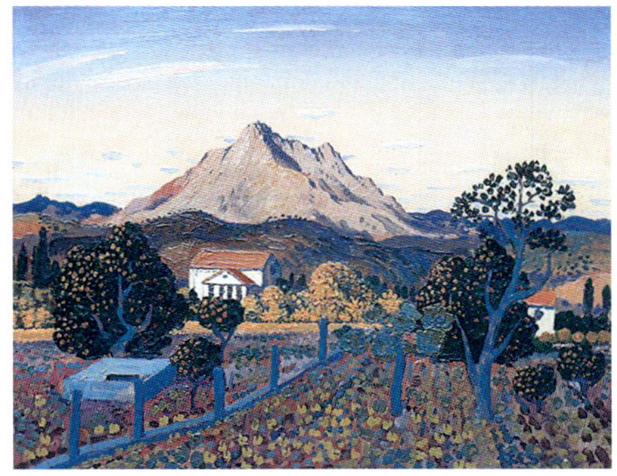
DL13.5

DL13.5
The Little Gardens / The Little Gardens, Cassis, France, 1913
ins: l.r.: Lees 13
Oil on panel
33 x 40.6 cm
prov: Chenil Gallery 1913–15; Redfern Gallery 1935; Mayor Gallery, London; Herbert Morton Hepworth, bequeathed to Leeds Art Gallery 1943
exh: Chenil 1913–14 (35), 1915 (89); Arts Council of Great Britain, London, *Landscape in Britain 1850–1950* 1983 (63)
notes: Tour Madeloc from the Banyuls market gardens

DL13.6
Pear Tree in Blossom / The Pear Tree / The Pear Tree, Provence, 1913
ins: l.r.: Lees 13; v.: [pencil sketch of hills]
Oil on panel
32.4 x 40.5 cm
prov: Chenil Gallery 1913–15; Private Collection; Sotheby's London Mar 1932 (139); Redfern Gallery 1932; purchased by the Knapping Fund for Tate 1939
exh: Chenil 1913–14 (52); Whitechapel 1914, loaned by Chenil Gallery (383); Chenil 1915 (93); Redfern 1932a (12); British Contemporary Art 1933, loaned by the Redfern Gallery (61); Redfern 1934 (16); Tate 1934–8, loaned by Rex Nan Kivell; Redfern 1939a (40); Tate, to Brussels, Amsterdam, Copenhagen, Paris, Berne, Vienna, Prague, Warsaw, Rome; *Modern British Pictures from the Tate Gallery, Continental Exhibition* Jan 1946–Feb 1947, as 'Poirier en Fleur' (43); *Modern British Pictures from the Last Fifty Years of British Painting 1897–1947*, May–Sep 1947; *Modern British Pictures from the Tate Gallery*, Sep 1947-Sep 1948
notes: Tour Madeloc from the Banyuls market gardens with an almond tree in blossom (personal communication with Yvon Berta-Maillol, grandson of Aristide Maillol, Banyuls, 2024)

DL13.7
Oriental Landscape / Tour Madeloc, c.1913
Oil on canvas
55.9 x 77.5 cm
prov: Cyril K. Butler 1925; Thos. Agnew & Sons; Mrs Saltonstall 1946, thence by descent
exh: NEAC 1925, Manchester, loaned by Cyril K. Butler (108)
notes: Reattributed in consultation with John Hoole (formerly JDI 318); Tour Madeloc from Banyuls facing north-west, relates to DL12.35

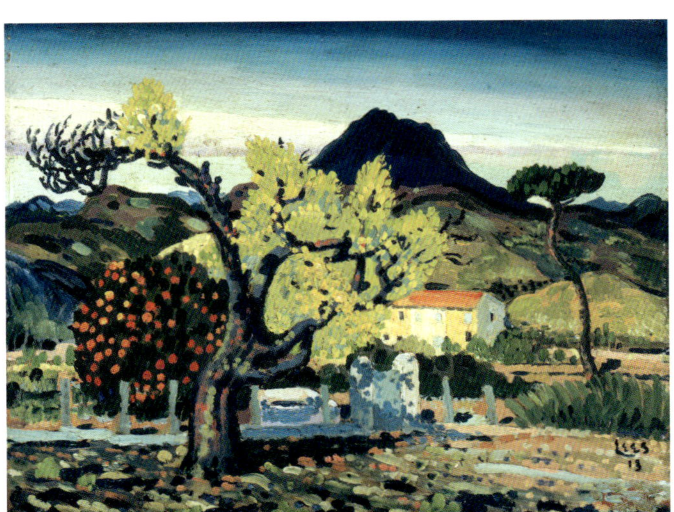

DL13.6

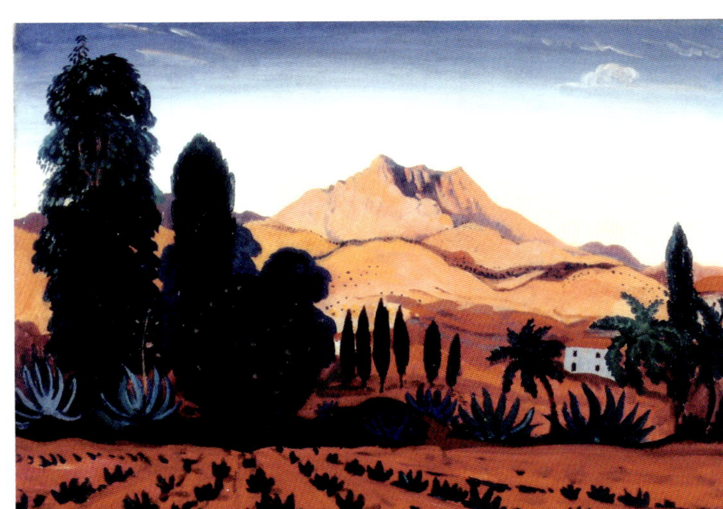
DL13.7

DL13.8
Two Drawings [upper], 1913
ins: l.l.: P.D.L.; l.r.: 1913
Print on paper
prov: In J. Middleton Murry (ed.), *The Blue Review*, 1(1), 1913

DL13.9
Two Drawings [lower], 1913
ins: l.r.: P.D.L. 1913
Print on paper
prov: In J. Middleton Murry (ed.), *The Blue Review*, 1(1), 1913
notes: DL and Lyndra; Tour Madeloc, hills and house as in DL13.7

DL13.10*
Fitzroy Square, December / Fitzroy Square under Snow, c.1913
Oil
prov: Redfern Gallery 1931, 1932, 1934, 1938, 1939; Randolph Schwabe (?)
exh: Redfern 1931c (1), 1932 (15), 1934 (19), 1938 (18), 1939a (26)

DL13.11
An Extensive Landscape with Houses, c.1913
ins: l.l.: Lees
Watercolour and gouache on paper
22.8 x 27.9 cm
prov: Sotheby's London Nov 2008; Brightwells, Leominster Jun 2013 (51)

DL13.12*
North Yorkshire Moors, c.1913
Oil on panel
15.5 x 25.5 cm
prov: Spink, Sydney Mar 1982 (207)
notes: Unresolved record

DL13.13**
Extensive Landscapes / Welsh Landscape / Extensive Valley Scene, c.1913
Oil on panel
27.9 x 49.5 cm
prov: Arthur Crossland; Christie's London Feb 1956, as 'Extensive Landscapes' attributed to JDI (149); Thos. Agnew & Sons 1956; Mr and Mrs J.O. Stanley-Clarke; Sotheby's London Mar 1973 (44); Colnaghi, London; Christie's London Nov 1989 (235), Jun 1992 (49); Private Collection; Christie's London Jul 2006 (84), Feb 2007 (56)
notes: Reattributed in consultation with John Hoole, formerly attributed to JDI

DL13.14*
Portrait of the Artist's Wife as a Young Woman, c.1913
Oil on canvas
43.2 x 28 cm
prov: W.H. Lane & Son, Penzance Jul 2000 (19)
notes: Unresolved record

DL13.15
Portrait of an Unknown Woman / The Lady Howard de Walden, c.1913
ins: v.: 22" x 16" [in pencil]
Pencil on paper
35.2 x 25.4 cm
prov: Brighton & Hove Museums, purchased 1979

DL13.16
Portrait of a Woman / Portrait of Artist's Wife, 1913–14
Pencil on paper
31 x 22.8 cm
prov: Redfern Gallery; Private Collection; Bridget McDonnell Gallery 2023–4
notes: Unknown model

DL13.17
The Model / The Young Model, 1913–14
Pencil on paper
29 x 22.5 cm
prov: Redfern Gallery 1948 (?); Private Collection; Bridget McDonnell Gallery; Private Collection
exh: Redfern 1948 (622)

DL13.18
Portrait of Artist's Wife, Lyndra, c.1913
Pencil on paper
29 x 22.5 cm
prov: Private Collection; Bridget McDonnell Gallery 2011; Private Collection

DL13.19
The Artist's Wife, Lyndra, 1913
ins: l.r.: Lees. 13
Pencil on paper
28 x 21.8 cm
prov: Redfern Gallery; John and Edward Barkes; Bridget McDonnell Gallery 1997; Private Collection
exh: Bridget McDonnell Gallery 1997 (21)

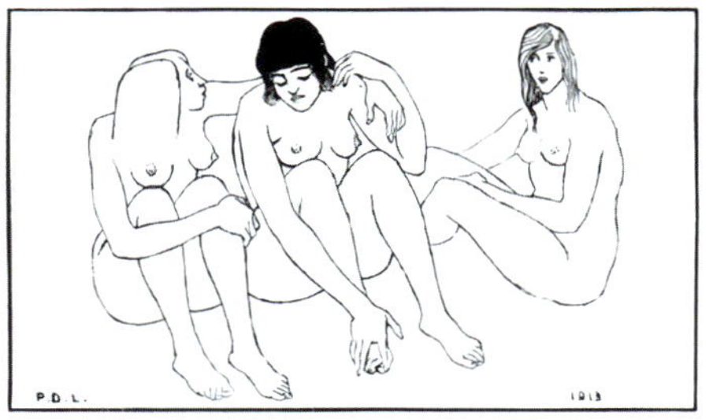

DL13.8

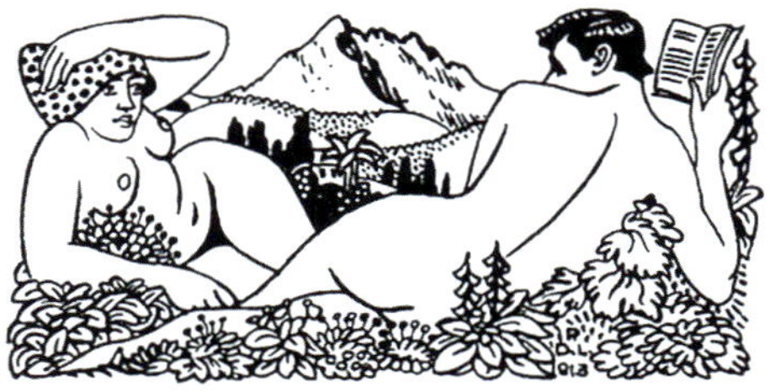

DL13.9

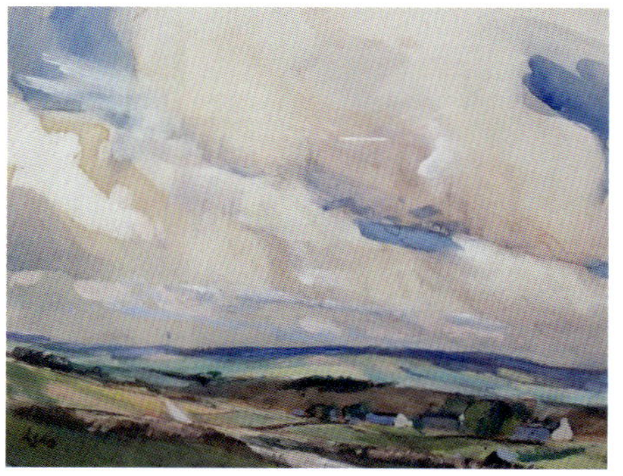

DL13.11

DL13.20
Profile, Lyndra / [Profile, Portrait of a Woman] / Portrait Study, c.1913
Pencil on paper
20.6 x 15.8 cm [image], 35.4 x 25.2cm [sheet]
prov: Deutsher 1978; National Gallery of Australia, Canberra, purchased 1979
exh: Deutsher 1978 (25); Sane 1997, loaned by the National Gallery of Australia (36)

DL13.21
Lyndra / Bust Portrait of a Young Woman / Untitled [Profile, Portrait of a Woman], 1913
ins: l.l.: D Lees. 12 [written over original erased signature and date: D Lees. 13]
Pencil on paper
30 x 23 cm
prov: Francis Bate (founder member, treasurer, secretary of NEAC), thence by descent; David Duggleby Auctioneers, Scarborough Sep 2018 (46); Sworders, London Apr 2021 (551); Abbott and Holder, London 2021–4 (8799); Private Collection

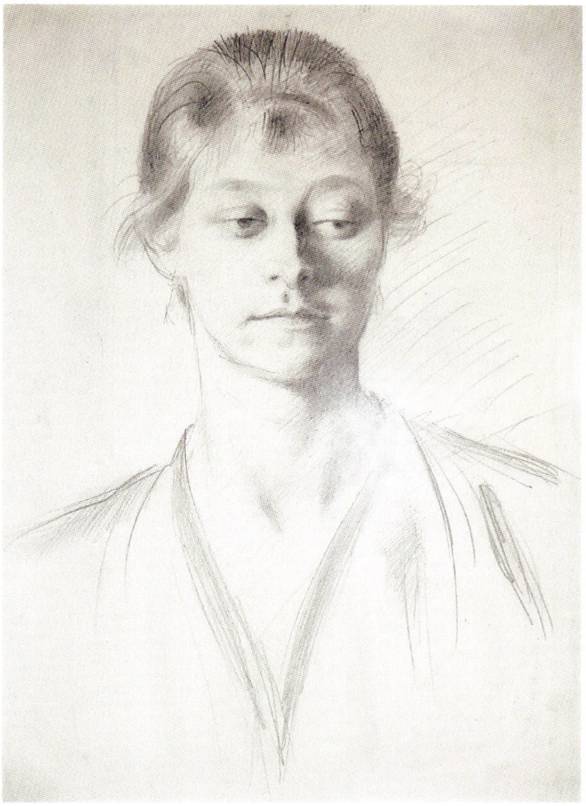

DL13.15

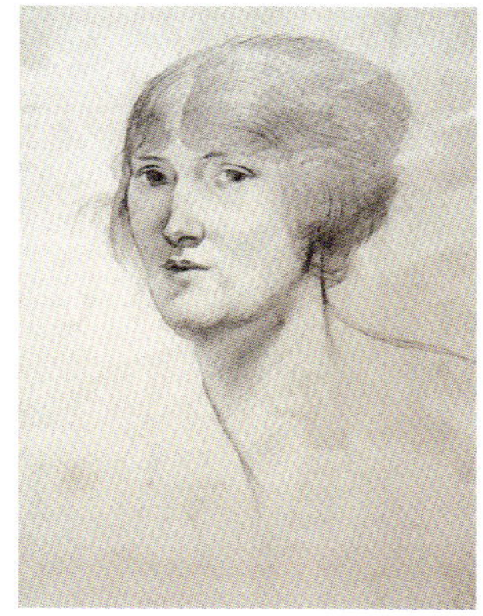

DL13.16

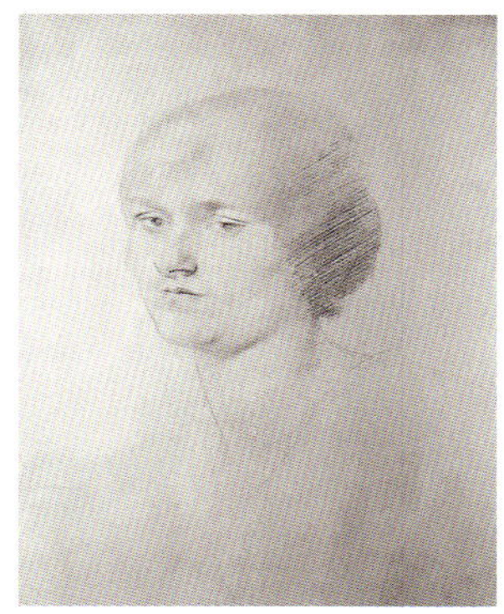

DL13.17

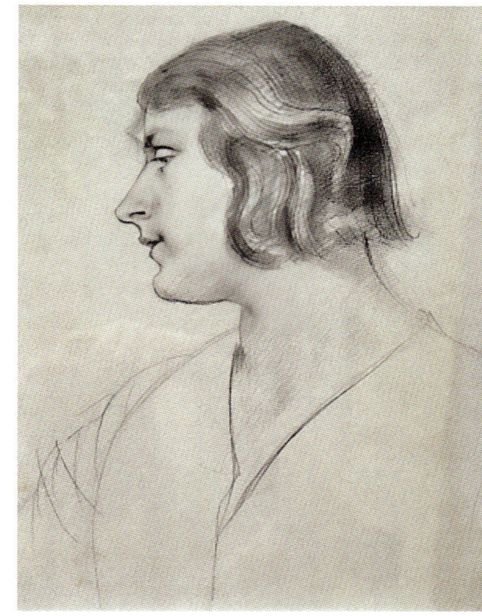

DL13.18

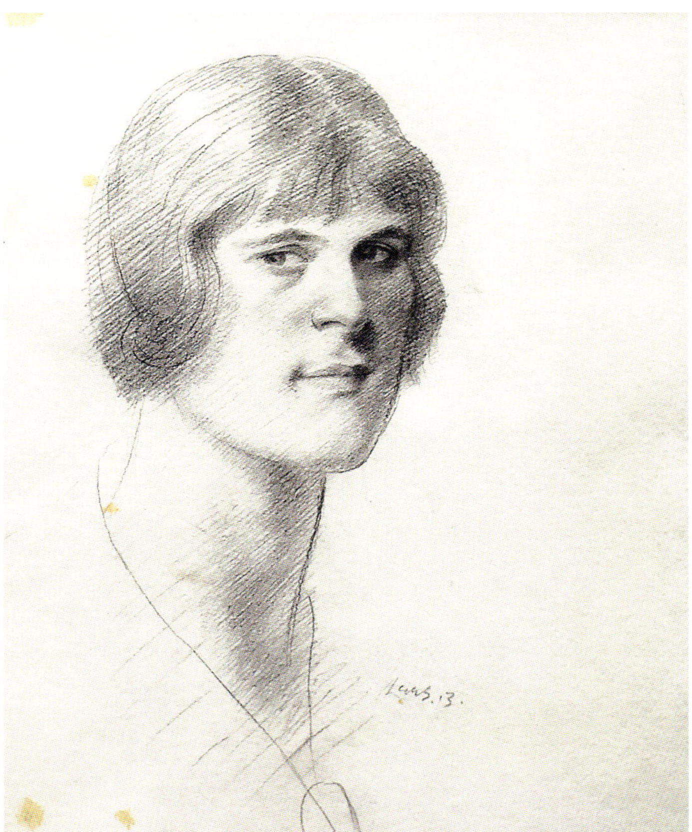

DL13.19

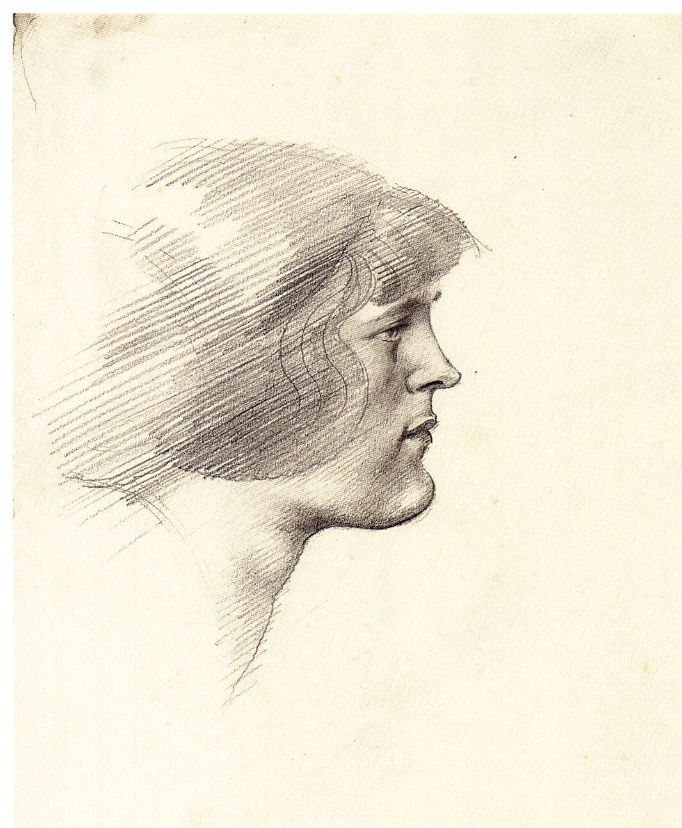

DL13.20

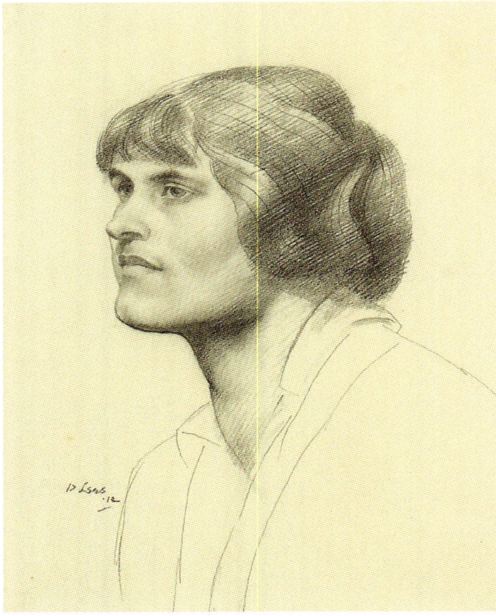

DL13.21

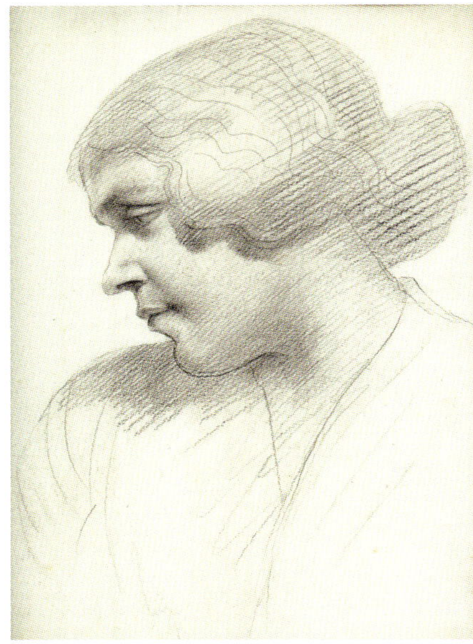

DL13.22

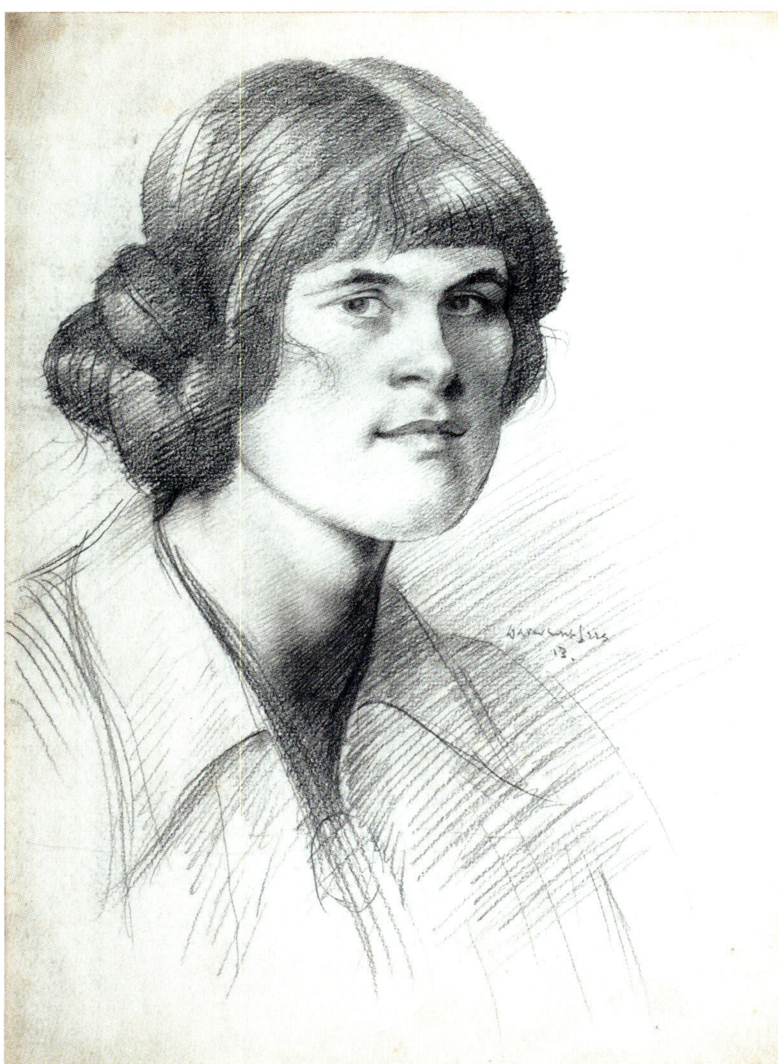

DL13.23

DL13.22
Portrait of a Young Woman / Portrait Study, c.1913
Pencil on paper
35.5 x 25.4 cm
prov: Rex Nan Kivell; Deutsher 1978; Colville Gallery, Hobart 2022; Private Collection
exh: Deutsher 1978 (18)
notes: Lyndra

DL13.23
Portrait of Lyndra, The Artist's Wife / Lyndra, Wife of Derwent Lees, 1913
ins: c.r.: Derwent Lees 13; v.: 7
Pencil on paper on panel
40.5 x 25.4 cm
prov: Belgrave Gallery, London Feb 1981 (2); Brighton & Hove Museum and Art Gallery (with assistance from V&A Purchase Grant Fund), purchased 1981

DL13.24**
Lyndra [profile, head turned slightly], 1 of 2, c.1913
Etching plate
prov: Print: Burstow and Hewett Abbey Mar 2024; Plate: Private Collection 2021

DL13.25**
Lyndra [profile, head turned slightly], 2 of 2, c.1913
Etching plate
prov: Private Collection 2021

DL13.26
The Orange Skirt, c.1913
ins: l.l.: [signature]
Oil on panel
48.9 x 29.2 cm
prov: Dowdeswell and Dowdeswell, London; Christie's London Feb 1917 (360); Redfern Gallery 1930, 1932, 1934
exh: Redfern 1930a (6), 1932 (11); British Contemporary Art 1933 (62); Redfern 1934 (6)
notes: Lyndra, Alderney Manor, Dorset

DL13.27 (see p.91)
Edith / Lyndra / White Dress, c.1913
Oil on panel
51 x 32.4 cm
prov: Chenil Gallery 1913–14; Redfern Gallery 1958; Anthony D'Offay Ltd, London; Fine Art Society; Christie's London Apr 1985; Lots Road Auctions, Chelsea Mar 2011 (344)
exh: Chenil 1913–14 (36); Redfern 1958 (33)
notes: Alderney Manor, Dorset

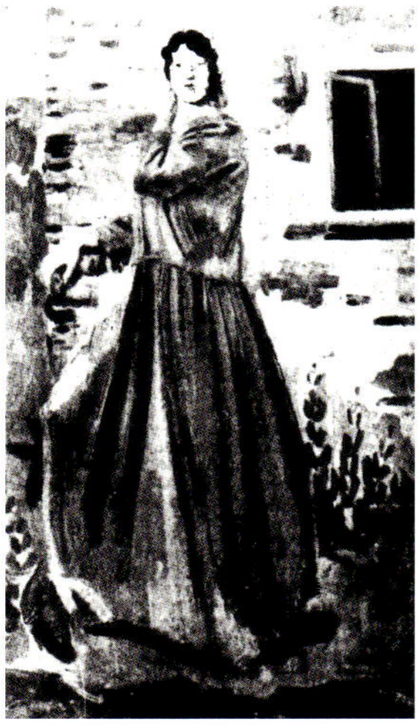

DL13.26

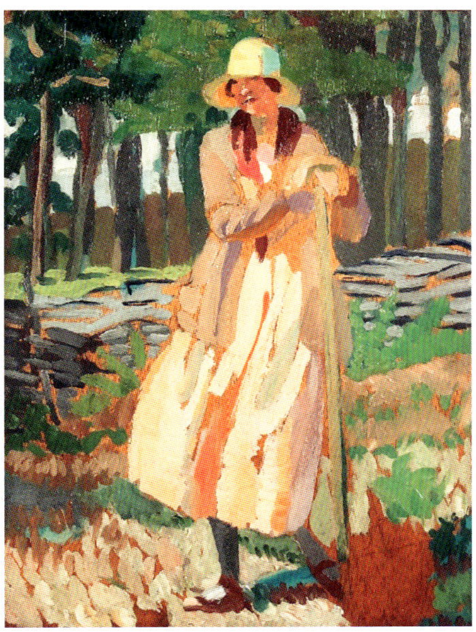

DL13.30

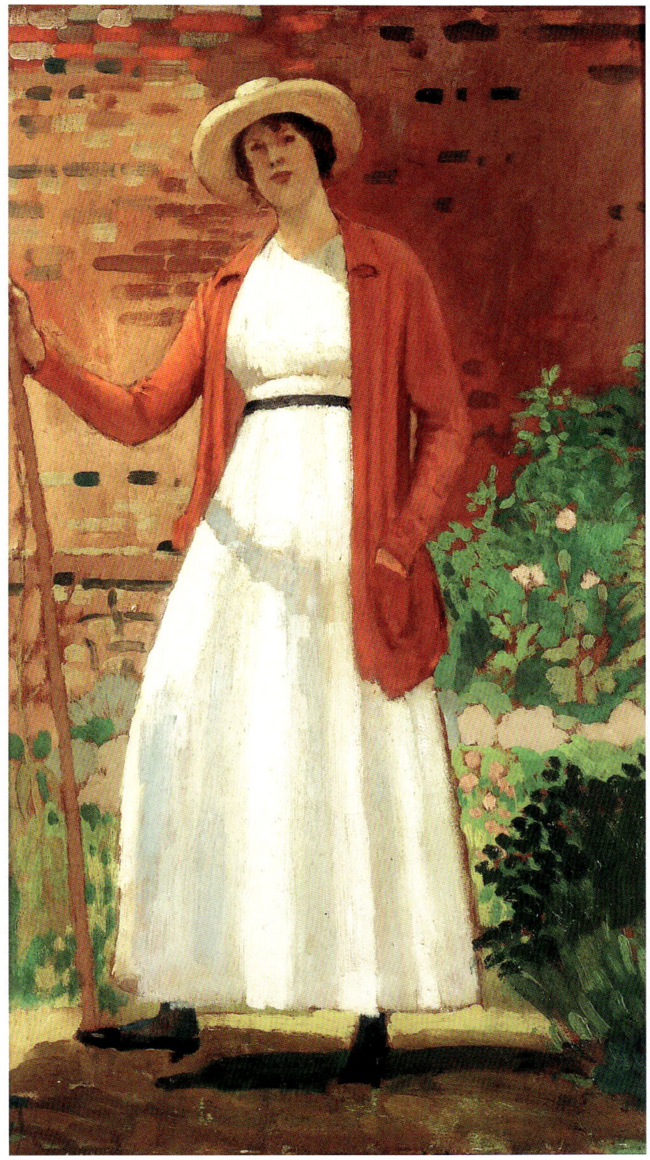

DL13.28

DL13.28
The Kitchen Garden / Lyndra in a Garden / The Orange Jacket, c.1913
Oil on panel
50.8 x 38.1 cm
prov: Rex Nan Kivell; J. Leger & Son Gallery, London 1963; Private Collection; Sotheby's London Dec 2006 (18), Nov 2007 (16); Roseberys, West Norwood Dec 2008; Private Collection; Christopher Kingzett Fine Art, London 2023; Piano Nobile, London 2024; Private Collection
exh: NEAC 54th 1915 (120); Piano Nobile, London, *Augustus John and the First Crisis of Brilliance* Apr–Jul 2024 (25)
notes: Alderney Manor garden, Dorset

DL13.29**
Lyndra / Dorelia, c.1913
ins: [signature]
Oil on panel
50.8 x 30.5 cm
prov: Sotheby's London Oct 1987 (109)
notes: Alderney Manor garden, Dorset

DL13.30
Lyndra in the Woods / Woman of the Woods, c.1913
Oil on panel
39.3 x 29.3 cm
prov: M.V.B. Hill, thence by descent; Dr Gourlay, Cambridge; Christie's London Jul 1967 (14); Fine Art Society; Chorley's, Gloucester Nov 2016 (240)
exh: Fine Art Society London Feb 1968 (3422)
notes: Alderney Manor, Dorset

DL13.31**
Lyndra Seated on a Sunny Bank / Girl Seated on a Sandy Bank / Lyndra in the Sun / A Dorset Heath, 1913
ins: l.l.: Lees 13
Oil on panel
33.7 x 40.6 cm
prov: Chenil Gallery 1913–14, 1915; Arthur Crossland; Redfern Gallery 1958; Christie's London Mar 1974 (111); Fine Art Society 1976; Private Collection
exh: Chenil 1913–14 (40), 1915 (98); Redfern 1958 (35); Fine Art Society London, Adelaide, *The Fine Art Society at the Adelaide Festival* 1976 (13); Fine Art Society London, *Centenary 1876–1976, Camden Town Recalled* Oct–Nov 1976 (90)
notes: Lyndra, the Blue Pool, Dorset

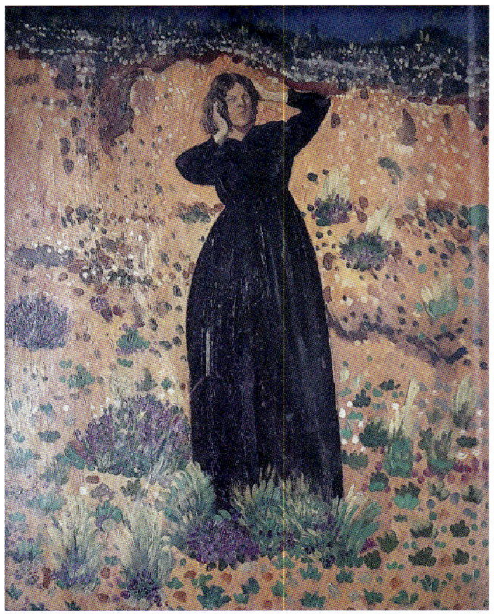

DL13.32

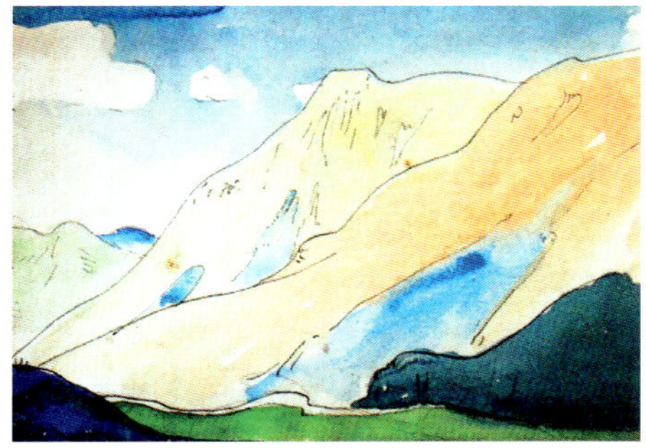

DL13.34

DL13.34
Study, The Blue Pool / Mountains / Mountain Landscape, 1913
Watercolour and pen on paper
24.1 x 34.3 cm
prov: Winifred Coombe-Tennant 1953; A.J.F. Coombe-Tennant 1961, thence by descent
exh: Graves Art Gallery, Sheffield, Glynn Vivian Art Gallery, Swansea, National Library of Wales, Aberystwyth Mar–May 1961, loaned by A.J.F. Coombe-Tennant (113); Glynn Vivian Art Gallery, Swansea 2008
notes: Reattributed in consultation with John Hoole (formerly JDI 313); sand mounds beside the Blue Pool, Dorset; likely study for DL13.35

DL13.32
Lyndra by the Blue Pool, 1913
ins: l.l.: Lees 13
Oil on panel
51 x 40 cm
prov: Nora (née Munro) and Gerald Summers, thence by descent

DL13.33
Lyndra in a Landscape, 1913
ins: l.l.: Lees. 13
Oil on panel
50.6 x 40.3 cm
prov: J. Leger & Son Gallery, London Oct 1947; NGV (through the Felton Bequest) purchased 1948
exh: NGV Melbourne International, *Travelling Exhibition no.1* 1950; National Gallery of South Australia, Special Exhibition, Adelaide Festival of the Arts, Melbourne, *British Painting 1900–1950* Mar 1966 (15); Sane 1997, loaned by NGV (17); NGV, *Night and Day 20th Century Painting* 2002; NGV Melbourne International Year, *Modern Britain 1900–1960* 2007–8; NGV, Gallery 8 2007–17
notes: Blue Pool, Dorset

DL13.35
The Sandhill / The Sand Hill / Lyndra in the Pyrenees / Lyndra in the Sandhills, Pyrenees, 1913
ins: l.l.: Lees 13
Oil on panel
41.7 x 52 cm
prov: Chenil Gallery 1913–14; Christie's London Dec 1917 (56); Private Collection; Christie's London Mar 1939 (108); Redfern Gallery 1939; Aberdeen Art Gallery (through the Murray Fund), purchased 1939
exh: Chenil 1913–14 (48); Redfern 1939c (8); Aberdeen Art Gallery Sep–Oct 1939 (20); Arts Council Scottish Committee 1952 (22); NEAC *Centenary Exhibition* 1986 (130); Ghent Museum, Belgium Oct 2007–Jan 2008 (204)
notes: Lyndra beside the Blue Pool, Dorset

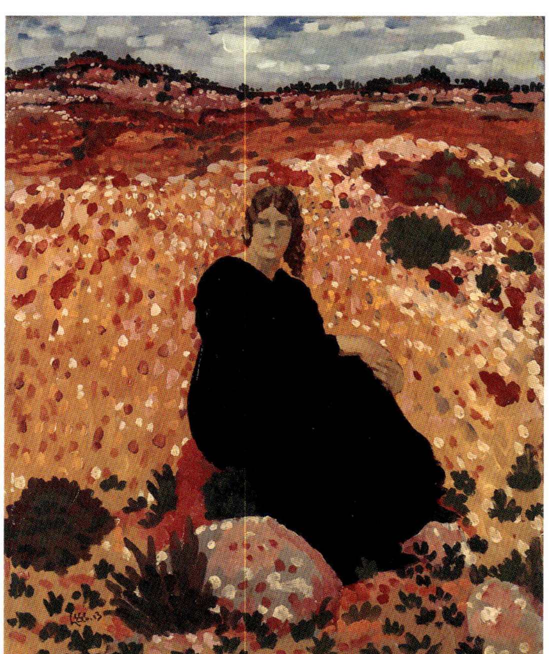

DL13.33

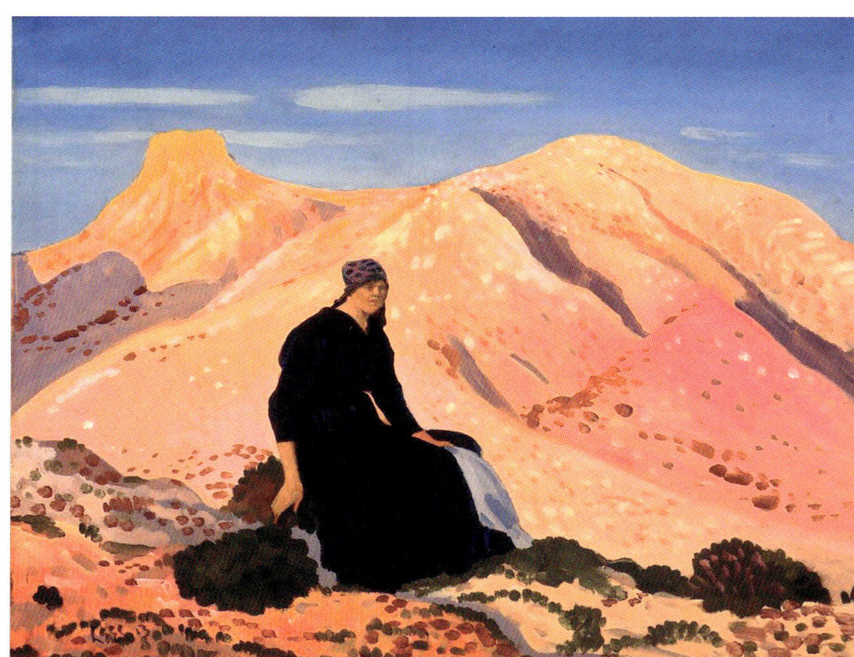

DL13.35

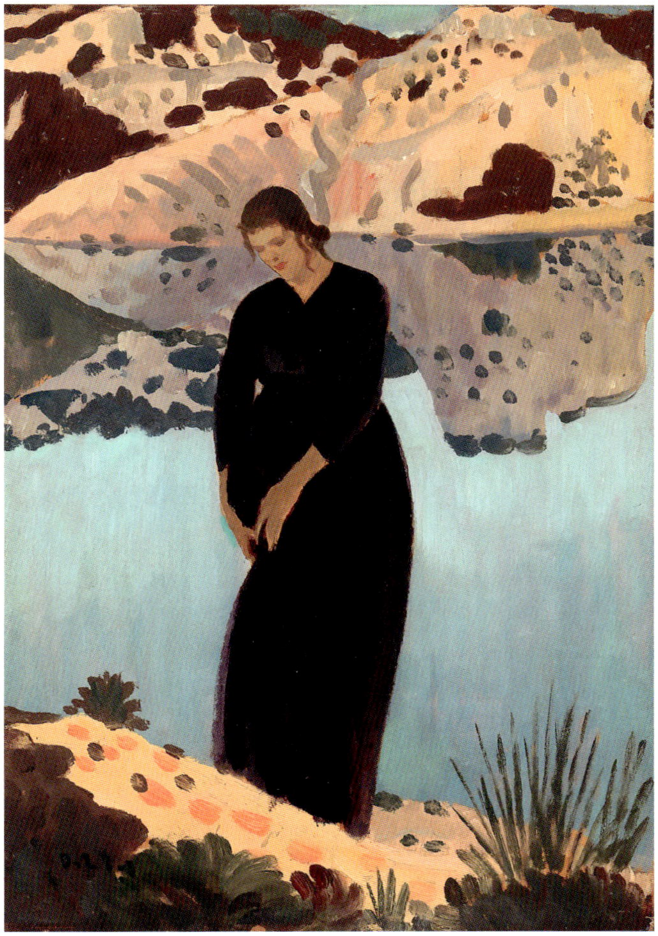

DL13.36

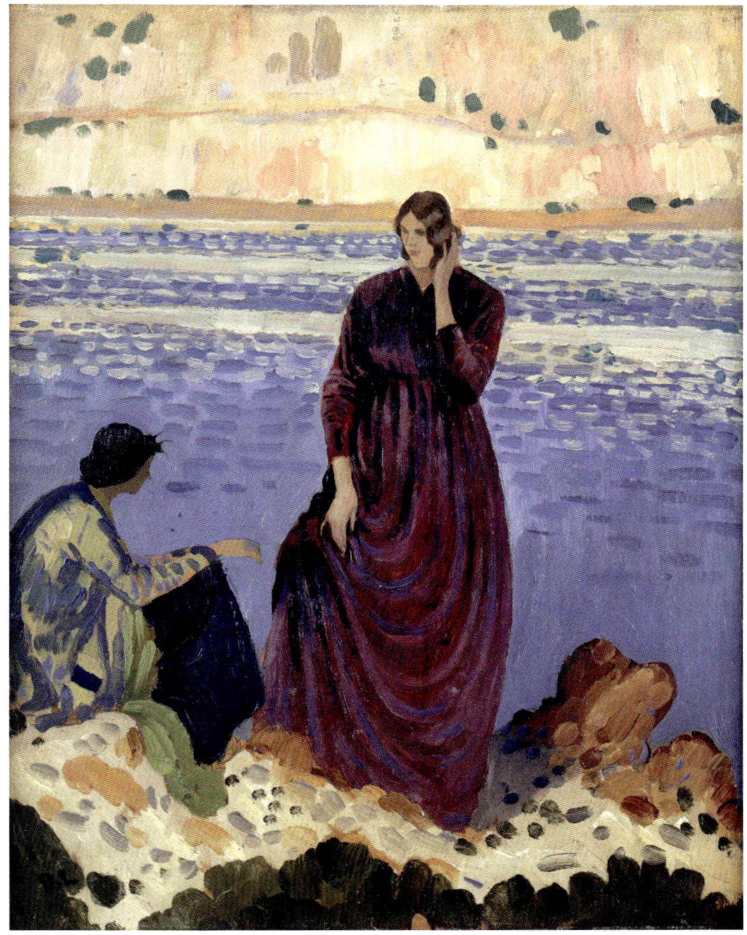

DL13.40

DL13.36
Lyndra at the Pool (Artist's Wife near the Blue Pool, Dorset) / Lyndra by the Blue Pool, 1913
ins: l.l.: D.L. 13
Oil on panel
39.5 x 29 cm
prov: Earl of Sandwich 1930; Sotheby's London Apr 1963; Mr and Mrs J.O. Stanley-Clarke; Sotheby's London Nov 1973 (24A); Fine Art Society 1974; National Gallery of Australia, Canberra, purchased 1976
exh: Redfern 1930a, loaned by the Earl of Sandwich (9); NEAC winter 1930 (66); British Contemporary Art 1933 (63); Empire Art 1934–5, loaned by the Earl of Sandwich (123); Redfern 1939a, loaned by the Earl of Sandwich (25); Fine Art Society London, *Face to Face* Dec 1974 (18); Fine Art Society London, Adelaide, *The Fine Art Society at the Adelaide Festival* 1976 (11)

DL13.37
Two Figures of Lyndra at the Blue Pool / Women at La Ciotat, 1913
ins: l.l.: Lees 13
Gouache, pen and ink on paper
24.4 x 36.2 cm
prov: Thos. Agnew & Sons Mar–Apr 1985 (96)
notes: The Blue Pool, Dorset

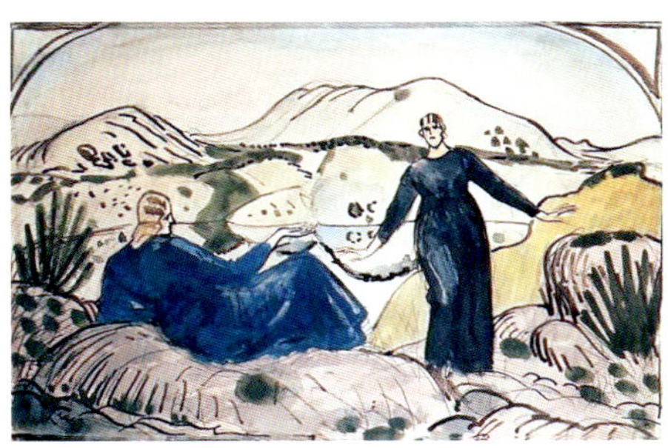

DL13.37

DL13.38 (see p.89)
Lyndra by the Blue Pool, Dorset / Lyndra / Lyndra at the Blue Pool, 1913
ins: l.r.: Lees 13
Oil on panel
39.4 x 50.1 cm
prov: Lady Katherine Parsons; Redfern Gallery 1934; Maurice Ingram; Redfern Gallery 1941; J. Leger & Son Gallery, London 1957; Art Gallery of South Australia, Adelaide (through the A.M. Ragless Bequest), purchased Aug 1957
exh: Redfern 1934 (1), 1939a, loaned by Maurice Ingram (42); Tate 1940, loaned by Maurice Ingram (101); Redfern 1941b, collection of the late Maurice Ingram (25); Sane 1997 (18); Art Gallery of South Australia, Adelaide, *Bohemian London* 1997 (44); NGV, *Modern Britain 1900–1960* 2007–8; Art Gallery of South Australia, Adelaide, *Making Nature* 2009
notes: In *South Australian Bulletin*, 19, Jan 1958, pp 1–7

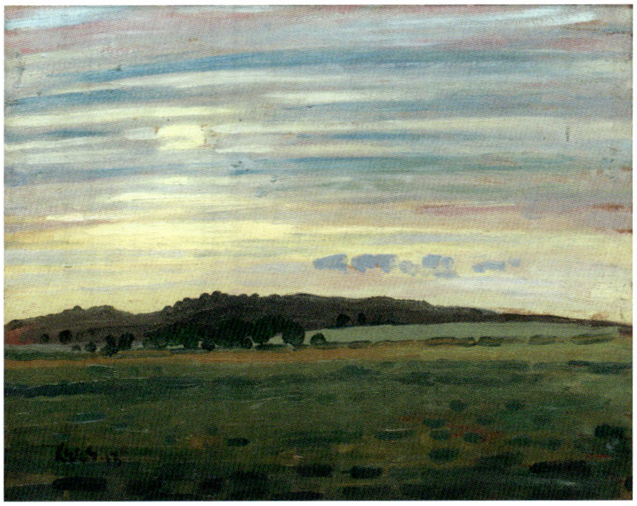

DL13.42

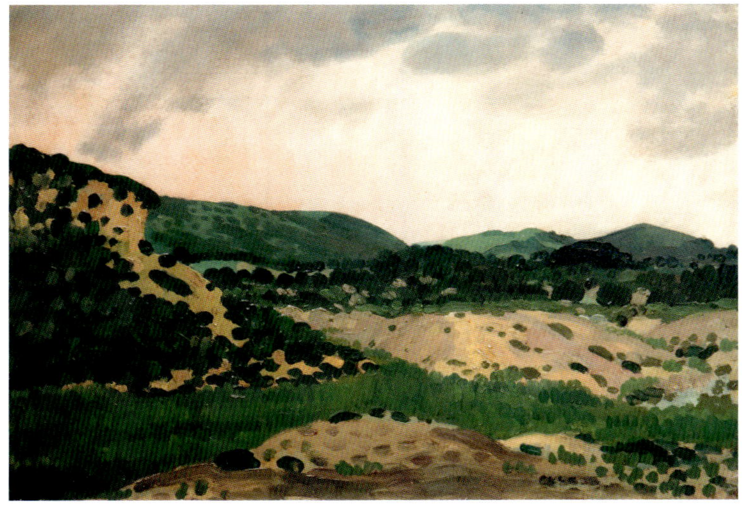

DL13.43

DL13.39*
Girl by the Pool / The Girl and the Pool, 1913
ins: l.l.: Lees 13
Oil on panel
34.3 x 24 cm
prov: Chenil Gallery 1913–14; John Quinn Collection; J.K. Byard 1927
exh: Chenil 1913–14 (56); Quinn 1927 (64)
notes: In Quinn 1927 sale catalogue, 'Neo-classical rendering of a maiden wearing an aubergine frock, reclining on a hill and holding a spray of flowers; before a sapphire-blue mirrored lake', p.32

DL13.40
Dorelia and Lyndra, The Blue Pool, Dorset / Two Women on Rocks by the Sea / Two Girls by the Shore / Two Maidens Standing in Lakeland Landscape, 1913
ins: l.l.: D.L. 13
Oil on panel
40.6 x 31.5 cm
prov: Henry Spencer Auctioneers, Retford May 1985 (194); Christie's London Mar 1986 (381)

DL13.41**
Nude at the Blue Pool / Seated Female Nude by the Sea / Female Nude Washing / Aphrodite Seated by the Shore / Bather, 1913
ins: l.r.: Lees 13
Pencil, black ink, watercolour, bodycolour on buff paper
35 x 23.5 cm
prov: Redfern Gallery 1946; Christie's London Mar 1995 (183); Bonhams London May 2000; Roseberys, West Norwood Nov 2001; Christie's London Jun 2002 (201) ; Private Collection; Lawrences Auctioneers, Bletchingley Apr 2025 (1020)
exh: Redfern 1946b (393)
notes: Lyndra, the Blue Pool, Dorset

DL13.42
Purbeck Hills / Aldbourne Landscape, 1913
ins: l.l.: Lees 13
Oil on panel
32.5 x 40.6 cm
prov: Chenil Gallery 1913–14; Redfern Gallery 1946; Arthur Tooth & Sons, London; Art Gallery of New South Wales, Sydney (through the Watson Bequest), purchased 1946
exh: Chenil 1913–14 (32); Redfern, *Contemporary Art Society Mixed Exhibition* Feb 1946 (239); National Gallery of South Australia, Special Exhibition, Adelaide Festival of the Arts, Melbourne, *British Painting 1900–1950* Mar 1966; Sane 1997, loaned by Art Gallery of New South Wales (19)
notes: Near Creech Barrow, Dorset

DL13.43
Creech Barrow, Dorset / Crick Barrow, Monmouthshire / Crich Barrow / Crech Barrow, 1913
ins: l.r.: Lees – 13
Oil on panel
33.6 x 42.3 cm
prov: Chenil Gallery 1913–15; Redfern Gallery 1930, 1934, 1939; John Sparrow; bequeathed to Birmingham Museums Trust 1992; Birmingham Museum and Art Gallery
exh: Chenil 1913–14 (46), 1915 (96); Redfern 1930a (16), 1934 (4), 1939a (32)
notes: Creech Barrow (r) and Knowle Hill ridge (l) from the Blue Pool, Dorset

DL13.44
The Blue Pool / The Blue Pool, Dorset, 1913
ins: l.l.: Lees
Oil on panel
33 x 40.5 cm
prov: Chenil Gallery 1913–14; Cyril K. Butler; Redfern Gallery 1939; Fairlie Harmar 1939–43; Mrs P. Cowlard 1946; Woolley & Wallis, Salisbury Apr 2004
exh: Chenil 1913–14 (38); Redfern 1930a, loaned by Cyril K. Butler (34), 1939a (43); National Gallery 1940, loaned by Fairlie Harmar (113); Roland, Browse & Delbanco, London, *The Lyrical Trend in English Painting* Mar–Apr 1946, loaned by Mrs P. Cowlard (31)

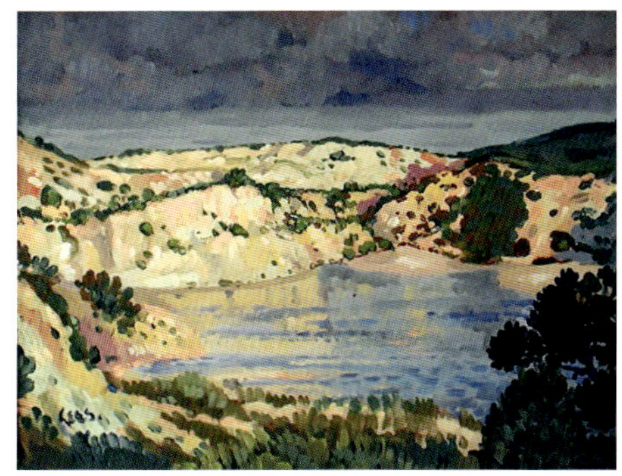

DL13.44

DL13.45
The Blue Pool / Reflections in Water, 1913
ins: l.l.: D.L. 13; v.: blue pool, Derwent Lees
Oil on panel
41 x 50.7 cm
prov: Chenil Gallery 1913–14; Redfern Gallery; Manchester Art Gallery, purchased May 1930
exh: Chenil 1913–14 (39); Redfern 1939a, loaned by Manchester Art Gallery (35); Aberdeen Art Gallery 1939; Leeds Art Gallery, *Picture of the Month* 1949; Derby Art Gallery 1956; Royal West of England Academy, Bristol, *Inquisitive Eyes: Slade Painters in Edwardian Wessex, 1900–1914* Feb–Jun 2016

DL13.46
The Blue Pool / The Blue Pool, Dorset / The Blue Pool, Dorsetshire, c.1913
ins: v.: The Blue Pool / sold to Mrs Vincent Massey, Feb. 1939 [on Redfern Gallery label]; Public Library and Art Museum, London Ontario, from the 1946–8 exhibition [on Elsie Perrin Williams Memorial Library label]; from the 1954 New Zealand exhibition [on Art Gallery of Hamilton label]
Oil on panel
31.4 x 41 cm
prov: Gieves Art Gallery, London 1928; G.P. Dudley Wallace 1930; Redfern Gallery 1932, 1939; Alice Massey (née Parkin) Feb 1939; Vincent Massey; gifted to the National Gallery of Canada, Ottawa (part of the Massey Collection of English Painting) Mar 1946
exh: Gieves Art Gallery, London Nov 1928 (2); Redfern 1930a, as 'The Blue Pool', loaned by G.P. Dudley Wallace (17), 1932 (10), 1939a (106); Tate, *A Collection of Contemporary English Painting* 1946 (28); National Gallery of Canada, Ottawa, Musée des Beaux-Arts, Montreal, Art Gallery of Ontario, Toronto, Art Gallery of Alberta, Edmonton, Vancouver Art Gallery, Industrial Exhibition Regina, Public Library and Art Museum, London Ontario, Winnipeg Art Gallery, Windsor Art Gallery, Owens Art Gallery at Mount Allison University Sackville, *The Massey Collection of English Painting, a Touring Exhibition Organized by the National Gallery of Canada* 1946–8 (30); Art Gallery of New South Wales, Sydney, NGV, Tasmanian Museum and Art Gallery, Hobart, Queen Victoria Museum and Art Gallery, Launceston, Art Gallery of South Australia, Adelaide, Public Library, Perth, Museum and Art Gallery of Western Australia, Perth, Queensland Art Gallery, Brisbane, National Art Gallery, Wellington, Auckland Art Gallery, Public Art Gallery, Dunedin, Robert McDougall Art Gallery, Christchurch, Honolulu Academy of Arts, California Palace of the Legion of Honor Fine Arts Museums of San Francisco, Vancouver Art Gallery, University of British Columbia, Vancouver, *The Massey Collection of English Painting, a Touring Exhibition Organized by the National Gallery of Canada* 1949–52 (32); Winnipeg Art Gallery, *British Pictures from the Massey Collection* 1952; Art Gallery of Hamilton, New Zealand, *Massey Collection of British Paintings* 1954; Confederation Centre of the Arts, Charlottetown, Dalhousie University Art Gallery, Halifax, Agnes Etherington Art Centre at Queen's University, Kingston, Mendel Art Gallery, Saskatoon, Art Gallery of Greater Victoria, Alberta College of Art, Calgary, Art Gallery of Alberta, Edmonton, *Massey Collection: Landscapes, a Touring Exhibition Organized by the National Gallery of Canada* 1966–7 (11); Sir George Williams University Art Galleries, Montreal, *Nineteenth- and Twentieth-Century English Painting: Works on Loan from the Permanent Collection of the National Gallery of Canada* 1974; Kelowna Art Gallery, Tom Thomson Art Gallery, Owen Sound, Beaverbrook Art Gallery, Fredericton, *The Changing Land: Modern British Landscape Painting 1900–1950, a Touring Exhibition Organized by the National Gallery of Canada* 2003–4 (17)

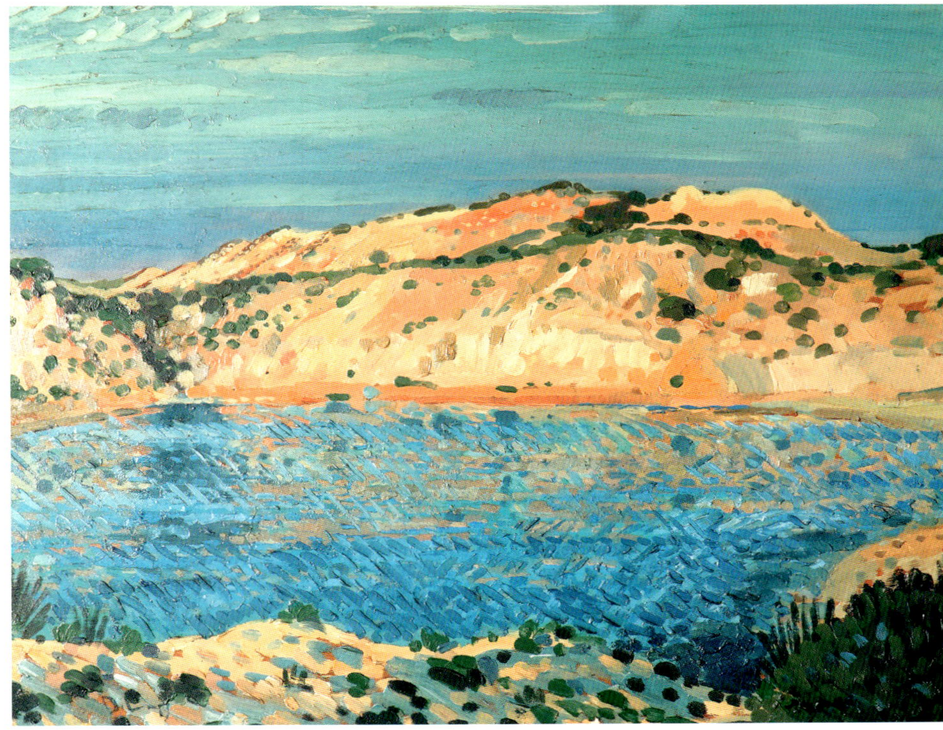
DL13.45

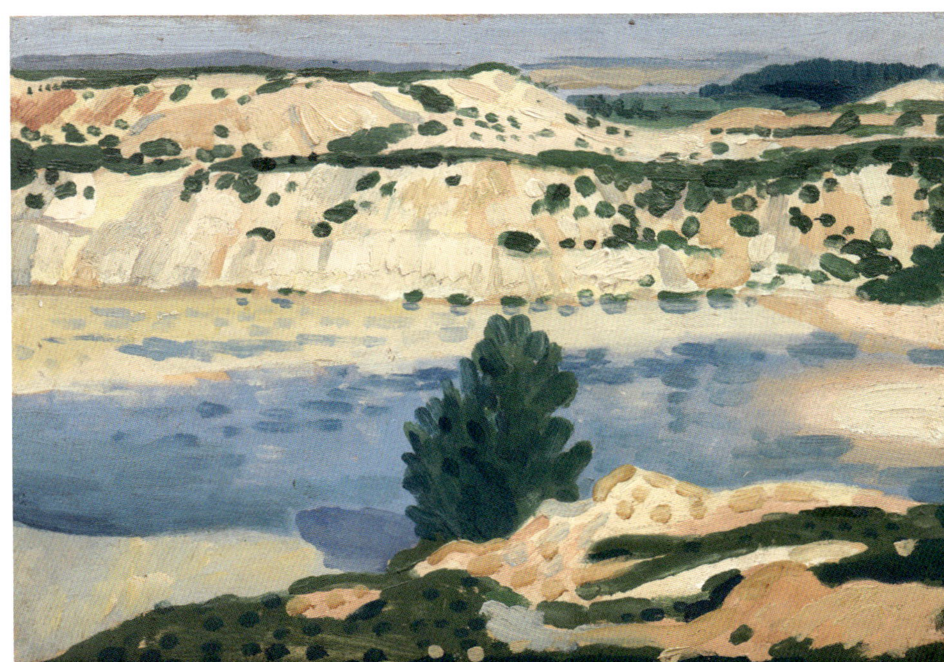
DL13.46

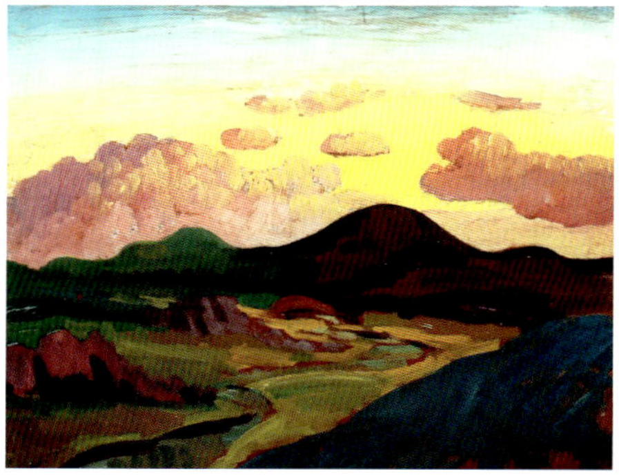

DL13.47

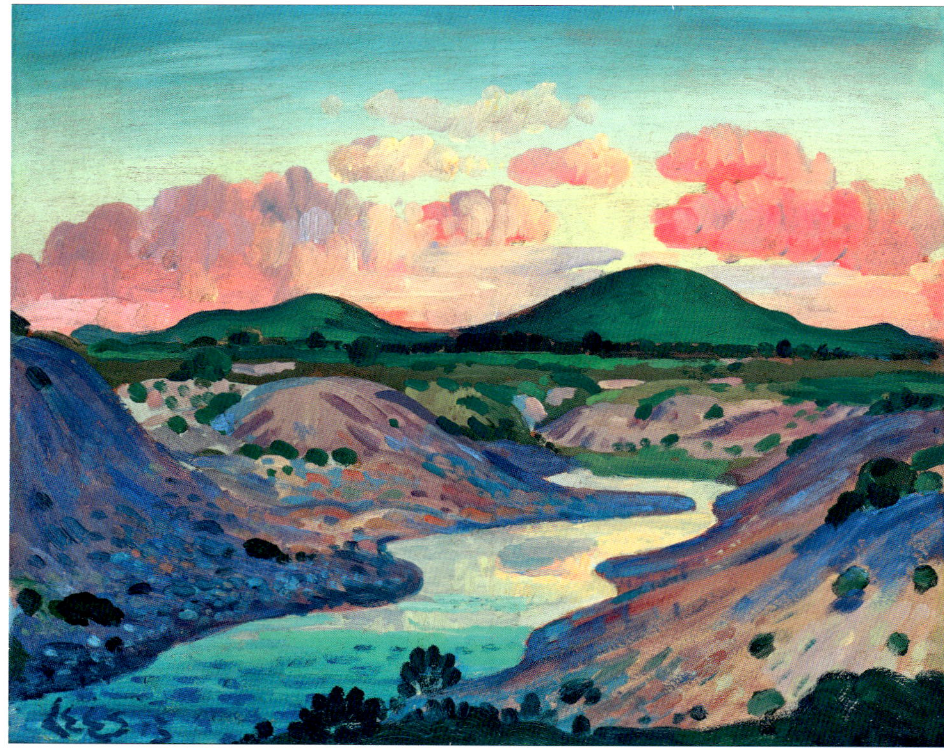

DL13.48

DL13.47
Study for Reflections / Evening, Sun Setting behind Arenig Fach / Arenig, Evening, 1913
Oil on panel
41 x 51 cm
prov: Museum of Modern Art, Machynlleth, Wales
exh: Museum of Modern Art, Machynlleth, Wales, as 'Evening, Sun Setting behind Arenig Fach' by JDI, Sep–Nov 2014
notes: Reattributed in consultation with John Hoole (formerly JDI 197); Creech Barrow (r) and Knowle Hill (l) from the Blue Pool, Dorset, study for DL13.48

DL13.48
Reflections / Reflections [Dorset 1913] / Reflections, The Blue Pool / Sunset in Wales / Sand Hills near the Blue Pool, Dorset / Sandhills, 1913
ins: l.l.: Lees 13; v.: [inscription] 'Sunset in Wales'; Sandhills [on Redfern Gallery label]
Oil on panel
32.4 x 40.7 cm
prov: Chenil Gallery 1913–14; John Quinn Collection 1927; Boylston Beal; Redfern Gallery 1934; Spink (K2 5291); Private Collection; Christie's London Oct 2021 (169)
exh: Chenil 1913–14 (44); Quinn 1927 (450); Redfern 1934 (13)
notes: Creech Barrow (r) and Knowle Hill (l) from the Blue Pool, Dorset; low water levels of summer 1913

DL13.49*
Dorset Scene, c.1913
Oil
prov: Edith Lees 1936
exh: Venice Biennale (English stand), as 'Dorset Scene', loaned by Mrs Edith Lees (while resident in Venice), 1936
notes: In De Sabbata, Massimo, 'Una mostra organizzata "in sordina": la Biennale di Venezia del' 1936', in Castellani, Francesca, and Charans, Eleonora (eds), *Crocevia Biennale*, Scalpendi, Milan, 2017, pp 85–98, 'the British authorities conceded an unofficial participation of works belonging to English collectors living in Italy, among the larger exhibition of the English stand' (translated by Paola Petrelli)

DL13.50
English Summer Landscape, 1913
ins: v.: Lees [pencil]
Oil on panel
20 x 25 cm
prov: Private Collection 1980s; Bridget McDonnell Gallery 1986, 1991; Lawsons, Sydney May 1999 (109), Dec 2000–May 2001; Private Collection
exh: Bridget McDonnell Gallery Apr–May 1986 (13), 1991 (19); Sane 1997 (16)
notes: Clay pit spoil mounds, the Blue Pool, Dorset; beside DL13.51

DL13.51
Pines and Heathland, Blue Pool, Dorset / Mediterranean Landscape, c.1913
ins: l.r: [signature, inscription]; v.: D. LEES 39 GRAFTON STREET. FITZROY SQ. W.
Oil on panel
21.5 x 26 cm
prov: Peter Nahum, London; Private Collection Jun 1988; Christie's London Jun 2000 (91); Private Collection
notes: Clay pit spoil mounds, the Blue Pool, Dorset; hill (c) as in DL13.50

DL13.52
The Gravel Pit / Sand-Dunes, Dorset Coast / The Quarry, c.1913
Oil on panel
31.8 x 40.6 cm
prov: Chenil Gallery 1913–14; Redfern Gallery 1934; Ivey-Selkirk Auction, Missouri Mar 2009; Private Collection
exh: Chenil 1913–14 (31); Redfern 1934 (15)
notes: Quarry site, the Blue Pool, Dorset

DL13.53*
Near Collioure, 1913
ins: [signature] 13
Watercolour, pen and black ink on paper
25.4 x 35.5 cm
prov: Leicester Galleries, London, 1969 (11); Sotheby's London Dec 1971 (117A); Christie's London Dec 1973 (139), Jun 1976 (160)
notes: In Southampton Art Gallery, Lees Artist's File – 'related watercolour' to DL13.2; Banyuls

DL13.54
An Aeroplane Passes / Amazement / Amazement – The First Aeroplane / The Aeroplane / Figures in a Field / Figures in Landscape, c.1913
ins: l.l.: Lees
Oil on panel
41 x 32.5 cm
prov: Redfern Gallery 1930, 1934, 1939, 1943, 1944, 1946, 1958; Private Collection; Leonard

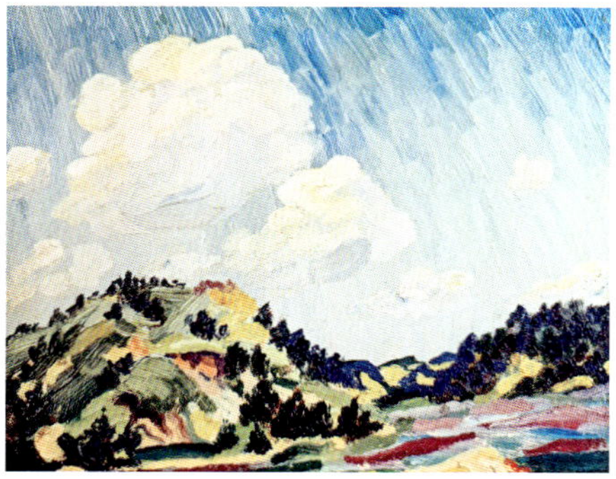

DL13.50

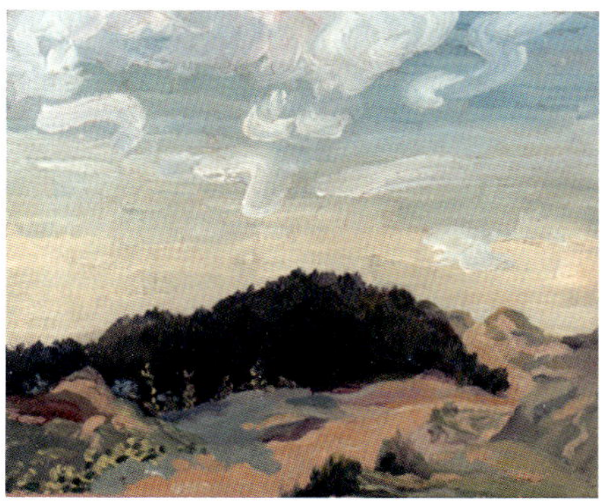

DL13.51

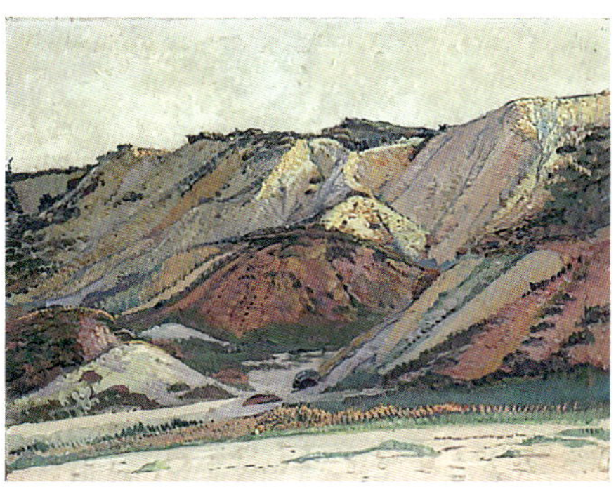

DL13.52

Joel, Melbourne Nov 1976 (204); Hogan and Deutsher (Block Gallery and Deutsher Galleries), Melbourne 1979 (48); Deutscher Sep 1984; Private Collection
exh: NEAC 58th 1917 (85); Redfern 1930a (10); British Contemporary Art 1933 (65); Redfern 1934 (34), 1939a (28), 1943 (92), 1944a (84), 1946b (48), 1958 (39); Block Gallery and Deutsher Galleries Jul–Aug 1979 (48); Sane 1997 (10)

DL13.55
The Sisters in Wales / The Sisters in Wales (sketch) / Sisters, c.1913
Oil on panel
41 x 32 cm
prov: Redfern Gallery 1934; Ferens Art Gallery, Hull, purchased 1934
exh: Redfern 1934 (22); Ferens Art Gallery loan, Grimsby Mar 1961, Dundee, *English Painting 1900–1950* 1979 (9); Edwardian Art 1987 (60); Cartwright Hall, Bradford, and Ferens Art Gallery, Hull Jun–Aug 1987 (60); Ferens Art Gallery, *Eye to Eye: The Ferens Portraits* Dec–Jan 1990; Ferens Art Gallery, *The Family* Nov 1995–Jan 1996; National Fishing Heritage Centre, Grimsby Jul 1996; Ferens Art Gallery, *From Steer to Spencer* Jun–Sep 2000; Ferens Art Gallery, *From Victorian to Edwardian* Jun–Sep 2009
notes: Likely study for DL13.54

DL13.56*
The Aeroplane, c.1913
Watercolour on paper
prov: Redfern Gallery 1944
exh: Redfern 1944a (48)
notes: Unresolved record

DL13.57*
Landscape with Figure, c.1913
Oil
exh: NEAC 52nd 1914 (81)
notes: Unresolved record

DL13.58
Woman in Chair, 1913
ins: v.: 1913
Ink and pencil on paper
50.8 x 35.5 cm
prov: Rex Nan Kivell; Deutsher 1978; Private Collection; Bridget McDonnell Gallery; Private Collection
exh: Deutsher 1978 (35)

DL13.59*
Portrait Study / Study for a Portrait, 1913
ins: v.: 1913
Pencil on paper
50.8 x 35.5 cm
prov: Redfern Gallery 1958; Deutsher 1978; Private Collection
exh: Redfern 1958 (47); Deutsher 1978 (31)
notes: Unresolved record

DL13.60*
The Morn, c.1913
Oil
prov: Chenil Gallery 1913–15
exh: Chenil 1913–14 (49), 1915 (94)
notes: Unresolved record

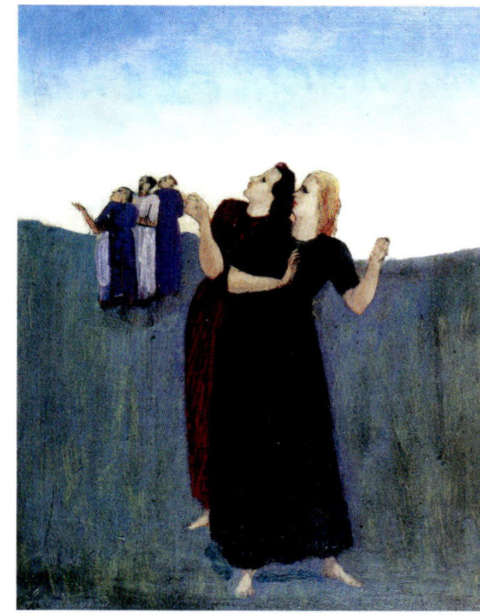

DL13.54

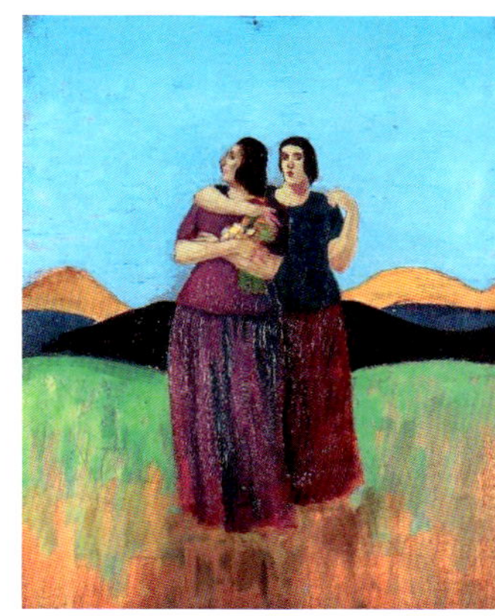

DL13.55

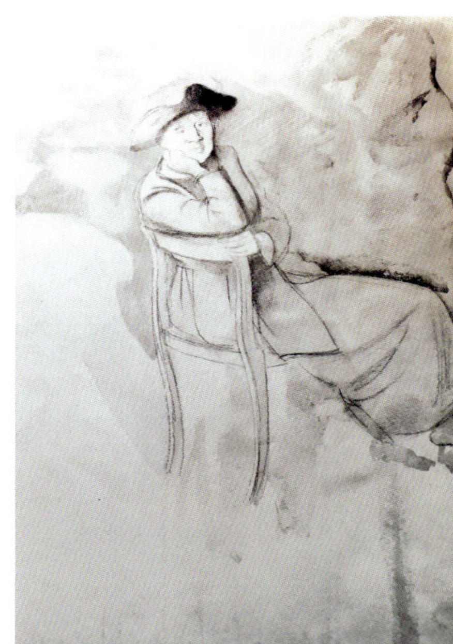

DL13.58

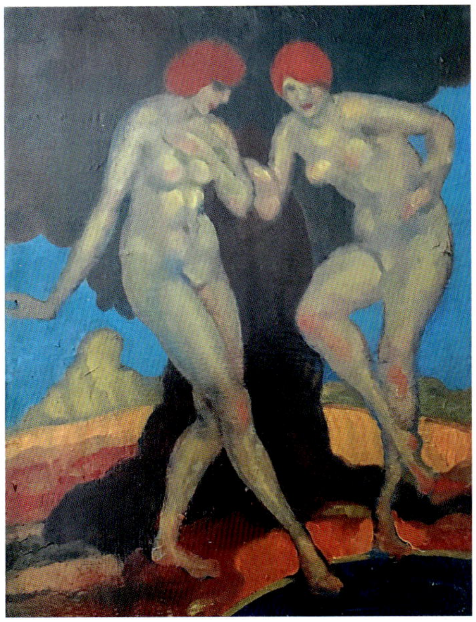

DL13.61

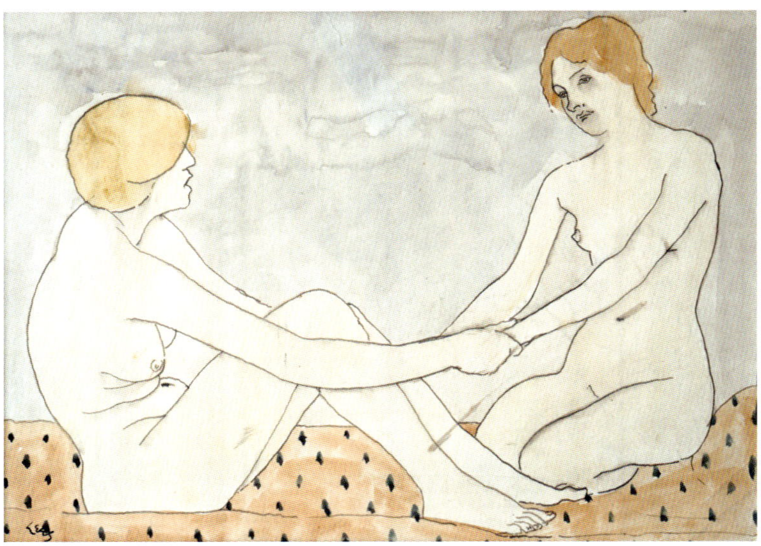

DL13.62

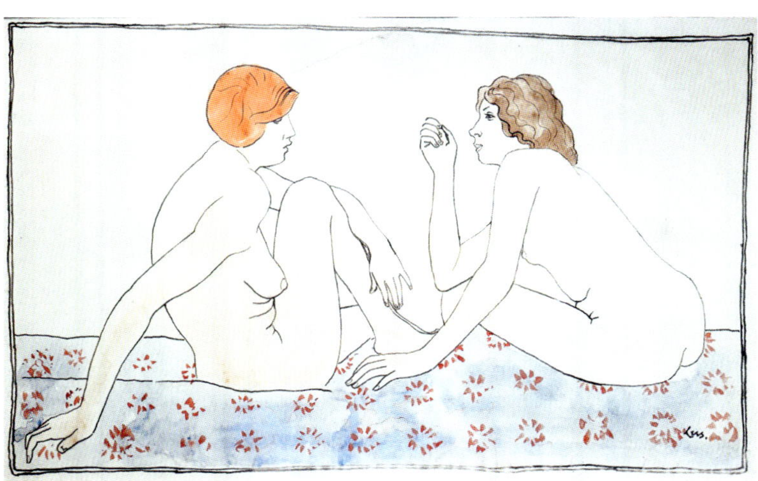

DL13.63

DL13.61
The Bathers / Two Nudes / The Red Bathing Caps / Two Nude Females Standing beneath a Tree Dipping their Toes in a Pool, 1913–14
ins: v.: Derwent Lees [on panel]
Oil on canvas on panel
28.9 x 21 cm
prov: Redfern Gallery 1934; Christie's London Sep 1989 (283B); Carfax Gallery, London; Denys Wilcox Fine Art (The Court Gallery, Taunton) Feb 2015; Private Collection
exh: Redfern 1934 (38)

DL13.62
Two Women / Two Girls, 1913–14
ins: l.l.: Lees
Watercolour and pencil on paper
25 x 35 cm
prov: Chenil Gallery 1913–15; The Alton Gallery, London; N. Podmore Jan 1991; Maynards Fine Art, Canada Jul 2021; Private Collection; Shapiro, Sydney Dec 2021 (287); Private Collection
exh: Chenil 1913–14 (47); Whitechapel 1914, loaned by Chenil Gallery (385); Chenil 1915 (90)
notes: Lyndra with Nora Summers (?)

DL13.63
Two Seated Women, 1913–14
ins: l.r.: Lees
Watercolour on paper
26 x 41 cm
prov: Christie's London c.1990; Private Collection
notes: Lyndra with Nora Summers (?)

DL13.64*
Corfe, c.1913
prov: Chenil Gallery 1913–14, 1915
exh: Chenil 1913–14 (60)
notes: Unresolved record

DL13.65
Coast Scene / Coast near Studland, Dorset / Studland, Dorset Coast / The Bathers (Coast Scene), 1913–14
ins: l.l.: Lees; v.: Coast Scene Derwent Lees N.E.A.C 1911
Oil on panel
20 x 29.3 cm
prov: Redfern Gallery 1934, 1947; Private Collection; *Contents of a Country Estate Auction* Victoria, Australia c.1989; Private Collection
exh: Redfern 1934 (31), 1947a; Sane 1997 (7)
notes: Likely Three Cliffs Bay, Gower Peninsula, Wales

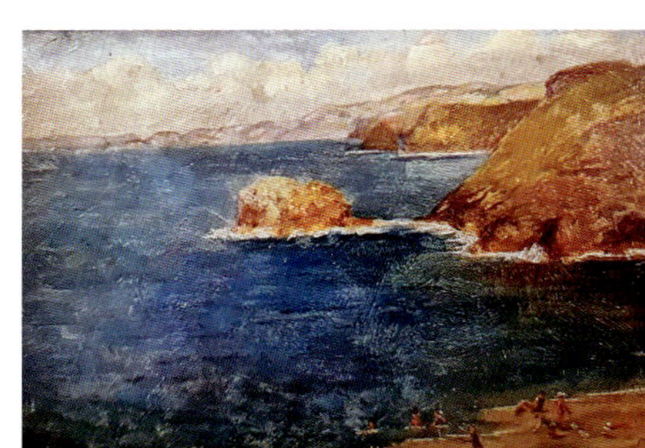

DL13.65

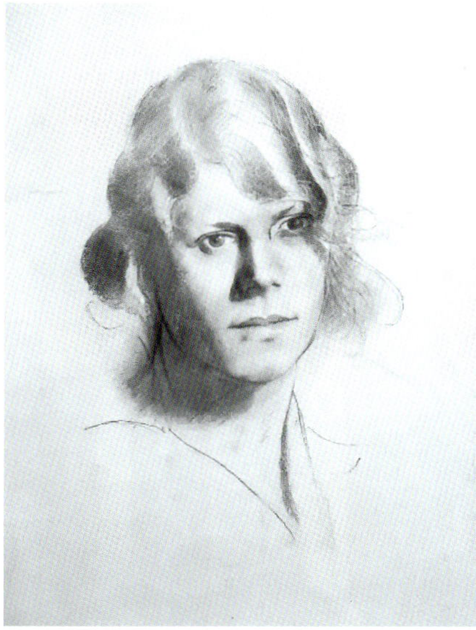

DL13.69

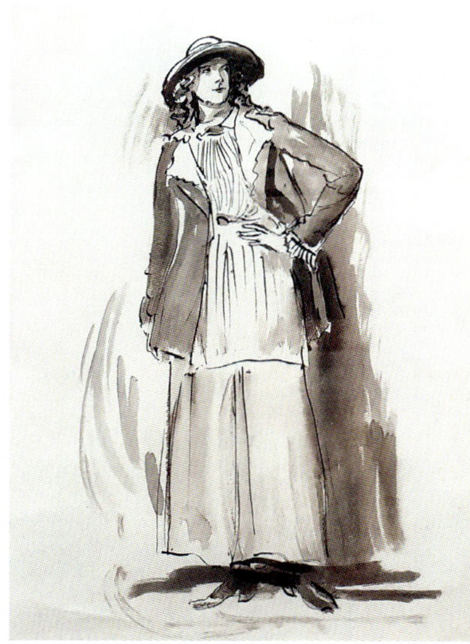

DL13.71

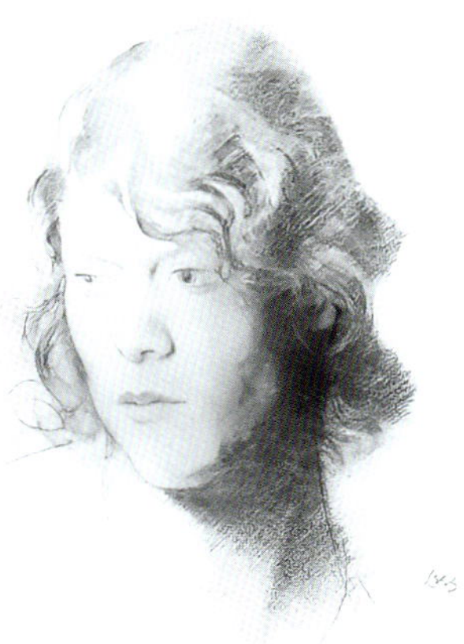

DL13.70

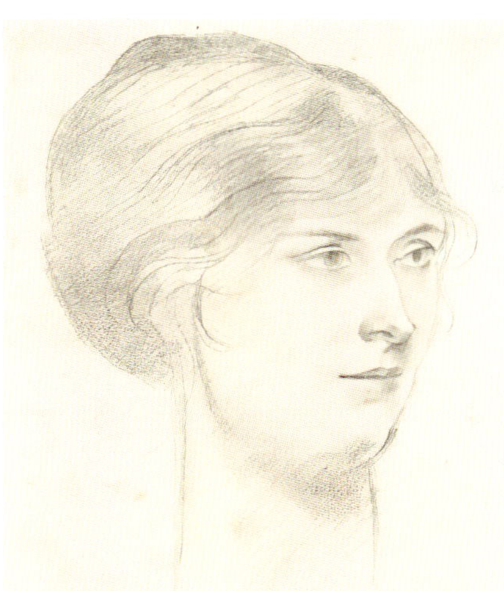

DL13.72

DL13.66*
The Shore, Dorset / Dorset Coast, c.1912–13
Oil on panel
25.4 x 34.9 cm
prov: Sir Michael Sadler 1934; Leicester Galleries, London 1944; Thos. Agnew & Sons; Frank Aldous Girling; Christie's London Mar 1974 (?), Feb 1975 (98), Jun 1980 (88)
exh: Redfern 1934, loaned by Sir Michael Sadler (14), 1939a, loaned by Sir Michael Sadler (36); Leicester Galleries, London, *Selected Paintings, Drawings, and Sculpture from the Collection of the late Sir Michael Sadler* Jan–Feb 1944 (80)

DL13.67*
Green Hill in Dorset / The Green Hill, c.1913
Watercolour on paper
prov: Redfern Gallery 1944, 1946
exh: Redfern 1944a (51), 1946b (524)

DL13.68 (see p.40)
Portrait Study / Portrait of Lyndra / Lyndra, c.1913
Pencil on paper
37 x 28 cm
prov: Redfern Gallery 1958; Bridget McDonnell Gallery c.2017; Private Collection
exh: Redfern 1958 (45)

DL13.69
Sketch of Lyndra, c.1913
Pencil on paper
31 x 24 cm
prov: Redfern Gallery; John and Edward Barkes; Bridget McDonnell Gallery 2002; Philip Stephenson 2025, gifted to Fitzwilliam Museum 2025
exh: Bridget McDonnell Gallery Dec 2002

DL13.70
The Artist's Wife / Portrait Study, c.1913
ins: l.r.: Lees
Pencil and crayon on paper
35.5 x 22.5 cm
prov: New Chenil Galleries c.1925–7; Redfern Gallery; Deutsher 1978; Christopher Day Bridge Street Gallery, Sydney 1982; Bridget McDonnell Gallery 1986; Lawsons, Sydney Nov 1990 (52); Polly Rumney; Raffan Kelaher & Thomas, Sydney 2023 (76); Private Collection
exh: Deutsher 1978 (29); Bridget McDonnell Gallery Feb–Mar 1986 (15)

DL13.71
Portrait of a Woman / Lyndra, c.1913
Ink and wash on paper
50 x 34 cm
prov: Rex Nan Kivell; Redfern Gallery; Deutsher 1978; John and Edward Barkes; Bridget McDonnell Gallery 1997, 2024
exh: Deutsher 1978 (30); Bridget McDonnell Gallery Oct 1997 (22)

DL13.72
Portrait of the Artist's Wife, 1913–14
Pencil on paper
23.5 x 19.5 cm
prov: Masterpiece Gallery, Hobart c.1998; The David and Susi Caddy Collection; Gibson's Auctions, Armadale Apr 2024 (86); Robin Gibson Gallery, Sydney 2024
notes: Unknown model

DL13.73*
Lyndra Posing, c.1913
Pencil on paper
47 x 31.7 cm
prov: Anthony D'Offay Ltd, London; Fine Art Society 1977; Private Collection

DL13.74*
The Little Stranger, c.1913
Panel
exh: Gieves Art Gallery, London Nov 1928
notes: In *The Times* (London), 'large decorative panel . . . apt to be scholastic', 8 Nov 1928, p.14

DL13.75*
Landscape
Watercolour
prov: Percy Withers 1939
exh: Redfern 1939a, collection of Percy Withers (118)
notes: Unresolved record

1914

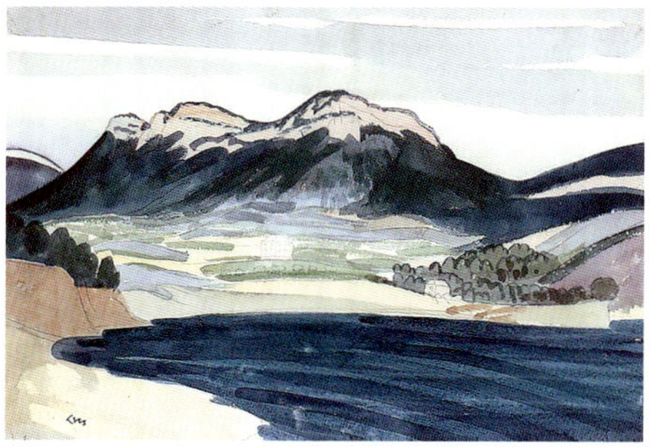

DL14.1

DL14.1
The Blue Bay, Mediterranean / A Mediterranean Bay / View of Banyuls, France, 1914
ins: l.l.: Lees
Watercolour and pencil on paper
24.2 x 33.7 cm
prov: Dr Mary Woodall; Thos. Agnew & Sons 1967 (130, stock no.28473); R.A. Bevan; Christie's London Apr 2011 (307); Abbott and Holder, London; Private Collection
exh: NEAC 55th 1916 (167)
notes: Cassis, study for DL14.4

DL14.2
A Bay – Cassis South of France / Cassis / Bay in the South of France / The Bay, South of France, 1914
ins: v.: (No.7) A Bay – C South of France (2)
Watercolour, bodycolour and pencil on paper
25.2 x 35.3 cm
prov: Redfern 1930–31; Laing, purchased Aug 1933
exh: Redfern 1930a (29), 1931b; British Contemporary Art 1933 (77); Shipley Art Gallery, *A Splash of Colour* Apr–Jun 1999; Laing, *Liquid Light: Painting in Watercolours: Beach and Ocean* Mar–Aug 2022
notes: In *Studio International*, 102, Jul–Dec 1931, p.277; reproduced in the *British Contemporary Art Catalogue*, 1933; study for DL14.4

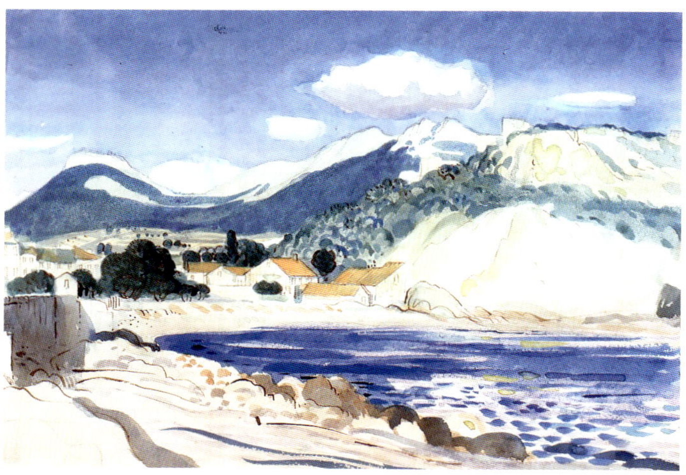

DL14.2

DL14.3 (see p.63)
Cassis Village and Bay / Coastal Landscape with a Village in a Cove / A Mediterranean Scene with a Village at the Edge of the Sea / The Bay, South of France / Bay in the South of France / Collioure, 1910 / Seaside Town, 1914
ins: l.r.: Lees [faded]
Watercolour, pen and brown ink on paper
24.1 x 34.3 cm
prov: Redfern Gallery 1934; Sotheby's London Feb 1972 (66), Jul 1972 (43); Christie's London Nov 1977 (215), Nov 1989 (234); Sotheby's Sussex Mar 1990; Private Collection, as 'Collioure, 1910' by JDI; Gorringe's, Lewes Mar 2022, as 'Collioure, 1910' by DL (424); Private Collection
exh: Redfern 1934 (50)
notes: Reattributed, formerly attributed to JDI; Cassis, study for DL14.4

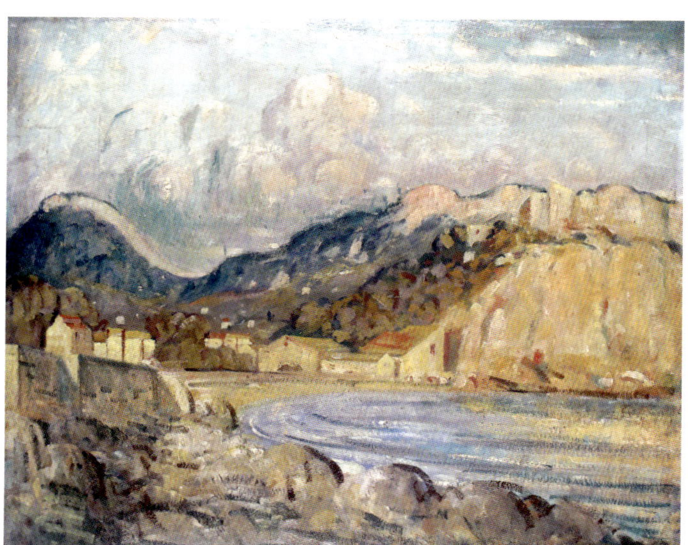

DL14.4

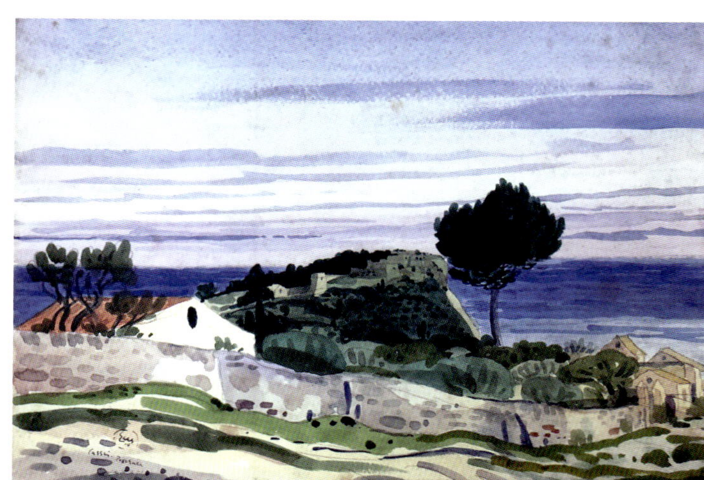

DL14.6

DL14.4
Town on Coast, South of France / Bay, South of France / Cassis, A View of a Bay / A Bay, the South of France, Cassis / Cassis / In the South of France, c.1914
ins: v.: A Bay the South of France Cassis Derwent Lees [pencil]
Oil on panel
63 x 76 cm
prov: Goupil Gallery 1930 (?); Redfern 1939, 1943; Sotheby's London May 1952 (104); Cogswell; Browse & Darby, London Jun–Jul 1989; Woolley & Wallis, Salisbury Jun 2014; Private Collection
exh: Goupil 1930 (74); Redfern 1939a (39), 1943 (116)
notes: From Plage du Bestouan, Cassis

DL14.5*
Boats at Anchor, c.1914
ins: [signature ?]
Oil on panel
25.4 x 35.6 cm
prov: Phillips, London Dec 1998 (152)
notes: Unresolved record

DL14.6
Cassis, Provence / Cassis, South of France, 1914
ins: l.l.: Lees 14 / Cassis. Provence [in cartouche]
Watercolour and pencil on paper
25.1 x 35.5 cm
prov: Arthur Edward Anderson, gifted to the Whitworth Institute (now The Whitworth, University of Manchester) 1929
exh: NEAC 51st 1914 (95) or (99)
notes: Castle headland, Cassis

DL14.7
Cassis, Provence / Cassis / Cassis, South of France, 1914
ins: l.l.: Lees. 1914 Cassis; v.: Port de Cassis Provence
Watercolour and pencil on paper
25.5 x 35.5 cm
prov: Redfern Gallery 1947 (?); Phillips, London Jun 1988; Sotheby's London Mar 1989 (113); Spink Jun 1989 (42)
exh: NEAC 51st 1914 (95) or (99); Redfern 1947b (359)
notes: Castle headland, Cassis

DL14.8*
The Castle, Cassis / Ruin on Cliff, Cassis / Ruin, Cassis, 1914
Watercolour on paper
prov: Redfern Gallery 1934; Mr and Mrs J.B. Priestley 1946–Nov 1951
exh: Redfern 1934 (51)
notes: Varying titles in Priestley collection papers

DL14.9 (see p.100)
Cap Canaille / Seascape with Headland, near Cassis / Cap Cauville, Cassis, South of France, 1914
ins: l.l.: Lees '14 / Cap Canaille / Cassis – Bouches du Rhone
Watercolour, pencil, pen and ink with surface scratching on paper
25 x 35.5 cm
prov: Arthur Edward Anderson; gifted to the Whitworth Institute (now The Whitworth, University of Manchester) 1929
exh: NEAC 51st 1914 (141); Empire Art 1934–5, as 'Seascape with Headland, near Cassis' (125); Royal Scottish Academy, *109th Annual Exhibition* Apr 1935
notes: Cap Canaille from the Cassis breakwater

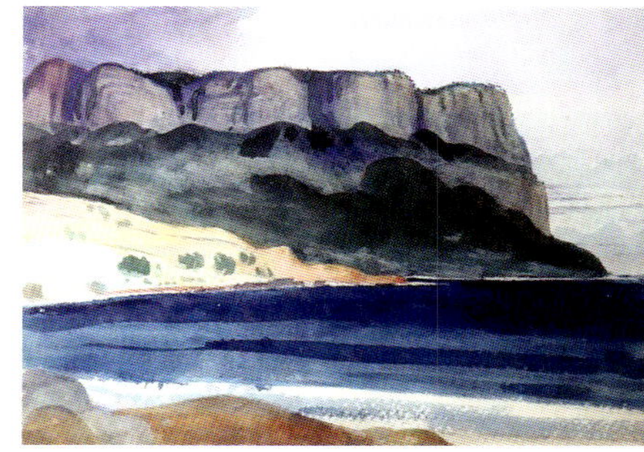

DL14.10

DL14.10
Cap Canaille, South of France, 1914
Watercolour on paper
24 x 34 cm
prov: Sotheby's London Dec 1964 (32); Thos. Agnew & Sons; Glynn Vivian Art Gallery, Swansea, purchased Mar 1966
notes: Cap Canaille from the Cassis breakwater

DL14.11
Landscape – Cassis / Cassis / Landscape near Cassis / Cassis, France, 1914
ins: l.l.: Lees 14 Cassis
Watercolour on paper
24.8 x 34.9 cm
prov: Redfern Gallery 1931, 1934; Arthur Knyvett-Lee 1934, thence by descent; Christie's London Mar 2016 (109)
exh: Redfern 1931a (27), 1934 (47); Empire Art 1934–5, loaned by Arthur Knyvett-Lee (126)
notes: In the *Evening Star*, 'rich harmonies of blue and green, combined with horizontal pattern in clouds and fields, make it a satisfying watercolour', 16 May 1934

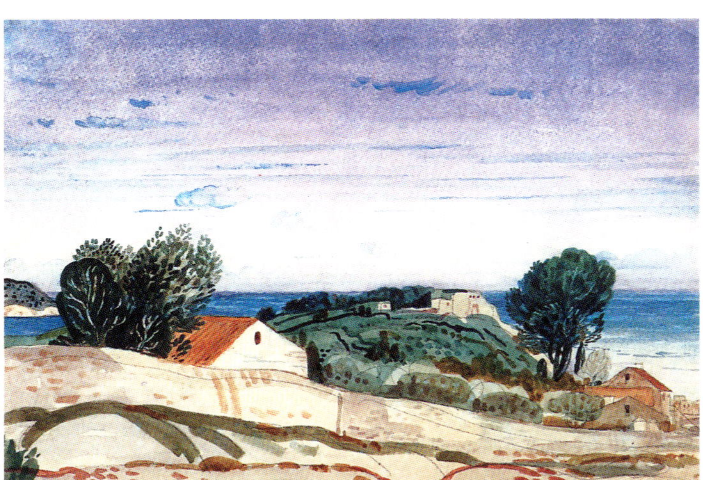

DL14.7

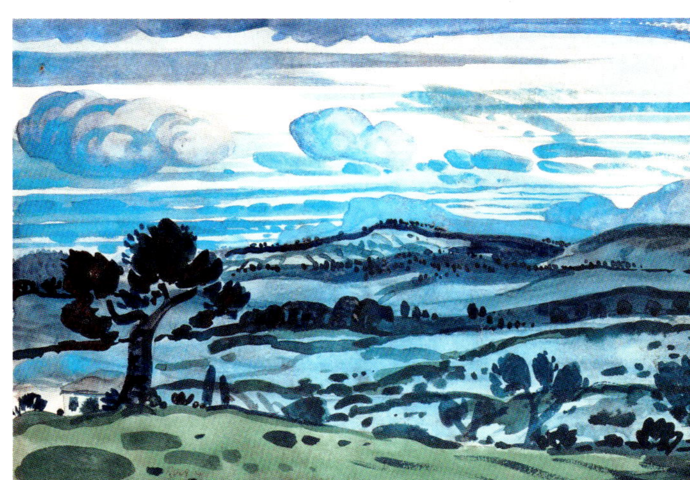

DL14.11

DL14.12
Coast at La Ciotat, France / Coast at Cavtat, Croatia / Cavtat / Coast at Cavtat, Yugoslavia, 1914
ins: l.r.: Lees
Watercolour and pencil on paper
28 x 38.5 cm
prov: Redfern 1939, 1942; Wilfrid A. Evill, bequeathed to Miss Honor Frost 1963; Sotheby's London Nov 1980 (170); Spink Jun–Jul 1981 (52, stock no.K3 7576); Sotheby's Olympia, London Jun 2005 (4), Jun 2011; Martyn Gregory, London; Christie's London, *The Martyn Gregory Collection of British Art*, Mar 2022 (183); Private Collection
exh: Redfern Gallery 1939a (115); British Council, London, *Allied Institutes* ('G.H.', 'P.H.') 1943; British Institute of Adult Education, Brighton Art Gallery and Museum, *Wilfrid Evill Memorial Exhibition* 1965 (99); Martyn Gregory, London, *A Foray into the 20th Century: Works by British Artists* Apr–May 2015 (41)
notes: Mistitled in the late 1930s; from Calanque du Mugel beach, La Ciotat

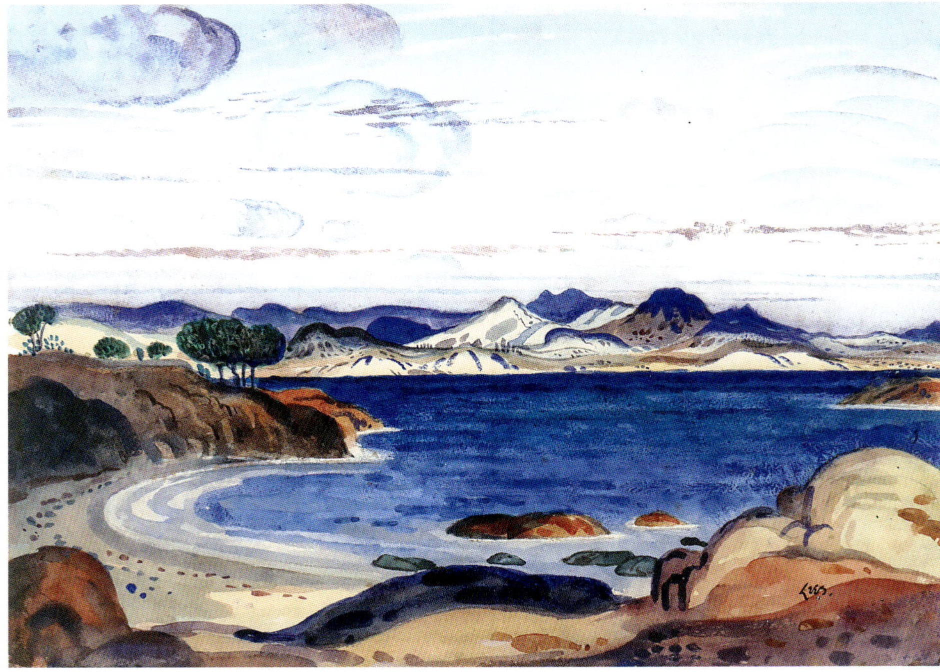
DL14.12

DL14.13
La Ciotat / La Ciolat, 1914
ins: l.l.: Lees La Ciotat [pencil]
Watercolour on paper
38.6 x 56.6 cm
prov: Lord Howard de Walden, purchased for the CAS Wales 1934, thence gifted to the National Museum of Wales (now Amgueddfa Cymru, Museum Wales) 1947
exh: NEAC 53rd 1915, as 'La Ciolat' (147); National Museum of Wales, *J.D. Innes* 1975 (384a)
notes: From Calanque du Mugel beach, La Ciotat

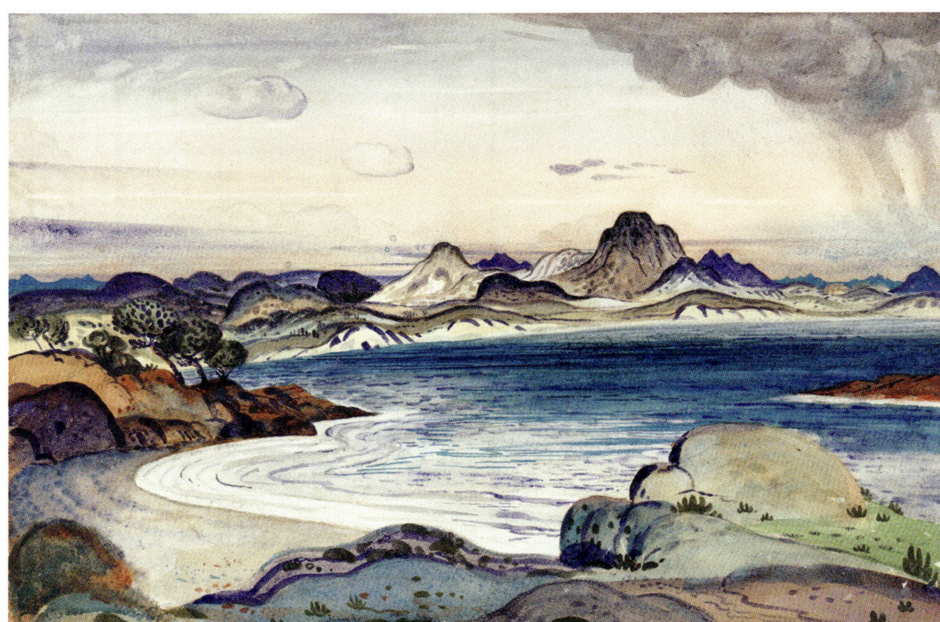
DL14.13

DL14.14*
Baie de la Ciotat, 1914
Pencil on paper
prov: Arthur Crossland 1939–56; Christie's London Feb 1956 (57, 1st of 2 in the lot); Piccadilly Gallery, London 1956
exh: Laing 1939 (184)

DL14.15
La Ciotat, South of France / Baie de la Crotat / Bair-de-la-Ciolat, Provence / Baie de la Ciotat, near Marseilles, 1914 / *Seascape / Lake*, 1914
ins: l.l.: Lees 14 / La Ciotat [in cartouche]
Watercolour and pencil on paper
25.2 x 35.5 cm
prov: CAS purchased 1928, as 'Seascape', thence gifted to the Whitworth Institute (now The Whitworth, University of Manchester) 1931 as 'Lake'
exh: NEAC 51st 1914 (94); Friday Club, London 1915 (106); Royal Scottish Academy, *109th Annual Exhibition* Apr 1935; Whitworth Art Gallery, Manchester, *British Artists in Europe*, Jan–Feb 1973 (60)
notes: From Anse du Sec, La Ciotat

DL14.16*
Boats at Ciotat / Boats on the Shore, La Ciotat, c.1914
Watercolour on paper
prov: Redfern Gallery 1948, 1949
exh: Redfern 1948 (361), 1949 (398)

DL14.17*
Bay and Mountains / Cassis / Coastal Landscape, Cassis, 1914
Oil on canvas
71.1 x 94.4 cm
prov: Cyril K. Butler 1925; Phillips, London Mar 1984 (117)
exh: NEAC 1925, loaned by Cyril K. Butler, Manchester (41), London (229); Redfern 1934, as 'Cassis', loaned by Cyril K. Butler (25)
notes: Cap Canaille, Cassis

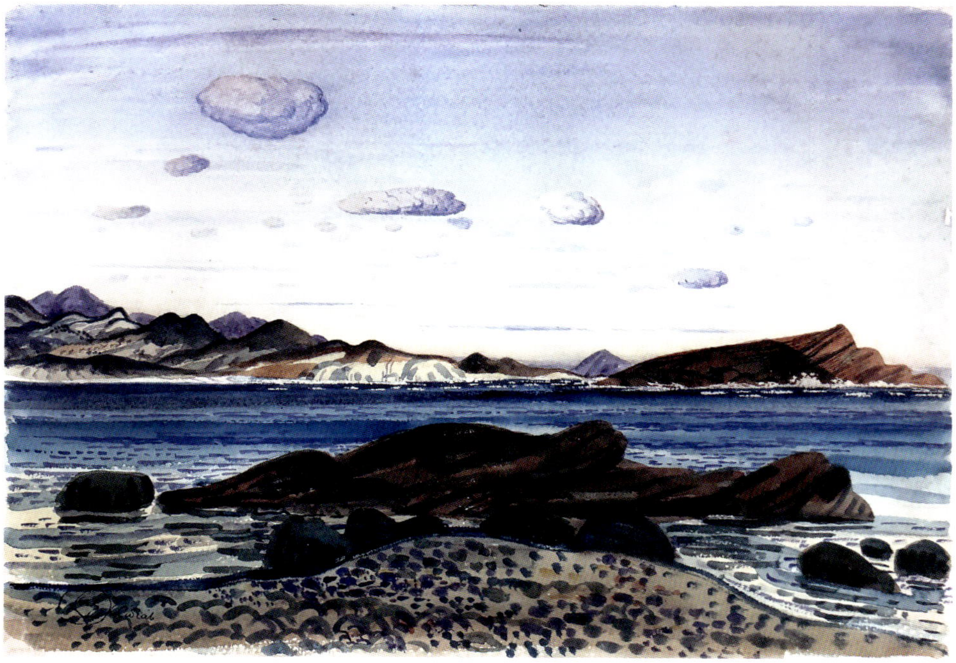

DL14.15

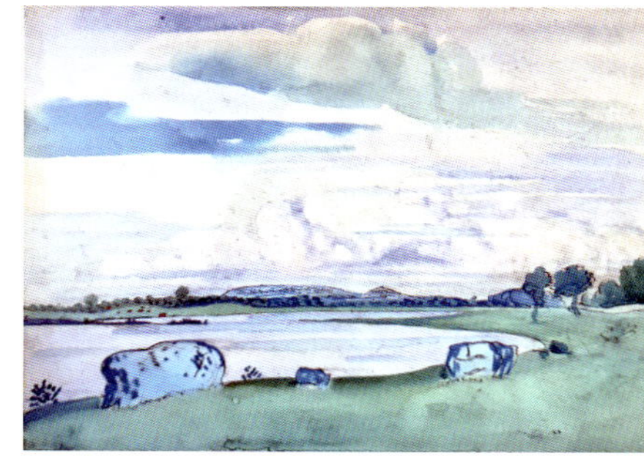

DL14.21

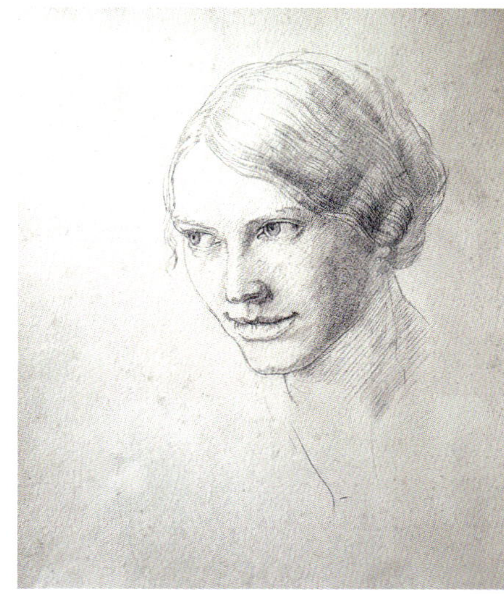

DL14.22

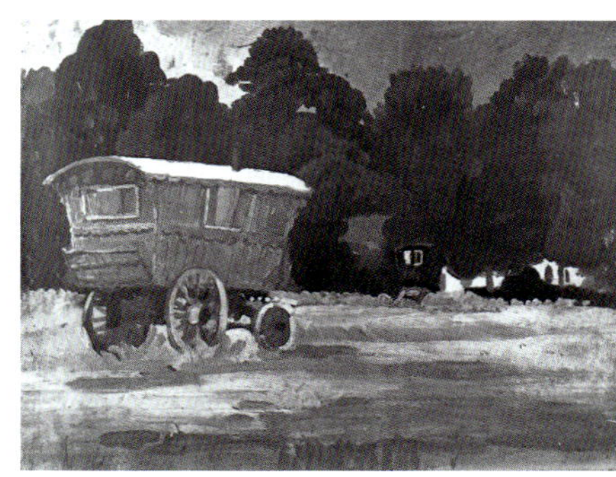

DL14.23

DL14.18 (see p.97)
Cartoon – Les Anciennes / Mothers and Children in a Landscape / Sketch for a Decoration, 1914
ins: l.l.: 1914
Oil over charcoal on paper glued to canvas
144.8 x 180.4 cm
prov: Mrs Edith Lees, stored at Alfred Stiles & Sons, London 1952; Slade School, London 1952 (request to store from Rex Nan Kivell for Mrs Edith Lees); UCL Art Museum
exh: NEAC 51st 1914, as 'Cartoon – Les Anciennes' (112); NEAC 55th 1916, as 'Sketch for a Decoration' (13) (?)
notes: Original charcoal exhibited 1914, overpainted in oil, c.1916; above Cassis town

DL14.19*
Near La Ciotat, c.1914
Watercolour on paper
prov: Redfern Gallery 1939
exh: Redfern 1939a (121)
notes: Unresolved record

DL14.20 (see p.105)
Rings Hill Cliff, Dorset, 1914
ins: l.l.: To G & M Summers – Souvenir de ballade d'automobile. May. 1914; l.r.: Ringshill Cliff Dorset Lees. 14
Watercolour on paper
25 x 35.5 cm
prov: Gifted to Nora (née Munro) and Gerald Summers by DL 1914, thence by descent
notes: Worbarrow Bay, Dorset

DL14.21
Lake / The Lake, Dorset, c.1914
Watercolour on paper
25 x 35.5 cm
prov: Redfern Gallery 1944; Christie's London mid-1990s; Private Collection
exh: Redfern 1944a (41)
notes: Creech Barrow Hill and former lake, East Creech, Dorset

DL14.22
Portrait of Nora Summers, c.1914
Pencil on paper
36 x 26.5 cm
prov: Gifted to Nora (née Munro) and Gerald Summers by DL c.1914, thence by descent

DL14.23
Caravans at Alderney, c.1914
Oil on panel
31.7 x 40.6 cm
prov: Redfern Gallery 1948, 1952, 1958; Graves Art Gallery, Sheffield; Christie's London Jun 1978 (76)
exh: Redfern 1948 (15), 1952 (296), 1958 (37)
notes: Similar to Augustus John's *Caravans at Dusk*

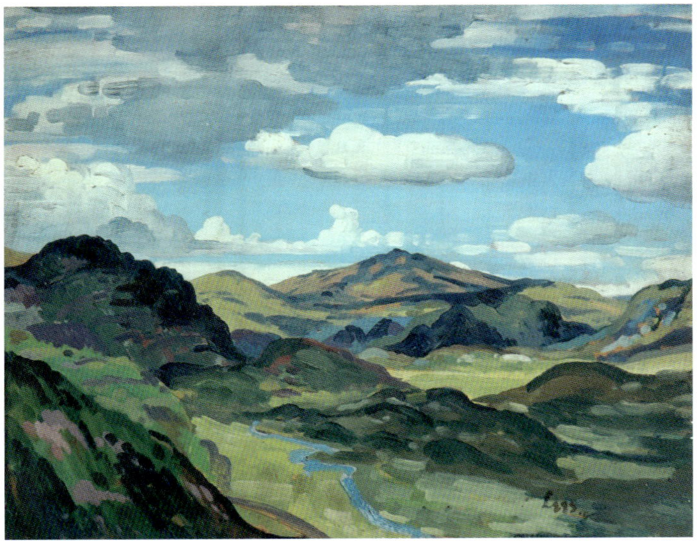

DL14.24

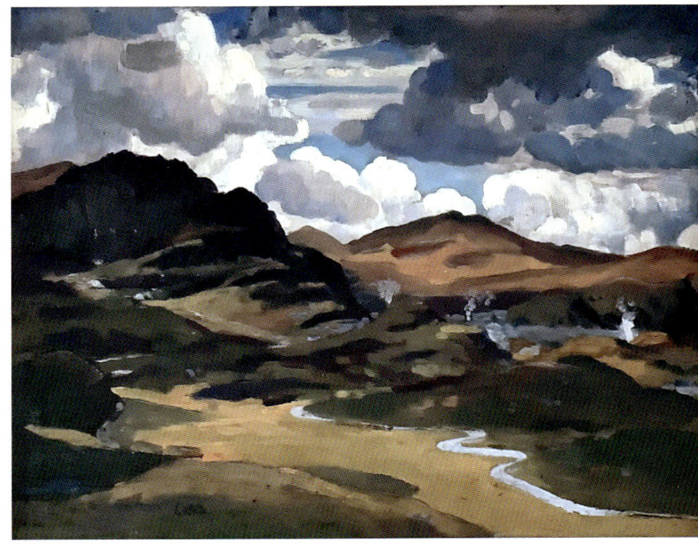

DL14.25

DL14.24
Valley of the Afon Tryweryn / Landscape / Landscape No.2, 1914
ins: l.r.: Lees 14
Oil on panel
39.5 x 51 cm
prov: Redfern Gallery 1928; Bradford District Museum, purchased Jan 1929; Corporation Art Gallery, Bradford 1939; Bradford Museum and Art Gallery 1939
exh: Cartwright Hall Gallery, Bradford, *Spring Exhibition* 1929 (254); Redfern 1939a, loaned by the Corporation Art Gallery, Bradford (37); Arts Council of Great Britain, London, 'Picture of the Month' year unknown
notes: Arenig Fach and Afon Tryweryn, North Wales

DL14.25
Welsh Landscape / Landscape No.4 / Welsh Landscape No.4 / Landscape, c.1914
ins: l.l.: Lees
Oil on panel
33 x 40.5 cm
prov: Redfern Gallery 1930; Earl of Sandwich; Beaux Arts Gallery, London 1946; Spink; Mayor Gallery, London; Christie's London Jun 1995 (107); Private Collection
exh: Redfern 1930a (1), 1934, loaned by the Earl of Sandwich (29); British Council, South America, loaned by the Earl of Sandwich, 1936
notes: Location as in DL14.24

DL14.26
Landscape No.3 / Welsh Landscape, 1914
ins: l.l.: Lees 14
Oil on panel
33 x 40.5 cm
prov: Redfern Gallery pre-1936; Woolley & Wallis, Salisbury, year unknown (15); Sotheby's London Jun 2004 (26); Private Collection
notes: Arenig Fach, North Wales

DL14.27
Welsh Landscape No.? / First Study of Welsh Mountains / Welsh Landscape, c.1914
ins: v.: Lees [pencil]
Oil on panel
25.4 x 35.6 cm
prov: Arthur Knyvett-Lee, thence by descent; Redfern Gallery 1958; Canterbury Auction Galleries Nov 2020
exh: Redfern 1958 (50)
notes: Arenig Fawr and Moel Llyfnant from Carnedd Iago, Nant Ddu, North Wales

DL14.28
Arenig Fawr / Hill in Wales / Capel-y-Ffin, Wales, c.1914
Oil on panel
32.4 x 40.7 cm
prov: Redfern Gallery 1947; Miss M. Garnett, thence by descent; Christie's London Jun 2014 (105); Browse & Darby, London 2014; Christopher Kingzett Fine Art, London c.2021; Private Collection
exh: Redfern 1947b (27)
notes: Arenig Fawr near Nant Ddu

DL14.29
The Rainbow, North Wales / Rainbow, Welsh Mountains / The Rainbow, Landscape in Wales, c.1914
ins: v.: The Rainbow, Wales
Oil on panel
32 x 39.5 cm
prov: Redfern Gallery 1930, 1932, 1934, 1939; Christie's London Oct 1979, Nov 1990
exh: Redfern 1930a (22), 1932 (18), 1934 (27), 1939a (110); Hull City Art Gallery, autumn 1942
notes: Arenig Fawr, North Wales

DL14.30*
Llyn-cwm-Orthin, Wales, c.1914
Oil
exh: Friday Club, London Mar 1915 (112)
notes: Unresolved record; lake above Tanygrisiau, North Wales

DL14.31*
The Moelwyn, Wales / Tan-y-Grisiau, c.1914
Oil
prov: Redfern Gallery 1930 (?)
exh: Friday Club, London 1915 (113); Redfern Gallery 1930a (25)
notes: Unresolved record

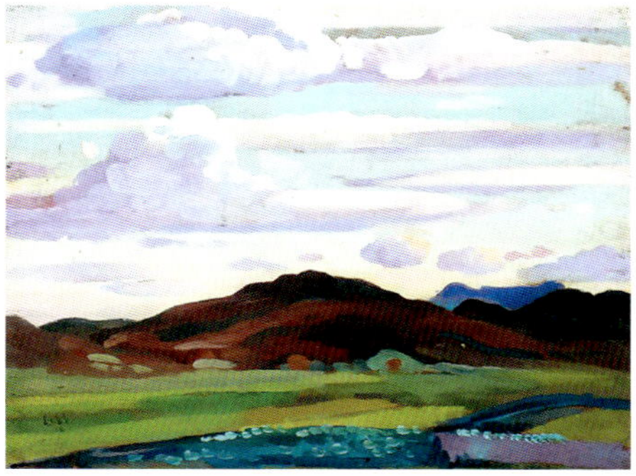

DL14.26

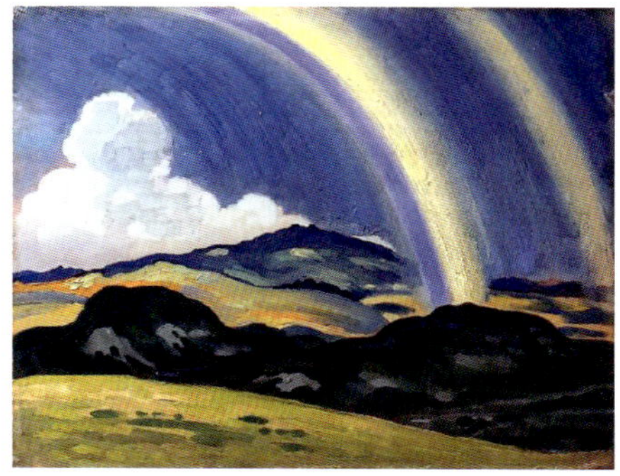

DL14.29

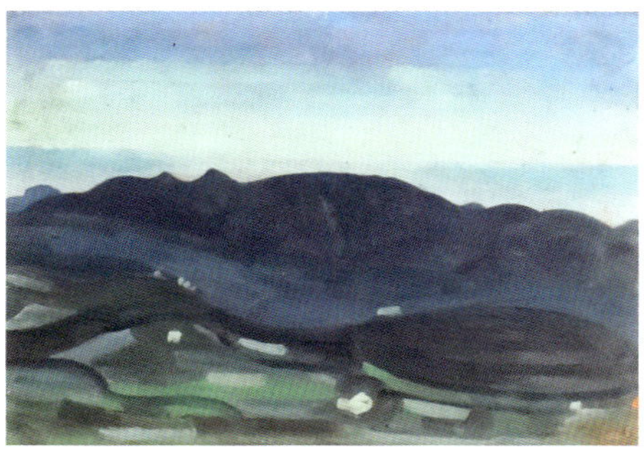

DL14.27

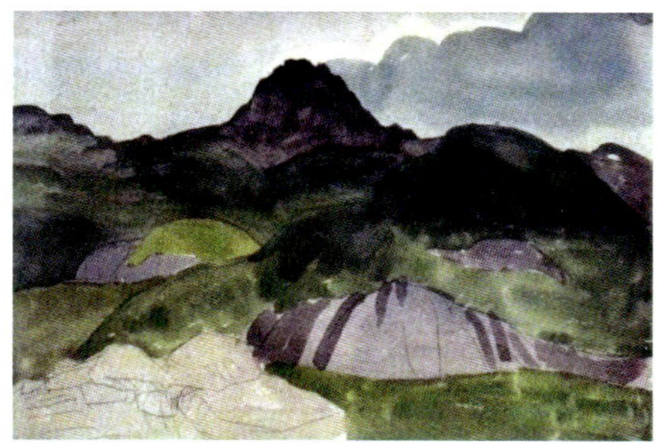

DL14.32

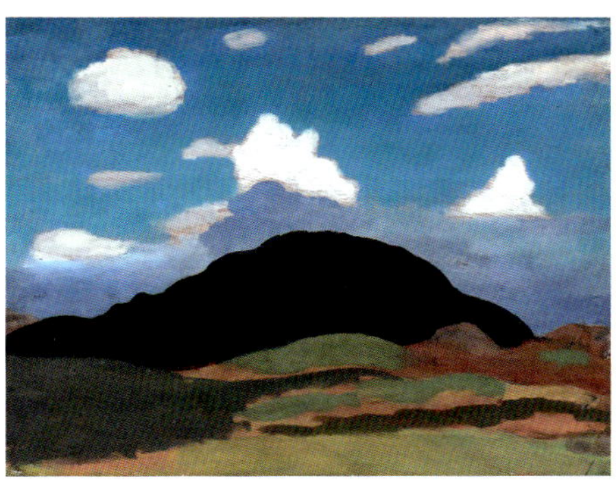

DL14.28

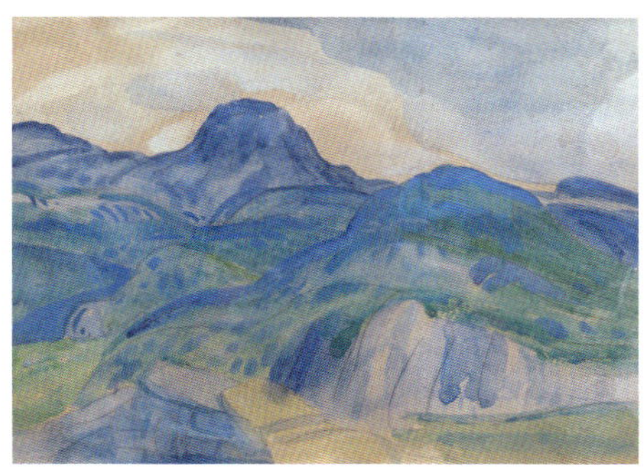

DL14.33

DL14.32
Moelwyn Mawr / Tan-y-Grisiau, c.1914
Watercolour and pencil on paper
24.8 x 33.7 cm
prov: Redfern Gallery 1938 (?); George Eumorfopoulos; Sotheby's London Oct 1946 (?); Sidney Meteyard; Norman Lupton, thence bequeathed to Leeds Art Gallery 1953
exh: Arts Council of Great Britain, London, *Three Centuries of British Watercolours* 1951 (94); Southampton Art Gallery (and tour), *J.D. Innes* 1977 (22); Welsh Arts Council 1982, 1983
notes: Reattributed in consultation with John Hoole, formerly attributed to JDI; possibly a study for DL14.31

DL14.33
Moelwyn Mawr / Tan-y-Grisiau, c.1914
Watercolour and pencil on paper
25 x 35 cm
prov: Mrs Euphemia Grove (née Forrest, then Lamb), thence by descent; Dr and Mrs Christopher Turton, thence by descent
notes: Reattributed in consultation with John Hoole, formerly attributed to JDI; possibly a study for DL14.31

DL14.34
Tan-y-Bwlch / Lyndra at Tan-y-Bwlch / The Yellow Skirt / Lady in Yellow Skirt, 1914
ins: l.r.: Lees 14
Oil on panel
50.7 x 38.3 cm
prov: Redfern Gallery 1930, 1932, 1934, 1939; Mrs Thelma Cazelet Keir 1939; John Martin & Co., Adelaide 1974; Sir Edward Hayward; Carrick Hill Trust, Adelaide (through the Hayward Bequest), purchased 1983
exh: Redfern 1930a, as 'Tan-y-Bwlch' (20), 1932, as 'Lyndra at Tan-y-Bwlch' (13), 1934 (5), 1939a, as 'The Yellow Skirt' (34); Arts Exhibition Bureau, Burlington Gardens, London, *The Camden Town Group* 1939; British Council, Fine Arts Committee, London, New York, Museu Nacional de Belas Artes, Rio de Janeiro, Museo Provincial de Bellas Artes, Cordoba, Argentina, *Allied Institutes* and *Allied National Centres* 1943; National Gallery of South Australia, Adelaide, *Royal Visit Loan Exhibition* Mar–Apr 1954; John Martin & Co., Adelaide Festival of the Arts 1974 (72); Art Gallery of South Australia, Adelaide, *Bohemian London* 1997 (45); Sane 1997, loaned by Carrick Hill (23); National Gallery of Australia, Canberra, Art Gallery of South Australia, Adelaide, *The Edwardians: Secrets and Desires* Mar–Sep 2004, loaned by Carrick Hill Trust (79)
notes: In *Studio International*, [full page illustration] as 'Lady in Yellow Skirt' (Mrs Thelma Cazelet Keir, MP), 126, Jul–Dec 1943, p.41; Lyndra above Tan-y-Bwlch railway station, North Wales

DL14.35
Lyndra by the Rocks / Lyndra and the Rocks, 1914
Oil on panel
52 x 39.5 cm
prov: Redfern Gallery 1930, 1931, 1932, 1939; Friends of Wakefield Art Gallery and Museums (through the Wakefield Permanent Art Fund) purchased for The Hepworth Wakefield 1945
exh: Redfern 1930a (8), 1932 (9), 1939a (41); Mostyn Art Gallery 1982–3 (58)
notes: Cwmorthin valley above Tanygrisiau, North Wales

DL14.36
Lyndra by the Pool / Lyndra, 1914
ins: l.l.: Lees 14
Oil on panel
50.9 x 40 cm
prov: Mrs Edith Lees; Redfern Gallery 1930; Robert H. Jackson; Manchester Art Gallery, purchased Dec 1937
exh: Redfern 1930a (5); Arts Council, North West Region, *25 Paintings from Manchester City Art Gallery* 1951; Glynn Vivian Art Gallery, Swansea, loaned by the Manchester Art Gallery 1952; Mostyn Art Gallery 1982–3 (60); Manchester Art Gallery, *Friends, Family and Other Animals* Jun 2023–Mar 2024
notes: In *The Studio*, 'harmonies of color, figure and simple landscape', 103, 1932, p.53; Tanygrisiau, North Wales

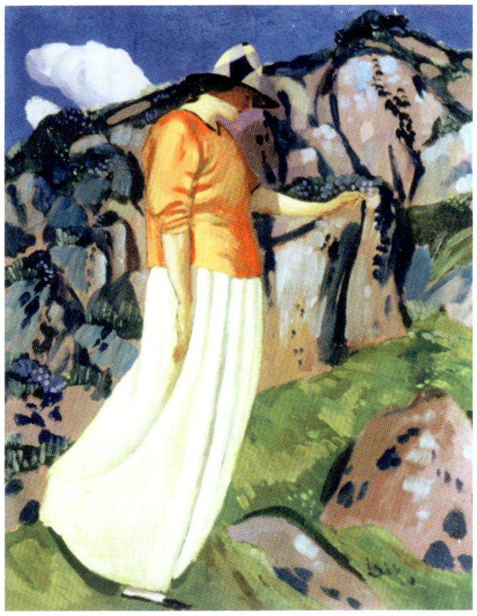

DL14.34

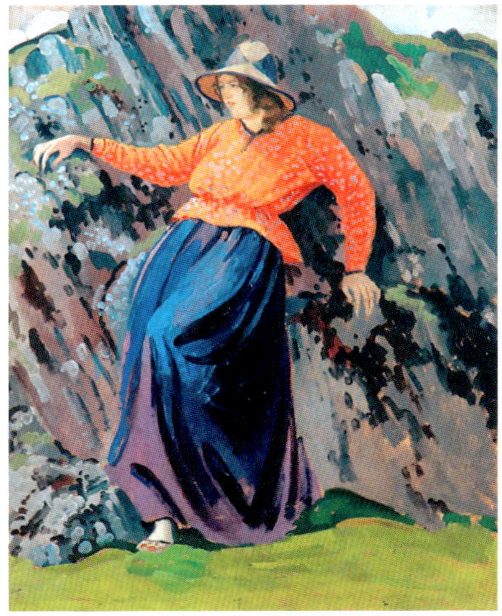

DL14.35

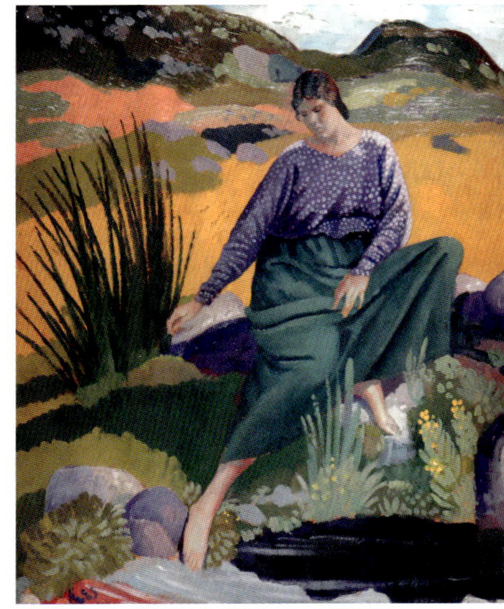

DL14.36

DL14.37
Lyndra in Wales / Figure by Pool, Tan-y-Grisiau, 1914
ins: l.r.: Lees 14
Oil on panel
39.3 x 50.4 cm
prov: Goupil Gallery Jun 1931, 1932 (?); Redfern Gallery 1947, 1949; Sir Keith (Arthur) Murdoch, Melbourne; Yeo Crosthwaite & Co. and McClelland, Melbourne 1953 (308); Queensland Art Gallery | Gallery of Modern Art, Brisbane (through the Maria Theresa Treweeke Bequest), purchased 1953
exh: Goupil 1931a (53); Goupil Gallery, London, *Summer Salon: London Group 29th Exhibition* autumn 1932; Redfern 1947b (144), 1949 (73); Queensland National Art Gallery, Brisbane, 1953 (43); National Gallery of South Australia, Adelaide Festival of Arts, Melbourne, *British Painting 1900–1950* 1966 (14); Sane 1997, loaned by Queensland Art Gallery (22)
notes: Tanygrisiau, North Wales

DL14.38
Lyndra at Tanygrisiau / Girl Seated / Lyndra, Tan-y-Grisiau / Lyndra at Tan-y-Griseau / Lyndra, 1914
ins: l.l.: Lees
Oil on panel
38.5 x 32 cm
prov: Redfern Gallery 1943, 1944, 1946, 1948; Museum of New Zealand Te Papa Tongarewa, Wellington (through the Harold Beauchamp Collection Fund), purchased 1957
exh: Redfern 1943 (98), 1944b (75), 1946c, 1948 (127); National Art Gallery, Wellington, *The First Fifty Years. British Art of the 20th Century from the Collection of the National Art Gallery* Oct 1981–Jan 1982; Sane 1997, loaned by Museum of New Zealand Te Papa Tongarewa (21); Museum of New Zealand Te Papa Tongarewa, Wellington, *Toi Te Papa Art of the Nation* Aug 2011–Mar 2012
notes: In *The Studio*, 132, Nov 1946, p.157; early Redfern Gallery labels as 'Girl Seated' and 'Lyndra at Tan-Y-Griseau'; above Tanygrisiau, North Wales

DL14.39
Lyndra, 1914
ins: l.l.: Lees 14
Oil on panel
49.8 x 38.5 cm
prov: Redfern Gallery 1930; Leeds Art Gallery (through the Leeds Art Collection Fund), purchased 1930
exh: Redfern 1930a (13); Temple Newsam House, Leeds, *Acquisitions of the Leeds Art Collection Fund (1913–1949)* 1949 (10); Sheffield and Aberdeen, *British Painting 1900–1960* 1975–6; Mostyn Art Gallery 1982–3 (59)
notes: Near Nant Ddu, North Wales

DL14.40
Portrait of a Lady in a Landscape / Lyndra (?), c.1914
ins: l.r.: Lees
Oil on panel
50.7 x 29.8 cm
prov: J. Leger & Son Gallery, London 1944 (?); Mr Ken Riddiford; Mrs P. Riddiford, Surrey, gifted to the Sarjeant Gallery, Te Whare o Rehua, Whanganui, New Zealand 1964
exh: J. Leger & Son Gallery, London, *Exhibition of Modern Paintings* Apr–May 1944, as 'Lyndra' (27) (?), *Exhibition of Old and Modern Masters* Sep 1944 (?); Sarjeant Gallery, Whanganui, *Silvermining: The Director Celebrates 25 Years at the Sarjeant Gallery* Oct 2000–Feb 2001; Whangarei Art Museum, *Über Kewel* Apr–Jun 2006; Sarjeant Gallery, Whanganui, *COLOUR* Jun–Nov 2010; Sarjeant Gallery, Whanganui, *A Few of our Favourite Things* Dec 2013–Mar 2014; Sarjeant Gallery, Sarjeant on the Quay, Whanganui, *125: Celebrating Women from the Collection* Sep 2018–Feb 2019; Sarjeant Gallery, online, *My Choice: Marie McKay* Dec 2022
notes: Near Nant Ddu, North Wales

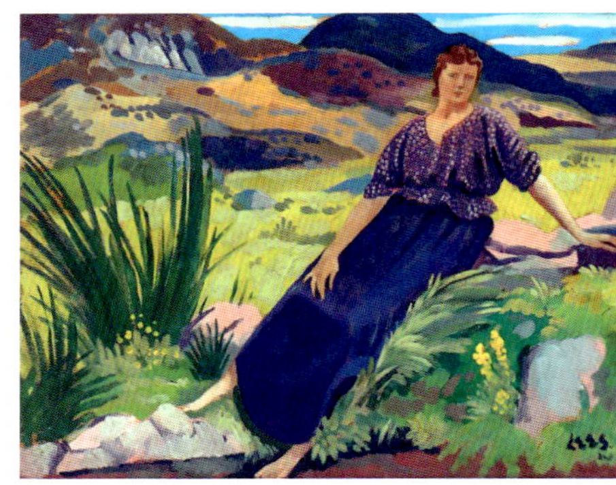

DL14.37

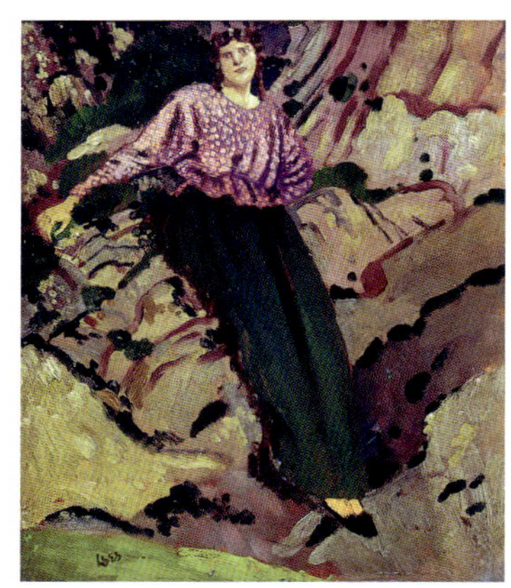

DL14.38

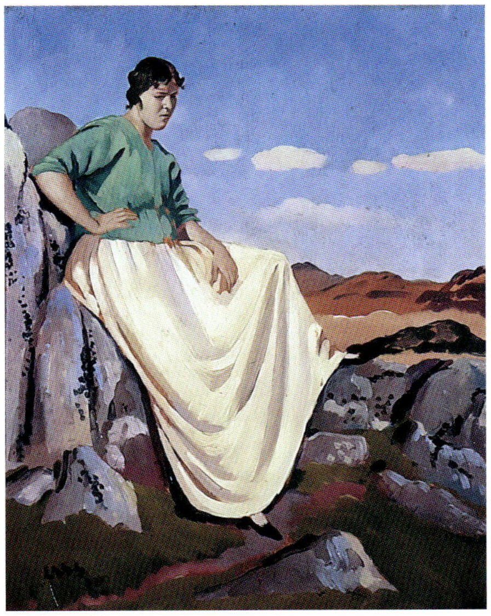

DL14.39

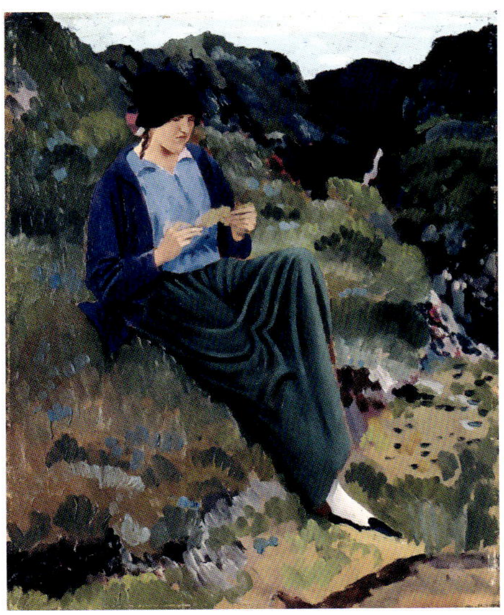

DL14.41

DL14.41
Girl in a Black Hat / Girl in Black Cap, c.1914
Oil on panel
41 x 32.1 cm
prov: Redfern Gallery 1930; Arthur Tooth & Sons, London (1988/4, 2136); A.J.L. McDonnell (advisor to the Felton Bequest 1947–64), presented to NGV by the National Gallery Society of Victoria 1949
exh: Redfern 1930a (2); Redfern Gallery, Hull, *British Artist's Exhibitions*, year unknown; Queensland National Gallery and Perth National Gallery, Jul 1952–Mar 1953; Sane 1997, loaned by NGV (12); NGV Melbourne International Year, *Modern Britain 1900–1960* 2007–8; NGV, Gallery 8 2003, Gallery 7 2014–16
notes: Lyndra at Cwmorthin, North Wales

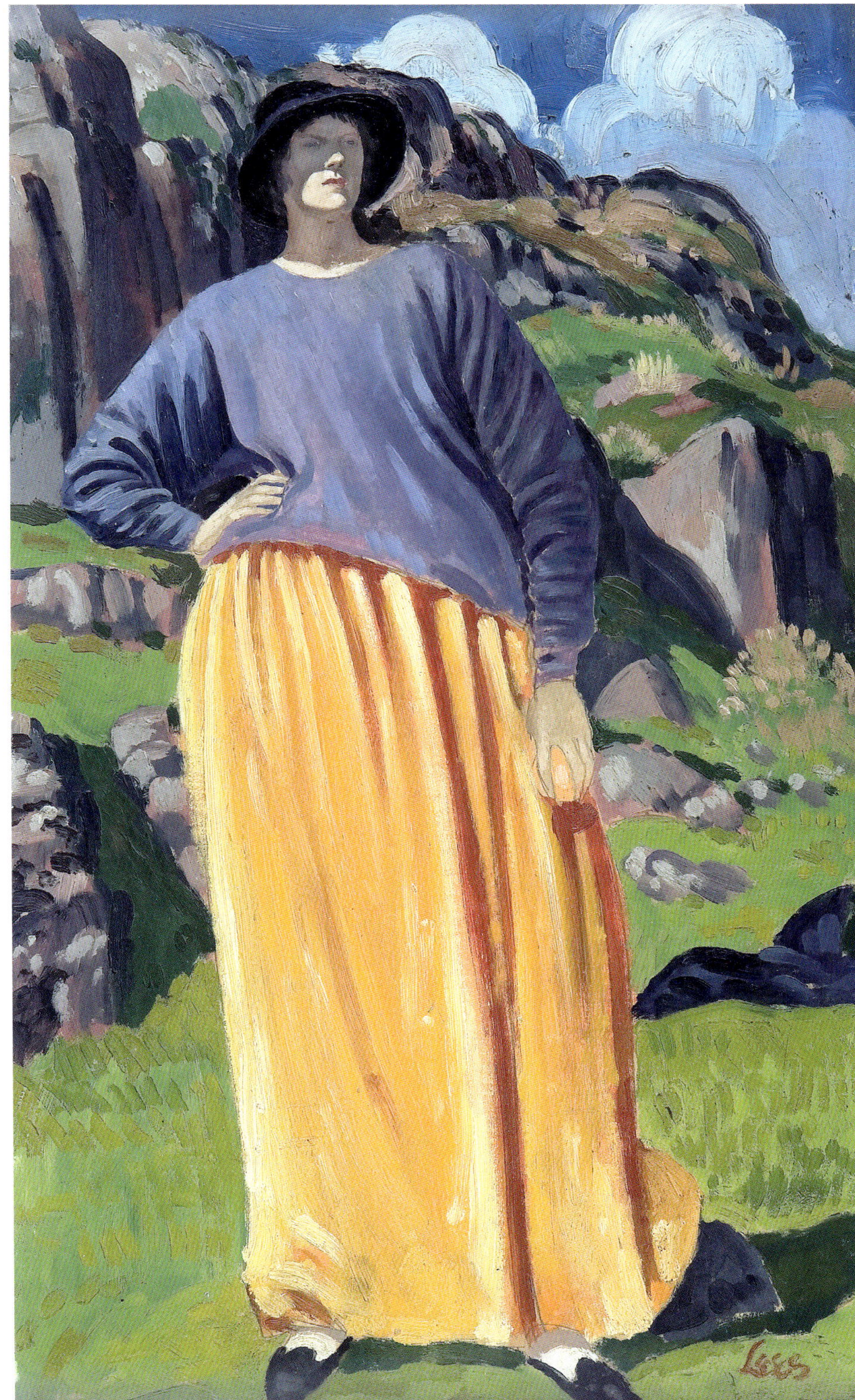

DL14.40

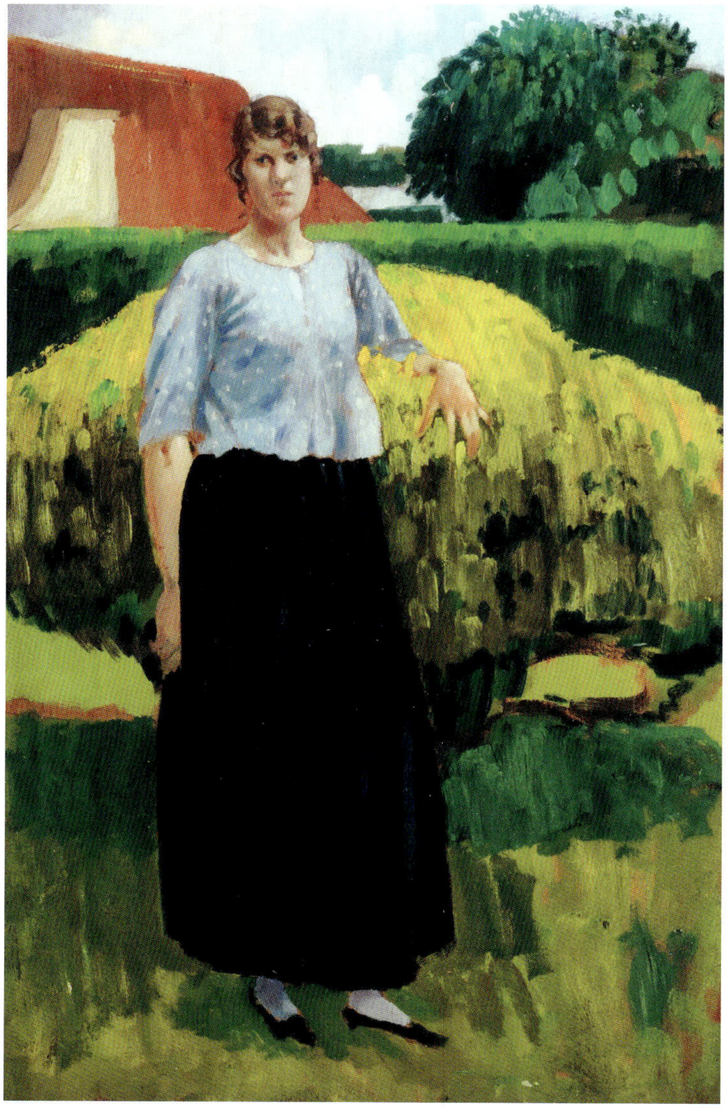
DL14.42

DL14.42
A Girl Standing by a Haycart, 1914–15
Oil on panel
49.5 x 31.7 cm
prov: Arthur Tooth & Sons, London (7530); Museums Sheffield, purchased 1969; Graves Art Gallery, Sheffield 1992
exh: Arts Council of Great Britain, Touring Exhibition, Southampton, Swansea, Ramsgate, Sheffield, Milton Keynes, *Semi-Detached: Pictures of People and Places* Apr–Oct 1984, loaned by the Graves Art Gallery; Millennium Gallery, Sheffield, *Beyond Bloomsbury: Life, Love and Legacy* Nov 2021–Feb 2022
notes: Lyndra

DL14.43
Portrait of a Girl / Seated Girl (?), 1914
ins: l.l.: Lees 14; v.: 21 Fitzroy Square [on handwritten note]
Oil on panel
51 x 39.5 cm
prov: Redfern Gallery 1930; Atkinson Gallery, Southport, purchased 1932
exh: NEAC 52nd 1914 (86); Redfern 1930a (3) (?)
notes: Lyndra, Tanygrisiau, North Wales

DL14.44
Lyndra in Wales / Portrait of the Artist's Wife, 1914
ins: l.l.: Lees 14; v.: [note inscribed by E.M.B. Ingram]
Oil on panel
32.7 x 40.6 cm
prov: Redfern Gallery 1937; Maurice Ingram 1937; bequeathed by Maurice Ingram to the Fitzwilliam Museum, Cambridge 1941
exh: Redfern Aug–Sep 1937, Sep–Oct 1937,

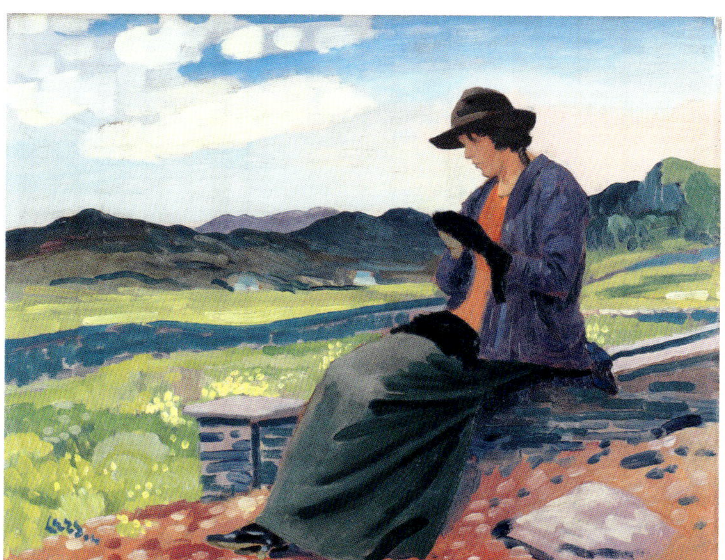
DL14.44

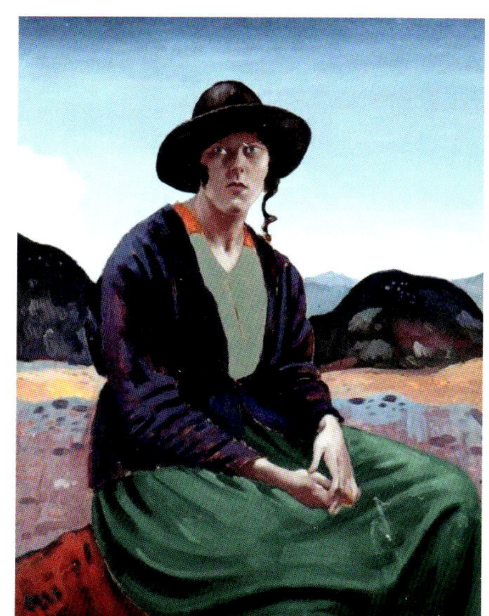
DL14.43

1939a, collection of Maurice Ingram (33); Tate 1940, collection of Maurice Ingram (104); Redfern 1941b, collection of the late Maurice Ingram (29); Lakeland Arts, Kendal, loaned by Fitzwilliam Museum, 2002
notes: v.: [note inscribed by Maurice Ingram] 'This is a picture of Mrs Derwent Lees darning a pair of Augustus John's socks (Told me by Mrs D. Lees July 1937. EMBI)'; Plas Brondanw, near Garreg, North Wales

DL14.45*
Beach Scene / The Beach / Coastal Scene, c.1914
Oil on panel
11.5 x 26.5 cm
prov: Christie's Melbourne Mar 1978 (491); Spink, Sydney Sep 1981 (162); Deutscher 1982, 1983; Geoff K. Gray, Sydney Nov 1983 (349); Rushton Fine Arts, Sydney Mar 1986; Leonard Joel, Melbourne Jul 1997 (527); Private Collection
notes: Unresolved record

DL14.46*
Cavtat, c.1914
Oil
prov: Redfern Gallery 1939
exh: Redfern 1939a (30), 1939d (137)
notes: Likely La Ciotat, France

DL14.47**
A Mediterranean Bay, 1914
Watercolour on paper
23 x 34.5 cm
prov: Redfern Gallery; Thos. Agnew & Sons; Spink; Sotheby's London Nov 1978 (58); Christie's London Jun 1995 (105), Jun 2008 (105); Private Collection
notes: From the Pointe du Matelad facing the Phare du Môle Neuf lighthouse-breakwater, La Ciotat

DL14.48*
Weymouth Bay / The Bay, Dorset, 1914
Oil
prov: Redfern Gallery 1932–4
exh: Redfern 1932 (14), 1934 (23)
notes: Unresolved record

DL14.49
Welsh Mountains and Lake, c.1914
Watercolour on paper
25.5 x 35.5cm
prov: A.G. Innes; Thos. Agnew & Sons (17751); E. W. Jenkinson; Margaret S. Taylor, thence by descent 2015; Private Collection; Olympia Auctions London, Mar 2025 (530)
exh: Graves Art Gallery Sheffield, Glynn Vivian Art Gallery Swansea, National Library of Wales Aberystwyth, lent by E.W. Jenkinson, Mar-May 1961 (70)
notes: Possibly related to DL11.9; Reattributed in consultation with John Hoole, formerly attributed to J.D. Innes; View of Moel Llyfnant across Llyn Tryweryn, North Wales

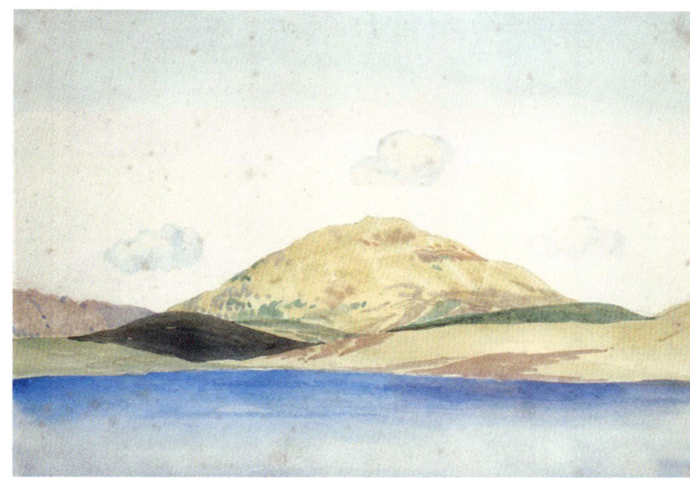

DL14.49

1915

DL15.1**
Lyndra, bust portrait, looking upwards holding tennis racket, c.1915
Etching plate
approx. 20.3 x 15.2 cm [plate]
prov: Private Collection
notes: Lyndra, likely at Aldbourne

DL15.2
London Public House / Public Bar, c.1915
ins: l.l.: Lees (?)
Pencil, ink wash and gum arabic on paper
22.2 x 26 cm
prov: Mrs Edith Lees; Redfern Gallery Mar 1963; Bonhams & Butterfields, San Francisco and Los Angeles Feb 2006 (7122); Private Collection
exh: Stafford 1939

DL15.3**
Woman in Long Coat / Standing Figure, c.1915
Ink and wash on paper
47 x 31.5 cm
prov: Rex Nan Kivell; Deutsher 1978; Josef Lebovic Gallery, Sydney Aug 1997 (76); Private Collection; Josef Lebovic Gallery, Sydney 2009–10 (79); Private Collection
exh: Deutsher 1978 (37)

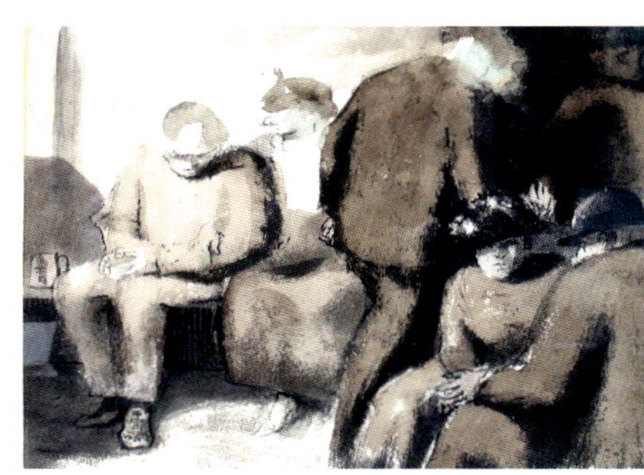

DL15.2

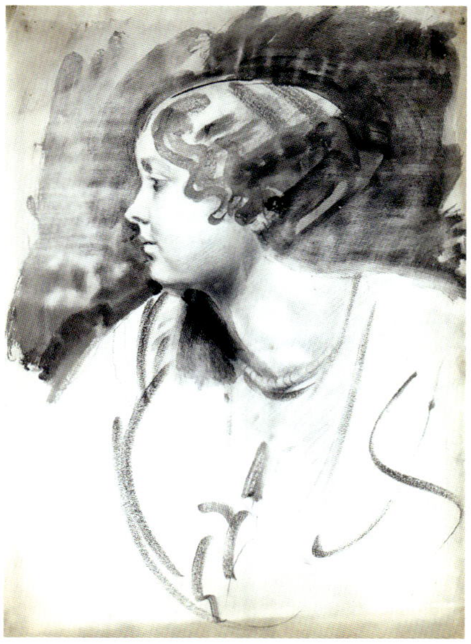

DL15.4

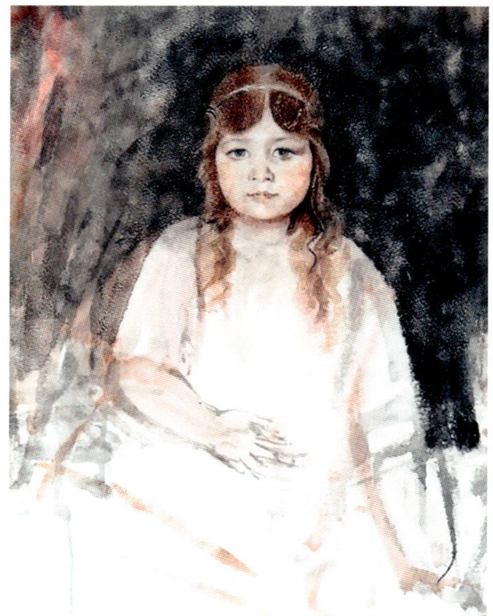

DL15.5

DL15.6
Portrait of Francis Helps / Portrait of an Unknown Man / Portrait of a Gentleman, c.1915
Pencil on paper
32.5 x 26 cm
prov: Mrs Edith Lees; Deutscher 1982; Masterpiece Fine Art Gallery, Hobart; Private Collection; Bridget McDonnell Gallery; Leonard Joel, Melbourne Feb 2005 (P175); Bridget McDonnell 2017; Private Collection
exh: Stafford 1939

DL15.7
Portrait of Francis Helps in Uniform / Francis Helps / Artist in 1915, c.1915
ins: l.l.: [pencil] 17 1/2 x 11 1/4
Watercolour and graphite on paper
47 x 29.8 cm
prov: Mrs Edith Lees; Suckling & Co., London; British Museum, London, purchased 1939
exh: Stafford 1939; British Museum, London, *Portrait Drawings, xv–xx Centuries* Jul–Dec 1974 (403)

DL15.4
Portrait Study: Woman with Head Turned to the Right / Head of a Girl / Portrait of a Young Girl, 1915–18
Ink, wash, brush and pencil on paper
50.7 x 35.6 cm
prov: Rex Nan Kivell; Deutsher 1978; National Gallery of Australia, Canberra, purchased 1979
exh: Deutsher 1978 (40); Sane 1997, loaned by the National Gallery of Australia (37)

DL15.5
Study of a Young Girl / Portrait Study / Portrait of a Young Girl, c.1915
Watercolour wash and pencil on paper
35.5 x 25.3 cm
prov: Redfern Gallery 1934; Rex Nan Kivell Collection; Belgrave Gallery, London; Deutsher 1976–8; Deutscher-Menzies Fine Art, Melbourne Aug 2002 (420); Masterpiece Gallery, Hobart Jun–Aug 2004; Mossgreen Auctions, Melbourne Oct 2015 (141); Lauder & Howard Antiques & Fine Art, Hobart Mar 2021; Private Collection
exh: Redfern 1934 (43); Deutsher 1978 (22); Sane 1997 (32)

DL15.8
Portrait Study / Portrait of a Girl, Head Turned, 1915
ins: v.: 1915
Pencil on paper
50.7 x 35.5 cm
prov: Rex Nan Kivell; Deutsher 1978; Private Collection
exh: Deutsher 1978 (33)

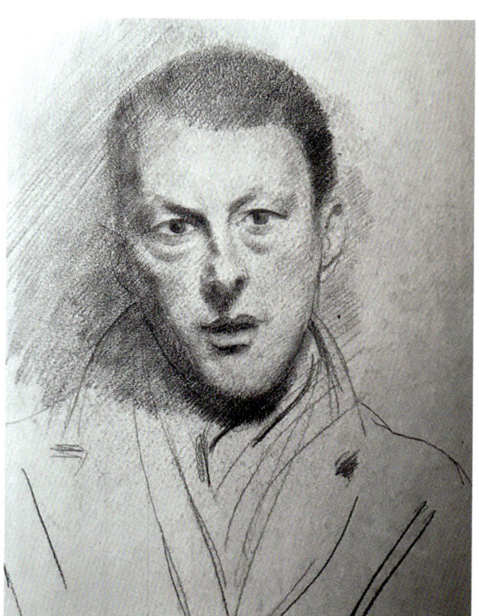

DL15.6

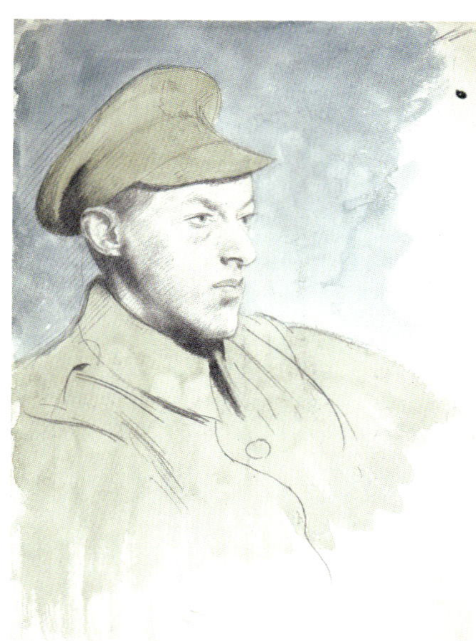

DL15.7

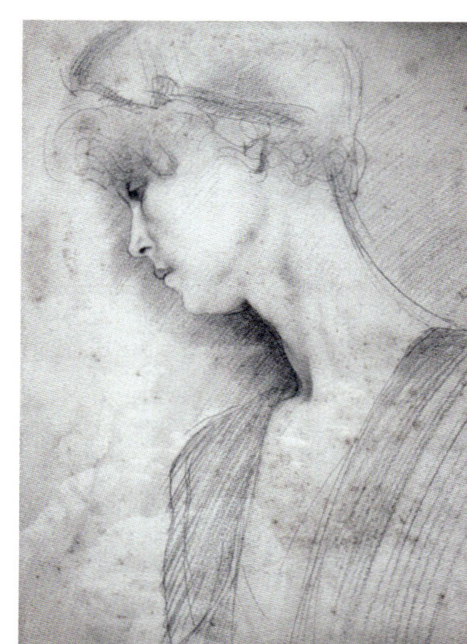

DL15.8

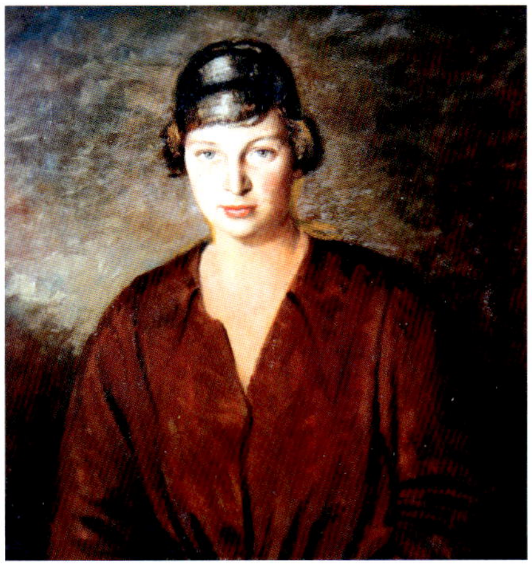

DL15.9

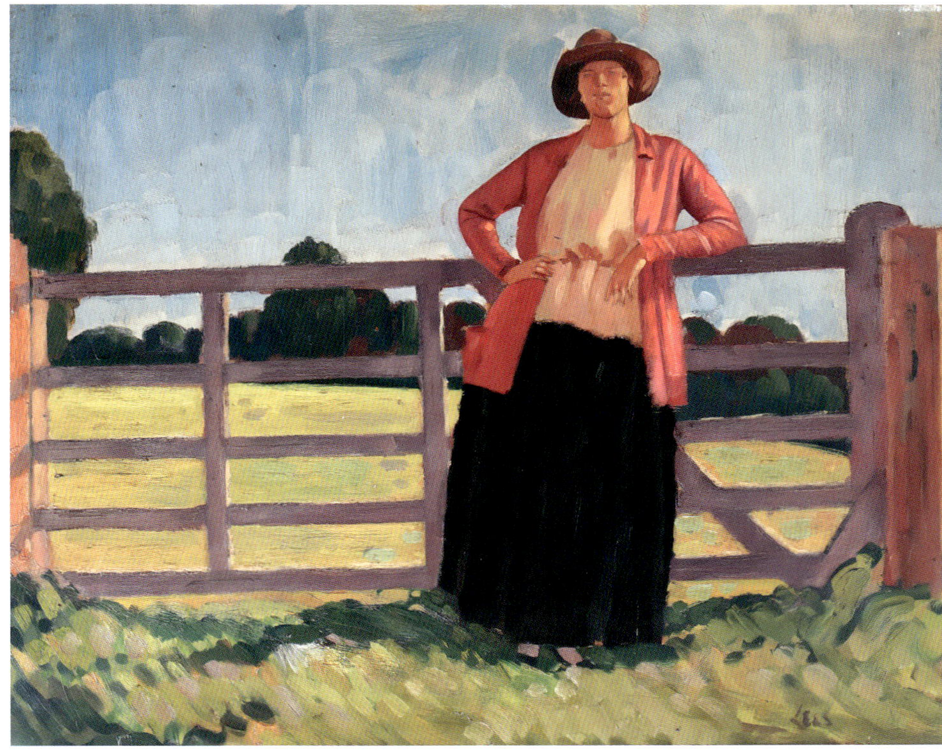

DL15.11

DL15.9
Girl in Brown / Portrait of a Young Woman, c.1915
Oil on canvas
56.9 x 51 cm
prov: T.W. Spurr & Son, London pre-Jul 1937; Private Collection 1952; Christie's London Jul 2012 (415); Bonhams Oxford Sep 2014; Lauder & Howard Antiques & Fine Art, Hobart 2020–21; Private Collection
exh: City of Bradford Art Gallery, Cartwright Hall, *Jubilee Exhibition: Fifty Years of British Art 1904–54* (loan 25) Mar–Jun 1954 (219); Guildhall Art Gallery, Art Exhibitions Bureau, London, *Trends in British Art* Jul–Aug 1954
notes: Possibly Lady Diana Manners

DL15.10*
Self Portrait, c.1915
Watercolour on paper
prov: Mrs Edith Lees 1939
exh: Redfern 1939a, loaned by Mrs Derwent Lees (122)

DL15.11
Lyndra at the Gate / Girl in Red Jacket / The Red Jacket, 1915
ins: l.r.: Lees
Oil on panel
39 x 51 cm
prov: Goupil Gallery Nov 1931; Redfern Gallery 1937, 1939–45; Bonhams London Mar 2004 (12)
exh: Goupil 1931b (111); Redfern 1937 (25), 1939a (102); British Council, British Pavilion, *Exhibition of Contemporary British Art*, New York World's Fair, 1939 (67), Museum of Fine Arts, Boston, 1940 (67), loaned by the Redfern Gallery; British Council, Museu Nacional de Belas Artes Rio de Janeiro, Museo Provincial de Bellas Artes Cordoba Argentina, Palacio de Bellas Artes Santiago Chile, *Exposicion de Arte Britanico Contemporaneo*, as 'Chaqueta Roja', loaned by the Redfern Gallery, 1940–43 (41); Redfern 1945b (637)

DL15.12
Lyndra, Sunset, Aldbourne / Lyndra Watching Sunset / Lyndra in Sunset, 1915
ins: v.: Mrs Lees 99 Warwick Road S.W.5 2.L.2.6 [on label], No 108, The Redfern Gallery Ltd, 20 Cork Street, Burlington gardens, Bond Street London W.1 [on label], loaned by Margaret S. Davies Gregynog Newtown Derwent Lees 'Lyndra. Sunset' [on label]
Oil on panel
41.1 x 32.4 cm
prov: Mrs Edith Lees; Redfern Gallery 1945, 1946, 1952; Miss Margaret S. Davies Jun 1952; bequeathed to the National Museum of Wales (now Amgueddfa Cymru, Museum Wales) Dec 1963
exh: Redfern 1945b (237), 1946b (192), 1952 (108)

DL15.13
The Thorn / The Manicure / Lyndra: The Thorn / Lyndra in a White Smock / Lyndra in a White Blouse, 1915
ins: v.: The Fine Art Society Limited, Est. 1876. Number 4860 Date: July 1979. Derwent Lees. 1885 – 1931, Lyndra in a White Smock [on label]; v.: Mrs Lees, 99 Warwick Rd, S.W.5. 2. L. 25 [on label]
Oil on panel
41.9 x 33.7 cm
prov: Mrs Edith Lees; R.F. Goldschmidt; Christie's London Jun 1941, as 'Thorn'; Adams 1941; Redfern Gallery 1941, 1945, 1958, 1963, 1964, 1966, 1967, 1968; Fine Art Society Jun–Jul 1979 (4860); Corporate Collection, Sydney; Shapiro, Sydney Dec 2006 (53); Christie's London May, Aug 2007 (523); Lynda Cotton Gallery, West Somerset 2017; Lawrence's Auctioneers, Crewkerne Apr 2021 (1561); Private Collection
exh: Redfern 1941a (21), 1945b (21), 1958 (38), 1963 (335), 1964 (406), 1966 (271), 1967 (314), 1968 (205); Fine Art Society London Jul 1979 (4860)
notes: Lyndra, Aldbourne

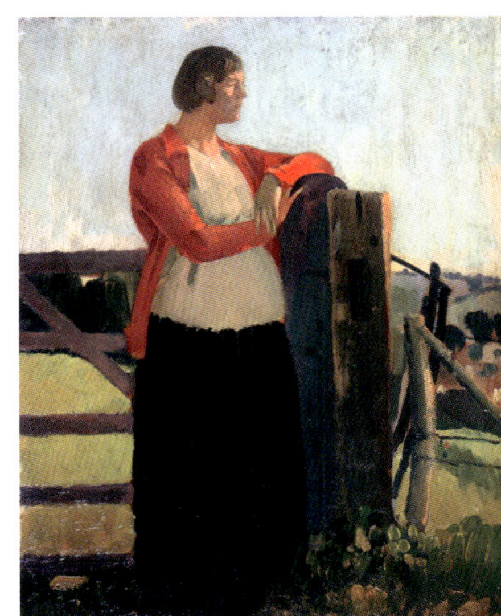

DL15.12

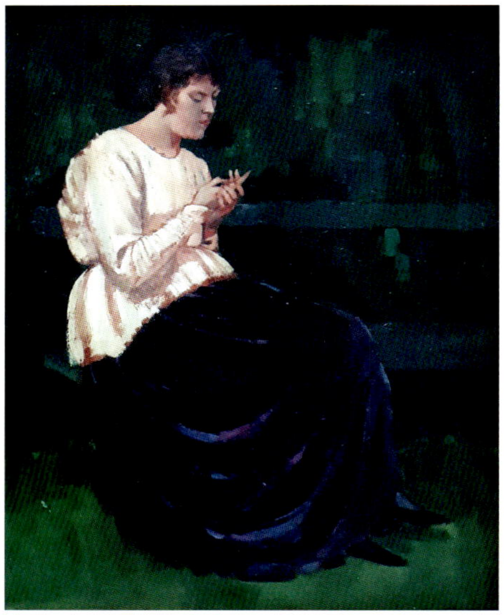

DL15.13

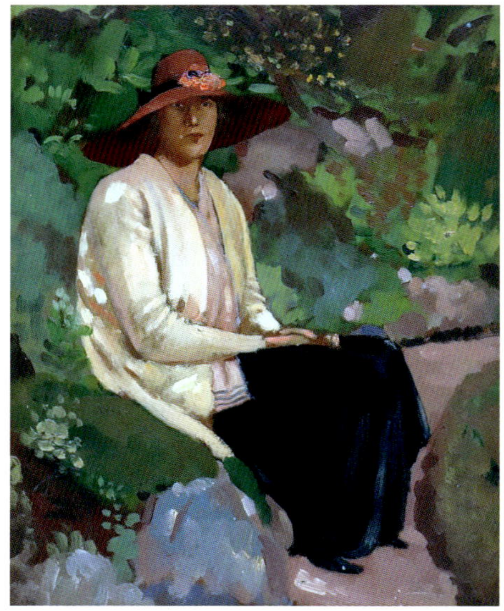

DL15.14

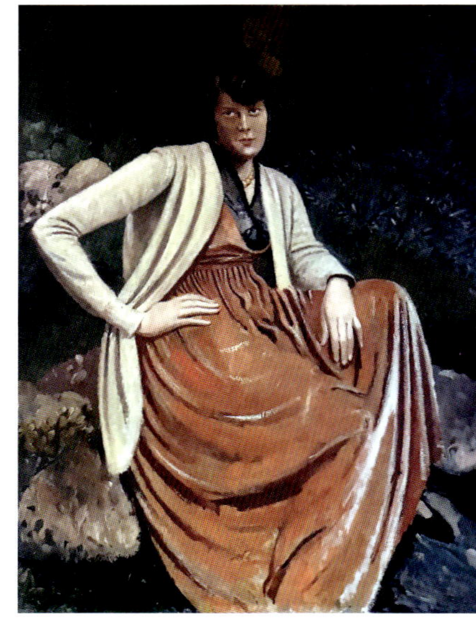

DL15.15

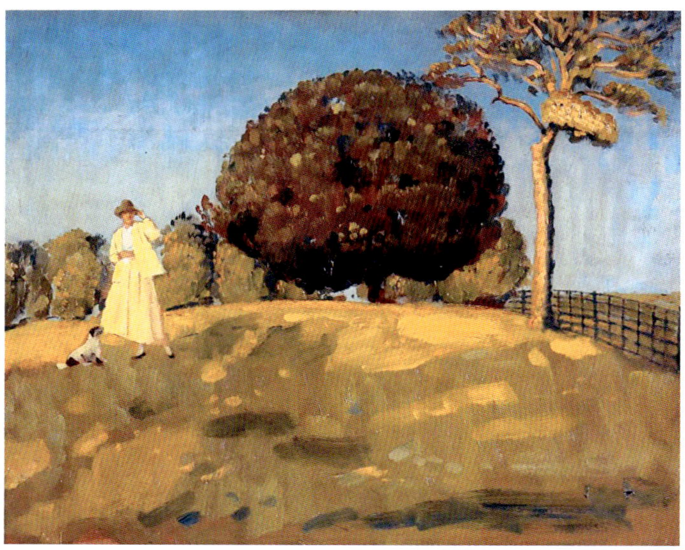

DL15.16

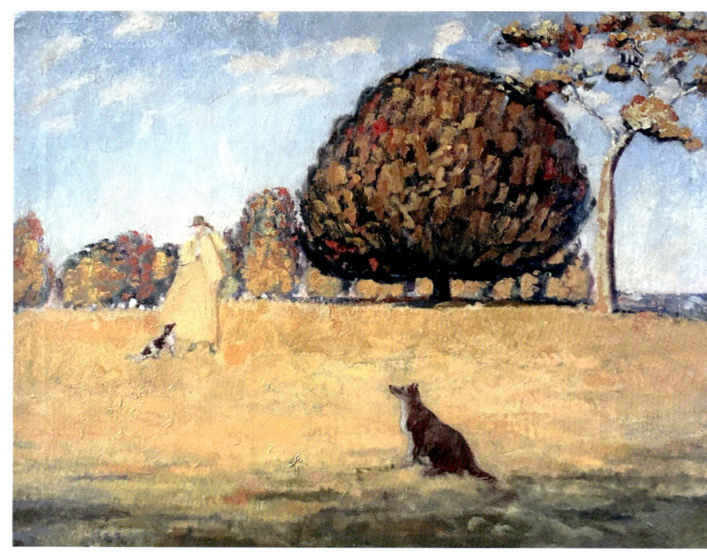

DL15.17

DL15.14
The Yellow Coat, 1915
Oil on panel
40 x 31.5 cm
prov: Redfern Gallery 1958; Fine Art Society 1971, 1974; Queensland Art Gallery | Gallery of Modern Art, purchased 1975
exh: NEAC 56th 1916–17, as 'The Yellow Coat' (92); Redfern 1958 (36); Fine Art Society 1971 (41); Fine Art Society London, *Face to Face* Dec 1974 (19); Sane 1997, loaned by Queensland Art Gallery (15)
notes: Lyndra, Aldbourne; location as in DL15.15 and DL15.36

DL15.15
Lyndra Seated in the Garden / Lyndra in the Garden / Portrait of the Artist's Wife / Portrait of the Artist's Wife Lyndra, Seated on a Bank / Seated Lady in a Garden / Lyndra, c.1915
ins: l.l.: Lees
Oil on canvas
111.6 x 87.6 cm
prov: Redfern Gallery 1958, 1964; Chelsea Gallery, London; Christie's London Nov 1977 (196); Belgrave Gallery, London 1978; Christie's London Jun 1982 (50); John Taylor's, Louth May 1984 (326); Sotheby's London May 1988; Private Collection
exh: Redfern 1958 (30), 1964 (402); Sane 1997, as 'Lyndra' (24)
notes: Lyndra, Aldbourne; location as in DL15.14 and DL15.36

DL15.16
The Round Tree, 1915
Oil on canvas
39.3 x 50.4 cm
prov: Redfern Gallery 1930, 1939; Aberdeen Archives, Gallery and Museum (through the Macdonald Bequest), purchased 1939
exh: Redfern 1930a (23), 1939a (108); Aberdeen Art Gallery Sep 2015–Jan 2016
notes: Lyndra, Aldbourne

DL15.17
An Autumn Wander / An Autumn Walk / An Autumn Walk, Elegant Woman with Dogs in a Parkland Setting, 1915
ins: l.l.: Lees
Oil on canvas
71 x 91.2 cm
prov: Roseberys, London Apr 2000; Sotheby's London Dec 2000 (84); Christie's London Jul 2001 (63), Sep 2001 (202); Denys Wilcox Fine Art (The Court Gallery, Taunton) Jan 2002; Private Collection
notes: Lyndra, Aldbourne

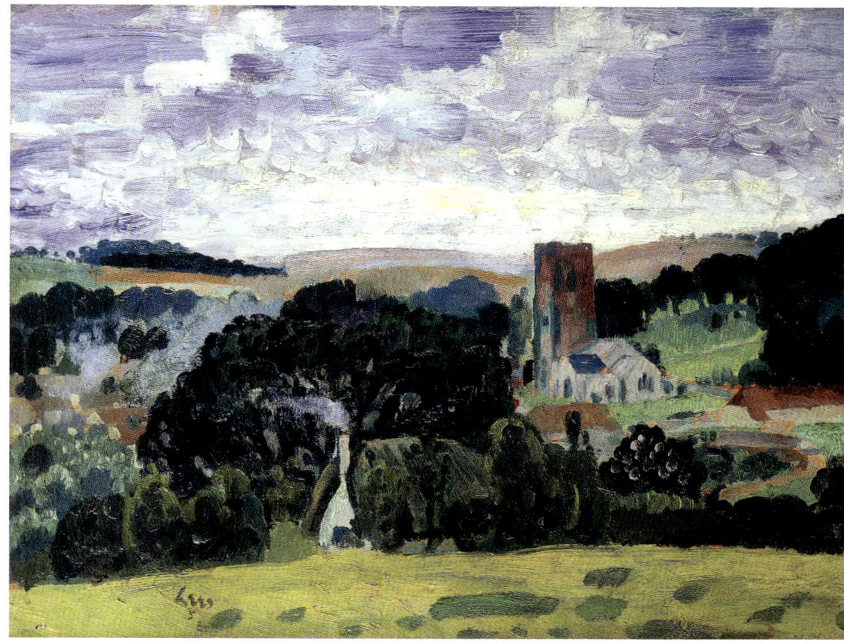

DL15.18

DL15.18
Aldbourne, Wiltshire / Aldbourne, Evening / Village and Church / A View of Oldbourne, 1915
ins: l.l.: Lees
Oil (on canvas) on panel
31.7 x 40 cm
prov: Goupil Gallery 1926, 1929; Lord Henry Cavendish-Bentinck 1931 (?); Sotheby's London May 1933 (92); Burrows; Redfern Gallery 1943, 1944, 1946, 1948; Sotheby's London May 1950 (149); Roland, Browse & Delbanco, London; Sotheby's London Dec 1970 (42); Christie's London Nov 1985
exh: Goupil 1926 (261), Aug 1929 (15); Redfern 1943 (15), 1944b (73), 1946b (239), 1948 (129)
notes: Above Oxford Street, Aldbourne

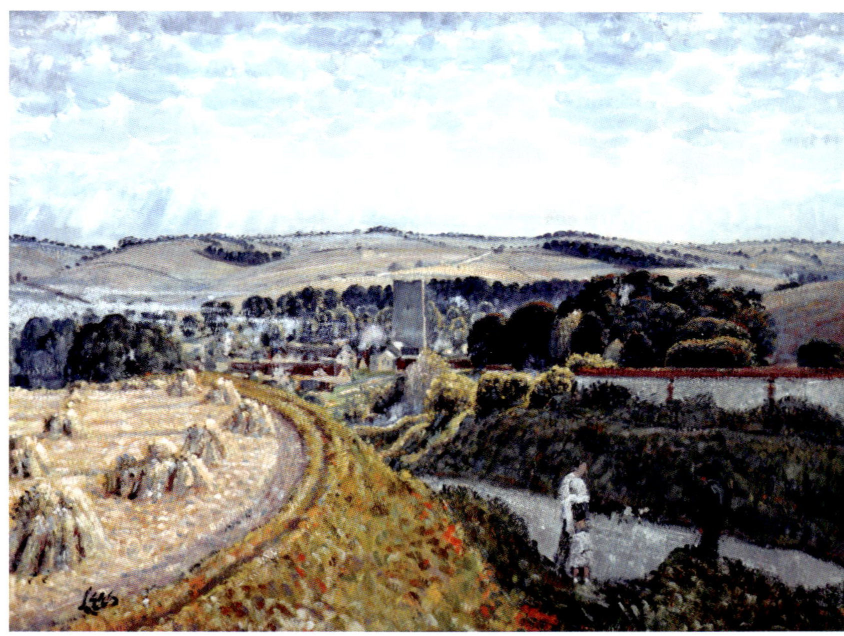

DL15.19

DL15.19
Aldbourne, 1915
ins: l.l.: Lees
Oil on canvas
71 x 91 cm
prov: CAS 1915, gifted to the Walker Art Gallery, Liverpool 1923
exh: NEAC 54th 1915 (105); Walker Art Gallery, Liverpool, *New Radicals: From Sickert to Freud* Jul–Sep 2004
notes: Lyndra and Charles or Ambrose McEvoy (?); above Oxford Street, Aldbourne

DL15.20*
Cornfield, Aldbourne / Cornfield, Aldbourne, Wilts / A Cornfield, Aldbourne, 1915
Oil on panel
38.1 x 49.5 cm
prov: Redfern Gallery 1930; Lord Ivor Spencer-Churchill 1934
exh: Redfern 1930a (24), 1934, loaned by Lord Ivor Spencer-Churchill (2)

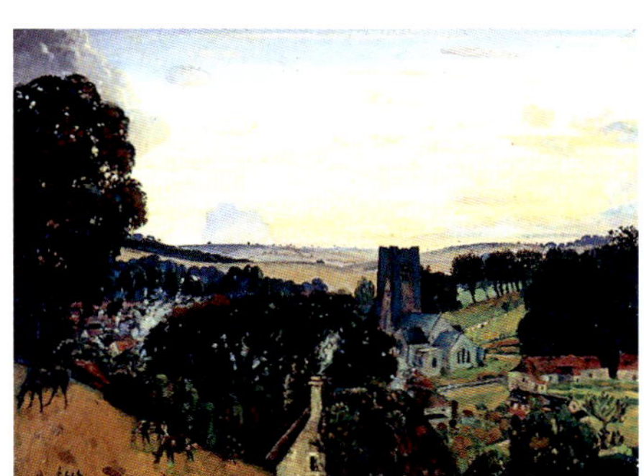

DL15.21

DL15.21
Aldbourne, Wiltshire / Aldbourne, Wilts., No.1 / Aldbourne, 1915
ins: l.l.: Lees
Oil on canvas
70.5 x 90.9 cm
prov: Redfern Gallery 1930; Lord Ivor Spencer-Churchill, gifted to the CAS 1936–7; thence gifted to Leeds Art Gallery 1937
exh: Redfern 1930a (27); Empire Art 1934–5, loaned by Lord Ivor Spencer-Churchill (124)
notes: Above Oxford Street, Aldbourne

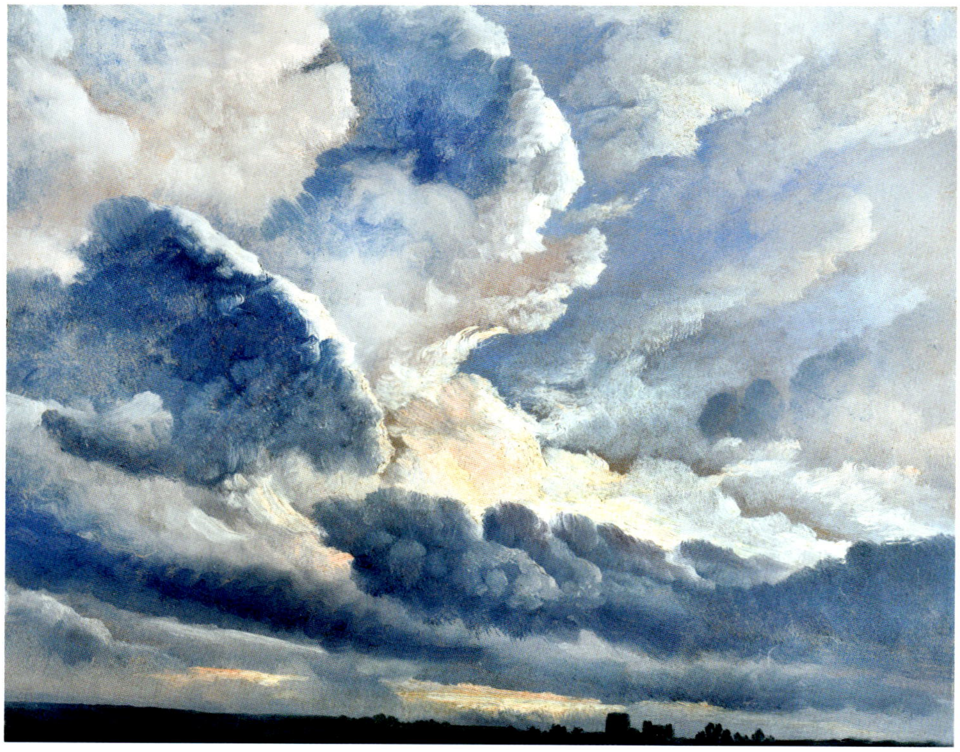

DL15.22

Leicester Galleries, London Aug 1989; Ewan Mundy Fine Art, Argyll Sep 1989; Private Collection
exh: Redfern 1958 (40); Fine Art Society 1971 (42); Fine Art Society, The David Paul Gallery, Chichester, *British Art 1800–1950* 1973 (39); Deutscher 1982 (50); Peter Nahum Ltd, London, *British Art from the Twentieth Century* Jul 1989
notes: Lyndra, Alderney Manor, Dorset

DL15.27**
The Straw Hat / Lyndra in a Straw Hat, c.1915
Oil on panel
40.5 x 32 cm
prov: Redfern Gallery 1944, 1947; Dr Harold Widdup; Hammer Gallery, New York; Redfern Gallery 1958, 1964; Sotheby's New York Mar 1993; Sotheby's London Mar 1994; Dreweatts (formerly Hamptons Fine Art), Godalming Jul 2003 (168); Denys Wilcox Fine Art (The Court Gallery, Taunton) Jul 2003; Private Collection
exh: Redfern 1944b, 1947a, 1958 (32), 1964 (403); Campbelltown Arts Centre, New South Wales, Joan Sutherland Performing Arts Centre, Penrith, Ivan Dougherty Gallery College of Fine Arts, University of New South Wales Sep–Nov 2006, Bundoora Homestead Art Centre, Melbourne Jun–Jul 2007 (280)

DL15.22
The Thunder Cloud, 1915
ins: l.l.: [signature, date]
Oil on canvas
30.4 x 24.5 cm
exh: NEAC 54th 1915 (97)
notes: Aldbourne village; location of work unknown

DL15.23*
The Road by the River c.1915
Oil on panel
29.2 x 39.3 cm
prov: Lord Henry Cavendish Bentinck, thence by descent to Lady Bentinck; Christie's London Apr 1940 (141); Angus 1940

DL15.24*
Otters, c.1915
Ink on paper
25.4 x 35.6 cm
prov: Rex Nan Kivell; Deutsher 1978; Private Collection
exh: Deutsher 1978 (8)
notes: Unresolved record

DL15.25
Lyndra in the Garden at Alderney / Lyndra in the Garden / Lyndra at Aldbourne / Lyndra: The Garden, Aldbourne, 1915
ins: l.l.: Lees – 15
Oil and pencil on panel
31 x 39.5 cm
prov: Rex Nan Kivell; Redfern Gallery 1945, 1946, 1947, 1948, 1949, 1952, 1958, 1963, 1964; Fine Art Society Feb 1972; Belgrave Gallery, London Feb–Nov 1981; Alex Reid & Lefevre, London 1980s; Christie's London Nov 1990 (65), Nov 1997 (8), Nov 1998 (185), Mar 1999 (3); Sotheby's London Apr 2017 (57); Woolley & Wallis, Salisbury Nov 2017 (291)
exh: Redfern 1945b (207), 1946b (41), 1947b (37), 1948 (20), 1949 (74); Birmingham City Gallery 1952, loaned by the Redfern Gallery (54); Redfern 1958 (30), 1963 (334), 1964 (401); Fine Art Society London Feb 1972 (4855)
notes: Lyndra, Alderney Manor, Dorset

DL15.26
The Artist's Wife Reclining / Lyndra Resting / The Artist's Wife / Artist's Wife with Hat / Girl Lying on a Rug / The Artist's Wife Lynda Reclining, 1915
ins: l.l.: Lees 15
Oil on panel
32.4 x 50.8 cm
prov: Redfern Gallery 1958; Deutsher Nov 1975; Deutscher 1982–9; Peter Nahum at the

DL15.28
Lyndra and Charlie / Lyndra and the Donkey / Lyndra with Donkey, 1915
ins: l.r.: LEES 15
Oil on panel
32.4 x 40.6 cm
prov: Redfern Gallery 1930, 1931, 1934; Lord Ivor Spencer-Churchill 1939; Redfern Gallery 1945, 1947; Mr and Mrs J.B. Priestley 1947–Sep 1951; Mrs D.A. Bannerman (formerly Mrs Priestley); Sotheby's London Dec 1967 (31), Dec 1970 (57); Fine Art Society 1971–6; Private Collection
exh: Redfern 1930a (19), 1930b (21), 1931c (21), 1934 (9); Empire Art 1939, loaned by Lord Ivor Spencer-Churchill (67); Redfern 1945b (171), 1947b (45); Fine Art Society 1971 (43); Fine Art Society London, Adelaide, *The Fine Art Society at the Adelaide Festival* 1976 (12); Sane 1997 (25)
notes: Alderney Manor, Dorset

DL15.29
The Artist's Wife, Lyndra, c.1915
Oil and pencil on paper, on canvas
60.7 x 40.5 cm
prov: Chelsea Gallery, London; Bridget McDonnell Gallery 1988, 2024
exh: Bridget McDonnell Gallery 2006 (16)
notes: Same chair as in DL12.14; likely DL's 21 Fitzroy Square studio

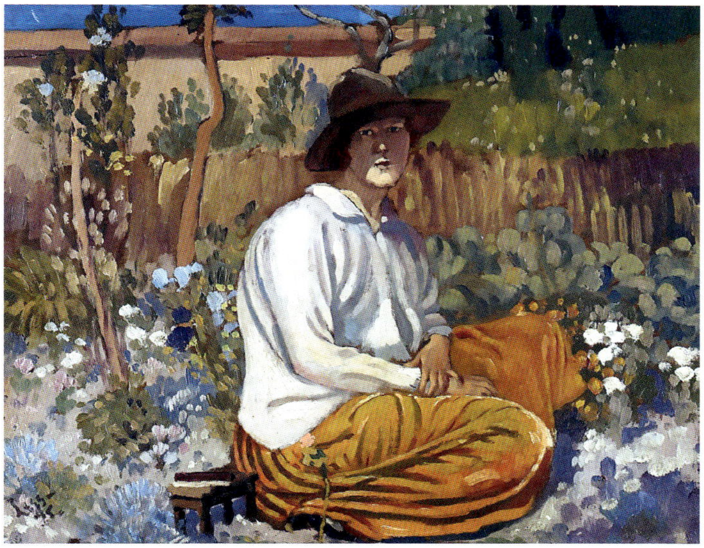

DL15.25

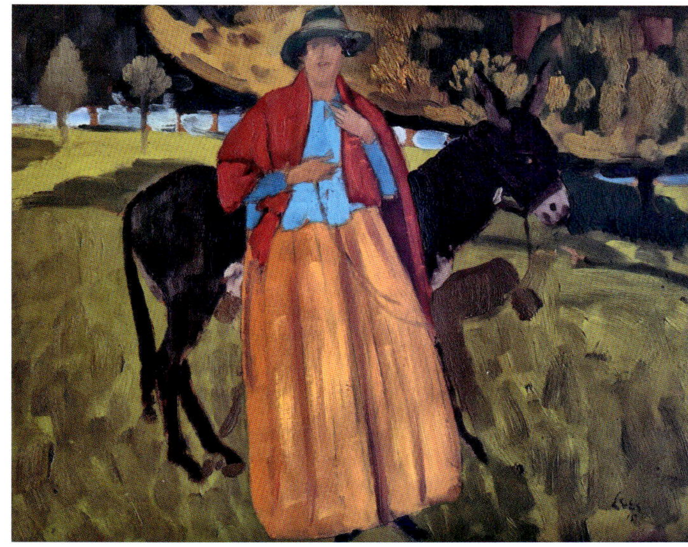

DL15.28

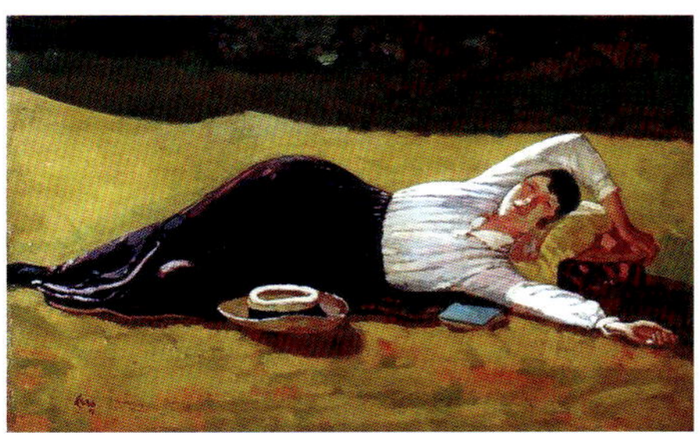

DL15.26

DL15.30
Lyndra, 1915
ins: c.r.: Lees 15 [pencil]
Watercolour on paper
61 x 45 cm
prov: Redfern Gallery; Private Collection; Gilty Restorers, Sydney 2023; Private Collection

DL15.31
Portrait of a Girl / Portrait of the Artist's Wife, 1915
Pencil and wash on paper
40 x 32.6 cm
prov: Redfern Gallery; Rex Nan Kivell Collection; Deutsher 1976–7; Belgrave Gallery, London; Sotheby's London May 1981 (102); Deutscher 1982; Private Collection 1992
exh: Sane 1997 (39)

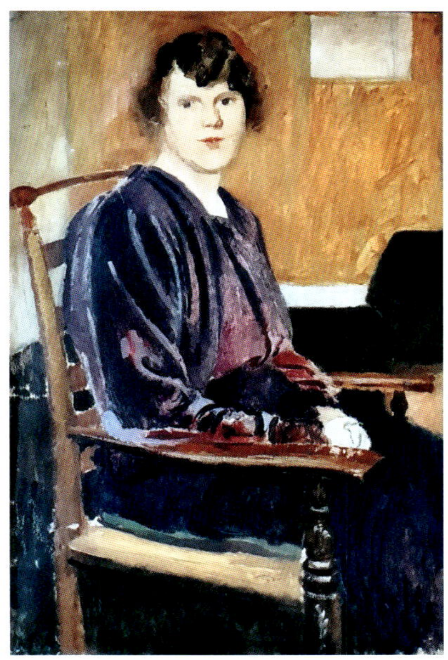

DL15.29

DL15.32*
The Artist's Wife / Lyndra, c.1915
Watercolour on paper
46 x 31 cm
prov: Redfern Gallery 1934; Ursula Hayward (Hayward Collection), thence by descent
exh: Redfern 1934 (49)

DL15.33*
Head of a Lady, 1915–18
Pencil on paper
33 x 26 cm
prov: Dowdeswell and Dowdeswell, London; Christie's London Feb 1917 (79)
notes: Unresolved record

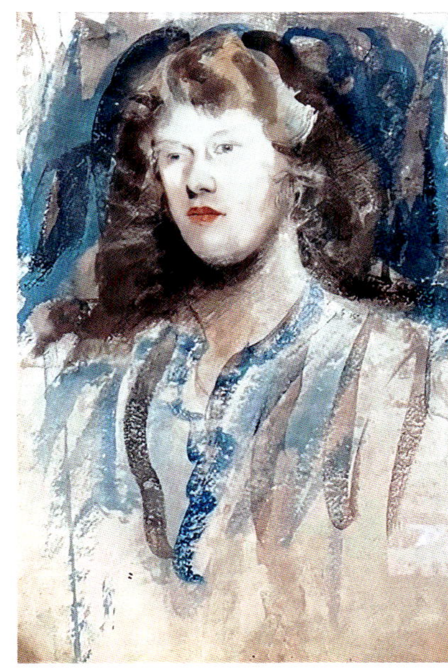

DL15.30

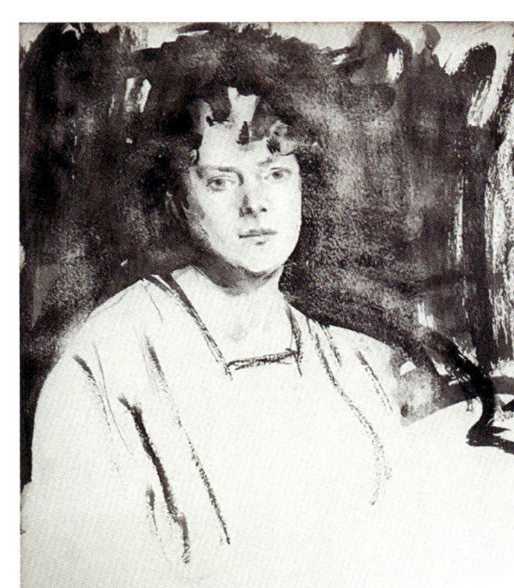

DL15.31

DL15.34*
Head of a Lady, 1915–18
Pencil on paper
prov: Dowdeswell and Dowdeswell, London; Christie's London Feb 1917 (2, 1st of 2 in the lot)
notes: Unresolved record

DL15.35*
The Artist's Wife, c.1915
Oil on card
30 x 40.5 cm
prov: Sotheby's London Mar–Apr 1976 (156)
notes: Unresolved record

DL15.36
Lyndra, 1915
ins: l.r.: Lees
Oil on panel
45 x 38 cm
prov: Private Collection, purchased from a London gallery 1940s, thence by descent
notes: Lyndra, Aldbourne; location as in DL15.14 and DL15.15

DL15.37
Aldbourne, Wilts. No.2 / Aldbourne, Wiltshire, 1915
ins: l.l.: Lees 15; v.: Snow on the Welsh Hills [on label]
Oil on panel
40 x 51 cm
prov: Redfern Gallery 1930; Lord Ivor Spencer-Churchill; Sotheby's London Mar 1961 (64); Thos. Agnew & Sons May 1961 (21733); Christie's London Nov 1985; Private Collection; Dreweatts, Newbury Jul 2024 (99)
exh: Redfern 1930a, as 'Aldbourne, Wilts. No.2' (26)

DL15.38*
A Cornfield, Aldbourne, 1915
Oil on panel
38.1 x 49.5 cm
prov: Christie's London May 1935; Baird

DL15.39*
Girl's Head, c.1915
Pencil on paper
prov: Dowdeswell and Dowdeswell, London; Christie's London Feb 1917 (2, 2nd of 2 in the lot)
exh: NEAC 55th 1916 (65)
notes: Unresolved record

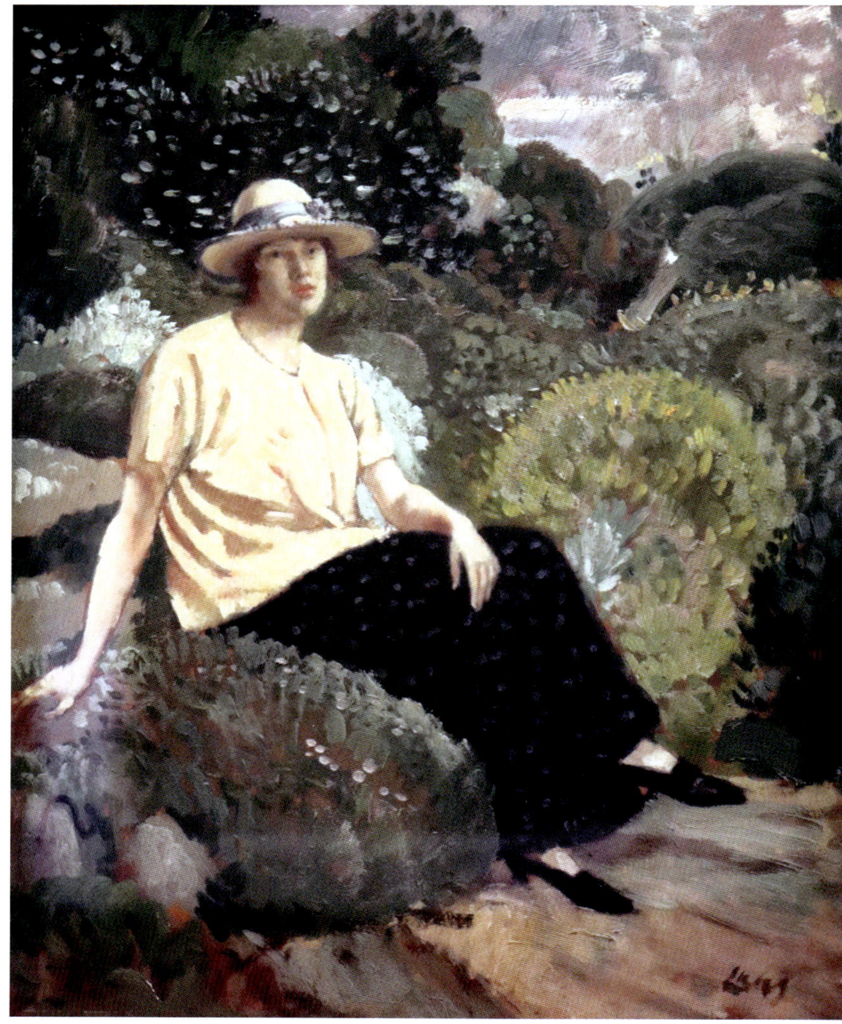

DL15.36

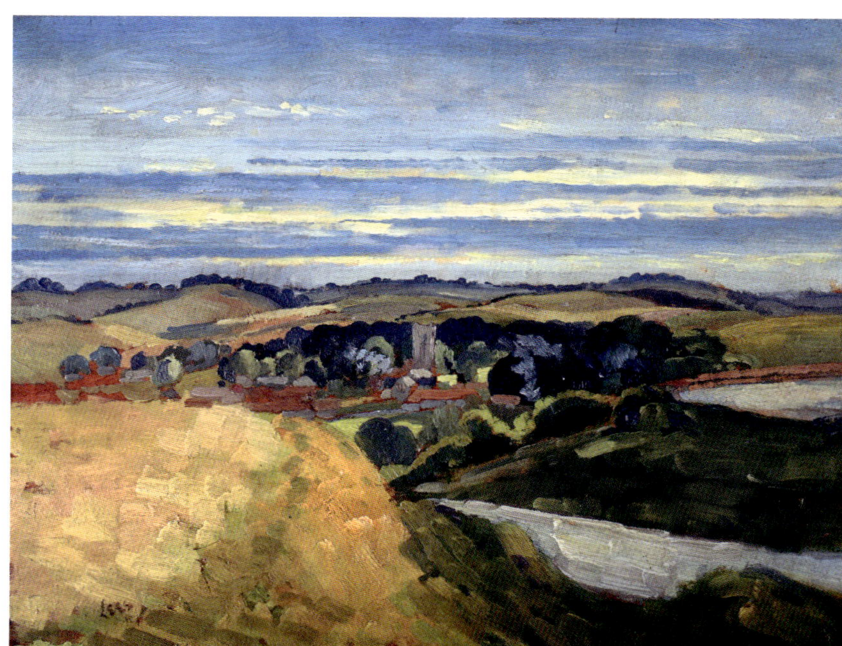

DL15.37

DL15.40*
The Weir, Freshford, c.1915
Watercolour
prov: Redfern Gallery 1944
exh: Redfern 1944a (49)
notes: Unresolved record; location of work unknown

DL15.41*
The House over the Hedge / A Tree by a House (?), c.1915
Oil on canvas
59.5 x 49.5 cm
prov: W. Wallis; R.G. Micklethwait; Sotheby's London Nov 1933 (44); Fielding 1933; Sotheby's London Dec 1963, collection of W. Wallis (42), Mar 1973 (48)
notes: 1930s ownership order unclear

DL15.42*
Lyndra at Aldbourne, c.1915
Oil on panel
24.1 x 31.7 cm
prov: Sotheby's London Apr 1951; Thos. Agnew & Sons 1951
notes: Unresolved record

1916

DL16.1*
Landscape with Trees / Trees in a Park, c.1916
Watercolour and pencil on paper
28 x 38.5 cm
prov: Rex Nan Kivell; Deutsher 1978; Belgrave Gallery, London; Sotheby's London May 1981 (99, 2nd of 3 in the lot)
exh: Deutsher 1978 (3)

DL16.2
Bourton / Village Street, Bourton / Village Street Scene, 1916
ins: v.: [pencil, on original stretcher] Derwent Lees Bourton
Oil on canvas
50.8 x 76.2 cm
prov: Cyril K. Butler 1916; Canterbury Auction Galleries Aug 2014; Burstow & Hewett, Battle 2017; Morris & Son, Woodbridge, Suffolk Aug 2017; Bloomsbury Fine Art, London Oct 2017; Private Collection
exh: NEAC 56th 1916–17, as 'Village Street, Bourton' (148)
notes: Loaned to the Tate, via the Goupil Gallery, for possible memorial exhibition Jun–Jul 1931; view along The Hill, Bourton

DL16.3 (see p.121)
Bourton Cross / Bourton-on the-Water / Bourton, 1916
ins: l.l.: Lees
Watercolour and ink on paper
23 x 33 cm
prov: Redfern Gallery 1958, 1964; John and Edward Barkes; Bridget McDonnell Gallery Feb–Mar 1986; Josef Lebovic Gallery, Sydney Jul 1997; Private Collection
exh: NEAC 56th 1916–17 (220); Redfern 1958 (41), 1964 (404); Bridget McDonnell Gallery, Feb–Mar 1986 (16)
notes: Bourton, Shrivenham

DL16.4
View across Roofs, Bourton, Berkshire / View across Roofs, Aldbourne, Wiltshire, 1916
Watercolour and pencil on paper
22.6 x 34.6 cm
prov: Redfern Gallery; Miss E.M. Plummer; Mrs W.B. Dalton; gifted to the Whitworth Institute (now The Whitworth, University of Manchester) Jun 1933
notes: St James' Church and Church Row houses from the Bourton House stable

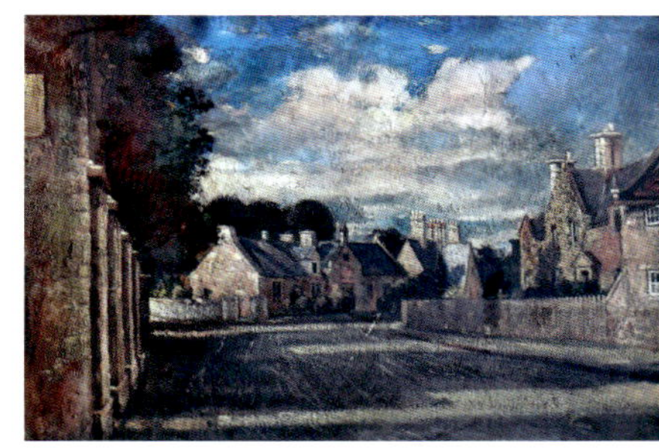

DL16.2

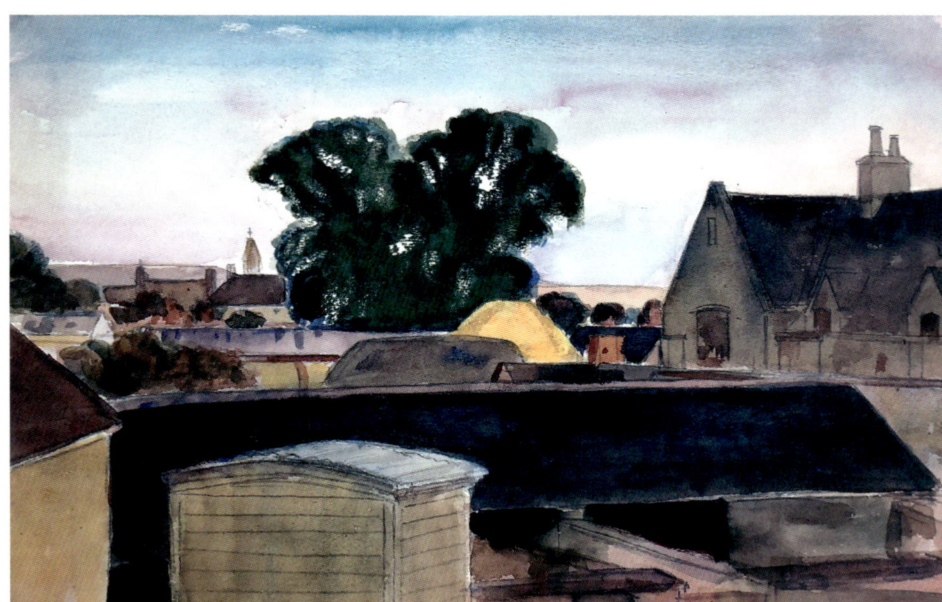

DL16.4

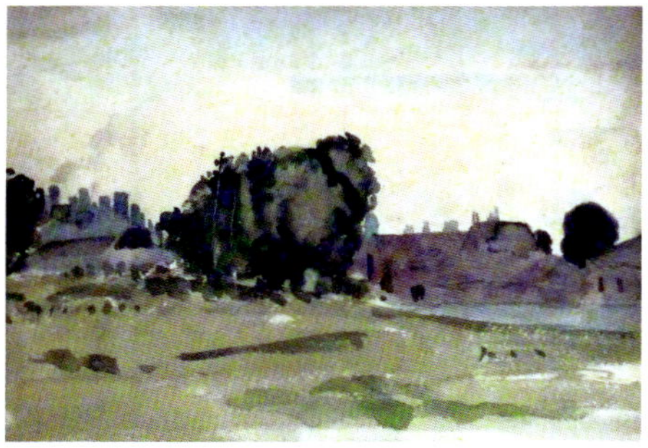

DL16.5

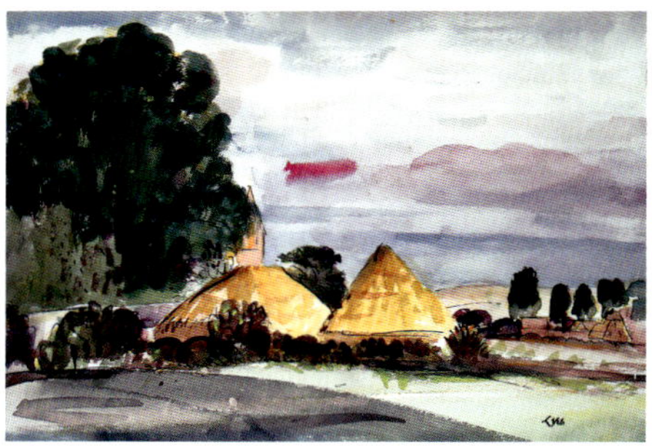

DL16.6

DL16.5
Bourton / Bourton-on-the-Water, 1916
Watercolour on paper
29.5 x 37 cm
prov: Redfern Gallery 1934; Bridget McDonnell Gallery 1993; Private Collection; the Hon. Christopher Legoe and Mrs Jenny Legoe, gifted to the Carrick Hill Trust Adelaide 2017
exh: Bridget McDonnell Gallery 1993 (28)
notes: Bourton House and Church Row houses with the old water tower right of centre tree

DL16.6
The Haystacks / Two Haystacks, 1916
ins: l.r.: Lees
Watercolour on paper
22.9 x 33.1 cm
prov: Sir Michael Sadler; R.E. Abbott (now Abbott and Holder), London; Winifred Coombe-Tennant, purchased 1953, thence by descent
exh: NEAC 56th 1916–17 (208)
notes: Opposite St James' Church, Bourton

DL16.7*
In a Rock Garden, 1916
ins: [signature]
73.5 x 49.5 cm
Oil on canvas
prov: Cyril K. Butler 1916; Lady Kendall Butler; Sotheby's London May 1946 (34)
exh: NEAC 56th 1916–17 (102)
notes: Loaned to the Tate, via the Goupil Gallery, for possible memorial exhibition Jun–Jul 1931; In Baron R.A. Butler of Saffron Walden, *The Art of the Possible: The Memoirs of Lord Butler*, Hamish Hamilton, London, 1971, p.12; garden at Bourton House

DL16.8*
Berkshire Landscape / Berkshire, c.1916
Watercolour on paper
prov: Redfern Gallery 1932, 1934, 1944, 1946
exh: British Contemporary Art 1933 (79); Redfern 1934 (44), 1944a (44), 1946b (433)
notes: Location of work unknown

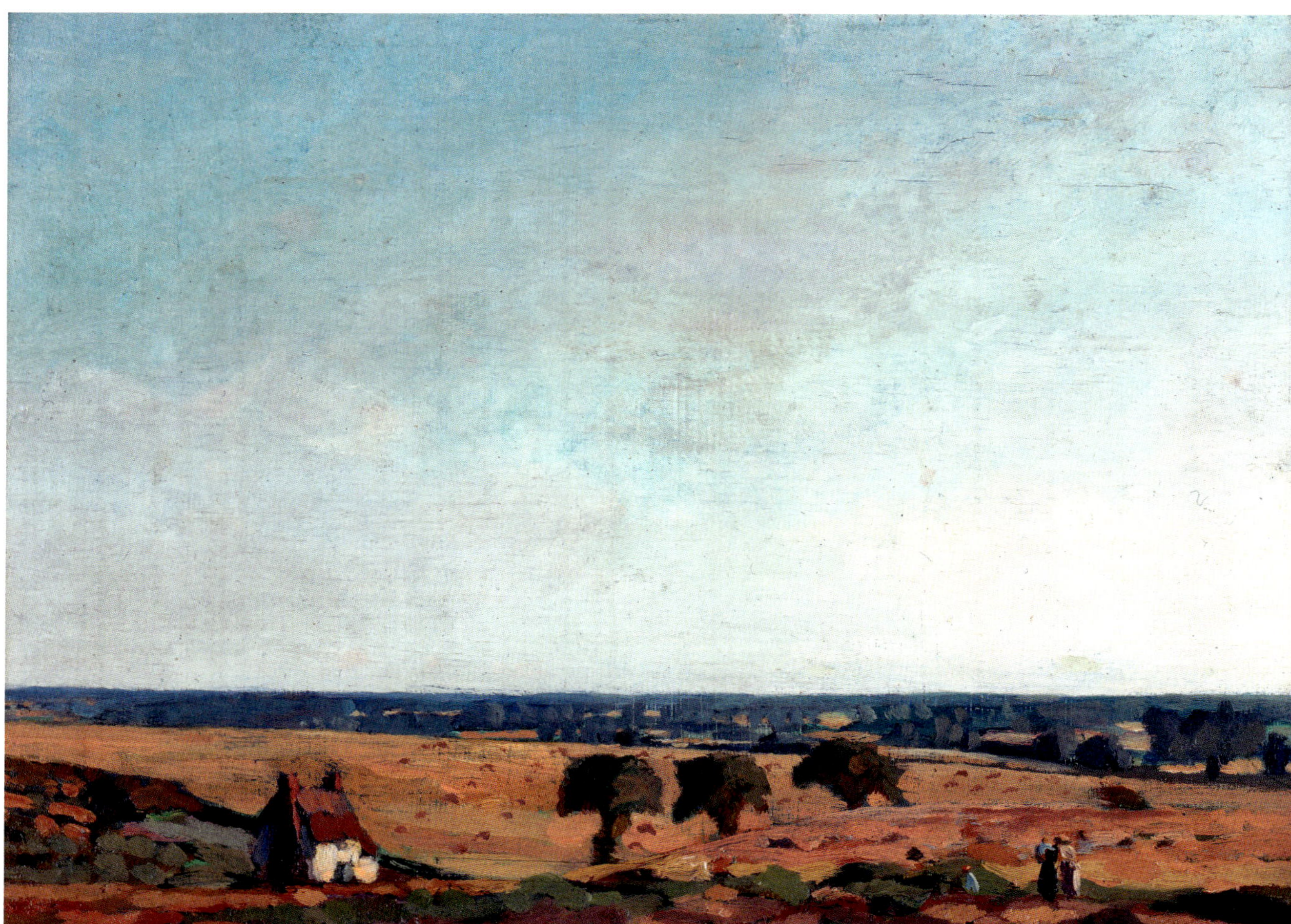

DL16.9

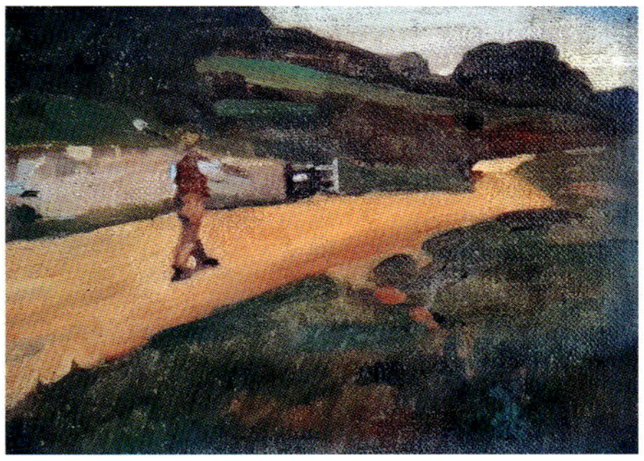

DL16.10

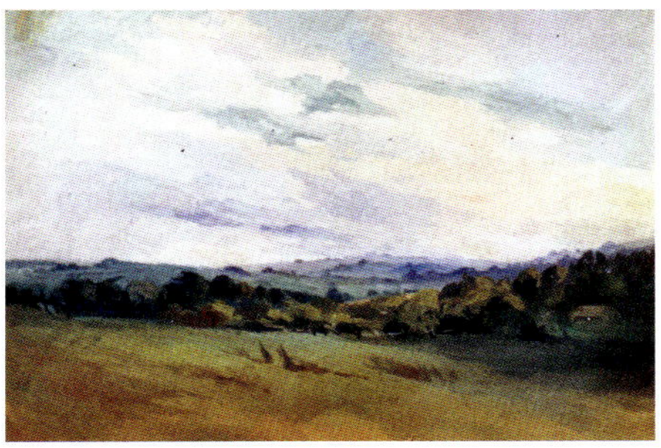

DL16.14

DL16.9
The Vista / Landscape, 1916
ins: v.: [signature]
Oil on panel
19.1 x 26.4 cm
prov: Dr Joseph Brown, gifted to The University of Melbourne 1987
exh: NEAC 56th 1916–17 (246); Sane 1997, loaned by The University of Melbourne Art Collection (6)
notes: Location as in DL16.10; from Idstone Road, Ashbury

DL16.10
The Bend in the Road / The Winding Road, 1916
Oil on canvas on panel
18 x 25 cm
prov: Wilfred A. Evill; Leicester Galleries, London; Private Collection; Jeffrey Sorrell 1970s–Mar 2023; Morris & Son, Woodbridge, Suffolk 2023; Private Collection
exh: NEAC 56th 1916–17 (235)
notes: Location and male figure as in DL16.9

DL16.11*
Road between Trees / A Wooded Driveway, c.1916
ins: v.: [signature]
Watercolour on paper
25.4 x 35.7 cm
prov: Rex Nan Kivell; Deutsher 1978; Belgrave Gallery, London; Sotheby's London May 1981 (99, 3rd of 3 in the lot)
exh: Deutsher 1978 (2) (?)

DL16.12*
Bourton Cross, 1916
Oil
prov: Cyril K. Butler
notes: Loaned to the Tate, via the Goupil Gallery, for possible memorial exhibition Jun–Jul 1931; Bourton, Shrivenham

DL16.13**
Portrait / Portrait of the Artist's Wife / Portrait of Mrs Derwent Lees, c.1916
ins: l.l.: Lees
Oil on canvas
91.5 x 71.2 cm
prov: Lady Kendall Butler; Sotheby's London May 1946 (42); Christie's London Nov 1976 (81); Sotheby's London Mar 1989 (93), Oct 1989; Sotheby's Sussex Jul 1990; Christie's London Mar 1997 (116); Woolley & Wallis, Salisbury Jun 2025 (485)
notes: Lady Louisa Kendall Butler

DL16.14
Landscape, c.1916
Gouache on paper
18 x 25 cm
prov: Rex Nan Kivell; Deutsher 1978; Bridget McDonnell Gallery 1993; Private Collection
exh: Deutsher 1978 (1); Bridget McDonnell Gallery May 1993 (14)

1917

DL17.1
The Drive / The Avenue / The Drive to the Asylum, 1917
ins: l.l.: Lees 17
Oil on canvas
40 x 47.5 cm
prov: Cyril K. Butler 1917; R.F. Goldschmidt; Christie's London Jun 1941; Thompson 1941; Phillips, London Sep 2000; Private Collection
exh: NEAC 56th 1916–17, as 'The Drive' (104); Empire Art 1934–5, as 'The Avenue', loaned by Cyril K. Butler (122); Campbelltown Arts Centre, New South Wales, Joan Sutherland Performing Arts Centre, Penrith, Ivan Dougherty Gallery College of Fine Arts, University of New South Wales Sep–Nov 2006, Bundoora Homestead Art Centre, Melbourne Jun–Jul 2007 (281)
notes: In Baron R.A. Butler of Saffron Walden, *The Art of the Possible: The Memoirs of Lord Butler*, Hamish Hamilton, London, 1971, p.12; Bourton House driveway joins Avenue Road, Bourton, Shrivenham

DL17.2*
Portrait, c.1917
exh: NEAC 57th 1917 (86)
notes: Unresolved record

DL17.3*
Portrait of a Lady, 1917–18
Pencil on paper
prov: Private Collection; Deutscher 1982 (?); Leonard Joel, Melbourne Feb–Jul (P142), Sep 2006; Private Collection

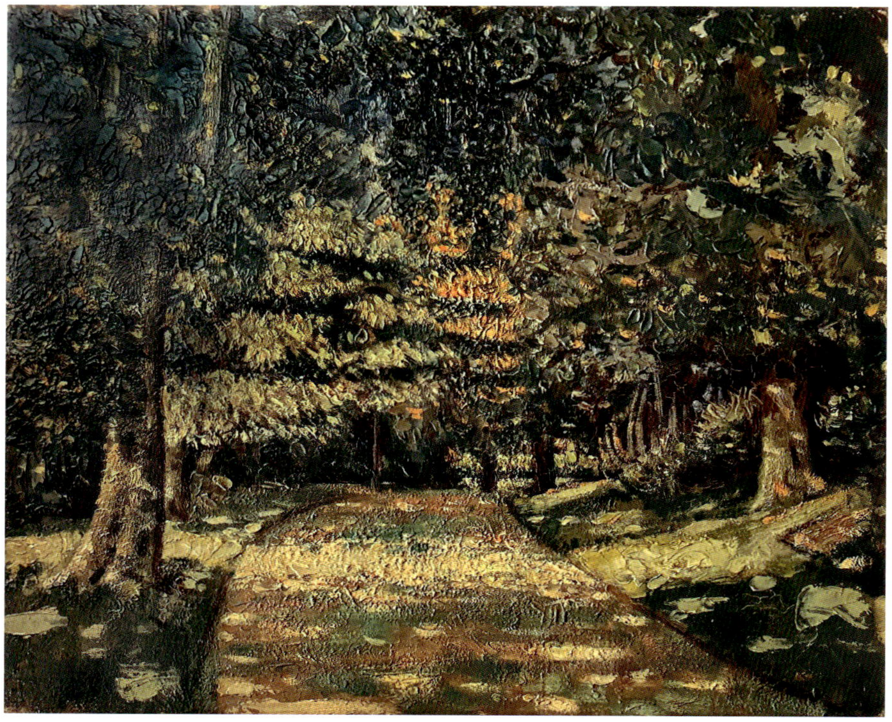

DL17.1

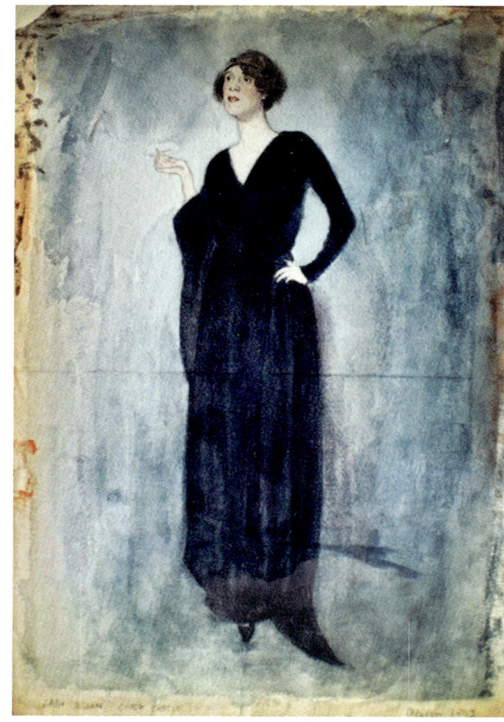

DL18.3

1918

DL18.1 (see p.127)
The Lady Howard de Walden, 1918
ins: u.r.: THE LADY HOWARD DE WALDEN; l.r.: By Derwent Lees Prov: Deutscher Gallery; Coll: Rex Nan Kivell
Watercolour wash and pencil on paper
35.2 x 25 cm
prov: Rex Nan Kivell; Deutsher 1978; Christie's Melbourne Apr 1992 (214); Private Collection; Burstow & Hewett, Battle Mar 2020; Private Collection
exh: Deutsher 1978 (21)
notes: Christie's Melbourne, catalogue 1992 'we are grateful to Lord Howard de Walden for confirming that this is a portrait of his mother. He remembers Derwent Lees staying at his family home'

DL18.2*
Shoreline, Dover / Dover, 1918
ins: [signature] 1918
Watercolour on paper
24.8 x 35.5 cm
prov: Frank Slade (?); Sotheby's London Nov 1931 (93); H.E. West 1931
exh: Tate, *Loan Exhibition of Works by P. Wilson Steer* Apr–Jul 1929
notes: Location of work unknown

DL18.3
Lady Ellen / Lady Ellis, c.1918
ins: l.l.: LADY ELLEN CHIRK CASTLE; l.r.: DERWENT LEES
Watercolour on paper
52.5 x 36.5 cm
prov: Redfern Gallery; John and Edward Barkes, London; Bridget McDonnell Gallery 1988; Private Collection
exh: Bridget McDonnell Gallery Feb–Mar 1988 (19)
notes: Margherita Scott-Ellis, Lady Howard de Walden

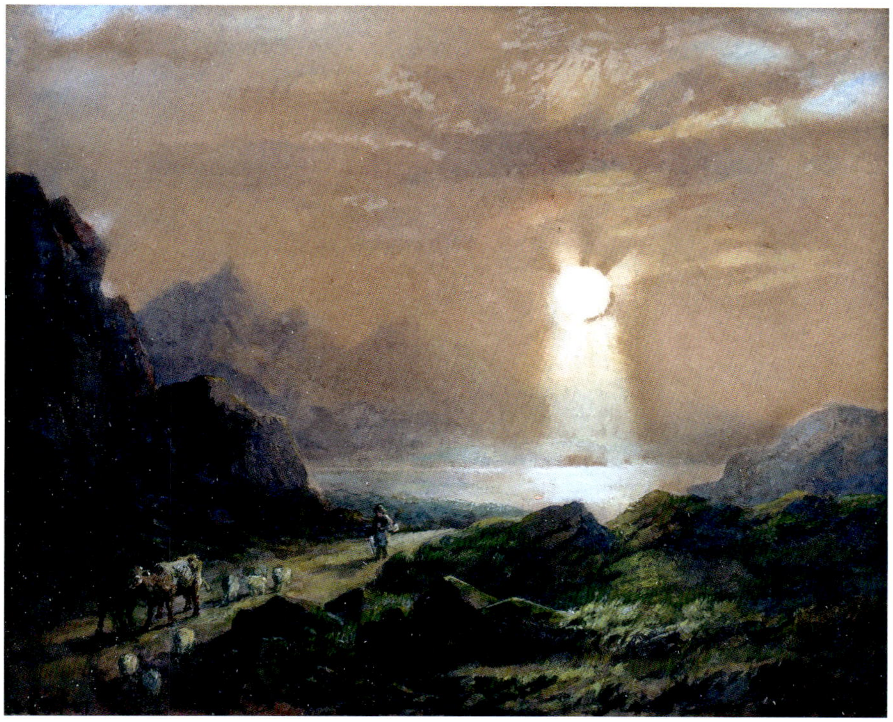

DL27.1

1919

DL19.1 (see p.132)
Derwent Lees / Self Portrait, c.1919
ins: Print 1 v.: u.l.: Self-portrait by Derwent Lees. Return to Redfern Gallery [pencil]
Etching on paper
17.5 x 12.2 cm [Print 1]
prov: Print 1: Redfern Gallery; National Portrait Gallery London, purchased 1987; Print 2: Denys Wilcox Fine Art (The Court Gallery, Taunton); Private Collection

1923

DL23.1*
A Sussex Landscape, 1923
ins: [signature] 1923
Watercolour on paper
27.3 x 36.2 cm
prov: Sotheby's London Nov 1931 (92); Fellowes 1931
notes: Location of work unknown

1927

DL27.1
Day's End / Pastoral, 1927
ins: l.l.: D Lees '27
Watercolour on paper
17 x 20 cm
prov: Phillips, London Sep 1991; Private Collection; Leski Auctions, Melbourne May 2021 (1066); Robin Gibson Gallery, Sydney

UNRESOLVED

Lrndra, c.1913
prov: Chenil Gallery 1913–14
exh: Chenil 1913–14 (50)

Woman in a Landscape
Watercolour on paper
21.5 x 30.5 cm
prov: Sotheby's Jun 1979

Small parcel of figure studies and a decorative design, various mediums and sizes; including 4 etchings, one signed, one inscribed
prov: Sotheby's London 'Catalogues of Sale A' 23 Jan 1980 (9)

Head of a Girl
Watercolour, pen and ink on paper
49.5 x 36 cm
prov: Christie's London Feb 1980

ACKNOWLEDGEMENTS

I am forever indebted to Peter Davies, David Murrell and David Lyons. Thank you for your unwavering support, patience and generosity.

I also owe a great debt to John Hoole, Gabriel and Leonie Summers, Gill Clarke, Stephen R. Johnson, Neil B. Maw, John Peel, James Trollope and Robert Winckworth.

I gratefully thank David Walsh, Steve Devereaux, Jarrod Rawlins and the Museum of Old and New Art (Mona, Australia) for their support in the book's production; and I warmly thank Nigel Farrow, Lucy Clark, Sarah Thorowgood, Rebeccah Williams and the Lund Humphries team, and Julie Gunz, for their unrelenting engagement in the pre- and post-production of the book.

I am enormously grateful to many people and organisations in Australia, New Zealand, England, Wales, France, USA, Canada, South Africa and Scotland. Friendships have blossomed with people I've never met. I thank you all: archive and library staff; curators and gallery managers; biographers and art historians; descendants of Derwent Lees, Nora and Gerald Summers, Lord and Lady Howard de Walden and Fred and Hannah Mayor; a journalist, rock climber, ecologist and standing-stone enthusiasts; artists and art collectors; local history associations, community groups and trusts.

RESEARCH

I gratefully acknowledge and thank:

In AUSTRALIA: Luisa Moscato (Archives, Melbourne Grammar School); Jack Ennis Butler (Research Library & Archives, National Gallery of Australia); Rachel Adams and Susanna Hennighausen (Library, University of Tasmania); Duncan McColl (Edmund & Joanna Capon Research Library, National Art Archives, Art Gallery of New South Wales); Nathaniel Williams (Rex Nan Kivell biographer); Bridget McDonnell (Bridget McDonnell Gallery, Melbourne); Geoffrey Williams and Robert Lees (Derwent Lees's descendants); Ellen Whitton and Katie Davies (Carrick Hill, South Australia); Henry Lew (art collector and author); Jane Clark, Jarrod Rawlins, Steve Devereaux, Jacqui Woolf, Caitlin Lawler and Mary Lijnzaad (Mona, Tasmania); Judy Gunning (Queensland Art Gallery | Gallery of Modern Art); Rowena Craic and Trish Stokes (Museums & Collections, The University of Melbourne); Monica Tran, Emma Round and Alice Rezende (National Gallery of Australia); Robyn Hovey (Art Gallery of Ballarat); Tansy Curtin and Ju Phan (Art Gallery of South Australia); Paola Petrelli (Italian research and translation); State Library of New South Wales; National Library of Australia; State Library Victoria; Queensland State Archives; Brisbane City Archives; State Library & Archive Service, Tasmania; University of Sydney Archives & Records Management; Museums of History New South Wales – State Archives; Deborah Lasky-Davison (Archive, ANZ Banking Group); The QVMAG Library; Bellerive Historical Society; Tasmania Club; Army Museum, Tasmania; Randwick City Council; Adelong Library; Adelong Alive Museum; Tumut Library; Sydney Grammar School; Brisbane Grammar School; The Kings School; Barker College; Launceston College Grammar School; St Andrews Cathedral School; Ipswich Grammar School; Toowoomba Grammar School.

And: Sarah Munks, Robert Littlewood, Louis Glowinski, Rob Jensen, Tom Easling, Brigita Ozolins, Steve Mallick, Lili Davies, Carol Devereaux, Rick Crossland, the late Nevin Hurst, Warren Boyles and Monica Lyons.

In NEW ZEALAND: Jennifer Jeffery and Tom Riley (Hocken Archives, Library, University of Otago); Jennifer Taylor Moore (The Sarjeant Gallery Te Whare o Rehua, Whanganui); Barbara Blake (Dunedin City Council Library); The Museum of New Zealand Te Papa Tongarewa; National Library of New Zealand; Presbyterian Research Centre Archives Knox College; Toitū Otago Settlers Museum, Dunedin City Council; Waitaki Museum & Archive; St Paul's Cathedral Dunedin; Christchurch City Libraries.

In ENGLAND: John Hoole (James Dickson Innes's co-biographer); Robert Winckworth (Special Collections, UCL Library Services); Gabriel and Leonie Summers (family of Nora and Gerald Summers); Gill Clarke (Randolph Schwabe's biographer); Thomas Seymour and Cilla Wills (family of Lord and Lady Howard de Walden and Gwendolyn van Raalte); James Trollope (Rudolph Ihlee's biographer); Stephen R. Johnson and the Reverend Vicar, The Friends of Horton Cemetery, Surrey; Neil B. Maw, the Shrivenham Heritage Society and the Paul Williams Collection; Isabelle Maxwell (Sotheby's London); Hannele Hellerstedt (Bonhams London); Elizabeth Comba, Clementine Swallow and Emma Lake (Christie's London); Kirstie Davidson (Browse & Darby); John Peel and Natasha Howes (Manchester Art Gallery); Sarah Charlton and Thomas Bailey (The Howard de Walden Estate Document Archive, London); Hannah Vollam and Jamilla Briggs (The Whitworth, Manchester); Ryan Finton and the Library & Archives staff (Tate, London); Nigel Walsh, Sarah Murray, Kirsty Young and Laura Claveria (Leeds Art Gallery); Erin Shields (Walker Art Gallery, National Museums Liverpool); Paul Cox (National Portrait Gallery); Peter Nahum (The Leicester Galleries); Rupert Maas (The Maas Gallery); Irving Grose (formerly of the Belgrave Gallery, London); Chin Yui Jasmine Lau (British Council); Dawn Ann Galer (Redbridge Museum & Heritage Centre); Camilla Riva (The Fine Art Society); Zara Moran (Research Centre, The National Gallery, London); Richard Morris (Morris & Son, Woodbridge, Suffolk); Paul Mayhew (Paul Mayhew Fine Art); Tom Edwards (Abbott and Holder Art Gallery); Luke Farey (Piano Nobile); Lauren Padgett (Bradford District Museums & Galleries); Clare Mitchell (Southampton City Art Gallery); Lucy Faithful (Brighton & Hove Museums); Andrea Fredrickson and Lucy Waitt (UCL Art Museum); Gemma Burns (Abbot Hall and Blackwell, Lakeland Arts); Sarah Richardson (Laing Art Gallery); Joanne Chamberlain (Southport Library, The Atkinson); Elizabeth Lindley (Sheffield Museums Trust); Martin Roberts (Herbert Art Gallery & Museum); Richard Jones (Mostyn Art Gallery); Kerri Offord (Ferens Art Gallery); Helen Sear (mixed-media artist); Victoria and Albert Museum, London; The British Museum; The Ashmolean Museum of Art and Archaeology; The Walpole Society; Sam Richardson (The Potteries Museum & Art Gallery); Steven Brindle and Kathryn Schofield (The Society of Architectural Historians of Great Britain); London Metropolitan Archives; Surrey History Centre; J.B. Priestley Library, University of Bradford; The Warburg Institute Library, University of London; Government Art Collection; The Contemporary Art Society; British Library; Bodleian Libraries, University of Oxford; Cambridge University Library; Artists Benevolent Fund;

Epsom & Ewell History Explorer; Surrey History Centre; The Art Society of Hull & East Riding; Aldbourne Heritage Centre; Liverpool Record Office; University Liverpool Special Collections & Archives; West Sussex Libraries; Richard Morris (Morris & Son); The Redfern Gallery.

And: Andrew Vaughan, John Barkes, David Boyd Haycock, Lydia Miller and Mary Nelson.

In WALES: Karen George (Chirk Castle, National Trust UK); Ellie Dawkins (Glynn Vivian Art Gallery); Neil Lebeter, Maddie Webb and Kay Kays (Amgueddfa Cymru, Museum Wales); Catrin Simon (ECS Carmarthen Library); Llanelli Reference Library; Margaret E. Jones (Archifdy Ceredigion Archives); the Llyfrgell Genedlaethol Cymru, National Library of Wales.

And: Peter Lord (art historian) and Jeff Towns.

In SCOTLAND: Keir Murray (Rozelle House, South Ayrshire Council).

In IRELAND: Trinity College Library, University of Dublin.

In CANADA: National Gallery of Canada; Beaverbrook Art Gallery; Archives, University of Toronto.

In the USA: Matt Rhoades and Abigail Lamphier (Yale Center for British Art); Charlotte DonVito and Anne H. Simmons (National Gallery of Art); Jan Howard (Rhode Island Design Museum); Terrie Wilson (Michigan State University); Beth (Milwaukee Public Library); Art Institute of Chicago Archives; National Gallery of Art; New York Public Library; The Frick Art Reference Library, New York; Balch Art Research Library; University of California Art History Department; John and Mable Ringling Museum of Art Library; Getty Research Institute Library; Penn State University Libraries; Los Angeles County Museum of Art; University of California Library network; Virginia Museum of Fine Arts; Ohio State University Fine Arts Library; Editor, Avery Index to Arch. Periodicals, Columbia University; University of Virginia Library; Billie Jane Baguley Library and Archives, Heard Museum; University of Georgia Art Library; University of Michigan Fine Arts Library; San Francisco Public Library; Print Council of America; Joseph C. Sloane Art Library | University of North Carolina at Chapel Hill; University of Delaware Library; Washington State University Library; Southern Illinois University Library; Christie's New York; Hawaii Pacific University.

In FRANCE: Collections Jacques Doucet, Institut National d'Histoire de l'Art, Paris; Marie-Andrée Calafat (Réseau des Bibliothèques de la Ville de Perpignan); Christine Argent (Directeur Général Adjoint, Perpignan Méditerranée Métropole); Claire Muchir (Directrice, Musée d'Art Moderne, Collioure); Les Amis du Musée d'Art Moderne, Collioure; Bibliothèque Nationale de France, Paris.

And: Jo Reed and Cléo Dankert.

In GERMANY: Silke Geiring (Bayerische Staatsbibliothek, Munich).

In SOUTH AFRICA: Phillipa van Stratten (Johannesburg Art Gallery); University of Pretoria Archives; Johannesburg Heritage Portal; Friends of the Johannesburg Art Gallery.

IMAGES

I warmly thank and gratefully acknowledge permissions granted by the museums, galleries, institutions, private collectors and copyright holders. My heartfelt thanks to David Murrell for his tremendous photographic and image work that contributed so much to this book. Dave's guidance, care, depth of knowledge and meticulous attention to detail have been invaluable.

Where possible, every attempt has been made to secure the owners' or holders' permission to reproduce an image. If there is insufficient data to determine a work's current location, it is recorded as 'Location of work unknown'. Some images have undergone a minor degree of digital editing. Specifically, this may include selective tonal adjustment; colour correction or enhancement; removal of reflections; cropping of unsuitable borders/ frames and edges; and image sharpening where appropriate, owing to the nature and quality of the image file obtained.

I thank the following people for kindly providing images or permitting access to images of works or other materials: Gabriel and Leonie Summers, Nigel Farrow, Andrew Vaughan, Henry Lew, John Hoole, Peter Lord, Geoff Williams, Robert Lees, Elliot Rubenstein, Tom Easling, Michael Jacobs, Robin Gibson, Carl Lykert and Robert Jensen.

GEOLOCATION

My deepest thanks and love go to my research ecologist husband Peter, who inadvertently joined (and never left) the research effort five years ago to geolocate Derwent's landscapes; identifying and resolving the location issues (see Appendix), compiling the landscape location maps and much of the catalogue data. His research was further enhanced by a dedicated group of volunteer geolocators. For this, we gratefully acknowledge and thank:

In BRITAIN: Neil B. Maw (Bourton, Shrivenham and Idstone, England); David Beeson, Gabriel Summers and Sarah Munks (Dorset and Cornwall, England); Steven Brindle and Kathryn Schofield, The Society of Architectural Historians of Great Britain (Kent, England); Keith Bowen, John Hoole and John Appleby (North Wales); and UK members of the Megalithic Portal.

In FRANCE: André Guerné, Yvon Berta-Maillol, Madeleine Claus and Pedro Soler, Florence and Hervé Bardon, Helen Sear and Andreas Ruethi (Banyuls-sur-Mer); Francoise Clotis, Annie and Francois Desclaux, Alexis Aloujes and Albert Hermandez (Collioure, Port Vendres, Perpignan); Christine Argent and Hervé Bardon (Prades, Vernet-les-Bains, the Cerdagne); Luc Fabre (Les Amis du Vieil Istres) and Etienne Sesmat.

IMAGE CREDITS

Every effort has been made to seek permission to reproduce the images in this book. Any omissions are entirely unintentional, and details should be addressed to the publishers.

Works by Derwent Lees. (Numbers in italics indicate 'DL' catalogue numbers.)
Abbott and Holder: *09.38, 12.3, 13.21, 14.1*; **Aberdeen Archives, Gallery and Museums**: *13.35, 15.16*; **Alamy**: *15.22* (and page 138); **Amgueddfa Cymru – National Museum Wales**: *14.13* (and page 92), *15.12*; **Art Gallery of Ballarat**: *08.4*; **Art Gallery of New South Wales**: *13.42*; **Art Gallery of South Australia**: *11.32* (and page 60t); **Art Institute of Chicago**, gift of Robert Allerton, 1925.536: *12.23*; **ART UK / National Museums Liverpool**: *15.19*; **Ashmolean Museum**: *11.53, 12.20* (and page 147); **Atkinson Art Gallery**: *14.43*; **Birmingham Museums Trust**: *13.43*; **The Blue Review** v.1, 1913: *13.8, 13.9*; **Bonhams**: *11.42, 12.15, 13.4* (and page 80t), *15.2, 15.9, 15.11, 16.14*; **Bradford Museums and Art Galleries / Bridgeman Images**: *14.24*; **Brighton & Hove Museums**: *11.24, 12.32, 13.15, 13.23*; **Brightwells**: *13.11*; **Bridget McDonnell Gallery**: *09.17, 09.18, 09.25, 09.30, 09.40, 10.9, 11.21, 11.63, 11.67, 12.39, 13.16, 13.17, 13.18, 13.19, 13.58, 13.68* (and page 40l); *13.69, 13.71, 15.6, 15.29, 18.3*; **Photo © British Council Collection**, London: *12.14*; **© The Trustees of the British Museum**: *11.27, 15.7*; **Brown University Archive**: *09.19*; **Browse & Darby**: *11.40*; **The Canterbury Auction Galleries**: *14.27, 16.2*; **Carrick Hill Trust**: *12.33, 14.34, 16.5*; **Christie's Images**: *07.23, 09.8, 09.20, 10.17, 10.49, 11.4, 11.23, 11.28, 11.38, 11.39, 11.43, 11.44, 12.5, 12.9, 12.12, 12.19, 12.25, 12.35, 13.1* (and page 81), *13.27* (and page 91), *13.30, 13.40* (and page 2), *13.48, 14.11, 14.12, 14.23, 14.25, 14.28, 14.29, 15.13, 15.18* (/Bridgeman Images), *15.25, 18.1* (and page 127); **Winifred Coombe Tennant** family: *11.22, 16.6*; **Christopher Kingzett Fine Art**: *11.47, 13.28*; **Deutscher and Hackett**: *10.6, 11.59, 15.5, 15.8*; **Dreweatts**: *11.50* (and front cover), *12.37, 12.41, 15.37*; **Tom Easling**: *15.28*; **Ferens Art Gallery: Hull Museums**: *11.5, 13.55*; **Fitzwilliam Museum**: *14.44* (and page 102); **Frick Art Reference Library**: *10.28*; **Gibson's Auctions**: *13.72*; **Ken Dickinson 2008, Glynn Vivian Gallery**: *14.10*; **Glynn Vivian Art Gallery / Bridgeman Images**: *11.2*; **Gorringe's**: *07.25*; **The Hepworth Wakefield**: *14.35*; **Herbert Art Gallery and Museum**: *08.25, 09.47*; **Michael Jacobs**: *15.36*; **Johannesburg Art Museum**: *11.31*; **The John Quinn Collection, American Art Association**, New York, 1926, p. 26: *12.31*; **© Laing Art Gallery, Tyne & Wear Archives & Museums**, Newcastle upon Tyne: *11.55, 14.2*; **Lawrences Auctioneers**: *08.24*; **Leeds Art Gallery / Bridgeman Images**: *10.26, 10.29, 10.31, 10.32* (and page 53t), *10.33, 13.5, 14.32, 14.39, 15.21*; **Henry Lew**: *10.13, 10.19, 11.17, 12.17, 12.18, 13.50, 13.54, 13.61, 13.65, 15.15, 15.17, 15.30*; **Lyon and Turnbull Auctions**: *10.10*; **Maas Gallery**: *09.26, 11.60*; **Manchester Art Gallery / Bridgeman Images**: *09.14* (and page 37), *09.29, 11.20, 11.51, 11.54, 13.45* (and page 82), *14.36*; **Martin Tinney Gallery**: *12.36*; **Mona**: *10.7*; **Richard Morris**: *11.71*; **Museum of Modern Art**, Machynlleth: *13.47*; **Museum of New Zealand Te Papa Tongarewa**: *14.38*; **Peter Nahum at The Leicester Galleries**: *11.8, 11.57, 13.51, 15.26*; **National Gallery of Australia**: *08.7, 09.6, 10.5, 10.15, 11.52, 12.24, 13.20, 13.36, 15.4*; **National Gallery of Canada**: *13.46*; **National Gallery of Victoria**: *08.12* (and page 38 and back cover), *13.33, 14.41*; **National Portrait Gallery**: *19.1* (and page 132); **Panter & Hall**: *09.4*; **Potteries Museum & Art Gallery**: *11.1* (and page 56); **N. Harth, Queensland Art Gallery | Gallery of Modern Art**: *09.27, 10.8, 14.37, 15.14*; **Raffan Kelaher & Thomas**: *13.70*; **Museum of Art, Rhode Island School of Design**: *09.9, 09.10*; *09.12, 10.18*; **Carl Lykert, Robin Gibson Gallery**: *11.26*; **Robin Gibson Gallery**: *27.1*; **© Royal Albert Memorial Museum and Art Gallery**, Exeter City Council: *09.11, 09.13*; **Rozelle House Galleries**: *12.6*; Collection of the **Sarjeant Gallery Te Whare o Rehua Whanganui**. Gift of Mrs P Riddiford, UK, 1964: *14.40*; **© Sheffield Museums Trust**: *14.42*; **Sotheby's**: *09.22, 10.20, 10.22, 10.27, 12.4, 12.34, 14.7, 14.26*; **South Australian Bulletin (AGSA)**, v.19, Jan 1958: *13.38* (and page 89t); **Southampton City Art Gallery**: *13.2*; **The Studio** v.108, 1934: *12.30* (and page 77b); **Sydney Mail**, 1933, p.24: *13.26*; **Tate**: *08.9, 09.1, 09.2, 09.3, 09.7, 09.15, 10.16, 12.26* (and pages 68 and 76t), *13.6*; Courtesy **Nikolaus Karlson, Thomas Agnew & Sons**, London: *13.37*; **UCL Art Museum, University College London / Bridgeman Images**: *07.1, 07.2* (and page 18), *07.3, 07.4, 07.5, 07.6, 07.7, 07.8, 07.9, 07.10, 07.11, 07.12, 07.13, 07.14, 07.15, 07.16, 07.17, 07.18, 07.20, 07.21, 07.24* (and page 23), *07.26* (and page 33), *14.18* (and page 97); **© Image: UK Government Art Collection**: *11.6*; Courtesy of the **University Art Collection, The University of Melbourne**: *11.58, 16.9* (and page 116); Courtesy of **University of New South Wales School of Art & Design / Henry Lew**: *17.1* (and page 128); **© Victoria and Albert Museum**, London: *10.23* (and pages 46 and 55), *10.30*; **Walker Art Gallery**: *12.10*; **Walpole Society**: *11.56*; **The Whitworth**: *08.5* (and page 30), *08.6, 14.6, 14.9* (and page 100), *14.15, 16.4*; **Woolley & Wallis**: *11.29* (and page 58t), *13.44, 14.4*; **Yale Center for British Art**: *12.22* (and page 158).

Other images
Amgueddfa Cymru – National Museum Wales: pages 33tl and 60bl; **Amgueddfa Cymru – National Museum Wales / Estate of Augustus John**: page 96; **Amgueddfa Gaerfyrddin / Carmarthenshire Museum**: page 58b; **Bridgeman Images / Estate of Augustus John**: page 65; **Bristol Museum and Art Gallery**: page 52; Courtesy of **Chris Beetles Gallery**, St James's, London: page 73; **Christie's Images**: page 49b; **Christie's Images / Estate of Augustus John / Bridgeman Images**: page 93; **Fitzwilliam Museum / Estate of Augustus John**: page 38l; **Gladys Beattie Crozier, The Slade School of Art**, 1912: page 20b; **Stephen R. Johnson**: page 143; Courtesy of **Neil B. Maw / Shrivenham Heritage Society and the Paul Williams Collection**: page 120t; **Melbourne Grammar School Archives**: page 13l; **La Tribune de l'Art / La Maison Ruffat**, Perpignan: page 33tr; Courtesy of **Lancashire County Council's Red Rose Collections**: page 67; **Museums of History New South Wales**: page 16; **National Library of Australia**: page 140; **New York Public Library**: page 83; **Piano Nobile Gallery / Estate of Augustus John**: page 40r; **Print Collectors Quarterly**, 1931 / **Estate of Augustus John**: page 131; **Seattle Star**: page 119; **The Sovereign Hill Museums Association**: page 9; **State Library Victoria**: pages 8, 13r; **Tasmanian Archives and Heritage Office**: page 10; **Tate**: page 72; **UCL Art Museum / Bridgeman Images**: page 45 and page 112; **UCL Digital Education**: page 122r; **UCL Library Services**: pages 20tl, 20tr, 27, 111, 113l, 113r, 112l; **© Victoria and Albert Museum**, London: page 109; **The Howard de Walden Estate**: pages 106, 125; **Wikimedia Commons**: page 21; **Zenodot Verlagsgesellschaft / Wikimedia Commons**: page 28.

INDEX

Page numbers in *italics* refer to reproductions; those in **bold** refer to the catalogue raisonné entries. Works not by Lees are indexed under the name of the artist. Lees's works are indexed alphabetically by title under the 'Lees, Derwent' entry and some works are grouped by subject rather than listed by title (see the catalogue raisonné for a complete list of all Lees's known works). All works are by Lees unless otherwise indicated.